INTRODUCTION TO
Adobe® Dreamweaver® CS6

Complete Coverage of the Adobe® Certified Associate Exam:
Web Communication using Adobe® Dreamweaver® CS6

AUTHOR	Jeremy Osborn
PROJECT MANAGER	Cheri White
VIDEO PRODUCTION	Chris Leavey
VP & PUBLISHER	Don Fowley
EDITOR	Bryan Gambrel
DIRECTOR OF SALES	Mitchell Beaton
EXECUTIVE MARKETING MANAGER	Chris Ruel
ASSISTANT MARKETING MANAGER	Debbie Martin
EDITORIAL PROGRAM ASSISTANT	Jennifer Lartz
SENIOR PRODUCTION MANAGER	Janis Soo
ASSOCIATE PRODUCTION MANAGER	Joel Balbin
CREATIVE DIRECTOR	Harry Nolan
COVER DESIGNER	Georgina Smith
TECHNOLOGY & MEDIA	Tom Kulesa, Wendy Ashenberg
TECHNICAL EDITORS	Cathy Auclair, Haziel Olivera, Greg Heald
ART DIRECTOR	Jennifer Smith

This book was set in Bembo by Spoke & Wheel with production and development services provided by American Graphics Institute. It was printed and bound by Courier Kendallville. The covers were printed by Lehigh Phoenix.

Founded in 1807, John Wiley & Sons, Inc. has been a valued source of knowledge and understanding for more than 200 years, helping people around the world meet their needs and fulfill their aspirations. Our company is built on a foundation of principles that include responsibility to the communities we serve and where we live and work. In 2008, we launched a Corporate Citizenship Initiative, a global effort to address the environmental, social, economic, and ethical challenges we face in our business. Among the issues we are addressing are carbon impact, paper specifications and procurement, ethical conduct within our business and among our vendors, and community and charitable support. For more information, please visit our website: *www.wiley.com/go/citizenship.*

ISBN 978-1-118-39406-9

Printed in the United States of America

10 9 8 7 6 5 4 3 2 1

Preface

Welcome to *Introduction to Adobe Dreamweaver CS6*. Part of Wiley's Adobe courseware series, this book is designed as a complete introduction to Adobe Dreamweaver for Creative Suite 6. With this series, we've set out to produce a series of textbooks that deliver compelling and innovative teaching solutions to instructors and superior learning experiences for students. Infused and informed by in-depth knowledge from Adobe Certified Experts and Dreamweaver professionals who have created many official training titles for Adobe Systems, and crafted by a publisher known worldwide for the pedagogical quality of its products, these textbooks maximize skills transfer in minimum time. Students are challenged to reach their potential by using their new technical skills as highly productive members of the workforce. This courseware was designed to ensure you receive the topical coverage that is most relevant to your personal and professional success.

Wiley's Adobe courseware Program

Wiley's Adobe courseware series is a complete program for instructors and institutions to prepare and deliver great courses on Adobe software technologies. With this courseware series, we recognize that—because of the rapid pace of change in the technology and curriculum developed by Adobe—there is an ongoing set of needs beyond classroom instruction tools for an instructor to be ready to teach the course. This courseware program endeavors to provide solutions for all these needs in a systematic manner in order to ensure a successful and rewarding course experience for both instructor and student via technical and curriculum training for instructor readiness with new software releases and a great set of tools for delivering instruction in the classroom and lab. All are important to the smooth delivery of a course on Adobe software, and all are provided with Wiley's Adobe courseware program. We think about this model as a gauge for ensuring that we completely support you in your goal of teaching a great course.

VIDEO TUTORIALS

Your *Introduction to Adobe Dreamweaver CS6* textbook comes with access to approximately 2 hours of online video tutorials. The video tutorials are designed to supplement each lesson in the book. These video tutorials are created and presented by the authors and demonstrate topics covered in each lesson or related topics that enhance your understanding of each lesson.

Illustrated Book Tour

Pedagogical Features

The Wiley Adobe courseware and textbooks for Adobe Creative Suite 6 are designed as complete introductory textbooks on a particular Adobe software product. The books are also designed to cover all the learning objectives for that product's related Adobe Certified Associate (ACA) exam. The ACA exam is industry-recognized and identifies skills and topics expected for entry-level positions. Each ACA exam item is referred to as an exam objective, and these objectives are highlighted throughout the textbooks. Many pedagogical features have been developed specifically for this courseware. Unique features of our task-based approach include a Lesson Skill Matrix that correlates skills taught in each lesson to the ACA objectives; Certification Ready exercises; and two levels of increasingly rigorous lesson-ending activities—Competency Assessment and Proficiency Assessment.

Presenting the extensive procedural information and technical concepts woven throughout the textbook raises challenges for the student and instructor alike. The Illustrated Book Tour that follows provides a guide to the rich features contributing to Wiley's Adobe courseware pedagogical plan. Following is a list of key features in each lesson designed to prepare students for success on the certification exams and in the workplace:

- Each lesson begins with a **Lesson Skill Matrix**. More than a standard list of learning objectives, the skill matrix correlates each software skill covered in the lesson to the specific ACA exam objective.
- Each lesson features a real-world **Business Case** scenario that places the software skills and knowledge to be acquired in a real-world setting.
- Concise and frequent **Step-by-Step** instructions teach students new features and provide an opportunity for hands-on practice. Numbered steps give detailed instructions to help students learn software skills. The steps also show results and screen images to match what students should see on their computer screens.
- **Illustrations** provide visual feedback as students work through the exercises. The images reinforce key concepts, provide visual clues about the steps, and allow students to check their progress.
- When the text instructs a student to use a particular tool, **tool images** are shown within the text.
- Important technical vocabulary is listed in the **Key Terms** section at the beginning of the lesson. When these terms are used later in the lesson, they appear in bold italic type and are defined. The Glossary contains all of the key terms and their definitions.
- Engaging point-of-use **Reader Aids** located throughout the lessons tell students why this topic is relevant (*The Bottom Line*) and provide students with helpful hints (identified with the words *Take Note*) or ways to expand their skills (identified using the text *Learning More*). Reader aids also provide additional relevant or background information that adds value to the lesson.
- **Certification Ready** features throughout the text signal students where a specific certification objective is covered. They provide students with a chance to check their understanding of that particular ACA exam objective and, if necessary, review the section of the lesson where it is covered. This courseware provides complete preparation for ACA certification.

- Each lesson ends with a **Skill Summary**, recapping the ACA exam skills covered in the lesson.
- Accompanying **video tutorials** for each lesson provide a visual way to see selected content from the each lesson presented by the authors.
- The **Knowledge Assessment** section provides a total of 20 questions from a mix of True/False and Multiple Choice, testing students on concepts learned in the lesson.
- **Competency Assessment** and **Proficiency Assessment** sections provide progressively more challenging lesson-ending activities.
- Integrated **Circling Back** projects provide students with an opportunity to renew and practice skills learned in previous lessons.
- The student companion website contains the **online files** needed for each lesson.

Illustrated Book Tour

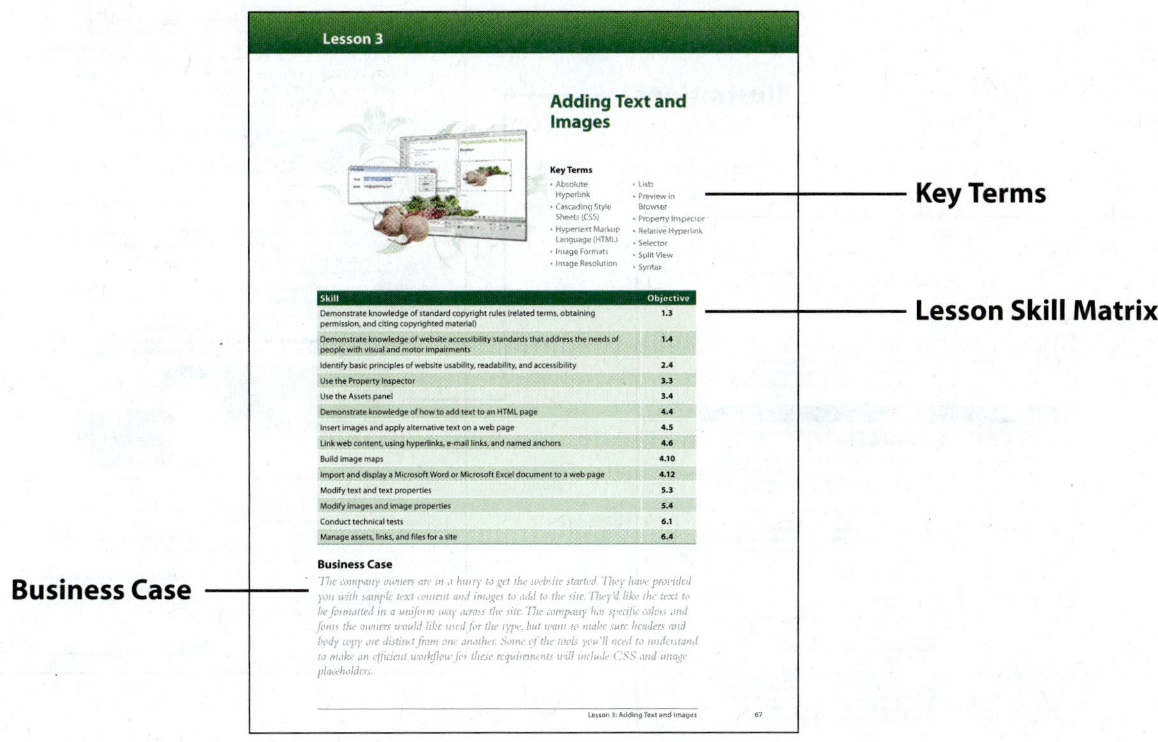

Lesson 3

Adding Text and Images

Key Terms

- Absolute Hyperlink
- Cascading Style Sheets (CSS)
- Hypertext Markup Language (HTML)
- Image Formats
- Image Resolution
- Lists
- Preview in Browser
- Property Inspector
- Relative Hyperlink
- Selector
- Split View
- Syntax

Skill	Objective
Demonstrate knowledge of standard copyright rules (related terms, obtaining permission, and citing copyrighted material)	1.3
Demonstrate knowledge of website accessibility standards that address the needs of people with visual and motor impairments	1.4
Identify basic principles of website usability, readability, and accessibility	2.4
Use the Property Inspector	3.3
Use the Assets panel	3.4
Demonstrate knowledge of how to add text to an HTML page	4.4
Insert images and apply alternative text on a web page	4.5
Link web content, using hyperlinks, e-mail links, and named anchors	4.6
Build image maps	4.10
Import and display a Microsoft Word or Microsoft Excel document to a web page	4.12
Modify text and text properties	5.3
Modify images and image properties	5.4
Conduct technical tests	6.1
Manage assets, links, and files for a site	6.4

Business Case

The company owners are in a hurry to get the website started. They have provided you with sample text content and images to add to the site. They'd like the text to be formatted in a uniform way across the site. The company has specific colors and fonts the owners would like used for the type, but want to make sure headers and body copy are distinct from one another. Some of the tools you'll need to understand to make an efficient workflow for these requirements will include CSS and image placeholders.

Lesson 3: Adding Text and Images 67

Key Terms

Lesson Skill Matrix

Business Case

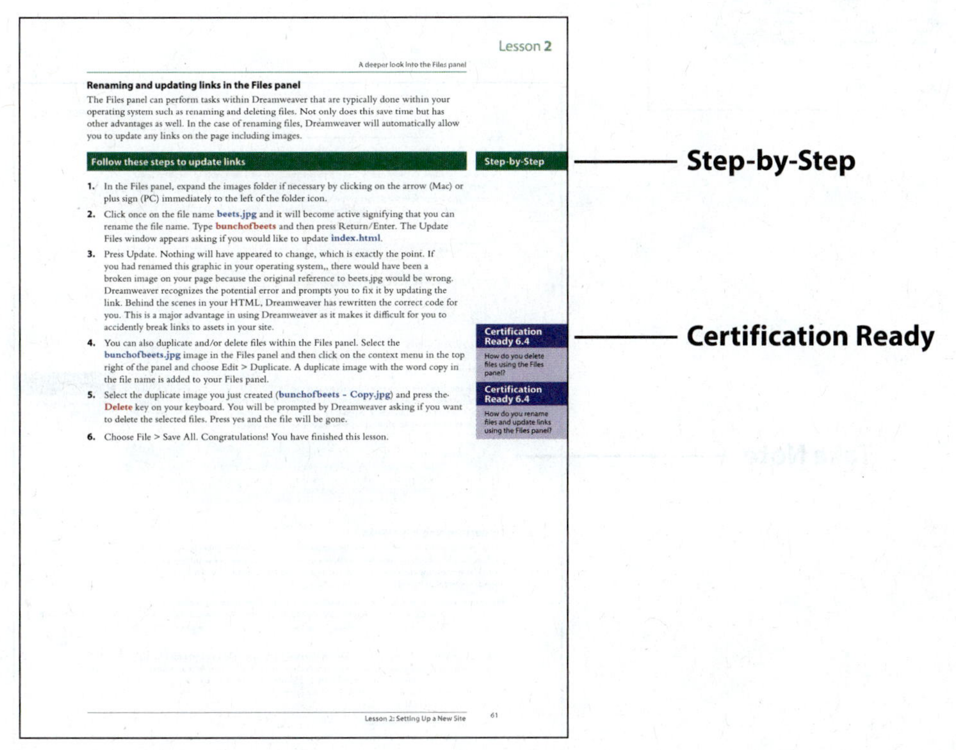

Lesson 2

A deeper look into the Files panel

Renaming and updating links in the Files panel

The Files panel can perform tasks within Dreamweaver that are typically done within your operating system such as renaming and deleting files. Not only does this save time but has other advantages as well. In the case of renaming files, Dreamweaver will automatically allow you to update any links on the page including images.

Follow these steps to update links — **Step-by-Step**

1. In the Files panel, expand the images folder if necessary by clicking on the arrow (Mac) or plus sign (PC) immediately to the left of the folder icon.
2. Click once on the file name **beets.jpg** and it will become active signifying that you can rename the file name. Type **bunchofbeets** and then press Return/Enter. The Update Files window appears asking if you would like to update **index.html**.
3. Press Update. Nothing will have appeared to change, which is exactly the point. If you had renamed this graphic in your operating system,, there would have been a broken image on your page because the original reference to beets.jpg would be wrong. Dreamweaver recognizes the potential error and prompts you to fix it by updating the link. Behind the scenes in your HTML, Dreamweaver has rewritten the correct code for you. This is a major advantage in using Dreamweaver as it makes it difficult for you to accidently break links to assets in your site.
4. You can also duplicate and/or delete files within the Files panel. Select the **bunchofbeets.jpg** image in the Files panel and then click on the context menu in the top right of the panel and choose Edit > Duplicate. A duplicate image with the word copy in the file name is added to your Files panel.
5. Select the duplicate image you just created (**bunchofbeets - Copy.jpg**) and press the **Delete** key on your keyboard. You will be prompted by Dreamweaver asking if you want to delete the selected files. Press yes and the file will be gone.
6. Choose File > Save All. Congratulations! You have finished this lesson.

Certification Ready 6.4
How do you delete files using the Files panel?

Certification Ready 6.4
How do you rename files and update links using the Files panel?

Lesson 2: Setting Up a New Site 61

Step-by-Step

Certification Ready

Illustrated Book Tour

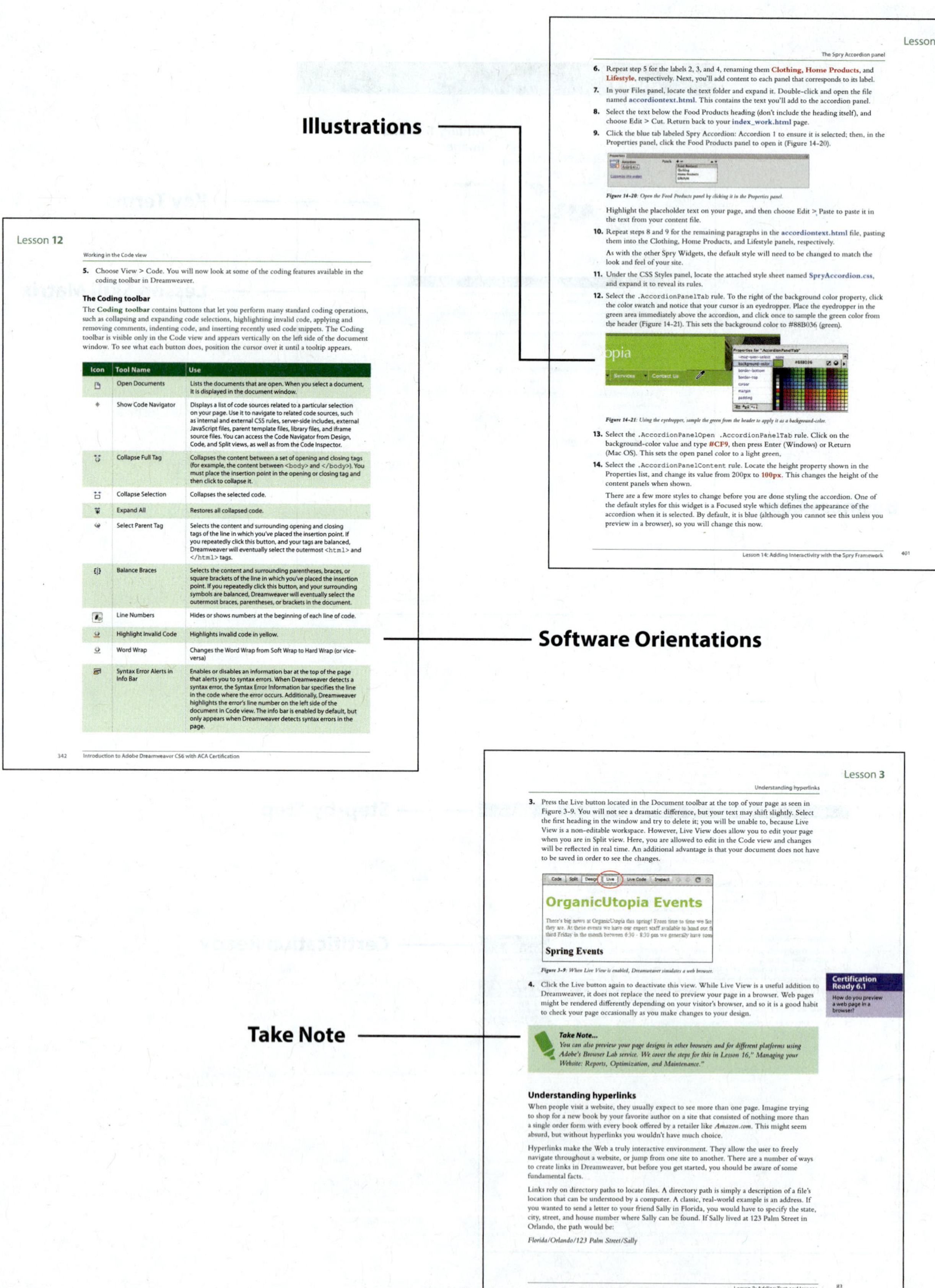

Lesson **14**

The Spry Accordion panel

6. Repeat step 5 for the labels 2, 3, and 4, renaming them **Clothing, Home Products**, and **Lifestyle**, respectively. Next, you'll add content to each panel that corresponds to its label.
7. In your Files panel, locate the text folder and expand it. Double-click and open the file named **accordiontext.html**. This contains the text you'll add to the accordion panel.
8. Select the text below the Food Products heading (don't include the heading itself), and choose Edit > Cut. Return back to your **index_work.html** page.
9. Click the blue tab labeled Spry Accordion: Accordion 1 to ensure it is selected; then, in the Properties panel, click the Food Products panel to open it (Figure 14-20).

Figure 14-20: Open the Food Products panel by clicking it in the Properties panel.

Highlight the placeholder text on your page, and then choose Edit > Paste to paste it in the text from your content file.

10. Repeat steps 8 and 9 for the remaining paragraphs in the **accordiontext.html** file, pasting them into the Clothing, Home Products, and Lifestyle panels, respectively.

As with the other Spry Widgets, the default style will need to be changed to match the look and feel of your site.

11. Under the CSS Styles panel, locate the attached style sheet named **SpryAccordion.css**, and expand it to reveal its rules.
12. Select the `.AccordionPanelTab` rule. To the right of the background color property, click the color swatch and notice that your cursor is an eyedropper. Place the eyedropper in the green area immediately above the accordion, and click once to sample the green color from the header (Figure 14-21). This sets the background color to #88B036 (green).

Figure 14-21: Using the eyedropper, sample the green from the header to apply it as a background-color.

13. Select the `.AccordionPanelOpen .AccordionPanelTab` rule. Click on the background-color value and type **#CF9**, then press Enter (Windows) or Return (Mac OS). This sets the open panel color to a light green,
14. Select the `.AccordionPanelContent` rule. Locate the height property shown in the Properties list, and change its value from 200px to **100px**. This changes the height of the content panels when shown.

There are a few more styles to change before you are done styling the accordion. One of the default styles for this widget is a Focused style which defines the appearance of the accordion when it is selected. By default, it is blue (although you cannot see this unless you preview in a browser), so you will change this now.

Lesson 14: Adding Interactivity with the Spry Framework 401

Lesson **12**

Working in the Code view

5. Choose View > Code. You will now look at some of the coding features available in the coding toolbar in Dreamweaver.

The Coding toolbar

The **Coding toolbar** contains buttons that let you perform many standard coding operations, such as collapsing and expanding code selections, highlighting invalid code, applying and removing comments, indenting code, and inserting recently used code snippets. The Coding toolbar is visible only in the Code view and appears vertically on the left side of the document window. To see what each button does, position the cursor over it until a tooltip appears.

Icon	Tool Name	Use
	Open Documents	Lists the documents that are open. When you select a document, it is displayed in the document window.
	Show Code Navigator	Displays a list of code sources related to a particular selection on your page. Use it to navigate to related code sources, such as internal and external CSS rules, server-side includes, external JavaScript files, parent template files, library files, and iframe source files. You can access the Code Navigator from Design, Code, and Split views, as well as from the Code Inspector.
	Collapse Full Tag	Collapses the content between a set of opening and closing tags (for example, the content between <body> and </body>). You must place the insertion point in the opening or closing tag and then click to collapse it.
	Collapse Selection	Collapses the selected code.
	Expand All	Restores all collapsed code.
	Select Parent Tag	Selects the content and surrounding opening and closing tags of the line in which you've placed the insertion point. If you repeatedly click this button, and your tags are balanced, Dreamweaver will eventually select the outermost <html> and </html> tags.
	Balance Braces	Selects the content and surrounding parentheses, braces, or square brackets of the line in which you've placed the insertion point. If you repeatedly click this button, and your surrounding symbols are balanced, Dreamweaver will eventually select the outermost braces, parentheses, or brackets in the document.
	Line Numbers	Hides or shows numbers at the beginning of each line of code.
	Highlight Invalid Code	Highlights invalid code in yellow.
	Word Wrap	Changes the Word Wrap from Soft Wrap to Hard Wrap (or vice-versa)
	Syntax Error Alerts in Info Bar	Enables or disables an information bar at the top of the page that alerts you to syntax errors. When Dreamweaver detects a syntax error, the Syntax Error Information bar specifies the line in the code where the error occurs. Additionally, Dreamweaver highlights the error's line number on the left side of the document in Code view. The info bar is enabled by default, but only appears when Dreamweaver detects syntax errors in the page.

342 Introduction to Adobe Dreamweaver CS6 with ACA Certification

Lesson **3**

Understanding hyperlinks

3. Press the Live button located in the Document toolbar at the top of your page as seen in Figure 3-9. You will not see a dramatic difference, but your text may shift slightly. Select the first heading in the window and try to delete it; you will be unable to, because Live View is a non-editable workspace. However, Live View does allow you to edit your page when you are in Split view. Here, you are allowed to edit in the Code view and changes will be reflected in real time. An additional advantage is that your document does not have to be saved in order to see the changes.

Figure 3-9: When Live View is enabled, Dreamweaver simulates a web browser.

4. Click the Live button again to deactivate this view. While Live View is a useful addition to Dreamweaver, it does not replace the need to preview your page in a browser. Web pages might be rendered differently depending on your visitor's browser, and so it is a good habit to check your page occasionally as you make changes to your design.

Certification Ready 6.1
How do you preview a web page in a browser?

Take Note...
You can also preview your page designs in other browsers and for different platforms using Adobe's Browser Lab service. We cover the steps for this in Lesson 16," Managing your Website: Reports, Optimization, and Maintenance."

Understanding hyperlinks

When people visit a website, they usually expect to see more than one page. Imagine trying to shop for a new book by your favorite author on a site that consisted of nothing more than a single order form with every book offered by a retailer like *Amazon.com*. This might seem absurd, but without hyperlinks you wouldn't have much choice.

Hyperlinks make the Web a truly interactive environment. They allow the user to freely navigate throughout a website, or jump from one site to another. There are a number of ways to create links in Dreamweaver, but before you get started, you should be aware of some fundamental facts.

Links rely on directory paths to locate files. A directory path is simply a description of a file's location that can be understood by a computer. A classic, real-world example is an address. If you wanted to send a letter to your friend Sally in Florida, you would have to specify the state, city, street, and house number where Sally can be found. If Sally lived at 123 Palm Street in Orlando, the path would be:

Florida/Orlando/123 Palm Street/Sally

Lesson 3: Adding Text and Images 83

Learning More

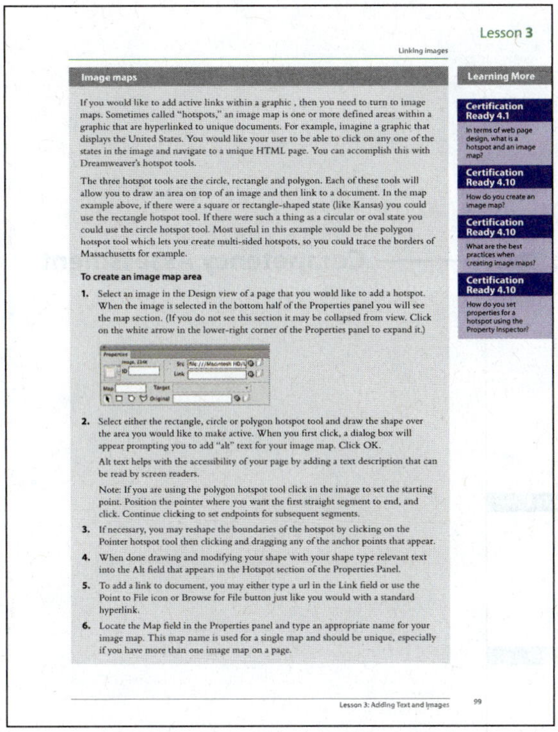

Lesson 3

Linking images

Image maps

If you would like to add active links within a graphic , then you need to turn to image maps. Sometimes called "hotspots," an image map is one or more defined areas within a graphic that are hyperlinked to unique documents. For example, imagine a graphic that displays the United States. You would like your user to be able to click on any one of the states in the image and navigate to a unique HTML page. You can accomplish this with Dreamweaver's hotspot tools.

The three hotspot tools are the circle, rectangle and polygon. Each of these tools will allow you to draw an area on top of an image and then link to a document. In the map example above, if there were a square or rectangle-shaped state (like Kansas) you could use the rectangle hotspot tool. If there were such a thing as a circular or oval state you could use the circle hotspot tool. Most useful in this example would be the polygon hotspot tool which lets you create multi-sided hotspots, so you could trace the borders of Massachusetts for example.

To create an image map area

1. Select an image in the Design view of a page that you would like to add a hotspot. When the image is selected in the bottom half of the Properties panel you will see the map section. (If you do not see this section it may be collapsed from view. Click on the white arrow in the lower-right corner of the Properties panel to expand it.)
2. Select either the rectangle, circle or polygon hotspot tool and draw the shape over the area you would like to make active. When you first click, a dialog box will appear prompting you to add "alt" text for your image map. Click OK.

   Alt text helps with the accessibility of your page by adding a text description that can be read by screen readers.

   Note: If you are using the polygon hotspot tool click in the image to set the starting point. Position the pointer where you want the first straight segment to end, and click. Continue clicking to set endpoints for subsequent segments.
3. If necessary, you may reshape the boundaries of the hotspot by clicking on the Pointer hotspot tool then clicking and dragging any of the anchor points that appear.
4. When done drawing and modifying your shape with your shape type relevant text into the Alt field that appears in the Hotspot section of the Properties Panel.
5. To add a link to document, you may either type a url in the Link field or use the Point to File icon or Browse for File button just like you would with a standard hyperlink.
6. Locate the Map field in the Properties panel and type an appropriate name for your image map. This map name is used for a single map and should be unique, especially if you have more than one image map on a page.

Learning More

Certification Ready 4.1
In terms of web page design, what is a hotspot and an image map?

Certification Ready 4.10
How do you create an image map?

Certification Ready 4.10
What are the best practices when creating image maps?

Certification Ready 4.10
How do you set properties for a hotspot using the Property Inspector?

Lesson 3: Adding Text and Images 99

Lesson 3

Skill Summary

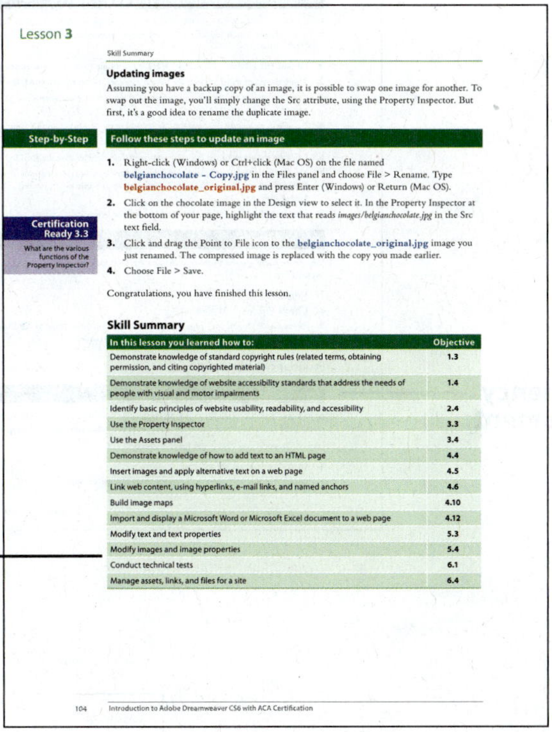

Updating images

Assuming you have a backup copy of an image, it is possible to swap one image for another. To swap out the image, you'll simply change the Src attribute, using the Property Inspector. But first, it's a good idea to rename the duplicate image.

Step-by-Step

Follow these steps to update an image

1. Right-click (Windows) or Ctrl+click (Mac OS) on the file named **belgianchocolate - Copy.jpg** in the Files panel and choose File > Rename. Type **belgianchocolate_original.jpg** and press Enter (Windows) or Return (Mac OS).
2. Click on the chocolate image in the Design view to select it. In the Property Inspector at the bottom of your page, highlight the text that reads *images/belgianchocolate.jpg* in the Src text field.
3. Click and drag the Point to File icon to the **belgianchocolate_original.jpg** image you just renamed. The compressed image is replaced with the copy you made earlier.
4. Choose File > Save.

Certification Ready 3.3
What are the various functions of the Property Inspector?

Congratulations, you have finished this lesson.

Skill Summary

Skill Summary

In this lesson you learned how to:	Objective
Demonstrate knowledge of standard copyright rules (related terms, obtaining permission, and citing copyrighted material)	1.3
Demonstrate knowledge of website accessibility standards that address the needs of people with visual and motor impairments	1.4
Identify basic principles of website usability, readability, and accessibility	2.4
Use the Property Inspector	3.3
Use the Assets panel	3.4
Demonstrate knowledge of how to add text to an HTML page	4.4
Insert images and apply alternative text on a web page	4.5
Link web content, using hyperlinks, e-mail links, and named anchors	4.6
Build image maps	4.10
Import and display a Microsoft Word or Microsoft Excel document to a web page	4.12
Modify text and text properties	5.3
Modify images and image properties	5.4
Conduct technical tests	6.1
Manage assets, links, and files for a site	6.4

104 Introduction to Adobe Dreamweaver CS6 with ACA Certification

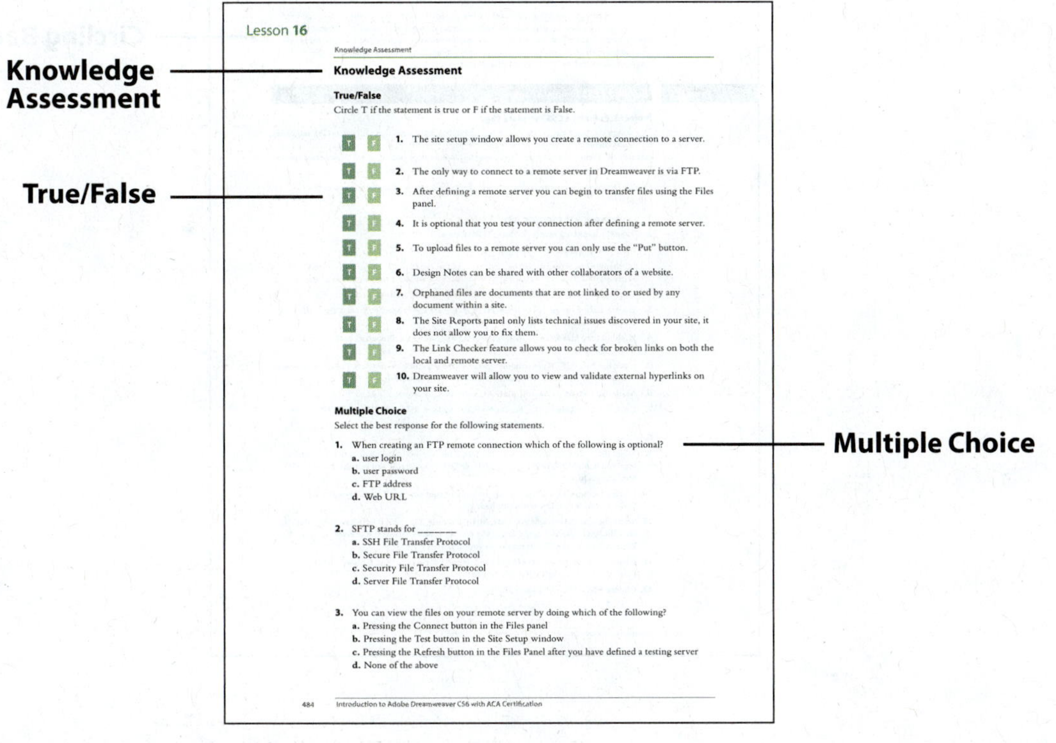
Knowledge Assessment

True/False

Lesson 16

Knowledge Assessment

Knowledge Assessment

True/False

Circle T if the statement is true or F if the statement is False.

T F 1. The site setup window allows you create a remote connection to a server.

T F 2. The only way to connect to a remote server in Dreamweaver is via FTP.

T F 3. After defining a remote server you can begin to transfer files using the Files panel.

T F 4. It is optional that you test your connection after defining a remote server.

T F 5. To upload files to a remote server you can only use the "Put" button.

T F 6. Design Notes can be shared with other collaborators of a website.

T F 7. Orphaned files are documents that are not linked to or used by any document within a site.

T F 8. The Site Reports panel only lists technical issues discovered in your site, it does not allow you to fix them.

T F 9. The Link Checker feature allows you to check for broken links on both the local and remote server.

T F 10. Dreamweaver will allow you to view and validate external hyperlinks on your site.

Multiple Choice

Select the best response for the following statements.

1. When creating an FTP remote connection which of the following is optional?
   a. user login
   b. user password
   c. FTP address
   d. Web URL
2. SFTP stands for ________
   a. SSH File Transfer Protocol
   b. Secure File Transfer Protocol
   c. Security File Transfer Protocol
   d. Server File Transfer Protocol
3. You can view the files on your remote server by doing which of the following?
   a. Pressing the Connect button in the Files panel
   b. Pressing the Test button in the Site Setup window
   c. Pressing the Refresh button in the Files Panel after you have defined a testing server
   d. None of the above

484 Introduction to Adobe Dreamweaver CS6 with ACA Certification

Multiple Choice

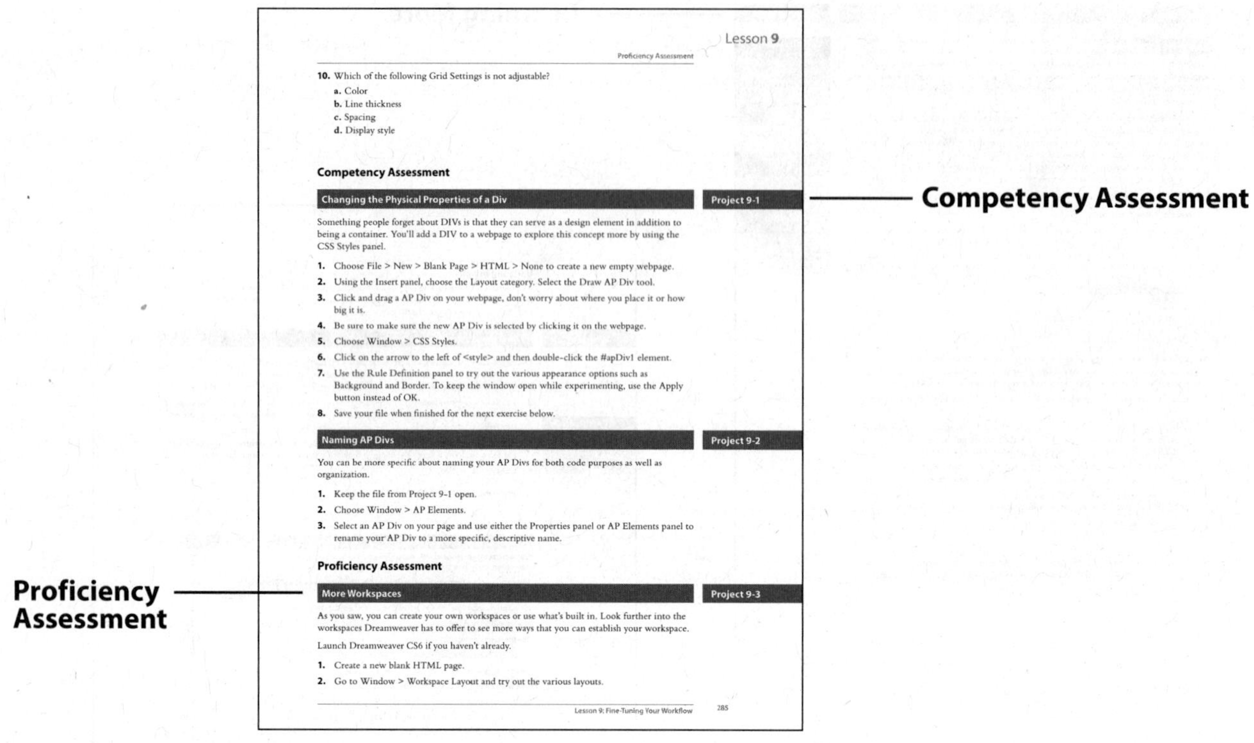
Lesson 9

Proficiency Assessment

10. Which of the following Grid Settings is not adjustable?
   a. Color
   b. Line thickness
   c. Spacing
   d. Display style

Competency Assessment

Changing the Physical Properties of a Div — **Project 9-1**

Something people forget about DIVs is that they can serve as a design element in addition to being a container. You'll add a DIV to a webpage to explore this concept more by using the CSS Styles panel.

1. Choose File > New > Blank Page > HTML > None to create a new empty webpage.
2. Using the Insert panel, choose the Layout category. Select the Draw AP Div tool.
3. Click and drag a AP Div on your webpage, don't worry about where you place it or how big it is.
4. Be sure to make sure the new AP Div is selected by clicking it on the webpage.
5. Choose Window > CSS Styles.
6. Click on the arrow to the left of <style> and then double-click the #apDiv1 element.
7. Use the Rule Definition panel to try out the various appearance options such as Background and Border. To keep the window open while experimenting, use the Apply button instead of OK.
8. Save your file when finished for the next exercise below.

Naming AP Divs — **Project 9-2**

You can be more specific about naming your AP Divs for both code purposes as well as organization.

1. Keep the file from Project 9-1 open.
2. Choose Window > AP Elements.
3. Select an AP Div on your page and use either the Properties panel or AP Elements panel to rename your AP Div to a more specific, descriptive name.

Proficiency Assessment

More Workspaces — **Project 9-3**

As you saw, you can create your own workspaces or use what's built in. Look further into the workspaces Dreamweaver has to offer to see more ways that you can establish your workspace.

Launch Dreamweaver CS6 if you haven't already.

1. Create a new blank HTML page.
2. Go to Window > Workspace Layout and try out the various layouts.

Lesson 9: Fine-Tuning Your Workflow 285

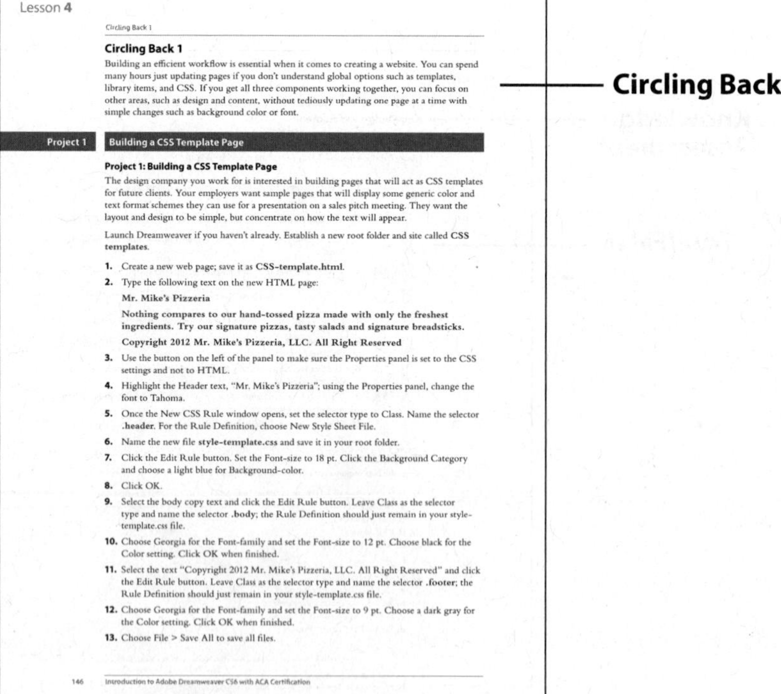
Lesson 4

Circling Back 1

Circling Back 1

Building an efficient workflow is essential when it comes to creating a website. You can spend many hours just updating pages if you don't understand global options such as templates, library items, and CSS. If you get all three components working together, you can focus on other areas, such as design and content, without tediously updating one page at a time with simple changes such as background color or font.

Project 1 — **Building a CSS Template Page**

Project 1: Building a CSS Template Page

The design company you work for is interested in building pages that will act as CSS templates for future clients. Your employers want sample pages that will display some generic color and text format schemes they can use for a presentation on a sales pitch meeting. They want the layout and design to be simple, but concentrate on how the text will appear.

Launch Dreamweaver if you haven't already. Establish a new root folder and site called **CSS templates**.

1. Create a new web page; save it as **CSS-template.html**.
2. Type the following text on the new HTML page:
   Mr. Mike's Pizzeria
   Nothing compares to our hand-tossed pizza made with only the freshest ingredients. Try our signature pizzas, tasty salads and signature breadsticks.
   Copyright 2012 Mr. Mike's Pizzeria, LLC. All Right Reserved
3. Use the button on the left of the panel to make sure the Properties panel is set to the CSS settings and not to HTML.
4. Highlight the Header text, "Mr. Mike's Pizzeria"; using the Properties panel, change the font to Tahoma.
5. Once the New CSS Rule window opens, set the selector type to Class. Name the selector **.header**. For the Rule Definition, choose New Style Sheet File.
6. Name the new file **style-template.css** and save it in your root folder.
7. Click the Edit Rule button. Set the Font-size to 18 pt. Click the Background Category and choose a light blue for Background-color.
8. Click OK.
9. Select the body copy text and click the Edit Rule button. Leave Class as the selector type and name the selector **.body**; the Rule Definition should just remain in your style-template.css file.
10. Choose Georgia for the Font-family and set the Font-size to 12 pt. Choose black for the Color setting. Click OK when finished.
11. Select the text "Copyright 2012 Mr. Mike's Pizzeria, LLC. All Right Reserved" and click the Edit Rule button. Leave Class as the selector type and name the selector **.footer**; the Rule Definition should just remain in your style-template.css file.
12. Choose Georgia for the Font-family and set the Font-size to 9 pt. Choose a dark gray for the Color setting. Click OK when finished.
13. Choose File > Save All to save all files.

146 Introduction to Adobe Dreamweaver CS6 with ACA Certification

Conventions and Features Used in This Book

This book uses particular fonts, symbols, and heading conventions to highlight important information or to call your attention to special steps. For more information about the features in each lesson, refer to the Illustrated Book Tour section.

File > Open Text separated by the greater than symbol (>) indicates instructions for using a menu to perform a task—with the first item indicating the menu to use and the second item indicating the menu choice. If the menu includes additional choices, more than one greater than symbol will be used to indicate the additional choices, such as File > Open > Recent Documents.

Certification Ready 3.1

Identify and label elements of the Dreamweaver interface.

Certification Ready

This feature signals the point in the text where a specific certification objective is covered. It provides you with a chance to check your understanding of that particular ACA objective and, if necessary, review the section of the lesson where it is covered.

Take Note...

Take Note reader aids provide helpful hints related to particular tasks or topics. These notes, set in green shaded boxes, provide pointers to information discussed elsewhere in the textbook or describe interesting features that are not directly addressed in the current topic or exercise.

ALT+Tab

A plus sign (+) between two key names means that you must press both keys at the same time. Keys that you are instructed to press in an exercise will appear in the font shown here.

Key Terms

Key terms appear in green.

Type My Name is

Any text you are asked to type on the keyboard appears in red.

BasicHTML.html

The names of data files will appear in blue for easy identification.

Instructor Support Program

Wiley's Adobe courseware program is accompanied by a rich array of resources that incorporate the extensive textbook visuals to form a pedagogically cohesive package. These resources provide all the materials instructors need to deploy and deliver their courses. The following resources are available online for download.

- The **Instructor's Guide** contains solutions to all the textbook exercises as well as chapter summaries and lecture notes. The Instructor's Guide and Syllabi for various term lengths are available from the Instructor's Book Companion Site (*http://www.wiley.com/college/sc/adobeseries*).
- The **Solution Files** for all the projects in the book are available online from our Instructor's Book Companion Site (*http://www.wiley.com/college/sc/adobeseries*).
- A complete set of **PowerPoint Presentations** is available on the Instructor's Book Companion Site (*http://www.wiley.com/college/sc/adobeseries*) to enhance classroom presentations. Tailored to the text's topical coverage and Skills Matrix, these presentations are designed to convey key Adobe Dreamweaver concepts addressed in the text.

  All images from the text are on the Instructor's Book Companion Site (*http://www.wiley.com/college/sc/adobeseries*). You can incorporate them into your PowerPoint presentations or create your own overhead transparencies and handouts.

  By using these visuals in class discussions, you can help focus students' attention on key elements of Dreamweaver and help them understand how to use it effectively in the workplace.
- The **Student Data Files** are available online on both the Instructor's Book Companion Site and for students on the Student Book Companion Site.
- To create a **complete certification solution**, this textbook can be bundled with Adobe Certified Associate exam vouchers and/or ACA practice tests from Certiport—available as a single bundle from Wiley. Providing your students with the ACA exam voucher is the ultimate workforce preparation.
- When it comes to improving the classroom experience, there is no better source of ideas and inspiration than your fellow colleagues. The **Wiley Faculty Network** connects teachers with technology, facilitates the exchange of best practices, and helps to enhance instructional efficiency and effectiveness. Faculty Network activities include technology training and tutorials, virtual seminars, peer-to-peer exchanges of experiences and ideas, personal consulting, and sharing of resources. For details, visit *www.WhereFacultyConnect.com*.

Wiley Faculty Network

VIDEO TUTORIALS

The Introduction to Dreamweaver CS6 textbook comes with access to approximately two hours of online video tutorials that accompany each lesson in the book. These video tutorials are designed to help your students to better understand certain topics covered within each lesson. The video tutorials do not replace the lessons and only cover select material the authors have selected to enhance the content being covered within the lesson. To obtain access to the video tutorials, go to *http://www.wiley.com/college/sc/adobeseries*.

Important Web Addresses and Phone Numbers

To locate the Wiley Higher Education Rep in your area, go to *www.wiley.com/college*, select Instructors under Resources & Events, and click on the Who's My Rep link, or call our toll-free number: 1+(888) 764-7001 (U.S. and Canada only).

Student Support Program

VIDEO TUTORIALS

Your Introduction to Dreamweaver CS6 textbook comes with access to approximately two hours of online video tutorials that accompany each lesson in the book. These video tutorials are accessible online and are hosted on Wiley Publishing's site. To obtain access to the video tutorials, go to *http://www.wiley.com/college/sc/adobeseries.* and search for Introduction to Dreamweaver. A broadband Internet connection is required to view the video tutorials.

Book Companion Website

The Students' Book Companion Site for this textbook (*http://www.wiley.com/college/sc/adobeseries*) includes any resources, exercise files, and web links that will be used in conjunction with this course.

Wiley Desktop Editions

Wiley Desktop Editions are innovative, electronic versions of printed textbooks. Students buy the desktop version for 50% off the U.S. price of the printed text and get the added value of permanence and portability. Wiley Desktop Editions provide students with numerous additional benefits that are not available with other e-text solutions.

Wiley Desktop Editions are NOT subscriptions; students download the Wiley Desktop Edition to their computer desktops. Students own the content they buy and keep it for as long as they want. Once a Wiley Desktop Edition is downloaded to the computer desktop, students have instant access to all of the content without being online. Students can also print the sections they prefer to read in hard copy. Students also have access to fully integrated resources within their Wiley Desktop Edition. From highlighting their e-text to taking and sharing notes, students can easily personalize their Wiley Desktop Edition as they are reading or following along in class.

CourseSmart

CourseSmart goes beyond traditional expectations providing instant, online access to the textbooks and course materials you need at a lower cost option. You can save time and hassle with a digital version of this book. The eTextbook option allows you to search for the most relevant content at the very moment you need it. To learn more go to: *www.coursesmart.com.*

WHY ACA CERTIFICATION?

The Adobe Certified Associate (ACA) credential has been upgraded to validate skills with the Adobe Creative Suite 6 system. The ACA certifications target information workers and cover the most popular business applications.

Adobe offers four areas in which to gain certification for entry-level skills: Web Communication using Adobe Dreamweaver, Rich Media Communication using Adobe Flash, Video Communication using Adobe Premiere Pro and Visual Communication using Adobe Photoshop. To learn more about becoming an Adobe Certified Associate and exam availability, visit *www.certiport.com/adobe.*

Preparing to Take an Exam

The workplace demand for digital media skills—creating, managing, integrating, and communicating information by using Adobe's dynamic multimedia, video, graphic, web, or design software—is on the rise. This new certification program will help educators effectively teach and validate digital communications skills while providing students with credentials that demonstrate real-world prowess to prospective employers.

What are the Benefits of Becoming Certified?

By certifying one's skills, individuals can validate their technical abilities and demonstrate proficiency. Adobe's associate-level certifications are based on research about digital communications skills required by industry, government, and education. The objectives reflect the foundation skills needed to be successful communicators in today's digital world.

In educational settings, industry-recognized certification programs ensure students and teachers are acquiring the knowledge and skills valued in today's workplace. For institutions seeking to keep curriculum vitalized and relevant, certification plays a critical role in bridging classroom learning to real-world application.

Preparing to Take an Exam

Unless you are a very experienced user, you will need to use a test preparation course to prepare for the test to complete it correctly and within the time allowed. Wiley's Adobe courseware is designed to prepare you with a strong knowledge of all exam topics. With some additional review and practice on your own, you should feel confident in your ability to pass the appropriate exam.

After you decide which exam to take, review the list of objectives for the exam. This list can be found in Appendix A at the back of this book. You can also easily identify tasks that are included in the objective list by locating the Lesson Skill Matrix at the start of each lesson and the Certification Ready sidebars in the margin of the lessons in this book.

To take the ACA test, visit *www.certiport.com/adobe* to locate your nearest testing center. Then call the testing center directly to schedule your test. The amount of advance notice you should provide will vary for different testing centers, and it typically depends on the number of computers available at the testing center, the number of other testers who have already been scheduled for the day on which you want to take the test, and the number of times per week that the testing center offers ACA testing. In general, you should call to schedule your test at least two weeks prior to the date on which you want to take the test.

When you arrive at the testing center, you might be asked for proof of identity. A driver's license or passport is an acceptable form of identification. If you do not have either of these items of documentation, call your testing center and ask what alternative forms of identification will be accepted. If you are retaking a test, bring your ACA identification number, which will have been given to you when you previously took the test. If you have not prepaid or if your organization has not already arranged to make payment for you, you will need to pay the test-taking fee when you arrive.

Test Format

All ACA certification tests are live, performance-based tests. There are no multiple-choice, true/false, or short-answer questions. Instructions are general: you are told the basic tasks to perform on the computer, but you aren't given any help in figuring out how to perform them. You are not permitted to use reference material other than the application's Help system.

Acknowledgments

Thank you to Nell Hurley, Tacy Trowbridge, Matt Niemitz, and Melissa Jones at Adobe for their encouragement and support in making this textbook the finest instructional materials for mastering the newest Adobe technologies for both students and instructors.

About the Author

Jeremy Osborn has more than 15 years of experience in Web and graphic design. He delivers training and professional development classes at American Graphics Institute. He is also the author of *HTML5 Digital Classroom* and the *Web Design with HTML and CSS* Digital Classroom, both published by Wiley. Jeremy holds an MS in Management from the Marlboro College Graduate Center and a BFA in Film/TV from Tisch School of the Arts at NYU.

Brief Contents

Contents

Contents

Lesson 5: Creating Page Layouts with CSS 149

Lesson 6: Advanced Page Layout 181

Lesson 8: Working with Tables 239

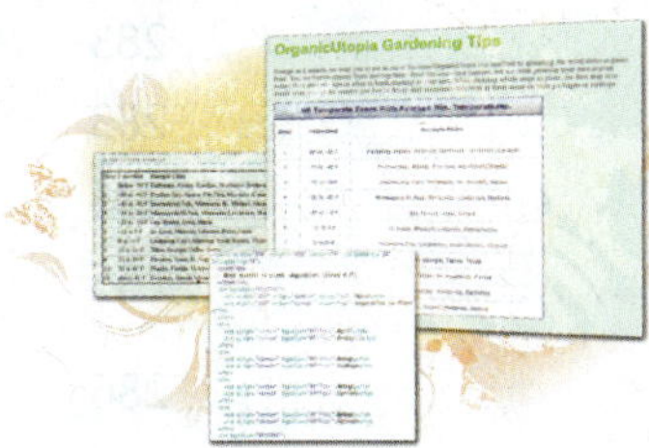

Lesson 9: Fine-Tuning Your Workflow 267

Contents

Lesson 13: Building Web Forms **355**

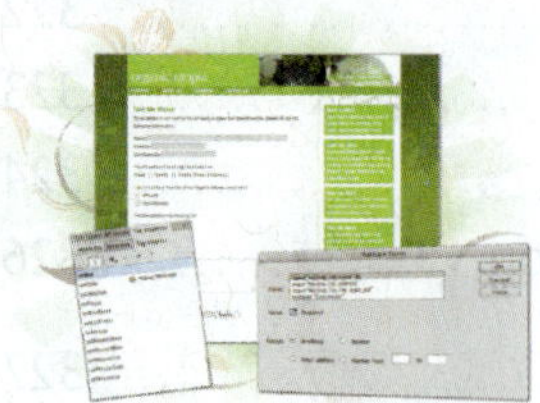

Lesson 14: Adding Interactivity with the Spry Framework 387

Lesson 15: Mobile Design and Layout 415

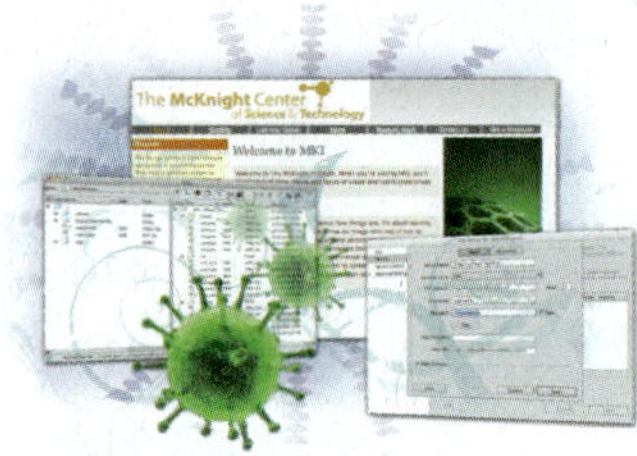

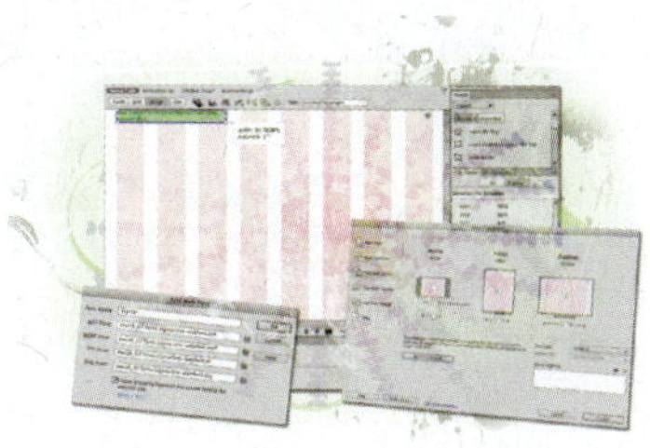

Dreamweaver CS6 Jumpstart

Key Terms

- Code Navigator
- Design
- HTML
- Live View
- markup language
- Server / Web Hosts
- Site Management
- Tag
- Workspace

Skill	Objective
Identify the purpose, audience, and audience needs for a website	1.1
Identify web page content that is relevant to the website purpose and appropriate for the target audience	1.2
Make website development decisions based on your analysis and interpretation of design specification	1.5
Understand project management tasks and responsibilities	1.6
Demonstrate general and Dreamweaver-specific knowledge of best practices for designing a website, such as maintaining consistency, separating content from design, using standard fonts, and utilizing visual hierarchy	2.1
Demonstrate knowledge of flowcharts, storyboards, and wireframes to create web pages and a site map that maintain the planned website hierarchy	2.5
Identify elements of the Dreamweaver interface	3.1
Use the Assets Panel	3.4
Create, title, name, and save a web page	4.3
Add text to a web page	4.4
Insert images and apply alternative text on a web page	4.5
Manage assets, links, and files for a site	6.4

Business Case

Organic Utopia is an organic food company that runs a small chain of supermarkets. It needs a website to advertise its services and products in order to gain exposure and compete with other stores of a similar nature. The owners at Organic Utopia want to display images of the company's food and provide more extensive information about the company itself, such as contact information, locations, and more. To better understand how to present these components on the website, you'll need to understand the basic overview to Dreamweaver's system.

Introduction

Before starting, make sure that your tools and panels are consistent by resetting your workspace. See "Resetting the Dreamweaver workspace" in the Starting Up section of this book.

Before you start, be sure to download the lesson files from *http://www.wiley.com/college/sc/adobeseries.*

You will work with several files from the dw01lessons folder in this lesson. Make sure that you have loaded the dwlessons folder onto your hard drive. See "Loading lesson files" in the Starting up section of this book.

Take Note...

If you want to get started and create a page, jump ahead to "Tag structure and attributes" later on in this lesson. Otherwise, the next few pages provide you with an overview of key capabilities and features of Dreamweaver CS6.

What is Dreamweaver?

Dreamweaver is an excellent web **design** and development tool for new and experienced users alike. Over the years it has become the preferred website creation and management program, providing a creative environment for both designers and developers. Whether you design websites, develop mobile phone content, or script complex server-side applications, Dreamweaver has something to offer.

Design and layout tools

Dreamweaver's many icon-driven menus and detailed panels such as the Insert panel (Figure 1-1) make it easy to insert and format text, images, and media (such as video files and Flash movies). This means that you can create attractive and functional web pages without knowing a single line of code—Dreamweaver takes care of building the code behind-the-scenes for you. Dreamweaver does not create graphics from scratch; instead, it is integrated with Adobe Photoshop CS6, so you can import and adjust graphics from within the application.

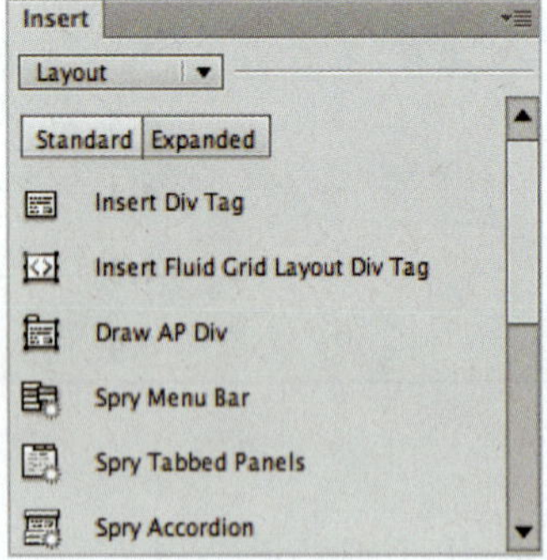

Figure 1-1: *The Insert panel features objects in several categories that let you easily add images, web forms, and media to your page.*

Site management and File Transfer Protocol

Dreamweaver has everything you need for complete **site management**, including built-in File Transfer Protocol (FTP) capabilities between a server and your local machine; reusable objects (such as page templates and library items); and site optimization tools (such as link checkers and site reports), so that you can ensure that your site functions properly and looks good. If you're designing your pages with Cascading Style Sheets (CSS), then the W3C Validation, the Browser Compatibility Check, and the CSS Advisor features will help you locate and troubleshoot any potential display issues that may occur across different web browsers.

Coding environment and text editor

Dreamweaver lets you work in a code-only view of your document (Figure 1-2) that acts as a powerful text editor. Features such as color-coding, indentation, and visual aids make Dreamweaver an excellent text editing or coding environment for web designers of any level.

```
<!DOCTYPE html PUBLIC "-//W3C//DTD XHTML 1.0 Transitional//EN"
"http://www.w3.org/TR/xhtml1/DTD/xhtml1-transitional.dtd">
<html xmlns="http://www.w3.org/1999/xhtml">
<head>
<meta http-equiv="Content-Type" content="text/html; charset=UTF-8" />
<title>Untitled Document</title>
<style type="text/css">
@import url("webfonts/plasdrip/stylesheet.css");
h1 {
    font-family: plasdrip;
    letter-spacing: .8em;
    font-weight: bolder;
    text-transform: uppercase;
    font-size: 118px;
}
</style>
</head>

<body>
<h1>Hello Jagger
</h1>
</body>
</html>
```

Figure 1-2: *Code view is a full-featured text editor that color-codes, tags, and scripts for editing that's easier to decipher.*

For more experienced developers, Dreamweaver supports popular coding and scripting languages, such as JavaScript, in addition to several server-side languages, including ColdFusion, PHP, and ASP.NET. Specialized insert menus and code panels help you build pages and applications in the language of your choice.

Take Note...

Scripting languages, such as those used to build interactive web pages or e-commerce sites, fall into two categories: client-side and server-side. Client-side languages (such as JavaScript) run in your browser, while server-side languages (such as ColdFusion) require that special software be installed on the server in order to run.

Mobile design and development features

The tools in Dreamweaver have evolved as the Web has evolved. The most recent versions of the application have numerous features designed to help make your website look and function well in the rapidly growing arena of mobile phones and devices. The Multiscreen Preview feature allows you to preview your pages in common screen sizes for smartphones and tablets and can be accessed by choosing Window > Multiscreen Preview (Figure 1-3).

Additionally, there is support for creating Media Queries, which are a CSS3 feature aimed at creating unique page layouts for different-sized screens. For more advanced users there is support for jQuery Mobile, which creates unique user interfaces for touchscreen devices. There is also support for creating native applications for iOS and Android operating systems with the new addition of the PhoneGap integration added in Dreamweaver CS6.

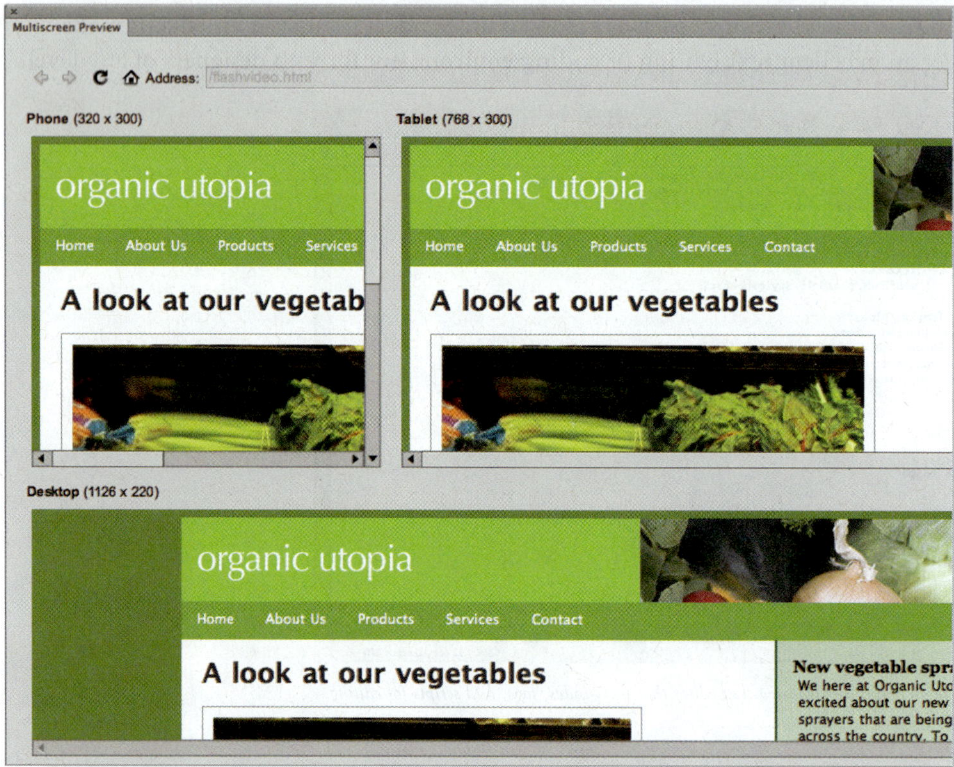

***Figure 1-3:** Multiscreen Preview allows you to test your pages in common screen sizes for mobile and other devices.*

Who uses Dreamweaver?

Dreamweaver's popularity is a result of its flexibility. Its ability to build a site from conception to launch—and provide continued maintenance afterward—makes it a preferred tool among industry professionals, businesses, and educational institutions. However, it remains easy and accessible enough for novice designers to get up-and-running quickly. It's not unusual to see Dreamweaver utilized for personal projects or by small businesses and media professionals, such as photographers and painters, to maintain a web presence.

Dreamweaver's workspace features

This book is dedicated to exploring, learning, and putting to use all that Dreamweaver has to offer. This section looks at some of the application's key features.

Four different points of view: When you work with a document, Dreamweaver lets you see your work in one of four views: Code, Split, Design, or Live view. Dreamweaver's default Design view lets you add elements to your page in a visual fashion, either by dragging objects onto the page from the Insert panel, or by directly adding text, image or multimedia content. More experienced web designers and coders can use the Code view to edit a document's **HTML** code and scripts directly, enhanced with easy-to-read color-coding and visual aids.

Certification Ready 3.1

What are the differences between Design view, Code view, Split view, and Live view?

For those who like something in between, the Split view provides a split-pane Design and Code view all at once as seen in Figure 1-4. You can easily change views at any time with a single click in the Document toolbar. The **Live view** is a type of "reality check" that allows you to view your page in a native web browser, eliminating the need to leave the program in order to preview your designs.

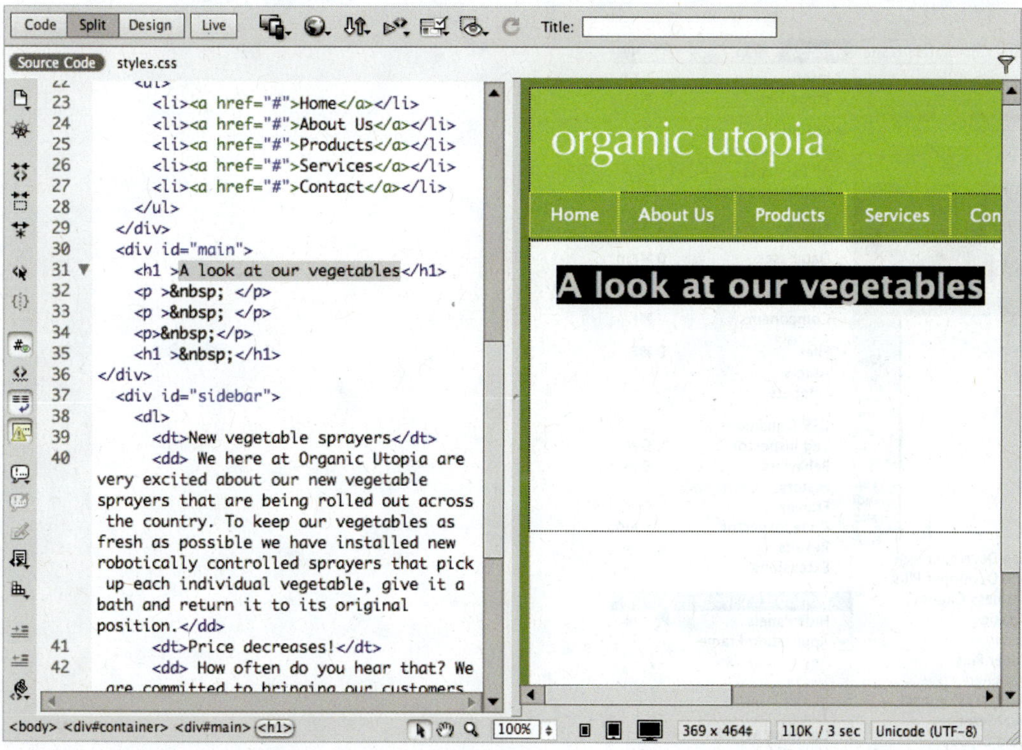

Figure 1-4: The Split view lets you edit your page visually while also seeing the code being created behind the scenes.

Built-in FTP: You can easily upload and download files to and from your web server using the Files panel's drag-and-drop interface. You can also use the Get/Put button at any time to post pages you're currently working on. In either case, there's no need for separate software. Dreamweaver also provides Check In/Check Out functionality and synchronization features; these allow multiple people to work more safely and efficiently on the same site.

Page and code object Insert panels: You can find intuitive icons for most common web page elements in a categorized Insert panel, from which you can add elements to your page with a single click. You can use additional panels to fine-tune any page element to ensure that you see exactly what you want. Included in the default Insert panel are tools for formatting text, building forms, and creating layouts. You can also customize a Favorites tab with your most-used icons.

Certification Ready 3.1

List six features of the Workspace Switcher.

Customizable workspace layouts: You can save combinations and positions of panels and toolbars for easy recall at any time. Save multiple **workspace** layouts for different users, or create different workspaces for specific tasks, such as coding or designing page layouts (Figure 1-5).

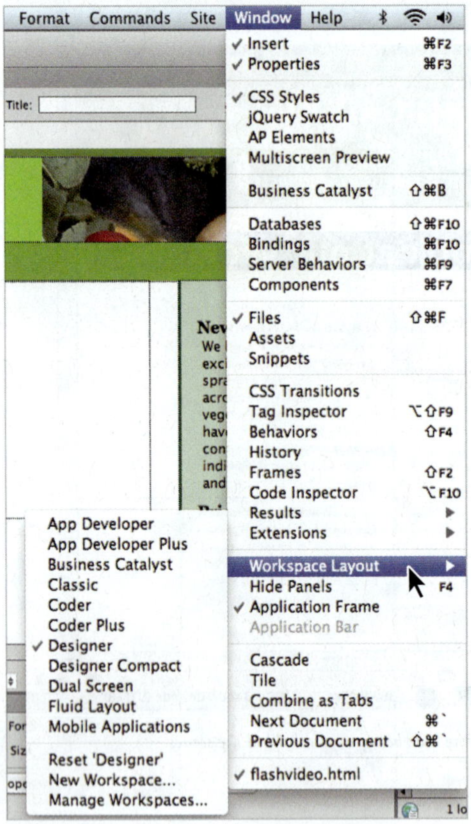

Figure 1-5*: You can choose a specific workspace layout in order to create an arrangement of panels that suits you best.*

Powerful visual aids: Take advantage of the precision you're accustomed to in other design programs through Dreamweaver's guides, rulers (Figure 1-6), measuring tools, and customizable positioning grid; many of these features are found and can be activated within the View menu. Dreamweaver's Design-Time style sheets let you customize the look of your page exclusively for the editing process, making layout quicker and easier without permanently altering the page's appearance.

***Figure 1-6**: Rulers, a document grid, and guides help you size and position page items with precision.*

CSS Styles panel: Take advantage of the vast design and formatting options that CSS provides through Dreamweaver's full-featured CSS Styles panel, which lets you create, edit, and manage styles on-the-fly from a single panel.

Certification Ready 3.4

What types of content can be accessed using the Assets panel?

The Assets Panel

Dreamweaver has an Assets Panel which can be accessed by clicking on the Assets tab or choosing Window > Assets. The Assets panel automatically catalogs different types of content and code from your site and allows you to easily locate and apply an asset by clicking and dragging or applying it. One example of how the Assets panel can be useful is colors. All colors that you use in a site are automatically listed in the Colors section, so if you would like to reuse a color that you have worked with previously it will automatically be available for you to apply.

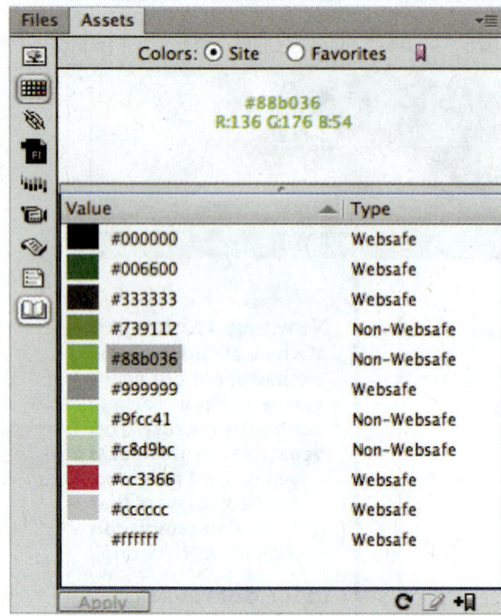

***Figure 1-7**: The Colors section of the Assets panel allows you to see colors used in a site and apply them to other objects.*

The Assets panel will allow you to access and reuse multiple types of content and code within your site (all of which you will learn more about throughout the book) including images, hyperlinks, Flash files, Shockwave movies, movie files, scripts, templates, and library items.

Live View and Live Code

Experience tells you that visual web editors often display differently than the browsers they're emulating. As script-driven interactivity gains popularity, the need to accurately design the different states of your page (including menus, panels, and interface elements), has become increasingly important. The static nature of the Design view in Dreamweaver often times does not meet users' advanced needs.

Dreamweaver's Live View mode (Figure 1-8) uses the WebKit rendering engine (which is also the basis for the Safari and Google Chrome web browsers), to give you a more accurate preview of your page in the same way that a browser would render it.

Figure 1-8: *Live View enables you to preview your page as if it were in a web browser.*

When you are in the Live View mode, the Live Code feature is enabled. Live Code allows you to see, in real time, how visually changing your page affects the code behind the scenes. If you have added interactive elements such as drop-down menus or accordion panels, then you can visually select an item on the page and see how the HTML code might be affected.

Also useful is the Freeze JavaScript button (or the F6 key). This feature freezes your page in a particular state (for example, with a menu locked open and a hover effect in place). You can then edit those interactive elements directly in Dreamweaver.

CSS Inspection and the Enable/Disable Feature

Another feature that is enabled when in Live View is the Inspect Mode. This mode allows users to peek at the visual model and structure of a page by hovering over elements on the page as seen in Figure 1-9. When hovering in Inspect Mode you can see the relationships between the HTML elements on your page and the styles assigned to them. This is useful because it dramatically shortens the time it takes to locate any given style for any given object on the page. However, when paired with the Enable/Disable feature, the Inspect Mode becomes even more powerful.

The Enable/Disable feature allows you to temporarily "turn off" an applied style on your page. This can be very useful when dealing with unfamiliar or complex designs where half the battle is simply understanding what styles are being used. Disabling a style will remove its properties so that you can visually observe the results. Keep in mind that disabling is always temporary, and that it is just as easy to restore the style by clicking Enable.

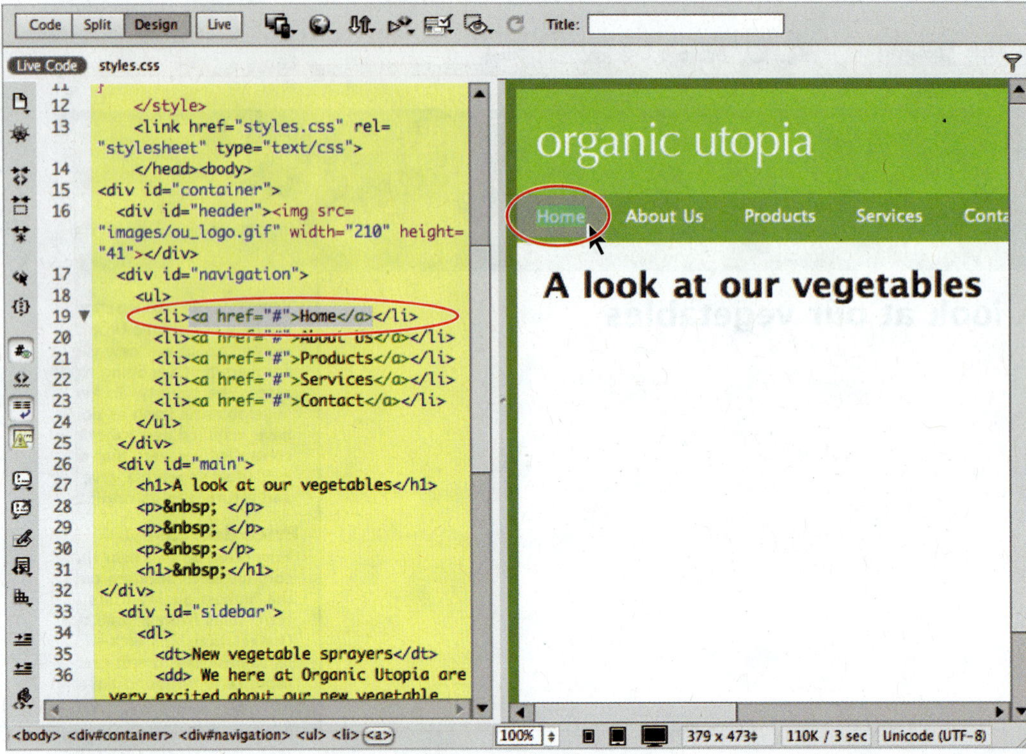

***Figure 1-9**: In the Inspect Mode, mousing over the elements in the Design view reveals the HTML and CSS code.*

Certification Ready 6.4

What is the Related Files toolbar used for?

Related files

Web-based projects are becoming more complex than ever before, and you often find that even a single page is composed of a variety of assets. These assets can include Cascading Style Sheets (CSS), external JavaScript files, and more. Dreamweaver CS6 has a feature that will help you become much more effective at designing and managing sites and applications with multiple assets.

The Related Files bar runs across the top of your document window, just below the document tabs as shown in Figure 1-10. The bar shows you all the various files that, when combined, create your finished page. You can switch between these files using the Related Files bar without losing the visual preview of their parent page. Design view (or Live View) always shows the parent file, but you can now edit any of the related files without losing their important visual context.

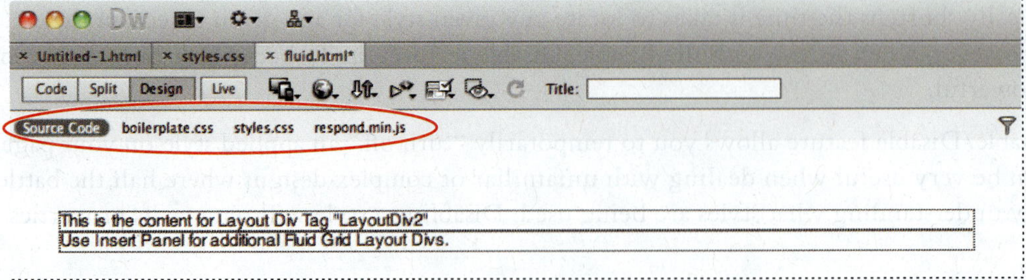

***Figure 1-10**: The Related Files bar shows you the various files that are part of your finished page.*

Code Navigator

The **Code Navigator** (✵) is a feature enabled in the Design view that appears when you hover over an element on the page. Clicking on the Navigator will let you see a quick summary of any CSS styles that have been applied (as seen in Figure 1-11), and if you choose to, you can click on the style in order to view the code directly. The benefit is that it is no longer necessary to manually hunt through your style sheets to find a specific rule; it's just a click away in Dreamweaver.

Certification Ready 3.1

What is the benefit of related files and the Code Navigator?

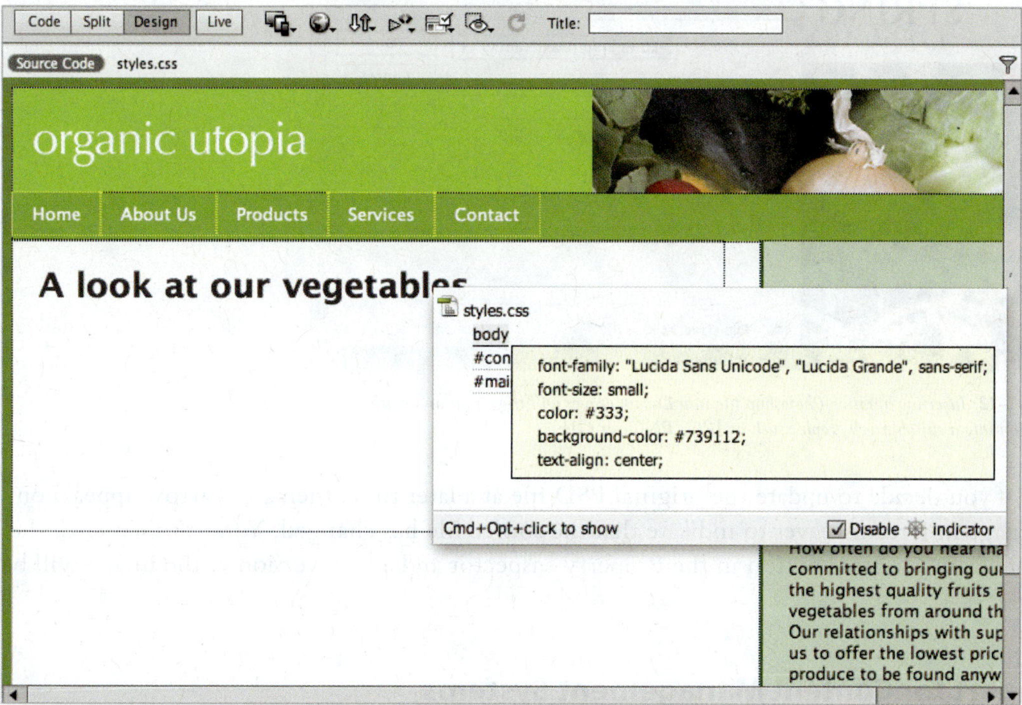

Figure 1-11: *The Code Navigator allows you to easily view the location and properties of your CSS styles in the Design View.*

Photoshop smart objects

Dreamweaver offers support for Photoshop smart objects, meaning you can drag a PSD file into a web page within Dreamweaver, optimize the image for the Web (as seen in Figure 1-12), and even resize it.

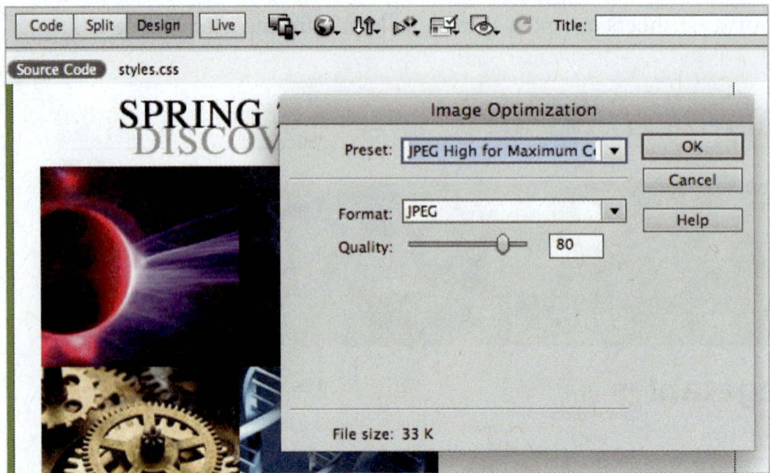

***Figure 1-12**: Inserting a native Photoshop file into Dreamweaver will trigger an automatic conversion into a suitable web graphic such as JPG, PNG, or GIF.*

Also, if you decide to update the original PSD file at a later time, then a red arrow appears on the image in Dreamweaver to indicate that the source file has changed. You can then click the Update from Original button in the Property Inspector and a new version of the image will be created.

Support for Content Management Systems

Enjoy authoring and testing support for content management systems like WordPress, Joomla! and Drupal. A CMS/blog software like WordPress provides users with an easy way to publish content online and has features such as automatic archiving and database integration. In the past, designers have been frustrated with creating the page designs for a CMS using Dreamweaver because these systems generally rely on a relatively complex combination of dynamic pages (often PHP) that could not be previewed in Dreamweaver. For designers or users who are not code-savvy, the complexity of these files can be daunting. Dreamweaver can now help you discover the related files needed to put together the pages in your CMS framework.

Dreamweaver does this by previewing the files of a CMS framework in the Design view (as long as you have a testing server defined), using the built-in Live View option. With this feature, Dreamweaver CS6 also lets you interact directly with a database, which means you can now test online forms, insert and modify database records, and more.

HTML5, CSS3, and PHP code hinting

For advanced users, there is now built in code-hinting support for HTML5 and CSS3 syntax as seen in Figure 1-13. This means the “library” of HTML and CSS syntax that is now available within Dreamweaver is larger than ever, which is a good sign for those designers and developers who need to build modern web pages.

Additionally, advanced users who use the scripting language PHP will be happy to learn that Dreamweaver CS6 now has improved support for PHP syntax. This includes code completion and syntax checking, as well as full support for all core functions, constants, and classes. PHP code hints have also been improved substantially.

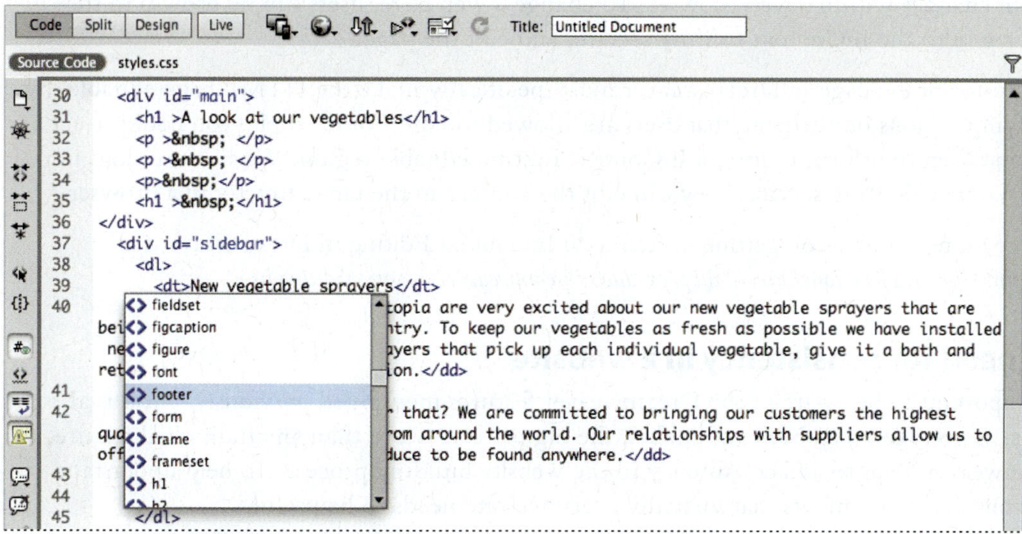

Figure 1-13: Dreamweaver provides support for HTML5, CSS3, and PHP code-hinting.

HTML and CSS Starter Pages

HTML and CSS Starter Pages have been around in Dreamweaver for a few versions now. These pages allow you to get a jumpstart on building page layouts by choosing from a variety of pre-built page layouts that you can subsequently modify. In Dreamweaver CS6, the code for these starter pages is new and improved for modern web browsers and comes with plenty of code commenting behind the scenes to help you start modifying your pages quickly. You can view starter pages by choosing File > New. The Layout column features a number of page layouts. CSS starter pages can also be found by clicking on the Page From Sample button.

Subversion

Dreamweaver has improved support for Subversion, a version control system similar to CVS and Visual SourceSafe (VSS). Subversion is typically used by companies to maintain a team environment on larger projects that require changes to be logged and versions to be controlled. Without Subversion, if you wanted to maintain versions, you would have to do the work yourself by maintaining folders and copies of previous versions. With Subversion, all files are kept on the Subversion server. Changes are tracked so that you can restore your project to any previous state. Subversion is enabled by choosing Site > New Site (or Site > Manage Sites), choosing Version Control and then clicking the Access menu and choosing Subversion.

Business Catalyst integration

Adobe's Business Catalyst is an online service that provides a variety of features such as online store/shopping cart capabilities, e-mail marketing, web form functionality, analytics extension, and more. With the Business Catalyst extension in Dreamweaver you can log-in to Business Catalyst and synchronize multiple sites at once. Dreamweaver can be used to access and edit the style module used on your Business Catalyst connected sites.

Certification Ready 4.5

What is the purpose and benefits to using InContext Editing?

InContext Editing

InContext Editing is another feature of Business Catalyst that allows any user to make simple content changes within a web browser. To change a web page, users simply browse to the page, log in to the InContext Editing service, and edit the page.

The creator of the page in Dreamweaver must specifically make the HTML page editable by specifying regions on the page that users are allowed to edit. For example, you could select a table and then transform it into an InContext Editing editable region. When a user logs into the InContext Editing service, they can edit the content in the table directly in a browser.

- For more resources on getting started with InContext Editing in Dreamweaver see *http://www.adobe.com/accessibility/products/dreamweaver/incontextediting.html*

The need for consistency in a website

It is important to be aware of the Dreamweaver features mentioned previously, but it is also important to take a step back and look at the big picture. More than any individual feature, Dreamweaver helps to add consistency to the website building process. To help understand this, consider the elements that virtually every website needs to be useful.

- **Consistent Page Layout**

When a visitor to a website navigates from page to page, there is an expectation that the layout remains the same. Of course there will be differences in appearance based on page content, but in general, aspects such as the height and width of columns should not change without reason.

- **Consistent navigation and user interface**

Users also expect the behavior, appearance and functionality of a website to be consistent. For example, a navigation link to the "Contact" section that works on one page but not another is very disconcerting and frustrating to a user. Any interactive elements such as buttons, menus, or accordion panels should act as expected and have a consistent look.

- **Consistent page color, text and link appearance**

In a similar fashion to layout and navigation, users can be thrown off or distracted when they navigate from one page to another and elements such as font size and color are suddenly different.

How Dreamweaver improves consistency

One of the main ways Dreamweaver can help prevent these issues is with the use of style sheets and, in particular, external style sheets. With an external style sheet you can define the rules for page layout (and other styles) in one single document. With proper use of a style sheet, the components of a page are defined in one central location and page layout, fonts, navigation and color all use a single set of style rules, thereby ensuring consistency.

Certification Ready 2.1

What are the attributes of a website that demonstrate consistency?

Certification Ready 2.1

What techniques are used to maintain consistency when building a website?

There are other features within Dreamweaver that can help your sites become more consistent:

- **Snippets, Library Items and Templates**

Dreamweaver has three features that can help you reuse components within your site. Snippets are small sections of code that you may want to reuse from page to page such as a table or a copyright notice. Library Items are similar to Snippets in that they are reusable, but unlike Snippets (which once placed on a page have no connection to the original) Library Items that you place on a page maintain a relationship with the original, allowing you to update multiple instances with a single change. Templates take the concept of reusability to the ultimate level and allow you to link multiple pages to one single master.

- **The Assets panel**

All websites have a collection of items that are constantly reused, such as colors, images, and links. The Assets panel collects many of these items automatically for you for to reuse. For example, instead of having to define that you want to save a particular color, Dreamweaver automatically scans your site for hexadecimal color code and stores it for you. Other categories in the Assets panel include media files such as video and Flash, scripts, library items, and templates.

Identifying your websites purpose, audience and audience needs

Certification Ready 1.1

What information determines purpose, audience and audience needs for a website?

When designing a website, an important question to ask is, "Why does this website need to exist?" It seems strange but a client might not be able to tell you exactly why they want a website. The answer, "Because everyone else has one," is not a good enough answer.

Imagine a carpenter who is hired by a homeowner to build a "structure" in their backyard, with little information provided about the final project. The carpenter needs to know the purpose of the structure. Do they want a shed? A bandstand? A garage? Just as structures have different purposes, so do websites. As a designer you should be able to define, or have the client define, the goal of the website in a simple sentence. For example, in this book, you will be designing a site called OrganicUtopia, a store that sells organic fruits and vegetables and has the following goal:

> *Help current and potential customers learn why they should shop at OrganicUtopia and to promote a healthy lifestyle.*

Although the designer may not have defined this objective, she can certainly contribute to the conversation. Here are some of the questions that might arise in discussing the functionality and design of such a site:

- Will the site be free? If yes, will there be advertising and is that something the designer needs to include in the layout?
- Is there a target audience in mind for the site and if so what is the typical occupation, sex, education, residence, race and computer literacy of this audience?
- What, if any, user interactions might there be on site. For example, can users submit recipes or simply browse existing ones?

In larger organizations, these conversations might also involve web developers, who would be responsible for any database functionality, along with the marketing department, the sales department, and other interested stakeholders. Even if these discussions take place before you, the designer, are brought into the project, you will want to have a good understanding of the goals of a website before you start any design work.

Certification Ready 1.2

How do you determine whether content is relevant to a website's purpose?

Certification Ready 1.2

How do you determine whether content is appropriate for the target audience?

Is your content relevant?

After defining the purpose of the site as well as the typical profile of a visitor, it is important to spend time thinking about, creating and organizing content. A web designer or developer is often more than just an "architect." Just as an architect needs to have a sense of what are good materials and bad materials, so must the designer and developer have a sense of what makes content work on the Web. You need to be able to communicate these concepts to a client. Here are some criteria for deciding whether content is relevant and/or appropriate for a website and its audience.

- **Page content should serve a single specific purpose**

When a user is on a page, they often know exactly what they are looking for. Whether they are reading an article, looking for a product, or trying to get in touch with you, your pages should contain content designed to serve a specific purpose

- **Content must be helpful and of practical use**

Too often, the creators of a website publish content without taking into consideration the context of the user and the format of the web. A good example of this is the press release. Press releases have been a standard tool for many years for distributing information about a new product or other notable aspects of a business. However, a press release is often not targeted toward customers but toward the media. (When is the last time you read a press release from beginning to end?) Consider the format you are delivering your content in. Are there hyperlinks to external sites? Could some or all the content be delivered as a chart, graph or even a video?

- **Organize your content**

It has been demonstrated that visitors to a website are more likely to scan a website rather than read every word. You can organize data by dividing it into chunks and using headings, subheadings, lists, tables, and images.

- **Sentence structure, grammar and typographical errors**

If a visitor notices basic writing errors in content, they will be under the impression that you don't care or not trustworthy. Evaluate if your sentences are clear and bring value to your message. Even reading copy out loud can uncover problems that can remain hidden onscreen. Many business websites have copywriters and proofreaders for a reason; you or your client may benefit from using a professional who can help shape your content.

Certification Ready 1.5

What is the relationship between end-user requirements and design and development decisions?

Certification Ready 1.5

What page elements are affected by end-user technical factors?

Making Design and Development decisions

Understanding the features of Dreamweaver is one thing, but understanding the needs of your users and how that will affect the design and development of your website is another. Before you begin work on your site, you should take some time to consider how your end-user's requirements could affect the decisions you make. The following items are some of the variables you need to take into account when designing a website:

- **Download Speed**

Although the rise of broadband Internet connections has been steadily increasing across the world, you need to take into account the experience of users who may not have the fastest connections. Although desktop connections may be getting faster, keep in mind that the rise of mobile web browsing means that the slower connection speed for mobile devices plays an important part. Many designers assign a limit on the total file size for an individual page. A conservative limit would be 100k per page; this excludes content that is high-bandwidth such as video.

- **Screen Resolution**

The number of screen sizes on the market is as wide as it has ever been, from small mobile screens (320 × 480 pixels) to large, high-resolution monitors (1920 × 1080 pixels and higher). Users are beginning to expect websites to function well at any size, and while there are technical solutions such as Dreamweaver's Fluid Grid layout, it is important that you decide which screen sizes you would like to target and start from there.

- **Support for JavaScript, plug-ins and multimedia**

Many modern web pages have features that are dependent on JavaScript and/or browser plugins such as Flash. You need consider the possibility of what happens in the scenario where the user does not have these features. It will be different for every technology; for example JavaScript is enabled by default in the majority of web browsers, even so, you should consider the scenario in which it is turned off or not functioning. Can your site still function without it? Is there some sort of fallback? Consider the role of Flash, a browser plug-in. Flash and Flash video is supported in more than 95% of all desktop browsers, but in the mobile browser landscape it is not supported in iOS (iPhone and iPad). Therefore, your mobile audience will have a drastically different experience unless you have some sort of fallback in place.

Project Management

Whether you are a single person responsible for an entire site from design to launch or part of a larger team, you should have a sense of the stages involved in the creation of a website and how long these stages last. Web design doesn't happen in a vacuum, there are usually clients involved and these clients have expectations. One way to define any project is to look at the following three variables; time, budget, and scope and think about how they are related.

- **Time**

Projects have deadlines, and for the sake of simplicity, let's consider the final deadline to be defined as the public launch of a site. Of course, throughout the evolution of a website there might be other deadlines, such a deadline for final designs, a deadline for all content to be approved, a deadline for final site navigation, and more.

- **Scope**

Scope is not only the size of a website (measured in page count) but also the type of features that are included. "Scope creep" is a phenomenon that occurs in many projects in which new features are requested or sometimes emerge for various reasons. For example, a client might suddenly ask for a calendar feature on their website. Designers, developers, and project managers generally expect some level of scope creep on a project and try to manage it as best as possible.

- **Budget**

Money and resources are an unavoidable part of the equation. No client has an unlimited budget; and expectations on the size and scope of a project are often related to the budget on hand.

As you may have guessed, these three variables are interconnected. For example, if the deadline for the launch of a site is fixed and a new feature is requested at the last minute, then we can imagine two scenarios: 1.) The budget needs to increase (because now those designers are working 12 hours a day until launch time to get things done!) 2.) If the budget is fixed (as well as the deadline) then the scope has to decrease, perhaps a certain feature is dropped and the time that is now freed-up is applied to the new calendar feature.

Learning More

Certification Ready 1.6

Identify deliverables that might be produced during the project.

The role of "deliverables"

The term "deliverables" is one that every web designer and developer should be familiar with. In general, deliverables are all the assets that you agree to create and hand over to your client (or another part of a team). Deliverables will include the final website, but often include other documentation or material in the earlier stages of a project. Examples of deliverables might include a site map, wireframes, a flow diagram, mockups, and a specification document describing one or more pages on a site. Although deliverables are more commonly associated with larger projects with multiple members on a team, they could easily be associated with a smaller project. For example, a solo web designer might create a simple one page website for a client. In addition to delivering and building the site, one of the deliverables would include a text document that includes the web hosting information (e.g., user name and password) as well as instructions that would allow the client to be able to update the site on their own. Defining deliverables is a crucial step at the beginning of a project, and is designed to ensure that everyone involved has a single point of reference to rely on.

Certification Ready 1.6

What items may appear on a project plan?

Certification Ready 1.6

What phases may appear on a project plan?

Certification Ready 1.6

What are common problems and issues in project management?

Project Phases

There will obviously be differences between small projects and large-scale ones, but there are still some commonalities worth discussing:

- **Defining a project plan**

Projects that are delivered on-time, on-budget and with all the requested features usually have had a solid project plan in place. A project plan might include clearly assigning tasks and responsibilities to various members of a team, assigning due dates and allocating resources (such as making sure machines are available for browser testing). In larger organizations, this role might fall upon a single person (appropriately known as a "project manager"). In smaller organizations, this role might also be the designer or another member of the team.

- **Planning and analysis**

All websites should have a reason for existing and serve the needs for one or more sets of users. The creator of a site should have a very good sense of this before moving further. Try to define the goal of a website in a single sentence, you may find this harder than you expect! Research and analysis into the needs of users is also crucial at this stage. Looking at any competing or similar websites is a natural and helpful thing to do, however be cautious of defining a goal that is not truly yours (or your clients').

- **Designing**

Designing a site does not mean opening Dreamweaver and beginning to create your pages. Typically, you might start the design process with a sketch. It is fast and easy to present a sketch to a client or team member and receive feedback which will help the design of the site evolve. Mockups are another tool to consider, a mockup might be a single page done in a program such as Photoshop, and attempts to convey color, type, and layout without moving into the realm of HTML and CSS yet.

- **Building**

The main subject of this book, the building of a site, involves organizing all the available content such as text and images into HTML (or a scripting language such as PHP), CSS and perhaps JavaScript. Additionally, a logical and usable navigation system (often referred to as information architecture) is needed.

- **Testing**

All sites should undergo a testing process before launch. Again, the amount of testing will vary depending on the scope of the project. Common tests include: checking a site for broken hyperlinks or images, checking page appearance on multiple browsers and platforms, checking for accessibility and readability. (There is also usability testing, which is best done toward the beginning or middle of a site's development cycle, not the end. Usability testing is a separate process that involves gathering feedback from unique users in order to help identify problems with site features or site goals).

- **Site launching and maintenance**

Site deployment (or "launching") is the final step and involves transferring site documents from a local or network system to a final destination or URL. Care must be taken here not to break site functionality or appearance during this transfer process. This can happen by forgetting assets such as style sheets, images or any other necessary document.

Flowcharts, storyboards and wireframes

There are important stages in the design process you should complete before writing a single line of HTML or CSS. If you begin designing visuals or building pages before you are prepared, you may end up discarding your original work. By using flowcharts, storyboards, and wireframes you can explore different design options and functionality quickly (and therefore less costly). Whether or not you use all three models generally depends on the size of the project. Larger projects that incorporate complicated elements, such as connection to a database, or use multiple features, will benefit from using all three models.

Certification Ready 2.5

What are flowcharts and why are they useful?

Certification Ready 2.5

What are storyboards and why are they useful?

Certification Ready 2.5

What are some items that appear on a website design storyboard?

Certification Ready 2.5

What are wireframes and why are they useful?

Flowcharts

Flowcharts provide a visual overview of how your website is organized. A flowchart does not attempt to document every single page in a site, it is more concerned with illustrating the primary navigation within a site as well as the relationships of pages. The term primary navigation relates to the hierarchy of a site. Hierarchy can be defined as the level of importance you assign to specific pages. For example, if you define the home page as the most important page, what is the second most important page? Or are there multiple pages with equal importance? This process of defining the hierarchy of pages as well the navigation of a site is often referred to as information architecture.

Flowcharts quickly and easily communicate the structure of a site to clients or other members on your team. Visually, you create a flowchart by creating boxes that represent pages (or collections of pages) and visually linking them together with lines. Depending on the size of your project, a flowchart could be as simple as a sketch on a notepad, or created in a program such as Visio or even Adobe Illustrator or InDesign.

Storyboards

Flowcharts abstractly illustrate a site's hierarchy and navigation, but say nothing about the content on the pages. Storyboards help you focus on the content on a page as well as provide a way to fine-tune your navigation and site structure. A storyboard consists of multiple pages based on those defined in the flowchart. Each storyboard is then filled out with navigation, a list of related links, a functional description of the page, images, text and some notes on content for that page. Although the storyboard is focusing on content it is not focused on design or page layout, this is traditionally the role of the wireframe discussed next.

A storyboard could be created by hand as a sketch or diagram, but is more often done digitally. Many people will choose to use Dreamweaver to create very basic HTML pages that function as storyboards although you could also use other applications such as Illustrator or InDesign.

Wireframes

The goal of a wireframe is to take you one step closer to your HTML and CSS designs but without committing to design decisions such as images, colors, and fonts. Wireframes are typically created in black and white or shades of gray, using placeholders. At this stage, organization of the content and the features of the site are still a priority, the goal is to allow time for feedback from clients or other members involved with the project. It is still easy to add or remove features to a site at this stage and much less expensive than when the site is in the process of being built!

Programs such as Adobe Fireworks allow you to quickly build interactive wireframes using a set of standard text and image placeholders as well as other common elements such as form controls, buttons, or video players.

Certification Ready 2.5

How can you determine whether or not a website followed the planned website hierarchy?

Testing your website's hierarchy

At the wireframe stage, it is possible that your original flowchart needs to be updated due to changes you discovered along the way. It is also possible that you may have strayed from your original hierarchy, perhaps by dropping or modifying elements in your navigation bar or other changes. You can always compare the flowchart to the wireframe and make sure pages are reflected but another way to determine if the planned hierarchy is being followed is by adding an element of interactivity. For example, by making working links in your navigation menus, you can confirm that your site navigation is logical and that a user can reach all pages from any other page or that no page becomes "orphaned." An orphaned page is a document that exists in your website but has no incoming links. At any point in the site-building process Dreamweaver can check for orphan pages by checking a site for broken links.

Take Note...

Checking a site for broken links is covered in Lesson 16 "Managing your Website: Reports, Optimization, and Maintenance."

How websites work

Before embarking on the task of building web pages (and in turn, a website), it's a good idea to know the basics of how websites work, how your users view them, and what you need to know to make sure your website functions and looks its best.

A simple flow chart

What happens when you type in a website address? Most people don't even think about it—they just type in a URL (Uniform Resource Locator) and the website appears. They most likely don't realize how many things are going on behind the scenes to make sure that pages gets delivered to their computer so that they can do their shopping, check their e-mail, or research a project.

When you type a URL or IP address in the address bar of a web browser, you are connecting to a remote computer (called a server), and downloading the documents, images, and resources necessary to render the pages you will view while on the site. Web pages aren't delivered as a finished product; your web browser is responsible for reconstructing and formatting the pages based on the HTML code included within the pages. HTML (Hypertext Markup Language) is a simple, tag-based language that instructs your browser how and where to insert and format pictures, text, and media files. Web pages are written in HTML, and Dreamweaver builds the HTML as you construct your page in the Design view.

An Internet Service Provider (ISP) enables you to connect to the Internet. Some well-known ISPs include Verizon, Comcast, and EarthLink. You view web pages over an Internet connection using a browser, such as Internet Explorer, Firefox, or Safari. A browser can decipher and display web pages and their content, including images, text, and video.

Domain names and IP addresses

When you type in a website address, you usually enter the website's domain name (such as *Wiley.com*). The website owner purchased this domain name and uses it to mask an IP address, which is a numerical address used to locate and dial up the pages and files associated with a specific website.

So how does the Web know what domains match up with what IP address, and in turn, with what websites? It uses a Domain Name Service (DNS) server, which makes connections between domain names and IP addresses.

Servers and web hosts

A DNS server is responsible for matching a domain name with its companion IP address. Think of the DNS server as the operator at a phone company who connects calls through a massive switchboard. DNS servers are typically maintained by either the web host or the registrar from which the domain was purchased. Once the match is made, the request from your user is routed to the appropriate server and folder where your website resides. When the request reaches the correct account, the server then directs it to the first page of the website, which is typically named index.html, default.html, or whatever the server is set up to recognize as a default starting page.

A **server** is a machine very much like your desktop computer, but it's capable of handling traffic from thousands of users (often at the same time!), and it maintains a constant connection to the Internet so that your website is available 24 hours a day. Servers are typically maintained by a web host. **Web hosts** are companies that charge a fee to host and serve your website to the public. A single server can sometimes host hundreds of websites. Web hosting services are available from a variety of providers, including well-known Internet service companies such as Yahoo!, and other large, dedicated hosting companies. It is also common for a large company to maintain its own servers and websites on its premises.

The role of web browsers

A web browser is an application that downloads and displays HTML pages. Every time you request a page by clicking a link or typing in a website address you are requesting an HTML page and any files that it includes. The browser's job is to reconstruct and display that page based on the instructions in the HTML code, which guides the layout and formatting of the text, images, and other assets used within the page. The HTML code works like a set of assembly instructions for the browser to use.

An introduction to HTML

HTML is what makes the Web work; web pages are built using HTML code, which in turn is read and used by your web browser to lay out and format text, images, and video on the page. As you design and lay out web pages in Design view, Dreamweaver writes the code behind the scenes that is necessary to display and format your page in a web browser.

Contrary to what you may think, HTML is not a programming language, but rather a simple text-based **markup language**. A markup language is a system for annotating (marking up) a document in syntax that is different than the plain text. HTML uses **tags**, or bracketed keywords, in order to format page content such as text or images. An example of a tag would be <p> which is the paragraph tag. Many tags also require a closing tag, which is the keyword preceded by a forward slash (/), for example </p>. HTML is not proprietary to Dreamweaver—you can create and edit HTML in any text editor, even in simple applications such as Windows Notepad and Mac OS X's TextEdit. Dreamweaver's job is to give you a visual way to create web pages without having to code by hand. If you like to work with code, however, Dreamweaver's Code view is a fully featured text editor with color-coding and formatting tools that make it easier to write and read HTML and other languages.

XHTML 1.0 Transitional

The language of HTML has continued to evolve over the years and there are a few different page types currently in use. Unless you specifically change it, the default page type that Dreamweaver creates is named XHTML 1.0 Transitional. To keep things simple for now, think of XHTML (which was introduced around the year 2000), as a stricter version of the

HTML language that was used to build the first web pages in the 1990s, when the Web was first created (for now, we'll refer to this as HTML 4.0, although the technical details are a bit more complicated). XHTML was designed to make web pages more compatible with newer platforms, such as mobile phones and handheld devices. XHTML combines elements of HTML and XML, a language used to describe data. XML, or Extensible Markup Language, has become a popular method of exchanging information among seemingly unrelated applications, platforms, and systems.

What's the difference?

The difference between HTML 4.0 and XHTML is not terribly dramatic. The structure of the language changes somewhat with XHTML in that it becomes stricter. Whereas HTML 4.0 was very forgiving of coding practices such as overlapping or unclosed tags, XHTML requires that all tags be closed and properly nested. HTML 4.0 doesn't care which case you use when constructing tags, but in XHTML, all tags must be lowercase.

Here's an example of how HTML and XHTML might differ. The break element is used to push or "break" content to the next line on a page. In HTML, you can do this by simply adding the opening tag `<br>`. In XHTML, all opening tags must also have a closing tag. The long way to do this would be `<br></br>`. However, there is special syntax in XHTML that lets you get away with less code, and this syntax is called self-closing. You can write tags to *self-close* by using a forward slash—making sure there is a space between the `br` and the forward slash—and then closing the bracket like so:

```
<br />
```

The result is a well-formed language that takes advantage of newer browsers and device platforms, while remaining compatible with older browsers. As noted previously, working with XHTML in Dreamweaver requires nothing more than creating a new page.

What about HTML5?

In 2004, a group of representatives from browser manufacturers, such as Opera, Mozilla, and Apple, and a group of working web developers formed an independent group called the WHATWG (Web Hypertext Application Technology Working Group). Their mission was to create a better HTML markup specification, designed to build the new type of web application without breaking backwards compatibility with existing browsers.

The term "HTML5" has grown to cover a number of developing web technologies such as CSS3, JavaScript as well as a number of related technologies such as Geolocation, Canvas, and Offline Storage. The use of HTML5 for mobile applications and websites has become particularly popular, since for many websites the ability to present multimedia can best be accomplished with the HTML5 `<video>` and `<audio>` tags. In fact HTML5 markup introduces several new tags designed to make the structure of a web page more logical. The most important of these new elements include `<footer>`, `<nav>`, `<section>`, `<aside>`, and `<article>` as well as other new elements that play a less important role such as `<hgroup>` and `<wbr>`. These new tags are aimed at making page layout more organized, standardized, and efficient for designers and developers.

Learning More

Certification Ready 4.1

What is the difference between HTML1.x, HTML4 and HTML5?

Certification Ready 4.1

What are some HTML5 capabilities?

Tag structure and attributes

This exercise is for users who are completely new to HTML and Dreamweaver, and it will cover basic concepts such as the role of tags in HTML documents. Tags in HTML define how the content on the page is presented.

Step-by-Step

Follow these steps to create a CSS rule

1. Launch Dreamweaver. Choose File > Open. When the Open dialog box appears, navigate to the dw01lessons folder. Select **BasicHTML.html** and press Open.
2. Select the Split button in the Document toolbar to see the layout as well as the code that makes up the page.

   In Figure 1-14 take a look at line 10 (indicated at the left edge of the Code panel). The text *My Bold Title* is inside a Strong tag, which is simply the word *strong* contained within angled brackets. Any words or characters inside these tags are formatted in bold, and appear as shown in the Design view.

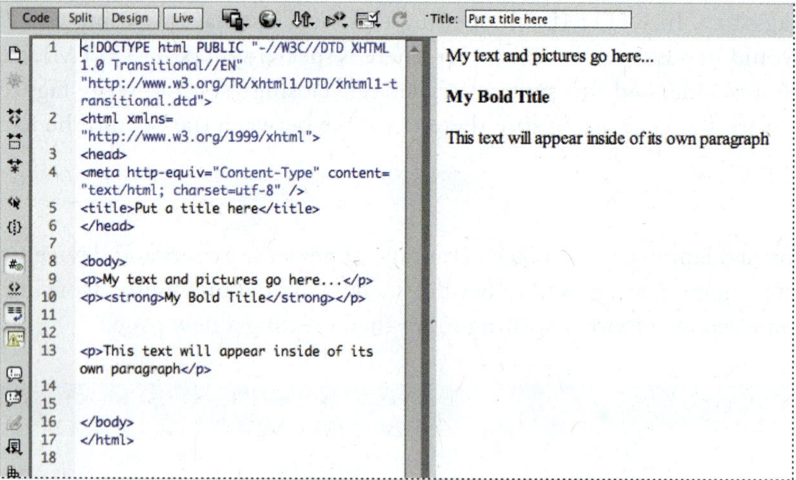

Figure 1-14: *A look at the code reveals the tags used to format text in your page.*

Tags can also accept CSS rules that specify additional information for how the tag should display the content. CSS rules may have one or more properties, such as size, color, or alignment. Take a look at the line that reads: *This text will appear inside of its own paragraph.* This line is enclosed in a *p* (paragraph) tag, which separates it from the other text by a line above and below. You can add a CSS class rule to this to align the text.

3. Highlight the entire line that reads: *This text will appear inside of its own paragraph* at the bottom of the Design view.

4. With the CSS button selected in the Property Inspector panel at the bottom of the page, locate the paragraph align buttons. Press the Align Center button (≣).

5. In the New CSS Rule dialog box seen here in Figure 1-15, type **.center** into the Selector Name text field, and press OK.

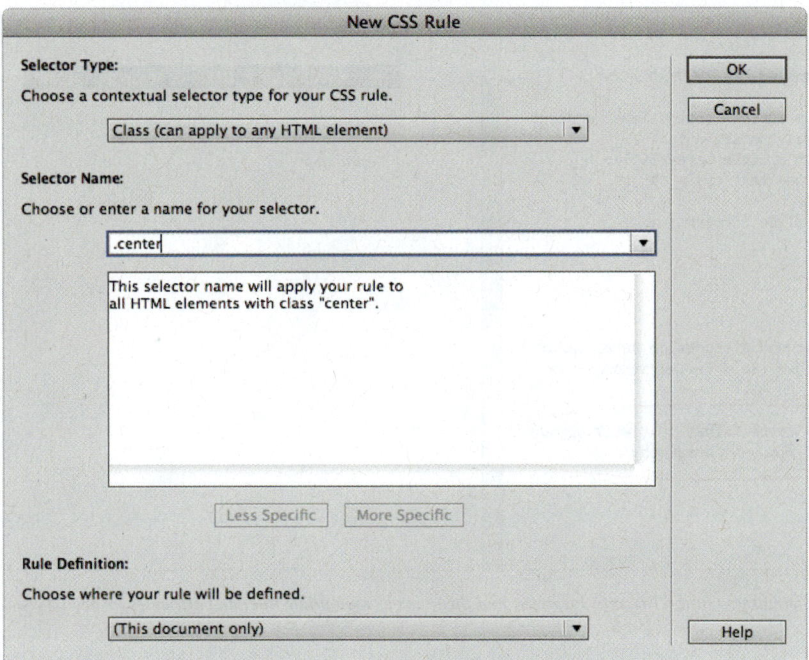

***Figure 1-15**: Name a newly created style in the New CSS Rule dialog box.*

6. The text is now centered. Take a look at the Code view as seen in Figure 1-16, and notice that the .center rule has been added to the opening <p> tag. This is not the only method of centering a paragraph using CSS, but it begins to introduce you to the practice of integrating HTML and CSS.

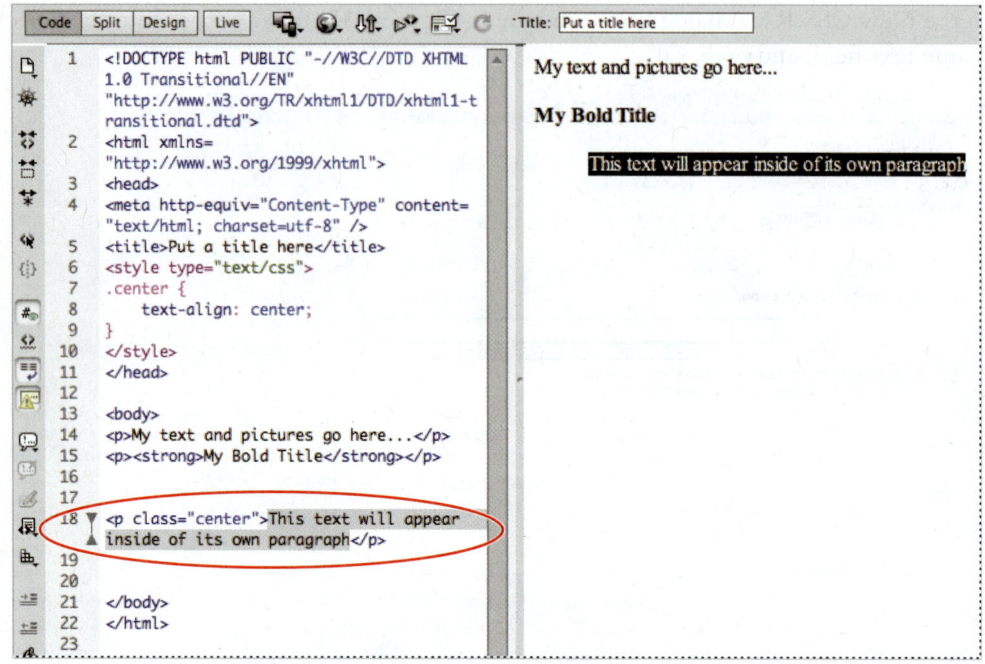

Figure 1-16: Align or format text in the Property Inspector, and then see the appropriate rules and attributes created in your code.

Take Note...

For more information on formatting text with CSS rules, please see Lesson 3, "Adding Text and Images."

7. Choose File > Save to save your work, then choose File > Close.

Certification Ready 2.1

What features in Dreamweaver are used to maintain page structure and content hierarchy?

The structure of an HTML document

In HTML a pair of tags is referred to as an "element." For example, in the last exercise you created a style for one of the paragraph elements on the page. HTML elements define the structure of a page as well as the content hierarchy (importance) and examples include headings, lists, images, tables, formatting such as the strong, small, and em tags and even the HTML documents themselves. The HTML element is the most fundamental element you will use. It is used to specify the beginning and end of HTML in a document:

```
<html></html>
```

The HTML element consists of two tags that contain two key sections of your web page: the head and the body. The head element of your page contains items that are not visible to your user, but are important nonetheless. Search engine keywords, page descriptions, and links to outside scripts or style sheets are all found in the head element. You create the head of the document inside the HTML tags using the <head> tags:

```
<html>
<head></head>
</html>
```

The body of your page is where all the visible elements of your page are contained. This is where you insert text, images, and other media. You define the body of the page using the <body> element:

```
<html>
    <head></head>
        <body>

            My text and pictures go here...

        </body>
<html>
```

Whenever you create a new HTML document in Dreamweaver, this structure is created automatically before you add anything to the page. Any visual elements you add to the page are added, using the appropriate HTML code inside the <body> element.

Placing images in HTML

You use some elements in HTML to place items, such as pictures or media files, inside a web page. The <img> element is the most common example; its job is to place and format an image on the page. To place an image and see the resulting code, follow these steps:

Follow these steps to place an image

Step-by-Step

1. Choose File > Open. When the Open dialog box appears, navigate to the dw01lessons folder. Select the **Images.html** file and press Open to edit the file.
2. As seen in Figure 1-17, click the Split button in the Document toolbar so that you're viewing both the layout and the code for your page. In the Design view portion of the Split view, click below the line of text to place your cursor underneath it. This is where you'll place a new image.

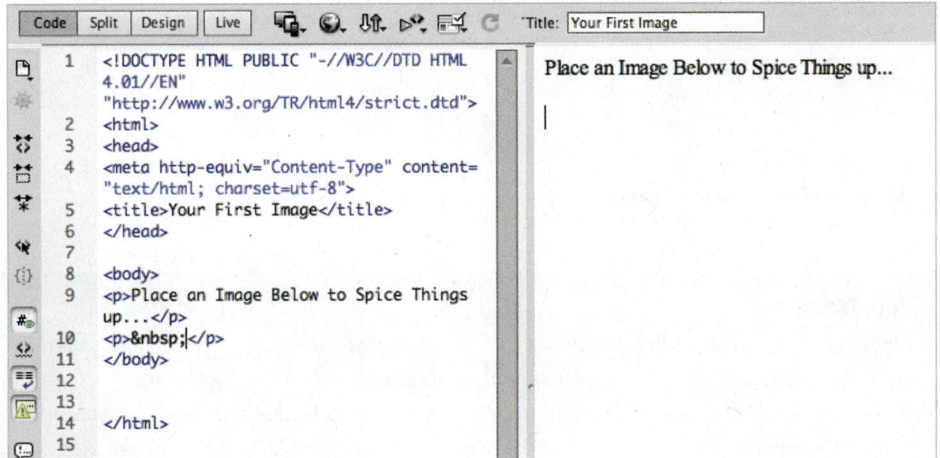

Figure 1-17*: Enter the Split view before you insert the image onto your page.*

3. From the Common category in the Insert panel on the right side of the screen as seen in Figure 1-18, click on the Images element and choose Image. When the Select Image Source dialog box appears, select the file named **gears.jpg**, located in the images folder within the dw01lessons folder and press OK (Windows) or Choose (Mac OS).

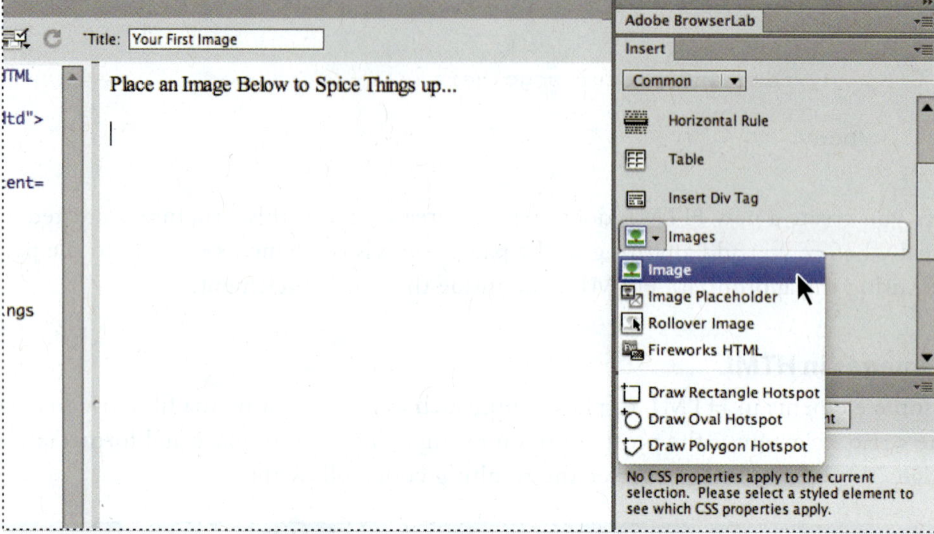

***Figure 1-18**: Choose Image from the Common tab in the Insert bar.*

4. When the Image Tag Accessibility Attributes dialog box appears as seen in Figure 1-19, type the words **Gears Image** in the Alternate text field, and press OK to place the image.

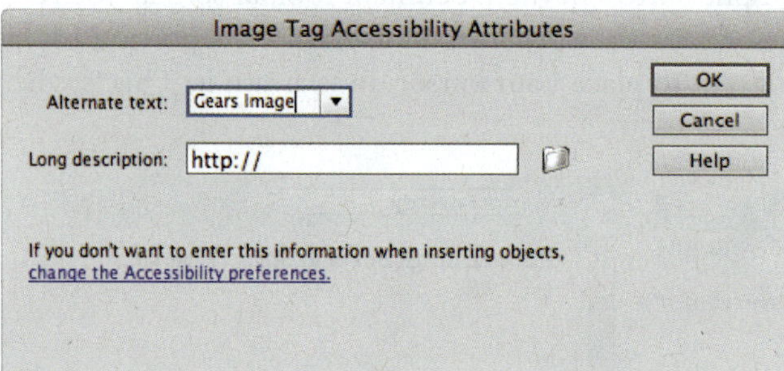

***Figure 1-19**: Attach alternate text to your image.*

Take Note...

The Image Tag Accessibility Attributes dialog box appears when you add images to provide additional information for users with special needs (such as the visually impaired). You should always provide each image with alternate text, but you can disable this panel by choosing Edit > Preferences (Windows) or Dreamweaver > Preferences (Mac OS). In the Accessibility category, uncheck the Images *option.*

5. The code shows that the HTML <img> element has been used to place the image. Click once on the image in the document window to select it. The Property Inspector at the bottom of the page displays and sets the properties for the image.
6. Choose File > Save to save your work, then choose File > Close.

   Note that in HTML, images and media are not embedded, but placed. This means that the elements contain additional information known as attributes, and values that point to the location of an image file, and may even contain other information such as the width and height values.

Colors in HTML

Certification Ready 3.1

Identify and label elements of the Dreamweaver interface.

In Dreamweaver's various panels and in your code, each color is referred to by a six-character code preceded by a pound sign. This code is called the hexadecimal code, and it is the system that HTML pages use to identify and use colors. You can reproduce almost any color using a unique hexadecimal code. For example, a lime green hexadecimal color is `#9F3` as seen in Figure 1-20.

The first, middle, and last two digits of the hexadecimal code correspond to values in the RGB spectrum. For instance, white, which is represented in RGB as R:255 G:255 B:255, is represented in HTML as `#FFFFFF` (255|255|255). Choosing colors is easy, thanks to a handy Swatches panel, which you can find in many places throughout the work area.

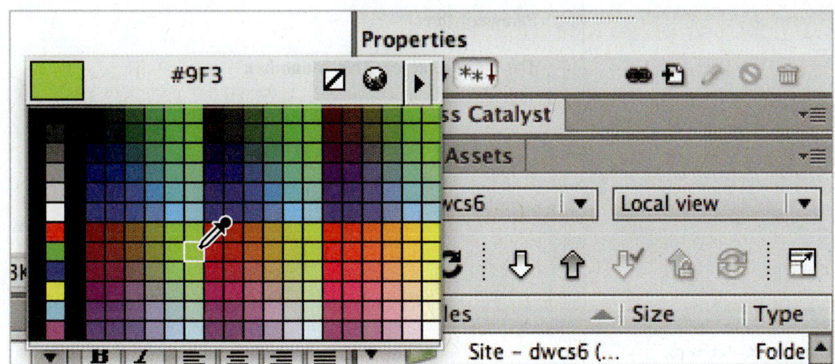

***Figure 1-20**: The Swatches panel makes it easy to work with colors.*

Take Note...

The color pickers in Adobe Photoshop and Illustrator also display and accept hexadecimal codes, making it easy to copy and paste colors between these applications and Dreamweaver.

Case sensitivity and whitespace rules

HTML is a flexible language that has very few rules regarding its own appearance. Based on how strictly you want to write it, HTML can be either very specific about whether tags are written in upper- or lowercase (called case sensitivity), or not specific at all. To see how HTML treats whitespace, follow these steps.

Step-by-Step

Certification Ready 4.4

What is the effect of pressing Return and pressing Shift+Return when typing text on an HTML page?

Follow these steps to see how HTML treats whitespace

1. Choose File > Open. When the Open dialog box appears, navigate to the dw01lessons folder. Select the **Whitespace.html** file, and then press Open.
2. If your file is not in Split view, press the Split button in the Document toolbar at the top of the page, so that you can view both the layout and the code as seen in Figure 1-21. The first three paragraphs have different amounts of space between them in the HTML but will be rendered on the page one after the other.

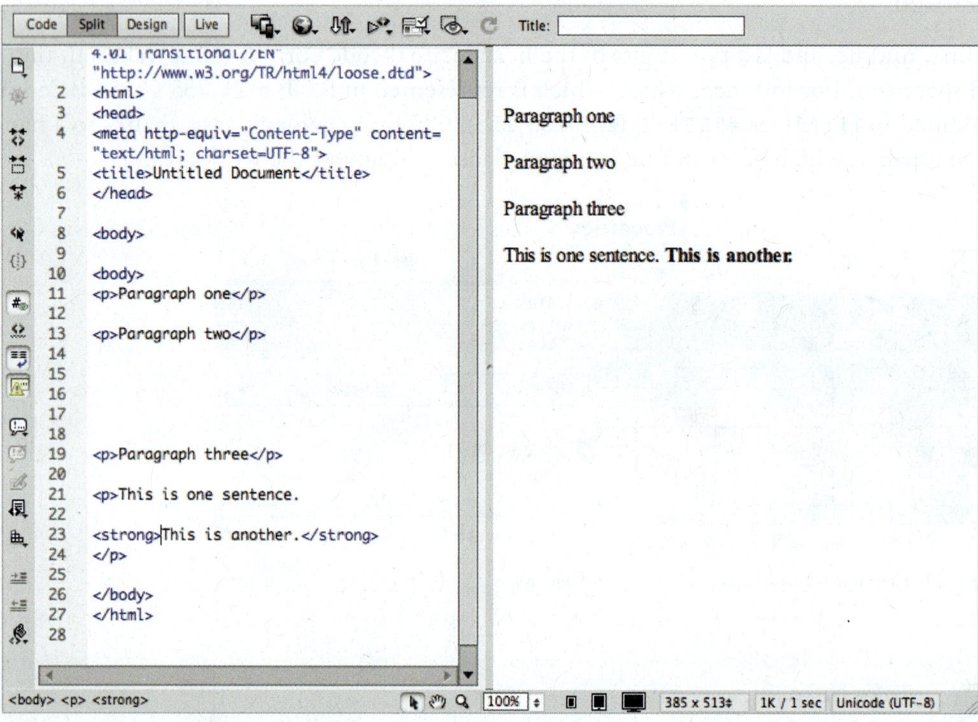

Figure 1-21: The browser ignores any whitespace between the paragraphs.

This tells you that whitespace and line returns are ignored by the browser. You have to begin making a distinction between code that is readable by humans versus the way a web browser interprets and renders code.

3. You will see there are a few different ways to format your text. In the Design view, click once after the sentence that reads, *This is one sentence*, and then press Shift+Enter (Windows) or Shift+Return (Mac OS) twice. This creates two line returns—you can see that each line return is created in your code by a
 (break) tag as seen in Figure 1-22. When rendered in the browser, the <br> tag adds blank lines between the sentences; however the sentences are technically within the same paragraph. This is sometimes referred to as a hard return. This method is actually not the ideal way to add new lines on your page, although it does occasionally come in handy.

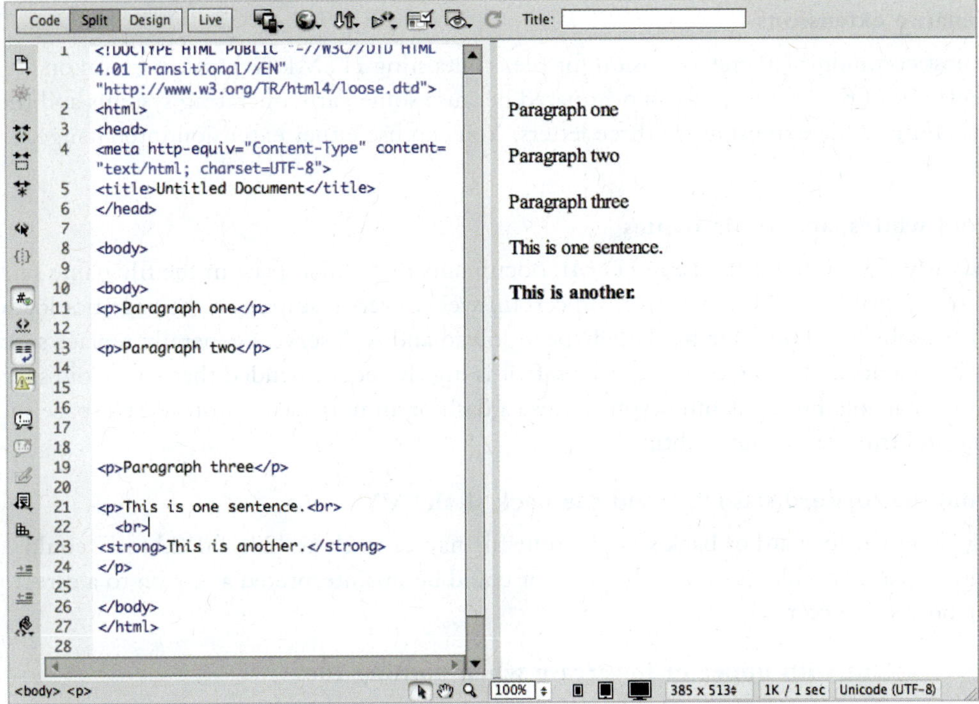

***Figure 1-22**: To create a line return, hold down the Shift key while pressing the Enter or Return key.*

4. To create a new paragraph, position your cursor before the phrase *This is another*, and press Enter (Windows) or Return (Mac OS). The text is separated by a line above and below, and is wrapped inside a set of <p> (paragraph) tags. This is the preferred method of adding paragraphs.

Take Note...

Other than a standard single space (such as the space used between words), several consecutive spaces created by the spacebar are ignored and are displayed as only one space in Design view and in a browser.

5. Choose File > Save to save your work then choose File > Close.

Certification Ready 4.3

What are the rules for naming HTML files?

Certification Ready 4.3

What are best practices for naming HTML files?

Certification Ready 4.3

What is the result of naming an HTML file index.htm(l) or default.htm(l)?

File name restrictions and conventions

Although HTML is very flexible, there are a few things to pay attention to. The following is a list of file naming restrictions (issues which may cause errors) and conventions (standard practice for designers and developers):

- **Forbidden Characters**

When you save your HTML files, stay away from using any of the following characters as they may cause problems in your file directory or when loading in a web browser: *&^%$#@!

- **Filename extensions**

The most common filename extension for files containing HTML is .html. A common abbreviation of this is .htm, which originated because some early operating systems and file systems limited file extensions to three letters. You can use either extension interchangeably these days.

- **Avoid whitespace in file names**

In the early days of the web, using HTML documents that had a space in the file name such as "about us.html" could cause errors on certain web servers resulting in the page not loading or other problems. This issue has largely been solved and web servers generally replace spaces with the characters %20. However, to be safe it is highly recommended that you avoid spaces in your file name. For readability you can use a dash or an underscore instead of a space such as "about_us.html" or "about-us.html".

- **Avoid the forward slash "/" and the back slash "\"**

Using either the forward or back slash in your file names (such as "2/6/2012.html" could potentially cause problems on a web server or could be misinterpreted as a path to a directory by the browser, server, or user.

- **Be consistent with upper or lowercase when naming files**

Many designers and developers have settled on using all lowercase for their file names (for example "contact.html" not "Contact.html" or "CONTACT.html". One reason for this that on certain servers directory and file names are case sensitive so this address: *http://www.mysite.com/myGreatSite.html* is not considered the same as *http://www.mysite.com/mygreatsite.html.* If you decide on a convention of consistently using lowercase, you can avoid the problem of creating errors with mixed case file names. Lowercase also has the benefit of being more readable, especially when compared to all uppercase.

- **Using "index.html" vs. "default.html"**

The file names "index.html" and "default.html" are used as the default file loaded by a web browser when it is sent to a directory (most familiarly as the home page of a website). The "index.html" convention has generally become the standard, although "default.html" will likely work on most servers.

Element hierarchy

HTML elements should have a well-formed hierarchy or nesting structure in order to make sure that everything displays as it should. The element at the top of the hierarchy is the `<html>` element, and every other element you create is contained within it. Elements such as the `<body>` end up nesting all the other elements on a page, such as the `<p>` (paragraph), `<img>` (image), and `<strong>` (bold) elements. In addition, structural elements (such as those that create divs, paragraphs, lists, and tables) hold more weight than formatting tags such as `<strong>` (bold) and `<em>` (italic). Take this line of code, for example:

```
<strong><p>Big bold paragraph</p></strong>
```

Although code such as this may work in certain browsers, it isn't structured well because the `<strong>` tag technically holds less weight than the `<p>` tag. The following code represents a better way to include the bold type:

```
<p><strong>Big bold paragraph</strong></p>
```

Dreamweaver generally does a great job of keeping tags properly nested or contained within each other. When you choose to manipulate the code by hand, you should always keep good coding techniques in mind.

Explorations in code

Although this book occasionally refers to the code for examples, hand-coding is not a primary goal of these lessons. The best way to learn how code represents the layouts you are building visually is to switch to the Code view and explore what's happening behind the scenes.

It's important to remember that every button, panel, and menu in Dreamweaver represents some type of HTML tag, attribute, or value; very rarely will you learn something that is unrelated or proprietary to Dreamweaver alone. Think of the Dreamweaver workspace as a pretty face on the HTML language.

A look at the Welcome Screen

A common fixture in most CS6 applications is the Welcome Screen, which is a launching pad for new and recent documents. In Dreamweaver, the Welcome Screen appears when the application launches or when no documents are open as seen in Figure 1-23. From the Welcome Screen, you can create new pages, create a new site, open a recent document, or use one of Dreamweaver's many starter pages or layouts.

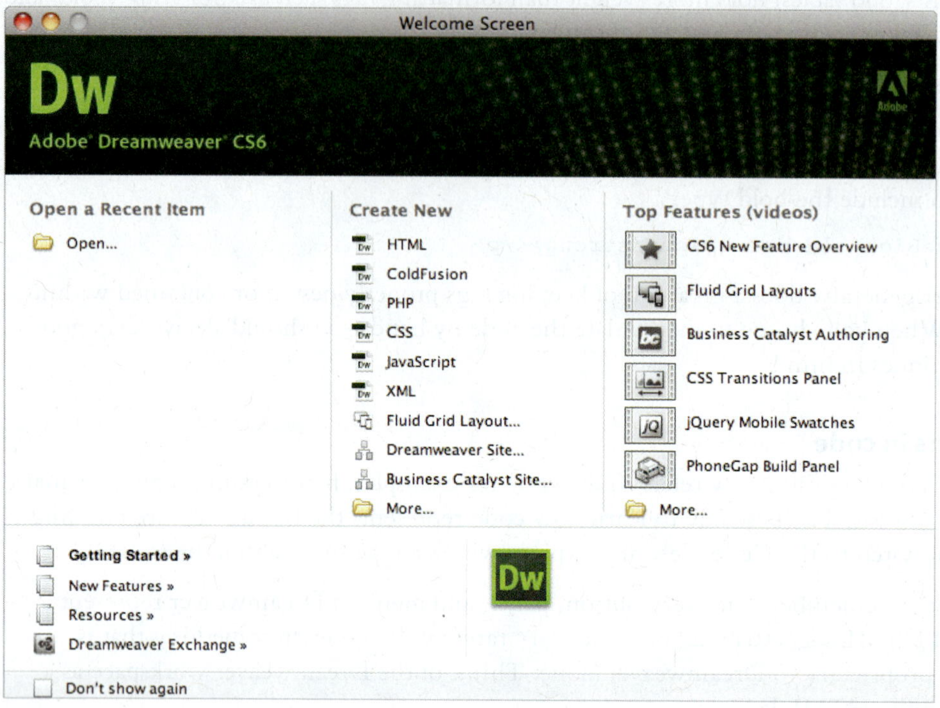

Figure 1-23: The Welcome Screen appears when you launch the application, or when no documents are open.

Here's what you'll find on the Welcome Screen:

Open a Recent Item: A list of the last few documents you worked on appears in the far left column, or you can browse to open a different file using the Open button at the bottom.

Create New: In addition to HTML pages, you can choose from a variety of new document formats, such as CSS, JavaScript, and XML. Dreamweaver is not just a web page-building tool, but also a superior text editor, making it ideal for creating many non-HTML files. You can also define a new Dreamweaver site using the link at the bottom, or choose the More folder for even more new file options.

Top Features (videos): On the far right side of the Welcome Screen, there is a column that contains link to videos of Top Features. These videos explore some of the new top features of Dreamweaver CS6, including Fluid Grid Layouts, Business Catalyst, and the CSS Transitions panel among others. The videos are located on Adobe's website, *adobe.com*, and when you click on one, Dreamweaver launches the site in your web browser to give you access to the video.

Creating, opening, and saving documents

The lessons throughout this book require that you create, save, and open existing files. You can accomplish most file-related tasks from the File menu at the top, or from the Welcome Screen that appears when you launch Dreamweaver.

Creating new documents

Dreamweaver creates text files most commonly in the form of HTML files (or web pages). It can also create files in a variety of text-based languages, including CSS, XML, JavaScript, and even Flash ActionScript.

You can create blank files that you build from the ground up, or you can get started with a variety of layout templates and themes as seen below in Figure 1-24. You can create new documents from the File menu or from the Welcome Screen. Here, you'll create a new page using the File menu.

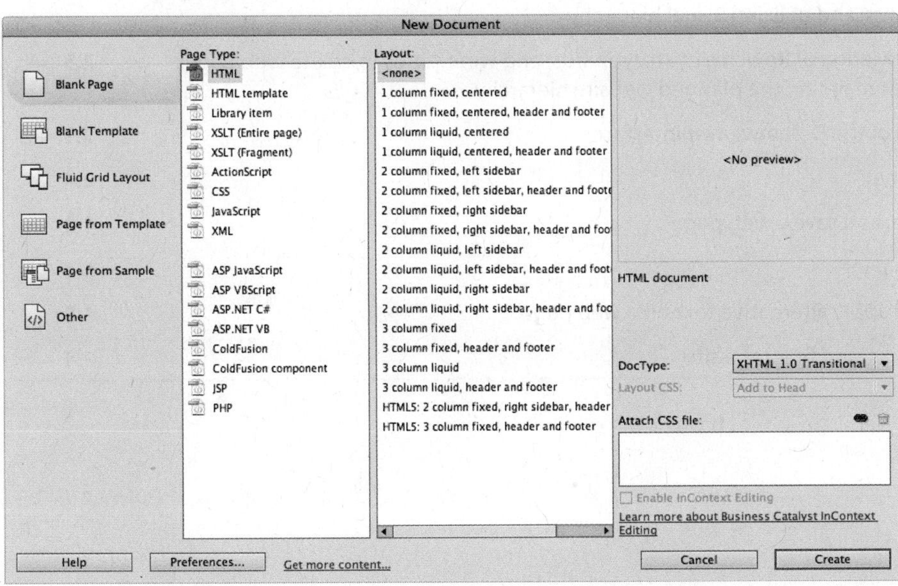

Figure 1-24: The New Document dialog box gives you a choice of new files in a variety of formats and templates.

Step-by-Step

Follow these steps to create a new document

1. To create a new document, choose File > New. The New Document dialog box appears.
2. Select Blank Page and under the Page Type column, choose HTML. Under Layout, choose <none> to start a new blank document. Leave the DocType drop-down menu at its default. Press Create.
3. Choose File > Save or File > Save As to start the process of saving your document.
4. When prompted, choose a location for your file and assign it a name. Note that you must save HTML files with an .html extension, or they will not be interpreted properly in a browser. This rule applies for files of any type (such as .xml, .css, and .cfm).

Learning More

Opening a recently opened document

To open a document you've worked on recently, Choose File > Open Recent or, from the Welcome Screen, select a document under the Open a Recent Item column.

Now that you've seen what Dreamweaver can do, it's time to put what you've learned into practice. Move to the next lesson so that you can begin building your first Dreamweaver site!

Skill Summary

In this lesson you learned how to:	Objective
Identify the purpose, audience, and audience needs for a website	1.1
Identify web page content that is relevant to the website purpose and appropriate for the target audience	1.2
Make website development decisions based on your analysis and interpretation of design specification	1.5
Understand project management tasks and responsibilities	1.6
Demonstrate general and Dreamweaver-specific knowledge of best practices for designing a website, such as maintaining consistency, separating content from design, using standard fonts, and utilizing visual hierarchy	2.1
Demonstrate knowledge of flowcharts, storyboards, and wireframes to create web pages and a site map that maintain the planned website hierarchy	2.5
Identify elements of the Dreamweaver interface	3.1
Use the Assets Panel	3.4
Create, title, name, and save a web page	4.3
Add text to a web page	4.4
Insert images and apply alternative text on a web page	4.5
Manage assets, links, and files for a site	6.4

Knowledge Assessment

True/False

Circle T if the statement is true or F if the statement is false.

T F **1.** The Multiscreen Preview feature in Dreamweaver allows you to preview what your website will look like in a browser, a tablet and a mobile phone all at the same time.

T F **2.** Dreamweaver will not allow the user to add a PSD file to their web page.

T F **3.** HTML can be created and edited in any text editor program.

T F **4.** Domain names such as *Wiley.com* cover up the actual IP address of the website.

T F **5.** CSS cannot be integrated with HTML.

T F **6.** HTML files can be saved without the .html extension.

T F **7.** The split button in the Document toolbar allows you to view both code and design at the same time.

T F **8.** In HTML, the word strong is associated with creating italicized text.

T F **9.** In XHTML, all tags must be lowercase.

T F **10.** XHTML is not compatible with mobile phones and other handheld devices.

Multiple Choice

Select the best response for the following statements.

1. Dreamweaver supports which of the following code languages:

a. ColdFusion
b. PHP
c. ASP.NET
d. All of the above

2. HTML uses _________ for placing and formatting content:

a. Brackets
b. Arrays
c. Tags
d. Photoshop

3. In HTML, a pair of tags is referred to as an:

a. Array
b. Composite
c. Block
d. Element

4. In the Image Tag Accessibility Attributes Dialog Box, Alternate text is used for:

a. Alphabetizing images
b. For users with special needs (such as the visually impaired)
c. Web browser image recognition
d. Archival purposes

5. The code used to refer to color values is called:

a. Hexadecimal code
b. CSS
c. CGI
d. Hexagonal code

6. Which category in the Insert panel allows you to insert an image on your webpage?

a. Forms
b. Data
c. Layout
d. Common

7. XHTML is a combination of HTML and:

a. XAML
b. XML
c. XCL
d. XTC

8. The <em> tag is used to format text in what way?

a. Bold
b. Italics
c. Height
d. Color

9. What other programs beside Dreamweaver allow you to set color according to a hexadecimal value?

a. Photoshop
b. Flash
c. Illustrator
d. All of the above

10. In HTML, which tag is commonly associated with the placement of images?

a. <img>
b. <imge>
c. <im>
d. <jpg>

Competency Assessment

Adding an Image Placeholder

Project 1-1

Let's say that you're building your first webpage but not all the images are ready to be placed on the page. The good news is that you can still work on your layout while your graphics guru finishes prepping the image. To work on your layout without finished graphics, you'll add an Image Placeholder.

1. Choose File > New > Blank Page > HTML > None to create a new empty webpage.
2. Choose Save and save the file as **placeholder.html**.
3. To add an Image Placeholder, go to the Insert panel and under the Common category chooses Images > Image Placeholder.
4. Fill in the following parameters in the Image Placeholder dialog window:

   Name: **Logo**

   Width: **250**

   Height: **100**

   Choose any color you'd like to use

   Alternate Text: **Company logo**

   Click OK.
5. Use the Properties panel for any further changes you'd like to make. Save the file when you're finished.

Gaining a Better Understanding

Project 1-2

There's always more than meets the eye when it comes to the various panels you'll encounter in programs like Dreamweaver. Fortunately, there's a way to learn more about panels themselves that's right in front of you!

1. Choose File > New
2. When the New Document panel opens, click the Help button located in the bottom left corner.
3. Examine the information in the Help section to learn more about the New Document panel and the various options that are available.

Proficiency Assessment

Project 1-3 Learning More About Code

Since you're in the first chapter, you're probably still a little new to the process of dealing with code. One thing that's important is to understand what the code is supposed to do, even if you don't know how to write it.

Dreamweaver provides a reference library that will help you understand more about code.

Get Ready. Launch Dreamweaver CS6 if you haven't already.

1. Go to Window > Results > Reference.
2. Take a look at the Book menu to see the different code reference books you have at your disposal.
3. Start investigating the various codes and their tag definitions.

Project 1-4 Turning off the Welcome Screen

Not everyone likes the Welcome Screen open every time they launch Dreamweaver. The Preferences will allow you to get in there and customize whether you want the Welcome Screen or not.

Get Ready. Launch Dreamweaver CS6 if you haven't already.

1. Go to Edit > Preferences (Windows) or Dreamweaver > Preferences (Mac OS).
2. Examine the Preferences to determine how to turn off the Welcome Screen when the program launches.

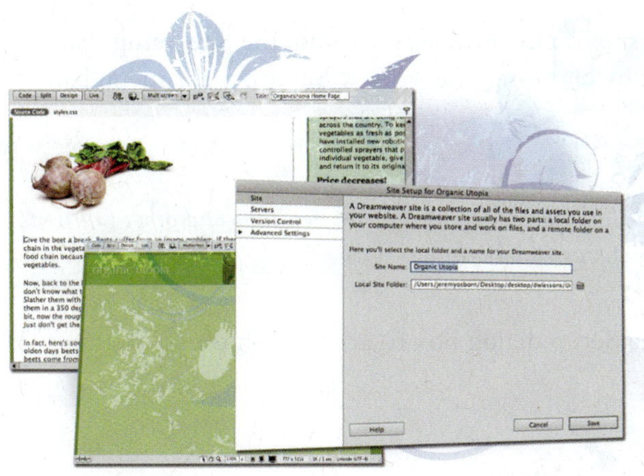

Setting Up a New Site

Key Terms

- Code View
- FTP
- Hexadecimal color
- Hyperlinks
- Page Properties
- Remote Folder
- Root Folder
- Server Name
- Site
- XHTML 1.0 Transitional

Skill	Objective
Identify elements of the Dreamweaver interface	3.1
Use the Files panel	3.5
Define a Dreamweaver site	4.2
Create, title, name, and save a web page	4.3
Set and modify document properties	5.1
Manage assets, links, and files for a site	6.4

Business Case

Organic Utopia needs a site designed for the company, and the owners need to establish the service that will host the site. Files will need to be uploaded to the host and access will be needed to make updates to the site, such as adding new pages. Your task requires that you understand how to set up site management, connect to a server, and create new pages.

Introduction

Before starting, make sure that your tools and panels are consistent by resetting your workspace. See "Resetting the Dreamweaver workspace" in the Starting Up section of this book.

You will work with several files from the dw02lessons folder in this lesson. Make sure that you have loaded the dwlessons folder onto your hard drive. See "Loading lesson files" in the Starting Up section of this book.

Creating a new site

In Dreamweaver, the term **site** refers to the local and remote storage locations where the files that make up a website are stored. A site can also include a testing server location for processing dynamic pages. To take full advantage of Dreamweaver's features, you should always start by creating a site. In Dreamweaver CS6, there is a new category called a Business Catalyst Site. Business Catalyst is a service that Adobe provides (for a fee) that allows you to connect your website with analytic software and other features. However, we do not cover setup of Business Catalyst sites in this book.

The easiest way to create a standard new site in Dreamweaver is to use the Site Setup dialog box. One way to access this dialog box is by choosing Site > New Site from the menu bar.

Take Note...
You can also use the Manage Sites dialog box to create a new site. This and other functions of the Manage Sites dialog box are discussed later in this book.

In this lesson, you begin by using the Site Setup dialog box to accomplish the following tasks:

- Define the site
- Name the site
- Define the local root folder
- Set up a remote folder
- Explore advanced settings
- Save the site

By default, the Site Setup dialog box opens with the Site Settings available. The options available here will help guide you through the essentials of defining your site. The Servers, Version Control, and Advanced Settings options allow you to set up local, remote, and testing servers directly.

Step-by-Step

Follow these steps to set up a new server

1. Launch Dreamweaver CS6, if it is not already open, then choose Site > New Site. First, you have to name the site. In the Site Name text field, type **Organic Utopia** as seen in Figure 2-1.

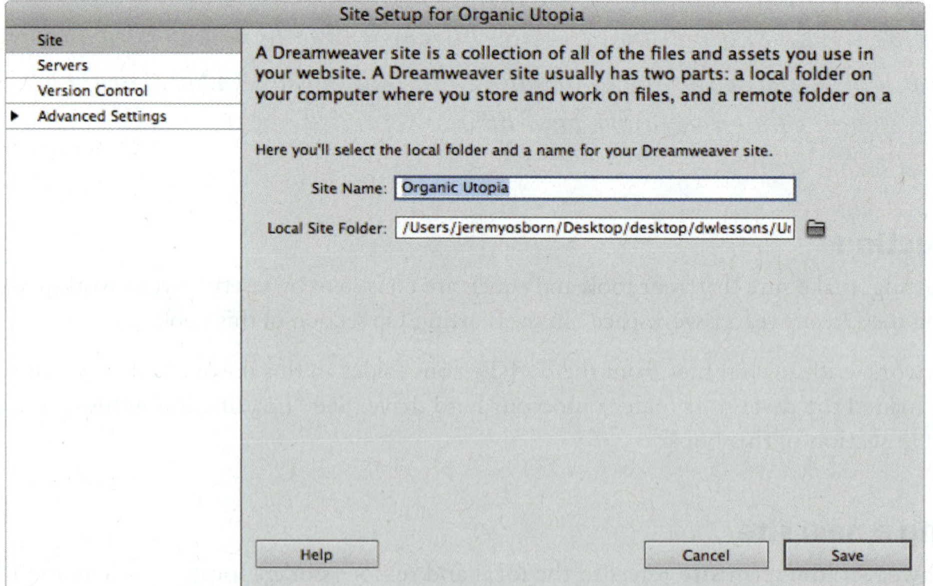

Figure 2-1: *Type the Site Name into the text field.*

Next, you need to set up a local root folder, which is where Dreamweaver stores the files with which you're currently working. The Local Site Folder field allows you to enter information regarding where you'll be working with your files during development.

Take Note...

To ensure that the links you set up on your computer will work when you upload the site to a web server, it is essential that you store all the site's resources in one main folder on your hard drive, then identify it within Dreamweaver. This is because the links will only work properly if all the site's elements remain in the same relative location on the web server as with your hard drive.

2. Click on the Folder icon (📁) to the right of the Local Site Folder text field to navigate to any pre-existing files. In the next step, you will locate the lesson files we have provided for this chapter.

If you did not click on this folder and click Save, Dreamweaver would simply create a new folder on your system where you could begin to create new pages in your site. In this case, you will be pointing to a pre-existing folder that already has files within it.

It is important to distinguish between adding a new site (which is what you are doing now) and creating a new site from scratch. In both cases, the important part is that Dreamweaver knows where this folder is on your system. This folder is known as the **root folder** and will always contain the content that will eventually be your website.

3. Navigate to your desktop and locate the dw02lessons folder you copied to your desktop earlier.

4. Select the dw02lessons folder. On the Windows platform, click Open to open this folder, then press Select (Windows). On the Mac OS platform, press Choose to choose this as your local root folder. The field now shows the path to your newly defined local root folder.

At this point, you have done the minimum amount of steps required to begin working on a site, however you will take a look now at some of the optional features within the Site Setup process.

5. Click on the Servers tab. This section allows you to define the remote server where your website will end up being hosted. Take a moment to read the heading in the dialog box. Note that it says you do not need to fill in this information to begin creating a website. It is only necessary if you are connecting to the Web.

You are not connecting to the Web in this lesson, but you should take a look at the screen anyway to understand the information needed.

6. Click on the + button and the Basic site settings window appears as seen in Figure 2-2. Here there are fields for **Server Name**, Connect Using, **FTP** Address, Username and Password, along with other options. These settings allow you to choose both a destination and a method (FTP being the most common) for Dreamweaver to use to transfer files.

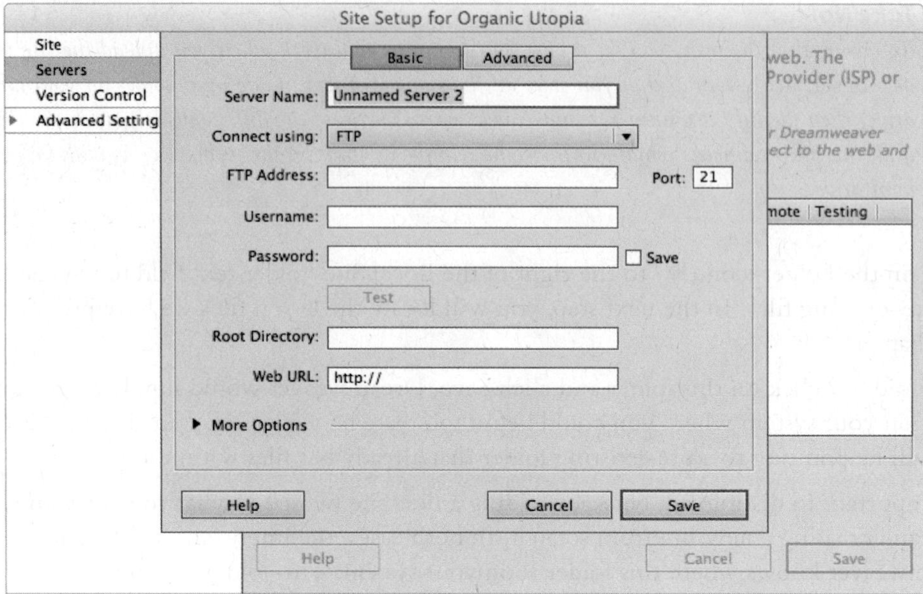

Figure 2-2: Set up access to your remote folder.

As noted earlier, this is an optional step, and you do not have to define your **remote folder** at this stage. Dreamweaver allows you to define your remote folder at a later time, such as when you're ready to upload.

7. Click on the Advanced tab. Click on the Server Model menu in the Testing Server section. Here there are choices for different scripting languages such as PHP and ASP pages. If you are an advanced user, this is where you would set up the connections to your testing server.

   Again, you won't be making any changes here, so press Cancel.

8. Click on the Version Control option on the left to access Subversion settings. Subversion, a VCS (or version control system), keeps track of changes made to files, enabling users to track changes and return to previous versions of any file. For this exercise, make sure the Access pull-down in this window is set to None, as you won't be using Subversion.

   You've now completed the site setup process, using basic settings. Don't close the Site Setup dialog box yet, though, as you'll now explore the options found under the Advanced Settings option.

Certification Ready 4.2

What is the definition for local site, remote site/folder, web server and root folder?

Version Control

Subversion is a system that requires a dedicated installation on a server. Once a Subversion SVN repository is installed, it allows multiple users to work with files in a powerful way. An example of a problem that Subversion solves is when two or more people on a team happen to be working on the same file. The Subversion system can prevent a file from being overwritten accidentally. Multiple versions of the same file are always saved and can even be compared and merged as needed. Additional features of Subversion include the ability to synchronize changes of files as well as the ability for a user to hide a file with File Cloaking, thereby preventing others from accessing it until ready.

Learning More

Certification Ready 6.4

How does one use file management techniques such as Subversion control and check-in/check-out when working in teams?

Advanced site-creation options

Chances are if you are new to Dreamweaver or web design you won't need these advanced settings. If you are in this category, press Save and skip to the Adding Pages section. Other users may be curious what these settings are and should proceed.

Follow these steps to explore the advanced settings for your site

Step-by-Step

1. Click on the arrow next to Advanced Settings in the Site Setup dialog box.
2. From the categories listed below Advanced Settings, choose Local Info as seen in Figure 2-3.

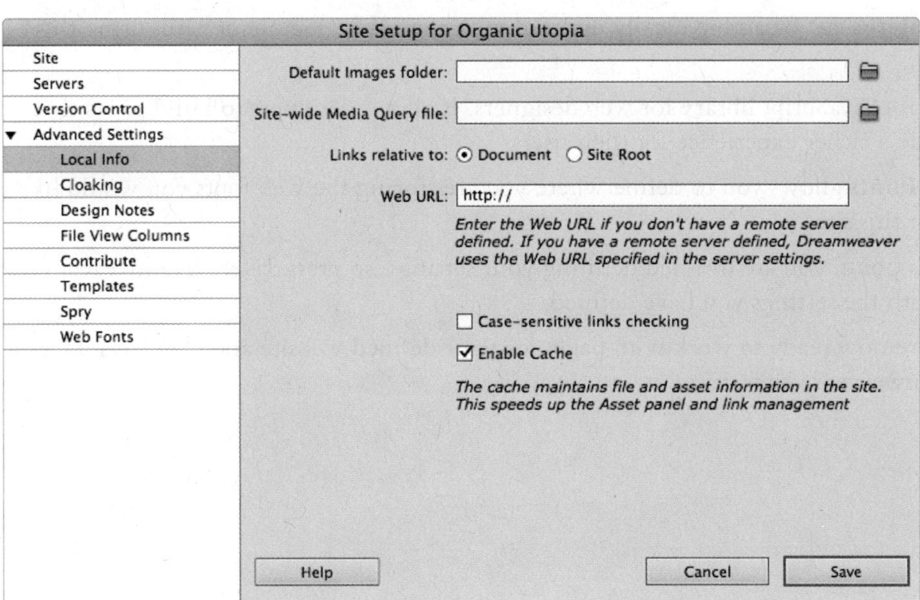

Figure 2-3: *Choose Local Info from Advanced Settings.*

The information you set in the Local Info window identifies your Default Images folder, what your links are relative to, and a web URL to be used if you don't have a remote server defined. One of the more important Local Info settings, though, is case-sensitive link checking.

The case-sensitive link checking feature ensures that your links will work on a Unix server, where links are case-sensitive. If you're using a Windows or Mac OS server, this doesn't matter as much, but it is a good idea to follow the strict naming and linking conventions of a Unix system in case you ever move your site to a different server.

Take Note...

A web server delivers web pages on the request of a client (such as a browser) using HTTP. There are different operating systems on web servers just as there are different operating systems on the desktop. In rare instances, these differences can affect the way your site works and this is why Dreamweaver provides options such as case-sensitive link checking.

If you happen to have already defined a CSS3 site-wide Media Query file, this is where you could redefine or modify it. (We cover the creation of site-wide Media Query files in Lesson 15, "Mobile Design and Layout.")

The remaining categories to the left of the Advanced tab of the Site Setup dialog box help to define your site's production, collaboration, and deployment capabilities. They include the following:

Cloaking allows you to specify file types or specific files that you do not want uploaded to the server.

Design Notes is a collaboration tool that keeps notes regarding the development of the page or site.

File View Columns is an organizational tool. If you want to share the custom columns with others, you must enable Design Notes as well.

Contribute is a separate application that enables users with basic word processing and web browser skills and little or no HTML knowledge to create and maintain web pages.

Templates can be automatically updated with rewritten document paths using this option.

Spry is a JavaScript library for web designers. It allows designers to build pages that provide a richer experience for their users.

Web Fonts allows you to define where you are storing the web fonts you would like to use for this site.

Certification Ready 4.2

What are the steps for defining a new Dreamweaver site using the Site Setup dialog?

3. At this point, you are finished defining your settings, so press Save. Dreamweaver creates a site with the settings you have defined.

You are now ready to work with pages for your defined website and take advantage of Dreamweaver's site features.

Adding pages

Dreamweaver contains many features to assist you in building pages for your site. For example, you can define properties for pages, including titles, background colors or images, as well as default text and link colors.

The first step for creating a new page correctly was taken when you defined the site in the last exercise. By defining the root folder, Dreamweaver will always create new pages in your site automatically. These pages are now visible in the Files Panel in the lower right of your screen as seen here in Figure 2-4.

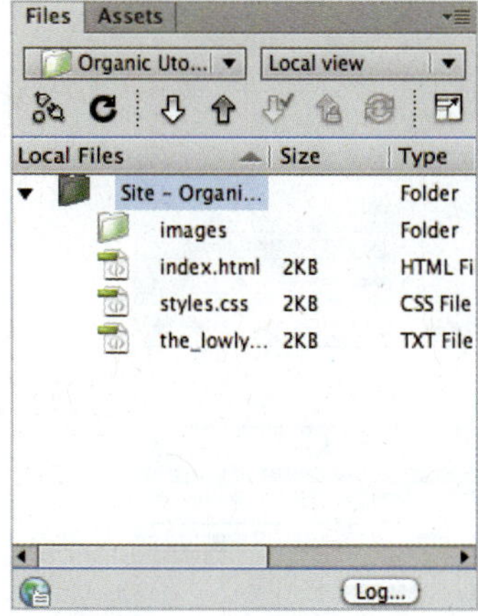

***Figure 2-4**: The Files panel.*

Take Note...

If your Files panel does not look the same as it does here, choose Window > Workspace Layout > Reset 'Designer.'

Adding pages

Step-by-Step

Follow these steps to add a new page

1. Choose File > New. The New Document dialog box opens as seen in Figure 2-5.

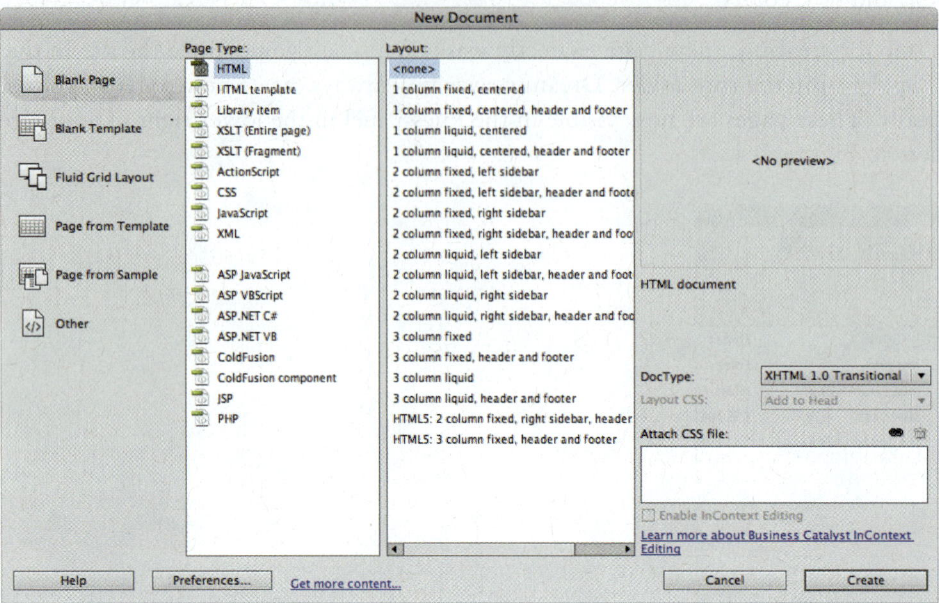

Figure 2-5*: Use the New Document dialog box to add a page to your site.*

2. You can create a new page using a predesigned layout, or start with a blank page and build a layout of your own. In this exercise, you'll start with a blank page and in later lessons, you will get a chance to explore some of the other options. Click on the Blank Page category on the left side of the New Document dialog box.
3. In the Page Type column, you can select the type of page you want to create (for example, HTML, ColdFusion, and so on). Select HTML if it is not currently selected.

   In the Layout column, you can choose to base your page on a prebuilt design. These predesigned layouts fall into one of three categories:

   Fixed creates a layout with columns that do not resize based on the user's browser settings. They are measured in pixels.

   Liquid creates a layout with columns that resize if the user resizes the browser window, but not if the user changes the text settings.

   HTML5 creates a fixed layout that uses the new HTML5 elements such as `<header>`, `<section>` and `<article>` among others.

4. Click on <none> in the Layout column to build the page without using a prebuilt layout.
5. Click on the DocType menu in the lower-right corner. This DocType drop-down menu (seen in Figure 2-6) defines the document type for different versions of HTML including HTML5. **XHTML 1.0 Transitional** is the default setting and is suitable in most cases, so be sure to bring it back to this option.

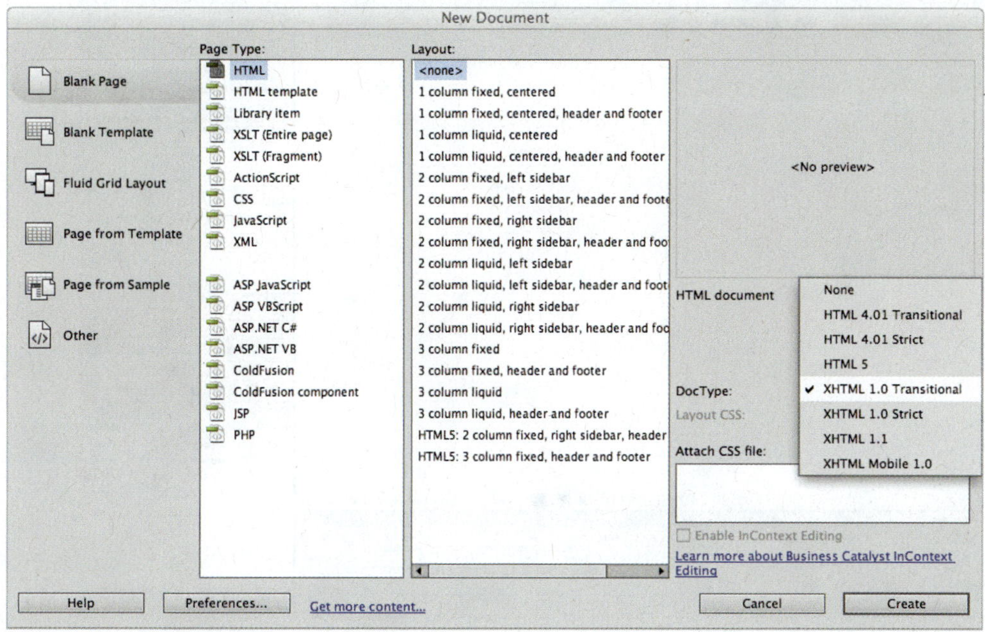

Figure 2- 6: Choose XHTML 1.0 Transitional as your DocType.

Take Note...

The Layout CSS and Attach CSS settings are irrelevant here, as you didn't choose a CSS-based layout for this page.

6. Press Create to create a new, blank HTML page. You will learn more about Workspaces a bit later, but to ensure you are working as we are, choose Window > Workspace Layout and choose Reset Designer. Your screen should now look like Figure 2-7. (Although if you are in Code View, you should switch to the Design view now.)

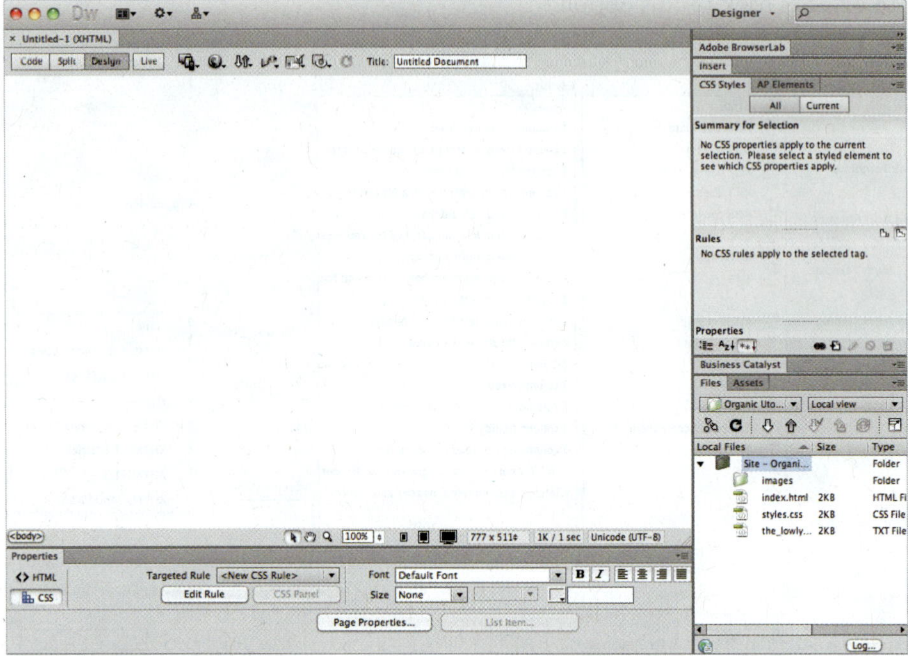

Figure 2-7: Your new, blank HTML page.

Saving a page to your site

You should get accustomed to saving pages to your local root folder early and often. It is very important that you store all your site's resources in one main folder on your hard drive so that the links you set on your computer will work when your site is uploaded to a server.

Step-by-Step

Follow these steps to save a page to your site

1. Choose File > Save.
2. In the Save As dialog box, Dreamweaver should have automatically opened your dw02lessons folder which was defined earlier in the Site Settings.

   If this is not the case, navigate to your desktop and locate the dw02lessons folder.
3. In the Save As text field, name your file **about_us.html**.
4. Click Save to save the page in your local root folder. In the Files panel note that the file about_us.html has now been added. Again, this is why site settings are so important in Dreamweaver, files are automatically saved and organized based on having a site definition.

Certification Ready 4.3

How do you create, save and name a new HTML page?

Defining page properties

Now that you've created a page in Dreamweaver, you'll use the **Page Properties** dialog box to specify its layout and formatting properties. For example, you can set page titles, background colors and images, text, and link colors, as well as other basic properties of every web page. You use this dialog box to define page properties for each new page you create, and to modify the settings for pages you've already created.

Follow these steps to create and modify settings for pages

Step-by-Step

1. To access the Page Properties dialog box, choose Modify > Page Properties, or use the keyboard shortcut Ctrl+J (Windows) or Command+J (Mac OS). The Page Properties dialog box appears, with the Appearance (CSS) category selected by default as seen in Figure 2-8.

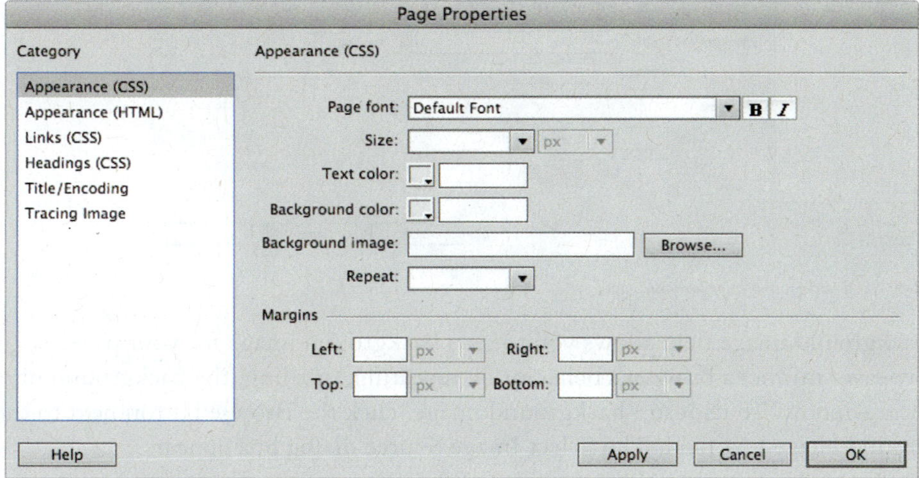

***Figure 2-8**: The Page Properties dialog box.*

Settings found in the Appearance (CSS) category will automatically create a Cascading Style Sheet that defines the appearance of your page. Using a CSS file to define these page properties adds flexibility to your design, as styling can be changed more easily, and more universally, than if your defaults are defined using HTML code.

2. The Page font and Size fields define the default appearance of text on your page. For now, leave these settings at their defaults. You'll be styling type with CSS in later lessons in this book.

3. The Text color option allows you to set a default color in which to render type. To set a text color, click on the color swatch next to Text; the Swatches panel appears. You can choose your default text color by clicking on the appropriate swatch from the Swatches panel. Try this by clicking on any color swatch, and press Apply to apply your desired default text color.

   You can also type the **hexadecimal** notation for your desired color into the text field. Type the hex code **666666** in the text field to specify a dark gray as the default text color.

Take Note...

You'll see the effects of this change later in this lesson, when you add text to your page using the Files panel.

4. Use the Background color option to choose a background color for your page. Click on the color swatch next to the Background text field; the Swatches panel appears. You can choose your background color by clicking on the appropriate swatch from the Swatches panel. Try this by clicking on any color swatch, then press Apply to see the results.

   You can also choose the background color by typing the hexadecimal notation for your desired color into the Background text field. Type the hex code **739112** in the Background text field (as seen in Figure 2-9), then press Apply to specify a green as the background color.

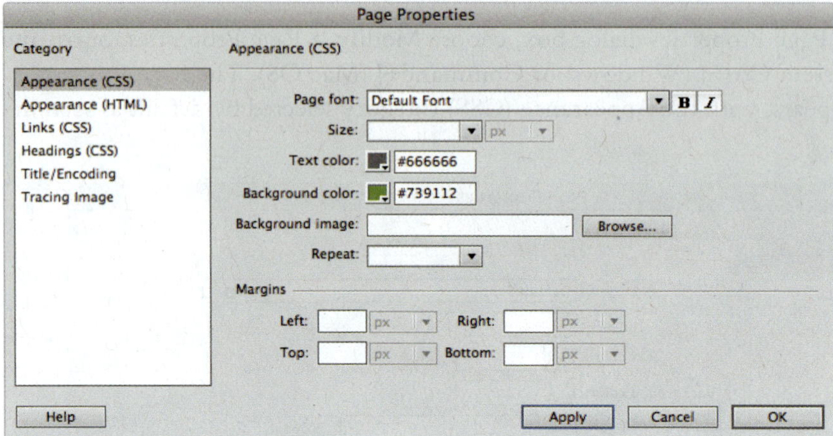

***Figure 2-9**: Set a background color for your page.*

5. The Background image field allows you to set a background image for your page. Dreamweaver mimics a browser's behavior by repeating, or tiling, the background image to fill the window. To choose a background image, click the Browse button next to the Background image text field. The Select Image Source dialog box appears.

6. Navigate to the folder titled "Images" within the dw02lessons folder and select **bg_gradient.gif** for your page background; then press Apply. You will see the background image, which is a gradient, appear on the page. Background images are tiled both horizontally and vertically by default, which is not appropriate for this image, so you will fix this with the Repeat property.

7. From the Repeat drop-down menu, choose repeat-x (as seen in Figure 2-10). Click Apply to see the change.

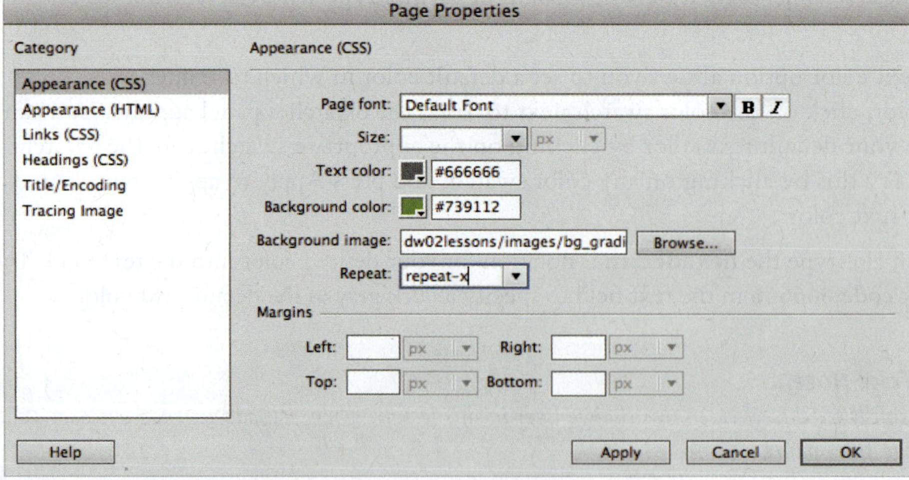

Figure 2-10 Choose a background image for your page (background.gif).

Take Note...

You can also type the path to your background image into the Background image text field.

8. By default, Dreamweaver places your text and images in close proximity to the top and left edges of the page. To build in some extra room between your page edges and the content on them, use the Margin settings in the Page Properties dialog box. In the Left margin text field, type **25** to place your content 25 pixels from the left edge of the page. In the Top margin text field, type **25** to place your content 25 pixels from the top edge of the page.

The Appearance (HTML) category in the Page Properties dialog box contains many of the same settings you just defined. Setting default page attributes with HTML code, however, is not recommended. Setting appearance with CSS is a better option.

The Links (CSS) category allows you to define the appearance of linked text within your document. For more information on creating **hyperlinks**, see Lesson 3, "Adding Text and Images."

9. Click on the Links category on the left-hand side and leave the Link font and Size settings at their defaults (same as Page font). This ensures that your hyperlinks will display in the same typeface and size as the rest of the text on your page.

10. Set the colors for your different link types in the following fields:

Link Color: Type **#fc3** for the default link color applied to linked text on your web page.

Visited links: Type **#ccc** for the color applied to linked text after a user has clicked on it.

Rollover links: Type **#f03** for the color applied to linked text when a user rolls over it.

Active links: Type **#ff6** for the color applied when the user clicks on linked text.

11. Because you're using CSS formatting, you can choose whether or not (and/or when) you want your links to be underlined. This is not possible with HTML formatting. Choose the default setting of Always Underline in the Underline style drop-down menu as seen in Figure 2-11.

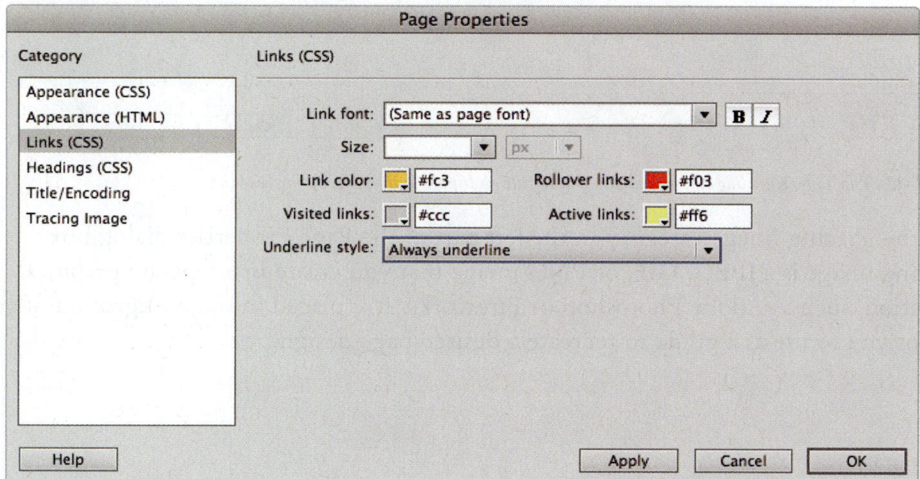

***Figure 2-11**: Choose default colors for links, visited links, and active links.*

The Headings (CSS) category allows you to define the font, style, size, and color of heading text within your document.

12. Click the Headings (CSS) category and leave the settings at their defaults for now. You'll be using CSS to style your heading text later in this book.

13. Click the Title/Encoding category to the left of the Page Properties dialog box to expose more settings. Most of these settings are better left alone unless you know what they do and why you need to change them, with the major exception of the first one: Title.

14. Type **Organic Utopia: About Us** in the Title text field as seen in Figure 2-12.

Certification Ready 4.3

What is the difference between document filenames and document or page titles?

Certification Ready 4.3

How do you assign a document or page title?

Take Note...

The document title is not the same thing as the document file name.The document title appears in the title bar of most browser windows and is also used when a user bookmarks a page. Document titles are used extensively by search engines to help categorize your page.

Leave the Document Type (DTD) set to XHTML 1.0 Transitional. This makes the HTML document XHTML-compliant.

Unicode (UTF-8) will likely be set as the default option. This specifies the encoding used for characters in your page, letting the browser know what to expect.

The Unicode Normalization Form is likely set to C (Canonical Decomposition). This setting is rarely changed unless you have a specific reason for changing it. Unicode Normalization Forms has to do with the way special characters such as glyphs are rendered on the screen.

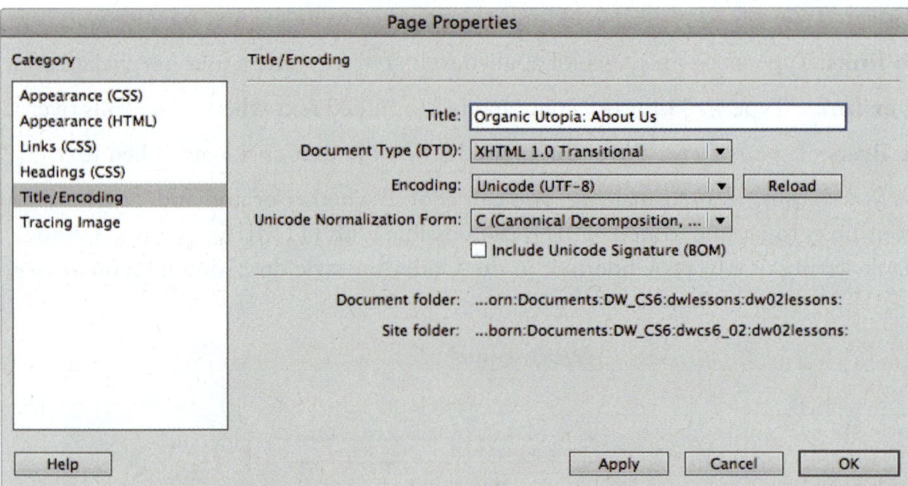

***Figure 2-12**: The Title/Encoding category allows you to title your page and/or specify the encoding used.*

15. Click the Tracing Image category in the left part of the Page Properties dialog box. A tracing image is a JPEG, GIF, or PNG image that you create in a separate graphics application, such as Adobe Photoshop or Fireworks. It is placed in the background of your page for you to use as a guide to recreate a desired page design.

16. Press the Browse button next to the Tracing image text field. You can also type the path to your image directly into this text field.

17. In the Select Image Source dialog box, navigate to your dw02lessons folder, and select the file named **tracing.gif** from the Images folder; then press OK (Windows) or Choose (Mac OS).

18. Set the transparency of the tracing image to 50 percent by sliding the Transparency slider to the left as seen in Figure 2-13.

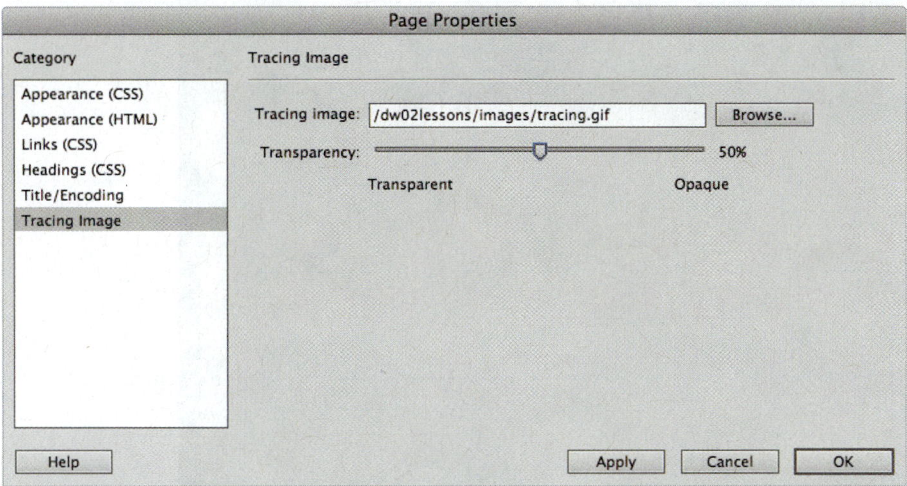

Figure 2-13: *Place a tracing image in the background of your page.*

19. Press Apply to see the results. Tracing Images can be useful tools for building layout. Oftentimes, you can import a page mockup created originally in Photoshop or another application and use it as a visual guideline.

20. When activated, the tracing image replaces any background image you've added to your page, but only in Dreamweaver. Tracing images are never visible when you view your page in a browser. Now that you have a sense of how the tracing feature works, you'll remove it. Select the path within the Tracing Image field and press Delete to remove it.

21. Press OK to close the Page Properties dialog box.

22. Choose File > Save. Now that you've finished setting up your page properties, you'll examine your page in Dreamweaver's three different work view modes.

Certification Ready 5.1

What are document properties that can be set or edited globally by using the Page Properties dialog box.

Certification Ready 5.1

How do you set or modify global CSS styles including those for text, links and background?

Work views

In this book's lessons, you'll do most of your work in the Design View, as you're taking advantage of Dreamweaver's visual page layout features. You can, however, easily access the HTML code being written as you work in the Design View, and use it to edit your pages through Dreamweaver's other work views. You'll switch views, using the Document toolbar (seen in Figure 2-14).

Figure 2-14: *The Document toolbar.*

Follow these steps to switch views

Step-by-Step

1. In the Document toolbar, press the Design view button, if it is not currently selected. Design view is a fully editable, visual representation of your page, similar to what the viewer would see in a browser (seen in Figure 2-15).

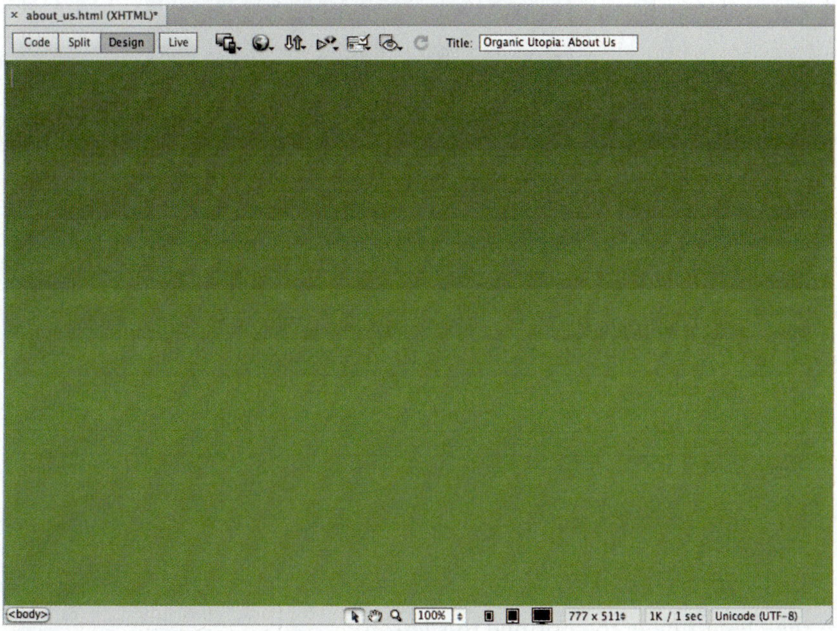

***Figure 2-15**: With Design view, you see your page as the viewer will see it.*

2. Click on the Code view button to switch to the **Code view** as seen in Figure 2-16. Your page is now displayed in a hand-coding environment used for writing and editing HTML and other types of code, including JavaScript, PHP, and ColdFusion.

```
× about_us.html (XHTML)*
Code | Split | Design | Live        Title: Organic Utopia: About Us

1  <!DOCTYPE html PUBLIC "-//W3C//DTD XHTML 1.0 Transitional//EN"
   "http://www.w3.org/TR/xhtml1/DTD/xhtml1-transitional.dtd">
2  <html xmlns="http://www.w3.org/1999/xhtml">
3  <head>
4  <meta http-equiv="Content-Type" content="text/html; charset=UTF-8" />
5  <title>Organic Utopia: About Us</title>
6  <style type="text/css">
7  body,td,th {
8      color: #666666;
9  }
10 body {
11     background-color: #739112;
12     background-image: url(../../dwcs6_02/dw02lessons/images/bg_gradient.gif);
13     background-repeat: repeat-x;
14 }
15 a:link {
16     color: #fc3;
17 }
18 a:visited {
19     color: #ccc;
20 }
21 a:hover {
22     color: #f03;
23 }
24 a:active {
25     color: #ff6;
26 }
27 </style>
28 </head>
29
30 <body>

<body>                                        1K / 1 sec   Unicode (UTF-8)
```

***Figure 2-16**: Code view shows the HTML code generated to display your page.*

3. Click on the Split view button to split the document window between the Code and Design views (Figure 2-17). This view is a great learning tool, as it displays and highlights the HTML code generated when you make a change visually in Design mode, and vice versa.

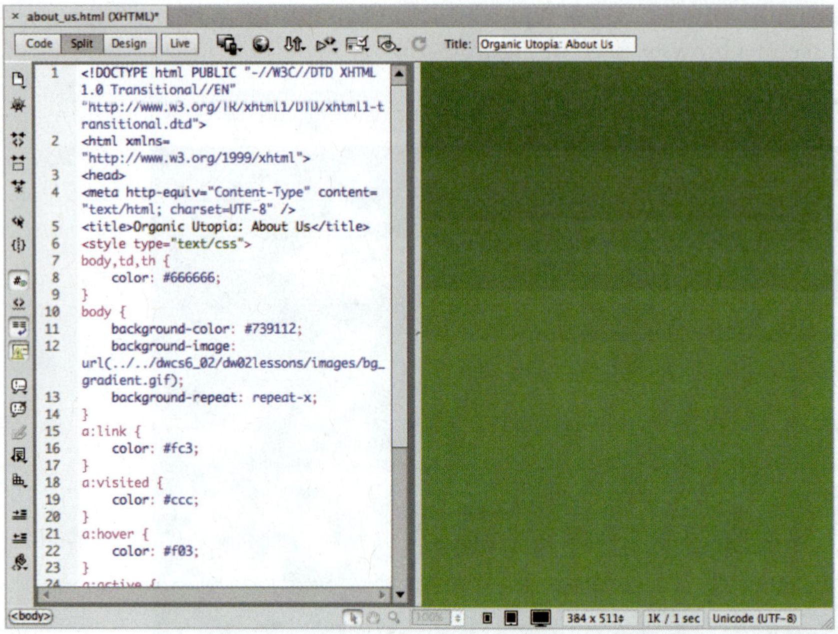

***Figure 2-17**: Use Split view to display your page in both modes at once.*

Certification Ready 3.1

What are the differences between Design view, Code view, Split view and Live view?

4. Switch back to the Design view to continue this lesson.

A deeper look into the Files panel

You have already seen how Dreamweaver populates the Files panel when you define a new site. However, the Files panel is more than just a window into your root folder; it also allows you to manage files locally and transfer them to and from a remote server. The Files panel maintains a parallel structure between local and remote sites, copying and removing files when needed to ensure synchronicity between the two.

The default workspace in Dreamweaver displays the Files panel in the panel grouping to the right of the document window.

When you chose to use the dw02lessons folder as your local root folder earlier in this lesson, Dreamweaver set up a connection to those local files through the Files panel.

Viewing local files

You can view local files and folders on the right side of your screen within the Files panel, whether they're associated with a Dreamweaver site or not.

Follow these steps to view local files — Step-by-Step

1. Click on the drop-down menu in the upper-left part of the Files panel, and choose Desktop (Windows) or Computer > Desktop folder (Mac OS) to view the current contents of your Desktop folder.
2. Choose Local Disk (C:) (Windows) or Mac HD (Mac OS) from this menu to access the contents of your hard drive.
3. Choose CD Drive (D:) (Windows) from this menu to view the contents of an inserted CD. On a Mac, the CD icon and the name of the CD appear in the menu.
4. Choose Organic_Utopia to return to your local root folder view.

Selecting and editing files

You can select, open, and drag HTML pages, graphics, text, and other files listed in the Files panel to the document window for placement.

Follow these steps to edit a file — Step-by-Step

1. Double-click on the **index.html** file, located in the Files panel. The page opens for editing. Click beneath the heading *The lowly beet.*
2. Click on the plus sign (Windows) or arrow (Mac OS) to the left of the images folder to expand it and then click and drag the **beets.jpg** image file from the Files panel to the index.html document window. If an Image Tag Accessibility Attributes dialog box appears, type **beets** inside the Alternate Text field and then press OK. The image is added to the open page.

Take Note...
If you have an image editor such as Photoshop or Fireworks installed on your computer, you can double-click on the **beets.jpg** *image file to open for editing and optimizing.*

3. Double-click on **the_lowly_beet.txt** in the Files panel to open it directly in Dreamweaver.
4. Choose Edit > Select All to select all the text in this file. You could also use the keyboard shortcuts, Ctrl+A (Windows) or Command+A (Mac OS).
5. Choose Edit > Copy to copy the text to the clipboard. You could also use the keyboard shortcuts, Ctrl+C (Windows) or Command+C (Mac OS).
6. Click on the **index.html** tab of the document window to return to the index page. Click on your page to the right of the image to place an insertion cursor, and press Return once to start a new paragraph.
7. Choose Edit > Paste. You could also use the keyboard shortcuts, Ctrl+V (Windows) or Command+V (Mac OS). The text has now been added to the open page, beneath the image, in the default text color you chose earlier (Figure 2-18).

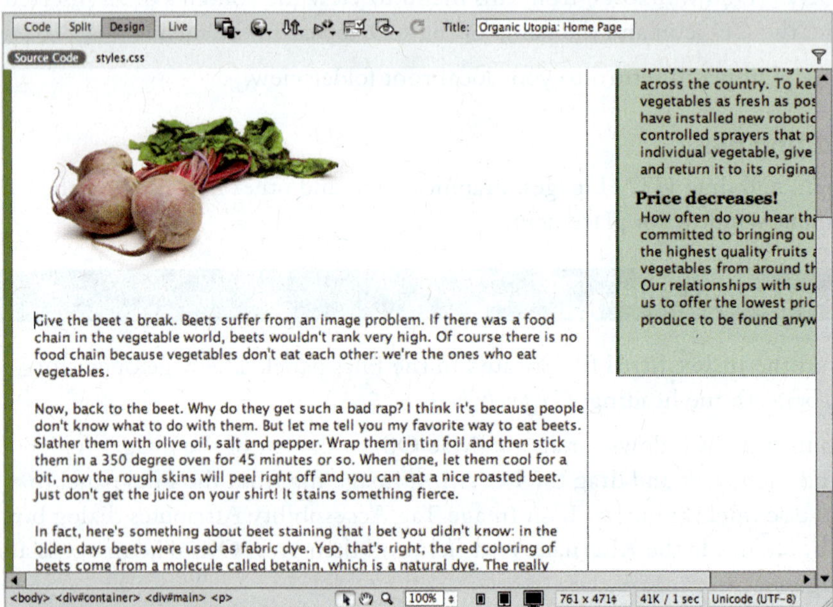

Figure 2-18: Paste the new text in the page.

Certification Ready 3.5

What is the Files panel used for?

8. Choose File > Save and then close this file.

Renaming and updating links in the Files panel

The Files panel can perform tasks within Dreamweaver that are typically done within your operating system such as renaming and deleting files. Not only does this save time but has other advantages as well. In the case of renaming files, Dreamweaver will automatically allow you to update any links on the page including images.

Follow these steps to update links

Step-by-Step

1. In the Files panel, expand the images folder if necessary by clicking on the arrow (Mac) or plus sign (PC) immediately to the left of the folder icon.
2. Click once on the file name **beets.jpg** and it will become active signifying that you can rename the file name. Type **bunchofbeets** and then press Return/Enter. The Update Files window appears asking if you would like to update **index.html**.
3. Press Update. Nothing will have appeared to change, which is exactly the point. If you had renamed this graphic in your operating system, there would have been a broken image on your page because the original reference to beets.jpg would be wrong. Dreamweaver recognizes the potential error and prompts you to fix it by updating the link. Behind the scenes in your HTML, Dreamweaver has rewritten the correct code for you. This is a major advantage in using Dreamweaver as it makes it difficult for you to accidently break links to assets in your site.
4. You can also duplicate and/or delete files within the Files panel. Select the **bunchofbeets.jpg** image in the Files panel and then click on the context menu in the top right of the panel and choose Edit > Duplicate. A duplicate image with the word copy in the file name is added to your Files panel.
5. Select the duplicate image you just created (**bunchofbeets - Copy.jpg**) and press the **Delete** key on your keyboard. You will be prompted by Dreamweaver asking if you want to delete the selected files. Press yes and the file will be gone.
6. Choose File > Save All. Congratulations! You have finished this lesson.

Certification Ready 6.4

How do you delete files using the Files panel?

Certification Ready 6.4

How do you rename files and update links using the Files panel?

Skill Summary

In this lesson you learned how to:	Objective
Identify elements of the Dreamweaver interface	3.1
Use the Files panel	3.5
Define a Dreamweaver site	4.2
Create, title, name, and save a web page	4.3
Set and modify document properties	5.1
Manage assets, links, and files for a site	6.4

Knowledge Assessment

True/False

Circle T if the statement is true or F if the statement is false.

T F **1.** In order to begin working on HTML files in Dreamweaver you must define a site first.

T F **2.** If you do not manually specify a local site folder when defining a site in the Site Setup window, Dreamweaver will automatically define one for you.

T F **3.** The Site Setup window only allows you to define a new site from scratch, to import an existing site you must use another method.

T F **4.** Whenever you define a site in Dreamweaver, it is mandatory to add Remote Server information.

T F **5.** When you first create a blank HTML page with no layout in Dreamweaver you are prompted to add page properties such as page font, text color, and background color.

T F **6.** It is not possible to have both a background image and a background color on a page.

T F **7.** A Tracing Image allows you to add a background image to your page and will show up when you preview the page in the browser.

T F **8.** Dreamweaver's Split View allows you to see the design of your page and the code of your page simultaneously.

T F **9.** Using the Files panel, you can see all local files and folders on your system, even if they are not part of a Dreamweaver site.

T F **10.** You can set the default style of links on a page using the Page Properties window.

Multiple Choice

Select the best response for the following statements.

1. Which of the following is true about defining a site in Dreamweaver?

a. It is mandatory.

b. It gives you access to list of page layouts such as 1 column, 2 column, 3 column and more.

c. New HTML files that you create are automatically saved into your defined site folder.

d. All of the above.

2. If you are asked to add FTP information for a defined site, in which of the following sections of the Site Setup panel would you do this?

a. Site

b. Servers

c. Version Control

d. Advanced Settings

3. If you needed to define a Testing Server, which of the following sections of the Site Setup panel would you need to access?

a. The Basic section of the Servers category

b. The Advanced section of the Servers category

c. The Local Site Folder section of the Site category

d. The Local Info category of the Advanced Settings category

4. One of the benefits of adding a Title to your page is what?

a. It is used when someone bookmarks your page in a browser.

b. It will appear in the title bar of most web browsers.

c. It helps with Search Engine Optimization.

d. All of the above.

5. In the Page Properties window, where would you use the Repeat menu?

a. In the Margins section of the Appearance (CSS) category

b. In the Heading Font section of the Headings category

c. In the Link Font section of the Links (CSS) category

d. In the Background Image section of the Appearance (CSS) category

6. Which of the following is NOT true about Tracing Images?

a. They must be created in a separate image editing application.

b. They are placed in the background of your page in the Design View.

c. You have control over the transparency of the image.

d. They are visible when you preview your page in the browser.

7. You would most likely access the Links (CSS) category of the Page Properties window to do which of the following?

a. Set default styles for hyperlinks in your page using Cascading Style Sheets.
b. Instruct Dreamweaver to automatically check for broken links.
c. Set default HTML styles for hyperlinks.
d. Set styles for your links in an external style sheet only.

8. The Files panel will allow you to do which of the following?

a. Add images to your page.
b. View the contents of the Documents folder on your system.
c. Provide access to both local and remote sites.
d. All of the above.

9. The Default DocType setting in Dreamweaver CS6 is which of the following?

a. XHTML 1.0 Transitional
b. HTML 1.0 Transitional
c. HTML5
d. XHTML 1.1

10. If you create new HTML page and then save it, which of the following is true?

a. It is automatically named index.html and then is visible in the Files panel.
b. It is automatically named default.html and then is visible in the Files panel.
c. It is automatically named home.html and then is visible in the Files panel.
d. You are prompted to name the file after which it is visible in the Files panel.

Competency Assessment

Project 2-1 Setting up a new site

You need to start building a website for a client, Serenity Spa, an upscale day spa that offers a full range of spa and beauty treatments for men and women. Start by creating the new site.

1. Choose Site > New Site. Name the site **Spa**. The Local Site Folder field will be displaying a path. Chances are this path will be pointing to a Documents folder, however it could be pointing to any number of locations on your system. You now will create a new folder on your desktop and point Dreamweaver to this folder in order to define the site.
2. Click on the folder icon to the right of the Local Site Folder field. The Choose Root Folder window appears. Locate your Desktop and then either click on the Create New Folder icon (Windows) or click on the New Folder button (Mac) and name it **Serenity_Spa**.
3. Click Open (Windows) or Choose (Mac OS) to open the new folder. You will now see the path to the Local Site Folder updated.
4. As you won't be uploading this site to a server the Servers section does not need to be filled out.
5. Click Save and confirm that your site is visible in the Files panel.

Creating a web page and setting page properties

Project 2-2

You have a site defined for your client Serenity Spa, you'll now create the first web page for your client's site and create some simple styles that will be used globally across the site.

1. Choose File > New. In the New Document window, choose HTML as the Page Type and <none> as the Layout. Leave all the other settings in that window at their defaults and press Create. Dreamweaver comes with a number of design templates to start the layout process for you. The <none> page is a simply a blank page with no layout or content.
2. Now, save the page to your root folder (also known as a directory). Choose File > Save, and be sure that the Serenity_Site directory is visible in the Save In field. In the dialog box, name the file **index.html** and press Save.
3. Now set the page properties. Choose Modify > Page Properties > Appearance to set background, text, and link colors. Select styles of your own choosing here.
4. Click on Title/Encoding in the Category list on the left, then enter a title for the web page—this will appear in the top bar of the page when it is viewed with a web browser, so you may want to use the name of the business as the title for the page: **Serenity Spa**.
5. Leave all other settings the way they are, and click OK. Save the file.

Proficiency Assessment

New Site

Project 2-3

You need to create a new website for a local Spa. Define a new site and add some default styles for the home page.

Get Ready. Launch Dreamweaver if it is not already running.

1. Choose Site > New Site to invoke the Site Setup dialog box, and use it to create a new local site called **Spa_Site** on your desktop.
2. Create a new page and make sure it is named **index.html**. Add some default text to the page such as **Welcome to our Spa!**
3. Select Modify > Page Properties and add a default background page color of blue-green and default text color of orange.
4. Add left and right margins of 100 pixels to your page.
5. Save all your files and close the site.

Project 2-4 Editing Site Settings

Setting up a new site is fine when you know all your settings. But what if you need to design a site that has no hosting information set up yet?

With the Manage Sites window, you'll be able to change site settings as well as add new sites.

Get Ready. Launch Dreamweaver CS6 if you haven't already.

1. Go to Site > Manage Sites.

2. Click New and add a new site. You may want to establish a couple of different practice root folders too.

3. Finish setting up your new site and continue to set up some additional practice sites.

4. Select a Site and click the Edit button to make further site changes.

Project 2-5 Exporting and Importing Site Settings

If you're working with more than one person or computer, you may end up having to share site information across several machines. Import and export your site settings instead of having to recreate the site each time.

Get Ready. Launch Dreamweaver CS6 if you haven't already.

1. Go to Site > Manage Sites.

2. Use the Export and Import features to share your site setup information from one computer to another.

Adding Text and Images

Key Terms

- Absolute Hyperlink
- Cascading Style Sheets (CSS)
- Hypertext Markup Language (HTML)
- Image Formats
- Image Resolution
- Lists
- Preview in Browser
- Property Inspector
- Relative Hyperlink
- Selector
- Split View
- Syntax

Skill	Objective
Demonstrate knowledge of standard copyright rules (related terms, obtaining permission, and citing copyrighted material)	1.3
Demonstrate knowledge of website accessibility standards that address the needs of people with visual and motor impairments	1.4
Identify basic principles of website usability, readability, and accessibility	2.4
Use the Property Inspector	3.3
Demonstrate knowledge of Hypertext Markup Language	4.1
Demonstrate knowledge of how to add text to an HTML page	4.4
Insert images and apply alternative text on a web page	4.5
Link web content, using hyperlinks, e-mail links, and named anchors	4.6
Build image maps	4.10
Import and display a Microsoft Word or Microsoft Excel document to a web page	4.12
Modify text and text properties	5.3
Modify images and image properties	5.4
Conduct technical tests	6.1
Manage assets, links, and files for a site	6.4

Business Case

The company owners are in a hurry to get the website started. They have provided you with sample text content and images to add to the site. They'd like the text to be formatted in a uniform way across the site. The company has specific colors and fonts the owners would like used for the type, but want to make sure headers and body copy are distinct from one another. Some of the tools you'll need to understand to make an efficient workflow for these requirements will include CSS and image placeholders.

Introduction

Before starting, make sure that your tools and panels are consistent by resetting your workspace. See "Resetting the Dreamweaver workspace" in the Starting Up section of this book.

You will work with several files from the dw03lessons folder in this lesson. Make sure that you have loaded the dwlessons folder onto your hard drive. See "Loading lesson files" in the Starting Up section of this book.

Before you begin, you need to create site settings that point to the dw03lessons folder. Go to Site > New Site, and name the site **dw03lessons**, or, for details on creating a site, refer to Lesson 2, "Setting Up a New Site."

Certification Ready 1.4

What is website accessibility?

Making text and images accessible

The Internet is a powerful tool allowing users from all over the world to access information remotely. However, there are often technical obstacles on a web page that prevent users with disabilities from accessing this information. There are a few different categories of disability types including Visual (Blindness, low vision, or color blindness), Hearing (Deafness), Motor (Inability to use a mouse, limited motor control, or response time) and Cognitive (Learning disabilities, inability to remember or focus on large amounts of information). Website accessibility, therefore is defined as the practice of providing equal access to the information and functionality of your website by people of all abilities and disabilities.

Certification Ready 1.4

Why should you consider accessibility in website design?

Include accessibility in the early plans of your website

Thinking about accessibility up-front in the design process is well worth your time. In addition to being the morally right thing to do, all websites strive to achieve the largest audience possible. Some estimates place the number of people in the population with some type of disability around 20%. This does not mean that all members of this group have difficulties accessing the Internet, but it is a large number nonetheless and excluding a group of people from accessing your site translates into lost sales and/or decreased visibility and publicity for your site.

In some scenarios, making your website accessible could also be the law. In the United States, there are laws that apply toward federally- or state-funded websites. These laws include the American with Disabilities Act, the Individuals with Disabilities Education Act and Sections 504 and Section 508 of the Rehabilitation Act of 1973. Many international laws also address accessibility.

Below you will find a list of some key principles of accessible design. Most accessibility principles can be implemented very easily and will not impact the overall "look and feel" of your website.

Certification Ready 2.4

What are some specific techniques used to make make a website accessible to viewers with visual and motor impairments?

Basic principles of website accessibility

So now that you've established what Accessibility is and why it matters, the question is how can you address these concerns on a practical level on your website. Throughout this book we will provide you explicit directions for using Dreamweaver for accessibility purposes, but a few general principles are in order:

- **Provide appropriate alternative text**

Alternative text provides a text alternative to non-text content in web pages such as images. It is useful for people who are blind or visually impaired and rely on a screen reader to have the content of the website read aloud.

- **Ensure users can complete and submit all forms**

Form elements (text field, checkbox, drop-down menus) should have a label using the `<label>` tag.

- **Label links**

Add a title attribute to your links. The title attribute contains descriptive information about the link (such as the destination) and can be read aloud by screen readers and appears in most browsers when a user hovers over a link.

- **Allow users to skip repetitive elements on the page**

You should provide a method that allows users to skip repeated elements on the page such as navigation. This can be accomplished by providing a "Skip Navigation" or "Skip to Content" link at the top of the page which jumps to the main section of the page.

- **Do not rely on color alone to convey information**

The use of color is a valuable tool in design, but do not use color to convey information. Users who are colorblind may not be able to perceive it and will be unavailable to screen readers

- **Keyboard equivalents**

The accesskey attribute can be added to certain form elements, including area, button, input, label, legend, and textarea.

Screen Readers

Certification Ready 2.4

What are the elements of a website that by default are not read by screen readers?

Screen reading devices are designed to read aloud the content of a page. It is easy to imagine how this can be done with text, but what about other elements such as images. How does a screen reader handle these? In HTML an image can be referenced in the code like so:

```
<img src="tree.jpg">
```

This is the simplest example of the image tag but this tag has support for an attribute called the alt attribute, whose job is to provide a text alternative for non-text objects, so within the code it looks like this:

```
<img src="tree.jpg" alt="Maple tree">
```

Strictly speaking, adding the alt attribute to images is optional. As you will see in later lessons, Dreamweaver prompts you to add the alt attribute every time you insert an image. However Dreamweaver does not do this for other elements on the page, they will require your attention for maximum accessibility. Objects such as hyperlinks, image maps, table data order, buttons, movies, and sound need extra help in order to be read by a screen reader. You'll learn some of these techniques throughout the book and in Lesson 16, "Managing your Website: Reports, Optimization, and Maintenance," you will learn how to run a test within Dreamweaver to check your pages for accessibility.

Certification Ready 2.4

What elements are used to improve website usability?

Website Usability

Accessibility and Usability are very closely related, but whereas accessibility is concerned with providing equal access to the information and functionality of your website, usability is concerned with removing the obstacles to the information on your site for your users. Some aspects of usability may seem obvious while other may not be so obvious. You will learn how to run a formal usability test in Lesson 16, but here are a few general principles:

- **Visual hierarchy**

Hierarchy is defined as organizing content into levels of importance. The tags in HTML can help you organize and group your content in logical ways and create a logical hierarchy. Headings, for example, come in six sizes (h1-h6). The heading 1 tag should contain the most important content on the page and using CSS font size and color you can direct your user's eye to this heading first.

- **Consistent location of repeatable items**

Place elements such as navigation menus, search boxes or any other content that is visible on all the pages in your site in the same place in order to avoid user disorientation.

- **File size (page load time)**

Be aware of how the file size of a page can effect the usability of a site, especially for those users who have slower connections. Be judicious when adding content that can affect page load time such as animation, video, or audio. Optimize your images to achieve the smallest file size possible without losing image quality. If the total file size of a page is more than 100k, be aware that users with slower connections (including mobile) may experience delays in page load.

- **Place the most important information above the fold**

In the world of print media the term "above the fold" referred to the top half of a newspaper where the most important information is located. A website obviously has no fold, but there is a vertical cut-off point beyond which the user must scroll. Scrolling doesn't have to be avoided, but there may be a point where it makes more sense to break a single long page into multiple pages and create links.

Certification Ready 2.4

What are text formatting guidelines that improve readability?

Improving readability

Text is a significant proportion of most web pages and arguably the most important component. Regardless of what type of website you have, it is important that you have an understanding of the basic rules of Readability. Readability on the Web is defined as how well your users can process the information within your content. Poor readability will drive users away from your site. Excellent readability allows users to efficiently read and absorb the information in your text. There are some basic concepts to be aware of that will help you create readable text:

- **Contrast**

One of the most important factors determining readability Good contrast largely goes unnoticed as it makes text easy on the eyes. Poor contrast forces the users eye to work hard and results in slower intake of information and possible abandonment of the site. Black text on a white background is the standard and most safe level of contrast. Be careful of any colored text on a colored background, especially for large blocks of text.

- **Font Size**

One of the most obvious elements determining readability The smaller the font, the harder is to read, but what are the guidelines? It is hard to define a single number because readability is partially based on other factors such as the target audience of your website and the amount of text within a given section. For body copy, the general rule of thumb is that anything less than 10 pixels for font size is too small for most readers. Consider the following fact: if you were to do no styling whatsover, the default web browser font size for a paragraph is 16 pixels. Therefore you should use your best judgement and consider all the other factors and stay within 10-16 pixels for the majority of your text.

- **Serif versus sans-serif**

A conservative way to choose fonts for your page is to use serif fonts (such as Times or Georgia) for your body copy and sans-serif fonts (such as Verdana or Trebuchet) for your headings. There has been some evidence that serif fonts are somewhat easier to read on the computer screen. However you should take this advice with a grain of salt, Verdana, for example is a sans-serif font that was specifically designed for readability on a monitor and works well as body copy.

- **Paragraph line-height and line length**

Line-height is the amount of space between the lines in a paragraph. Too much line-height can cause the reader to lose their place in the text. Too little line-height causes text to look cramped and can frustrate the reader. Line length refers to how long a line of text is. If line length is too long the user works hard to stay on track and they often lose their place. If line length is too short the user has to retain infomation as their eye skips to the next line and they can also lose their place.

- **Organization of content**

On the web the user is often "scanning" your text instead of truly reading it. The web tends to be more about information seeking rather than the more focused reading of a magazine article or a book. To make your copy scannable, you should make good use of headers and hierarchy and provide focus points to guide the user through the content. Examples of focus points include using lists of information where necessary, using images to break up content and taking the factors mentioned above (font-size, color, paragraph spacing) into account.

Typography and images on the Web

Dreamweaver CS6 offers some convenient features for placing images and formatting text. In this lesson, you'll be working with a few pages within a site and adding some photos and text to a simple page for a fictional store.

Adding text

You should already have created a new site, using the dw03lessons folder as your root. In this section, you'll be adding a headline and formatting the text on the events.html page.

Follow these steps to add text to a page | **Step-by-Step**

1. If it's not already open, launch Dreamweaver CS6.
2. Make sure your dw03lessons site is open in the Files panel. If not, open it now.

Certification Ready 4.4

How do you add text to an HTML page?

3. Double-click on the **events.html** file in your Files panel to open it in the Design view. Without any formatting, the text seems random and lacks purpose. First, you'll add a headline to give the first paragraph some context.
4. Click to place your cursor in front of the word *There's* in the first paragraph. Type **OrganicUtopia Events** and press Enter (Windows) or Return (Mac OS) to create a line break as seen in Figure 3-1.

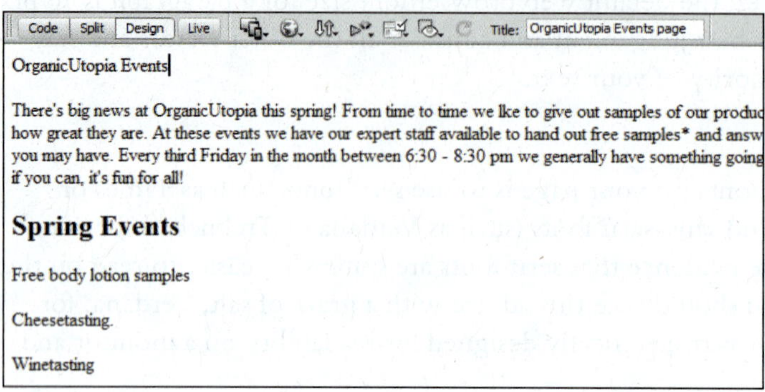

Figure 3-1: *Typing the words* ***OrganicUtopia Events*** *and then putting them on their own line.*

5. Click and drag to highlight the phrase you just typed. You will now format your text using the **Property Inspector**. Located at the bottom of the screen, the Property Inspector allows you to format your text using a combination of HTML and CSS. HTML stands for Hypertext Markup Language, and CSS stands for Cascading Styles Sheets. You will learn much more about the use of HTML and CSS in the next lesson; however, you will need to have a basic understanding of these two languages in order to use the Property Inspector to format your text.

6. Locate the Property Inspector at the bottom of your screen; there are two buttons immediately below the word "Properties." If necessary, click on the HTML button to see your HTML formatting options. Choose Heading 1 from the Format drop-down menu. The text gets larger and becomes bold. By default, the style of any HTML text formatted as Heading 1 is generic: the color is black and the font-family is Times New Roman (Figure 3-2).

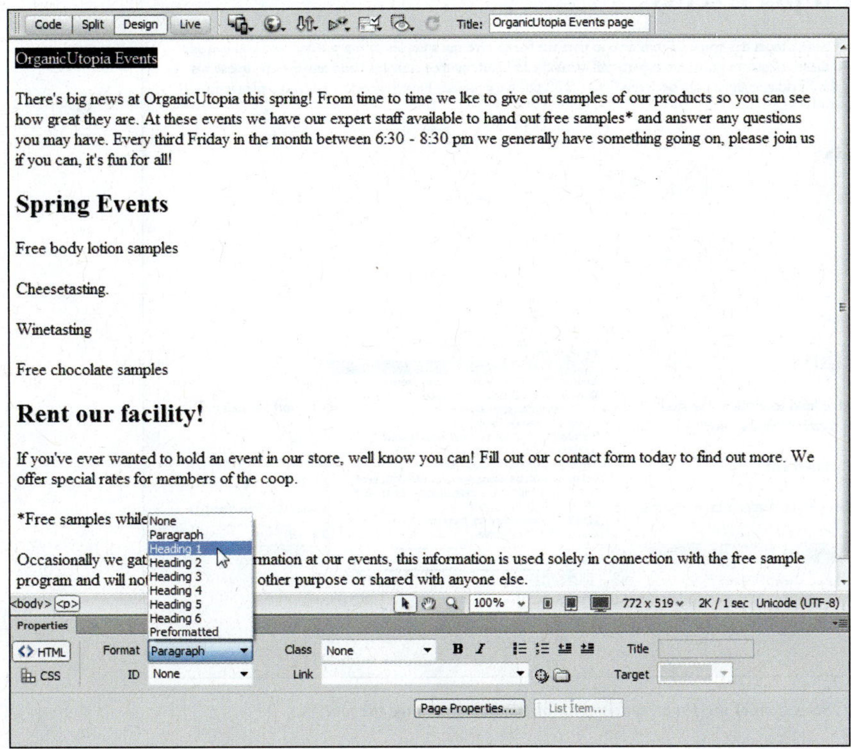

Figure 3-2: Use the Format drop-down menu in the Property Inspector to make the selected text a level-1 heading.

Although you are working in Dreamweaver's Design view, you have actually changed the HTML code for this page. Page content such as text is wrapped in opening and closing tags, and everything between these two tags is formatted according to the rules of these tags. The text OrganicUtopia Events originally had an opening and closing tag defining it as a paragraph. The code looked like this:

```
<p>OrganicUtopia Events</p>
```

The first <p> is the opening tag for a paragraph, and the second </p> is the closing tag for a paragraph. A pair of opening and closing tags in HTML is called an element. So in the previous step, you changed the formatting of the text from a paragraph element to a Heading 1 element, and the HTML code changed to this:

```
<h1>OrganicUtopia Events</h1>
```

Headings are important structural elements in HTML. The largest heading is H1, and the subsequent headings become smaller with H2, H3, and so on. For the next step, you will format this text in order to change the font style of this heading to Arial; however, you will not be using HTML to accomplish this, but rather CSS.

7. Click anywhere inside the heading OrganicUtopia Events; you do not need to have it selected. In the Property Inspector, click on the CSS button to access the formatting options. Choose Verdana, Geneva, sans-serif from the Font drop-down menu as seen in Figure 3-3.

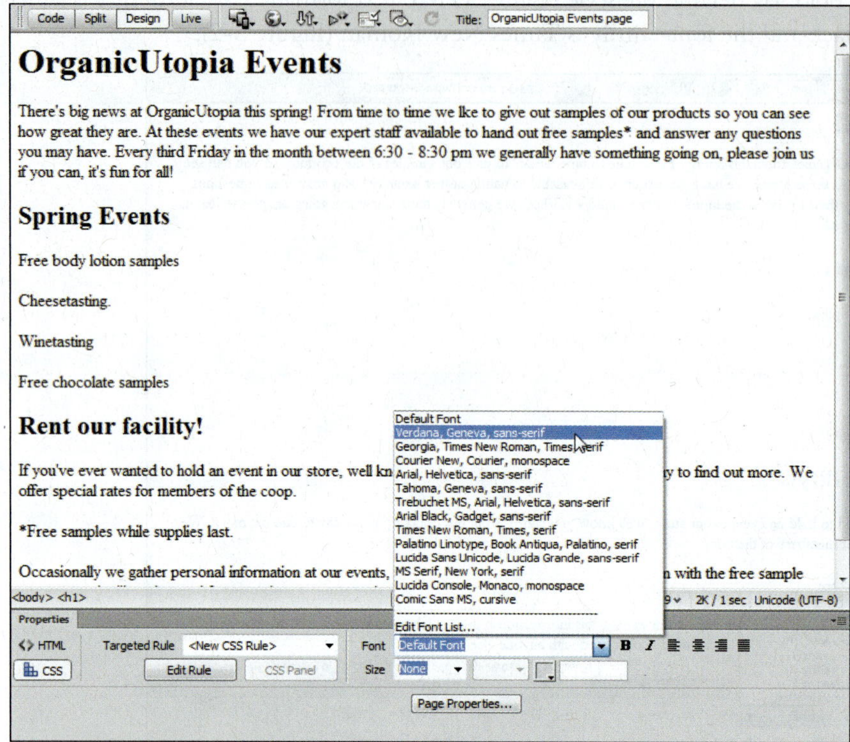

Figure 3-3: The CSS section of the Property Inspector allows you to change the font.

The New CSS Rule dialog box appears.

8. From the Selector Type drop-down menu, choose Tag. In the Selector Name text field, the selector h1 has been chosen for you (Figure 3-4). Dreamweaver does this because you placed your cursor inside the text formatted as H1.

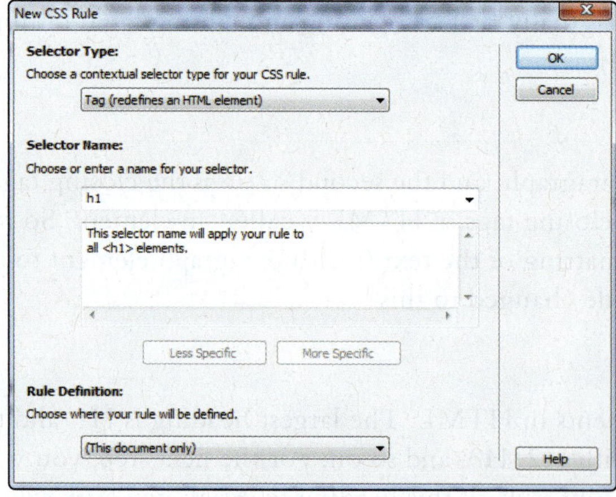

Figure 3-4: The New CSS Rule dialog box appears the first time you style text.

Press OK. Your heading is now styled in Verdana.

The role of the font stack

Dreamweaver allows you to format text in a way that is similar to desktop publishing and word processing applications, but there are important differences to keep in mind. When you chose the styling, Verdana, Geneva, and sans-serif, they were listed together as one option in the Font drop-down menu. When a web page is rendered in a browser, it uses the fonts installed on the user's computer. Assigning multiple fonts allows you to control which font is used if the person viewing your page doesn't have a specific font installed. In this case, if the user doesn't have Verdana, Geneva displays instead. Sans-serif is included as the last option in case the user doesn't have either Verdana or Geneva. A generic font family (either sans-serif or serif) is listed at the end of all the options in the Font drop-down menu.

The Font drop-down menu has a list of default font-families, however you can also create a custom font-stack by choosing the Edit Fonts option and in the Edit Font List window that appears, select one or more option from the list of Available fonts and add them to the Chosen fonts list and then click OK. You will now have a custom font list that will always be available in the Fonts menu within the Property Inspector.

Learning More

Certification Ready 5.3

How do you create a custom stack font using the Edit Font list command in the Properties Inspector or for the font-family property in the CSS rule definition dialog box?

Additional text formatting options

There are additional HTML text formatting options, some of them may not be used frequently but you should know that they exist. Try selecting text on your page and using some of the following formatting.

- **Blockquote**

The `blockquote` element will take selected text and indent it slightly to the right, thereby setting it off visually from the rest of the page. (Choose Insert > HTML > Text Objects > Blockquote.)

Certification Ready 5.3

How do you indent text to set off a block quotation?

- **Abbreviation**

The abbreviation element allows you to describes an abbreviated phrase.

By marking up abbreviations you can give useful information to browsers, spell checkers, translation systems, and search-engine indexers.

You will now change the text color using the Property Inspector.

9. Highlight *OrganicUtopia Events* and click on the Text Color button to the right of the Size drop-down menu. When the Swatches panel appears (Figure 3-5), hover over the color swatches. At the top of the Swatches panel, a different hexadecimal color value appears for each color. When you locate the value labeled #9C3 (an olive green), click once to apply the color.

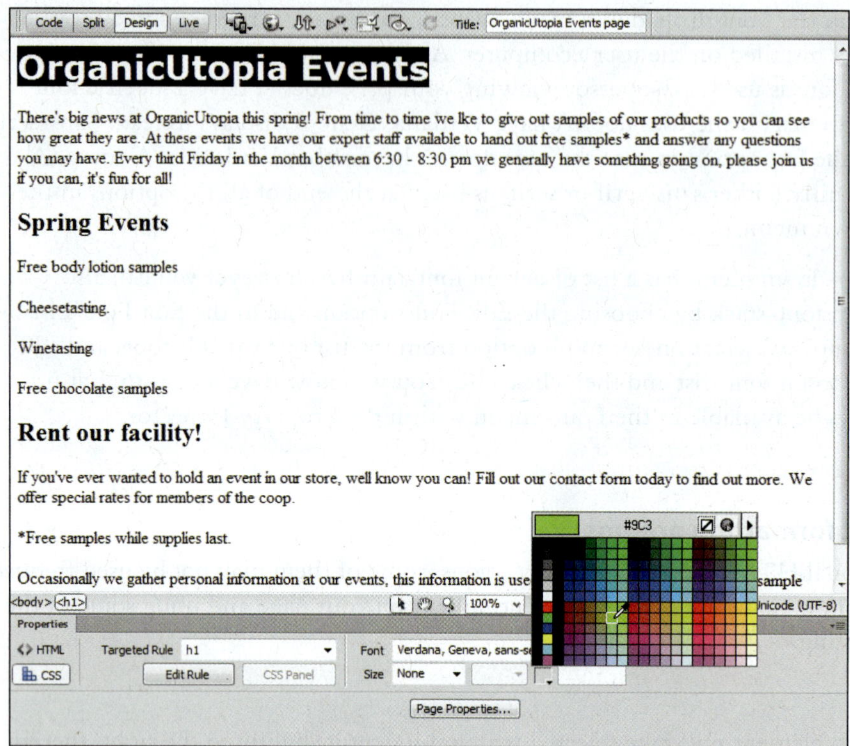

Figure 3-5: *Click on the Text Color swatch and choose the #9C3 color from the swatches.*

10. Choose File > Save. Keep this file open for the next part of this lesson.

Importing Word and Excel documents

You cannot import Microsoft Word or Excel documents directly into Dreamweaver, those file formats are not supported. There are two useful methods, however for bringing in the content from these documents.

Microsoft Word

- If you have Microsoft Word on your system, you may open the file and then save it as Plain Text (.txt) and then open this file directly in Dreamweaver by choosing File > Open. Keep in mind that .txt files do not support Microsoft Word styles so any formatting will be lost. In many cases, however, this is preferable as you will have finer control over the name and properties of the styles you create in Dreamweaver.
- The other method for importing is by copying selected text in Microsoft Word (by choosing Edit > Copy) and then switching to Dreamweaver and choosing Edit > Paste Special. The Paste Special dialog box gives you multiple options for how you would like the text to be formatted when you click OK.

In general, if you would like no styles to be transferred you would select the "Text Only" option or the "Text with Structure"option. If you would like to carry over styles from Word you should try either the "Text with structure plus basic formatting" or the "Text with structure plus full formatting" options. Keep in mind that if you import styles from Microsoft Word they are automatically converted to CSS styles and these are not always logically named or useful. We highly recommend not attempting to import styles form Word unless necessary.

Microsoft Excel

- If you have Microsoft Excel on your system, you may open the file and then save it in a delimited format such as a comma separated value file (.csv) and then open this file directly in Dreamweaver by choosing File > Open. If you open a .csv file directly, the data appears as plain text. Oftentimes a more useful option is to choose File > Import Tabular Data in which case you can format the data into an HTML table and maintain the row and column structure. (An exercise outlining these steps can be found in Lesson 8, "Working with Tables.")
- The other method for importing data is by copying selected text in Microsoft Excel (by choosing Edit > Copy) and then switching to Dreamweaver and choosing Edit > Paste Special. As in the examples listed above for Microsoft Word, you may choose to bring in data as plain text or with structure and formatting styles. The primary difference here is that if you choose to bring in data with the "structure" options, the data will be pasted as a table.

Linking to Microsoft Word and Excel files

- You can link elements such as text or images to Word and Excel documents as well. Simply select the object you would like to link and then choose Insert > Hyperlink. In the Hyperlink window, click on the Folder icon in the Link section and navigate to a Word or Excel document. It is important that this file already be located within your current site folder (just like any other asset such as images or video). Keep in mind that a visitor who clicks on this link online will need some method of opening Word or Excel files.

Learning More

Certification Ready 4.12

How do you add Word or Excel content to a web page?

Certification Ready 4.12

What are the correct settings to use when importing a Word document, based on the content in the document?

Certification Ready 4.12

How can you link to a Word or Excel document from a web page?

An introduction to styles

You have styled the first element on your page by first formatting the text as a Heading 1 in HTML, and then you changed the font and color using CSS. It's important to realize that every change you make in the Design view creates or modifies the code. In the next exercise, you'll begin to explore the HTML and CSS code behind the Design view. To help put this exercise in context, a little background on HTML and CSS is in order.

The HTML language has been around since the dawn of the Web. It's easiest to think of **HTML** as the structure behind the pages that are rendered in your web browser. An HTML page at its most basic is a collection of text, images, and sometimes multimedia such as Flash or video files. The different sections of a web page, such as a paragraph, a heading, or a list, are all elements.

CSS is also a language, but it has not been around as long as HTML. In many ways, CSS was created in order to allow HTML to do what it does best: create the structure of a page, but not style. CSS is a simple language that works in combination with HTML to apply style to the content in web pages, such as text, images, tables, and form elements. CSS uses rules, or style instructions, that the HTML elements on your page follow. The most important thing to remember is that HTML and CSS are two separate languages, but they are very closely aligned and work together very well.

In the last exercise, you were introduced to this interplay between HTML and CSS. There was an HTML element for the Heading 1 formatting. In the code it looks like this:

```
<h1>OrganicUtopia Events</h1>
```

That was the HTML element. The CSS rule that defines the appearance of the *<h1>* element looks like this:

```
h1 {
    font-family: Verdana, Geneva, sans-serif;
    color: #9C3;
}
```

CSS has a different **syntax** than HTML. In HTML, tags are defined by angled brackets, and you have opening tags, `<h1>`, and closing tags, `</h1>`. In CSS code, you are not working with tags at all, instead you use selectors. In the CSS code above, the h1 is referred to as the **selector** because it is selecting the HTML element and then declaring some rules for its appearance. Because you've established that HTML and CSS are two separate languages and have different syntax, it's important that you see where this code lives in your web page. You will do this by changing Dreamweaver's workspace.

This exercise is intended to help you understand the relationship between HTML and CSS code that is created in Dreamweaver, and is not necessarily the way you will always work in the program. Many people will work in the Design view most of the time, but the Split view you are about to use is very helpful for learning the languages of HTML and CSS.

Follow these steps to format text using CSS

Step-by-Step

1. Click on the Split button in the Document toolbar at the top of your page to open up the Split view. The **Split view** allows you to see your code and the design of your page simultaneously.
2. Click quickly three times in the paragraph beneath OrganicUtopia Events in the Design view. In the Code view the text is highlighted between the opening and closing paragraph tags as seen in Figure 3-6. As noted above, this is referred to as the paragraph element.

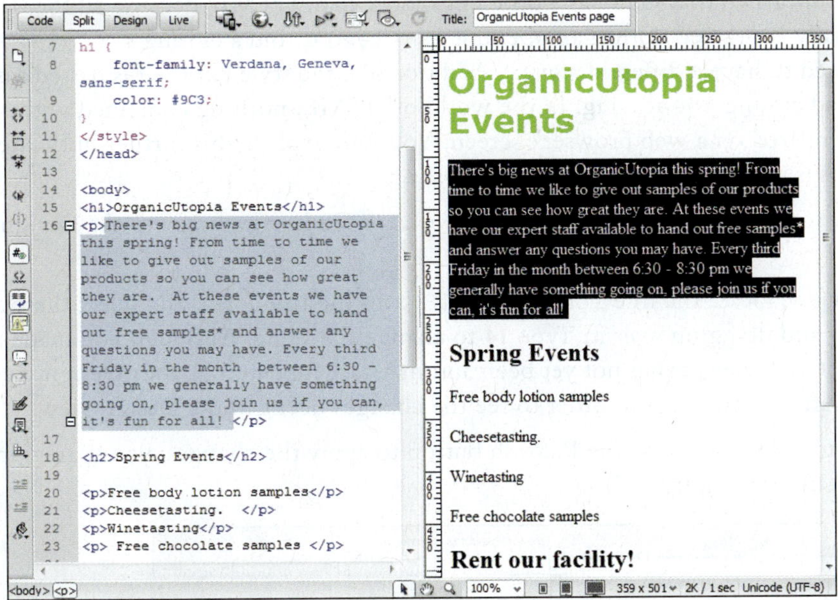

***Figure 3-6**: A paragraph highlighted in the Split view.*

You will now change the font size of your paragraphs.

3. Make sure you have CSS selected in the Property Inspector at the bottom of your page and choose 18 from the Size drop-down menu. The New CSS Rule dialog box appears again. This dialog box appears because it is the first time you have attempted to style a paragraph. After you define the properties, all text formatted as a paragraph will appear as indicated.
4. From the Selector Type drop-down menu, choose Tag. Since there are different categories of CSS rules, Dreamweaver wants to know which one you would like to use. You will stick with Tag for now (as you did in the last exercise). In the Selector Name text field, the selector p has been chosen for you because your cursor was inside a paragraph. Press OK to apply the changes; in this case, the font size is set to 18 pixels. Now let's look at the CSS code that is defining this font size.
5. Within the Code view of the split screen is all the HTML and CSS code that defines the appearance of this page. On the right side of the Code view, scroll up by clicking on the up arrow or by clicking the scroll bar and dragging upward. Toward the top of the page, you are looking for a few lines of code that look like this:

Certification Ready 5.3

How do you change font, font size, and color?

```
<style type="text/css">
h1 {
    font-family: Arial, Helvetica, sans-serif;
    color: #9C3;
}
p {
    font-size:18px;
}
</style>
```

Between the two <style> tags are all the CSS rules you have created up to this point. Previously, you learned that CSS has a different syntax than HTML: because all the CSS rules are actually contained within an opening <style> tag and a closing </style> tag, they are allowed to have a different syntax. Additionally, the style tag itself is nested inside an opening and closing <head> tag. In the world of HTML, nothing contained within head tags is rendered on a web browser's screen. You will explore this further in the next lesson, but this is referred to as an internal style sheet.

You will now see that changes made in Dreamweaver's Code view apply to the Design view as well.

6. In the Code view, locate the line `font-size:18px` in the rule for `p`, and select the value 18 by clicking and dragging over it. Type **14** to change the value. Although you made a change in the Code view, it has not yet been automatically updated in your Design view. You need to refresh your page in order to see the changes occur in the Design view.

7. In the Property Inspector, press the Refresh button to apply the changes; your paragraph text becomes smaller (Figure 3-7).

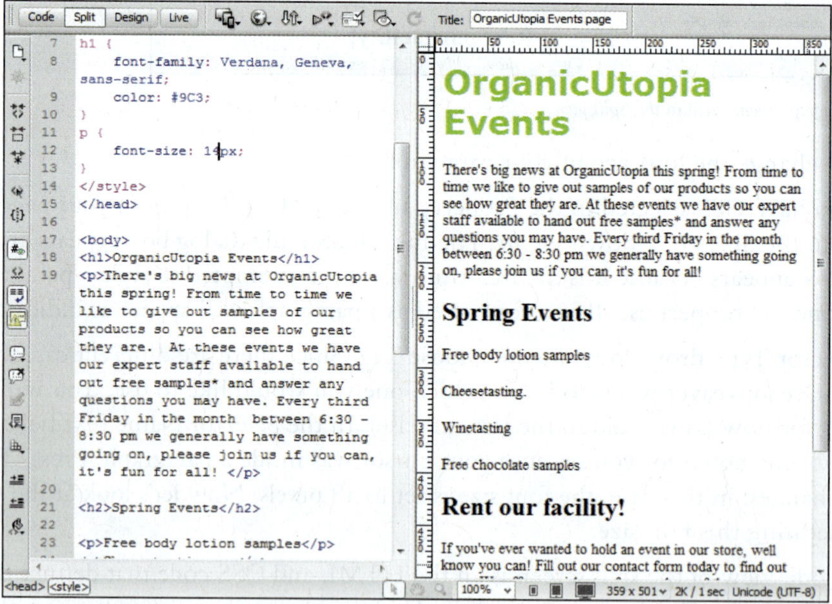

Figure 3-7: *Changes made in the Code view are reflected in the Design view after pressing the Refresh button.*

Take Note...

You can also click once inside the Design view for the page to refresh automatically.

On the Web, font sizes are specified differently than they are in print. The numerical choices in the Size drop-down menu refer to pixels instead of points. Also, the xx-small through larger options may seem oddly generic if you are accustomed to the precision of print layout. Because web pages are displayed on a variety of monitors and browsers, relative measurements can be a useful way for designers to plan ahead for inevitable discrepancies in the rendering of pages.

8. Click inside the first paragraph in the Design view. You will now change the color of the paragraph slightly to a dark gray rather than the default pure black. In the Property Inspector, click on the color swatch, and in the top-left corner, locate the dark gray swatch, which is hexadecimal color #666. Click on the swatch to apply the color. Notice that not only does the appearance in the Design view change, but in your Code view a new line of CSS has also been created (color: #666).

   Working in the Split view can be a great way to learn about hand-coding without diving in completely. Even if you're not quite comfortable editing code, keeping an eye on the code that Dreamweaver writes for you can give you a better understanding of how things like CSS affect your web pages.

9. Click the Design view button to return to Design view.

10. Choose File > Save. Keep this file open for the next part of this lesson.

Certification Ready 5.3

How do you apply a paragraph style to a paragraph of text?

Take Note...

For a more in-depth look at Cascading Style Sheets see the Web Design with HTML and CSS Digital Classroom *book available in electronic and print formats.*

Previewing pages in a web browser

Viewing your pages in the Design view is helpful, but visitors to your site will be using a web browser to access your site. In Lesson 1, "Dreamweaver CS6 Jumpstart," you learned how browsers use HTML code to render a page. Unfortunately, not every browser renders HTML code in exactly the same way, so it's important to test-drive your pages in a number of different browsers to check for inconsistencies and basic functionality.

Next, you'll use Dreamweaver's **Preview in Browser** feature to see how the OrganicUtopia site looks in a web browser.

Previewing pages in a web browser

Step-by-Step | **Follow these steps to preview your page in a web browser**

1. With **events.html** open in Dreamweaver, choose File > Preview in Browser (Figure 3-8) and select a browser from the available options. This list varies, depending on the browsers you have installed on your hard drive.

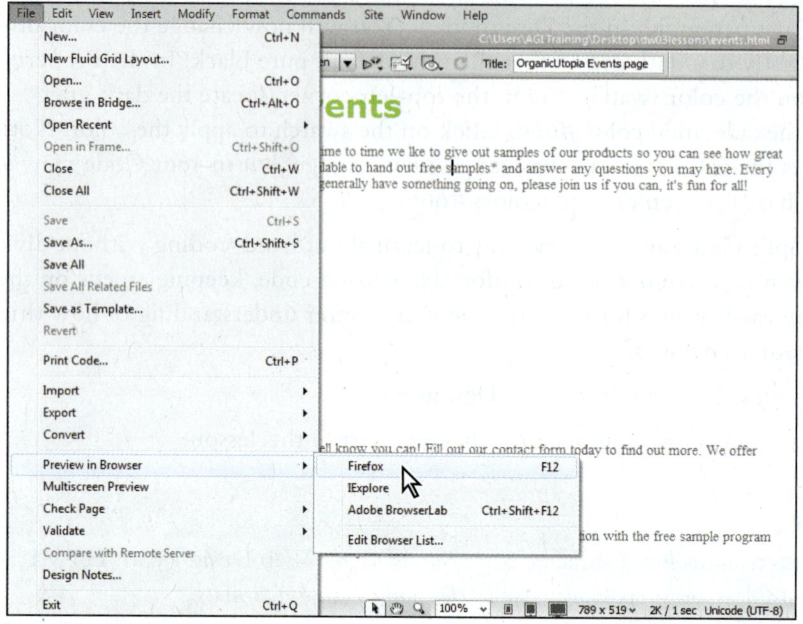

Figure 3-8: Preview in Browser allows you to see how a selected browser would render your page.

Take Note...

The options found under File > Preview in Browser can be customized by choosing File > Preview in Browser > Edit Browser List.

2. When events.html opens in the browser of your choice, look for differences between the Design view preview and the version rendered by your browser. At this stage, there shouldn't be anything too surprising, but there may be subtle differences in spacing and font style. Close your web browser.

   There is another method to preview your pages: the Live View feature. Live View allows you to preview your page without having to leave the Dreamweaver workspace. You can think of Live View as a browser within Dreamweaver (in fact, it is the same WebKit rendering engine found in browsers such as Apple's Safari and Google's Chrome, among others).

3. Press the Live button located in the Document toolbar at the top of your page as seen in Figure 3-9. You will not see a dramatic difference, but your text may shift slightly. Select the first heading in the window and try to delete it; you will be unable to, because Live View is a non-editable workspace. However, Live View does allow you to edit your page when you are in Split view. Here, you are allowed to edit in the Code view and changes will be reflected in real time. An additional advantage is that your document does not have to be saved in order to see the changes.

***Figure 3-9**: When Live View is enabled, Dreamweaver simulates a web browser.*

4. Click the Live button again to deactivate this view. While Live View is a useful addition to Dreamweaver, it does not replace the need to preview your page in a browser. Web pages might be rendered differently depending on your visitor's browser, and so it is a good habit to check your page occasionally as you make changes to your design.

Certification Ready 6.1

How do you preview a web page in a browser?

Take Note...

You can also preview your page designs in other browsers and for different platforms using Adobe's Browser Lab service. We cover the steps for this in Lesson 16, "Managing your Website: Reports, Optimization, and Maintenance."

Understanding hyperlinks

When people visit a website, they usually expect to see more than one page. Imagine trying to shop for a new book by your favorite author on a site that consisted of nothing more than a single order form with every book offered by a retailer like *Amazon.com*. This might seem absurd, but without hyperlinks you wouldn't have much choice.

Hyperlinks make the Web a truly interactive environment. They allow the user to freely navigate throughout a website, or jump from one site to another. There are a number of ways to create links in Dreamweaver, but before you get started, you should be aware of some fundamental facts.

Links rely on directory paths to locate files. A directory path is simply a description of a file's location that can be understood by a computer. A classic, real-world example is an address. If you wanted to send a letter to your friend Sally in Florida, you would have to specify the state, city, street, and house number where Sally can be found. If Sally lived at 123 Palm Street in Orlando, the path would be:

Florida/Orlando/123 Palm Street/Sally

This simply means that inside Florida, inside Orlando, in the house numbered 123 on a street named Palm Street, you can find a person named Sally. Hyperlinks follow the same logic:

www.somewebsitesomewhere.com/photos/mydog.jpg

This URL address is a link to a JPEG image named mydog.jpg, which is inside a folder named photos on a website named *somewebsitesomewhere.com*.

Creating hyperlinks

Later in this lesson, you'll be creating a gallery page to showcase some of the sample products mentioned in the main paragraph. Before you work on that page, you'll link it to the home page by creating a hyperlink. If you are not already in Design view, select Design view now.

Step-by-Step

Follow these steps to create a hyperlink

1. In the Property Inspector, click on the HTML button to access the HTML properties.
2. In the first paragraph, highlight the word products in the second sentence.
3. In the Property Inspector, type **products.html** in the Link text field (Figure 3-10). Press Enter (Windows) or Return (Mac OS). The highlighted word automatically becomes underlined. It is important to note that we have created this page for you and it is currently inside your site folder, you are simply linking to it.

Figure 3-10: *Type* **products.html** *into the Link text field in the Property Inspector.*

4. Choose File > Save and then File > Preview in Browser.
5. Click on the new products link. The products page appears in your browser window. This is because a previously existing page named products.html was located in this folder.

   Now visitors can easily navigate to the products page, but what happens when they want to go back to the events page? It looks like you'll need another link.
6. Return to Dreamweaver and double-click on **products.html** in the Files panel. Click to the right of the word Produce and press Enter (Windows) or Return (Mac OS) to create a new line. Choose Insert > Hyperlink to open the Hyperlink dialog box.

   The Hyperlink dialog box is one of the many ways to create a link in Dreamweaver. It offers all the options found in the Property Inspector, with a few additions.

7. Type **Events** in the Text field as seen in Figure 3-11.

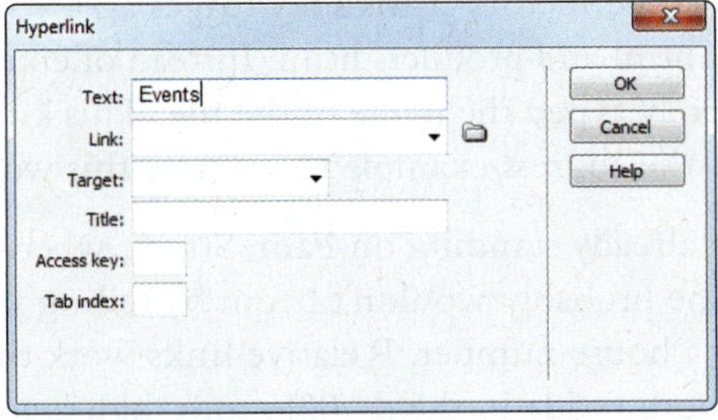

Figure 3-11: *The Hyperlink dialog box is one of the many ways to create links in Dreamweaver.*

8. Click on the Browse button to the right of the Link text field to open the Select File dialog box. The dw03lessons folder you defined as the root for this site should be selected for you by default. If not, click the Site Root button. Select **events.html** and press OK (Windows) or Open (Mac OS).
9. Click inside the Title field and type **Organic Utopia events page**. Titles are strictly optional for hyperlinks, but they improve accessibility for users with assistive technologies, such as Screen Readers. Additionally, adding titles to your hyperlinks can also improve your site's search engine rankings. Click OK to commit the changes; notice that a link to events.html has been created for you using the text entered into the Text field in the Hyperlink dialog box.
10. Choose File > Save and keep this file open for the next part of this lesson.

Named Hyperlink Anchors

In addition to linking from one page to another, you can also link to a specific location on a page. This is most useful on pages with lots of content. Imagine a page that has a list of the 100 best restaurants in the world and you would like to link to number 99 on this page. You could add a named anchor to this item and then create a hyperlink sending a user directly to the section.

To create and link to a Named Anchor

1. Place your cursor in front of the first letter of the page element you would like to link to.
2. Choose Insert > Named Anchor or click the "Named Anchor" icon in the "Common" toolbar.
3. Give your anchor a name; type **best99**.
4. Click OK. Named anchors appear as a small anchor icon in the Design view and as `<a name="best99">` in the Code view.
5. To link to the named anchor you need to select the element you want linked (such as a text).
6. In the Properties Inspector, use the Point to File icon and drag it to the name anchor. You could also type in the anchor name within the Link field of the Properties Inspector, like so **#best99**.

Learning More

Certification Ready 4.6

How do you create and link to a named anchor?

Relative versus absolute hyperlinks

After reading about the fundamentals of hyperlinks and directory paths a few pages ago, you may be surprised by the simplicity of linking events.html and products.html. Instead of entering a long directory path in the Link text fields, you merely typed the name of the file. This kind of link is called a **relative hyperlink**. Let's go back to the address example to see how this works.

Remember Sally from Orlando? Imagine you were already standing on Palm Street, where she lives. If you called her for directions to her house, she probably wouldn't begin by telling you how to get to Florida. At this point, all you need is a house number. Relative links work the same way. Because events.html and products.html both reside in the dw03lessons folder, you don't need to tell the browser where to find this folder.

Now you'll create an absolute link that will allow visitors to access the Adobe website to learn more about Dreamweaver CS6.

Step-by-Step

Certification Ready 4.6

What are hyperlinks and what are the differences between the various types?

Certification Ready 4.6

How do you link text and images to another website?

Follow these steps to create an absolute hyperlink

1. Click on the **events.html** tab above the Document toolbar to bring the page forward. Scroll down to the bottom of the page if necessary. Using the Design view window, create a new line at the bottom of the page after the text that reads "Occasionally we gather...", and type **This page was created with Adobe Dreamweaver**.
2. Highlight the words Adobe Dreamweaver and in the Common section of the Insert panel on the right side of the screen, click on the Hyperlink icon to open the Hyperlink dialog box (Figure 3-12).

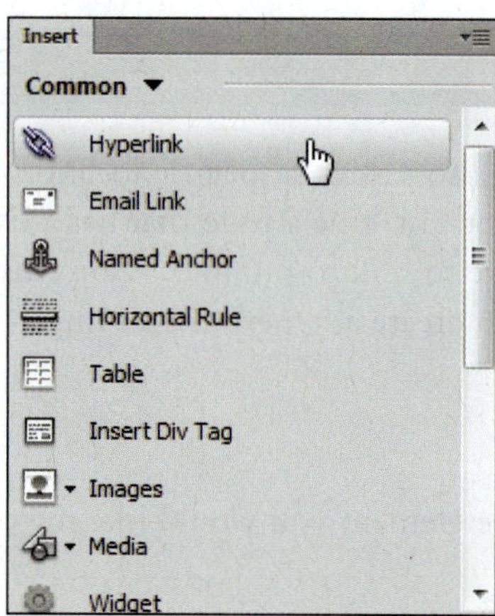

Figure 3-12*: The Hyperlink icon in the Insert panel is another convenient way to create links.*

3. The Hyperlink dialog box opens. Notice that Adobe Dreamweaver has been entered into the Text field for you. In the Link text field, type **http://www.adobe.com/products/dreamweaver.html**. Make sure to include the colon and the appropriate number of forward slashes.

The **absolute hyperlink** *http://www.adobe.com/products/dreamweaver.html* instructs the browser to find a website named *adobe.com* on the World Wide Web. Then the browser looks for a file named dreamweaver.html located inside a folder named products.

Take Note...

You do not have to type the absolute hyperlinks if you have the website open in your browser. In your web browser, select the address in the address bar, copy it, and then paste it into the Link field in Dreamweaver.

4. Choose `_blank` from the Target drop-down menu (Figure 3-13). Choosing the `_blank` option will cause the hyperlink to the Adobe website to open in a new, blank browser window or tab (depending on the browser).

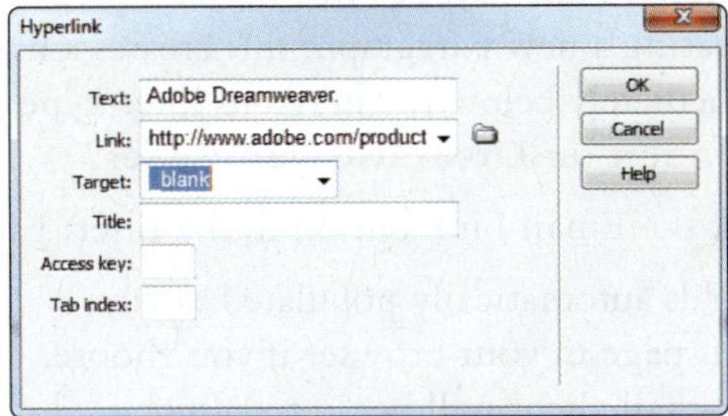

Figure 3-13: *Set the target window for the hyperlink to open in a blank browser window or tab.*

Take Note...

The Target attribute

The target attribute in HTML specifies where to open a linked document. There are four possible values for this attribute

- **`_blank`** Opens the linked document in a new window or tab
- **`_self`** Opens the linked document in the same frame as it was clicked (this is default)
- **`_parent`** Opens the linked document in the parent frame
- **`_top`** Opens the linked document in the full body of the window

Certification Ready 4.6

How do you target links?

5. Press OK to close the Hyperlink dialog box. Choose File > Save, then File > Preview in Browser, or press the Preview/Debug in Browser button (●) in the Document toolbar.
6. Click on the Adobe Dreamweaver text. Unlike the Events and Products links you created earlier, this link causes your browser to open a new tab or window, and it is pointing to an external web page on the Internet.
7. Close your browser and keep this file open; you will be adding to it in the next exercise.

Linking to an e-mail address

Absolute and relative links can be used to access web pages, but it's also possible to link to an e-mail address. Instead of opening a new web page, an e-mail link opens up the default mail program on a visitor's computer and populates the address field with the address you specify when creating the link. As you may imagine, this kind of link can work differently depending on how your visitors have configured their computers.

In the previous part of this lesson, you gave the visitor a link to some information on Dreamweaver. Now you'll link them to an e-mail address where they can get some information on learning Dreamweaver from the folks who wrote this book.

Step-by-Step

Follow these steps to create a link to an e-mail address

1. Place your cursor at the end of the last line, then hold down your Shift key and press Enter (Windows) or Return (Mac OS). Instead of creating a new paragraph, this creates a line break, or a soft return, and the text begins immediately below the previous line. Type **Contact info@agitraining.com for information on Dreamweaver classes**.
2. Highlight the text *info@agitraining.com* and click the Email Link button in the Insert panel.
3. The Email Link dialog box opens with both fields automatically populated as seen in Figure 3-14. Press OK. You may preview this page in your browser if you choose. Remember that if you click on the link, your e-mail client will begin to launch.

Certification Ready 4.6

What is a hyperlink, e-mail link and named anchor?

Certification Ready 4.6

How do you link text or images to an e-mail address?

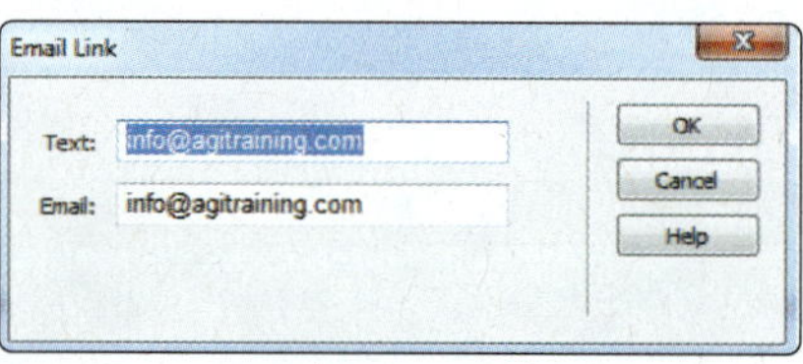

***Figure 3-14**: The Email Link dialog box allows you to link to an e-mail address.*

Creating lists

Bulleted lists may be familiar to you if you have worked with word processing or desktop publishing applications. **Lists** are a helpful way to present information to a reader without the formal constraints of a paragraph. They are especially important on the Web. Studies indicate that people typically skim web pages instead of reading them from beginning to end. Creating lists will make it easier for your visitors to get the most from your website without sifting through several paragraphs of text.

Follow these steps to create a list in HTML

Step-by-Step

1. On the **events.html** page, click and drag to highlight the four lines below Spring Events.
2. Make sure you have the HTML button selected in the Property Inspector at the bottom of your page, and click the Unordered List button (Figure 3-15). The highlighted text becomes indented, and a bullet point is placed at the beginning of each line.

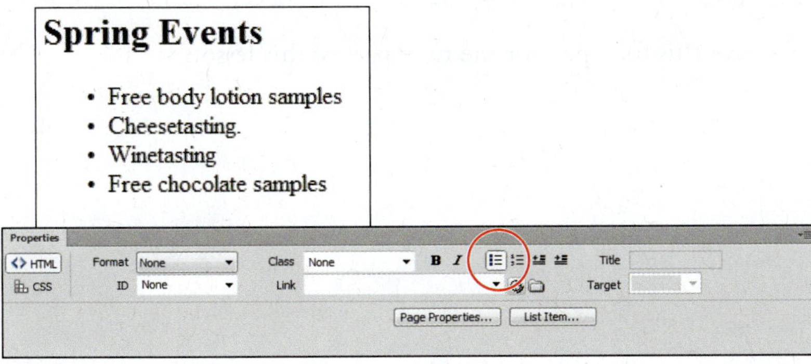

Figure 3-15: Use the Unordered List button in the Property Inspector to create a bulleted list.

3. Click the Ordered List button to the right of the Unordered List button. The bullets change to sequential numbers.
4. Choose Format > List > Properties to open the List Properties dialog box. Choose Bulleted List from the List type drop-down menu to return to your first style of list. The Numbered List and Bulleted List options in the List type drop-down menu also allow you to switch between ordered and unordered lists.
5. From the Style drop-down menu, choose Square as seen in Figure 3-16. This changes the default circular bullets to square bullets. Press OK to exit the List Properties dialog box.

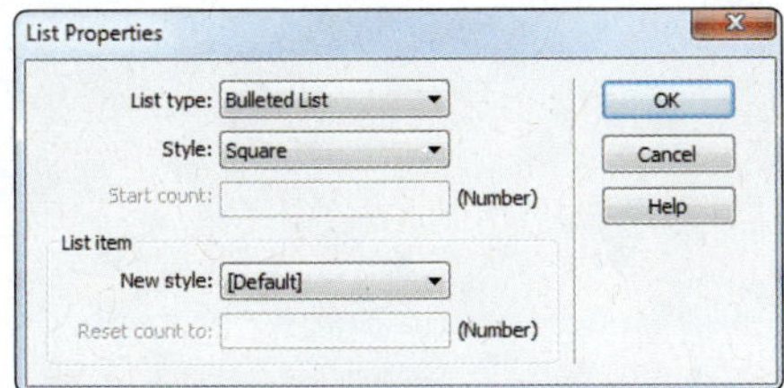

Figure 3-16: Change the bullet style to square in the List Properties dialog box.

You may have noticed that the four lines of text in your list have lost their style. They are slightly larger than your paragraphs and they are black, not dark gray. This is because a style has been defined for paragraphs, but not an unordered list. You will now create a new CSS rule for the appearance of all unordered lists in the document.

6. With all four lines still highlighted, click on the CSS button in the Property Inspector at the bottom of your page. Click on the arrow to the right of the Size field. Choose 14 from the Size drop-down menu in the Property Inspector. The New CSS Rule dialog box appears. This dialog box appears because it is the first time you have attempted to style an unordered list. After you define the properties, all text formatted as an unordered list will appear the same.

Certification Ready 5.3

How do you create unordered and ordered lists and set the properties for a list by using the Property Inspector?

7. From the Selector Type drop-down menu, choose Tag. In the Selector Name text field, the selector `ul` has been chosen for you; `ul` is the HTML tag for an unordered list. If `ul` is not chosen for you, type **ul** inside this text field. Press OK to apply the changes; in this case the font size is set to 14 pixels. Now you need to change the color of the unordered list to match the color of your paragraph.

Certification Ready 5.3

What are ordered, unordered, and defintion lists?

8. In the Property Inspector, if the Targeted Rule drop-down menu does not read ul, choose ul from the menu. Click on the color swatch and in the top-left corner of the colors panel, locate the dark gray swatch, which is hexadecimal color #666. Click on the swatch to apply the color.

9. Choose File > Save. Leave this file open for the next part of this lesson.

Creating a Definition list

Ordered and Unordered lists are used frequently in web pages. There is a third type of list in HTML that is used less frequently called a Definition list. A Definition list is a list of terms and corresponding definitions

Example:

Professional sports teams of Boston
Boston Red Sox
Boston Celtics
Boston Bruins

Definition lists have a slightly more complex structure than either ordered or unordered lists. In the example above, "Professional sports teams of Boston" is the definition term (which uses the dt tag) and the three teams are each definition descriptions (using the dd tag). So in HTML, the example looks like this:

```
<dl>
   <dt>Professional sports teams of Boston</dt>
         <dd>Boston Red Sox</dd>
         <dd>Boston Celtics</dd>
         <dd>Boston Bruins</dd>
   </dt>
</dl>
```

The formatting of Definition lists are also different than either ordered or unordered lists. The definition description(s) for any given definition term will be indented one level by default, making it visually clear that the description is a sub-category of the term.

To create a definition list

1. Place your cursor on a new line where you would like to add the list and choose Insert > HTML > Text Objects > Definition List.

   Type your definition term (this is the dt tag).

2. If you would like the next line to be a Definition Description, press Return and Dreamweaver will automatically add one (this is the dd tag). Alternatively if you wanted another Definition Term on the second line instead of a Definition Description, you could choose Insert > HTML > Text Objects > Definition term.

Learning More

Certification Ready 5.3

How do you create definition lists?

Using the Text Insert panel

There are a number of ways to format text in Dreamweaver. One method you haven't explored yet is the Text Insert panel. Because most of the options available in the Text Insert panel are also available in the Property Inspector, you may find it more convenient to use the Property Inspector for common tasks. However, you should be aware of the Characters menu located in the Text Insert panel. One of the most common items in the Characters menu used on the Web is the copyright symbol, ©. You will now insert a copyright notification at the bottom of your Events page.

Step-by-Step

Follow these steps to insert a text character

1. Click to the left of the sentence *This page was created with Adobe Dreamweaver* and type **2012** and then add a space.
2. Click before the text 2012 to insert your cursor.
3. Click on the menu at the top of the Insert panel on the right side of your page and choose Text. Scroll all the way to the bottom of the resulting list and click on Characters to open a menu (Figure 3-17). Choose the Copyright symbol from the list to add it to the beginning of the line.

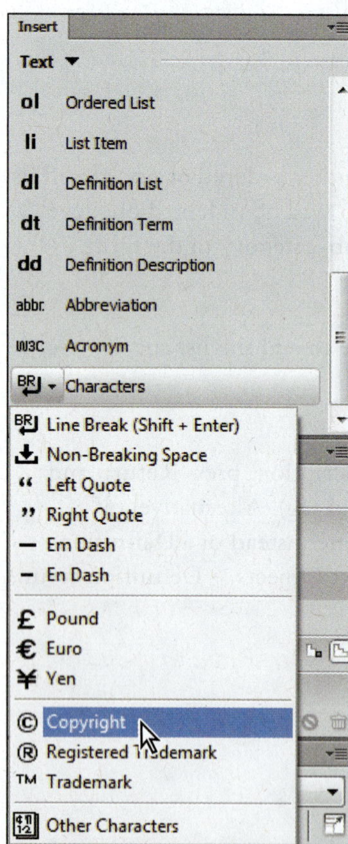

Figure 3-17: *The copyright symbol can be inserted from the Character menu.*

4. Highlight the last two lines on your page, beginning with the newly inserted copyright symbol and ending with Dreamweaver classes. You are going to set these two lines apart from the rest of the page by italicizing them. Layout considerations such as headers and footers will be discussed throughout the following lessons in this book, but for now you can use the Text options in the Insert panel to italicize these two lines.

5. Scroll to the top of the Text options in the Insert panel and click the Italic option.

Take Note...
You could have also used the Italic button in the Property Inspector. Additionally, you could have selected the text and chosen Insert > HTML > Text Objects to accomplish the same thing.

6. Choose File > Save.

Paying attention to copyright

Anyone who publishes content to the Web needs to be aware of the legal issues involved. In general, unless you have created the content yourself (such as text, images, video, music or any other media) you will need the permission of the creator. There are some exceptions to this principle, although they are very rare.

Certification Ready 1.3
How do you use copyright terms correctly?

Certification Ready 1.3
How do you identify when permission must be obtained to use copyrighted material?

Certification Ready 1.3
What methods used to indicate content as copyrighted?

- **Intellectual property**

Refers to unique content for which a set of exclusive rights are recognized under law. Under intellectual property law, owners are granted certain exclusive rights to a variety of intangible assets, such as musical, literary, and artistic works; discoveries and inventions; and words, phrases, symbols, and designs.

- **Copyright**

Copyright is one type of Intellectual Property and is a legal concept giving the creator of original work exclusive rights to it, usually for a limited time. There are certain standards for labeling content that is copyrighted, such as the copyright symbol (©) or the word "copyright" or adding the date of publication on the content. It is important to note that the lack of a copyright on content (such as an image) does not mean that there is no copyright. The author of a creative work is automatically assigned a legal copyright regardless of whether there is a label or not.

- **Fair Use Doctrine**

Fair use is a doctrine that permits limited use of copyrighted material without acquiring permission from the rights holders. General examples of this would include news reporting, commentary, criticism, and for some educational purposes. There are some general guidelines for determining whether content can be used as fair use. For more information on this, visit:

http://fairuse.stanford.edu/Copyright_and_Fair_Use_Overview/chapter9/9-b.html

So how does this all affect you, the web designer? As stated earlier, do not use content on your site unless you are sure you have permission from the creator. If you have any questions about whether something can be used, hold off until you have consulted someone with legal background.

- **Derivative work**

A derivative work is material that is "based on or derived from" another work such as a painting of a scene from a movie.

You may not distribute a derivative work of a work under copyright without the original author's permission unless the content meets certain criteria of fair use.

A web designer, for example, might take a famous photograph and apply a Photoshop filter to it. Chances are this image will still remain under copyright even though it has been altered slightly.

Learning More

Certification Ready 1.3

What are the proper methods for citing websites, images, sounds, video, and text from the Internet?

Citing a website or other content from the Internet

The World Wide Web is built on hyperlinked documents which makes it easy for you to link to or embed content from other websites. An informal citing of material can be a mention in your text, e.g., "On April 24, 2012, *Newsweek* had listed on its website…".

If a more formal citation is required you can follow these guideline examples below. The web is not like a print publication so try to include relevant information such as the date visited or modified:

1. "Adobe Privacy Policy," Last updated on July 14, 2009 *http://www.adobe.com/misc/privacy.html*
2. "5 easy ways to make money on the Internet," YouTube, accessed April 20, 2012 *http://www.youtube.com/watch?v=oHg5SJYRHA0*

Inserting images

Images are an essential part of most web pages. Just as lists make content friendlier and more accessible, images help to give your visitors the rich, visual experience that they've come to expect on the Web. However, before you learn to insert images, you will briefly learn about web graphics.

Image resolution

Image resolution is defined as the number of pixels in a digital image, typically as "width × height". Your original image has an absolute number of pixels and if you need to resize it, this is most often done in an image editing program such as Photoshop. While it is possible to resize images with Dreamweaver, it's generally not a good idea. Specifying the width and height of an image in the Property Inspector changes the display size of the image, but it does not resample the image the way a graphic processing application like Photoshop does. For example, a JPEG image that is 150 pixels by 150 pixels might have a file size of 30k. You could resize this image in Dreamweaver by 50% and the result would be a thumbnail image displayed at 75 pixels by 75 pixels. However, even though the image is visually smaller, the file size remains the same. A visitor to your website still must download the 30k file and this translates to slower loading time for the image (and possibly the page) and a potentially poor user experience, especially if they have low bandwith.

Certification Ready 4.5

What image file types can be viewed in all browsers?

Certification Ready 4.5

What are the different image file types and what are their uses?

Image formats

The three most common **image formats** on the Web are JPEG, GIF, and PNG. While an exhaustive description of how each of these formats compresses data is beyond the scope of this book, a general overview can help you avoid some common pitfalls.

The JPEG format was created by a committee named the Joint Photographic Experts Group. Its sole purpose is to compress photographic images. Specifically, it uses lossy compression, which means that it selectively discards information, to reduce the size of a file. When you save a JPEG, you decide how much information you are willing to sacrifice by selecting a quality level. A high-quality image preserves more information and results in a larger file size. A low-quality image discards more information, but produces a smaller file size. The goal is to reduce file size as much as possible without creating distortion and artifacts.

Because JPEGs were designed to handle photographic images, they can significantly reduce the size of images containing gradients and soft edges, without producing noticeable degradation. However, reproducing sharp edges and solid areas of color often requires a higher quality setting.

The GIF format was created by CompuServe. GIF is an acronym for Graphics Interchange Format. Unlike the JPEG format, GIFs do not use lossy compression. Instead, GIFs rely on a maximum of 256 colors to reduce the size of images. This means that images with a limited number of colors can be reproduced without degradation. Logos, illustrations, and line drawings are well-suited to this format. Unlike JPEGs, GIFs excel at reproducing sharp edges and solid areas of color. However, because photographic elements such as gradients and soft edges require a large number of colors to appear convincing, GIF images containing these elements look choppy and posterized.

The PNG format has become increasingly popular on the Web in recent years because it incorporates many of the best features of JPEGs and GIFs. The PNG format is closer to GIFs in that it offers lossless compression and comes in two categories: 8 bit and 24 bit. This means it can be used quite effectively for simple graphics as well as continuous tone photographic images. A PNG also offers better transparency features than a GIF, most significantly the support of alpha channels. For many years the adoption of PNGs (especially the use of the transparency) was held back because Internet Explorer 6 ignored the transparency. As the number of people using that browser continues to decline, the PNG format is being used more frequently. For more information on web graphics see the *Web Design with HTML and CSS Digital Classroom* book, which is available in both print and electronic formats.

Creating a simple gallery page

Now that you have a better understanding of the types of images that are appropriate for use on your website, it's time to build the products.html page that you linked to earlier in this lesson.

Follow these steps to create a gallery page

Step-by-Step

1. Double-click on **products.html** in the Files panel or click on the tab, as it's still open. Place your cursor after the word Produce and press Enter (Windows) or Return (Mac OS) to create a new line.
2. Choose Insert > Image. The Select Image Source dialog box appears. If your site folder does not open automatically, click the Site Root button, and then double-click the images folder. Select **beets.jpg** and press OK (Windows) or Open (Mac OS).
3. When the Image Tag Accessibility Attributes dialog box appears, type **Beets** in the Alternate text field. Press OK.

Certification Ready 4.5

How do you add alternative text to images?

Take Note...

The Alternate text field in the Image Tag Accessibility Attributes dialog box corresponds to the Alt attribute of an <img> tag. Including a description of the inserted image in this field is not technically necessary, but it is good practice. It provides information about the images to visually impaired visitors using screen readers. Also, Alt text is displayed in place of images on some handheld devices, and browsers where images are disabled.

4. Click on the Split button in the Document toolbar to view the code that was written by Dreamweaver when you inserted beets.jpg (Figure 3-18). An <img> tag was created, with four attributes. The src attribute is a relative link to the .jpg file in your images folder. The alt attribute is the alternate text you specified in the last step. The width and height attributes are simply the width and height of the image, and these have automatically been added by Dreamweaver. Press the Design button to return to this view.

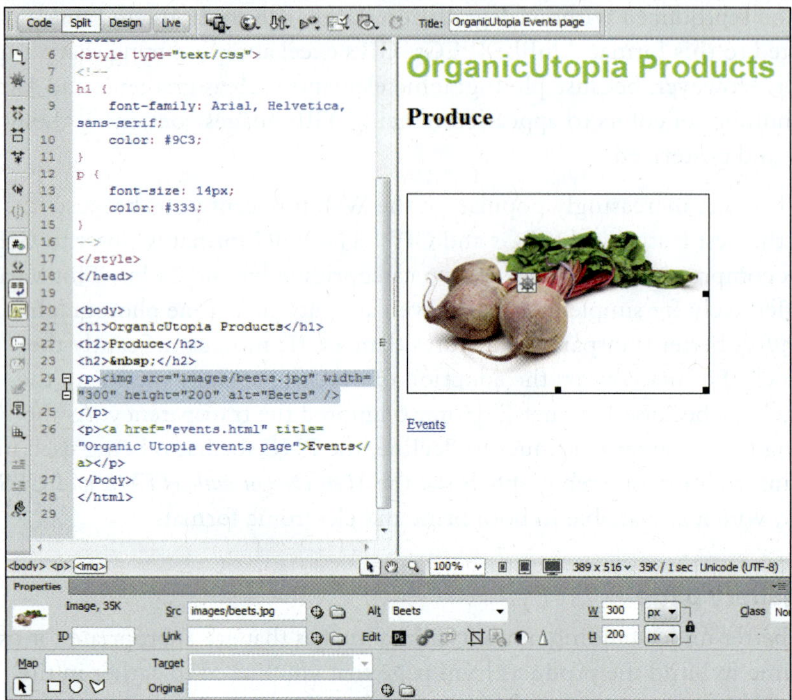

***Figure 3-18**: Dreamweaver creates an <img> tag with a number of attributes when you insert an image.*

Certification Ready 5.4

How do you scale an image?

Take Note...

Although you can scale an image in Dreamweaver, you need to be very careful doing so. The width and height attributes of an image are automatically pulled from the dimensions of your web graphic You can scale a graphic in Dreamweaver two ways: 1.) By modifiying the Width and Height values of a selected image within the Properties panel or 2.) Clicking and dragging one of the corners of a selected image in the Design view.

In general, it is highly recommended that you not scale an image using either of these two techniques. It is easy to distort an image using these techniques and the recommended practice is to use an image editor such as Photoshop to do your scaling and then replace the image.

5. Double-click on the images folder in the Files panel to reveal its contents. In the document window, click to the right of the beets image and press Enter (Windows) or Return (Mac OS) to create a new line. Click and drag cucumbers.jpg from your Files panel directly below the beets image in the Design view. When the Image Tag Accessibility Attributes dialog box appears, type **Cucumbers** into the Alternate text field. Press OK.

6. Click to the right of the cucumber image to place your cursor, and press Enter (Windows) or Return (Mac OS) to create a new line. To add the last image, you'll use the Insert panel on the right side of your page. Click the menu at the top of the Insert panel and choose Common from the list. Click on the Images: Image option (Figure 3-19), and the Select Image Source dialog box appears.

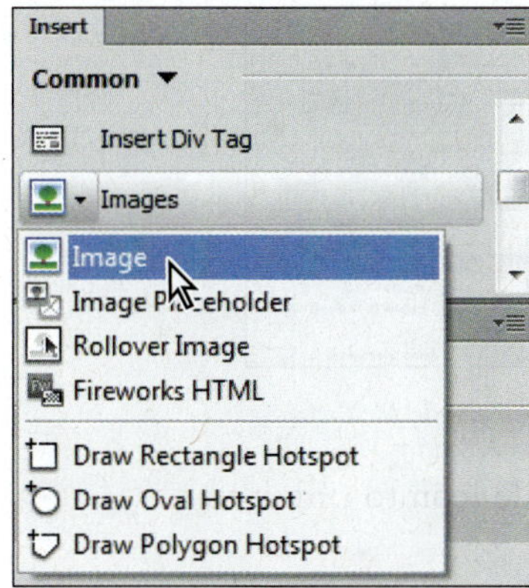

***Figure 3-19**: Choose Image from the Images drop-down menu in the Common section of the Insert panel.*

7. Navigate to the images folder if necessary, select the **eggplants.jpg** image, and press OK (Windows) or Open (Mac OS).
8. Type **Eggplants** in the Alternate text field of the Image Tag Accessibility Attributes dialog box, then press OK.
9. Choose File > Save and leave products.html open for the next part of this lesson.

Certification Ready 4.5

What are the steps for inserting images on a web page?

Linking images

Often, gallery pages on the Web contain small thumbnail images that are linked to larger, high-resolution images. Like many web conventions, there are practical reasons for this format. Because all the images on a gallery page must be downloaded by visitors in order to view the page, small images are necessary to keep the page from taking too long to load. Additionally, a user's screen isn't large enough to accommodate multiple large pictures at one time. Giving your visitor a way to preview which pictures they would like to see on a larger scale makes the page more user friendly and interactive.

Follow these steps to link images in your gallery page

Step-by-Step

1. In **products.html**, click on the image of the beets to select it. In the Property Inspector, type **images/beets_large.jpg** into the Link text field. Press Enter (Windows) or Return (Mac OS).

   Manually typing in the link is one way to link to the image, but can introduce errors. Here is a second method using Dreamweaver's Point to File feature.

Certification Ready 6.4

What are the different methods you can use to link files?

2. Click on the image of the cucumbers to select it. In the Property Inspector, locate the Point to File icon (⊕) next to the Link text field. Click and drag this icon into the Files panel as seen in Figure 3-20. An arrow with a target at the end follows your cursor. As you hover over items in the Files panel, they become highlighted. Release the mouse while hovering over the **cucumbers_large.jpg** file.

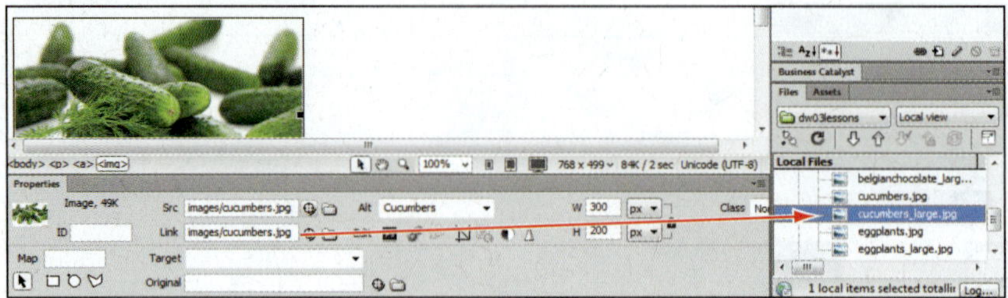

***Figure 3-20**: With the Point to File feature, you can simply click and drag to create a link.*

Certification Ready 4.6

How do you link text and images to another web page of the same site?

3. Select the image of the eggplants and use the Point to File icon to link it to **eggplants_large.jpg**.

4. Choose File > Save, and then File > Preview in Browser. Click on the thumbnails to see the large versions of each image. You'll have to use your browser's back button to get back to the products page. If you had an HTML page that you wanted to link to, you could do that as well.

Image maps

If you would like to add active links within a graphic , then you need to turn to image maps. Sometimes called "hotspots," an image map is one or more defined areas within a graphic that are hyperlinked to unique documents. For example, imagine a graphic that displays the United States. You would like your user to be able to click on any one of the states in the image and navigate to a unique HTML page. You can accomplish this with Dreamweaver's hotspot tools.

The three hotspot tools are the circle, rectangle and polygon. Each of these tools will allow you to draw an area on top of an image and then link to a document. In the map example above, if there were a square or rectangle-shaped state (like Kansas) you could use the rectangle hotspot tool. If there were such a thing as a circular or oval state you could use the circle hotspot tool. Most useful in this example would be the polygon hotspot tool which lets you create multi-sided hotspots, so you could trace the borders of Massachusetts for example.

To create an image map area

1. Select an image in the Design view of a page that you would like to add a hotspot. When the image is selected in the bottom half of the Properties panel you will see the map section. (If you do not see this section it may be collapsed from view. Click on the white arrow in the lower-right corner of the Properties panel to expand it.)

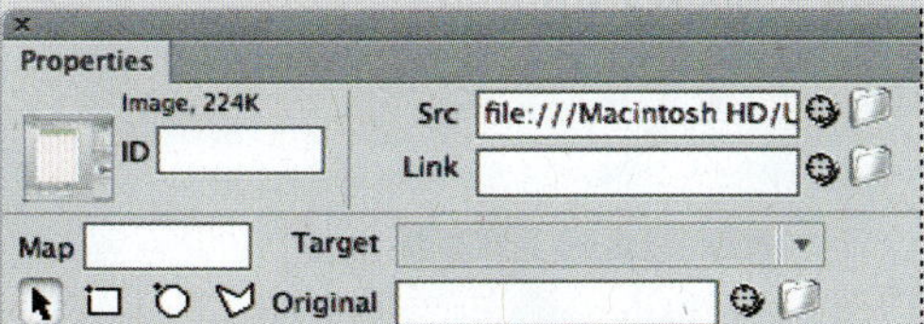

2. Select either the rectangle, circle or polygon hotspot tool and draw the shape over the area you would like to make active. When you first click, a dialog box will appear prompting you to add "alt" text for your image map. Click OK.

   Alt text helps with the accessibility of your page by adding a text description that can be read by screen readers.

   Note: If you are using the polygon hotspot tool click in the image to set the starting point. Position the pointer where you want the first straight segment to end, and click. Continue clicking to set endpoints for subsequent segments.

3. If necessary, you may reshape the boundaries of the hotspot by clicking on the Pointer hotspot tool then clicking and dragging any of the anchor points that appear.
4. When done drawing and modifying your shape with your shape type relevant text into the Alt field that appears in the Hotspot section of the Properties Panel.
5. To add a link to document, you may either type a url in the Link field or use the Point to File icon or Browse for File button just like you would with a standard hyperlink.
6. Locate the Map field in the Properties panel and type an appropriate name for your image map. This map name is used for a single map and should be unique, especially if you have more than one image map on a page.

Learning More

Certification Ready 4.1

In terms of web page design, what is a hotspot and an image map?

Certification Ready 4.10

How do you create an image map?

Certification Ready 4.10

What are the best practices when creating image maps?

Certification Ready 4.10

How do you set properties for a hotspot using the Property Inspector?

Using image placeholders

Often, you will want to start building web pages before you have all the final content available. This happens regularly in professional situations where different people may be responsible for preparing images, writing copy, and creating the site. Next, you'll build a second section in the products.html page that will eventually include a collection of chocolate pictures.

Step-by-Step

Follow these steps to create an image placeholder

1. In Dreamweaver, on the **products.html** page, place your cursor to the right of the eggplants image, and press Enter (Windows) or Return (Mac OS) to create a new line.
2. Type **Chocolate**, then press the HTML button in the Property Inspector and choose Heading 2 from the Format drop-down menu. Place your cursor at the end of the word Chocolate and press Enter/Return to create a line below this new heading.
3. Choose Insert > Image Objects > Image Placeholder. When the Image Placeholder dialog box appears, type **belgianchocolate** in the Name text field, **300** in the Width text field, and **200** in the Height text field. Leave the Color set to the default and the Alternative text field blank. Press OK to exit the dialog box.

   A gray box with the name belgianchocolate appears as seen in Figure 3-21. This box is simply an `<img>` tag with an empty Src attribute. If you are new to web design, it's important to note that placeholders are not required, but they are useful in allowing you to visualize a page when you don't have images available. Now you'll insert an image into the placeholder by setting the Src attribute in the Property Inspector.

Figure 3-21: *The belgianchocolate image placeholder.*

4. With the belgianchocolate image placeholder selected, click and drag the Point to File icon to the right of the Src text field and locate the **belgianchocolate.jpg** image. The image of the Belgian chocolate replaces the gray box.
5. In the Property Inspector, use the Point to File icon of the Link text field to link belgianchocolate.jpg to **belgianchocolate_large.jpg**. Choose File > Save and leave this file open for the next part of this lesson.

Editing images

Although it's best to make adjustments to your images using a professional graphics-editing program like Adobe Photoshop, sometimes that's not an option. Dreamweaver offers a number of editing options, including an Edit link that allows you to quickly open a selected image in the graphics editor of your choice.

Take Note...

The Edit button can be customized in the File Types/Editors section of the Preferences dialog box, found under the Dreamweaver drop-down menu. You can use this section to add or subtract programs from the list of available editors, and set programs as the primary choice for handling specific file extensions.

Adjusting brightness and contrast

Now you'll use Dreamweaver's Brightness and Contrast button to lighten up the eggplants image on your products page.

Follow these steps to edit an image

Step-by-Step

1. Click on the **eggplants.jpg** image in products.html to select it, then click on the Brightness and Contrast button in the Property Inspector as seen in Figure 3-22.

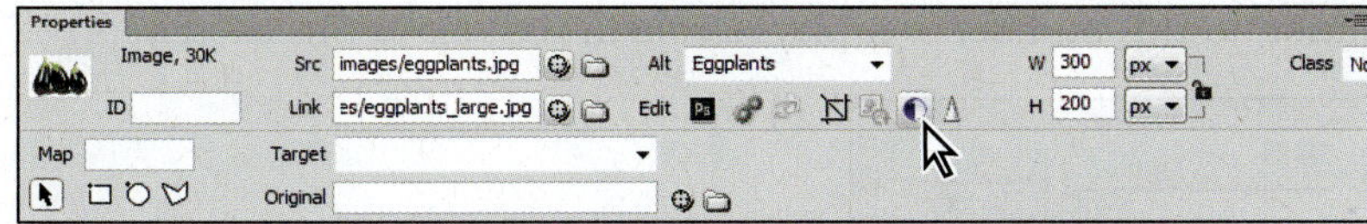

Figure 3-22: *Select the Brightness and Contrast button in the Property Inspector.*

   A warning dialog box appears, indicating that you are about to make permanent changes to the selected image. Press OK.

2. When the Brightness/Contrast dialog box appears, drag the Brightness slider to 20 or type **20** in the text field to the right of the slider.
3. Drag the Contrast slider to 10 or type **10** in the text field to the right of the slider.
4. Click the *Preview* checkbox in the lower-right corner to see the original photo. Click the Preview checkbox again to see the changes. Press OK.

Take Note...

While changing the brightness and contrast is very convenient in Dreamweaver, you should be sure you are not performing the corrections on the original, as these changes are destructive.

Optimizing images

In most cases, if you need to have fine control over the appearance of your graphics, you should open an image editor designed for that purpose. Both Dreamweaver and Photoshop are made by Adobe, and you'll see some of the integration between the two in this exercise. However, sometimes you will just want to make a quick-and-easy change to a graphic. In this scenario, you can use the Edit Image Settings option in the Property Inspector.

You'll use this feature to change the optimization of the belgianchocolate.jpg image, but before you make any permanent changes, you'll duplicate this image in the Files panel. It's good practice to save copies of your image files before making permanent changes. Later, you'll use this backup copy to undo your changes.

Step-by-Step | **Follow these steps to optimize an image**

1. In the Files panel, click on the **belgianchocolate.jpg** file to select it. From the Files panel menu (▾≡), select Edit > Duplicate. A new file named *belgianchocolate - Copy.jpg* appears in the list of files inside the images folder.
2. Click on the **belgianchocolate.jpg** image in the document window to make sure it is selected, then click the Edit Image Settings button (⚙) in the Property Inspector at the bottom of your page. The Image Optimization window appears (Figure 3-23). This window allows you to either choose from a number of compression presets, or to create your own. Currently, the format is set to JPEG because Dreamweaver recognizes the type of file you have selected. Notice in the bottom-left corner that the file size is listed; in this case, 31k. Pay attention to this number as it plays a role in the rest of this exercise.

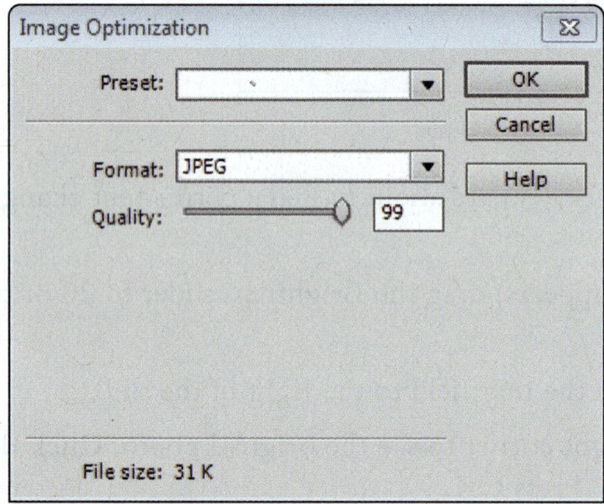

Figure 3-23*: The Image Optimization window appears when you click on the Edit Image Settings button.*

3. Click the preset menu and choose GIF for Background Images. The optimization settings appear. Click the Color menu and choose 4. The image of the chocolate changes to a preview of these settings, and the image has become flat with most of the detail removed. Notice that the file size has changed to 3K.

   This tells you that you would achieve a tremendous reduction in file size, but it would occur at the expense of image quality. In fact, the GIF file format is not generally suited for photographic images. You will now try a custom setting.

4. Click the Format menu and choose JPEG from the list. You now have a slider for quality, the default value is 80 and you can see the file size has changed to 9K. Drag the slider to the left to a quality of 10 and notice that the image quality changes instantly. Again, this is too drastic a trade-off. Drag the quality slider to 90. The image looks slightly better than it did at a quality of 80, and you have a file size of around 14K (which is approximately 50% of the original image).

   Click OK to commit the change. Note that this method of optimization is risky if you do not have a backup. (Recall the backup created in step 1.)

Certification Ready 5.4

What are the capabilities and limitations of editing or modifying images in Dreamweaver?

5. You can also choose to do your optimization in Photoshop. Click the cucumbers image, and then in the Property Inspector, click the Photoshop icon if available (Figure 3-24). Note that you must have Photoshop installed for this icon to be visible. As noted earlier, you can always change the photo editor that Dreamweaver uses by opening Edit > Preferences > File Types/Editors (PC) or Dreamweaver > Preferences > File Types/ Editors (Mac), and then changing the application associated with images.

Certification Ready 5.4

How do you edit static and interactive assets with Fireworks, Photoshop, and Flash from inside Dreamweaver?

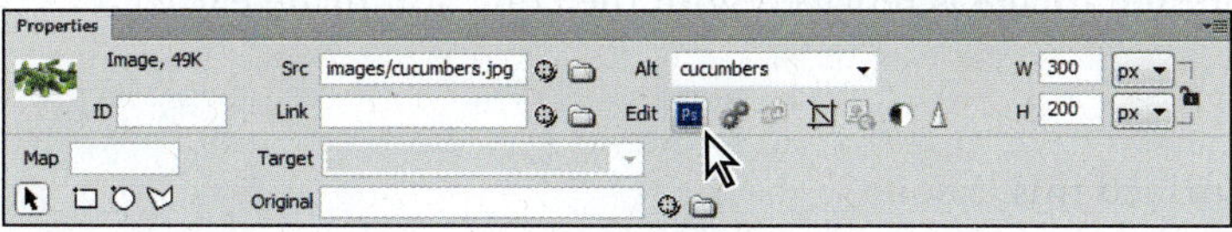

***Figure 3-24**: Click on the Photoshop icon to launch Photoshop.*

   In addition to integration with Photoshop images, Dreamweaver will also integrate with Fireworks and Flash assets as well. PNG assets will be associated with Fireworks by default and SWF files can be associated with Flash's FLA format in a similar manner.

6. The image will open in Photoshop, and then you can make any changes you want, as well as use the more in-depth controls of the Save for Web feature. We will not walk through that process now, so you can close this image and return to Dreamweaver.

Photoshop Smart Objects

Learning More

Photoshop's .psd format is not a valid file type for the web, however you can insert a .psd file using Dreamweaver's Smart Objects feature. Inserting a native Photoshop file into Dreamweaver will trigger an automatic conversion into a suitable web graphic such as JPG, PNG, or GIF. The original PSD file is still linked, however, and the converted.

Smart Objects are labeled with a unique icon in Dreamweaver's design view.

If the source Photoshop file is modified for any reason then a red arrow appears on the image in Dreamweaver to indicate that the file has changed. You can then click the Update from Original button in the Property Inspector and the latest version of the image will be updated.

Certification Ready 4.5

How do you use Photoshop Smart Objects?

Updating images

Assuming you have a backup copy of an image, it is possible to swap one image for another. To swap out the image, you'll simply change the Src attribute, using the Property Inspector. But first, it's a good idea to rename the duplicate image.

Step-by-Step

Follow these steps to update an image

1. Right-click (Windows) or Ctrl+click (Mac OS) on the file named **belgianchocolate - Copy.jpg** in the Files panel and choose File > Rename. Type **belgianchocolate_original.jpg** and press Enter (Windows) or Return (Mac OS).
2. Click on the chocolate image in the Design view to select it. In the Property Inspector at the bottom of your page, highlight the text that reads *images/belgianchocolate.jpg* in the Src text field.
3. Click and drag the Point to File icon to the **belgianchocolate_original.jpg** image you just renamed. The compressed image is replaced with the copy you made earlier.
4. Choose File > Save.

Certification Ready 3.3

What are the various functions of the Property Inspector?

Congratulations, you have finished this lesson.

Skill Summary

In this lesson you learned how to:	Objective
Demonstrate knowledge of standard copyright rules (related terms, obtaining permission, and citing copyrighted material)	1.3
Demonstrate knowledge of website accessibility standards that address the needs of people with visual and motor impairments	1.4
Identify basic principles of website usability, readability, and accessibility	2.4
Use the Property Inspector	3.3
Demonstrate knowledge of Hypertext Markup Language	4.1
Demonstrate knowledge of how to add text to an HTML page	4.4
Insert images and apply alternative text on a web page	4.5
Link web content, using hyperlinks, e-mail links, and named anchors	4.6
Build image maps	4.10
Import and display a Microsoft Word or Microsoft Excel document to a web page	4.12
Modify text and text properties	5.3
Modify images and image properties	5.4
Conduct technical tests	6.1
Manage assets, links, and files for a site	6.4

Knowledge Assessment

True/False

Circle T if the statement is true or F if the statement is false.

T F **1.** Unless you are using web fonts, when a web page is rendered in a user's browser it can only display fonts installed on the user's computer.

T F **2.** In order to change the formatting of a paragraph element to a heading 1 element you should first make sure you are not in the CSS mode of the Property Inspector.

T F **3.** In order to define the color of a heading 1 element for the first time in a document you should be in the HTML mode of the Property Inspector.

T F **4.** The structure of a web page is defined by paragraphs, headings, lists, forms (and much more). Technically, these are all called objects.

T F **5.** By default in Dreamweaver CS6, HTML defines the style of a page and CSS defines the structure.

T F **6.** You can create hyperlinks in Dreamweaver using the Insert panel.

T F **7.** You can import Photoshop documents (.psd) into Dreamweaver CS6.

T F **8.** Dreamweaver's Live View allows you to see the design of your page and the code of your page simultaneously.

T F **9.** When you create an unordered list in Dreamweaver, each list item is automatically given a bullet point.

T F **10.** You can adjust the brightness and contrast of a web graphic directly in Dreamweaver instead of having to adjust it in an image editing program such as Photoshop.

Multiple Choice

Select the best response for the following statements

1. Which of the following headings are the largest?

- **a.** h6
- **b.** h4
- **c.** h2
- **d.** h1

2. In an internal style sheet, style rules are defined where?.

- **a.** Within `<style>` tags nested in the head section of a page
- **b.** Within `<style>` tags nested in the body section of a page
- **c.** Within `<style>` tags located in a separate document and linked from the HTML page
- **d.** None of the above

3. You have just opened a new document with no pre-existing styles and would like to make sure that all the paragraphs on your site are the same color. How would you do this using the Property Inspector?
   a. Select a paragraph, make sure you are in the CSS panel, click a color swatch and choose a color, then define a New CSS Rule.
   b. Select a paragraph, make sure you are in the HTML panel, click a color swatch and choose a color.
   c. Make sure you are in the CSS panel, click a color swatch and drag it onto any paragraph, then define a New CSS Rule.
   d. All of the above.

4. If you wanted to create a link on your page to an external website the type of link you would create would be a/an ________ link.
   a. absolute
   b. relative
   c. anchor
   d. directory

5. Which of the following image formats does not support transparency?
   a. PNG
   b. GIF
   c. JPG
   d. All of the above

6. Which of the following is true about creating e-mail hyperlinks?
   a. When a user clicks on an e-mail hyperlink it will open a new page.
   b. When a user clicks on an e-mail hyperlink the browser will attempt to connect to a mail program.
   c. The designer/developer of the site must create an e-mail form or else when the user clicks on an e-mail hyperlink nothing will happen.
   d. You cannot create e-mail hyperlinks.

7. When you attempt to insert a Photoshop file (.psd) to an HTML page in Dreamweaver CS6, what happens?
   a. You receive an error. Photoshop files cannot be added to HTML pages.
   b. The Image Preview window appears.
   c. The Image Optimization window appears.
   d. The Save for Web window appears.

8. Which of the following is true about Dreamweaver CS6's Live View?
   a. When turned on, your view changes to the Split view automatically.
   b. When turned on, you cannot edit your page in the Design view
   c. When turned on, you cannot edit your page in the Split view
   d. All of the above

9. What does the command File > Preview in Browser > Edit Browser List do?

a. Allows you to add or remove the browsers used to display your web pages

b. Automatically scans your local system for available web browsers

c. Automatically scans your system and identifies browsers that need to be updated

d. None of the above

10. Where would you look in the Dreamweaver CS6 interface in order to add a Copyright symbol to your page?

a. The Snippets panel

b. The Property Inspector

c. The Tag Chooser

d. The Insert panel

Competency Assessment

Adding Text to a page

Project 3-1

You are beginning work on a website for Serenity Spa and need to add and format some text to the page.

1. Open the **index.html** file located in the dw03lessons folder.
2. Click with your cursor in the Design pane. Type the words **Serenity Spa**.
3. Click and drag to highlight the words you just typed. In the Property Inspector, make sure the button on the far left side is set to HTML. Choose Heading 1 from the Format drop-down menu, then click on the CSS button in the Properties panel and choose Georgia, Times New Roman, Times, serif from the Font drop-down menu.
4. Click on the Selector type menu and choose the Tag option. Dreamweaver should automatically pick up the h1 Selector Name.
5. Click OK to apply the change.
6. Center the text horizontally by clicking on the Align Center icon on the Property Inspector.
7. Click anywhere in the Design pane to deselect the text.
8. Let's add some text to the page: insert the cursor at the end of the heading text and press Return.
9. Enter the following text: **Welcome to your urban oasis. Relax and let us pamper you with our professional facials, massages, body wraps, and reflexology.**
10. Save the page and leave it open for the next exercise.

Project 3-2 Adding hyperlinks

You need to add hyperlinks to the Serenity Spa website so users can navigate to other websites that provide products and services that may interest users.

1. Use the **index.html** file from the last project (3-1). Place your cursor at the end of the welcome message. Hit Return.
2. Type this list, pressing Return at the end of each item:
   - The Body Holiday
   - Destination Relaxation
   - Spa Vacations
3. Format this text as an unordered list by selecting the text, then clicking on the Unordered List icon on the Property Inspector. You can also choose Format > List > Unordered List.
4. Highlight the first item on the list, The Body Holiday. In the Property Inspector, type a URL into the Link field in the Property Inspector that begins with **http://www**.

   Pull down the Target menu and select `_blank`, so the linked page will open in a new window. Create hyperlinks for the other two items on the list.
5. Save the page and preview it in your web browser. Test the links to see if they work properly. If not, go back and check to be sure you entered the URLs correctly in the Link field on the Property Inspector.

Proficiency Assessment

Project 3-3 More Characters

There are those special characters like the copyright symbol that are used routinely, but what about the symbols that are a bit off the beaten path?

Dreamweaver allows for the insertion of numerous special characters.

Get Ready. Launch Dreamweaver CS6 if you haven't already.

1. Create a new blank HTML page.
2. Go to the Insert panel and select the Text category.
3. In the Characters pop-up menu, select Other Characters to examine the options you have available.

Project 3-4 And More Editing

While Dreamweaver isn't the most powerful image editing program in the world, it's nice that it offers some of the basics.

Get Ready. Launch Dreamweaver CS6 if you haven't already.

1. Create a new webpage and insert an image.
2. Crop the image after selecting it using the options found in the Properties panel.
3. Choose File > Save and save this file into your lesson folder.

Styling Your Pages with CSS

Key Terms

- CSS
- CSS Classes
- CSS IDs
- CSS Rules
- CSS Styles
- Contextual Selectors
- Div Tags
- External Style Sheets
- Inheritance
- Internal Style Sheets
- Pseudo-class
- Rule Definition

Skill	Objective
Demonstrate general and Dreamweaver-specific knowledge of best practices for designing a website, such as maintaining consistency, separating content from design, using standard fonts, and utilizing visual hierarchy	2.1
Set and modify document properties	5.1
Organize web page layout with relative and absolutely-positioned div tags and CSS styles	5.2
Modify text and text properties	5.3
Use CSS to implement a reusable design	5.8

Business Case

The owners at Organic Utopia are discovering that they'd like to have more elaborate text in terms of how the text is presented on the screen. They'd like to have list items that stand out on their own aside from the body copy, and they'd like the hyperlinks to be a bit more prominent with the use of custom colors. Another thing they'll need is the ability to modify the text globally. To build the workflow for this, a more in-depth understanding of style sheets is going to be necessary, especially the ability to create external style sheet files.

Introduction

Before starting, make sure that your tools and panels are consistent by resetting your workspace. See "Resetting the Dreamweaver workspace" in the Starting Up section of this book.

You will work with several files from the dw04lessons folder in this lesson. Make sure that you have loaded the dwlessons folder onto your hard drive. See "Loading lesson files" in the Starting Up section of this book.

Before you begin, you need to create site settings that point to the dw04lessons folder. Go to Site > New Site, or, for details on creating a site, refer to Lesson 2, "Setting Up a New Site."

What are Cascading Style Sheets?

In the last lesson you had a brief introduction to Cascading Style Sheets (CSS); now you will dive in a bit deeper. **CSS** is a simple language that works alongside HTML to apply formatting to content in web pages, such as text, images, tables, and form elements. Developed by the World Wide Web Consortium (W3C), CSS creates rules, or style instructions, that elements on your page follow. There are three locations for CSS: 1) An **internal style sheet** where the styles are located directly within the `<head>` section of an HTML document, 2) inline styles (the CSS is located side by side with your HTML tags), or 3) An **external style sheet** where styles are located in an external file that can be linked to any number of HTML pages. If you completed Lesson 3, you have had experience with the first option.

A style sheet is a collection of **CSS rules**; typically, rules that belong to a specific project, theme, or section are grouped together, but you can group rules in any way you want. You can place style sheets directly within your page using the `<style>` tag or in an external .css file that is linked to your document with the `<link>` tag. A single page or set of pages can use several style sheets at once.

You can apply CSS rules selectively to any number of elements on a page, or use them to modify the appearance of an existing HTML tag. Each CSS rule is composed of one or more declarations. A declaration contains both a property and a value. Examples of properties include color, width, and font size. Examples of values for these properties are green, 450px, and 12px, respectively. Dreamweaver's **CSS Styles** panel lets you easily view and modify any of these properties and values and change the appearance of your page in real time.

This sample rule is composed of three declarations that control the color, typeface, and size of any text to which it's applied. In the simplest example, the CSS rules define the appearance of an H1 or heading element:

```
h1 {
    color: red;
    font-family: Arial,Helvetica,Sans-serif;
    font-size: 28px;
}
```

Here is the result of the preceding code snippet applied to text:

CSS-styled text shown in the Design view.

CSS rules can affect properties as simple as typeface, size, and color, or as complex as positioning and visibility. Dreamweaver uses CSS as the primary method of styling page text and elements, and its detailed CSS Styles panel makes it possible to create and manage styles at any point during a project.

The different levels of CSS

Just like HTML, CSS is an evolving language. The "rules" for how to use a language such as HTML or CSS are contained in a master document called a specification. There is no single specification for CSS, instead it has been broken down into levels. Currently there are 3 levels of CSS commonly referred to as CSS1, CSS2 and CSS3. It is important to have a passing knowledge of these levels as it will impact what design features you can reliably use in your page designs.

CSS1

The specification for how to use CSS was first released to the world in 1996 with this version and although many of the fundamentals of the language are the same, most people consider CSS 1.0 to be obsolete and rely on the CSS 2.0 specification.

CSS2

CSS2 builds on CSS1 and with few exceptions all valid CSS1 style sheets are valid CSS2 style sheets. Anyone building a website in the 21st century has most likely used the CSS2 specification (There is also a CSS 2.1 specification). However, the main consideration to keep in mind is that just because something is defined in the specification does not mean it has always worked in web browsers. For example a concept called "Css child selectors" was introduced in this specification but browsers such as Internet Explorer 6 did not support it correctly (or at all). Therefore, although officially included in the specification, in real world use CSS child selectors were avoided until there was a wider level of browser support. (Internet Explorer 7 and above do support CSS child selectors.)

CSS3

CSS3 is the latest version of CSS and includes many features that are either completely different than those or CSS2 or are improved features found in CSS2. For example CSS3 media queries (covered in Lesson 15 "Mobile Design and Layout") were completely new whereas CSS3 border radius improves the functionality of the border property introduced in CSS1 and CSS2. CSS3 is still very much a work in progress and although many of the features can be relied on to work in modern browsers there are also many that do not work in any browser reliably or have partial support.

Additional Resources

http://www.w3.org/TR/CSS/

The official and definitive look at the three levels of CSS including all the specifications for everything related to CSS1, CSS2 and CSS3

http://www.quirksmode.org/css/contents.html

A table that compares the list of CSS2 selectors and the level of support for different browsers.

Learning More

Certification Ready 2.1

What are the different levels of CSS and what are the different features and capabilities of CSS2 and CSS3?

CSS replaces inefficient HTML styling

Before CSS came along, you styled text on a page using the `<font>` tag in HTML; you could wrap this tag around any paragraph, phrase, or tidbit of text to apply color, or to set the font size and typeface. Although it was reliable, it was also very inefficient. Imagine a page with 10 paragraphs. Using the `<font>` tag, you would have to add the `<font>` tag 10 times, even if the color, size, and typeface values were exactly the same. Although the <font> tag is not in use as much anymore, you should still understand how it works. You will now open an HTML document in which the list is styled using the <font> tag.

Step-by-Step

Follow these steps to get an idea of the inefficiency of HTML-only code

1. In your Files panel located in the lower-right corner of your screen, locate and double-click the HTML file named **FontTagList.html** to open it in the document window.
2. Press the Code View button in the Document toolbar at the top of the document window. Notice that the <font> tag is used to style the items in the bulleted list (Figure 4-1).

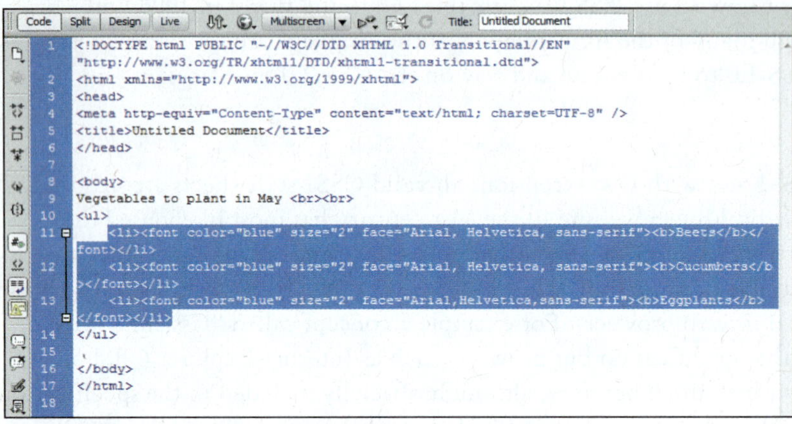

***Figure 4-1**: Here, a <font> tag is used to format each bullet point. If you add more bullet points, you'll need to use more <font> tags to keep the style of those bullets consistent with the others.*

As you can see, there's a lot of repetition in this code.

3. Press the Design View button on the Document toolbar. Position your cursor at the end of the last bulleted item, press Enter (Windows) or Return (Mac OS) to add a new bullet point, and type **Peppers**. You see that the text reverts to the default typeface, size, and color as seen in Figure 4-2. You would have to add a new <font> tag with the same attributes as the others to get it to match. If you wanted to change an attribute such as the color for all the bullet points, you would have to adjust each tag separately. In early versions of Dreamweaver, there were actually ways to perform global changes using HTML; however, these were sometimes tricky to control, and CSS offers a better solution in any case.

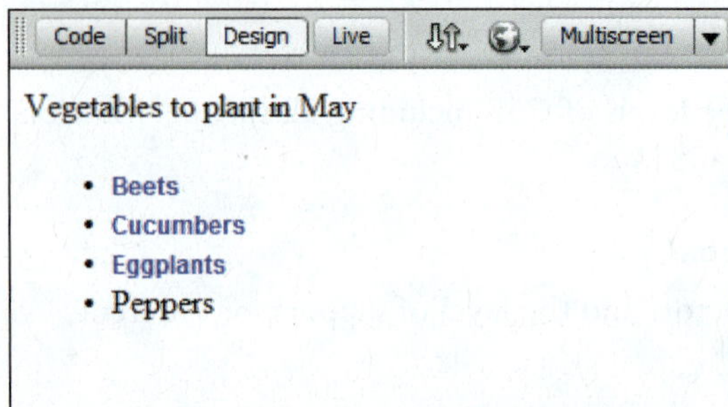

***Figure 4-2**: You may lose the formatting between bullet points when using <font> tags.*

Certification Ready 2.1

What are Cascading Style Sheets (CSS)?

4. Choose File > Save to save your work, then choose File > Close.

The benefits of CSS styling

CSS introduces a new level of control and flexibility far beyond the <font> tags in HTML. A significant benefit of CSS is the ability to apply consistent formatting of elements across one or all pages in a website. In the following exercises, you will learn a few different ways to create CSS rules that affect the style of your text. The first method you will explore involves creating tag- or element-based style rules. If you completed Lesson 3, you saw this method used to format text. This type of rule alters the appearance of an existing HTML tag, so the tag and any content that appears within it always appears formatted in a specific way. Instead of having to add a <font> tag around the contents of each new bullet point in a list, it would be easier for you to set a rule that states that items in a list should always be blue, for example.

Follow these steps to get an idea of the benefits of CSS

Step-by-Step

1. Locate and double-click the file named **CSSList.html** from the Files panel to open it.
2. Press the Design View button in the Document toolbar if necessary. The list that appears onscreen, unlike the one you saw in the previous example, is formatted without the use of <font> tags, and uses only CSS.
3. Position your cursor after the last bulleted item and press the Enter (Windows) or Return (Mac OS) key to create a new bullet point. Type in **Peppers**. The new text matches the bullet points above it.
4. Press Enter/Return again to add a fifth bullet point, and type **Okra**.

   No matter how many bullet points you add, the formatting is applied automatically every time.
5. Select Split view at the top of the document window so that you can see both code and design (Figure 4-3):

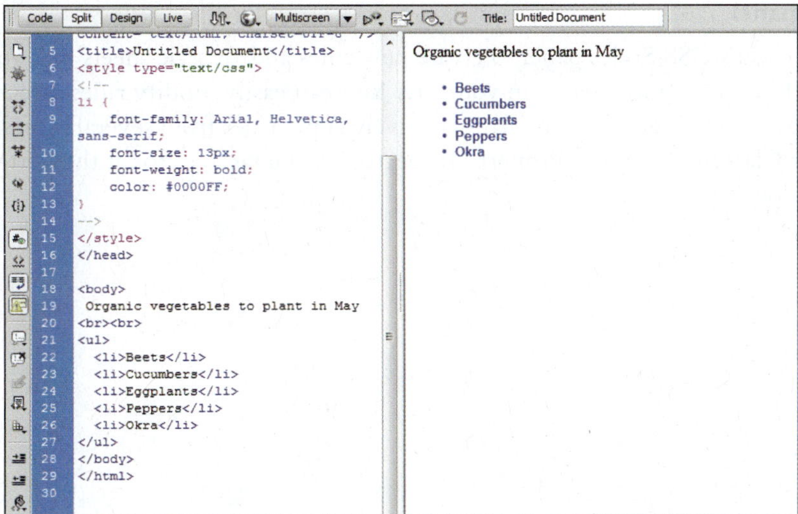

***Figure 4-3**: CSS allows you to define a style rule for a list item. All list items on this page will be blue.*

   What you'll notice is the absence of any formatting tags like the <font> tags you saw in the last exercise. In this example, you have several list items; however, all the styling information, such as the font-family, size, font style, and color, is being defined in one place: the CSS rule for the <li> tag.

6. If necessary, scroll to the top of the page and you'll see the code that makes this possible:

```
<style type="text/css">
<!--
li {
    font-family: Arial, Helvetica, sans-serif;
    font-size: 13px;
    font-weight: bold;
    color: #0000FF;
}
-->
</style>
```

Certification Ready 2.1

What are the benefits of using CSS styles?

Certification Ready 5.8

What are the advantages of using CSS for design?

In the code above, a CSS selector (seen here as `li`) is being used to define the style of all list items. It's almost like a dress code for all `<li>` tags; they know that when they are used on the page, they must look a certain way. Best of all, if you need to modify their appearance, you make your changes to that single style rule at the top of the page. You will get a chance to do this shortly; however, let's take a step back and look at how CSS is controlled in Dreamweaver.

7. Choose File > Save to save your work, then choose File > Close.

How do you create CSS rules in Dreamweaver?

In this exercise, you will take a tour of Dreamweaver's CSS controls. If you haven't worked with CSS before, this is a chance to learn a bit more about how it works. If you have worked with CSS previously, this section will help you understand the Dreamweaver interface and how it applies to familiar concepts. Regardless of your comfort level with CSS, you won't be making any changes, merely getting familiar with features that you will be using in later exercises.

You work with CSS rules in a few ways in Dreamweaver:

Using the CSS Styles panel

You can use Dreamweaver's CSS Styles panel to create new rules and/or style sheets that you can place directly within one or more pages in your site. You can easily modify rules directly from the CSS Styles panel. Furthermore, you can selectively apply rules from several places, including the Style or Class menu on the Property Inspector, or the tag selector at the bottom of the document window.

The CSS Styles panel has two buttons labeled All and Current. You'll get a chance to explore these shortly. In Figure 4-4, you are seeing the panel in the All view.

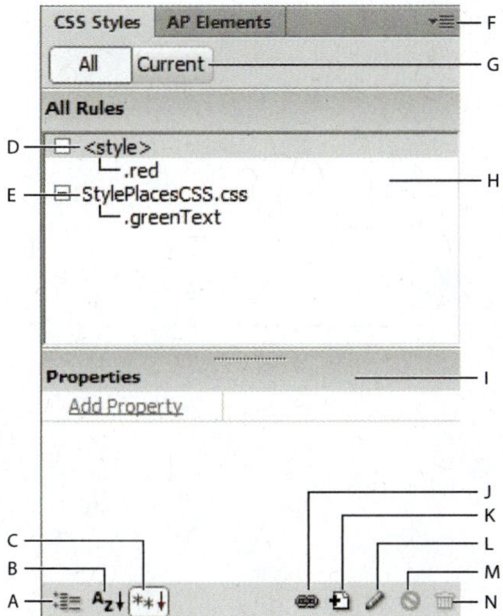

Figure 4-4*: Launch the CSS panel by choosing Window > CSS Styles.*
A*. Show Category View.* ***B****. Show List View.*
C*. Show Only Set Properties.* ***D****. Internal Style Sheet.*
E*. External Style Sheet.* ***F****. CSS panel menu.*
G*. Switch to Current Selection Mode.* ***H****. Rules pane.*
I*. Properties pane.* ***J****. Attach Style Sheet.*
K*. New CSS Rule.* ***L****. Edit Style Sheet.*
M*. Disable/Enable CSS Property.* ***N****. Delete/Unlink.*

To ensure that you are seeing the same panels we are, you'll reset your workspace. Choose Window > Workspace Layout > Designer. Then choose Workspace Layout > Reset 'Designer' to make sure the panels are reset.

To free up more screen space, double-click the Business Catalyst tab to close it. This expands the CSS Styles panel. Click the File panel tab at the bottom of the screen to expand it.

Follow these steps to use the CSS Styles panel

Step-by-Step

1. Double-click the **StylePlaces.html** document in your Files panel to open it, and click the Design View button, if necessary.
2. Click in the first line, *Hi there! I'm styled with an INLINE style!*
3. Press the Current button in the CSS Styles panel. A summary pane lists the CSS properties for the current selection. Depending on your monitor resolution you may not have enough room to see all the information in this panel. You can adjust the different panel groups by hand.

4. Place your cursor at the bottom of the CSS Styles tab group. A black double-arrow cursor will appear as seen in Figure 4-5. You can now click and drag downward to lengthen this panel.

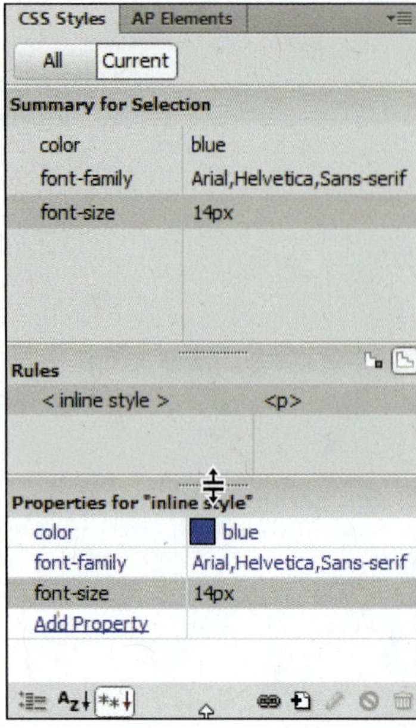

Figure 4-5 You can expand a panel by clicking and dragging the edges.

Take a few moments to read through this panel and absorb the summary. Don't worry too much about each detail; you'll have plenty of time to familiarize yourself with this panel. It hopefully makes sense that the properties of the first paragraph are the color blue, the font-family Arial, and the font size of 14 pixels.

5. Click on the second paragraph and notice that the color property changes to red. Click on the third paragraph and notice that the color property changes to green. The current selection always lists the properties of the selected text.

6. Press the All button in the CSS Styles panel to return to this view. You will toggle between these two views often. The Current view allows you to see the specific CSS properties and values of a selected object. The All view gives you an overview of all the styles associated with the document.

Creating styles using the Property Inspector

Whenever you format text directly on your page using the Property Inspector, Dreamweaver saves your settings as a new rule, which you have to name in your document. Rules that Dreamweaver creates appear in your CSS panel, where you can easily modify or rename them.

Follow these steps to create a style using the Property Inspector

Step-by-Step

1. Click in the second paragraph, *Hi there! I'm styled with an embedded, or INTERNAL style sheet!*
2. In the Property Inspector at the bottom of the screen, press the HTML button if necessary. This paragraph is styled using a CSS class named red. You'll learn more about classes and how to create and modify them shortly.
3. Press the CSS button in the Property Inspector. You can see some of the properties of this rule here in the Inspector (Figure 4-6), and you can also create and modify them here as you did in the previous lesson.

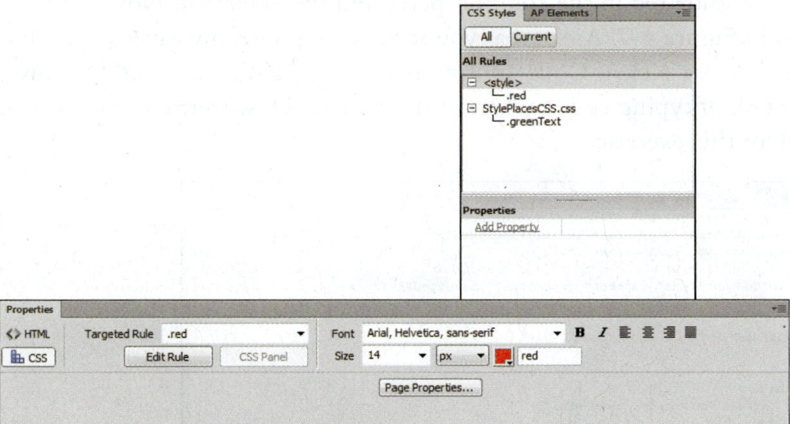

Figure 4-6: *CSS styles are automatically created when you format text with the Property Inspector.*

4. In the CSS styles panel, you should be in the All view. If not, click this button now. If the style labeled .red is visible, click it now. (If it is not visible, click the + sign to the left of the `<style>` label.) Compare the Property Inspector with the CSS Styles panel: they are displaying the exact same information at the moment. However, as your styles become more complex, you will see that the Property Inspector only shows you the most common styles, whereas the CSS Styles panel always shows you all of them.

In the Code view

CSS rules can also be created and modified directly in the Code view. Editing CSS in Dreamweaver's Code view offers a great degree of control and is often called *hand-coding*. Many coders and designers prefer hand-coding because of this control, but it's not for everyone. For example, when you work in the Code view misspellings or an incomplete knowledge of CSS syntax can easily break a page.

Step-by-Step

Follow these steps to display the Code view

1. Click in the second paragraph if you are not currently inside it. Press the Code view button to view your page in Code view. If you haven't worked with code previously, see if you can locate the second paragraph of HTML. (It has the class named "red.")
2. On the left side of the screen, notice that the line numbers are running from top to bottom; when working with code, each line has its own number, making it easy to refer to and locate objects.

   On line 10, select the value red in the color property and then delete it. Now type **#CE1A30** as seen in Figure 4-7. As soon as you start typing, Dreamweaver's code-hinting appears, giving you a color picker. Code-hinting is a form of assistance from Dreamweaver that can make the task of typing code by hand a little easier. However, you can also ignore it, and you should for this exercise.

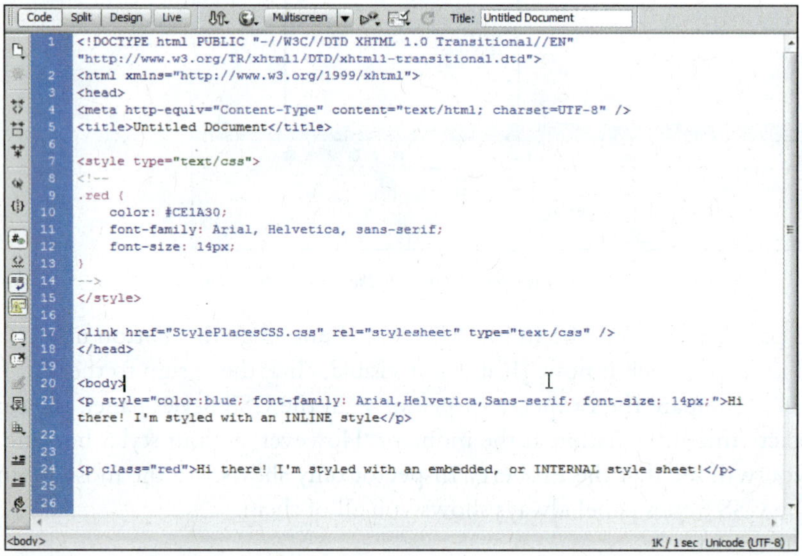

```
Code | Split | Design | Live | Multiscreen | Title: Untitled Document
1  <!DOCTYPE html PUBLIC "-//W3C//DTD XHTML 1.0 Transitional//EN"
   "http://www.w3.org/TR/xhtml1/DTD/xhtml1-transitional.dtd">
2  <html xmlns="http://www.w3.org/1999/xhtml">
3  <head>
4  <meta http-equiv="Content-Type" content="text/html; charset=UTF-8" />
5  <title>Untitled Document</title>
6
7  <style type="text/css">
8  <!--
9  .red {
10     color: #CE1A30;
11     font-family: Arial, Helvetica, sans-serif;
12     font-size: 14px;
13 }
14 -->
15 </style>
16
17 <link href="StylePlacesCSS.css" rel="stylesheet" type="text/css" />
18 </head>
19
20 <body>
21 <p style="color:blue; font-family: Arial,Helvetica,Sans-serif; font-size: 14px;">Hi
   there! I'm styled with an INLINE style</p>
22
23
24 <p class="red">Hi there! I'm styled with an embedded, or INTERNAL style sheet!</p>
25
26
<body>                                                   1K / 1 sec Unicode (UTF-8)
```

Figure 4-7*: Modifying the CSS color property in Code View.*

3. Press the Design view button. The text is still red, however it is using a hexadecimal color instead of a keyword. The danger of adding CSS properties by hand of course, is that if you mistype the value you may get a different color or no color at all.

Working with the Code Navigator

The Code Navigator allows you to view the CSS properties directly in the Design view through a small pop-up window. Additionally, it allows you to click on a property and edit it directly in the Split view.

Follow these steps to use the Code Navigator

Step-by-Step

1. Press Alt (Windows) or Command+Option (Mac OS) and click on the third paragraph. A small window appears, listing the properties of the CSS rule applying to this paragraph. The window lists the name of the style sheet, as well as the rule `.greenText`.
2. Place your cursor over the `.greenText` class, and the properties appear in a yellow pop-up window as seen in Figure 4-8. This feature allows you to quickly view the properties without needing to move to the CSS Styles panel or go into Code view.

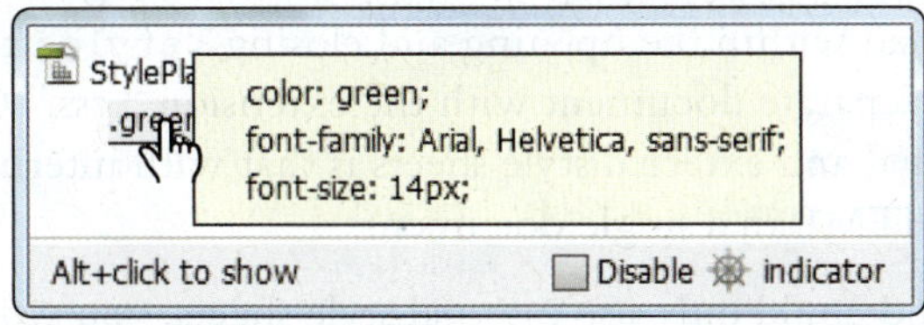

Figure 4-8: *The Code Navigator displays the CSS rules applied to a paragraph.*

Understanding Style Sheets

The term Cascading in Cascading Style Sheets alludes to the fact that styles can live in three different places, each of which has its strengths and weaknesses. You've actually been working with all three types of styles in the last exercise. The first paragraph is being defined with an inline style, the second with an internal style sheet, and the third with an external style sheet.

Inline styles

An inline style is a set of CSS properties defined directly in an HTML tag using the style attribute. These are slightly less common because you can't reuse them easily, and reusability is one of the major benefits of CSS. Nevertheless, inline styles are a part of the CSS language, and you should know what they are.

Follow these steps to create an inline style

Step-by-Step

1. In the file **StylePlaces.html** click three times rapidly to select the first paragraph.
2. Press the Split view button, and notice that your selected text is nested inside a paragraph or <p> element; however, the CSS style rules for color, font-family, and font-size are contained directly inside the opening paragraph tag (Figure 4-9). This is called an inline style because the CSS rules are not separated from the HTML.

Although inline styles are part of CSS, they are used infrequently. They present many of the same problems as the older <font> tags in HTML. They only apply to one tag at a time and are not easily reusable. So when are they used? Inline styles are useful when an internal or external style sheet may not be available; a good example of this is HTML-based e-mail. They are also used in certain situations to override other styles, but you will learn more about this later.

```
21  <p style="color:blue; font-family:
    Arial,Helvetica,Sans-serif; font-size
    : 14px;">Hi there! I'm styled with an
    INLINE style</p>
```

Figure 4-9*: An inline style places rules within a HTML opening tag.*

Internal versus external style sheets

Internal style sheets are CSS rules that are contained directly within a document, using the <style> tag. The entire style sheet is contained within the opening and closing <style> tags. External style sheets are style rules saved in a separate document with the extension ".css." One of the fundamental differences between internal and external style sheets is that with internal style sheets, the CSS rules apply only to the HTML in a single document.

For example, if you had a ten-page website and could only use internal style sheets, you would essentially have ten style sheets: one per page. If you made a change on one page and then needed to make the other pages look the same, you would have to either copy or redefine internal styles from page to page—not an enjoyable prospect.

External style sheets, by contrast, have CSS rules located in one single document. You can attach .css files, or external style sheets, to an unlimited number of HTML pages. This method is extremely flexible: if a style rule such as the font-color for a paragraph is changed in the external style sheet, all paragraphs in the site are instantly modified, whether it be two pages, ten pages or 100 pages.

In Dreamweaver, when you create a new style, the default behavior is to use an internal style sheet. In many ways, a web browser doesn't care which type of style sheet you use; it renders the page exactly the same. There are certain situations when an internal style sheet makes more sense than an external style sheet and vice-versa. You will explore this in more detail in later exercises, but first you need to know how to determine whether a style is internal or external.

Step-by-Step

Follow these steps to determine if a style sheet is internal or external

1. Open **StylePlaces.html** if you do not already have it open and click the Design View button to enter the Design view. In the CSS Styles panel, click on the All button if necessary. In the top half of the screen you will see a listing for <style> and one for **StylePlacesCSS.css**. The first line is the internal style sheet, and the second is for the external style sheet.
2. If necessary, click the arrow to the left of the plus sign (Windows) or the arrow (Mac OS) to the left of the <style> option, and it expands to show you the rule for the class red. Again, if necessary, click the arrow to the left of **StylePlacesCSS.css** to expand this and see the rule for the class `.greenText`. You may have noticed that the listing for the inline style is not here; only rules for internal and external style sheets are visible in All mode.

   In the last exercise, you used the Code Navigator to view the CSS rules applied to a paragraph. You can also use the Code Navigator to quickly determine where the CSS rules are located.

3. Back in Design view, Alt+click (Windows) or Command+Option+click (Mac OS) inside the second paragraph to open the Code Navigator. The window reads StylePlaces.html and the class `.red` is indented below it as seenin Figure 4-10. If a style is located inside an HTML document, as it is in this case, it must be an internal style.

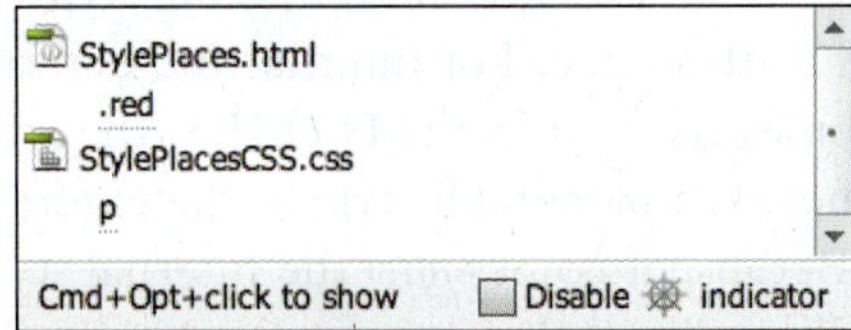

Figure 4-10*: The Code Navigator has located the origin of this CSS rule to be in StylePlaces.html.*

4. Place your cursor over the `.red` class, and all the properties appear; this is a quick way to determine the properties.
5. Click on the `.red` rule, and Dreamweaver's Split view opens, sending you directly to the internal style. An experienced hand-coder might use this to directly edit the rule as you did earlier, although you will not be making any changes at this point. Now you will look at the external style sheet again using the Code Navigator.
6. Alt+click (Windows) or Command+Option+click (Mac OS) in the third paragraph to open the Code Navigator.
7. This time, the Code Navigator window lists **StylePlacesCSS.css** first. If a style is located inside a .css document, as it is in this case, it is an external style. Place your cursor over the `.greenText` class, and all the properties appear.
8. Click on the `.greenText` class, and in the Split view, the external style sheet **StylePlacesCSS.css** appears (Figure 4-11). Doing this actually opens the external style sheet, which is a separate document.

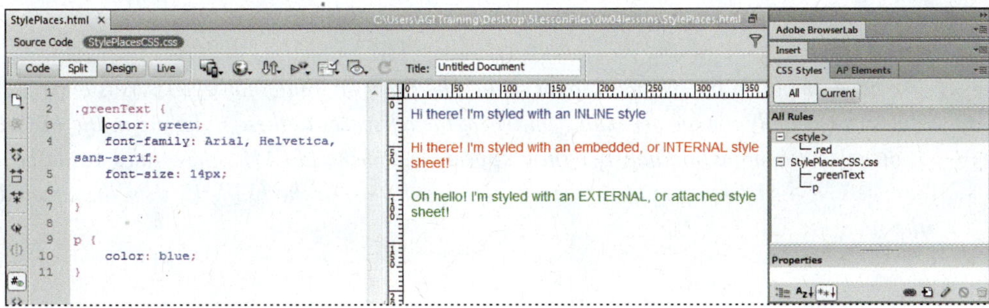

Figure 4-11*: An External Style Sheet is a separate document with the extension .css.*

To return to the original HTML document, press the Source Code button immediately to the left of the button labeled **StylePlacesCSS.css**.

9. Choose File > Save All. Close this document for now. Choosing *Save All* saves not just the HTML document but the external stylesheet at the same time.

Understanding why they're called Cascading

You have learned how CSS integrates with HTML, and that there are three categories of styles: inline, internal, and external. Additionally, you have seen that an HTML document, such as the one from the last exercise, can contain all three types. Now you'll begin to explore when you might use one type over the other. A good way to look at this is to ask the question: Which one of the three style types is most dominant?

To help you picture this, consider the following situation: you have a paragraph, or more accurately, a <p> tag in your document, and you have the three style types (inline, internal, and external). Each one targets the <p> tag with the same property (color, for example) but they all have different values. So which one wins? The answer is the inline style, which is the most dominant because it is closest to the HTML source. The strength of competing styles is largely related to where the style is in relation to the HTML source. For internal and external styles, if they have competing rules, whichever style comes last within the HTML is the strongest. So in the following scenario, imagine that there is a paragraph style in the external style sheet (styles.css) declaring paragraphs to be blue. Because it comes *after* the internal style sheet's rule for red paragraphs, the external style sheet "wins" and the paragraph is blue.

```
<style type="text/css">
p {
   color: red;
}
</style>
<link href=" styles.css" rel="stylesheet" type="text/css" />
```

However it is equally possible that the author of the HTML has arranged the styles in a different order:

```
<link href=" styles.css" rel="stylesheet" type="text/css" />
<style type="text/css">
p {
   color: red;
}
</style>
```

Certification Ready 2.1

What are CSS best practices?

Here, the paragraphs will be red because the internal style sheet comes last in the HTML code. There is no default order of styles in the documents that Dreamweaver creates, so you do need to be aware of this rule.

Take Note...

We have simplified the relationship for now. The strength of internal styles versus external styles can actually change depending on where the references to these styles are in the HTML. If the reference to the internal style sheet appears last in the HTML, these rules would be strongest. If the reference to the external style appears last in the HTML, then these would be the strongest.

Creating and modifying styles

You will now get a chance to begin working more deeply with CSS. In this exercise, you'll be picking up where you left off in the last lesson with the events page for the OrganicUtopia website. In that lesson, you covered the creation of new CSS rules; however, you essentially worked with just one category of CSS rules, the element or tag-based rules. In all instances from the last lesson, you defined the properties for a tag, such as `<h1>`, `<p>`, and `<ul>` (unordered lists). You will now explore how to create classes and IDs. First, a brief review of the styles you used in the last lesson for tag styles.

A tag style assigns rules directly to a specific HTML tag to alter its appearance. You can attach tag styles to any tag from the <body> tag down; as a matter of fact, when you modify page properties (Modify > Page Properties) to change default text formatting and background color, you are using a tag style assigned to the <body> tag.

The most basic tag styles are very straightforward. For instance, when you create a **rule definition** for the <p> (paragraph) tag, all paragraphs appear the same. The limitations begin when you want to customize one specific paragraph to appear different from the others. You will explore some solutions to this dilemma; for now, keep in mind that tag styles are a great way to ensure consistency across multiple elements and pages where specific tags are used, such as lists, tables, and paragraphs.

Follow these steps to modify a style

Step-by-Step

1. Double-click the **events.html** file in the Files panel to open it. This page has already had its Heading 1, paragraph, and list styled. You will now style the Heading 2.
2. In the Design view, click inside the heading *Spring Events.* This is already formatted as a Heading 2 for you.
3. Click the CSS button in the left side of the Property Inspector; this allows you to define the properties of the Heading.
4. Choose 18 from the Size drop-down menu on the Property Inspector, and the New CSS Rule dialog box appears. From the Choose a **contextual selector** type for your CSS rule drop-down menu, choose Tag. In the Selector Name text field, the selector h2 has been chosen for you as seen in Figure 4-12. Dreamweaver does this because you placed your cursor inside the text formatted as h2. Press OK. Now you can add additional properties, and Dreamweaver adds them to the definition of the h2 tag.

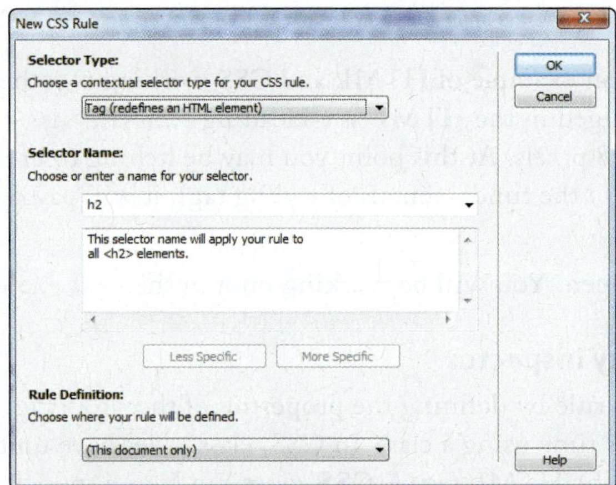

Figure 4-12*: Defining a Heading 2 for the first time causes the New CSS Rule dialog box to appear.*

5. In the Property Inspector, click on the color swatch to choose a color for your text from the Swatches panel that appears. Select a dark green. The color #390, located in the top row, is used in this example. Your heading now changes to green. You have just styled the font-size and color of the <h2> tag. At this point, all text formatted as h2 appears this way. You will now format the last heading in the page in order to see this.
6. Click inside the text, *Rent our facility.* In the Property Inspector, click the HTML button. You need to toggle into this view because you now want to change the HTML formatting, not the CSS.

7. In the Property Inspector, note that the Format for this text is currently set to None. From the Format drop-down menu, choose Heading 2 (as seen in Figure 4-13) to see your text change.

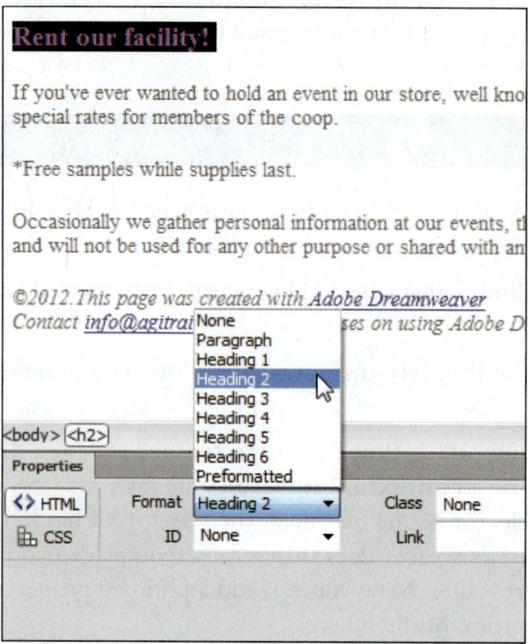

Figure 4-13: *Formatting text as a Heading 2 assumes the properties of the CSS rule.*

What you have seen in this exercise is an example of HTML and CSS working together with a tag style. In this case, all text tagged in the HTML as a Heading 2 or `<h2>` is defined by the CSS rule as green and 18 pixels. At this point you may be itching to create more complex layouts; if you understand the fundamentals of styling tags, it will pay off as you move to the next level of CSS.

8. Choose File > Save but keep this file open. You will be working on it in the next exercise.

Creating a class style with the Property Inspector

In the last exercise, you created a new CSS rule by defining the properties of the `<h2>` tag. Now you will create another CSS rule, this time using a class. In CSS, class styles have unique names and are not associated with any specific HTML tag. A **CSS class** can have a specific style that can be applied to one or more elements in your website. So you might create a class called `holidayText`, for example, and the properties of this class might be a single rule defining the font-color. Once the class is created, this text could then be applied to a table, paragraph, heading, or form element simultaneously. So on Halloween, if you change the property of the font-color to orange, all text that is defined by the `holidayText` class is orange, and on Valentine's Day, if you change the property of the font-color to red, it all changes to red.

In this exercise, you will create a class for the copyright text at the bottom of the page in order to distinguish it from the rest of the page.

Follow these steps to create a class style

Step-by-Step

1. Locate the paragraph at the very bottom of your page, click immediately before the copyright symbol, and then drag across until the two lines are selected.
2. Press the CSS button in the Property Inspector if necessary; note that this text has a size of 14 pixels and a dark gray color. This is because these are paragraphs and the CSS rules for paragraphs in this document currently have these properties. You will now format all this text with a different size and font, and then add a background color. First notice the section of the Property Inspector labeled Targeted Rule and note that it is set to <New CSS Rule> as seen in Figure 4-14.

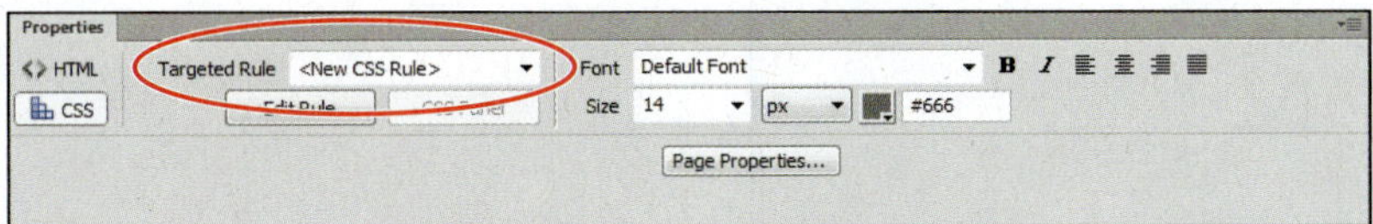

***Figure 4-14**: The Targeted Rule is set to* <New CSS Rule>.

Because CSS is so flexible, you often have many options for styling. Here, Dreamweaver is telling you that a new rule will be created. The other option is that you could update the paragraph rule that already exists. You can see this option by clicking the menu and noting the "p" rule in the Cascade section. For now, make sure that New CSS Rule is still selected.

3. In the Property Inspector, click on the drop-down menu for Size and change the size from 14 pixels to 10 pixels. The New CSS Rule dialog box appears. The default choice for Selector Type is Class, which is what you would like to use. Classes, unlike the Tag styles you have been using, must be named; additionally, you must name the class, as Dreamweaver does not do it for you.

Take Note...

Older versions of Dreamweaver automatically assigned generic names to new classes, such as `.style1`, `.style2`, *and so on. In recent versions of Dreamweaver when it comes to styles, users are now required to name CSS classes. Although this may seem to be an extra step, it is a good one. By being forced to assign names to styles, users are more aware of the code they are generating, which makes their web pages easier to maintain.*

4. In the Selector Name field, type copyright. As you type, notice that Dreamweaver adds the text, This selector name will apply your rule to all HTML elements with class "copyright." (Figure 4-15) This is Dreamweaver's way of helping you understand how your new class can be applied.

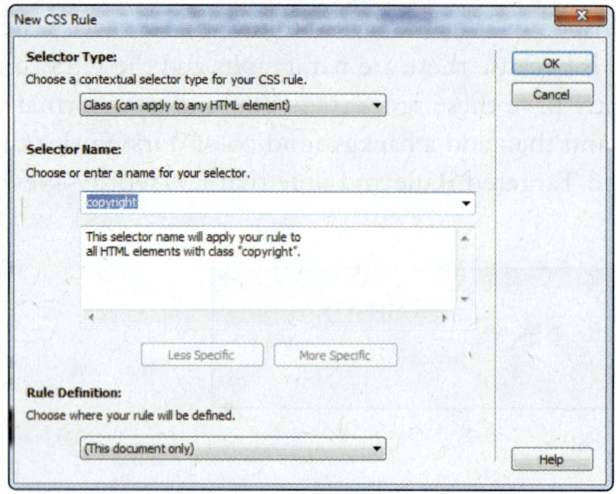

Figure 4-15*: Set the rules for the new* `copyright` *class.*

5. Press OK. You now see the text formatted at 10 pixels. Once the class is created, you can add other properties.

6. Click once in the first line of the copyright text. Notice in the Property Inspector, in the Targeted Rule section, the menu is now set for .copyright. This is important, as it confirms that you are modifying the class, not creating a new rule or modifying the paragraph tag style. In the Property Inspector, choose Verdana, Geneva, sans-serif from the Font menu to add this property to the copyright class. Now you'll add a new line of text and apply the copyright class to it.

Certification Ready 5.2

How do you create CSS rules in the Property Inspector?

7. Place your cursor at the end of the last line of the paragraph and press Enter (Windows) or Return (Mac OS) to add a new line. Type the following text: **All images on this website are the copyright of Glenn "The Hodge" Hodgkinson.** Notice that the text is still using the copyright style. If you wanted to remove this class for any reason, you could click on the Targeted Rule drop-down menu and choose Remove Class.

Creating and modifying styles in the CSS Styles panel

Using the Property Inspector is a quick-and-easy way to create and apply styles and make some basic formatting choices; however, the number of style choices in the Property Inspector is very limited. To take advantage of the full power of CSS, you will begin to dive into the CSS Styles panel. In this exercise, you'll explore some of the powerful options that CSS has at its disposal. The first thing you'll do is change the background color of your page by adding a new style to the body tag.

Follow these steps to create a style in the CSS Styles panel

Step-by-Step

1. At the top of the CSS Styles panel in the upper-right corner of your screen, make sure the All tab is active, and locate `<style>` underneath; if it is not currently expanded, click the arrow to see the list of current rules in your document. You will now add a new rule for the body tag in order to change the background color.
2. Click the New CSS Rule icon ( ) at the bottom of the CSS Styles panel. This displays the same dialog box you are accustomed to working with, just accessed from a different location. From the Choose a contextual selector type for your CSS rule drop-down menu, choose Tag. Previously, you have accepted the automatic choices in the Selector Name section, but in this case, you need to instruct Dreamweaver that you would like to create a new rule for the body tag.
3. From the Choose or enter a name for your selector drop-down menu, select body. Press OK. The CSS Rule definition dialog box appears as seen in Figure 4-16. This dialog box gives you access to the numerous styling options available in CSS.

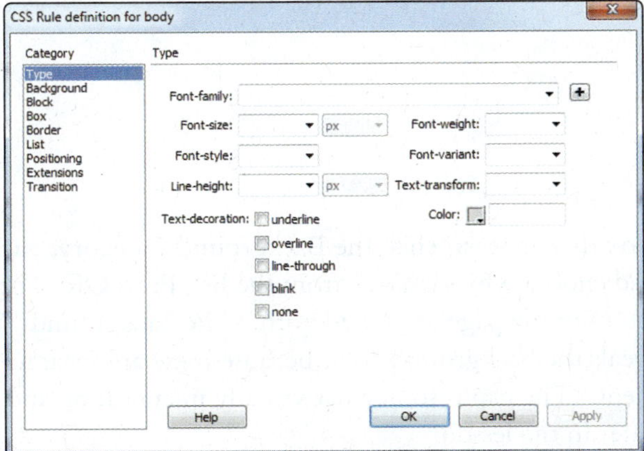

***Figure 4-16**: Creating a new rule for the body tag launches the CSS Rule definition dialog box.*

4. In the left Category column, select Background to access the Background properties. In the field for Background-color, type in the following hexadecimal number: **#E0F0E4**. The background color does not apply automatically. Press the Apply button in the bottom-right corner to preview the new background color.
5. Press OK to confirm the background color. You will now change the background color for the copyright class at the bottom of the page.

6. In the list of rules in the CSS Styles panel, double-click the .copyright class as seen in Figure 4-17 to edit these properties.

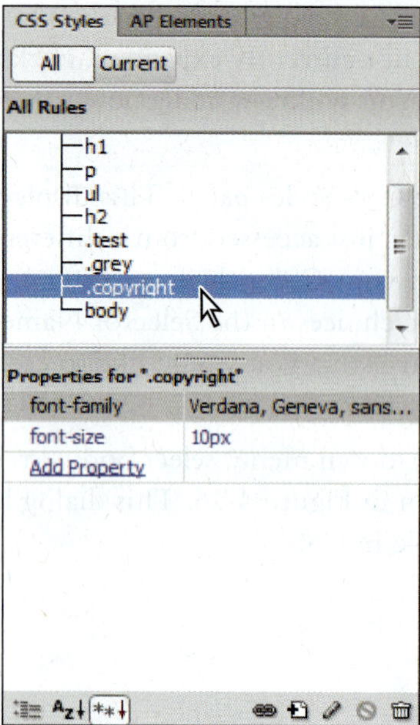

Figure 4-17: Double-clicking a style in the style window opens the CSS Rule definition dialog box.

7. In the CSS Rule definition dialog box that appears, click the Background Category, click on the Background-color swatch, and choose white (#FFF) from the list. Press OK. The two copyright paragraphs at the bottom of the page are styled with white backgrounds. The gap between the two paragraphs reveals the background color because these are separate paragraphs, and are both block elements. The gap is somewhat visually unappealing and is something you will be fixing a bit later in the lesson.

Advanced text formatting with CSS

Text on the Web is necessarily limited due to the fact that designers cannot assume that fonts they choose in Dreamweaver will be available to the user. There is a small set of fonts that designers can use that are essentially guaranteed to be on all users' systems. Given this limitation, you can use some of the properties in CSS to give your text a distinctive look. In this exercise, you will work with the line spacing of your paragraphs and lists, and the letter spacing of your headings.

Take Note...

The limitations on web fonts are slowly changing, and in Dreamweaver CS6, there is now a new feature that allows you access to a wider range of font choices. For now, it is still important to learn the basics. We cover the new web fonts feature in Lesson 7, "CSS3 Transitions and Web Fonts."

Follow these steps to explore advanced text formatting with CSS

Step-by-Step

1. In the CSS panel, double-click the rule for `p` (paragraph) to open the CSS Rule definition dialog box. You will now override the default line-height for your paragraphs. If you have a print background, you may be familiar with leading, which is the amount of space between the lines in a paragraph. Line-height is the same thing as leading.
2. In the Line-height field, type **20**; the value is automatically set for pixels. Press Apply, and you will see the space between your paragraph lines increase. Extra line-height can often make your text more readable, so it is great that you have this option in CSS. However, a problem may arise if you change the font-size. For example, setting the fixed value of 20 pixels looks good with 14-pixel type, but what if you were to later change the font-size of your paragraph? The 20-pixel line-height would look strange. A more flexible way to assign line-height is to use a percentage.
3. From Line-height drop-down menu to the right of the text field, choose percent (%). Change the value from 20 to **120**, (as seen in Figure 4-18) and press Apply. You won't actually see a dramatic difference because the end result is similar, but by assigning the line-height to 120 percent, your initial font-size isn't as important. There will always be the height of the line plus 20 percent extra, no matter what the font-size is. Press OK.

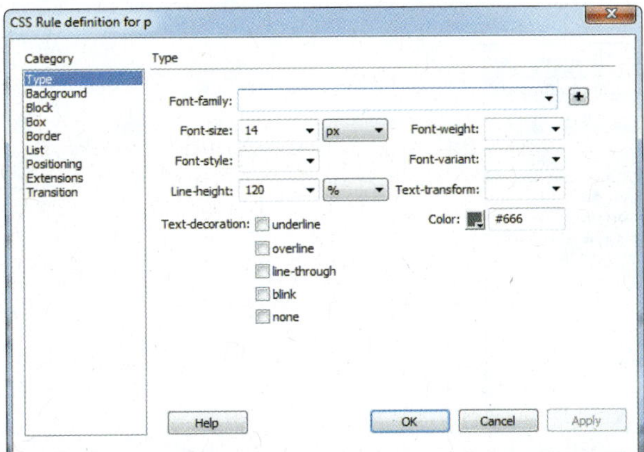

***Figure 4-18**: Changing the line-height value of a paragraph to a percentage is more flexible than using pixels.*

Notice that the list under Spring Events did not change. This is because the line-height property applies solely to paragraphs, not lists. If you want to make this list appear the same, you could always apply the same value of line-height. However, you will be adding extra space between the lines to make the list stand out from the rest of the page.

4. In the CSS Styles panel, double-click on the `ul` rule. The CSS Rule definition dialog box appears. In the field for line-height, type **150**; then from the drop-down menu to the right, select percentage (%). Press OK, and you now have extra space between your list items. Now you'll style your Heading 2 element.

5. In the CSS Styles panel, double-click the h2 rule. In the Text-transform section, click the menu, and from the list, choose uppercase. Press Apply, and you will see your two headings, *Spring Events* and *Rent Our Facility!*, transform to uppercase. This helps your headings stand out and is a lot faster than retyping these headings by hand. Now you'll add some space between all the letters.

Take Note...

Transforming your text to uppercase is just a style; in the HTML, your original text still has the standard formatting. One of the few times this might be an issue is if your web page is being viewed without a style sheet; older cell phones and PDAs with web browsers do not fully support style sheets (or use them at all), and so your text would appear lowercase as it is in the HTML.

6. Select the Block category in the CSS Rule definition dialog box. Block styles generally control the way text is displayed in the browser. In the field for Letter-spacing, type **5**; then choose px from the drop-down menu to the right. Press Apply, and the two headings are extended. Each letter pair has 5 pixels of space between them. Press OK. When used well, letter-spacing can make your headings more readable and unique as seen in Figure 4-19.

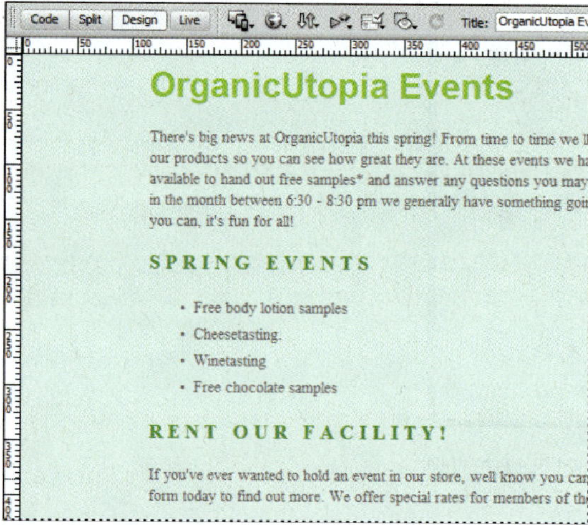

Figure 4-19: *Adding letter-spacing and uppercasing to your headings can make them stand out.*

Fine-tuning page appearance with contextual and pseudo-class selectors

CSS allows you to create styles that are targeted at specific HTML elements on your page. Understanding these techniques is crucial if you want to gain control over the appearance of your page. Look at the Spring Events list on your page: lines 1 and 4 both begin with the word Free. Let's say you wanted to emphasize this word to attract your user's attention. You could simply bold the word, but what if you not only wanted to bold it, but change the color as well. It would be possible to create a class to do this, but there is another option that has some useful benefits called *contextual selectors*.

Dreamweaver actually refers to contextual selectors, which is the official CSS term for them, as *compound selectors*. Despite the terminology, they are very powerful and important to understand.

Contextual selectors apply formatting to tags and classes when they appear in a specific combination. For instance, you often have separate rules for the <p> (paragraph) and `<strong>` (bold) tag, but what if you want a rule for `<strong>` tags that are used inside <p> tags? Contextual selectors can handle this; for instance, you can designate that any text inside a `<strong>` tag must be red, unless it is used within a <p> tag, in which case it should be blue. This breathes new life into your tag styles by multiplying the number of times you can use them in conjunction with each other.

Step-by-Step

Follow these steps to create a selector

Certification Ready 5.3

How do you apply emphasis to text by using the Insert menu or the Property Inspector?

1. In the first line of the Spring Events list, select the word *Free*. Click the HTML button in the Property Inspector, then press the Bold button. (This actually creates a `<strong>` tag in the HTML.) Using the example from above, let's say that simply bolding this wasn't enough and you wanted to add some color.
2. Press the CSS button in the Property Inspector; then click the menu for Targeted Rule and choose <New CSS Rule>. You must do this; otherwise, when you choose a color, you will target the whole list, which is not what you want.
3. Click the color swatch in the Property Inspector and choose the dark green swatch in the top row, #030. The New CSS Rule dialog box appears.

4. From the Choose a contextual selector type for your CSS rule drop-down menu, choose Compound (based on your selection). In the Selector Name field, the text *body ul li strong* appears as seen in Figure 4-20. This may look strange at first, but it's logical if you read it from left to right. The body tag is the ancestor, or parent, of the `ul` tag. The strong tag is referred to as a descendent selector. In other words, your style will only apply to strong tags, which are nested in a list item (which is nested in the unordered list, and so on).

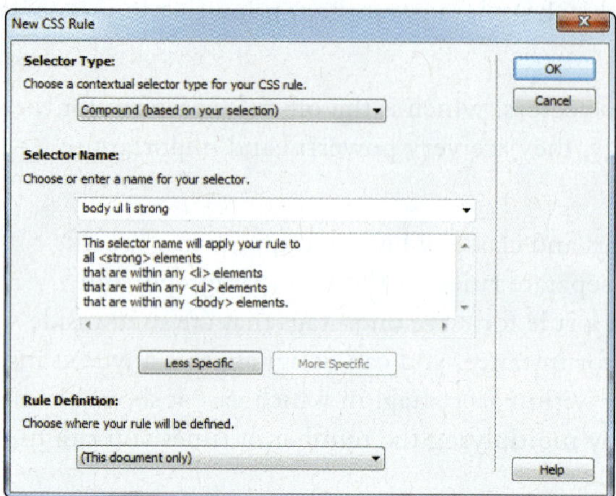

***Figure 4-20**: Set the Selector Type to Compound to create a contextual selector.*

Take Note...

In the official specification of CSS, the term "descendent selectors" is used to define this ability to select elements that are descendents of another element in the document.

Dreamweaver includes the body element in this rule, but it's not necessary. Technically speaking, body is the ancestor of all tags in a document, so Dreamweaver wants to include it. There's no harm in leaving it as is, but it is a little redundant. In any case, you have the option to shorten this code manually.

5. Below the Selector Name section, click the Less Specific button, and the list of rules is shortened to *ul li strong*. This has no effect on the behavior of the rule. Press OK. The word Free is now bold and dark green. Deselect the text to see the final result. The rule is in place, and anything that is bold inside a list will have this appearance. You can see this now by bolding the word Free in the fourth line of the list.

Certification Ready 5.3

How do you align paragraphs?

6. Press the HTML button in the Property Inspector. Select the word Free in the fourth line and then press the Bold button in the Property Inspector. The word takes on the same appearance. Bolding anything else in the list causes it to have the same appearance, while bolding anything not in a list has only the default effect.

Styling hyperlinks

You're slowly beginning to pull together a page with a color theme to it, even if there is no layout *per se*. A frequently asked question when people are learning to create web pages is how to style the hyperlinks on a page. This can be accomplished with CSS, although there are some precautions. Since the early days of CSS, the default style for unvisited hyperlinks has been a bright blue with an underline and a purple color with an underline for visited hyperlinks. An argument can be made that users might be confused by hyperlinks that do not fit this mold. On the other hand, many designers like being able to color their hyperlinks to match the rest of their page. Regardless of the debate, it's important to understand how to do this.

Technically speaking, hyperlinks live in a category called a **pseudo-class**. A pseudo-class selector affects a part or state of a selected tag or class. A state often refers to an item's appearance in response to something happening, such as the mouse pointer rolling over it. One of the most common pseudo-class selectors is applied to the <a> tag, which is used to create hyperlinks. You'll now create a pseudo-class selector to affect the appearance of hyperlinks on the events.html page in different states:

Follow these steps to style a hyperlink — **Step-by-Step**

1. Click the products link in the first paragraph, and then choose New from the CSS Styles panel menu to create a new rule. The New CSS Rule dialog box appears.
2. From the Choose a contextual selector type for your CSS rule drop-down menu, choose Compound. In the Selector Name section, click to open the drop-down menu to the right of the selector field. You will have different selectors appearing at the top of your menu; this is because Dreamweaver is attempting to create a compound rule, but in fact you are only interested in the last four options, which are `a:link`, `a:visited`, `a:hover`, and `a:active`. Choose a:link (as seen in Figure 4-21), which affects the appearance of a hyperlink when it hasn't yet been visited. Press OK.

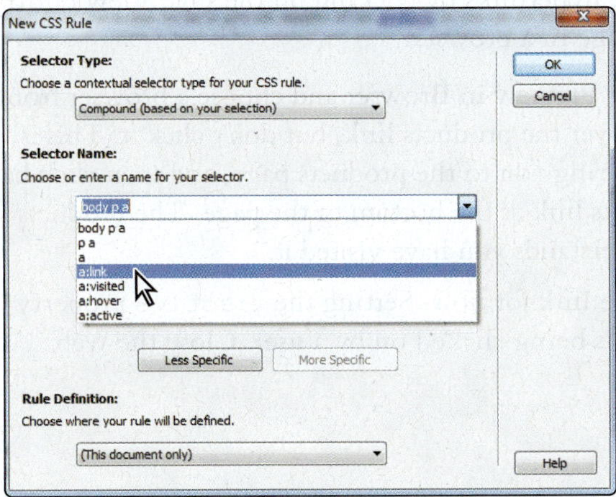

***Figure 4-21**: Set the Selector type to* Compound *and choose* a:link *from the Selector menu.*

3. The CSS Rule definition dialog box appears. Under the Type category, click the color swatch next to Color and choose the green shade you used in the previous exercise (#030). Press OK, and the products link in the first paragraph as well as the two links at the bottom of the page are now green instead of blue. Now you'll set the style for hover links, or `a:hover`.

4. Make sure that the products link in the first paragraph is selected and once again, choose New from the CSS Styles panel menu and the New CSS Rule dialog box opens. You will leave the state for the visited link alone for now. In this case, the default purple is fine. You will now change the state for `a:hover`, which defines the color of a hyperlink when a user places their cursor over it.
5. From the Choose a contextual selector type for your CSS rule drop-down menu, choose Compound. In the Selector Name section, choose `a:hover` from the drop-down menu, then press OK.
6. From the Type category, click the color swatch next to Color and select the bright orange approximately in the center of the Swatches panel (#C60). In the Text-decoration section, mark the last checkbox labeled *none* as seen in Figure 4-22. This removes the underline from the hyperlink for the hover state only. Press OK.

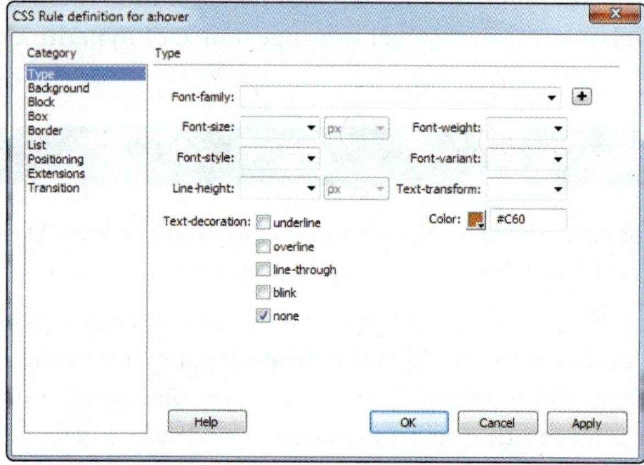

***Figure 4-22**: Set properties for a:hover, or the appearance of hyperlinks when the mouse pointer rolls over them.*

You can preview the appearance of the hyperlinks by clicking on the Live View button in the Application bar or opening your page in a browser.

Certification Ready 5.8

How do you use the different selector types such as descendent selectors, classes, the tag selector, pseudo class selectors and group selectors?

7. Choose File > Save; then choose File > Preview in Browser and choose a browser from the list to launch it. Place your cursor over the products link, but don't click it. This is the hover link. Click the products link to bring you to the products page, and then click back to the events page by clicking the Events link at the bottom of the page. The products link is now purple because the browser understands you have visited it.

   You will leave off styling the `a:active` link for now. Setting the `a:active` property defines the way a link appears when it is being clicked on by a user. Close the web browser.

Div tags and CSS ID selectors

Your page is coming along nicely on the style front, as you have used quite a bit of CSS, but looking at your page, it's fair to say that it is still lacking a cohesive style. All your various headings and paragraphs, as well as your list, are floating about on the page, and with the exception of the copyright text at the bottom of the page, it's difficult at a single glance to get a sense of where one section ends and another begins. It's time to add more structure to your page through the use of the **`<div>` tag** and more control of your CSS with ID selectors. **CSS ID** styles can be applied to any HTML element in a document. All class styles are displayed in the CSS Styles panel with a hash tag [#] preceding their name and in the Style pop-up menu of the text Property inspector. Unlike Class styles, ID styles can only be used one time per page.

Let's look at the structure first. It would be nice to gather the text on the bottom of your page, starting with the line, *Occasionally we gather...*, and then the two paragraphs below, and put it all into a single section. You could then take this new section and style it separately from the rest of the page. This is possible with the <div> tag. In this exercise, you will begin by creating a footer ID.

Follow these steps to create a div tag

Step-by-Step

1. Click and drag to select all the text from the line, *Occasionally we gather...*, down to the bottom of the page. You will be grouping these three paragraphs together.
2. Immediately above the CSS Styles panel is the Insert tab. Click on this once to open the Insert panel. If the drop-down menu is not set to Common, select Common from the menu now. In the Common section, press the Insert Div Tag ( ) button, and the Insert Div Tag dialog box opens as seen in Figure 4-23. In the Insert section, the default choice is *Wrap around selection*; this is exactly what you want to do, so leave this option as is.

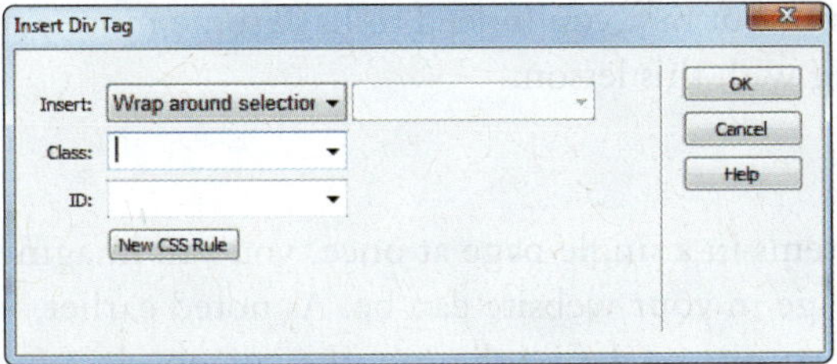

***Figure 4-23**: Press the Insert Div Tag button in the Common section of the Insert panel.*

A <div> tag by itself doesn't do anything until some CSS properties are attached to it. In other words, unlike other HTML tags, which often have a default visual effect in the browser (think of headings), the <div> tag has no effect on your rendered page unless you specifically instruct it to. You will now get to do this.

3. In the field labeled ID, type **footer**. Just like classes, IDs should have good, descriptive names to help identify them. You'll now apply a background color of white to the entire block of text you selected. Notice that there is a field for class as well. Classes and IDs are very similar. The difference between them is that classes can be used multiple times on different elements on a page, whereas an ID can only be used once. In this case, an ID is appropriate because there is only one footer on this page.
4. Click the New CSS Rule button. You don't need to change anything here; just confirm that you are creating an ID with the name footer. The footer name is preceded by the pound sign (#). This is the main difference between ID names and class names. If this were a class named footer, it would be named `.footer`. Press OK, and the CSS Rule definition dialog box appears.

Certification Ready 5.1

What are the different uses for global CSS rules and CSS rules for div tags?

Certification Ready 5.2

How do you define, modify and check CSS rules?

5. Select the Background category, then click the Background-color swatch. Choose the pure white swatch (#FFF) and press OK. Press OK again to close the Insert Div Tag dialog box. In Dreamweaver's Design view, a box has appeared around the text and there is now a white background unifying the footer text as seen in Figure 4-25.

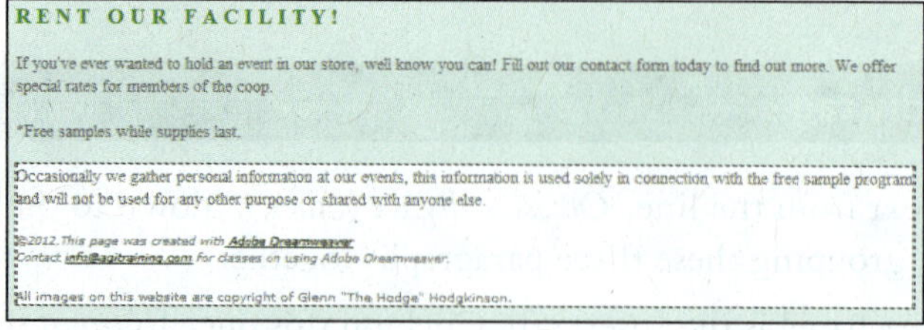

Figure 4-24: *Set the Background-color to* #FFF *in the CSS Rule definition dialog box.*

If you haven't guessed by now, these are the first steps toward page layout with CSS. A footer is a common element on most pages, and there are a few other obvious ones as well: headers, sidebars, and navigation bars to name a few. You'll begin working with these page structures more deeply in upcoming lessons, but first you'll need to have some more control of the CSS rules that you've been working with this lesson.

Internal versus external style sheets

Now that you've seen how to modify a few items in a single page at once, you can imagine how powerful a style sheet shared by every page in your website can be. As noted earlier, when you create new CSS rules, you have the opportunity to define them in the current document or in a new CSS file. A collection of rules stored in a separate .css file is referred to as an external style sheet. You can attach external style sheets to any number of pages in a site so that they all share the same style rules.

So far, you've created internal, or embedded, styles. This means you wrote the style rules directly into the page using the `<style>` tag. Although you can format a page with an internal style sheet, this method is not very portable. To apply the same rules in another page, you have to copy and paste the internal style sheet from one page to another. This can create inconsistency among pages if the same rule is updated in one page and not the other.

To utilize the true power of style sheets, you need to create an external style sheet that any or all pages on your site can share. When you change an external style, pages linked to that style sheet are updated. This is especially handy when working with sites containing many pages and sections.

You can create external style sheets in the following ways:

- Move rules from an internal style sheet into a new CSS file.
- Define styles in a page in a new document using the New CSS Rule panel.
- Create a new CSS document from the Start page or File menu.

Now you will export internal styles from your events.html page into a separate CSS file so that other pages may share them.

Follow these steps to create an external CSS style sheet

Step-by-Step

1. With the **events.html** document open, expand the style sheet shown in the CSS Styles panel so that you can see all the rules you have created. If you have limited screenspace, double-click the Insert panel to collapse it. Also remember you can expand a pane by clicking the bottom edge and dragging down.
2. Click the first rule below the `<style>` tag at the top of the panel and then scroll down if necessary to locate the last rule. Shift+click the last rule in the panel so that all the rules are selected. In the upper-right corner, press the CSS Styles panel menu button (▾≡) and choose Move CSS Rules (Figure 4-26).

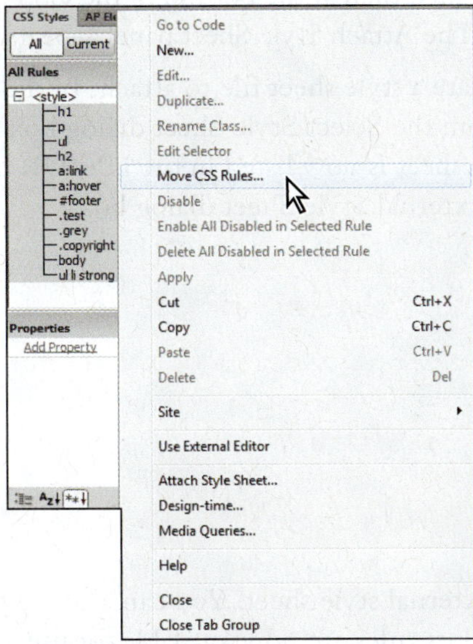

***Figure 4-26**: Select All rules in your style sheet and then choose Move CSS Rules.*

3. The Move CSS Rules dialog box appears, asking if you want to move the styles to an existing or a new style sheet. Select A new style sheet and press OK.
4. A Save Style Sheet dialog box appears, asking you to choose a name and location for the new file that is about to be created. Name it **mystyles**, navigate to the root folder of your site (dw04lessons folder), and choose Save.
5. Look inside your CSS Styles panel and note that the new style sheet, **mystyles.css**, is listed and all the rules are nested within. The internal style sheet (shown as `<style>`) is still in your document, but it contains no rules. You can always click the plus sign (Windows) or arrow (Mac OS) to the left of mystyles.css to collapse or expand it.

Attaching an external style sheet to your page

Dreamweaver automatically made the new external style sheet available to the current page by attaching it. However, you will have to link this style sheet to other pages in your site to use it. You can accomplish this with the Attach Style Sheet command in the CSS Styles panel.

Step-by-Step

Follow these steps to use an external CSS style sheet in your page

1. Double-click the **products.html** file from the Files panel. This page is a version of the products page you created in Lesson 3, "Adding Text and Images." You will now link your new style sheet to this page.
2. If necessary, click the All button in the CSS Styles panel, then at the bottom of the CSS Styles panel, click the Attach Style Sheet icon ( ). The Attach Style Sheet panel appears.
3. Next to File/URL, click the Browse button to locate a style sheet file to attach. In the dw04lessons folder, select the **mystyles.css** file from the Select Style Sheet dialog box and press OK (Windows) or Open (Mac OS). The stylesheet is now listed in the File/URL field (Figure 4-27). Press OK to close the Attach External Style Sheet dialog box.

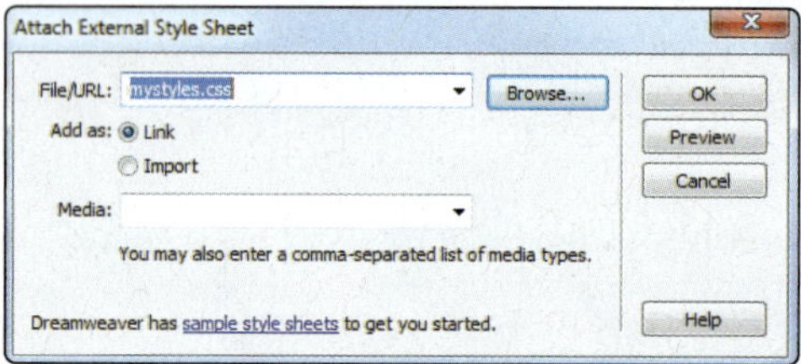

***Figure 4-27**: Adding an external style sheet.*

Certification Ready 5.8

How do you create inline styles and external style sheets?

The page refreshes with the styles defined in the external style sheet. You can also see that the CSS Styles panel shows that mystyles.css and all its rules are now available for use and editing.

Modifying attached style sheets

Because an attached style sheet appears in your CSS Styles panel, you can modify any of its rules and the changes will apply across other pages that share that style sheet. You'll be another step closer to layout now by modifying the body property in order to add some margins to your page.

Step-by-Step

Follow these steps to modify an external style

1. If necessary, in the CSS Styles panel, click the plus sign (Windows) or arrow (Mac OS) to the left of **mystyles.css** and double-click the body rule. The CSS Rule definition dialog box opens.

2. Click the Box category and deselect the checkbox labeled *Same for all* in the Margin column as seen in Figure 4-28.

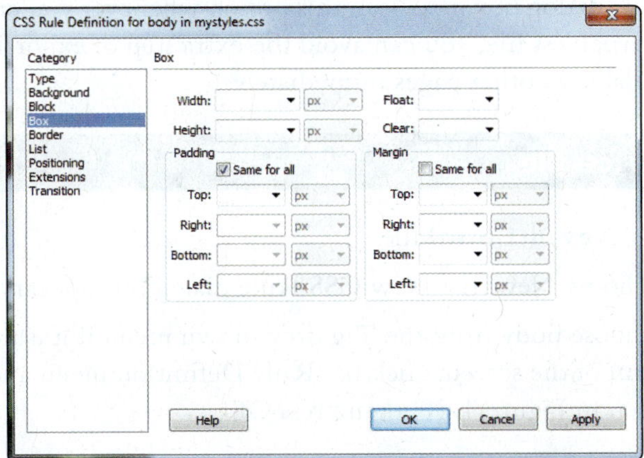

Figure 4-28: *Deselect the checkbox in the Margin section of the Box category.*

Because CSS is based on a box model, it treats every element as a container. Because the <body> tag is the largest container, if you modify its margins, it affects all the content on the page. You'll specifically be changing the left and right margins to create a more centered layout.

3. In the Margin field labeled Right, type **15**, and choose % from the drop-down menu.

4. In the Margin field labeled Left, type **15**, and choose % from the menu (Figure 4-29). Press OK, and your content shifts toward the center.

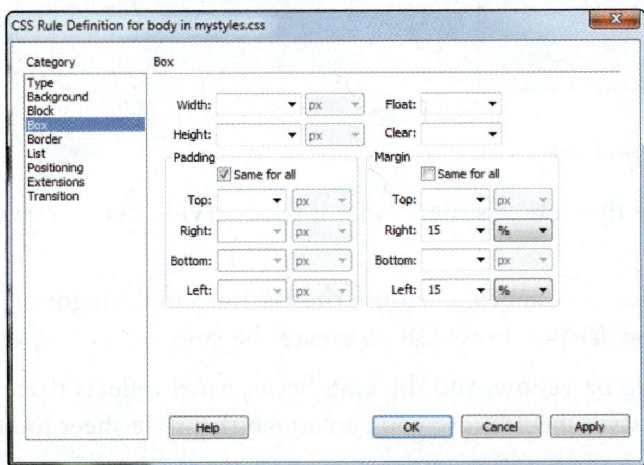

Figure 4-29: *Change the left and right margin for body to 15 percent.*

5. Choose File > Save All, and then preview your page in the browser. You are able to navigate between the products page and the events page using the hyperlinks in each document. Shorten the width of your browser, and notice that the content adjusts accordingly. There will always be 15 percent space to the left of content in the browser window and 15 percent to the right, thereby centering your content. Open the events.html file in your web browser to see how this page's appearance is now being controlled by the external style sheet. When done, close the browser.

Creating a new .css file (external style sheet)

Although it's easy to move styles to a new .css file, you can also create styles in a new .css file from the beginning. The New CSS Rule dialog box gives you this option whenever you create a new rule. By creating styles in an external .css file, you can avoid the extra step of exporting them later and make the style sheet available to other pages immediately.

Step-by-Step

Follow these steps to create a new .css file

1. In the Files panel, double-click on the **event1.html** file.
2. From the CSS Styles panel menu, choose New; the New CSS Rule dialog box appears.
3. Set the Selector Type as Tag, and choose body from the Tag drop-down menu if it is not automatically selected. At the bottom of the screen, click the Rule Definition menu and choose (New Style Sheet File) as seen in Figure 4-30; then press OK.

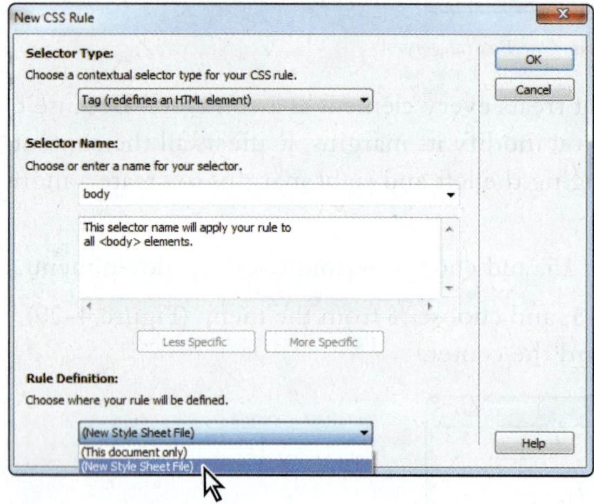

Figure 4-30: Creating a new external style sheet from scratch.

Certification Ready 5.8

How do you use CSS to set properties for text and HTML tags?

Certification Ready 5.2

How do you use external style sheets?

4. You are prompted to name and save the new .css file. Name it **morestyles.css** and save it in the root folder of your site.
5. When the CSS Rule definition dialog box appears, choose the Background category. Set the background color to light yellow, **#FFC**. Press OK to create the rule.

   Your page's background color should be yellow, and the CSS Styles panel reflects that the style was created in a new external style sheet. Now you can attach this style sheet to any other page in your site.
6. Choose File > Save All.

Learning More

More details on CSS

Inheritance

When you nest one rule inside another, the nested rule **inherits** properties from the rule in which it's contained. For instance, if you define a font-size and font-family for all <p> tags, then it carries over to a class style used within the paragraph. This paragraph may not specify values for either property. It automatically inherits the font-size and font-family from the <p> tag selector.

CSS rule weight

What happens if two classes of the same name exist in the same page? It is possible to have two identically named styles, either in the same style sheet or between internal and external style sheets used by the same page. Along the same lines, it is possible to have two rules that both apply to the same tag. If either of these cases exists, how do you know which rule is followed?

You know which rule is followed based on two factors: weight and placement. If two selectors are the same weight (for instance, two tag selectors for the body tag), then the last defined rule takes precedence.

If a rule of the same name is defined in both an internal and external style sheet in your document, the rule from the last defined style sheet takes precedence. For instance, if an external style sheet is attached to the page anywhere after the internal style sheet, the rule in the attached style sheet wins.

Skill Summary

In this lesson you learned how to:	Objective
Demonstrate general and Dreamweaver-specific knowledge of best practices for designing a website, such as maintaining consistency, separating content from design, using standard fonts, and utilizing visual hierarchy	2.1
Set and modify document properties	5.1
Organize web page layout with relative and absolutely-positioned div tags and CSS styles	5.2
Modify text and text properties	5.3
Use CSS to implement a reusable design	5.8

Knowledge Assessment

True/False

Circle T if the statement is true or F if the statement is false.

T F **1.** CSS styles can be located in three locations: inline, internal and external.

T F **2.** You can use multiple external style sheets per document.

T F **3.** The `<font>` tag is the best way to effectively style paragraphs of text on a page.

T F **4.** You can apply CSS styles from both the CSS Styles panel as well as the Property Inspector.

T F **5.** You can modify CSS styles from both the CSS Styles panel as well as the Property Inspector.

T F **6.** You can only create a new CSS rule from the CSS Styles panel.

T F **7.** The role of the Code Navigator in Dreamweaver CS6 is to identify all the possible styles you can use for any given selection.

T F **8.** The div tag in HTML has no visual properties by default.

T F **9.** If you modify the paragraph style in an external style sheet, only paragraphs in pages that link to that style sheet will be affected.

T F **10.** You can attach an external style sheet in the CSS Styles panel.

Multiple Choice

Select the best response for the following statements

1. A CSS rule is is composed of one or more __________ such as color and font-size (among others).

a. elements
b. tags
c. properties
d. objects

2. The following CSS selector is an example of what type of CSS syntax: a:link

a. A compound selector
b. A pseudo-class
c. A hyperlink
d. A tag selector

3. Which of the following is not a part of CSS syntax?

a. A tag selector
b. An ID selector
c. A Class selector
d. A Div selector

4. You can create a new style sheet using which of the following techniques?

a. By choosing "Move Rules" from the context menu of the CSS styles panel
b. From the Dreamweaver CS6 Welcome Screen
c. From the Rule Definition menu within the New CSS Rule panel
d. All of the above

5. Why would you use the Move CSS Rules command?

a. To create an inline style
b. To create an internal style sheet
c. To create an external style sheet
d. All of the above

6. Why would you use "Text-decoration: none" for a hyperlink style?

a. To remove the underline from a hyperlink
b. To change the default color of a visited link
c. To change the default color of an active link
d. To change the default color of a hover link

7. What would the following css selector (p strong) allow you to do in a style?

a. Create the same style for both paragraph and strong elements.
b. Create a specific style for strong elements that are nested within paragraph elements.
c. Create a style for all strong elements in a page.
d. Create a style for all paragraph elements in a page.

8. What are the default colors for hyperlinks?

a. Blue for unvisited links and gray for visited links
b. Purple for unvisited links and gray for visited links
c. Blue for unvisited links and purple for visited links
d. Purple for unvisited links and blue for visited links

9. There are ___ special categories of styles for hyperlinks

a. two
b. three
c. four
d. five

10. You could increase the amount of space between the text in your paragraph using which of the following CSS styles?

a. Leading-transform
b. Text-transform
c. Letter-spacing
d. None of the above

Competency Assessment

Project 4-1 Using class styles

As the designer for Serenity Spa, you need to create a class style that colors text red to help identify products on sale.

1. Open the **index.html** file located in the lesson folder.
2. In the CSS Styles panel, click the panel menu button in the upper-right corner and select New. You can also click on the New CSS Rule button at the bottom-right portion of the window.
3. In the New CSS Rule dialog box, ensure that Class is selected as the Selector Type. Enter the name .sale in the Name field (classes start with a dot as the first part of the name). Make sure that "This document only" is selected as the Rule Definition and press OK.
4. In the CSS Rule Definition dialog box, click on the Color swatch, and choose a red. Click OK.
5. In the Design pane, insert your cursor at the end of the welcome text. Press Return, then type in these items, each on its own line.
   - Massages
   - Facials
   - Body Scrubs & Wraps
6. Format this text as an unordered list by selecting the text, then clicking on the Unordered List icon on the Property Inspector. You can also choose Format > List > Unordered List.
7. In the Properties panel, click on the HTML button if necessary. Select the three bulleted lines of text. Use the Class drop-down menu and choose the sale class. You'll see the text in the Design pane assume the red attributes you assigned to the `.sale` style.
8. Save the file but keep it open, you'll be using it for the next exercise.

Project 4-2 Creating and applying Cascading Style Sheets

As the designer of the Serenity Spa website you need to add a second page to your website and attach a style sheet to it so that the styles you've already created will carry over to your new page. First we'll save the style sheet from the index.html file.

1. With the **index.html** file used in Exercise 4-1 open, choose Window > CSS Styles.
2. In the CSS Styles panel, click on the `.sale` style that you just created.
3. From the CSS Styles panel menu, choose Move CSS Rules. In the dialog box that appears, select A New Style Sheet and press OK.

4. Name the file **spa.css** and save it to the root folder of your website
5. Now create a new page for the site and attach the style sheet. Choose File > New.
6. In the Blank Page category of the New Document dialog box, select HTML as the Page Type and <none> as the Layout. Leave all the other settings as is, and click Create. Save the file as newpage.html.
7. If the CSS Styles panel is not open, open it (Window > CSS Styles). Click on the menu icon in the upper right corner of the panel, then scroll down to select Attach Style Sheet.
8. In the dialog box, click on the Browse button and select the **spa.css** file from the site's root directory, then click OK. Leave all the other settings in the box at their defaults and press OK.
9. The styles you created for the **index.html** page should now appear in the CSS Styles panel for the **newpage.html** page. Save the file.

Proficiency Assessment

Practicing with Styles

Project 4-3

To see the various design options available through CSS, we suggest further exploration. As you'll see, there's only so much you can cover for an exercise as there are a myriad of choices for how you choose to utilize the alternatives available through CSS.

Get Ready. Launch Dreamweaver CS6 if you haven't already.

1. Create a new blank HTML page.
2. Type out some text on your webpage.
3. Connect one of the .css files you created earlier, open the CSS Styles panel and continue to explore the settings.

Dreamweaver CSS Sample Pages

Project 4-4

Dreamweaver has some pre-built CSS styles to start with in case you're new to the process and are looking for some ideas.

Get Ready. Launch Dreamweaver CS6 if you haven't already.

1. Choose File > New.
2. From the New Document window, select Page from Sample, then CSS Style Sheet and start trying out the various choices available.

Circling Back 1

Building an efficient workflow is essential when it comes to creating a website. You can spend many hours just updating pages if you don't understand global options such as templates, library items, and CSS. If you get all three components working together, you can focus on other areas, such as design and content, without tediously updating one page at a time with simple changes such as background color or font.

Project 1 **Building a CSS Template Page**

Project 1: Building a CSS Template Page

The design company you work for is interested in building pages that will act as CSS templates for future clients. Your employers want sample pages that will display some generic color and text format schemes they can use for a presentation on a sales pitch meeting. They want the layout and design to be simple, but concentrate on how the text will appear.

Launch Dreamweaver if you haven't already. Establish a new root folder and site called **CSS templates**.

1. Create a new web page; save it as **CSS-template.html**.
2. Type the following text on the new HTML page:

   Mr. Mike's Pizzeria

   Nothing compares to our hand-tossed pizza made with only the freshest ingredients. Try our signature pizzas, tasty salads and signature breadsticks.

   Copyright 2012 Mr. Mike's Pizzeria, LLC. All Right Reserved
3. Use the button on the left of the panel to make sure the Properties panel is set to the CSS settings and not to HTML.
4. Highlight the Header text, "Mr. Mike's Pizzeria"; using the Properties panel, change the font to Tahoma.
5. Once the New CSS Rule window opens, set the selector type to Class. Name the selector **.header**. For the Rule Definition, choose New Style Sheet File.
6. Name the new file **style-template.css** and save it in your root folder.
7. Click the Edit Rule button. Set the Font-size to 18 pt. Click the Background Category and choose a light blue for Background-color.
8. Click OK.
9. Select the body copy text and click the Edit Rule button. Leave Class as the selector type and name the selector **.body**; the Rule Definition should just remain in your style-template.css file.
10. Choose Georgia for the Font-family and set the Font-size to 12 pt. Choose black for the Color setting. Click OK when finished.
11. Select the text "Copyright 2012 Mr. Mike's Pizzeria, LLC. All Right Reserved" and click the Edit Rule button. Leave Class as the selector type and name the selector **.footer**; the Rule Definition should just remain in your style-template.css file.
12. Choose Georgia for the Font-family and set the Font-size to 9 pt. Choose a dark gray for the Color setting. Click OK when finished.
13. Choose File > Save All to save all files.

Page Background and Hyperlinks

Project 2

Text is generally consistent globally, but background colors of pages might change from one page to the next. For example, each of the main categories of the site might be visually represented by a different color. Hyperlinks should generally be the same color to avoid confusing the reader, but you might need to make exceptions based on background color.

1. **CSS-template.html** should still be open from the previous exercise.
2. Choose Modify > Page Properties.
3. Under Appearance (CSS), set the Background color to a pale yellow, such as #FF9. Choose Apply to see the change and keep the window open.
4. Click Links (CSS) and choose a link color for each of the link color options. Set the Underline style to Show underline only on rollover. Click OK.
5. Save your work.

Attaching an external style sheet

Project 3

Now that the basic page and CSS file is set up and ready to go, make sure you understand how to connect that .css file to another page, should the need arise.

1. Create a new webpage and save it as **page1.html**.
2. Add the following text to your page:

   Mr. Mike's Subs

   Nothing compares to our sandwiches and subs made with only the freshest ingredients. Try our signature Italian sub or the tasty Meatball Supreme.

   Copyright 2012 Mr. Mike's Pizzeria, LLC. All Right Reserved
3. Choose Window > CSS Styles.
4. Click the Attach Style Sheet button at the base of the CSS Styles panel.
5. Click the Browser button in the Attach External Style Sheet window and find the **style-template.css** file.
6. Select first line, "Mr. Mike's Subs"; use the Properties panel to apply the header class style. Select the last line of text "Copyright 2012 Mr. Mike's Pizzeria, LLC. All Right Reserved" and use the Properties panel to apply the footer class style.
7. Choose File > Save All to save your work.

Creating Page Layouts with CSS

Key Terms

- Absolute Positioning
- AP Div
- Box Model
- Border property
- Cross-browser Compatible
- Margins
- Padding
- Relative Positioning

Skill	Objective
Demonstrate general and Dreamweaver-specific knowledge of best practices for designing a website, such as maintaining consistency, separating content from design, using standard fonts, and utilizing visual hierarchy	2.1
Organize web page layout with relative and absolutely-positioned div tags and CSS styles	5.2

Business Case

The Organic Utopia website is starting to get more complex. The company owners have decided to go with a more visually-engaging layout that includes adding text over images. Their idea of the design also includes separate text blocks, and they'd like to add more distinctive borders to separate one body of text from another. DIVs are a great tool for accomplishing these tasks.

Introduction

Before starting, make sure that your tools and panels are consistent by resetting your workspace. See "Resetting the Dreamweaver workspace" in the Starting Up section of this book.

You will work with several files from the dw05lessons folder in this lesson. Make sure that you have loaded the dwlessons folder onto your hard drive. See "Loading lesson files" in the Starting Up section of this book.

Before you begin, you need to create site settings that point to the dw05lessons folder. Go to Site > New Site, or, for details on creating a site, refer to Lesson 2, "Setting Up a New Site."

The CSS Box model

CSS positions elements within a page using the **Box model**, which refers to the fact that all HTML elements have default boxes that you can choose to style. You can think of a box as a container for text, images, media, tables, and other content. In most cases, the width and height of a box is determined by the amount of content; however, you can also assign an explicit width and height to any box. Additionally, each box can have its own optional padding, margin, and border settings (described in detail shortly).

Toward the end of Lesson 4, "Styling Your Pages with CSS," you began to explore page structure through the use of the HTML <div> element. The Box model in CSS applies to all elements in HTML but is often paired with <div> tags. The <div> element, in conjunction with CSS rules, can be freely positioned, formatted, and even told how to interact with other boxes adjacent to it. You can also stack and overlap <div> containers, opening the door to flexible and creative layouts that are not possible with HTML alone.

This lesson dives deeper into the many uses of the <div> element. If you have jumped directly to this lesson, it is highly recommended that you understand the basic concepts in Lesson 4, "Styling Your Pages with CSS," before starting this one.

Take Note...

If you've worked with layout applications such as InDesign, the idea of creating and positioning containers for page content should be very familiar to you. Boxes created with the <div> tag can be thought of as analogous to the text and image frames you create in InDesign.

Certification Ready 5.2

What are the different div tag attributes and what are they used for?

The basics of CSS margins, padding, and borders

The Box model allows each element on a page to have unique margin, padding, and border settings (Figure 5-1).

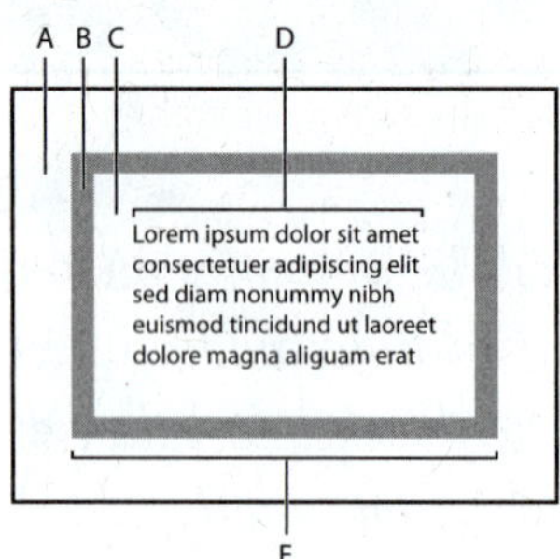

Figure 5-1: ***A.*** *Margin.* ***B.*** *Border.* ***C.*** *Padding.* ***D.*** *Content width.* ***E.*** *Visible width.*

Margins refer to the transparent area surrounding the box, which you set using the margin group of CSS properties. Margins can play an essential role in creating distance between a box and the content surrounding it (such as other boxes), or the boundaries of the page itself. You can set margins for all sides at once or uniquely for each side.

Padding is the distance between the inside edge of the box and its contents. By setting padding, you create space between the box and any text, images, or other content that it contains. You set padding using the padding group of CSS properties, and, like margins, you can set padding for all four sides of a box at once or for each side individually.

The **border property** of a box is transparent by default, but you can add width, color, and a border style for decoration or definition around boxes. Borders sit directly between margins and padding, and define the actual boundaries of the box. You set borders using the border group of CSS properties and, like margins and padding, you can define borders for all four sides at once or for each side individually.

You can incorporate each property into any style rule and attach it to a box, similar to the way you've attached classes to paragraphs and tables in previous lessons.

Reviewing the <div> element

As mentioned earlier, when exploring and creating page layouts with CSS, you will frequently encounter and use the <div> element. The <div> element creates areas or divisions within an HTML document; you can place page content such as text and images directly within sets of <div> tags. Dreamweaver enables you to create CSS-driven page layouts using the Insert Div Tag and Draw **AP Div** buttons in the Insert panel; both of these features use <div> tags to create areas of layout, but do this in different ways.

Reviewing the ID selector

In Lesson 4, "Styling Your Pages with CSS," you learned about the different selector types in CSS: classes, tags, pseudo-class selectors, and IDs. In this lesson, IDs take center stage and become an essential part of working with CSS boxes and positioning. An ID is a special selector type created for a unique element using the same name within a page, and it's meant for one-time use only. ID rules appear within a style sheet and are preceded by a pound sign (#), in contrast to classes, which are preceded by a period character (.).

Because IDs can be used only once per page, they are ideal for setting properties that need to be specific to a single element, such as positioning information. In other words, page elements such as headers or columns occupy a specific position on the page, such as top, right, left, and so on. When creating layouts using the Insert Div Tag button, Dreamweaver requires you to create or assign an ID rule for each box created. When drawing boxes with the Draw AP Div button, Dreamweaver automatically creates a unique ID rule that contains positioning, width, and height information for that specific box.

Because the <div> element has no display attributes, it is given its properties by either an ID or a class, or both. Dreamweaver has a bias; therefore, the program is more likely to use CSS IDs for layout. Think of an ID as a set of instructions that give a <div> its unique appearance and behavior (as DNA does to a human being). An ID rule is matched to a <div> using the tag's ID attribute as seen in Figure 5-2.

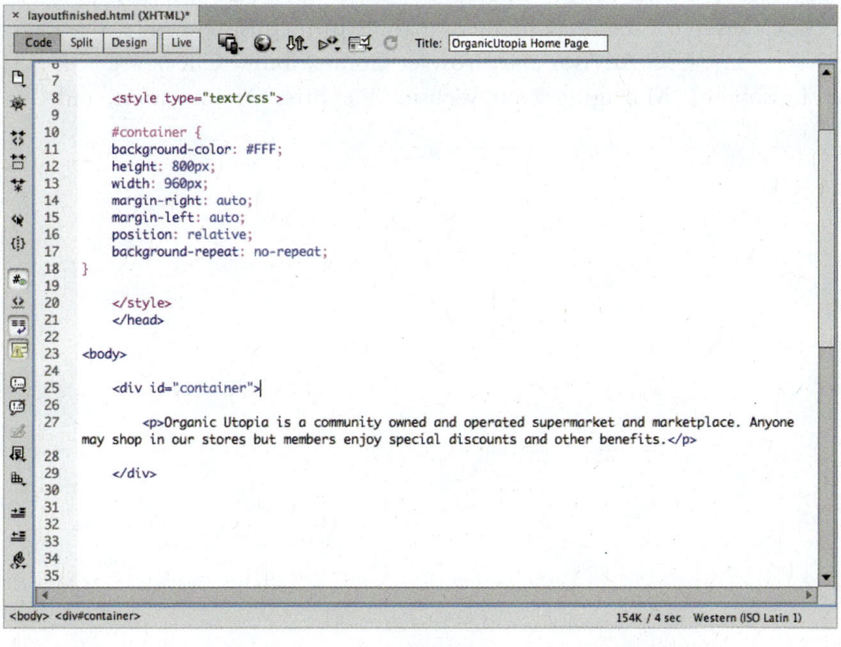

```
× layoutfinished.html (XHTML)*
Code | Split | Design | Live        Title: OrganicUtopia Home Page
7
8     <style type="text/css">
9
10    #container {
11    background-color: #FFF;
12    height: 800px;
13    width: 960px;
14    margin-right: auto;
15    margin-left: auto;
16    position: relative;
17    background-repeat: no-repeat;
18  }
19
20    </style>
21    </head>
22
23  <body>
24
25    <div id="container">
26
27        <p>Organic Utopia is a community owned and operated supermarket and marketplace. Anyone
    may shop in our stores but members enjoy special discounts and other benefits.</p>
28
29    </div>
30
31
32
33
34
35
<body> <div#container>                154K / 4 sec  Western (ISO Latin 1)
```

***Figure 5-2**: The Code view shows the style sheet and <div> tag that create the container.*

Learning More

Tables or CSS for layout?

Certification Ready 5.2

What are the advantages of using div tags instead of tables for page layout?

When CSS first appeared as a tool for layout (in the early 2000s), a debate started within the web design community about the best approach to creating page layouts, because designers could use either CSS or HTML tables. The argument went something like this: Many designers felt like tables were the wrong tool for the job and CSS, with its box model, should be adopted as the primary method for positioning page content. Designers in favor of tables asserted that tables are more reliable in older browsers and easier and quicker to build. For the most part, the argument has been resolved: CSS layout is now regarded as the industry standard for creating page layouts.

Here is a brief overview of what you need to know:

Tables: Although fewer sites are being built from scratch in tables these days, there remain countless websites that were built with them and are still on the Web being updated and maintained. Designers who find themselves having to maintain a tables-based site would do well to understand their behavior. Also, HTML email often relies on the use of tables due to the limited capabilities of email readers.

Tables' limitations include the following: You are restricted to its cell-based structure, and to achieve more complex layouts, you need to nest several levels of tables. Tables also add extraneous code to pages and can present difficulties in accessibility for devices such as screen readers.

CSS: CSS positioning has been around for many years. However different browsers have chosen to support it at varying and inconsistent levels. At this point, CSS positioning has a set of Best Practices that are widely known and used across the web design and development industry. If you need your sites to work reliably in older browsers, testing is still necessary to expose potential inconsistencies.

The CSS Advisor and Browser Compatibility Check features in Dreamweaver CS6 benefit designers who want to use CSS more extensively. These tools flag and help troubleshoot any CSS-related items that may be incompatible or inconsistent in commonly used browsers. The CSS Advisor and Browser Compatibility Check are discussed in detail in Lesson 16, "Managing Your Website: Reports, Optimization, and Maintenance."

Creating a centered container for your page

The goal of this lesson is to create the home page for the Organic Utopia site. This page will look like the thumbnail in Figure 5-3.

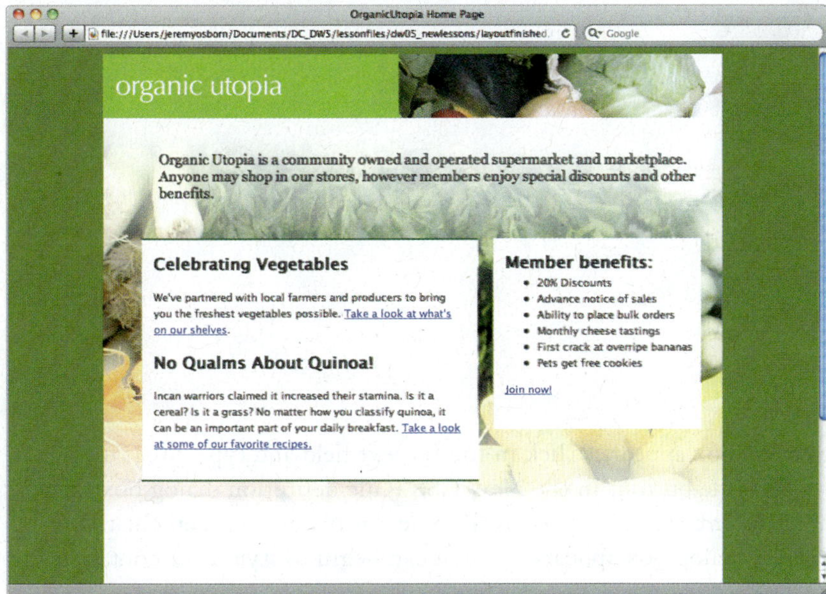

Figure 5-3: *The completed layout you will be creating in this lesson.*

The home page will be a different design and layout than the rest of the site (this layout is covered in more detail in Lesson 6, "Advanced Page Layout."), and you will start by creating a container that will end up nesting the other sections of your page such as the header, sidebar and other elements. This container will have a fixed width of 960 pixels and also be centered within the browser window.

This container will use a combination of relative positioning and automatic margins to achieve the centering effect. Relative positioning allows you to position this box relative to the body of the page, and the automatic margins will force the fixed-width container to stay centered regardless of the browser window's width.

Follow these steps to create a centered container

Step-by-Step

1. In the Files panel, navigate to the dw05lessons folder and double-click the **layout.html** file to open it. This document has been partially prepared for you, with a background color and a page title added. Additionally, the default font, font color, and font size have been defined as Lucida Sans, grey, and small, respectively. Your first step will be to add a box, which will become your main column of text.
2. If it's not already visible, open the Insert panel by choosing Window > Insert. The Insert panel features a list of objects that can be added to your pages easily.

3. In the bottom-left corner of your document window, click the <body> tag. Remember, the body tag encloses all the other tags within a page. You will now create a new <div> element that will function as a container for the other layout elements. In the Insert panel, click the Insert Div Tag button (Figure 5-4).

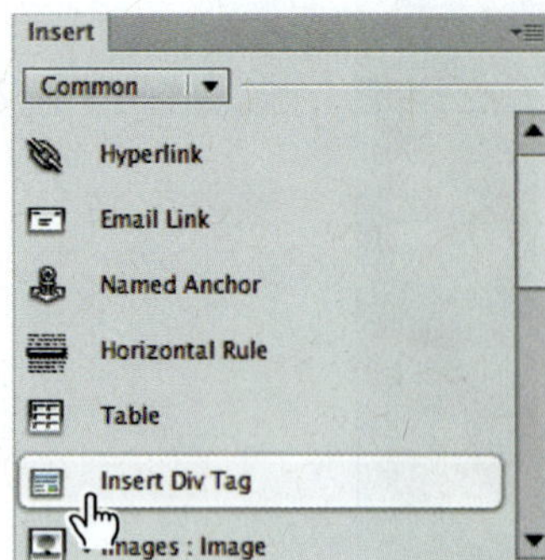

Figure 5-4: *Click the Insert Div Tag to add a container div element.*

4. The Insert Div Tag dialog box appears. Click in the ID text field and type **container**, then click the New CSS Rule button. In the New CSS Rule definition dialog box that appears, make sure that `#container` is listed as the Selector Name and then click OK. The CSS Rule definition dialog box appears and you can begin to style your container div.

5. Select the Box listing in the Category column on the left side of the dialog box. In the Width text field, type **840** and make sure px (pixels) is selected from the drop-down menu to the right. For Height, type **800** in the text field. In the Margin section, uncheck Same for All, then, from the Right margin drop-down menu, choose auto. Choose auto from the Left margin drop-down menu as seen in Figure 5-5.

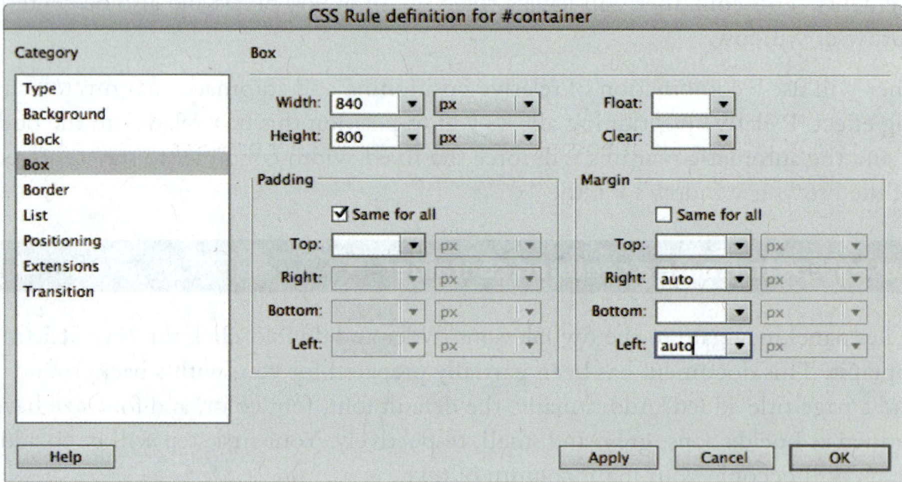

Figure 5-5: *Choose the settings for the* `#container` *element.*

You'll explore using margins in more depth, but by setting a margin value of auto to the left and right side of the container, you are instructing the browser to put equal amounts of space on the right and left sides. The end result will be a box that is centered within the browser window.

6. Select the Background category on the left side of the dialog box, then click the Background-color swatch and choose the white (#FFF) swatch. This adds a background color of white to your entire container, separating it from the background.

Certification Ready 5.2

How do you insert a div tag in standard mode?

7. Select the Positioning category on the left side of the dialog box and choose relative from the Position drop-down menu. This is key to the success of your next steps. By setting the position of the container to relative you will be able to position the page elements using the container as a frame of reference. Press OK in this dialog box, as well as OK for the Insert Div Tag dialog box that is still open.
8. Choose File > Save, then choose File > Preview in Browser. Your container will be centered in the middle of your browser window and Dreamweaver's default placeholder text is aligned in the top left of your container (Figure 5-6). (Occasionally, we have noticed Dreamweaver does not add this placeholder text; if this is the case for you, return to Dreamweaver, click within the container, and then type **content for id "container" Goes Here**.)

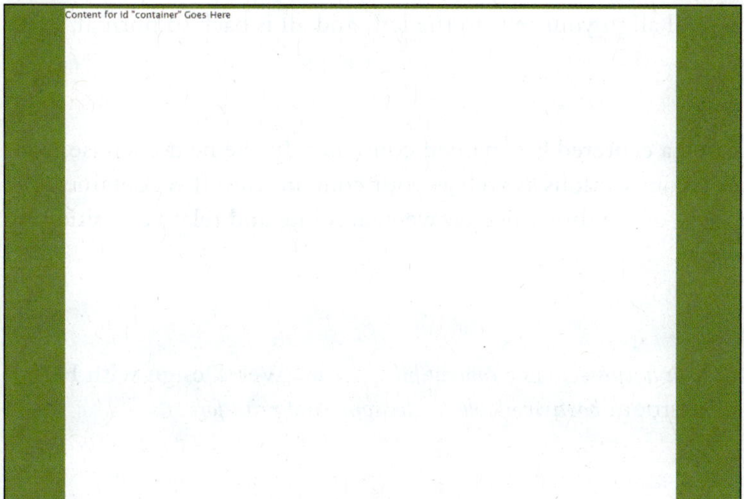

Figure 5-6: *With position set to relative and auto margins the container element will always be centered.*

Resize the browser width; the container stays centered until the window is narrower than 840 pixels, at which point the box is cropped. Close your browser. If your container div did not appear centered, it is possible you are using an older browser. Even if your container div is centered, there are a few additional steps you will now add to ensure the page centers in older browsers.

Making layouts cross-browser compatible

If you are new to web design, welcome to the world known as CSS hacks. In an ideal world, all web browsers would render HTML and CSS using the same set of rules, and all web pages would look the same, regardless of the browser. Unfortunately, this is not the case. **Cross-browser compatibility** is the term used to identify how a web page functions and appears on the multiple web browsers and operating systems used by your target audience. For example, older web browsers such as Netscape 4 and Internet Explorer 4 do not render CSS positioning particularly well. More modern browsers have their own set of quirks as well. In certain cases, additional rules can be added to the CSS that make the page work. These fixes are never ideal because they require additional code and sometimes create more problems than they solve; however, they are necessary if you want your pages to look similar across browsers.

Step-by-Step

Follow these steps to fix a cross-browser compatibility problem

1. With **layout.html** open, double-click the body rule in the CSS Styles panel to edit its properties. In the CSS Rule definition dialog box, select the Block category and choose center from the Text-align drop-down menu. Press OK.

   This fixes a problem that exists with version 6 (and earlier) of Internet Explorer regarding automatic margins. Although this fixes the bug, it creates another problem in that it will center all text on your page (you can see this currently in your container). So, in order to fix that problem you must create another rule to counteract this one.

2. Double-click the `#container` rule in the CSS Styles panel. In the CSS Rule definition dialog box, select the Block category on the left, and then choose left from the Text-align drop-down menu. This will align your text to the left, and all is back to normal. Press OK to accept these changes.

3. Choose File > Save.

   In this exercise you created a centered box named container. In the next exercise, you will place all your other layout sections as well as your content, into this container. Before doing this, a brief overview of the difference between absolute and relative positioning may help.

Take Note...

For a more in-depth look at cross-browser compatibility see the Web Design with HTML and CSS Digital Classroom *book available in electronic and print formats.*

Absolute versus relative positioning

Absolute positioning: An element that is set to absolute strictly follows the positioning values given to it, relative only to its containing element. The containing element can be another div or the page itself. Absolutely positioned elements are pulled out of the normal flow of HTML content, and regardless of what surrounds them (for example, text content or neighboring divs), they always appear at the exact coordinates assigned to them.

Figure 5-7 is an example of a div absolutely positioned within another div. The larger div (Box #1) is the containing element, and so any positioning values assigned to Box #2 are relative to the element boundaries of Box #1.

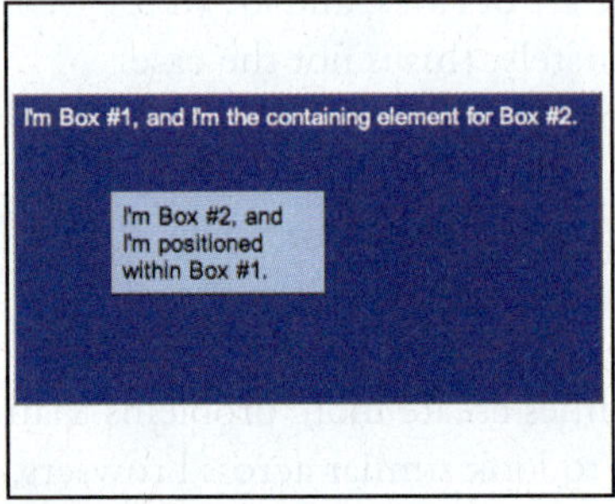

Figure 5-7*: Box #2 is contained, or nested, within Box #1.*

Adding additional content to the containing box (#1) has no effect on the nested div. It remains positioned outside the flow of HTML as seen in Figure 5-8.

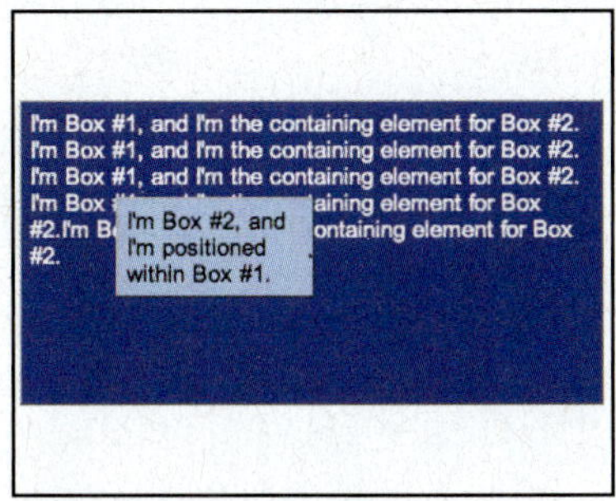

Figure 5-8: Box #2 remains in position even with added content in Box #1.

Relative positioning: A relatively positioned element accepts values for position properties such as top and left, but it also takes the normal flow of neighboring HTML content into account. In Figure 5-9 are the same boxes and values shown in the preceding two figures; the only difference here is that the position property for Box #2 has been set to relative instead of absolute.

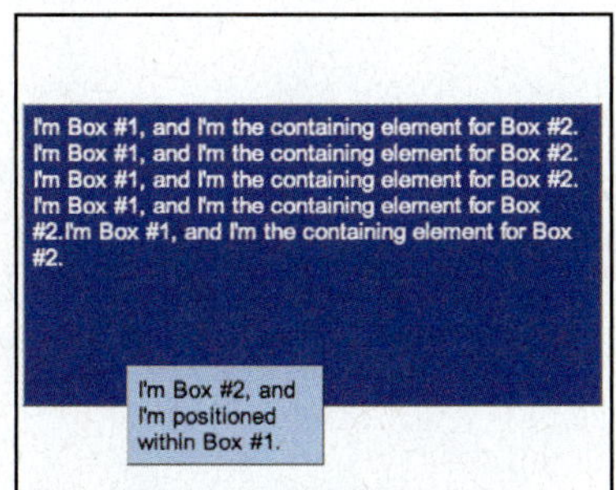

Figure 5-9: Box #2 is still offset, just as before, but it's being displaced by the content before it.

Although it appears that the top and left values have changed, they haven't. Unlike absolutely positioned elements, relatively positioned elements stay within the normal flow of HTML content, which means that they can be displaced by the elements (in this case, the text) surrounding them. In this example, Box #2 is still 50 pixels from the top and 50 pixels from the left, but its point of reference is the end of the preceding text content, not Box #1.

Positioning items relatively is useful when you want an item to flow with the items surrounding it. Figure 5-10 shows five divs nested inside a larger div to create a menu.

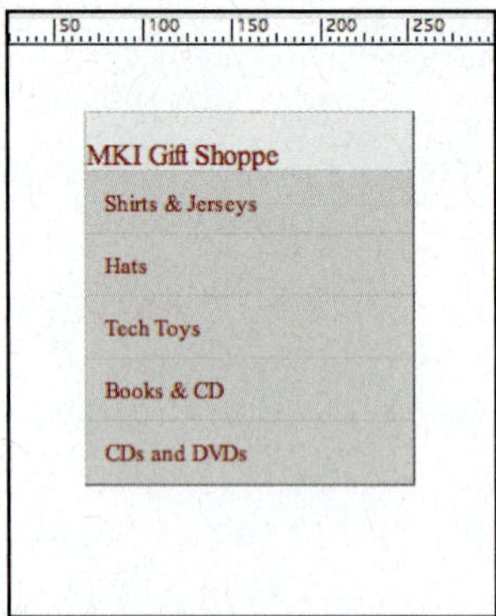

Figure 5-10: *All menu items are positioned relative to one another, and so they fall into place based on each other's position.*

The same example is shown in the Figure 5-11, with the position set to absolute for all menu items. The result is a collapse of the menu—all the menu items are trying to occupy the same place at the same time, without regard for their neighbors.

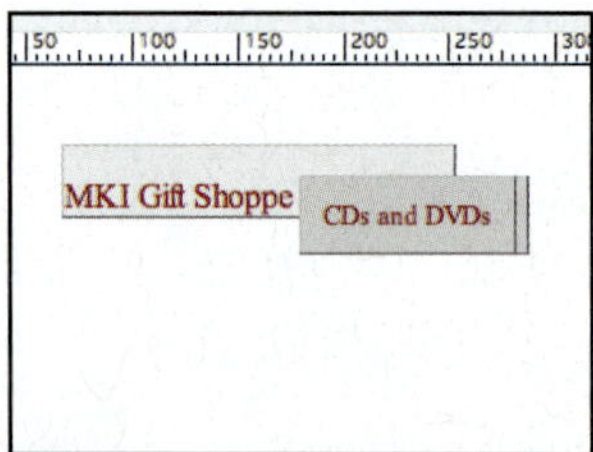

Figure 5-11: *When set to absolute, the menu items stack on top of one another, because they all must be at the same place, regardless of the elements that surround them.*

Take Note...

The files used for these examples are located in the dw05lessons folder, and are named absolute_relative.html and relative_menu.html. Open them in Dreamweaver and explore the code to further your knowledge.

Certification Ready 5.2

What are the differences between absolute, relative, fixed and static positioning?

Any element, or, in this case, any box, can have the position property applied, and one of five possible values can be set: absolute, fixed, relative, static, or inherit. The two most commonly used are absolute and relative, and although both can accept positioning properties such as top and left; they are rendered differently, even with identical positioning values.

Positioning content with AP Divs

Now that your container is centered on the page, you'll need to add boxes to hold content within the container. The easiest and most visual way to place boxes in Dreamweaver is with the Draw AP Div button. An **AP Div** is Dreamweaver's name for absolutely positioned div elements and is represented in the Design View as a box into which you can add text and/or other elements such as images or media. An AP Div is placed exactly where you draw it, using the page as its point of reference by default; after drawing, you can reposition it precisely.

For this exercise, you'll want your AP Divs to be positioned using the container as their point of reference. To change the default behavior of AP Divs as you draw them, an additional step is required. This step will ensure that your AP Divs are nested inside the container div.

1. In the **layout.html** document, choose Edit > Preferences (Windows) or Dreamweaver > Preferences (Mac OS) and then choose the AP Elements category. Click the checkbox labeled Nesting (Figure 5-12). This ensures that the new boxes you create will be nested inside the container. Click OK.

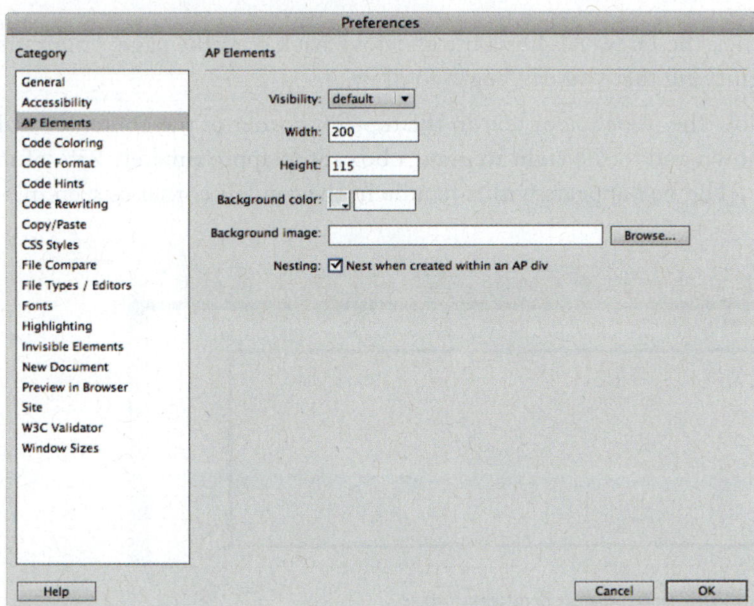

Figure 5-12: *Set your Preferences so that new AP Elements automatically nest when inside your container.*

Creating a header section with the Draw AP Div

You have already created a container that is centered within your page; now you'll add the other layout elements, starting with the header. The Draw AP Div tool allows you to add boxes within your pages manually. Once a box is added, you can style it with CSS (change the width and height, add background color and more) and you can also add content such as text or images.

Step-by-Step

Follow these steps to create an AP div

1. In the Insert panel, click the drop-down menu and choose Layout (Figure 5-13).

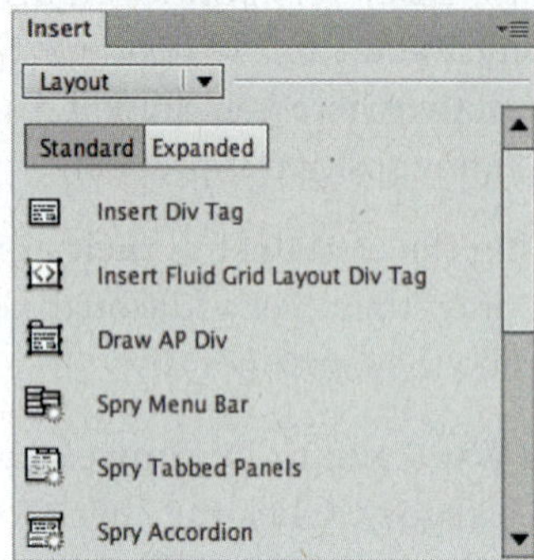

Figure 5- 13: The Layout section of the Insert panel displays the available layout icons.

2. In the Insert panel, click the Draw AP Div button. Move back over the page; your cursor is now a crosshair signifying that you can begin to draw.
3. Place your cursor below the placeholder text in the top-left corner of the container and then click and drag down and to the right to draw a box. Stop approximately 25% of the way down the screen. The box appears with a handle in the top left corner as seen in Figure 5-14.

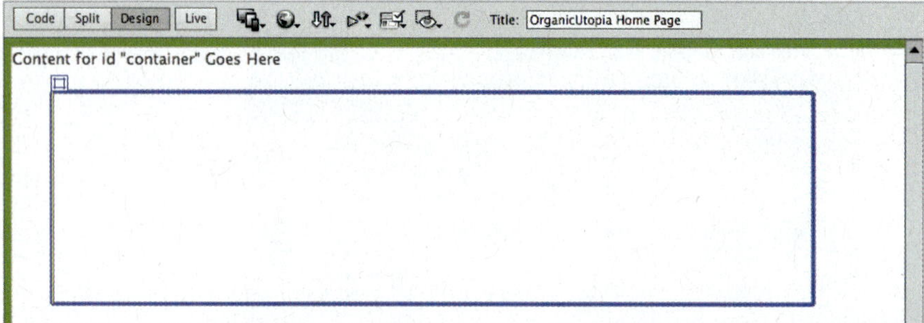

Figure 5- 14: The newly created AP Div has a handle in its top-left corner.

4. Click the selection handle in the top-left corner of the AP Div and click and drag the box around the screen to see how you can position the box manually. Notice in the Property Inspector that the properties for your box are displayed and dynamically change as you move it; currently just the Left and Top position (L and T) will change. Your settings will likely be different than those in the figure.

   Click inside the Bg color text field, type **#9fcc41**, and then press Enter (Windows) or Return (Mac OS) to apply the color, which is a yellow-green shade (Figure 5-15).

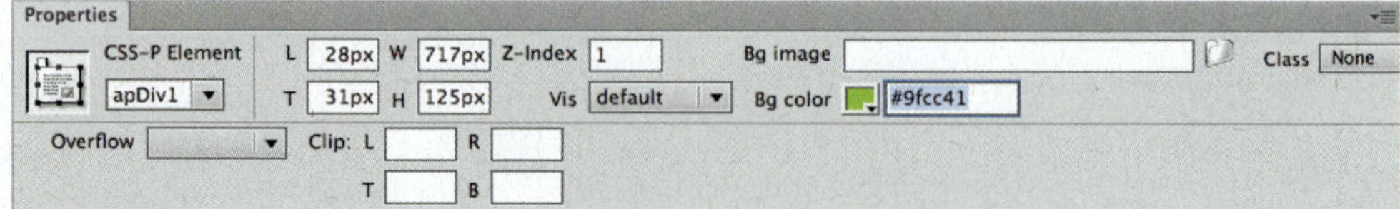

***Figure 5-15**: The Property Inspector displays the properties of the AP Div and allows you to set its background color.*

You will now position this box to become your header.

5. In the bottom-left corner of the Property Inspector, locate the CSS-P Element text field. It is currently named apDiv1. Select the text within this text field and type **header**.

   When Dreamweaver creates new AP Divs, it gives them the default names of apDiv1, apDiv2, and so on. You can, and most often should, rename these, simply because the default name is nondescriptive and unhelpful. Keep in mind that functionally, this is exactly the same step as the previous exercise when you named the div "container." In both cases you are creating a CSS ID behind the scenes.

6. Select the placeholder text Content for id "container" Goes Here and delete it. You are about to create your header at the top of the page and you don't need this content.

7. If you currently do not have rulers visible, choose View > Rulers > Show. Click the edge of the header div again, and pay careful attention to the L (Left) and the T (Top) values.

   You will now position the header to the top-left corner of the container using the Property Inspector.

8. In the Property Inspector, type **0px** into the L (Left) text field and press Enter (Windows) or Return (Mac OS). The box moves and the left side of the box is positioned horizontally at 0 pixels. Type **0px** into the T (Top) text field and press Enter (Windows) or Return (Mac OS). The top of the box is positioned vertically at 0 pixels as seen in Figure 5-16.

   Be sure to type the number and the px value (i.e., **100px**) together in order for position to be valid.

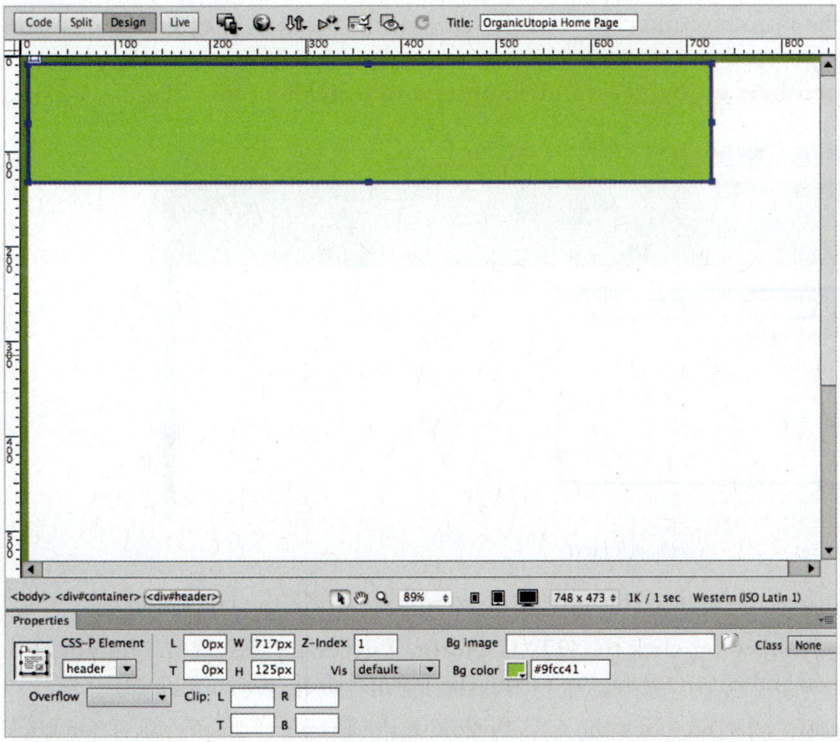

Figure 5-16: With Top and Left values both set to 0px the header is aligned to the top-left corner of the container.

9. You also need to set the width of this header. Again, you could do this manually by dragging the edges of the header box, but this is not precise. It is better to use number values and match the width of the header to the width of the container.

   In the Property Inspector, type **840px** for the W value and **80px** for the H value.

10. You can add content to the box by simply typing in it. Click inside the box on the workspace and type **Organic Utopia**. You'll be replacing this with the logo a bit later, for now this will serve as a placeholder.

11. Choose File > Save to save your work, and then preview your page by choosing File > Preview in Browser or by pressing the Preview/Debug in browser button (🌐) at the top of the document window. Close the browser when finished.

Adding an introduction section to your page

Now you can add additional sections to your page. The first section you'll add is a box below the header where you'll format an introductory paragraph to state the mission of the site, and grab the user's attention.

Step-by-Step

Follow these steps to create an introduction section

1. In the Insert panel, click the Draw AP Div object and draw a box below your header. Don't worry about the exact size of the box, but make the width about half the header and roughly twice the height.

   A good habit to get into is renaming your AP Divs immediately after they are created.

2. Click the edge of the new div and in the CSS-P Element text field, type **intro** and press Enter (Windows) or Return (Mac OS).

3. Click inside the intro box and type the following text: **Organic Utopia is a community owned and operated supermarket and marketplace. Anyone may shop in our stores but members enjoy special discounts and other benefits.** (Figure 5-17)

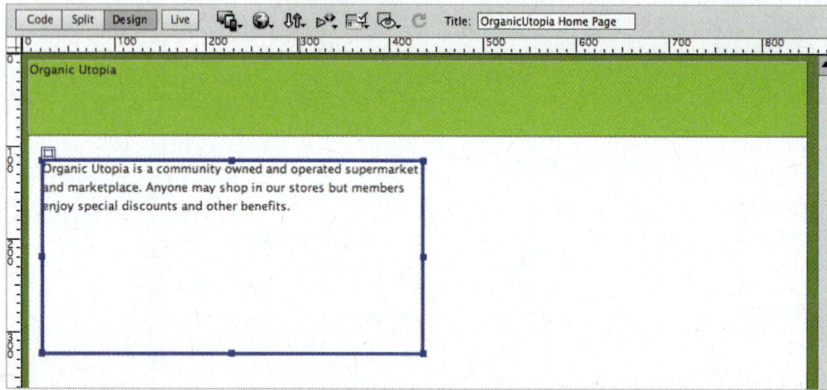

***Figure 5-17**: The `#intro` AP Div with added text.*

   Now you'll format the text in this box using techniques from the last lesson.

4. In the Property Inspector, click the HTML button if necessary. Select and highlight the text you entered and choose Paragraph from the Format drop-down menu.

5. With the text still selected, click the CSS button in the Property Inspector. Then click the Font drop-down menu and choose the Georgia, Times New Roman, Times, serif family. The New CSS Rule definition dialog box will open. The Selector Type will be compound. The Selector Name is `#container #intro p`. Press the Less Specific button to set the selector to `#intro p`.

   Press OK and the change is applied.

6. In the Property Inspector, click the Size drop-down menu to change the font size and choose the keyword large. Your text size will enlarge as seen in Figure 5-18.

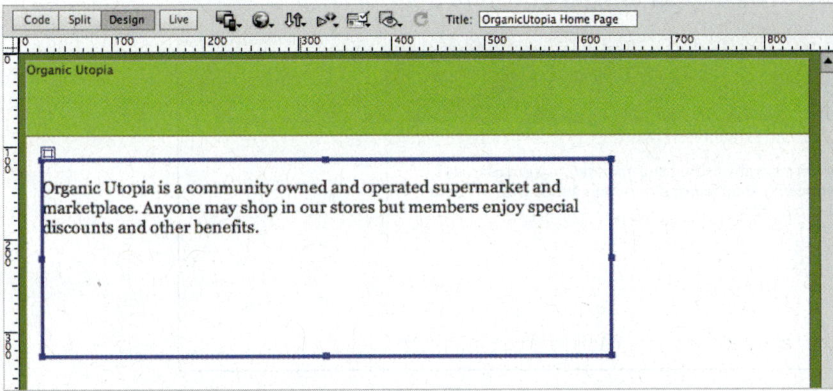

Figure 5-18*: Set the paragraph text inside the intro box to Georgia and large.*

Depending on how large you made your intro box, you will likely need to adjust the width and height of the box.

7. Click the edge of the intro box to activate it and then click any of the anchor points on the box to adjust the width and height. We used a width of **720px** and a height of **130px**. Click anywhere on the background of the page to deselect the intro div.

Adding images to your layout

Before you add the remaining sections of your page, you'll add images to both the header and container sections of the page. First, you'll add a background image of vegetables to the right side of your header.

Follow these steps to insert a background image

Step-by-Step

1. In the CSS Styles panel double-click the `#header` rule to open the CSS Rule definition dialog box. Click the Background category. In addition to the background color, you can also add CSS background images.

2. In the Background image section, press the Browse button. In the select Image Source dialog box, navigate to the images folder within the dw05lessons folder and select **veggies.jpg**. Press OK (Windows) or Choose (Mac OS). Press Apply and you will see the image tiled across the header. (If you see a Missing Profile message click OK.)

   By default, background images in CSS have this tiled effect, so you will need to add additional properties in order to remove the tiling and position the image to the right.

3. From the Background-repeat drop-down menu, choose no-repeat. From the Background-position (X) drop-down menu, choose right. Press OK and you see the image now aligned to the right side of the header as seen in Figure 5-19.

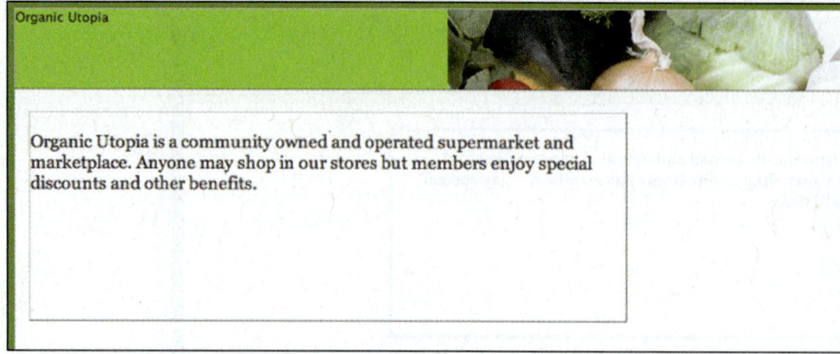

***Figure 5-19**: Background images can be added and positioned to a* `<div>` *element.*

A background image is controlled by CSS, and you can only have one background image per element. So in order to have two images inside the header, you'll add the Organic Utopia logo as an inline element. This means the logo is being added to the HTML code, not the CSS.

4. Select the Organic Utopia placeholder text in the `#header` div and delete it. Then choose Insert > Image. In the Select Image Source dialog box, navigate to the images folder within the dw05lessons folder and select **ou_logo.gif**. Press OK (Windows) or Open (Mac OS). Type **OrganicUtopia Logo** into the text field when asked to add an Alternative text tag, and then press OK. The image appears in the top-left corner of the header. You will position this image away from the sides of the header box later in the lesson. (If you receive a Missing Profile message, click OK.)

Take Note...

When working with images, follow this rule of thumb: HTML inline images should be used for content; CSS background images should be used for decoration. One way to test this rule is to imagine the impact on the page if the image were not displayed. In the example above, the image of the vegetables is not essential, so the website would not be adversely affected if the image is not displayed; however, the logo is important, so it should be considered content, not decoration.

Photoshop integration

Often the images used in your web page need to be modified in Photoshop before they integrate well with your design. Photoshop and Dreamweaver are integrated in a few ways. In this exercise, you will see how Dreamweaver can optimize .psd files when you insert them into your page.

Follow these steps to insert and optimize a .psd image | **Step-by-Step**

1. In the CSS Styles panel, double-click the `#container` rule. Click the Background category and choose the Browse button in the Background-image section. In your dw05lessons folder, open the artwork folder. Choose the **veggiebackground.psd** file and press OK (Windows) or Open (Mac OS) The Image Optimization dialog box appears (Figure 5-20).

   This dialog box appears because you have chosen a .psd file to import and this is not a valid file format for the Web. Dreamweaver triggers the Image Optimization dialog box, which allows you to optimize the graphic and save it in a more appropriate format.

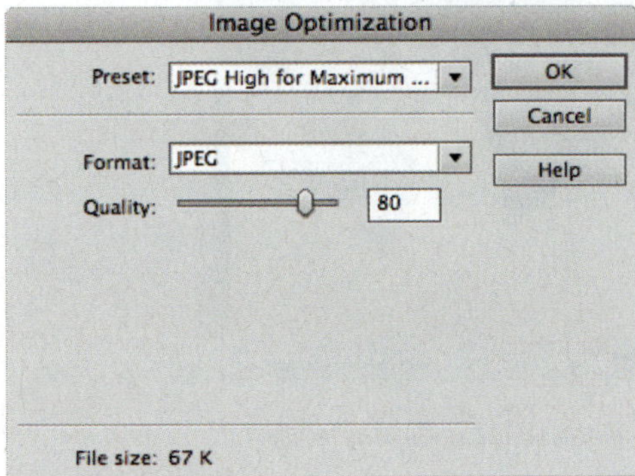

***Figure 5-20**: Importing a .psd file into Dreamweaver will trigger the Image Preview, allowing you to save as a web graphic.*

2. Click the Preset menu and choose "JPEG high for Maximum Compatibility" if it is not already selected. Slide the Quality slider to **1** and notice that the preview of the image on your page becomes pixelated. Reducing the quality results in a smaller file size, but going too low results in unacceptable loss of detail.
3. Drag the Quality slider to **70**, and notice that the quality improves dramatically. As with most compression, the goal is to find a good balance between small file size and image quality.
4. Click OK, and then navigate to the images folder in the dw05lessons folder and double-click it. In the URL section, notice the path images/veggie_background.jpg. It's important to understand that you are saving a copy of the original PSD file as a JPEG in this step. Click Save and you now have a link to the new background image.
5. Click the Background-repeat drop-down menu and choose no-repeat, and then click OK.

Adding Main and Sidebar content areas

Now you'll add two more sections to your page: a main column, which will feature the latest news from our fictional company Organic Utopia and a sidebar column, which features incentives for visitors to become members.

Step-by-Step

Follow these steps to create a content area

1. In the Insert panel, click the Draw AP Div button, then place your cursor below the intro box and click and drag down and to the right as seen in Figure 5-21. As you are drawing the AP Div notice there are width and height values that are updated in the Status Bar on the bottom right of your document window

FIgure 5-21: The width and height of an AP Div are updated in the Status bar as you draw the div.

Make the AP Div roughly 450px wide by 200px high. Don't try to get the exact dimensions, as it is very difficult to be precise when drawing. You can always fine-tune the width and height in the Property Inspector.

2. Click the border of the div and in the CSS-P Element text field rename the div to **main**. Next, click the Bg color swatch in the Property Inspector and from the color swatches that appear, choose white.
3. Click the Draw AP Div button again and draw another box to the right of the Main div. Make this one approximately the same height, and the width should be about 240. Again don't worry about the exact dimensions for now.
4. Click the border of the new div and in the CSS-P Element text field, type **sidebar** to rename the AP Div. Click the Bg color menu and make this background white as well.

You'll now make sure the top edges of the two boxes are lined up.

5. Click the handle on the top-left of the main div and reposition it to the following left and top values: L (Left) should be **35** and T (Top) should be **260** as seen in Figure 5-22.

***Figure 5-22**: Setting the Left and Top values of an AP Div.*

6. Click the top-left edge of the sidebar div and type **260** for the Top value. You can use the left and right arrows on your keyboard to nudge the div horizontally. We ended up with a Left value of **515**.

   With the top values the same for both boxes, the top edges line up. Once the boxes are lined up, you can always move them as a unit by selecting and dragging or nudging them.

7. Click the edge of the main div to select it and then Shift+click the sidebar. With both boxes selected, press your up arrow keys to move both boxes upward. There is no right value here, use your judgment and push the two boxes closer to the intro text.

Adding additional content and styles

Up to this point, you've been working with the base structure of your layout. Now it's time to add additional content in the form of text so that you can see how your layout works with real content, and make any necessary changes.

Follow these steps to add new content

Step-by-Step

1. Double-click the **main_content.html** file in the Files panel to open it. This is text that has already been formatted; all that is necessary is to copy and paste it into your layout.

2. Choose Edit > Select All and then choose Edit > Copy. Close the **main_content.html** document. In the **layout.html** document, click inside the main div and choose Edit > Paste. The content appears styled as Lucida Grande as seen in Figure 5-23 because there is a rule in the body defining the font-family; however, there are no CSS rules yet for headings or paragraphs.

Figure 5-23: *The results of copying and pasting the main_content.html page into your main div element.*

You pasted more content than can fit inside this box, which is why the text is flowing outside the boundaries of the container. In fact, what you are seeing is one of the disadvantages of using AP Divs. Defining the width and height of a box in pixels creates an inflexible container. One solution to this is simply to expand the size of the box.

3. Click the bottom of the blue border for the div and drag it down slightly, the box will automatically expand to fit the existing content.

   Now you'll add the content to the member benefit section.

4. Double-click the **memberbenefits_content.html** file in the Files panel. Choose Edit > Select All and then choose Edit > Copy. Close the **memberbenefits_content.html** document. In the **layout.html** document, click inside the sidebar and choose Edit > Paste.

5. Click the bottom of the sidebar div and drag it down slightly to expand the box to fit the content.

Setting margins and borders

As you learned earlier, CSS uses the Box model for elements, and as such, each element can be given unique margins, padding, and borders, either for decorative or practical purposes.

Now that you have content inside your columns, it is clear that you need to do some fine-tuning. Your text and logo are crowded against their respective div elements and you should make them more pleasing and readable. Technically, you can start anywhere, but in this exercise, you'll start at the top of your page and work down.

Follow these steps to create settings for margins and borders **Step-by-Step**

1. Select the Organic Utopia logo in the header. In the CSS Styles panel, press the New CSS Rule button (+). The New CSS Rule dialog box appears and the Selector Name, `#container #header img` is selected. Since the rule gets more specific from left to right, ultimately you are targeting the <img> tag located inside the header div, which is inside the container div. Click OK.
2. In the CSS Rule definition dialog box that appears, select the Box category on the left. If necessary, move the dialog box to see the logo. Uncheck the Same for All checkbox in the Margin section. In the Top text field, type **20** and press Apply. The logo is pushed down 20 pixels from the top of the header div, because there is now a 20-pixel margin applied to the top of the image.
3. In the Left margin text field, type **15** and press OK. Adding a 15-pixel left margin pushes the logo to the right. Now you'll add similar margins in the main column.
4. Click anywhere inside the heading Celebrating Vegetables in the main column. In the CSS Styles panel, press the New CSS Rule button. In the New CSS Rule dialog box, make sure the selector name reads `#container #main h2`. Press OK.
5. In the CSS Rule definition dialog box, select the Box category, and uncheck the Same for All checkbox in the Margin section. In the Left text field, type **15** as seen in Figure 5-24 and press OK.

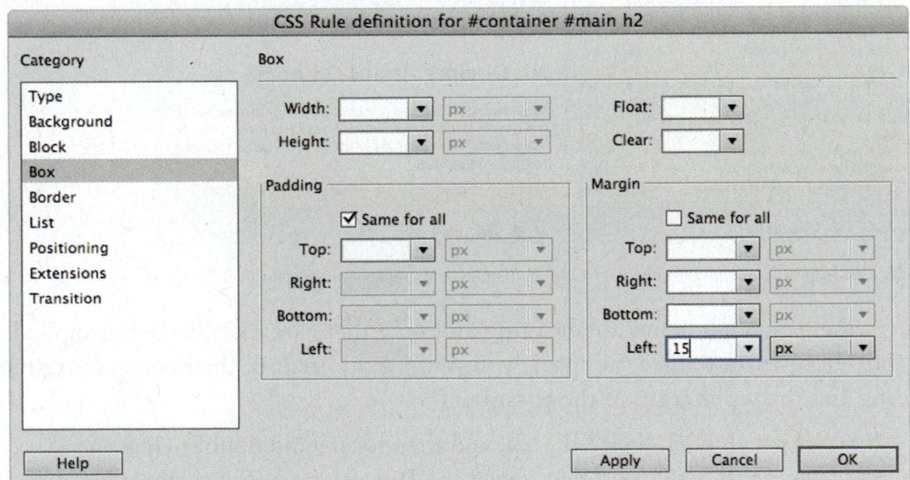

Figure 5-24: Applying a left margin of 15 to the main heading.

6. Click inside the paragraph below the Celebrating Vegetables heading. In the CSS Style panel, press the New CSS Rule button and in the New CSS Rule dialog box, make sure that `#container #main p` is highlighted in the Selector Name text field. Press OK.

7. In the CSS Rule definition dialog box, select the Box category from the left column, and uncheck the Same for All checkbox in the Margin section. In the Left and Right text fields, type **15**. You need to add both left and right padding because the text fills the main container. Press OK.

Overriding default margins in CSS

If you are new to Dreamweaver and/or CSS, an important concept is that of default margins. Web browsers will apply default margins to most block elements unless there is a value overriding them. So paragraphs and headings, for example, will have space between them even if you haven't set a value. You can see this space by using Dreamweaver's Inspect feature.

Step-by-Step

Follow these steps to override the default margins in CSS

1. In your document window, click the Live View button to cause the Live Code and Inspect buttons to appear. Click the Inspect Mode; Dreamweaver will prompt you to change your workspace settings. Press "Switch Now" to change your settings to the Split Code view. Now you can hover over elements on your page and see the normally invisible margins.
2. Place your cursor over the Celebrating Vegetables heading. The yellow highlight shows the margins being applied to this element as seen in Figure 5-25.

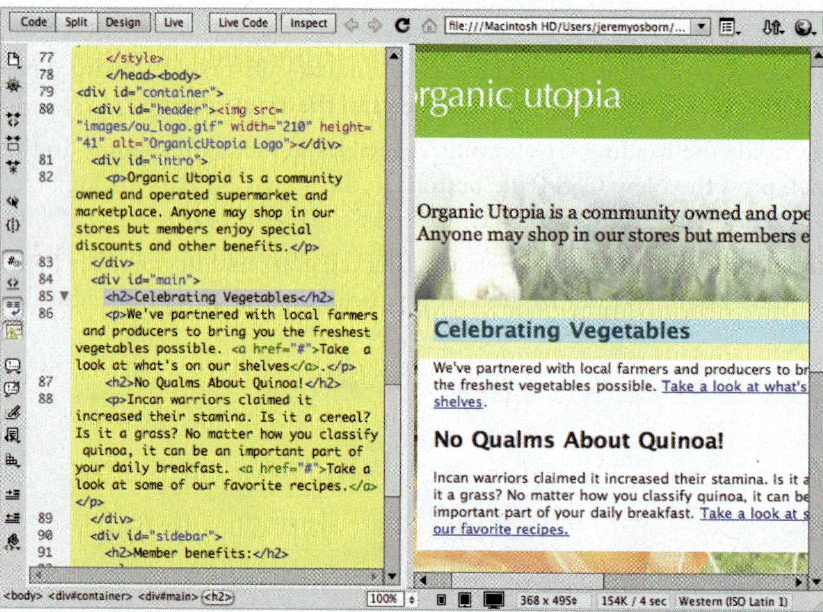

Figure 5-25: The Inspect feature in Dreamweaver CS6 highlights the margins of an element in yellow.

Hover over the paragraph below the heading and note there are margins being applied here as well. In order to reduce the space, you will need to reduce the bottom margin of the heading and the top margin of the paragraph.

3. In the CSS Styles panel, click the "All" tab, and then locate and double-click the `#container #main h2` style and then select the Box category. Set the bottom margin value to **0 px** and press OK.
4. Place your cursor over the heading. Note that the bottom margin is gone (in other words, there is no yellow border). You now need to set the top margin of the paragraph to 0 as well.

5. In the CSS Styles panel, double-click the `#container #main p` style and select the Box category. Set the top margin value to **0 px** and press OK. Now all the paragraphs in the main column shift upward.
6. Click the Live View button to de-activate this mode, and then click the Design button to return to your default mode.

Certification Ready 5.2

How do you define, modify and check CSS rules?

Take Note...

Because margins and padding are invisible, many designers resort to applying either background colors or borders to elements at the beginning of the layout process. This helps to understand the relationship between various sections on the page. The Inspect button in Dreamweaver partially removes the need to do this, but you may still find the original technique useful.

Adding borders to elements

The ability to add borders to elements is a great feature in CSS. Because of the CSS Box model, almost anything can be styled with borders: div elements, headings, lists and more. Additionally, the style, width and color of these borders can be set globally or for any given side.

Follow these steps to add a CSS border

Step-by-Step

1. In the CSS Style panel, double-click the `#main` style and then click the Border category to begin setting these properties.
2. In the Style category uncheck the Same for all checkbox. Click the Top menu and choose solid. Then click the Bottom menu and choose solid.

   In the Style menu, note the other options available. Styles such as dotted and dashed are the most reliable styles. For various reasons the other options such as groove, ridge, etc. are not particularly well-supported in older browsers and you should use them sparingly.
3. In the Width category, uncheck the Same for all checkbox and click the Top menu. Note that you can also choose keywords here for thin, medium or thick. Select (value) and then type **2**. The default value is px. Click the Bottom menu and type **2**.
4. In the Color category, uncheck the Same for all checkbox and in both the Top and Bottom fields type **#063** (Figure 5-26). This is a dark green color.

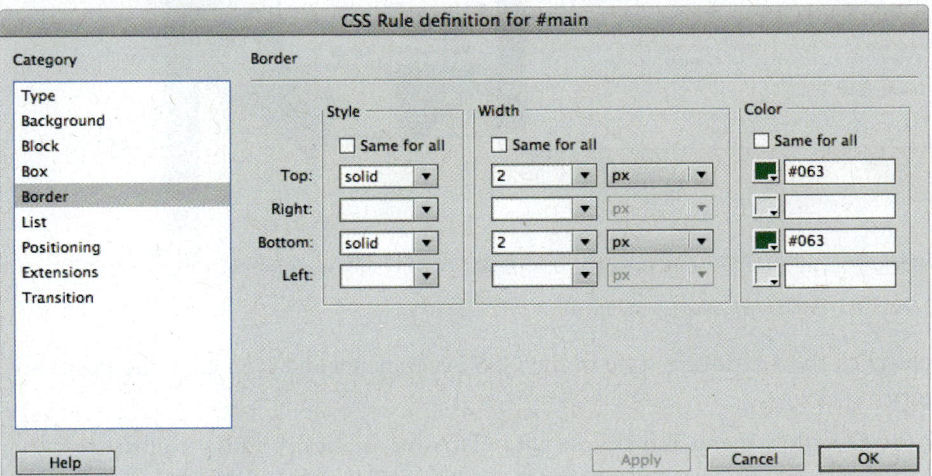

***Figure 5-26**: Setting border styles for the top and bottom of the Main div element.*

Click OK in the CSS Rule definition dialog box.

The borders will be hard to see since the div is still selected.

Certification Ready 5.2

How do you modify div tag attributes?

5. Choose File > Save All and preview the results by choosing File > Preview in Browser. Take a moment to admire your layout. You're almost done; however the last step is to future proof your page layout.
6. Close the browser and return to Dreamweaver.

Future proofing your layout

Absolutely positioning the elements of your page layout is very stable and reliable, but it also has some fundamental limitations. You have already seen what happens when there is more content than can fit inside a box: the box overflows resulting in unattractive content. You have also seen one solution, which is simply to expand the size of the box. Even this is not an ideal solution though. Content on the Web changes constantly; text is added and removed, images are inserted and so on. The designer of the page may have little or no control over this, especially if they are handing a website off to a client who will eventually be updating and modifying the site.

To help strengthen your layout for future modification, you can use a CSS property called overflow. This will help you prevent the worst-case scenario of text that breaks your layout as it overflows its container. For this exercise, you'll apply overflow to the Members Benefits sidebar.

Step-by-Step

Follow these steps to add a scrollbar

1. Click the bottom edge of the sidebar and then drag the bottom of the box upward until half of the list items are overflowing out of the box as seen in Figure 5-27.

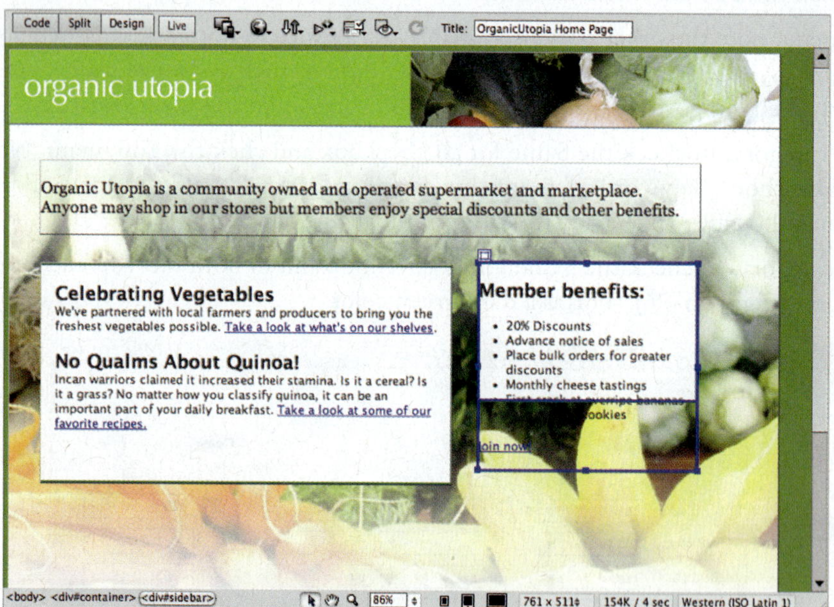

***Figure 5-27**: Text that is overflowing over the sidebar.*

2. Double-click the `#sidebar` style in the CSS Styles panel and then click the Positioning category.
3. Click the Overflow menu and choose auto. This automatically adds scrollbars to any `<div>` element that has more text than can fit inside. Click OK. You will see in Dreamweaver's design view that the box has snapped to fit the original height.

4. Choose File > Save, then File > Preview in Browser. Your div now has a scrollbar. While it may not be an ideal solution if you do not like scrollbars, at least it doesn't break the layout. Close the browser and return to Dreamweaver.

The pros and cons of Absolutely Positioned CSS layouts

You will now take a look at the limitations and weaknesses of the layout you have just created. Absolutely positioned layouts in Dreamweaver are the quickest and easiest way to get a web page up and working, however, as noted earlier they are not the most flexible.

In this exercise, we hope to point out some of the limitations of Absolutely Positioned layouts so that you can judge for yourself whether they fit all your needs or whether you need to be looking at the next step of creating pages using more advanced layout techniques, which are covered in Lesson 6, "Advanced Page Layout."

To illustrate this, you will take a look at your existing layout with the premise that someone has asked you to make the entire container larger and also switch the position of the two columns on your page.

Follow these steps to work more with AP divs

Step-by-Step

1. In the Design view, click the edge of your `#container` div to select it and in the Property Inspector, change the Width from **840** to **960**. The container width expands but when adding this extra 120 pixels of space, your header and the other sections are no longer well-aligned.

   Your background image is now also too narrow. This cannot be easily resolved in Dreamweaver. You would have to go back to Photoshop, resize the image, and export it again. For now, you'll simply turn it off temporarily.

2. In the CSS Styles panel, click the `#container` style, and click the All button if necessary. Now select the background-image property. Click the Disable/Enable CSS Property button (⊘) at the bottom of the panel (Figure 5-28) to turn off this image for now.

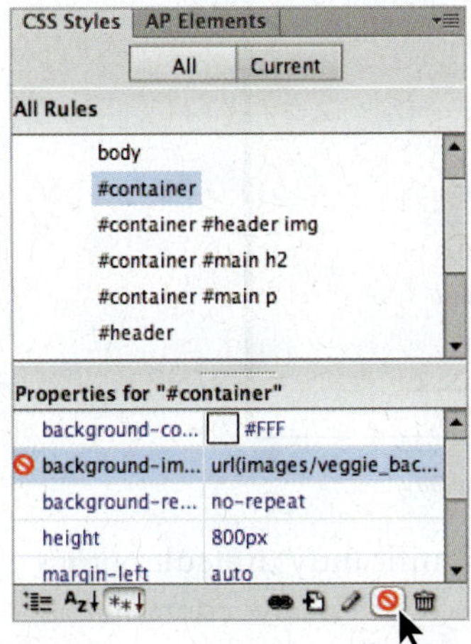

Figure 5-28: Clicking the Disable/Enable CSS Property button removes the style for the background image.

   With the background image temporarily removed, it is easier to see the structure of your layout.

3. Click the right edge of the header and drag it to the right to expand the width. Drag the header beyond the container and notice it is easy to break your layout. This is because absolutely positioned elements don't interact with the other elements on the page; you need to manually adjust them.
4. In the CSS Property Inspector, set the W (Width) value of the header to **960**. It must match the width of the container exactly. Although you'll also notice that the background image of the vegetables remains flush right.
5. Click the edge of the intro box, and, using your arrow keys, nudge it to the right until it is centered within the page.

   Now you need to switch the position of the main and sidebar divs.

Certification Ready 5.2

How do you display overlapping content on a web page using div tags?

6. Click the edge of the main div and use your arrow keys to nudge it to the right. Notice that it overlaps your sidebar. This is due to the behavior of absolutely positioned elements allowing them to occupy the same space on the page.

Take Note...
The property that controls which element is highest in the stacking order is called the z-index. Dreamweaver sets this property automatically when you create AP Divs. Elements with the higher z-index value will always "win" and be visible over elements with a lower z-index. You can also modify z-index values if you choose to adjust this.

7. Click the edge of the sidebar div and using your arrow keys nudge to the left until it reaches the original position of the main div.

   You may need to nudge the position of the two boxes until you are satisfied with their position. Additionally, feel free to adjust the width of the boxes if needed (Figure 5-29).

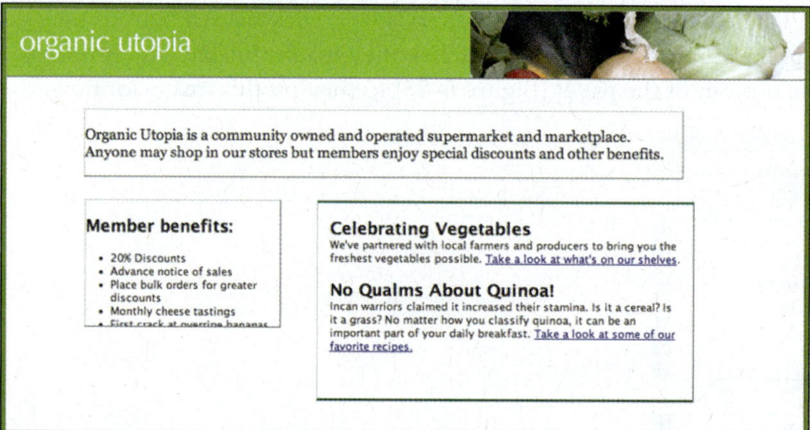

***Figure 5-29**: Switching the position of the two boxes requires you to move them manually.*

Adjusting the width of the layout and the columns is not significantly difficult but it's also not very efficient. Wouldn't it be nice if expanding the width of the container automatically readjusted the columns within the new space? In fact, there are techniques you can use to accomplish this. They are called float-based layouts and you will learn these techniques in the next lesson. For now, save and close the files.

Printing web pages

Whether it is desktop or mobile, web pages are meant to be delivered on screens first and foremost, however printing should not be an afterthought.

In the earlier days of the web, browsers would often print a web page based on a straight conversion of pixels to inches. This meant that in order to safely include your content on a standart 8½ × 11 inch piece of paper your website would have to be about 600 pixels wide if using a fixed-width layout. Because this is a very restrictive width for screens, this technique is rarely used today.

Virtually all web browsers today (and most recent browsers) will scale a web page automatically. This is a function of the browser and overrides the designer's intent. You can experiment with your own layout and your current web browser to see the results.

Another option is to create a special "print stylesheet". This can be done by adding a reference to a separate style sheet in your head section as follows:

```
<link rel="stylesheet" href="print.css" type="text/css"
media="print" />
```

The name "print.css" is arbitrary here, you can name this anything you would like. The important part of this code is the media="print" attribute and value. This tells the web browser to use this style sheet when printing.

To learn more about print style sheets visit: *http://www.alistapart.com/articles/goingtoprint/*

Learning More

Certification Ready 2.1

How will page layout and CSS design decisions affect how a web page will print?

Congratulations, you have finished Lesson 5, "Creating Page Layouts with CSS."

Take Note...

For a more in-depth look at Cascading Style Sheets see the Web Design with HTML and CSS Digital Classroom *book, and for a discussion of CSS3 and HTML5 see the* HTML5 Digital Classroom *book. Both of these titles are available in electronic and print formats.*

Skill Summary

In this lesson you learned how to:	Objective
Demonstrate general and Dreamweaver-specific knowledge of best practices for designing a website, such as maintaining consistency, separating content from design, using standard fonts, and utilizing visual hierarchy	2.1
Organize web page layout with relative and absolutely-positioned div tags and CSS styles	5.2

Knowledge Assessment

True/False

Circle T if the statement is true or F if the statement is false.

T F **1.** The CSS Box model applies only to div elements.

T F **2.** The CSS box model allows you to control the style of a border on a div element.

T F **3.** CSS margins refer to the distance between the inside edge of a box and its contents

T F **4.** You can set padding for all four sides of a box simultaneously as well as each side individually

T F **5.** In the Design view, the only way to add a div element to your page is using the AP Div button in the insert panel

T F **6.** You can only create a new CSS rule from the CSS Styles panel

T F **7.** One of the benefits of AP divs is that they are flexible and adapt to the size of the browser window by default.

T F **8.** In order to visually see the margins and padding on a page in Live View, you must click on the Inspect button

T F **9.** You can manually position an AP div by dragging it on the page in Design view.

T F **10.** Adding the overflow property with the value auto to a div will add scrollbars if there is too much text to fit in the div

Multiple Choice

Select the best response for the following statements

1. Jeff is adding 10 pixels of margin for all four sides of a div element. How will this affect it?

a. 10 pixels of space will be added to all four sides, inside the border of the div

b. 10 pixels of space will be added to all four sides, outside of the border of the div

c. 10 pixels of space to all four sides, inside the border of the div, but only if there is a border value

d. None of the Above

2. The default border style of a div element is ______

a. The color black, solid and 2 pixels wide
b. The color white, solid and 2 pixels wide
c. None
d. The color black, dashed and 2 pixels wide

3. For layout purposes, it is common to pair __________ with HTML Divs

a. CSS IDs
b. CSS classes
c. Both CSS IDs and classes
d. CSS pseudo-classes

4. Which of the following is true about absolutely positioned elements?

a. An absolutely positioned element is relative only to its containing element.
b. An absolutely positioned element must always be nested inside a relatively positioned element
c. An absolutely positioned element remains part of the default flow of an HTML page.
d. All of the above

5. When you draw an AP div in Dreamweaver CS6 you can do which of the following within the Property Inspector?

a. Rename the ID name
b. Manually enter positioning values
c. Change the background color
d. All of the above

6. Which of the following is true about CSS background images?

a. They can only be positioned using pixel values
b. They do not support transparency
c. They are repeated horizontally and vertically by default
d. They are also referred to as "inline" images.

7. When using the CSS Rule definition window in Dreamweaver CS6, in order to add a border style to just the bottom of an element, you must first do what?

a. Select the element you would like to style in the Design view
b. Uncheck the "Same for all" checkboxes for Style, Width and Color
c. Select the Bottom style label
d. None of the Above

8. If you have a page layout that is completely dependent on AP divs, which of the following is a potential drawback?

a. Two (or more) AP divs can occupy the same space resulting in a visual overlap
b. AP divs do not accept CSS background images
c. AP divs must be set with an Overflow value of Auto in order to appear on the page
d. AP divs can only be resized by hand in the Design view

9. If you wanted to see the appearance of your page without a background image, the best way to do this is _______
   a. Select the background image on the screen and press Delete
   b. Save a copy of your page and then select the background image on the screen and press Delete.
   c. Remove the background-repeat property to a value of no-repeat.
   d. Use the Disable/Enable CSS Property button

10. The process of integrating Photoshop images into a Dreamweaver page is called ________.
   a. Compressing
   b. Resampling
   c. Optimizing
   d. You cannot integrate Photoshop files into a page in Dreamweaver

Competency Assessment

Project 5-1 Using AP Divs for layout

As the designer for Serenity Spa, you need to quickly build the framework of a layout for a new page for your site.

1. Choose File > New. When the New Document panel appears, choose Blank Page > HTML, then press Create.
2. Choose File > Save. When the Save As dialog box appears, navigate to your site folder and type **gallery.html** in the Name text field. Press Save.
3. Choose the Layout category in the Insert panel. Locate and select the Draw AP Div button. Move back over the page; the cursor changes to a crosshair.
4. Click and drag to draw a box in the upper left-hand corner. The box appears with a tab on the top-left edge and handles on all sides and corners that can be used to resize the box.
5. Select the entire box by clicking the tab in its top- left corner. The Property Inspector displays all of the options for your box, including its current width, height, and position. Select the Bg color swatch and select a background color for the box from the Swatches panel.
6. You can add text to the box by simply typing in it. Click inside the box and type Gallery. Center the text in the box.
7. Save the file but keep it open for the next exercise

Project 5-2 Creating Overlapping boxes with AP Divs

As the designer of the Serenity Spa website you need to create a photocollage effect with overlapping images. You will use AP Divs and the Z-index feature to do this

1. On the **gallery.html** page, use the Draw AP Div tool, click and drag to draw a rectangle that is about one-sixth of the size of the entire page. Select the box by clicking on the tab in the upper left corner, and copy and paste it three times. Distribute the boxes around the page.

2. Place your cursor in one of the boxes. Click on the Common category of the Insert bar, and select the Image icon.
3. Choose one of the images in the images folder and press OK. The image will now appear inside the box. If you need to resize the image, click on the image itself, put your cursor on one of the handles, hold down the Shift key, and drag the handle to resize the image. To resize the box, select the box by clicking on the tab in the upper left corner, then click on one of the box handles and drag until the box is the size you want.
4. Follow the procedure outlined above to add images to the other three boxes on the page. The boxes should overlap.
5. Now, select each box, one at a time, and look at the z-index in the Property Inspector. Change the z-index of each box, assigning each one a different number, 1 through 3. Notice how the overlapping of the boxes changes as you assign the z-index numbers to them. Find the box that is at the back of all of the others, select it, and give it a z-index of 7. Absolutely positioned elements with a higher z-index will visually appear on the top.
7. Save the file.

Proficiency Assessment

Creating Tables

Project 5-3

Even though tables are considered an antiquated design concept these days, they can still be used for a quick, simple website layout if your project calls for it.

Get Ready. Launch Dreamweaver CS6 if you haven't already.

1. Create a new blank HTML page.
2. Choose Insert > Table
3. Choose from the settings offered and click OK. Use the Properties panel to alter the appearance of the table.
4. Keep the file open for the next exercise.

Comparing Divs and Tables

Project 5-4

If you're still on the fence about the pros and cons of divs and tables, put a div on the page with your table and hold one up against the other.

Get Ready. Launch Dreamweaver CS6 if you haven't already.

1. Continue with the file above.
2. Add a div to your page and try adding content to both the table and the div along with modifying their physical properties to draw a more educated comparison.

Advanced Page Layout

Key Terms

- CSS Floats
- Clear Property
- Column Layouts
- List-based Navigation
- List Item

Skill	Objective
Demonstrate general and Dreamweaver-specific knowledge of best practices for designing a website, such as maintaining consistency, separating content from design, using standard fonts, and utilizing visual hierarchy	2.1
Demonstrate knowledge of page layout design concepts and principles	2.3
Use CSS to implement a reusable design	5.8
Conduct technical tests	6.1

Business Case

The Organic Utopia site requires a consistent column layout. The trouble is that setting up columns on a webpage isn't a matter of dragging and dropping objects anywhere on the webpage; there are some rules dictated by the code. Getting more in-depth knowledge about CSS and DIVs will help with this process.

Introduction

Before starting, make sure that your tools and panels are consistent by resetting your workspace. See "Resetting the Dreamweaver workspace" in the Starting Up section of this book.

You will work with several files from the dw06lessons folder in this lesson. Make sure that you have loaded the dwlessons folder onto your hard drive. See "Loading lesson files" in the Starting Up section of this book.

Before you begin, you need to create site settings that point to the dw06lessons folder. Go to Site > New Site, or, for details on creating a site, refer to Lesson 2, "Setting Up a New Site."

Graphic design elements and principles

In web design, page layout can be divided into two categories: the aesthetics of a page and the underlying CSS and HTML code that renders the page in the browser. You'll have time to explore the code side later in the chapter but first here is a brief overview of design concepts that will help you understand the elements of a page.

Certification Ready 2.3

What are the relevant graphic design elements and principles in page layout?

- **Line, shape and form**

The line is one of the most basic elements in a page layout. Lines are used to divide space and separate content. Shape describes two-dimensional space, the three basic shapes are square, triangle and circle. Form is the three-dimensional version of a shape. So if the shape is square, then the form would be a cube.

- **Color, contrast and texture**

Color is a complex subject, but at its essence, color evokes reactions in people. You can use color to help visually organize your layout or use color as an accent on the page to attract the user's eye. Contrast is the technique of creating visual differences on the page, this could be placing two different colors side by side but contrast could also be the juxtaposition of two different shapes, typefaces or images. Texture in web design is always implied through the style of design (since there is no physical texture on a screen!). The visual texture of a background graphic or a pattern in your layout can help control the perception of the user. A leopard skin texture for a banking site, for example, would not likely inspire confidence to the user.

- **Emphasis, movement and balance**

Emphasis is the technique of making a specific element stand out to the eye. Movement is the technique of simulating motion or using graphical elements (such as arrows) to help direct the eye. Balance is the state of a page in which the design is clearly arranged in a planned, visual pattern.

- **Unity, proximity and repetition**

Unity is the feeling of "completeness" achieved when at least two or more components of your page have something in common such as color or other style. Proximity is the closeness or distance of individual design elements. Repetition is when a page element occurs more than a few times.

- **Rule of thirds**

A well known composition principle (also seen in photography, film and other disciplines) in which a page (or image) is divided into 9 imaginary equal parts (two equally-spaced horizontal lines and two equally-spaced vertical lines), and important compositional elements are placed along these lines or their intersections. This technique tends to create more interesting layout than simply centering the content would.

- **White space**

The absence of text and graphics is known as white space. Properties such as margins, space between columns and paragraphs can all be adjusted to achieve a form of balance. Too little white space and a page is cramped, busy and hard to read. Too much white space and a page can feel empty, lacking content and call attention to itself.

- **Alignment**

Alignment in page layout design is the technique of keeping related objects such as text and images, in line. Alignment is one of the keys to keeping the user's eye focused on the content.

Symmetry

Symmetry is when the weight of a page layout is evenly distributed around a central vertical or horizontal axis, for example if a page is split into two equal columns. Horizontal and vertical symmetry are the two most common forms, but there is also diagonal symmetry in which the central axis is a diagonal line. Radial symmetry occurs when objects are rotated in a certain direction around a point, in nature you might see radial symmetry in the spiral of a seashell. Asymmetry is when the weight of a page layout is not evenly distributed around a central axis.

Certification Ready 2.3

What are some examples of horizontal symmetry, vertical symmetry, diagonal symmetry, radial symmetry, and asymmetric layout?

Avoid these mistakes in your page designs

It takes experience to become a great visual designer, until you come more experienced you are likely to make some mistakes along the way. There are a few simple guidelines or "best practices" that you can follow that will help you create page designs that avoid the worst of these mistakes

- Don't use color merely for decoration. Color has the ability to evoke feeling and draw attention to a page element such as a heading or a section of a page. But color can be abused if it is too bright or saturated.
- Avoid extraneous graphics. Just as with color, imagery can draw attention to a section of a page. If an image is relevant then this is fine, however don't add graphics just to fill up space on a page.
- Page design should be consistent across the site. Even if your website has many sections and pages, these pages should feel unified. The contact page of your site might only be a single column whereas your home page has three columns, but they should both still feel as if they are part of the same family. This can be accomplished by using consistent page elements such as heading sizes, font colors, and graphics.

Learning More

Certification Ready 2.3

What are examples of page designs that violate design principles or best practices?

Layout with AP divs versus layout with floats

In this lesson, you'll learn an advanced method of layout in Dreamweaver using CSS boxes that are floated as columns. Unlike the inflexible nature of AP Divs, floated layouts can accommodate additional content more easily, and once you learn how to use them, they will allow you to use more creative layout options.

You may be asking: why are there two methods of layout in Dreamweaver, and why am I learning both? To understand this, it helps to keep in mind that historically Dreamweaver has been designed for use in the Design view (in other words, not working in code). As you will soon see, the **CSS `float`** property that you will be using to create columns was not truly designed to be a tool for layout, and requires a good understanding of CSS to be useful.

Floated layouts are trickier to control and understand than AP Divs. Additionally, older web browsers such as Internet Explorer 6 have well-documented bugs and quirks that can prevent floated layouts from rendering correctly. To address these problems, coding techniques known as "browser hacks" have been developed over the years. The browser hacks involve adding additional code targeted toward one browser in order to make the pages look the same.

In Dreamweaver, it is likely that the program leans toward using the more reliable and easier-to-manipulate AP Divs because of its traditional user base. However, as users of Dreamweaver seek to duplicate some of the sophisticated sites they see online, they really have no choice but to work with floats. As you walk through this lesson, it is important to keep in mind that you do not necessarily have to choose between absolutely positioned layouts and floated layouts. Layouts that combine both AP Divs and floated layouts are commonplace and combine the strengths of both.

Layout with AP divs versus layout with floats

In addition to the two layouts described above, Dreamweaver CS6 has added a third category of layouts: "fluid layouts." The fluid layout feature represents the latest development in web design and development: creating web pages designed to adapt to screens of different sizes. You will have the opportunity to work with this feature at the end of the lesson; however, you should note that this form of layout is not for everyone, so understanding the fundamentals of float-based layouts is still the recommended path for most Dreamweaver users.

To start creating more sophisticated and flexible layouts, you will first need to have a good understanding of the `float` property.

Creating a floated image

One of the reasons the `float` property in CSS was created was to allow for the appearance of text to wrap around an image. This concept was borrowed from print design, where the effect is standard practice and often called text wrap or runaround. In CSS, this effect is achieved by allowing elements following a floated element in the HTML markup to surround the element, effectively changing position. This behavior also makes it possible to create columns on a page, although this may not have been the original intent of the rule.

In this exercise, you will learn the basics of using the `float` property by applying it to an image in order to wrap text.

Step-by-Step

Follow these steps to create a floated image

1. From the dw06lessons site, open the **floatimage.html** page. You will see a page with a large paragraph block of text. Click in the middle of the paragraph, immediately before the sentence, "We also have added recyclable shopping bags."
2. Now choose Insert > Image and in the Select Image Source dialog box, choose the image **recycle_bag.gif** from the images folder, and choose OK. In the Alt text field, type **shopping bag** and click OK. The image has width and height dimensions of 81 × 101 pixels and is inserted as a block inside the paragraph as seen in Figure 6-1.

***Figure 6-1**: An image with default styling placed inside a paragraph.*

The amount of space between the two sentences is determined by the height of the graphic. This is the default flow of HTML when an inline image is inserted into a paragraph.

You'll now wrap the text around the image by applying the `float` property to the shopping bag graphic.

3. Make sure the image is still selected and then click the New CSS Rule button in the CSS Styles panel. Click the menu for Selector Type and choose Class. In the Selector Name text field, type **.floatimage** and click OK.
4. In the CSS Rule definition dialog box, click the Box category, then click the Float drop-down menu and choose right. Click OK.
5. Make sure the shopping bag graphic is still selected; if it is not, do so now. Look at the Property Inspector, there is a Class drop-down menu, which by default is set to None (Figure 6-2).

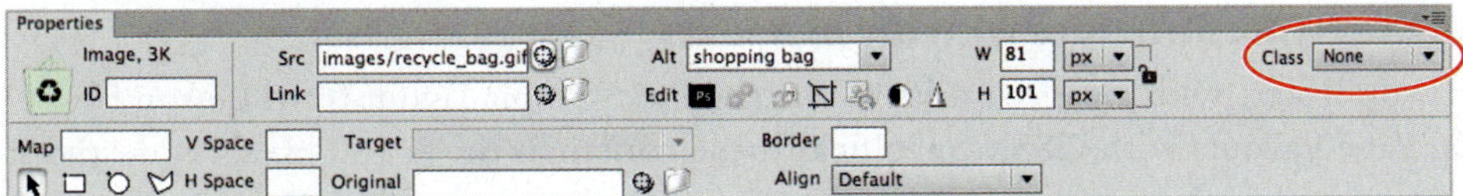

***Figure 6-2**: The default Class is set to* None.

From the Class drop-down menu, choose floatimage as seen in Figure 6-3. With the class applied, the image will now be removed from the flow of the text and be pushed far right to the edge of the container.

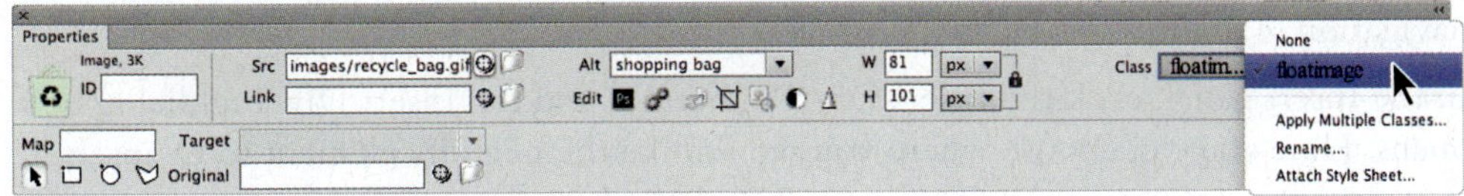

***Figure 6-3**: Change the Class to* floatimage.

6. In the CSS Styles panel, double-click the `.floatimage` rule. In the Box category, click the Float drop-down menu and change the value from right to left, then press OK.

   The image now floats to the left and the text wraps around it. This wrapping behavior is extremely important to keep in mind as you work with floated elements. You can float elements to the left or right only.

7. In the CSS Styles panel, double-click the .floatimage rule and in the Box category uncheck the Same for All checkbox for the Margin, then type a value of **10** for the Top and **10** for the Right. Make sure the unit is pixels. Press OK. The image now is set off from the text, adding needed space (Figure 6-4).

***Figure 6-4**: Set the Margin for the image.*

8. Choose File > Save, and then File > Preview in Browser to see the results in your browser. This technique is a simple and useful application of the `float` property. The next step is to apply this same concept to other elements, not just images. In the next exercise, you will float div elements to create columns. Close your browser and then close the floatimage.html document.

Creating columns with HTML and CSS

One of the most important aspects of working with floated elements is understanding how they interact with their surrounding elements. This relationship is easy to understand when you have an object with a fixed width and height such as the shopping bag graphic from the last exercise. When floated elements are objects that are not fixed in size, such as a column which is defined by the amount of text inside, things can get interesting.

Creating the HTML Structure with div elements

To begin, you'll start with a page similar to the Organic Utopia layout from Lesson 5, "Creating Page Layouts with CSS." Specifically, the container div is 960 pixels wide and styled to be centered within the browser. The header has one inline image (the Organic Utopia logo). You will first define the structure of the page by adding div elements for the various sections.

Step-by-Step

Follow these steps to structure an HTML document with divs

1. In the Files panel, double-click the **layout.html** page. Your first step will be to add the navigation section.
2. In the Insert panel, click the Insert Div Tag button, and the Insert Div Tag dialog box opens. Here you can choose where you would like the new div element to be inserted. You need the navigation div element to follow the header.
3. In the Insert Div Tag dialog box, click the Insert drop-down menu. Select the After tag option, then in the drop-down menu to the right, choose `<div id="header">`. Type **navigation** in the ID text field, then press the New CSS Rule button (Figure 6-5).

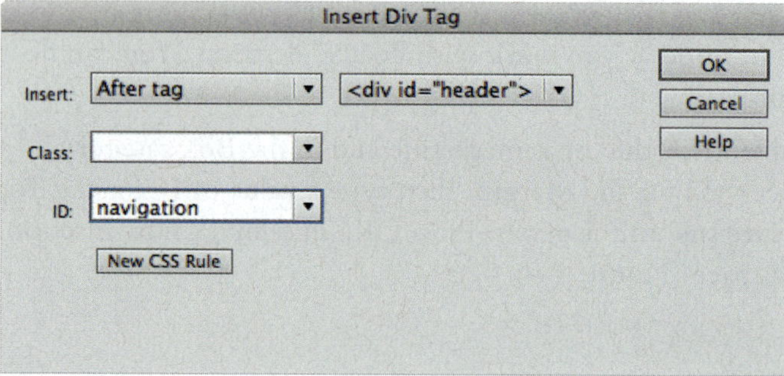

Figure 6-5: Set the properties in the Insert Div Tag dialog box.

The New CSS Rule definition dialog box opens. Click OK. You will now add a few simple styles to the navigation div.

4. In the CSS rule definition dialog box, click the Background category and type **#88b036** into the Background-color text field to add a green background color. Then click the Box category and type **100** in the Width text field, then from the drop-down menu to the right choose %. Click in the Height text field and type **36**, and leave the value set to px. Click OK. Click OK again in the Insert Div Tag dialog box. Your navigation section now spans across the width of the container.

You'll now add three div elements for the main and sidebar columns, as well as the footer. These next three steps are essentially variations on step 3: You are adding structural elements to your page and giving the elements good names to begin styling them.

5. Click the Insert Div Tag button in the Insert panel. Click the Insert drop-down menu and choose the After Tag option, and then in the drop-down menu to the right choose `<div id="navigation">`. Type **main** in the ID text field and then click OK.

6. Click the Insert Div Tag button in the Insert panel. Click the Insert drop-down menu and choose the After Tag option, then in the drop-down menu to the right, choose `<div id="main">`. Type **sidebar** in the ID text field and then click OK.

   The last section you will add will be for the footer at the bottom of the page.

7. Click the Insert Div Tag button in the Insert panel. Click the Insert drop-down menu. Select the After Tag option, then in the drop-down menu to the right choose `<div id="sidebar">`. Type **footer** in the ID text field, click the New CSS Rule button, then click OK. You will be adding a background-color style now so you can more easily see how the footer interacts with the two columns.

8. In the CSS Rule definition dialog box for the footer, click the Background category and in the Background-color text field, type **#CCC** to add a light gray. Click OK, and then click OK again in the Insert Div Tag dialog box. You now have the main sections of your page (Figure 6-6), and you now have to start setting the widths of the columns.

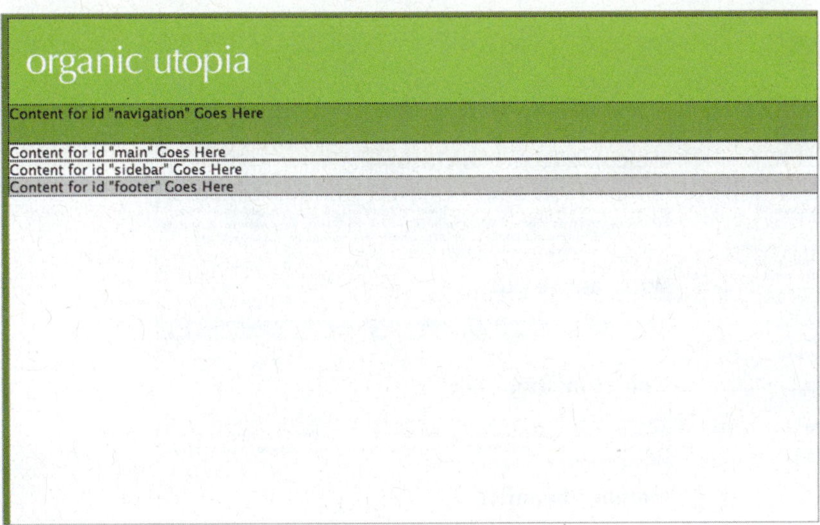

***Figure 6-6**: The main sections of your web page are now created.*

Setting the width and floating the columns

With the basic structure of your page set up in HTML, you will now set the width of the main and sidebar columns and float them using CSS. You will return to the navigation bar in a later exercise.

Follow these steps to float the columns and set the width — **Step-by-Step**

1. In the CSS Styles panel, click the New CSS Rule button and the New CSS Rule window appears. If the Selector Type menu is not set to ID, click on the menu and choose this option, then click on the Selector Name menu and from the list that appears choose main and then click OK.

2. In the CSS Rule definition dialog box that appears, click the Box category, and then type **600** inside the Width text field. From the Float drop-down menu, choose right. Click OK and you will see the main column moves to the right and the sidebar column moves up to fill in the remaining space. Now you'll add some content to see how it fits into the column.
3. In the Files panel, double-click the **main_content.html** page. Select all the text on this page, then press Ctrl+C (Windows) or Command+C (Mac OS) to copy it. Close the file, then select the placeholder text in the main div and press Ctrl+V (Windows) or Command+V (Mac OS) to paste. The column expands to accommodate all the content. Notice that the footer appears to be behind the main column. This is a result of the floated properties you just added. You'll take a look at this shortly, but first you will style the sidebar.
4. Click inside the sidebar div, then in the CSS Styles panel, click the New CSS Rule button. Press the Less Specific button once, and the Selector Name reads `#sidebar`. Click OK, and in the CSS Rule definition dialog box, click the Box category. In the Width text field, type **360**. From the Float drop-down menu, choose left. Click OK. Visually, very little will change, but the two columns now have explicit widths and both are floating.
5. In the Files panel, double-click the **sidebar_content.html** page. Select all the text on this page and copy it. Close the file, and then click inside the sidebar div and paste, replacing the placeholder text. The sidebar expands to fit this content, which is a definition list (Figure 6-7).

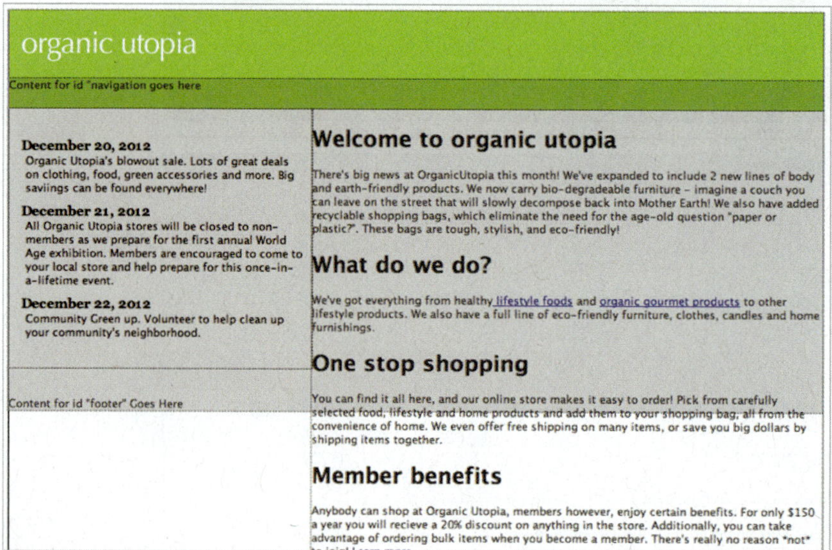

Figure 6-7: The sidebar section is floated to the left and has a width of 360. The main section is floated to the right and has a width of 600.

Take Note...

We have cheated a bit in this exercise and created pre-existing styles for the sidebar content. Many of the techniques for modifying the margins of elements have been covered in earlier lessons. If you're curious, you may look at the styles for the `<dl>` *and* `<dd>` *elements within the styles panel or the code view to see the details.*

What may be most confusing is the behavior and appearance of the footer div. As noted earlier, it appears to be behind your two columns. The reason for this has to do with the nature of floated elements. Floated elements are removed from the default flow of HTML and since both columns are floated, the footer ignores them and moves up directly below the navigation section. This is also why the height of the footer has expanded. From the perspective of the footer, there are no columns to interact with so it assumes its default behavior.

In order to push the footer below the columns, you need to add another CSS property to the footer called `clear`.

Using the clear property

When you apply the **`clear` property** to an object, you are essentially adding a rule that says *No floated elements are allowed on either side of me.* In fact, you can specify whether the left, right or both sides can have floated elements. You'll try two different options in order to understand the `clear` property better.

Follow these steps to use the clear property — Step-by-Step

1. In the CSS Styles panel, double-click the `#footer` style, and click the Box category. From the Clear drop-down menu, choose right. Click OK. This puts the footer box on the bottom of the page. You may need to scroll down to see it.

   Although this seems to do the trick, there is a potential pitfall. You set the clear value to right, but what would happen if the content in the main column were shorter than the content in the sidebar? Understanding the answer to this question will go a long way toward your understanding of floats and clears, so you'll do a short experiment.

2. In the main div, select the last three paragraphs and headings and then delete them. With less content in this column now, the footer still behaves the same and stops at the bottom of the main column, but the sidebar is longer now so the footer overlaps it as seen in Figure 6-8.

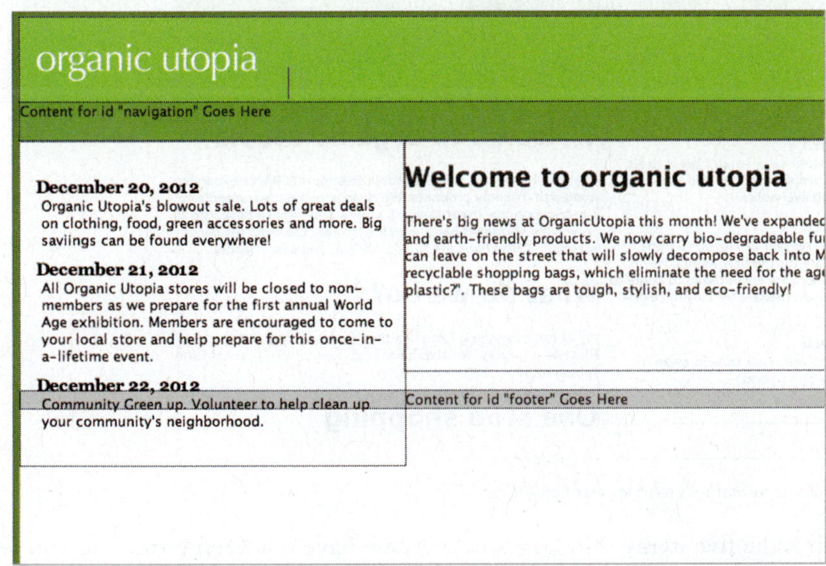

***Figure 6-8**: Select and delete the last three paragraphs and headings in the "Main" div.*

   Of course, you could fix this by switching the value of the `clear` property from Right to Left. This would prevent the footer from being next to the sidebar, but the problem is that you may never know which column will have the most content, so the safest solution is to apply the `clear` property to both sides.

3. Choose Edit > Undo Delete to bring the content back into the main div.

4. In the CSS Styles panel, double-click the footer style and from the Clear drop-down menu choose both, then click OK. The footer div will now always be at the bottom because no floated elements are allowed to the left or the right.

Creating a list-based navigation bar

Floats can not only be used for simple image wrapping and creating columns, but also to create navigation. Here you'll start creating a **list-based navigation** that uses CSS. This is a great way to create easily editable navigation bars that are also search engine-friendly because they use text instead of images. Additionally, you can think of navigation as simply a list of links to other pages, so it makes sense to use the list element. The first step is to add the content and then style the **list items** and the navigation element.

Step-by-Step **Follow these steps to create a navigation bar using list items**

1. Select the placeholder text in the navigation div and then click the HTML button in the Property Inspector, if necessary. Click the Unordered List button (⁝≡) and the text will become the first bullet in an unordered list.
2. Replace the placeholder text by typing **Home**, and then press Return. This adds a new list item. Add the following navigation sections pressing Return after each one: **About Us**, **Products**, **Services**, **Contact**. Your layout will appear to break as the list items are added (seen in Figure 6-9). Don't worry; you will be using float properties to turn this list into a horizontal navigation bar.

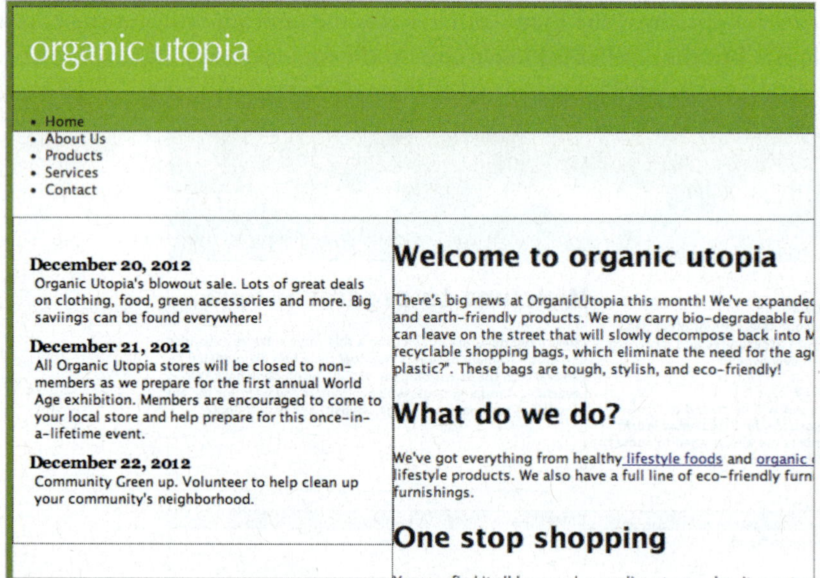

Figure 6-9: Add the list items that will serve as your navigation.

You will now link the five items. The pages in this case have not been created so you will use a placeholder link for each item.

3. Select the Home list item, click inside the Link text field in the Property Inspector and type # and then press Enter (Windows) or Return (Mac OS). This symbol creates a placeholder hyperlink. Repeat this step for each list item until all five are hyperlinked.

   Now you'll apply the `float` property and turn this vertical list into a horizontal one.

4. Click the `<li>` element in the tag selector as seen in Figure 6-10.

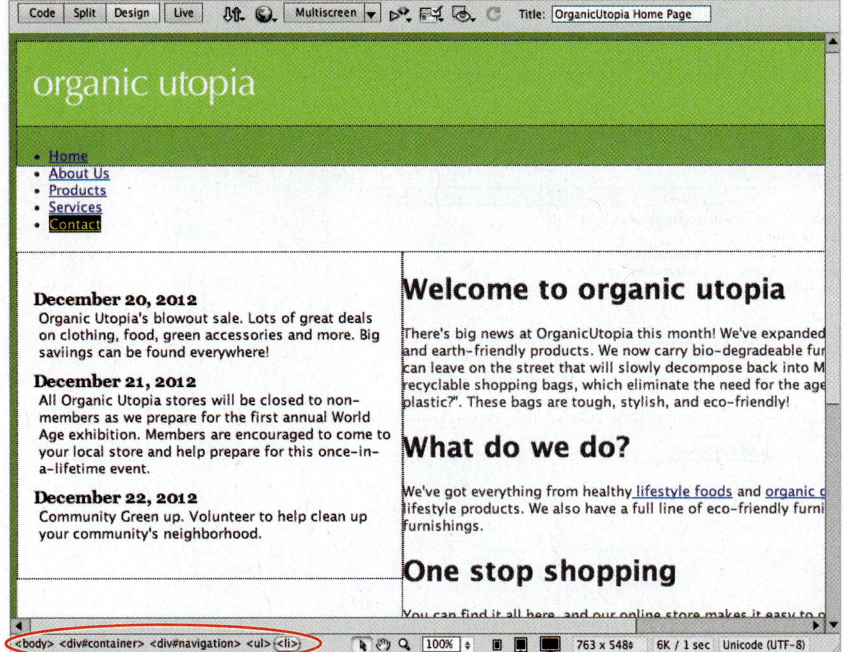

Figure 6-10: Select the `<li>` element in the tag selector.

   Click the New CSS Rule button in the CSS Styles panel and choose Less Specific so the Compound Selector reads `#navigation ul li`. Click OK.

5. In the Box category, from the Float drop-down menu, choose left. Press the Apply button, and you will see that your list items are now stacked horizontally rather than vertically. By applying the `float` property, you have overridden the list items' default behavior. However, there is still more work that you need to do.

6. Click the List category, then from the List-style-type drop-down menu, choose none. This removes the bullet points from each list item. Click OK.

   You still need to do more work; specifically, you need to create styles for the `<a>` element that is for hyperlinks You'll style the appearance and position of these links now.

7. Click inside any link in the navigation, and then in CSS Styles panel, click the New CSS Rule button. The selector type is compound, but unnecessarily complex; press the Less Specific button so the Selector Name is set to `#navigation ul li a`, as seen in Figure 6-11 and then click OK.

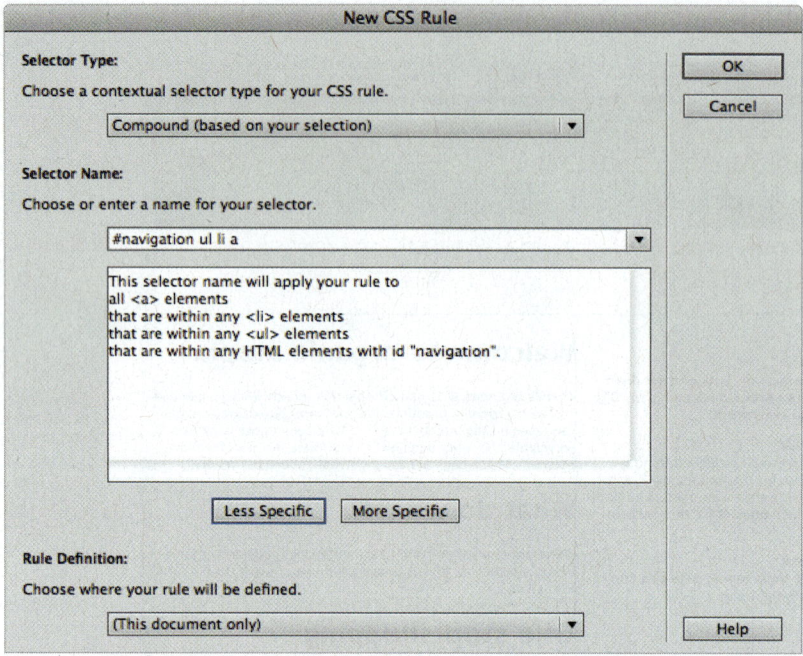

***Figure 6-11**: Create a new CSS rule for the navigation hyperlinks.*

8. In the Type category, check the Text-decoration checkbox labeled none. This will remove the default underline below your hyperlinks. Click the Color swatch and choose white.

9. Click the Box category and uncheck the Same for all checkbox for Padding. Type **8 px** for the top and bottom values, and **15 px** for the left and right values (Figure 6-12). Press Apply to see the space added between each hyperlink.

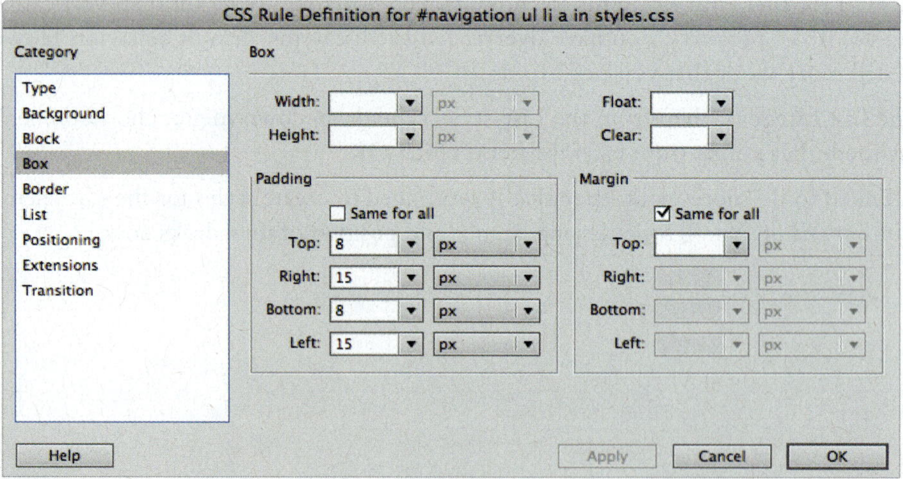

***Figure 6-12**: Apply padding to the hyperlink styles to create more space between your navigation.*

10. Click the Block category, and then from the Display drop-down menu, choose block. This property and value changes the appearance of the list item: it expands and also allows the entire block to be clickable, not just the text. Click OK.

    You're almost finished; however, your navigation links are currently overlapping the boundaries of the green navigation bar. This is because of some default margins—a topic you have run into before. In this case, the default margins of the unordered list are the culprit.

11. Click anywhere inside the navigation, if necessary, and then click the `<ul>` tag in the Tag Selector. Then, click the New CSS Rule button in the CSS Styles panel. Press the Less Specific button, making sure the selector reads `#navigation ul`, and then click OK.

12. In the CSS Rule definition dialog box, click the Box category and type **0** for Margin and Padding (Figure 6-13). Click OK and the hyperlinks are now centered within the navigation element.

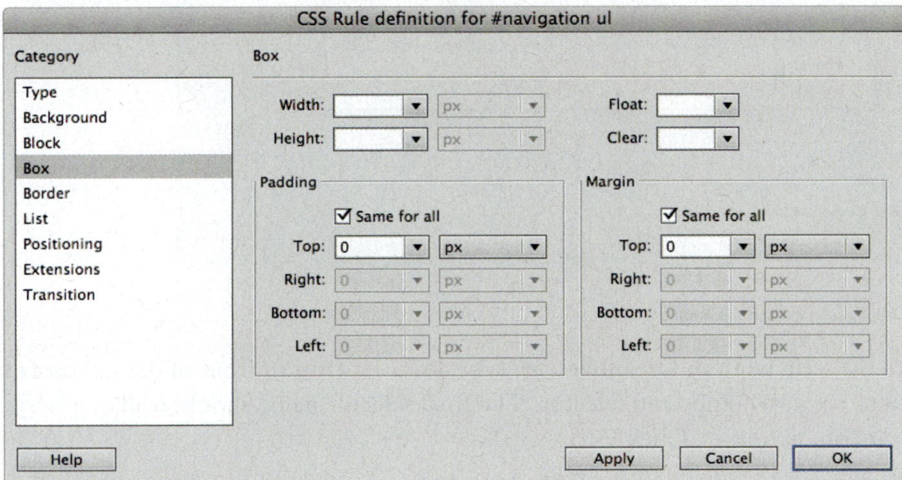

***Figure 6-13**: Set the margins for the navigation to give it a more defined look.*

The last piece to add is a little interactivity. Say that when the user mouses over any one of the navigation links, you would like it to change color. This improves usability by letting the user know the links are active. You can do this with the `hover` property for hyperlinks.

13. Click within any link, then click the New CSS Rule button in the CSS Styles panel. In the New CSS Rule dialog box, choose the `a:hover` property from the drop-down menu to the right of the Selector Name text field as seen in Figure 6-14.

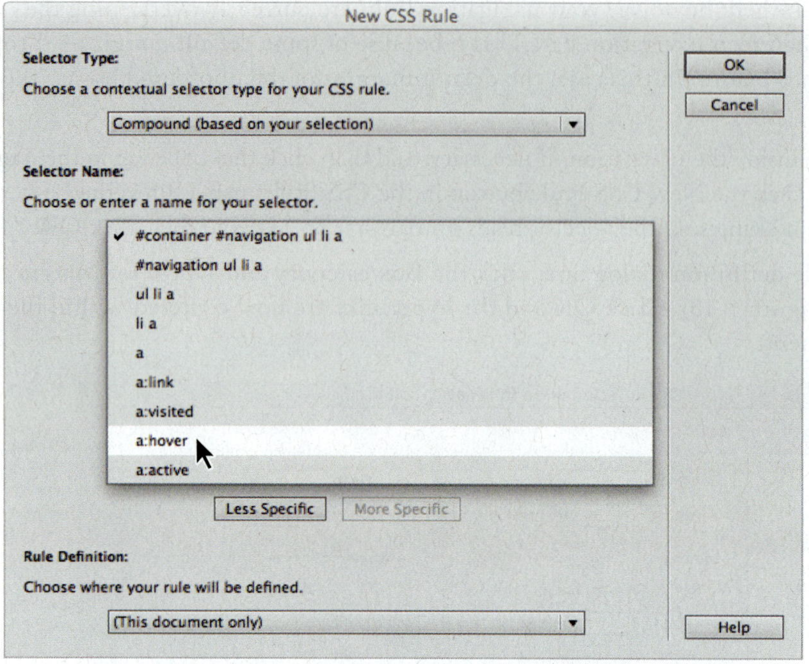

Figure 6-14: *Select the* `a:hover` *property.*

To make the style work in Dreamweaver, type **#navigation** in front of the `a:hover` property to create a compound selector. The final selector name should read `#navigation a:hover`. Click OK.

14. In the Background category of the CSS Rule definition dialog box, click in the Background-color text field, and type **#9FCC41**. This is the same green as the header. Click OK.

15. Save your document and choose File > Preview in Browser to see your list-based CSS menu. Be sure to mouse over the links to see the hover effect as seen in Figure 6-15.

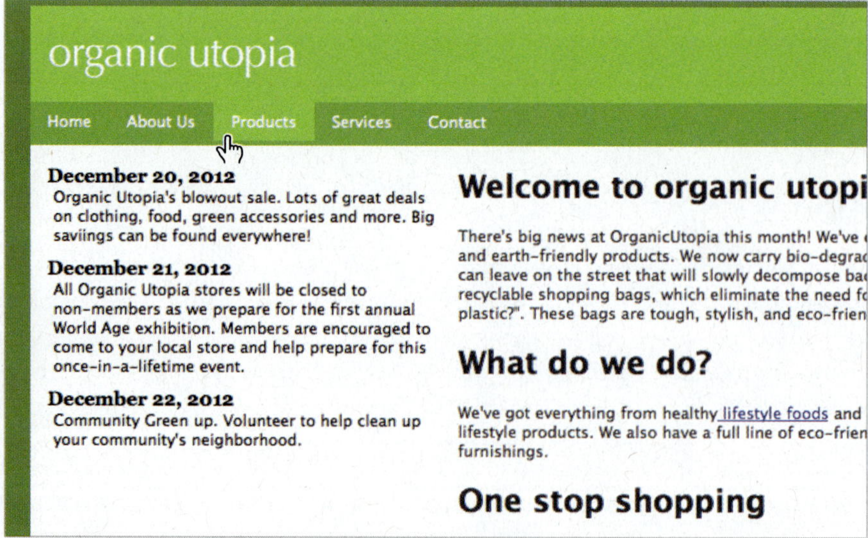

Figure 6-15: *Creating a style for the* `a:hover` *property produces a color rollover effect when the user's cursor is on a link.*

Changing column layout and size

Another benefit of using floated containers for layout is that they are very easy to modify. For example, perhaps you would like to experiment with your sidebar being on the right rather than the left, or perhaps you would like to experiment with changing the width of the entire layout. This can all be accomplished with a few easy modifications of the styles.

Follow these steps to edit column layout and size

Step-by-Step

1. In the CSS Styles panel, double-click the `#main` style. Click the Box category, change the Float value from right to **left**, and then click OK. This pushes the main box over to the left of the container and the sidebar slips to the right.
2. In the CSS Styles panel, double-click the `#sidebar` style, click the Box category, change the Float value from left to right, and then click OK. There will be no visual change in this case, but it does ensure that the sidebar is flush against the container as seen in Figure 6-16. That's it! Two simple style changes create a completely different layout.

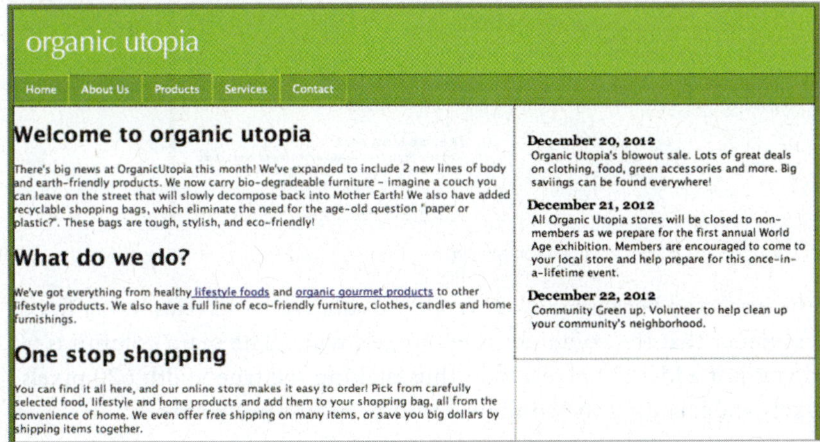

Figure 6-16*: Change the Float value of the* `#sidebar` *style from left to right.*

If you'd like to change the overall width of your page layout you can do this by modifying the `#container` div.

3. In the CSS Styles panel, double-click the `#container` style and click the Box category. Change the Width from 960 to **1100** and then press Apply. This expands your container, and because your columns are floating, they will both remain aligned to their respective sides. For the purpose of this exercise, the original value of 960 is better, so type this value back again. For now, the important part is to understand the concept.
4. While you are here, select the Height value and delete it, leaving it empty. Having a fixed height is useful at the beginning of the layout progress, but it should be removed at some point in order to accommodate more content. Click OK.

   Fine-tune your page: currently, the main column is aligned flush left against the container and the text is too close to the edge of the container. This is a common layout problem; you will now look at some techniques designed to help you create your own custom layouts and to better understand the behavior of floated elements.

5. Double-click the `#main` style in the CSS Styles panel, and then click the Box category. Uncheck the Same for all checkbox for Margin, type **20** inside the left margin, and then click OK. Notice that this change had the desired effect of adding space between the main column and the surrounding container. However, there is another effect: the sidebar has now "slipped" down below as seen in Figure 6-17.

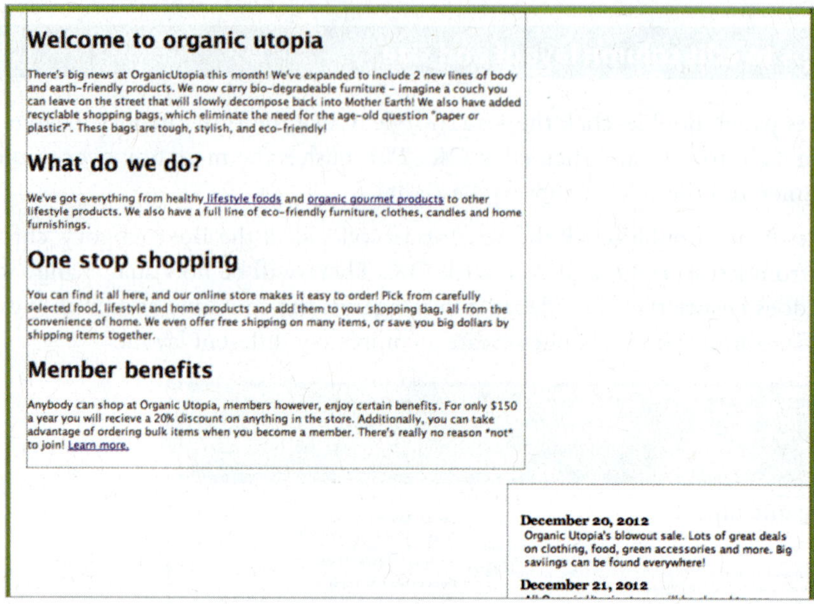

Figure 6-17: Adding 20 pixels of left margin to the `#main` *column.*

This effect is to be expected because you are trying to squeeze two boxes into a fixed width space. Remember that the container is 960 pixels wide. The main column is 600 pixels wide, and you just added 20 pixels to it, thus making the true width 620 pixels. The sidebar is 360 pixels wide; adding the combined widths results in 980 pixels.

This is a common dilemma with fixed width layouts, but as long as you understand the relationships, it is easy to fix. In this case, you'll try reducing the width of the main column.

6. Double-click the `#main` style in the CSS Styles panel, and then click the Box category. Change the width from 600 to **580** and press Apply. The width is reduced and the sidebar slips back up.

   However, you can take this a bit further: the columns are actually very close to each other. You can add more space by reducing the width of the main section even further.

7. Type **550** as the width, and then click OK. You now have an additional gap of space between the main section and the sidebar.

Take Note...

Keep in mind that you could have decreased the width of the `#sidebar` *style if you preferred to keep the width of the* `#main` *column intact. There are no set rules for how to do this correctly. Layout in CSS becomes interplay between width, margins, padding, and content; every page has slightly different requirements. Just be sure to keep track of all these relationships in your own designs, since it can get confusing as you add more elements.*

Creating the appearance of equal height columns

There is now another part of your layout that you need to pay attention to: the column height. Currently, the main column is longer than the sidebar; visually this isn't really a problem because neither column has a background color, so the whole page appears white. But what happens if your design requires that explicit columns be defined by color? In this exercise, you'll look at one solution for this issue.

Follow these steps to create columns of equal height — **Step-by-Step**

1. In the CSS Styles panel, double-click the rule for the sidebar div. Click the Background category, then, in the Background-color text field, type **#C8D9BC**.
2. Click the Border category. Uncheck the Same for all checkboxes for Style, Width and Color. In the row labeled Left, choose solid in the Style column's drop-down menu, and type **2** in the Width columns text field. In the Color column's text field, type **#060**. Click OK. The background color and border properties are now added to the sidebar (Figure 6-18).

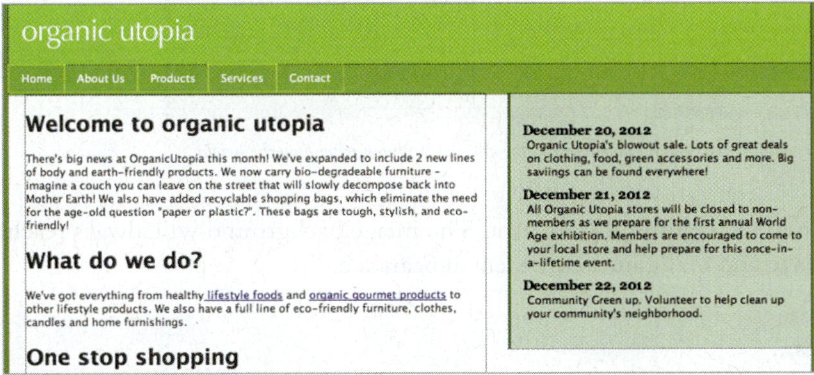

***Figure 6-18**: Set the border for the* `#sidebar` *div.*

The problem with the column is an aesthetic one. A column sometimes looks better when it spans to the bottom of the page rather than cutting off abruptly. Additionally, if you are using this layout throughout your site, every page will likely have different amounts of content. As a user moves from page to page, this would create irregular page appearance, as the column height jumps up and down based on the amount of content. To solve this, you'll add a background image to the container div, which simulates the appearance of the column from top to bottom.

3. In the CSS Styles panel, double-click the rule for the container div. Click the Background category, and for the Background-image property, press the Browse button and locate the **container_bg.gif** file in the images folder. Click Choose (Windows) or Open (Mac OS).

   This graphic is 960 pixels wide (which matches the width of your container), but it is only 2 pixels high. Essentially, it is a thin horizontal slice of the page and includes the sidebar color and green border.

4. From the Background-repeat drop-down menu, choose *repeat-y*. This ensures the graphic will only be tiled from top to bottom. Click OK and you will now see your columns filled in as seen in Figure 6-19.

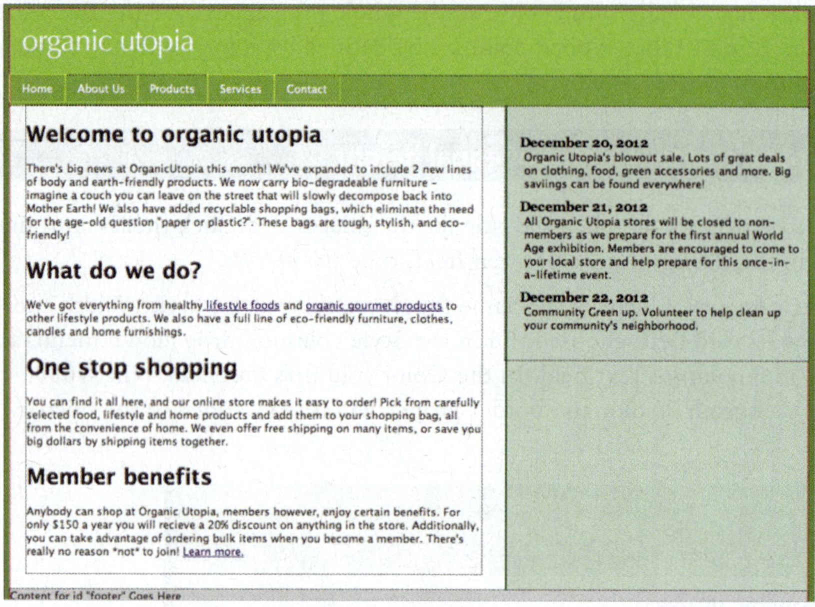

Figure 6-19*: A "fake column" background image creates the effect of a column extending the height of the page.*

Now, the length of the column is irrelevant. The image background will always reach the bottom of the page and maintain a consistent appearance.

> ***Take Note...***
> *Although this technique is useful, it relies on your layout being finalized. If the width of your container or the position of any of your columns changes, you must then change the background image. Additionally, other changes, such as the color of a column or any padding adjustments may also require you to modify your background image. For this reason, you should wait until the small changes and adjustments to your layout are complete before making a column background.*

How to create a fake column background in Photoshop

Learning More

The easiest way to make the fake column background is if you happen to have a mockup of your website as an image file or as a Photoshop file with layers. However, if you don't have a mockup, you need to be more creative. Here's how we created our page background.

1. Preview your web page in the browser. Look to make sure you have a clear cross-section of your columns from left to right. If there is any text or images in the column, you may need to go back to Dreamweaver and remove them temporarily.
2. Using your system's screen capture program, capture your screen. In the Mac OS, this can be done with the keyboard shortcut, Command+Shift+3. In Windows, use the Print Screen button to capture.

   In the case of the Mac OS, this will create a png file that will be saved to your desktop. In the case of Windows, this will copy the screen image to your clipboard.
3. In Photoshop, either open the screen capture image directly (Mac OS) or if in Windows, choose File > New, then press OK and press Ctrl+V.
4. Click the Rectangular Marquee tool, then in the Options panel, change the style from Normal to Fixed Size. Type in a width of **840 px** and a height of **2 px**. If your original layout has a different width, you will need to change this width value to match.
5. Click anywhere in the image with the Marquee tool to add a floating selection. Using your arrow keys, you must line up the selection exactly with the edges of the container. If the selection is even 1 pixel off it will result in a mismatch between the image and the real HTML columns.
6. Choose Image > Crop, then choose Save for Web and Devices to save it as a gif, jpg or png. Try to optimize the image in order to make it as small as possible. For example, in our case, we saved it as a gif using only four colors.

Browser compatibility

Up to this point, the concepts of creating a layout with floats and clears have made sense. There may have been some unusual or unexpected behaviors, but for the most part, once you understand the rules, you can begin to think about how you can apply this to your own designs. That's the good news. The bad news is that the expected behavior of CSS boxes takes a bad turn when we factor older browsers such as Internet Explorer 6 into the equation.

Due to certain rendering bugs in the browser, the behavior of floated elements can be hard to predict, and in some situations can completely "break" a layout. Web designers and developers have addressed this unfortunate behavior over the years by adding code fixes for Internet Explorer 6 to their style sheets, or by coming up with scripting solutions.

Adding code for IE 6

In the layout you have built, there is a code fix you will need to add to make the layout function well in IE 6. The problem is that the footer div that you cleared will not always be pushed below your columns. The bug that causes this can be fixed by "faking" a height for the footer. In general, IE 6 doesn't like floated elements that have no height, so this fix can solve many problems.

Step-by-Step

Follow these steps to account for IE 6 in your code

1. In the CSS Styles panel, double-click the `#footer` style, and in the Box category, type **1** for Height. Then click the drop-down menu and choose % as seen in Figure 6-20.

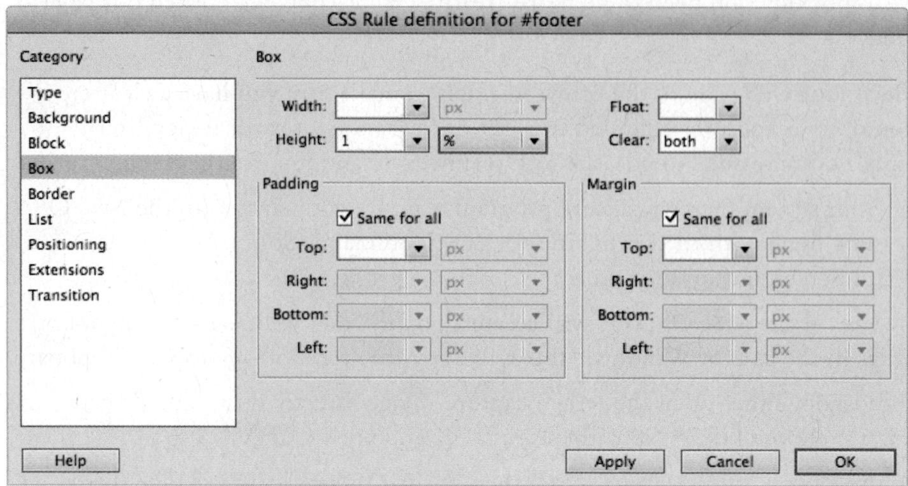

***Figure 6-20**: Set the Height for the `#footer` div.*

IE 6 needs this height value to prevent the layout from breaking.

2. Click OK and although you will not see any change, the layout is now fixed in IE. This fix might not have seemed too difficult, but more complex layouts will reveal other potential problems, especially when floats become involved. There is also the question as to whether you need to add the fix at all for this particular browser; however, this is a separate issue.

3. Choose File > Save to save your work.

Learning More

Do I need to optimize for Internet Explorer 6?

As of this writing, Internet Explorer 6 is a ten-year-old browser, and Internet Explorer 7, 8, and 9 have been released. Each version has improved the rendering of CSS, and in any case, the latest statistics have shown that use of Internet Explorer 6 has dropped down below 1% in the United States. (Although it is still far larger in other parts of the world. See *www.ie6countdown* for specific details.)

For many years, the extra code and troubleshooting involved in solving layout issues with Internet Explorer 6 was a significant problem that added time to the development process. Although this issue is no longer as relevant, the general problem of browser compatibility has not gone away. There are still differences between the way browsers interpret pages. However, in the year 2012, many of these issues have to do with evolving technology, such as CSS3 and HTML5, a topic we cover in more depth in the chapters "Mobile Design and Layout," and "CSS3 Transitions and Web Fonts."

Applying finishing touches

You'll now tidy up some loose ends with your layout. Specifically, you'll add a background image to your header, and then move the rules in your current style sheet to an external style sheet so you can use these styles for other pages in your site.

Follow these steps to add the finishing touches to your layout

Step-by-Step

1. In the CSS Styles panel, double-click the `#header` style to open it. Choose the Background category and then click the Browse button for Background-image. Navigate to the images folder located in your dw05lessons folder, choose **veggies.jpg** and then click Open.
2. Click the background-repeat menu and choose no-repeat. Click the `Background-position(x)` property and choose right. Click OK. Notice that the veggies image has been applied to the right side of your header as seen in Figure 6-21.

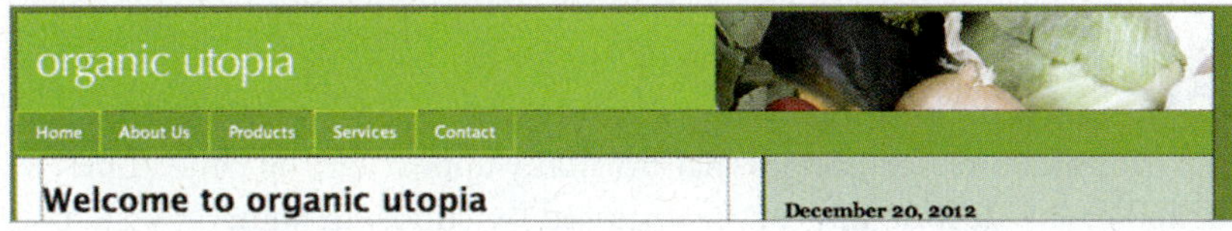

***Figure 6-21**: Adding a background image to the header.*

Now you will move all the style rules to an external style sheet so you can use these styles on new pages.

3. In the CSS Styles panel, be sure the All button is selected, click the first style (body), scroll down, and then Shift+click the last style (`dd`). This will select all the styles for the page.
4. Click the panel menu (·≡) at the top right corner of the CSS Styles panel, and choose Move CSS Rules.
5. Click the radio button labeled A new style sheet and click OK. You'll be prompted to save your style sheet. Type **styles** in the Save As text field and click OK (Windows) or Save (Mac OS). You now have an external style sheet that can be attached to new or existing pages in your site. (If you receive a message saying that duplicate names are being copied, confirm the save, don't cancel.)
6. Choose File > Save All.

Testing CSS layouts across browsers

Certification Ready 6.1

How do you test CSS layouts across web browsers?

Your layout may be looking good in Dreamweaver's Design view but you always need to test your layout in the real world of browsers. The general process looks something like this:

- Never rely solely on the design view. Preview your pages in Dreamweaver's Live view first. Live view is the quickest way to see your final design as it will appear in a browser.
- If you have multiple browsers on your system preview your page in these browsers and you may discover discrepancies that require you to refine your layout.
- In order to test your layout in browsers that you may not have access to, consider using a service such as Adobe Browserlab which allows you to check your layout in a number of different browsers as well as other platforms.

For more specifics on using Adobe BrowserLab refer to Lesson 16.

Learning More

Certification Ready 5.8

How do you troubleshoot CSS issues by using Visual Aids?

Troubleshooting CSS issues with Visual Aids

Dreamweaver has a few visual aids built-in to help you understand the CSS box model and how it affects your page.

CSS Layout Outlines

Displays the outlines of all CSS layout blocks on the page. This visual aid is turned on by default and can be accessed by choosing View > Visual Aids > CSS Layout Outlines.

CSS Layout Box Model

Displays the box model (padding and margins) of selected CSS layout block. This visual aid is turned on by default and can be accessed by choosing View > Visual Aids > CSS Layout Box Model

CSS Layout Backgrounds

Displays temporarily assigned background colors for individual CSS layout blocks, and hides any other background colors or images that normally appear on the page. This visual aid is not turned on by default and can be accessed by choosing View > Visual Aids > CSS Layout Backgrounds.

Creating more sophisticated layouts

The two-**column layout** you created represents a good foundation for a website. You would refer to this as a "Two-column fixed-width layout with a header and footer." However, you may be looking for more options. For example, what about a three-column layout, or a liquid layout in which the content adjusts to the width of the browser (also referred to as a flexible or fluid layout)? It is beyond the scope of this book to walk through all these options. However, Dreamweaver does offer a way to create different layouts on-the-fly. You can choose from a gallery of new layouts whenever you create a new page.

Follow these steps to choose a new layout

Step-by-Step

1. Choose File > New and make sure HTML is selected as the Page Type. In the Layout column, the None option is the default, but you can also choose from a number of pre-made options.
2. Choose the 2 column liquid, left sidebar, header and footer option. Notice that a small thumbnail with a description of the layout appears as seen in Figure 6-22. Click Create.

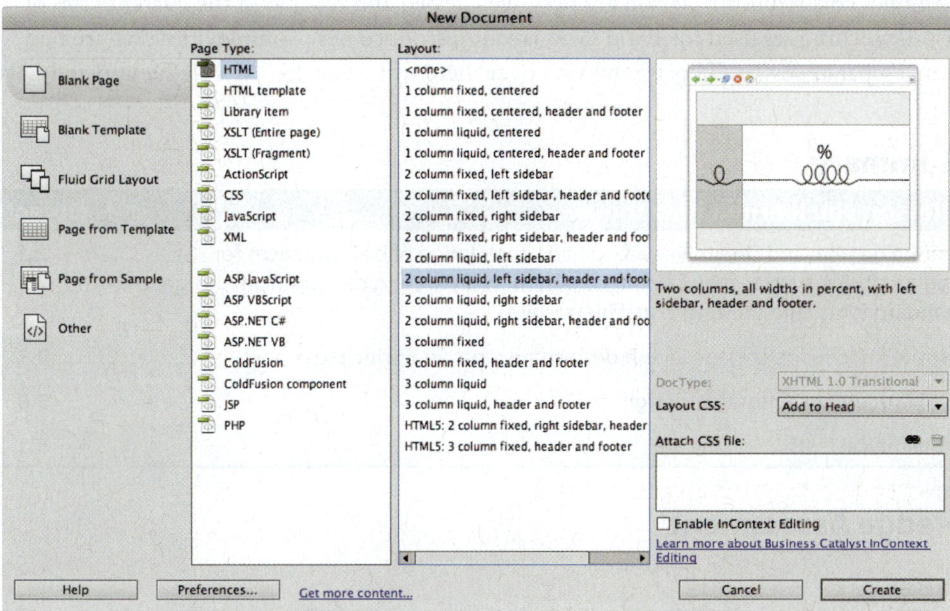

Figure 6-22: The thumbnail preview of the two-column layout.

3. Choose File > Save As and when prompted, save this file as **2col_liquid.html**. Choose File > Preview in Browser and adjust the width of the browser and you will see that the width of the container page adjusts, as well as the content within. Unlike the layout you created earlier, you might choose this layout because it is more adaptable for different sized monitors.

   Take a moment to read the text in this page. It mentions that the code for this page has been commented. You'll take a look at this code now, in order to better understand the pros and cons of using these pre-generated pages.

   Close the browser and return to Dreamweaver.
4. Click the Code View button and scroll to the top if necessary. The code in light gray represents comments that describe virtually every line of the CSS. So why is there a need to comment this file so heavily? To make a long story short, the code in this file is very robust and is optimized for cross-browser display. This means there are styles that address various bugs across different browsers, as well as other relatively advanced CSS code.

   This presents a dilemma: You will benefit most from these templates only as long as you know how to modify them. In order to modify them effectively, however, you need to understand the rules of HTML and CSS relatively well. There is a limit to how far a WYSIWYG (What You See Is What You Get) application can take you in learning these rules.

   This should not stop you in exploring these page layouts. They are extremely useful, and can be incredible time-savers. Just be aware that reverse-engineering how a page works can also be time-consuming, and that the answers may lie in the rules of HTML and CSS, and not in the Dreamweaver application.
5. Choose File > Close All and save any files if prompted.

Certification Ready 5.8

How do you use CSS Starter Layouts?

Certification Ready 2.1

What are fixed and flexible page sizing and when should they be used?

Dreamweaver Fluid Grid Layout

A new feature in Dreamweaver CS6 is the addition of Fluid Grid Layouts. This is a system for creating websites that are alternatively known as adaptive or responsive, meaning that the layout of your pages changes depending on the size of the user's screen. The model for this form of layout is in many ways radically different than the techniques presented in this lesson. Fluid Grid Layout uses a combination of HTML5, CSS3, and JavaScript to create layouts that are optimized for mobile devices and monitor screens of different sizes.

The techniques covered in this lesson are very well-tested and reliable in the current crop of web browsers; the techniques used for Fluid Grid layout introduce new complexities that are best covered in a separate lesson. This is why we cover them in Lesson 15 "Mobile Design and Layout."

Skill Summary

In this lesson you learned how to:	Objective
Demonstrate general and Dreamweaver-specific knowledge of best practices for designing a website, such as maintaining consistency, separating content from design, using standard fonts, and utilizing visual hierarchy	2.1
Demonstrate knowledge of page layout design concepts and principles	2.3
Use CSS to implement a reusable design	5.8
Conduct technical tests	6.1

Knowledge Assessment

True/False

Circle T if the statement is true or F if the statement is false.

T F **1.** AP divs are more flexible layout tools than CSS floats.

T F **2.** You can manually resize a CSS floated div in the Design view clicking and dragging the edges of the container.

T F **3.** You can manually resize a CSS floated div in the Design view by typing values for width and height in the Property Inspector.

T F **4.** You would use the CSS clear property on an image to create a "text wrap" effect on your page.

T F **5.** The default orientation for list items is vertical.

T F **6.** If there is no height property, the height of a div is dictated by its content.

T F **7.** Floated layouts are generally more flexible and adaptable than Absolutely Positioned layouts.

T F **8.** You can create the appearance of a hyperlink on text without actually linking to another document.

T F **9.** The most flexible and easy to edit navigation bars are image-based.

T F **10.** Any element on the page can be floated or cleared directly in the Property Inspector without the need for creating a CSS style.

Multiple Choice

Select the best response for the following statements

1. Which of the following are valid values for the CSS float property?

a. left, right, none
b. left, right, center, none
c. left, right, top, bottom, none
d. left, right, center, top, bottom, none

2. You are in the New CSS Rule window and Dreamweaver has automatically created the following rule: `#navigation ul li a`. If you pressed the Less Specific button, what would the result be?

a. `#navigation`
b. `ul li a`
c. `a`
d. None of the above

3. The CSS float property would allow you to ________

a. Create a horizontal navigation bar
b. Create thumbnail images
c. Reset the margins of any given element
d. None of the above

4. Which of the following statements best describes what happens when the CSS style `clear:both` is applied to an image?

a. The image will always remain below the previous element on the page.
b. No floated elements are allowed on either side of the image.
c. All margins are automatically reset on the image.
d. The image is removed from the default flow of HTML.

5. You could create a rollover effect on a hyperlink by creating a style for which of the following pseudo-classes?

a. `a:link`
b. `a:visited`
c. `a:hover`
d. `a:active`

6. Which of the following is true about CSS background images?

a. They can only be positioned using pixel values.
b. They do not support transparency.
c. They are repeated horizontally and vertically by default.
d. They are also referred to as "inline" images.

7. If you needed the background color of a div-based column to stretch to the bottom of a container, which of the following techniques could you use?
   a. Set the height value of the div-based column to 100%.
   b. Set the height value of the div-based column to auto.
   c. Apply a customized background image to the column or its container and repeat it vertically.
   d. Apply a background-color to the div-based column and set the v-space to 100%.

8. The menus for Float and Clear are found in which category of the CSS rule definition window?
   a. Type
   b. Block
   c. Box
   d. Positioning

9. If you wanted to remove the underline style from a hyperlink which category would you choose in the CSS rule definitions window
   a. Type
   b. Border.
   c. Positioning
   d. List

10. If you wanted to use one of Dreamweaver's pre-created three column layouts where would you start?
    a. The New Document window
    b. The Insert Panel
    c. File > Browse in Bridge
    d. Choose Site > Modify Site

Competency Assessment

Project 6-1 Floating an image

As the designer for the Serenity Spa website, you have been asked to create a "text wrap" effect on a page.

1. Open the page as **float.html** located within your lesson folder.
2. Click once at the beginning of the first paragraph. Now choose Insert > Image and in the Select Image Source dialog box, choose the **relaxing.jpg** image from your lesson folder.
3. Make sure the image is still selected and then click the New CSS Rule button in the CSS Styles panel. Click on the menu for Selector Type and choose Class. In the Selector Name text field, type **.floatimage** and click OK.
4. In the CSS Rule definition dialog box, click on the Box category, then click on the Float drop-down menu and choose right. Click OK.

5. In the Property Inspector, there is a Class drop-down menu, which by default is set to None.
6. Click on the Class drop-down menu, choose floatimage. With the class applied, the image will now be removed from the flow of the text and be pushed far right to the edge of the container.
7. In the CSS Styles panel, double-click the .floatimage rule and in the Box category uncheck the Same for All checkbox for the Margin, then type a value of 10 for the Top and 10 for the Right. Make sure the unit is pixels. Press OK. The image now is set off from the text, adding needed space.
8. Choose File > Save but keep this file open for the next exercise.

Creating columns with floats

Project 6-2

You need to begin creating the basics of a two-column layout for your website, Serenity Spa.

1. In the Files panel, double-click on the **float.html** page if it is not already open from the last exercise. Your first step will be to add a div container. Click at the beginning of the first paragraph and press Return a few times to add space. Then click once at the very top of the page.
2. In the Insert panel, click the Insert Div Tag button, and the Insert Div Tag dialog box opens. Here you can choose where you would like the new div element to be inserted.
3. In the Insert Div Tag dialog box, make sure the Insert drop-down menu is set to At insertion point (which is the default).
4. Type **sidebar** in the ID text field, then press the New CSS Rule button.
5. The New CSS Rule definition dialog box opens. Click OK. You will now add a few simple styles to the main div.
6. In the CSS rule definition dialog box, click on the Background category and type **#999** into the Background-color text field to add a gray background color. Then click on the Box category and type **250** in the Width text field, and make sure px is the value.
7. Click the Float menu and choose Right. Click OK. Click OK again in the Insert Div Tag dialog box. Your sidebar appears with placeholder text.
8. Click on the **relaxing.jpg** image to select it. Cut the image. Click once inside the sidebar and paste the image. Select the text on the page and then cut and paste it into the sidebar column. Click on the Insert Div Tag button in the Insert panel. Click on the Insert drop-down menu and choose the After Tag option, and then in the drop-down menu to the right choose `<div id = "sidebar">`. Type main in the ID text field and then click OK. This adds a new empty div.
9. Now you'll style the main column. Click once inside the main div and then in the tag selector at the bottom left, click on the div#main tag.
10. In the CSS Styles panel, click New Style. The #main id should be picked up in the Selector Name field. Click OK. Click on the Background-color property and choose a light tan color. Click on the Box category and for the Width type **600** and then click on the Float menu and choose left.
11. Save your page.

Proficiency Assessment

Project 6-3 Three Columns

Take it up a notch with your layout practice by using a three column layout. If you're wondering about sites that employ 3 columns, you can take a look at *www.apple.com* as an example.

Get Ready. Launch Dreamweaver CS6 if you haven't already.

1. Create a new blank HTML page.
2. Employ the methods you used earlier to add divs to your page.
3. Adjust accordingly with CSS.

Project 6-4 Background images for Divs

So far with divs, you've seen their colored backgrounds and how to make them clear. Another option is to use a background image for the div as a pattern. Use the image **recycle_bag.gif** located in this lesson's images folder as a background image for this exercise.

Get Ready. Launch Dreamweaver CS6 if you haven't already.

1. Create a new blank HTML page. Add a div to the page.
2. Use the CSS styles options to assign an image to the background of the div.

CSS3 Transitions and Web Fonts

Key Terms

- Browser Font Support
- CSS3
- CSS Transitions
- CSS Web Fonts
- Easing
- Font Licensing
- Timing Function

Skill	Objective
Add animation and interactivity to content	4.8
Organize web page layout with relative and absolutely-positioned div tags and CSS styles	5.2
Modify text and text properties	5.3

Business Case

The Internet has evolved quite a bit since its inception. Among the new tricks we can do are transitions for page elements. The Organic Utopia owners have chosen to be on the cutting edge and employ this technology to set them apart from their competitors, who are still relying on more conventional approaches. The owners also want to use custom fonts for their company's website—something that was not practical just a few years ago, but now is. Using CSS3 capabilities in Dreamweaver CS6, you'll be able to create dynamic transitions and incorporate any font that the client wants.

Introduction

Before you begin, reset your workspace to ensure your tools and panels are consistent. For more information, see "Resetting the Dreamweaver Workspace" in the Starting Up section of this book.

In this lesson, you will work with several files from the dw07lessons folder. Make sure that you have loaded the dwlessons folder onto your hard-drive. For more information, see "Loading lesson files" in the Starting Up section of this book.

Before you can proceed with the exercises in this section, you need to create site settings that point to the dw07lessons folder. Go to Site > New Site, or for details on creating a site, refer to Lesson 2, "Setting Up a New Site."

Understanding the role of CSS3

Cascading Style Sheets is a separate language from HTML; however, both languages are constantly evolving. The original CSS1 specification was released in 1996 and included many of the basic CSS properties used today, such as background-color, font-family and so on. Over the years, new versions of CSS have emerged with revisions and additions to the original specification. **CSS3** is the latest version of the language and offers a number of new CSS properties that give designers new tools for adding style to their pages.

The details of the evolution of CSS are not as important as understanding the key issue: browser support. Although CSS3 offers a number of exciting and useful features, designers and developers need to know which features the different web browsers can reliably support. There are a tremendous number of new features in CSS3, and these features have different levels of browser support. Some features you can use today very reliably, others may not be supported for years. The architects of CSS3 have broken up the language into categories called "modules"; examples include Backgrounds, and Borders and Animation, among others. In this lesson, you'll learn how to use CSS Transitions from the Animation module, and Web Fonts from the CSS Fonts module.

Certification Ready 4.8

What tools are used for creating animation and interactive content?

Other tools for animation and interactivity

CSS3 transitions are just the latest option for creating interactive and animated elements on the Web. You will be looking at other techniques including Flash animation (Lesson 10, "Adding Flash, Video, and Sound Content") and JavaScript (Lesson 14, "Adding Interactivity with the Spry Framework"). The decision as to which version to use is based on a number of factors including your target audience and any technical limitations. We discuss these limitations in more detail in the relevant lessons, but here is a brief overview:

- CSS3 transitions are best suited for user inteface elements such as buttons and navigation bars, however they are not visibile on all browsers, particularly older ones. But CSS3 transitions are extremely well-supported on modern mobile browsers and are often the best option for that audience.
- JavaScript animation and interactivity are more reliable than CSS3 transitions for browsers on the desktop and generally work well for mobile. They are not optimized for mobile however and more complex JavaScript animation may be harder to style with CSS.
- Flash animation can give you more creative freedom than either CSS3 or JavaScript animation and capabilities such as the drawing tools and the other features of the Flash authoring program is far more capable than anything found in CSS3 or JavaScript . The current trend, however, is to move away from using Flash for user interface animation and to reserve it for dedicated animation projects such as animated movies and games. A large reason for this has to do with lack of support for Flash content on mobile devices such as the iPhone and iPad.
- Adobe Edge is one of a few applications that promises a workflow allowing you to create animations whose output is CSS3 code, not the SWF format (used in Flash). Adobe Edge has a timeline editor very similar to Adobe Flash Professional and allows you to add motion to graphics and HTML elements. When working with Edge, you are working directly with HTML files and the animation is created with CSS3 code. This means that you could create a page in Dreamweaver, open this page within Edge, and then create a sophisticated animation. When complete, the animation requires no special browser plugin, just a modern browser that supports CSS3.

Certification Ready 4.8

How do you use Adobe Edge workflow for creating animations that will be placed into HTML5 web pages?

Adding a CSS Transition

CSS Transitions in Dreamweaver CS6 offer you a way to create simple animations on your page using only CSS. This is in contrast to the traditional method of creating effects, such as image rollovers, using JavaScript or Flash.

The basic concept of **CSS Transitions** is this: an object is animated by changing a property (or properties) over time. For example, in the following exercise you will start with a box that has its height property set to 350 pixels. You will then animate the height property down to 50 pixels over a period of two seconds. The result will be a slow collapsing effect when the user places their cursor over the box.

You'll start with a simple example file, and then in a later exercise, you will apply CSS transitions to the Organic Utopia layout.

Follow these steps to create a CSS transition

Step-by-Step

1. Open the **07_csstransitions.html** document. Currently, this page has a single style rule for the ID `#box`. You should take a look at these styles before proceeding.
2. In the Design view, click the edge of the box to select it. To be sure that you have the actual box selected, check for the blue outline that will appear around the box, which confirms that it is selected. In the CSS Styles panel, click the All button if necessary, and then click the `#box` style. This will expose the properties currently used. (If your Properties panel does not look like Figure 7-1, click on the "Show only set properties" icon in the lower-left corner of the CSS Styles panel.)

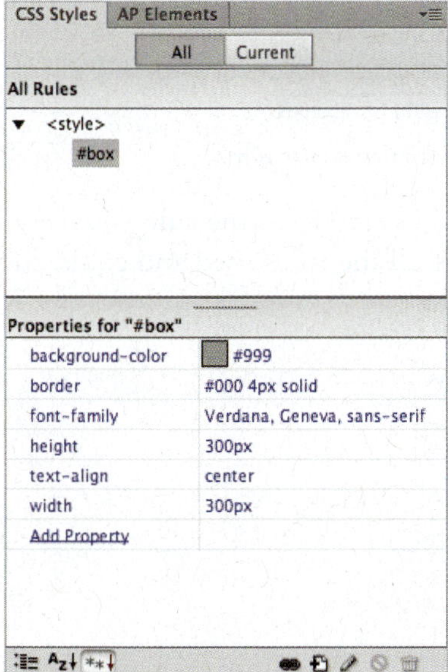

Figure 7-1: *The CSS properties associated with the CSS ID* `#box`.

The properties used here are `background-color`, `border`, `height`, `width`, `font-family`, and `text-align`. All these properties (and many more within CSS) can be animated using transitions.

Pay particular attention to the `height` property and the value, currently set to 300 pixels. You will now create a single transition that will animate the height of the box from the original 300 pixels to a more narrow height.

3. Choose Window > CSS Transitions to open the CSS Transitions window. This window lists all the existing transitions used in a document, and also allows you to Create, Remove, and Edit transitions.

4. Click the + sign in the upper-left of the CSS Transitions window; the New Transition window appears (Figure 7-2).

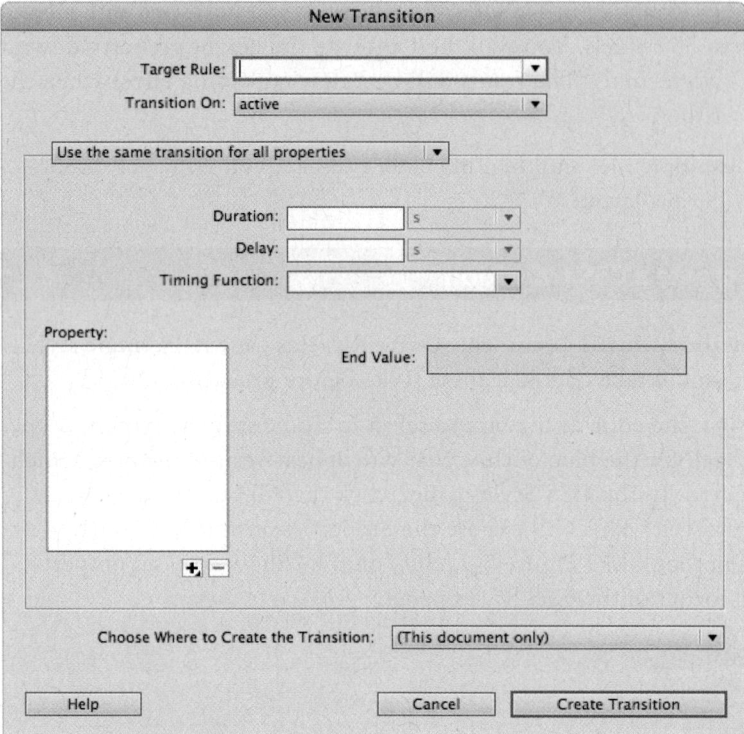

Figure 7-2: The New Transition window offers a number of options for you to create transition effects.

5. Click the Target Rule menu. The only choice available is for `#box`, the rule you examined in Step 2. In more complex documents, you would see all the rules used and could choose any of them. Choose `#box` from this drop-down menu.

6. Click the Transition On menu to see all the options available as seen in Figure 7-3. A transition starts in one state and then moves to another, but something must trigger the transition. This menu lists the various options: active, checked, disabled, enabled, focus, hover, indeterminate, and target. You'll learn more about these options shortly.

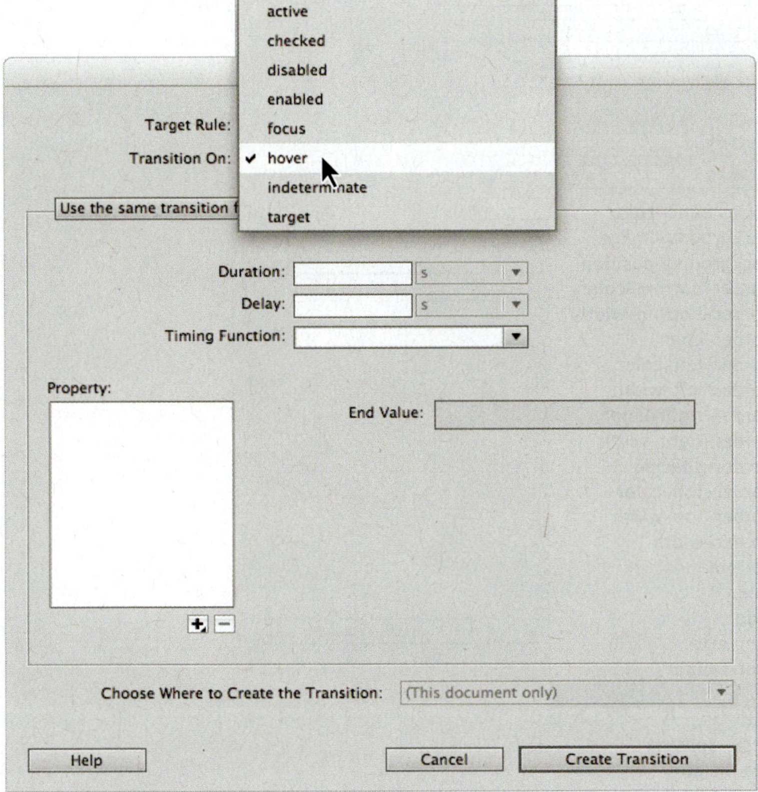

Figure 7-3*: The options available within the Transition on menu.*

7. Choose the Hover option.
8. Click inside the Duration field and type 2.

   CSS Transitions provide a way to control the speed of animation changes for one or more CSS properties. In this instance, you are stating that you want this transition to last two seconds. You will return to the two other options—Delay and Timing Function—in the next exercise, but first you need to define which property you want to animate.

9. Click the + sign at the bottom of the Property section. A menu appears with the entire list of CSS properties you can control. Select the height property as seen in Figure 7-4.

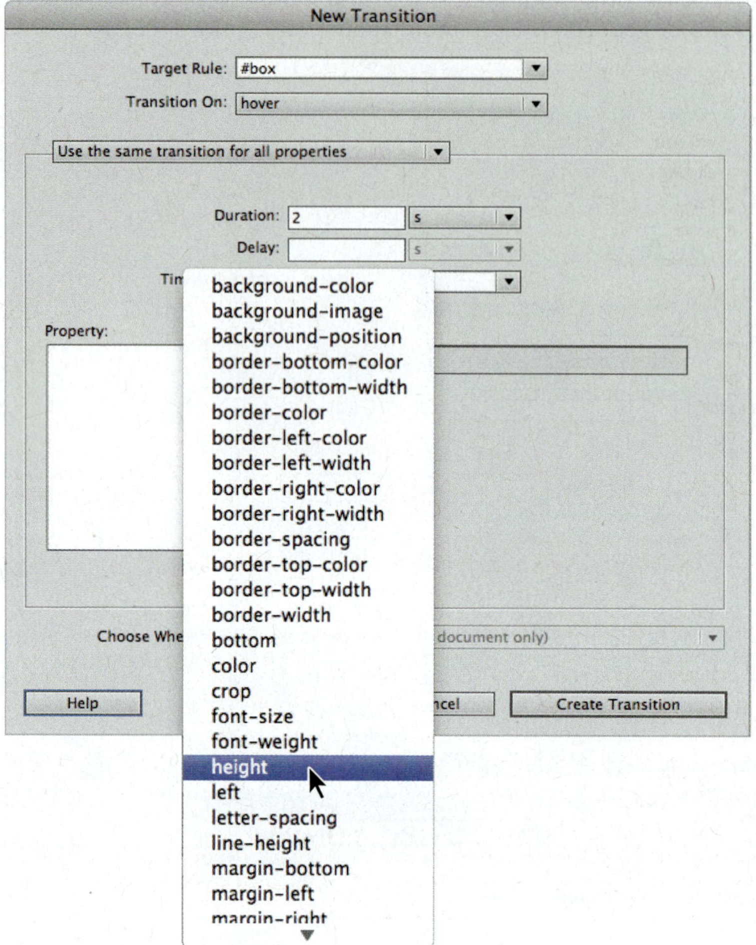

Figure 7-4*: Choose the height property from the available list of CSS properties.*

Take Note...

As this list shows, you cannot animate every single CSS property. For the official list of available properties visit:
http://www.w3.org/TR/css3-transitions/#animatable-properties-10

10. Click inside the field labeled End Value, type **50**, and make sure the menu to the right remains on pixels (px). The starting height of the box is 300 pixels; using this transition, you will change it to 50 pixels over a period of two seconds when the user hovers over the box.

    Click the Create Transition button to add it.

11. Choose File > Save As, type **07_csstransitions_work** in the File name and click Save to save this file in the dw07lessons folder. Choose File > Preview in Browser.

    Place your cursor inside the top of the box; you will see the box animate from the original height of 300 down to 50 pixels. As you move your cursor off the box, it begins to animate back to its original height as seen in Figure 7-5.

Figure 7-5: *When the user hovers over the box, it animates from a starting height of 300 pixels to an ending height of 50.*

This is a very basic example of a single CSS transition. In the next exercise, you will add more transitions and learn how to edit your existing one.

12. Close both the browser window and the original **07_csstransitions.html** page. Return to Dreamweaver. Keep the **07_csstransitions_work.html** file open, since you'll be working with it in the next exercise.

What if you can't see the transition?

Learning More

You might not be able to see the transition effect in the last exercise if your web browser does not support the transition property. The support for CSS3 Transitions is relatively new and not all properties are equally supported across all browsers, specifically the most popular versions of Internet Explorer 6, 7, 8, and 9.

At the time of this writing, Microsoft has indicated that Internet Explorer 10 is scheduled to support CSS Transitions. The following online resource provides a useful table to help you see the level of support for CSS Transitions for past, present, and future (planned) browsers.

http://caniuse.com/#feat=css-transitions

Modifying a CSS Transition

Now that you have seen how a CSS Transition works, you'll now see how to modify the existing transition speed, add a delay, and adjust the timing of the animation using a feature called Easing.

Before you get started with the modifications, you'll take a quick look at the CSS code that Dreamweaver creates in the background.

Step-by-Step

Follow these steps to modify a CSS transition

1. Click the Code View in your document and locate the `<style>` section at the top; specifically, the `#box` rule. Notice that there are five lines of code that were created by adding the transition, starting with `-webkit-transition: all 2s;` and ending with `transition: all 2s;` (Highlighted in Figure 7-6).

```
8   #box {
9       background-color: #999;
10      height: 300px;
11      width: 300px;
12      font-family:Verdana, Geneva, sans-serif;
13      border:#000 4px solid;
14      text-align: center;
15      -webkit-transition: all 2s;
16      -moz-transition: all 2s;
17      -ms-transition: all 2s;
18      -o-transition: all 2s;
19      transition: all 2s;
20  }
21
22  #box:hover {
23      height: 50px;
24  }
```

***Figure 7-6**: The generated transition CSS that was created by Dreamweaver.*

Five lines of code may seem like a lot; however, each line is exactly the same code, and each targets a specific web browser. The code `-webkit-transition: all 2s;` begins with a "vendor-specific prefix" to target Webkit browsers such as Apple Safari and Google Chrome. The code `-moz-transition: all 2s;` targets Mozilla browsers (Firefox). The next two lines, `-ms-transition: all 2s;` and `-o-transition: all 2s;` target Microsoft and Opera browsers.

The last line, `transition: all 2s;` is the "official" CSS3 property name for transitions. The reason for having five lines of almost-identical code is that each browser has its own timeline for supporting a new CSS3 property. For example, Google Chrome may have required the prefix `-webkit` in version 8.0. When it becomes evident that transitions are working reliably and are well-liked by designers, Google Chrome might choose to drop the requirement for the prefix in version 10.0. The goal is for all browsers to eventually support the "official" property transition; the only reason to use the vendor-specific ones would be to provide support for older browsers.

2. Look below the code for the #box style; you will see the style #box:hover. This code represents the trigger you set for the transition in the last exercise.

3. Click the Design view to toggle back to your page. Most likely, you will not need to modify the CSS transition code by hand, but you should understand where you can find it within the CSS, and understand some of the underlying concepts.

4. In your CSS Transitions window, click hover and then press the Pencil icon (✐) to edit the transition (Figure 7-7).

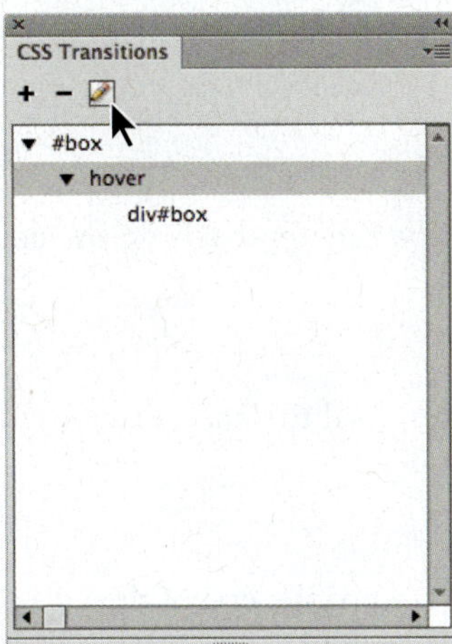

Figure 7-7: Select hover and then click the Pencil icon to edit a transition.

The Edit Transition window opens, allowing you to modify the values you created in the last exercise.

Take Note...

You can also double-click hover *or* div#box *to open this window.*

5. Select the value 2 inside the Duration field and type **0.5**. This will change the duration from two seconds to half a second.

6. Click inside the Delay field, type **1**, and make sure the menu to the right is set to s (for second). Delaying a transition simply means the transition will not begin until one second after the user hovers over the box.

7. Notice that there is a value in the **Timing Function** field set to ease. This is the default setting, so while you didn't set this in the last exercise, Dreamweaver fills it in as though you had.

Learning More

What is easing?

Easing is a term well known in computer animation that you might have seen before, particularly if you have used Adobe Flash. **Easing** allows you to vary the speed of a transition over time. For example, you may want an animation to start off slow and then speed up, or perhaps the reverse: start off quickly and then slow down.

Dreamweaver CS6 has six options for easing:

Linear

Maintains a constant speed for the duration of the transition.

Ease

The animation starts slowly, accelerates, and then slows down when approaching the end of the transition.

Ease-in

The animation begins slowly, and then progressively accelerates until the end of the transition.

Ease-out

The animation starts quickly, and then progressively slows down until the end of the transition.

Ease-in-out

The animation starts slowly at the beginning, maintains a steady rate in the middle, and then slows down toward the end of the transition.

Cubic-bezier(x1,y1,x2,y2)

Allows you to create a custom animation using the cubic bezier model. A sample value might be `cubic-bezier(0.4,0.2,0.8,0.7)`. This particular example would result in an animation that starts off slowly and speeds up toward the end of the transition.

8. Click the Timing Function menu and choose `ease-out` (Figure 7-8). The ease-out timing will cause the animation to start off quickly and then slow down. (Note that this effect will be difficult to see with the new half second duration.)

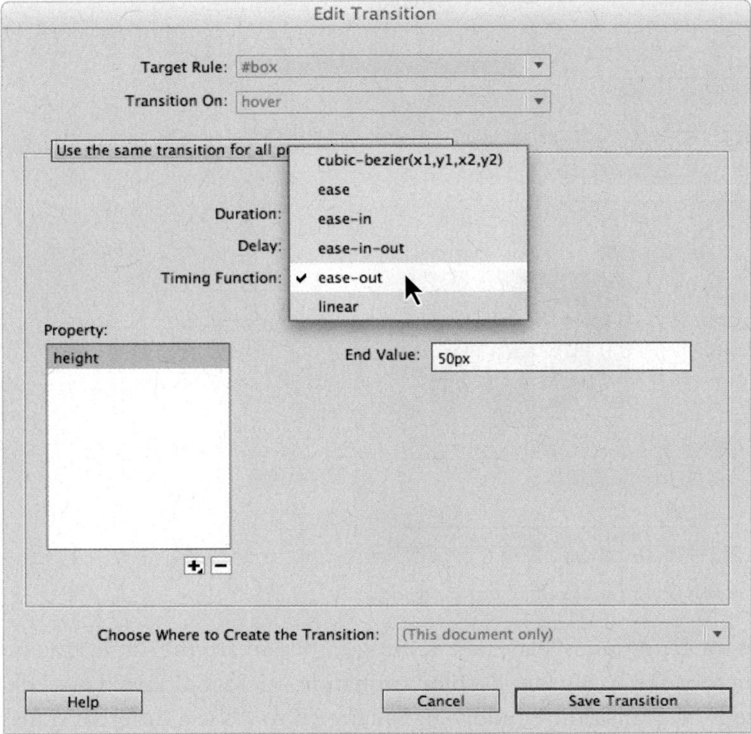

Figure 7-8: *Choose ease-out from the menu of Timing Functions.*

9. Click the + sign at the bottom of the Property section. You will now animate a second property to go with the height transition.

10. Choose background-color from the list, and then click the End-Value swatch; the color picker appears. Choose a dark pink color, such as `#C36` (Figure 7-9).

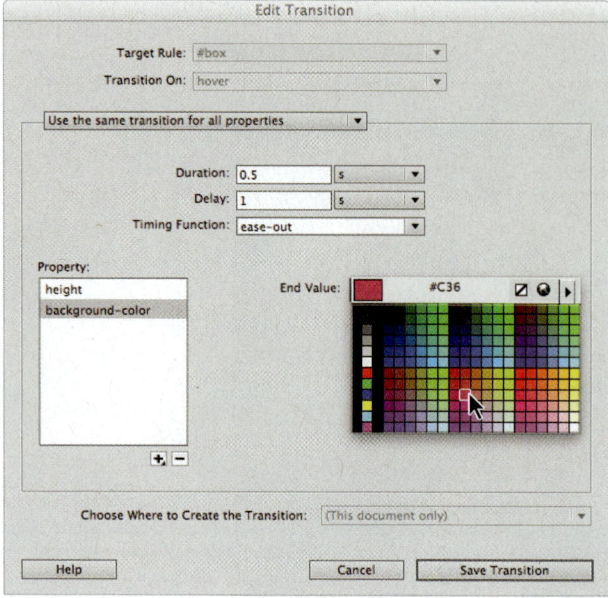

***Figure 7-9**: Choose a dark pink color for the* `background-color` *property.*

Notice that the values for Duration, Delay, and Timing Function are the same. If you want to create separate values for the background-color animation, you would need to click the menu at the top of the Edit Transition window and change it to "Use a different transition for each property."

11. Click Save Transition, and then choose File > Save. Preview the page in your browser and place your cursor at the top of the box as seen in the second image in Figure 7-10. Remember that there is a one-second delay that you added in Step 5; after this delay, the box will change height rapidly and simultaneously fade from gray to pink.

Take Note...

CSS3 transitions are supported in all major browsers except Internet Explorer. The current release of Internet Explorer is version 9 (as of this writing), however the next version (10) will support CSS3 transitions. For a detailed look at browser support visit: http://caniuse.com/#feat=css-transitions.

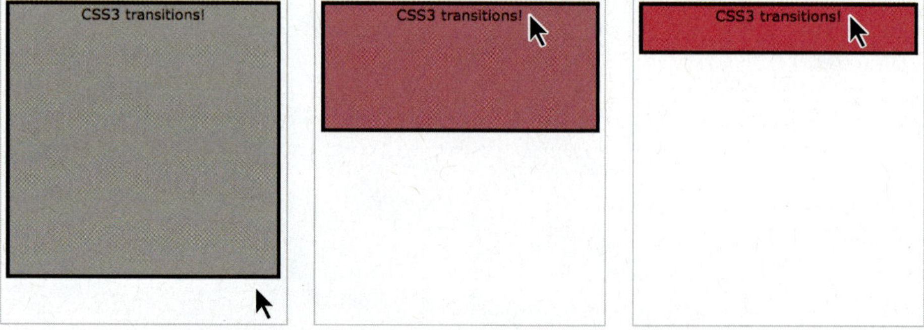

***Figure 7-10**: After a delay of one second, the box quickly reduces its height and animates its background color.*

12. Close the browser as well as the **07_csstransitions_work.html** file.

In these two exercises, you learned the fundamentals of CSS Transitions on a sample file. Now you'll apply what you've learned to a more realistic layout.

Adding CSS Transitions to a navigation menu

User interface elements such as navigation bars, menus, or buttons are great to use with CSS Transitions. Subtle animation can add an extra bit of sophistication and style to your pages.

Follow these steps to create a navigation menu with CSS Transitions

Step-by-Step

1. Open the **07_nav_transition.html** document by double-clicking it in the Files panel.

2. Choose File > Preview in Browser to view this page in the browser. Hover over the navigation as seen in Figure 7-11 to see the default styles. The effect you are seeing is a traditional CSS2 hover effect, the background color of a list item changes to a lighter green when the cursor is hovering over it. However, the change is instant, in CSS2 syntax, you have no control over how long it takes to go from the darker green to the lighter green. In CSS3 syntax, you do have this control using transitions. You will add a transition to make the hover effect more interesting.

Figure 7-11: The current hover effect is either on or off.

Close the browser and return to Dreamweaver.

3. If your CSS Transitions window is not currently open, do so now by choosing Window > CSS Transitions.

4. Click the + sign to open the New Transition window, and then click the Target Rule. Choose the `#navigation ul li a` style as seen in Figure 7-12. (This is currently the style for list items that are also hyperlinks inside the navigation div.)

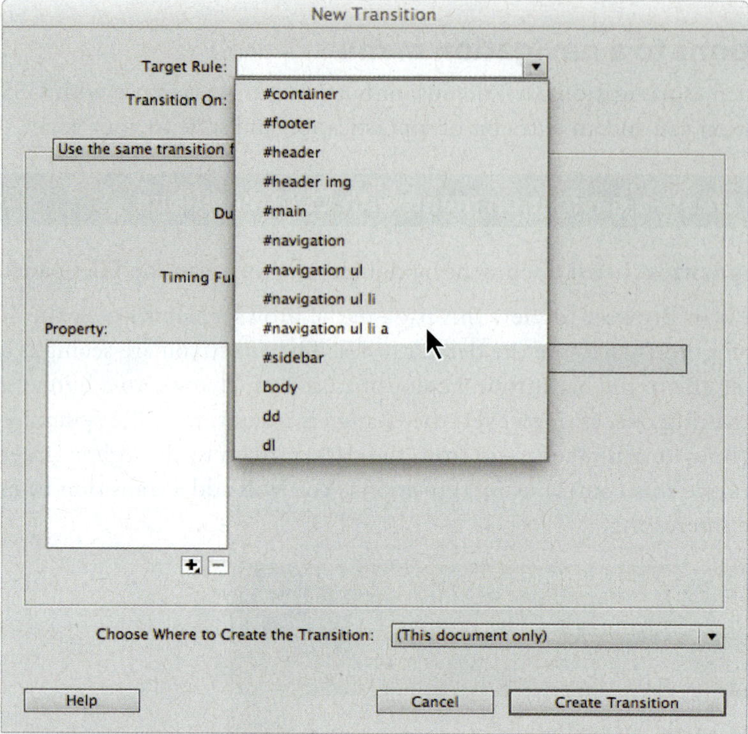

Figure 7-12: Choose the `#navigation ul li a` *style from the menu.*

5. Click the Transition On menu and choose hover.

6. Click the + sign in the Property section and choose `background-color` from the list. For Duration, type **400**; click the menu to the right and change it from s to ms (milliseconds). Leave the delay set to 0. For the Timing Function, choose ease-in-out and for the End Value, type **#9FCC41**. (This color matches the one currently used.)

   You'll now combine another effect by changing the foreground color of the text inside the navigation.

7. Click the + sign in the Property section and choose `color` from the list. By default, this second property is inheriting all the values added for the first value. You want more control, so you'll have to define separate rules for this `color` property.

8. At the top of your New Transition window, click the menu and change it to Use a different transition for each property (Figure 7-13).

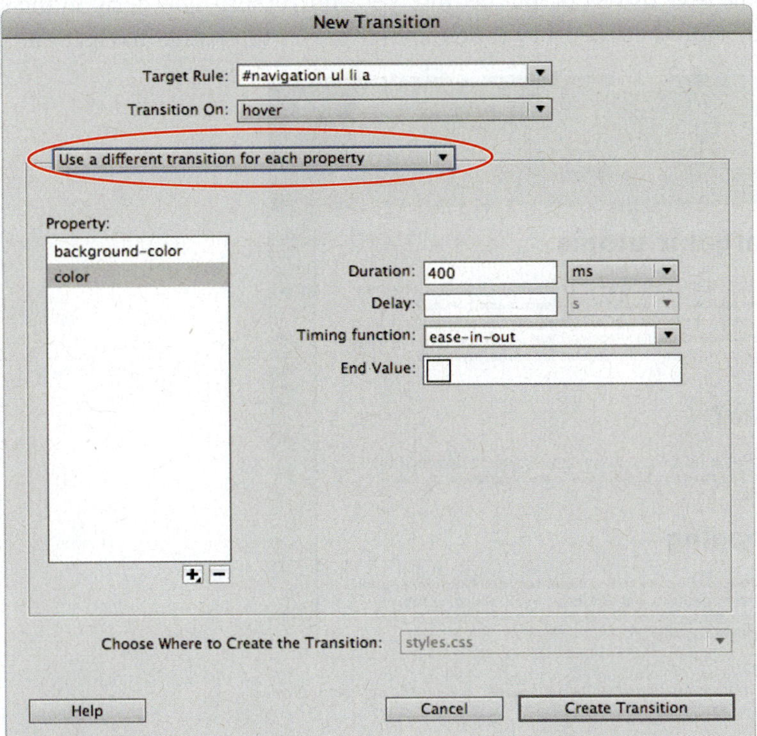

Figure 7-13: *You must specify whether you want to set different transitions for each property.*

9. Make sure the color property is selected. In the Duration field, type **500**; click the menu to the right and choose ms if it is not already selected. In the Delay field, type **100**; click the menu to the right and choose ms. Leave the Timing Function set to ease-in-out. Lastly, click the End Value swatch and choose the dark green value `#060`.

   Click Create Transition. Notice that your CSS Transitions panel now reads [5 instances] for hover. This automatically reflects the number of list items in your navigation.

10. Choose File > Save All, and then preview your page in the browser. Hover over the navigation as seen in Figure 7-14 and you will see the navigation background color fade up and down slightly. The text also fades, but because you added the 100ms delay in the last step, it creates a subtle fading effect every time the user moves to another navigation.

Figure 7-14*: Adding two separate transitions for the navigation: one for the background color, the other for the color of the text.*

11. Close your browser. Choose File > Close All. Close the CSS Transitions window. You are done with this lesson file.

Using CSS3 for web page layout

In the preceding exercise you learned one small aspect of CSS3 (transitions). However there are other elements of CSS3 that have enormous potential to change the way designers work with page layout and elements such as drop-down menus, accordion panels and other user interface controls.

Currently, the most reliable method of creating these types of page components is to use a combination of HTML, CSS and JavaScript (and perhaps image files for textures or gradients). This is the technique you will learn in Lesson 14 "Adding Interactivity with the Spry Framework." Using some or all the following features found in CSS3 you could create similar controls without any JavaScript or image files.

- **CSS3 Shapes**

Using a combination of the CSS3 border-radius property and CSS3 transforms it is possible to create basic primary shapes such as circles, rectangles, diamonds, arrows and more. These can be used instead of graphics to create the components of a navigation bar, for example.

- **CSS3 Gradients**

The CSS3 gradient feature can replace the type of linear and radial gradients currently created in applications such as Illustrator and Photo-shop. The linear-gradient property could be applied to button or navigation menu background for example.

- **CSS3 `:target` selector**

Not all of CSS3 is related to visual styling. Improvements in functionality are also part of the specification. For example the CSS3 pseudo-lector named :target. This feature is similar to the existing :hover pseudo-selector (which defines what happens when a user places their cursor over a link). The :target pseudo-selector allows you to target sections of an element (such as a paragraph) and do something to it such as turn its visibility off or on. In terms of page components you could use :target to create a tabbed system on your pages, something that today is most often accomplished with JavaScript.

There are many more areas of CSS3 to explore, the dilemma with all these cool features comes down to browser support. If you decide to use any CSS3 features (especially those that provide significant functionality such as a menu) you need to take a hard look at the current state of browser support for the feature and look into using fallbacks if the feature is not supported.

Certification Ready 5.2
How do you use CSS3 to organize the layout of web page?

The basics of web fonts

The limited choice of fonts for the Web has been a problem for many years. (The way fonts work on the Web was outlined in Lesson 3, "Adding Text and Images.") The core issue is that if you define a specific font in your CSS and a visitor to your site does not have that font, a substitute font is used. If you do not specify any font-family at all, the default font will be Times New Roman. Unfortunately, the list of fonts that are guaranteed to be installed on all users' computers is very small. As a result, over the years designers have looked for alternatives and workarounds to this limitation, but none of these techniques have had overwhelming success.

Certification Ready 5.3
What do viewers see if they do not have the selected font installed or if "Default Font" is selected as the font type?

However, there is now an accepted technique called Web Fonts in Dreamweaver CS6; technically, this is a feature of CSS3 called `@font-face`. The use of web fonts has gained industry support from designers and developers, and more importantly, from companies that make and license fonts. Simply put, **CSS web fonts** allow you to embed any font within a page by declaring the font you want to display and placing this font on your web server. When a user visits your site, their browser renders the page using this font wherever specified. Adding web fonts is a straight-forward process in Dreamweaver CS6; however, there are some details (technical and legal) that you need to be aware of.

Adding web fonts to your site

In this exercise, you will add the web font "Droid Sans Bold" (which is licensed for web use) to your website, embed that font so that it is available for use on a page, and then style a heading with the new web font.

Follow these steps to style text using a web font

Step-by-Step

1. Open the **07_webfonts.html** document by double-clicking it in the Files panel.

   There are a few steps you should take before adding a web font. In this example, you will style the first heading, "Welcome to organic utopia." You should first understand where the current style comes from.

2. In the Design view, click anywhere inside the heading, "Welcome to organic utopia." You can easily determine this is a Heading 1 element in two ways: 1) The tag selector indicates this is an <h1>; and 2) In the HTML section of the Property Inspector at the bottom of your page, you can see that Heading 1 is the value of the Format (Figure 7-15).

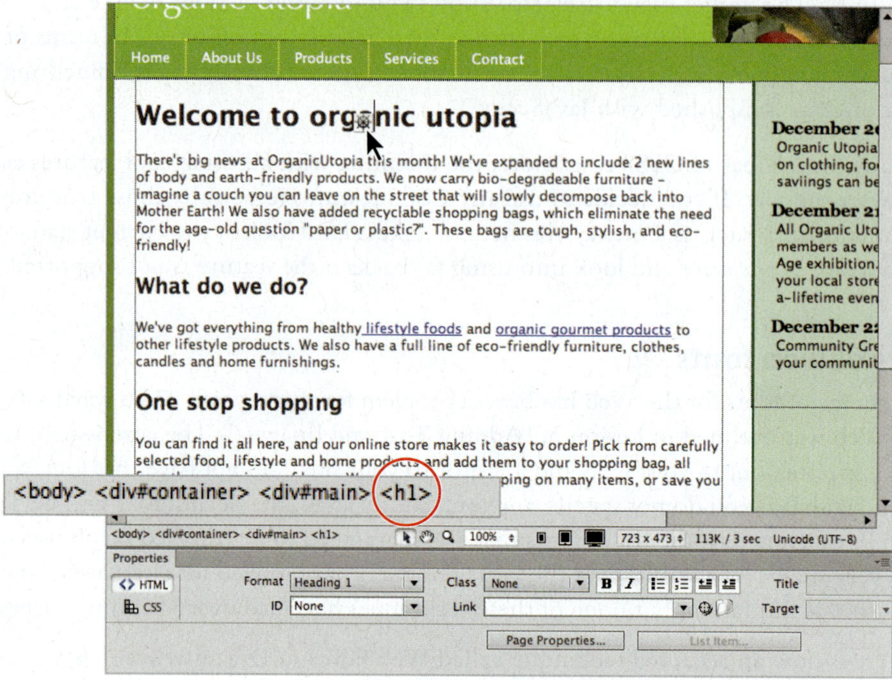

Figure 7-15: You can identify this element as a Heading 1 using either the Tag Selector or the Property Inspector.

You should also determine the style that is currently used for the heading.

3. Click the <h1> tag in the tag selector to highlight the tag. In the CSS Styles panel, click the Current tab. Adjust the height of the Rules and Properties sections inside the CSS Styles panel as needed.

You are looking for the rules used to style this heading, and there are three: `body`, `#container`, and `#main`. This tells you that there is no CSS style for an h1 on this page. Click the `body` rule as seen in Figure 7-16.

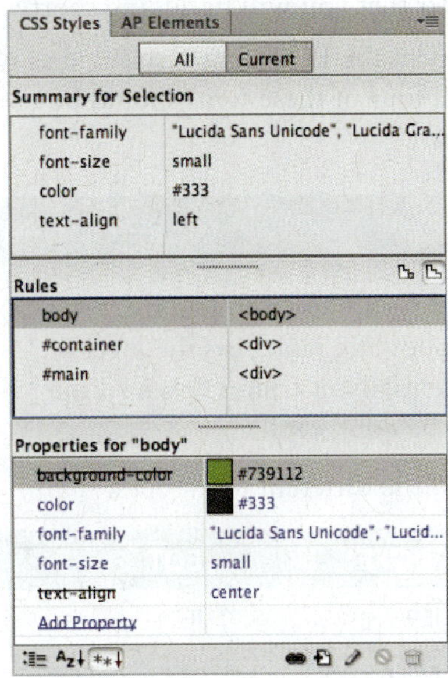

Figure 7-16: *Identifying the styles applied to the h1.*

The body rule indicates that the following properties are used: a `color` of *#333*; the `font-family` *"Lucida Sans Unicode," "Lucida Grande," sans-serif*; and the `font-size` *small*. Remember that the word "cascading" is part of Cascading Style Sheets, and you are seeing that effect here. The font Lucida Sans is defined in the body, and because there are no other styles for h1, the cascade is in effect, so it inherits the color and font-family styles.

Lucida Sans is a font that is extremely common on most users' computer systems; you'll now add a web font that is not so common.

4. Choose Modify > Web Fonts; the Web Fonts Manager window opens. This dialog box will allow you to embed fonts that are located in your system.

5. Click Add Font; the Add Web Font dialog box appears (Figure 7-17).

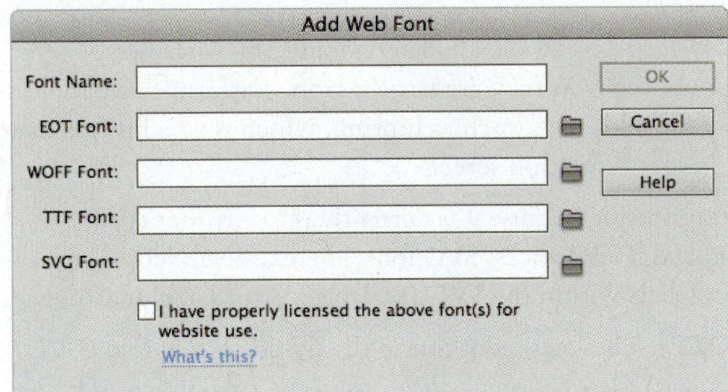

Figure 7-17: *The Add Web Font dialog box allows you to point to web fonts on your system.*

6. Click inside the Font Name field and type **Droid Sans Bold**. This typeface was created specifically as an open-source font for screen use and we have provided it for you in your lesson folder.

7. Click the Folder icon immediately to the right of the field labeled EOT Font; the Open window appears. Navigate within your dw07lessons folder to the web fonts folder and locate the file **DroidSans-Bold-webfont.eot**. The only files you are allowed to select are .eot files. There are actually additional font files in this folder that you will be adding shortly.

8. Choose **DroidSans-Bold-webfont.eot** and click Open; the EOT font is selected as well as the other three options: WOFF, TTF, and SVG. All four of these fonts should be used to ensure maximum compatibility across all web browsers.

Learning More

Browser Font Support

The use of web fonts has been complicated because you cannot use a single font format and have it supported across all browsers. The following table lists the level of **browser font support** for the different font types. Essentially, it comes down to the need to include them all if you want your font styles to be consistent.

The following table lists the various levels of support for the different font-types:

BROWSER	OTF & TTF	SVG	WOFF	EOT
IE	IE9	—	IE9	IE5+
FIREFOX	FF3.5	FF3.5	FF3.6	—
CHROME	Chrome 4	Chrome 0.3	Chrome 5	—
SAFARI	3.1	3.1	—	—
OPERA	Opera 10.00	Opera 9	—	—
iOS	—	iOS 1	—	—
ANDROID	2.2	—	—	—

- **OpenType (OTF)**: A widespread font format that is heavily supported by the industry. Initially developed as a collaboration between Adobe and Microsoft, one of the primary advantages of OpenType is cross-platform support. However, there are additional typesetting features, including glyph support, that make OpenType fonts the primary font of choice for professional font foundries.
- **TrueType (TTF)**: Originally developed by Apple and later adopted by Microsoft, TrueType fonts are still widely in use today as they are largely cross-platform compatible and also offer sophisticated typesetting controls, such as hinting, which is a technique that improves the quality of the font in low resolution screens.
- **SVG**: A vector-based format that is notable because it is currently the only font type supported by Apple's iOS for iPod and iPad devices. SVG fonts are text documents that define the font outlines as vector objects within the SVG (Scalable Vector Graphic) language.
- **Web Open Font Format (WOFF)**: The latest addition to the world of web fonts, WOFF has the potential to become a standard for web fonts, since it is in the final stages of being recommended as a standard by the World Wide Web Consortium (W3C). One of the key benefits of WOFF is the ability to heavily compress the font files and optimize them for distribution over an Internet connection.
- **Embedded OpenType (EOT)**: A variation on OpenType created by Microsoft and largely supported only by Internet Explorer. EOT has a variety of copy-protection features built-in, designed to prevent copying of fonts.

9. Click the checkbox labeled, "I have properly licensed the above font(s) for website use." This is a required step and will be explained in more detail at the end of this lesson.

10. Click OK. You will now see Droid Sans Bold listed in your Available Web Fonts (Figure 7-18).

    Click the Done button in the Web Fonts Manager.

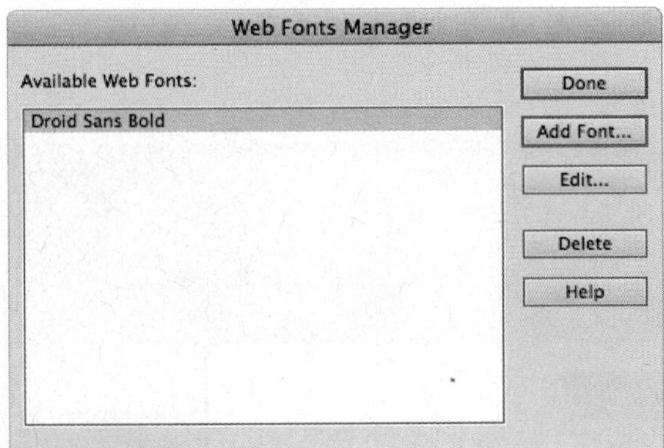

***Figure 7-18**: The Web Fonts Manager lists the available fonts for your current site.*

At this point, your new web font, Droid Sans Bold, has been made available to all existing pages and any new pages in the current site. Additionally, this web font will be available to any document in Dreamweaver, even if it is part of another site.

Font Licensing

Learning More

Understanding the rules of **font licensing** is an important part of using web fonts. You can technically add a font to a page, but this does not mean you are always *allowed* to. The fonts on your system may have specific licenses that only let you use them in print or for other specific uses. Even if you have paid for a font, this still does not necessarily mean you have paid for the web license of this font. You will need to ensure that you are allowed to use the fonts you add with the Web Font Manager.

For more information on web font licensing issues, visit the Web Font Licensing FAQ from the Adobe Type Team:

http://blogs.adobe.com/typblography/web-font-licensing-faq

Styling your heading with a web font

In addition to the legal licensing limitations involved with web fonts, there is also an aesthetic consideration. Not all fonts are designed to be rendered on the screen. The creators of a typical font are often more concerned with how the font renders in print or how the font looks at small sizes versus large sizes (or vice-versa). The web font you are using, Droid Sans Bold, was specifically designed to render well on small and large screens alike. Many designers still feel the majority of web fonts work best as headings rather than as large blocks of body text in paragraphs. This is a matter of interpretation and will likely change as more fonts are released for web use.

In this exercise, you will style your main heading with your new web font option.

Styling your heading with a web font

Step-by-Step

Follow these steps to style a heading with a web font

1. Make sure you have clicked inside the Heading 1 labeled, "Welcome to organic utopia." In the tag selector, make sure you click the `<h1>` tag as seen in Figure 7-19.

This highlights your Heading 1 and makes it easier for Dreamweaver to understand that you want to target this style.

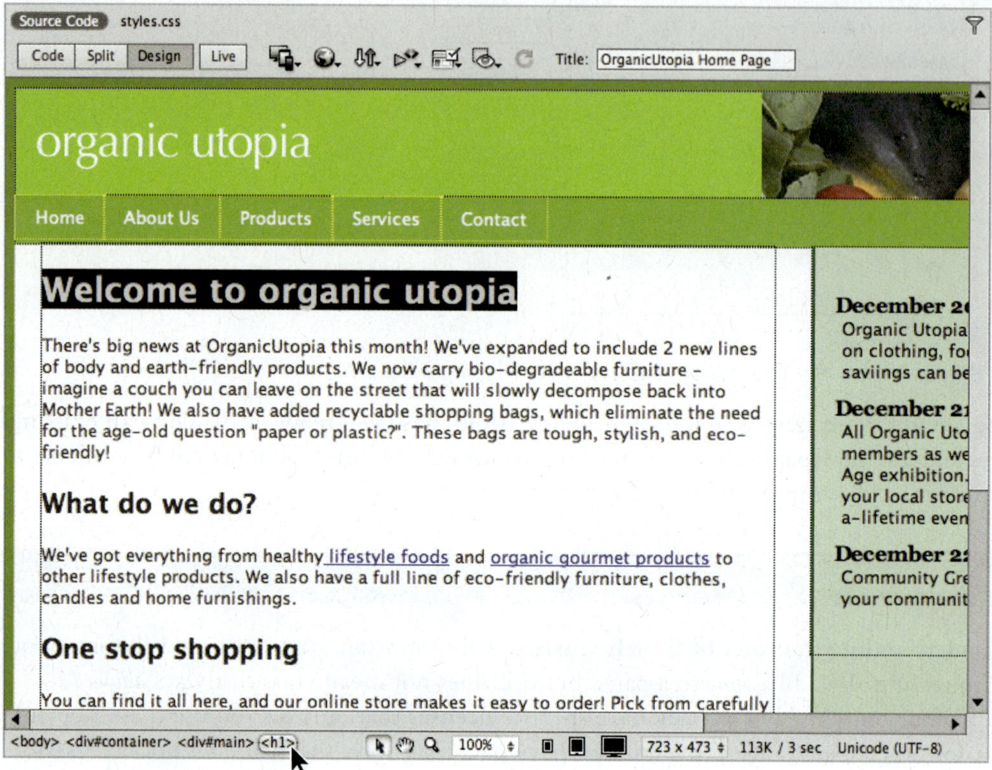

***Figure 7-19**: Click the* `<h1>` *tag in the Tag Selector to select the top heading.*

2. Click the CSS button in the Property Inspector if you are not currently in this view. Now click the Font menu; toward the bottom of this list, you will see Droid Sans Bold. Select this choice to apply it, and the New CSS Rule window will appear because there has not been a style defined for a `<h1>` element yet.

3. Click the Selector Type menu and choose Tag. Dreamweaver will recognize you have selected an h1 element, so this is the style that will be created. In other words, all Heading 1 elements will have the Droid Sans Bold font style. If Dreamweaver is attempting to create a Compound selector, press the Less Specific button until only `h1` remains in the Selector Name field as seen in Figure 7-20.

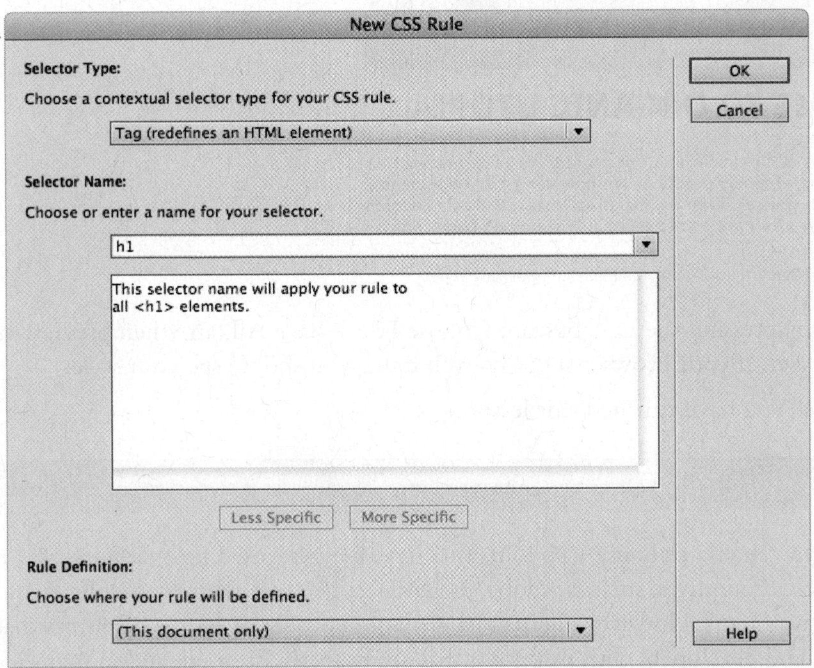

Figure 7-20*: Although you have applied the web font style, it may not be reflected in the Design view.*

4. Click OK. You have just applied the font style to your heading, but you might not see this change in your Design view. This is a limitation for some web fonts; you will only see an accurate view in the browser or in Dreamweaver's Live View.

5. Click Dreamweaver's Live View; you will see your heading set in Droid Sans Bold. You may not notice the difference immediately because Droid Sans and Lucida Sans are fairly similar; however, if you compare the letter "g" in the word organic to the letter "g" in the heading further down the page (One stop shopping), you will see the difference.

   You can still use certain CSS formatting to make the web font-styled heading more distinctive. You'll now add a style to make the heading uppercase.

6. In the CSS Styles panel, choose All and locate the stylesheet.css link. Notice that `@font-face` is listed. You will likely never modify this style—it is simply worth pointing out that is has been created. Double-click this `h1` rule to open the CSS rule definition window.

7. Click the Text-transform menu and choose uppercase. Click OK to apply it, and now your Live View updates to show your new heading (Figure 7-21).

***Figure 7-21**: Your web font-styled heading now has an uppercase style.*

Certification Ready 5.3

How do you reference font libraries in a web page?

8. Exit Live View by pressing the Live button. Choose File > Save All, and then preview your page in the browser. If your browser supports web fonts, you should see your style.

   Congratulations! You have finished this lesson.

Learning More

Where can I get more fonts?

As noted earlier, you should only use web fonts that have been licensed for that purpose. Many individual font foundries, such as Adobe and Monotype, have their own policies and systems for using web fonts. However, there are a growing number of online resources that provide designers and developers with web fonts that are properly licensed, and in many cases, are free or open-source. You should explore these options, but be aware that you may not find your favorite fonts listed here.

Fontsquirrel

This site offers a number of free fonts that are licensed for commercial work. The site is also a good resource for creating your own web fonts using the `@font-face`.

www.fontsquirrel.com

Google Web Fonts

Google Web Fonts provides a large number of free open-source fonts for use in your projects. It also provides a convenient way to sort and filter through the numerous options.

www.google.com/webfonts

Skill Summary

In this lesson you learned how to:	Objective
Add animation and interactivity to content	4.8
Organize web page layout with relative and absolutely-positioned div tags and CSS styles	5.2
Modify text and text properties	5.3

Knowledge Assessment

True/False

Circle T if the statement is true or F if the statement is false.

T F **1.** Transitions are part of CSS3 and Web fonts are part of CSS2.

T F **2.** CSS Transitions can replace some of the same functionality of animation created in Flash and/or JavaScript.

T F **3.** CSS Transitions require triggers.

T F **4.** CSS transitions provide a way to control the speed of animation changes for one or more CSS properties.

T F **5.** CSS transitions can only be applied to a single property for a target rule.

T F **6.** Web Fonts use a feature of CSS3 called `@font-family`.

T F **7.** The Web Fonts Manager allows you to locate fonts on your system suitable for embedding.

T F **8.** One of the benefits of Web Fonts is you can use a single font format and it will be supported across all browsers.

T F **9.** To preview Web Fonts inside of Dreamweaver CS6 you must use the Live View.

T F **10.** You must confirm that you have properly licensed web fonts for website use before Dreamweaver will allow you to add them to your site.

Multiple Choice

Select the best response for the following statements

1. CSS3 provides new properties that allow you to improve the style of your websites. Which of the following is the most important factor to consider?

a. Dreamweaver CS6 only supports some of the CSS3 features.

b. CSS3 features cannot be created entirely in Dreamweaver's Design View and require you to directly work within the Code View.

c. CSS3 properties have different levels of support amongst web browsers; therefore some features may not work correctly or at all.

d. All of the above.

2. A client would like you to use a specific font on the website you are designing for them. Which of the following needs to happen before you can embed the font in the page?

a. You need to convert the font to the proper font formats.

b. You need to research if the font is licensed for web use.

c. You need to research if the hosting company supports Web Fonts.

d. You need to create a separate folder within your site folder exclusively for the web fonts.

3. Which of the following are valid alternatives to CSS3 transitions for creating interactive animated elements on a web page?
    a. JavaScript
    b. Animated jpegs
    c. Image Maps
    d. All of the above.

4. CSS transitions can best be described as which of the following?
    a. Animating an object by changing one or more CSS properties over time.
    b. A technique for creating image rollovers without JavaScript.
    c. The ability to assign more than one CSS property to an HTML div element.
    d. The ability to gradually change from one set of CSS styles to another using keyframes.

5. Which of the following statements is true regarding CSS transitions?
    a. You can only use CSS transitions with the following CSS properties: color, background-color, height and width.
    b. You can only use CSS transitions with specific set of CSS properties.
    c. You can use CSS transitions with all CSS properties.
    d. None of the above.

6. Easing is a term best described as which of the following?
    a. The ability to vary the speed of a CSS transition over time.
    b. The ability to change the length of a CSS transition.
    c. The ability to delay the start of a CSS transition.
    d. The ability to apply two or more CSS properties to a transition.

7. CSS3 web fonts differ from the traditional CSS font-family property in what way?
    a. With CSS3 web fonts the user does not have to have the specified font installed on their system in order for it do display.
    b. CSS3 web fonts use a single font format and have better support across all browsers.
    c. CSS3 web fonts are better optimized for mobile viewing.
    d. All of the above.

8. What is a limitation of Web Fonts in Dreamweaver CS6?
    a. You will only see an accurate display of the web font in the browser or Live View.
    b. You will only see an accurate display of the web font in the browser or Design View.
    c. You will only see an accurate display of the web font in the browser or Multiscreen Preview.
    d. You will only see an accurate display of the web font in the browser.

9. In order to change the appearance of text that uses a Web Font to uppercase you would do which of the following?

a. Manually set the type to uppercase by typing with Caps Lock on.
b. Modify the text-transform property.
c. Modify the font-style property.
d. Modify the font-variant property.

10. Which of the following is not a valid font-type for the web?

a. OpenType (OTF)
b. Embedded PostScripr (EPS)
c. TrueType (TTF)
d. Web Open Font Format (WOFF)

Competency Assessment

Floating an image

Project 7-1

A colleague asks you to demonstrate one of the CSS3 transitions.

1. Open the **07_csstransitions.html** document and choose File > Save As and name this document **07_7-1.html**.
2. Choose Window > CSS Transitions to open the CSS Transitions window.
3. Click the + sign in the upper-left of the CSS Transitions window.
4. Click the Target Rule menu. Choose `#box`.
5. Click the Transition On menu and choose the Hover option. Then click inside the Duration field and type **1**.
6. Click the + sign at the bottom of the Property section. A menu appears with the entire list of CSS properties you can control. Select the border-width property.
7. Click inside the field labeled End Value, type **8px**. Click the Create Transition button to add it.
8. Choose File > Save and then Choose File > Preview in Browser. Place your cursor inside the box; you will see the box border animate from the original height of 4 up to 8 pixels.

Project 7-2 Styling a heading with a web font

You have added a web font to your page and styled a heading 1 with Droid Sans Bold. You will now style your heading 2 with the same font but use a different style.

1. Choose File > Open and open the **07_webfonts.html** document in your lesson folder. You added the web font, Droid Sans, to this document and styled the H1 as Droid Sans in the lesson. Choose File > Save As and save this as **07_webfonts_7-2.html**.
2. You will now style the Heading 2 in this document as Droid Sans as well. Click inside the Heading 2 labeled, "What do we do?" In the tag selector (at the lower-left of your document window), make sure you click the <h2> tag.
3. Click the CSS button in the Property Inspector if you are not currently in this view. Now click the Font menu; toward the bottom of this list, you will see Droid Sans Bold. Select this choice to apply it, and the New CSS Rule window will appear because there has not been a style defined for a <h2> element yet.
4. Click the Selector Type menu and choose Tag. H2 should automatically appear, if it does not, type **h2**.
5. Click OK. You have just applied the font style to your heading, but remember that there is a limitation for some web fonts; you will only see an accurate view in the browser or in Dreamweaver's Live View.
6. Click Dreamweaver's Live View; you will see your two heading 2s set in Droid Sans Bold. You'll now add a style that will capitalize every first letter of words in the heading.
7. In the CSS Styles panel, choose All and double-click the h2 rule to open the CSS rule definition window.
8. Click the Text-transform menu and choose capitalize. Click OK to apply it, and now your Live View updates to show your new heading.
9. Exit Live View by pressing the Live button. Choose File > Save All, and then preview your page in the browser. If your browser supports web fonts, you should see your style.

Proficiency Assessment

Comparing Fonts in Various Browsers

Project 7-3

Just because you can do something doesn't mean that you should. With relation to fonts, the more complicated it is, the trickier it can be when different computers are involved. Try comparing fonts in different browsers and platforms to see more.

Launch Dreamweaver CS6 if you haven't already.

1. Create a new blank HTML page.
2. Add some of the more off-beat fonts on your system and create some text to show those fonts.
3. See how the page translates in different browsers and if possible on a Windows-based machine as well as a Mac.

Page Transition Speeds

Project 7-4

The speed in which your transition occurs can create a different feel to the design of the webpage. Trying more settings will show you how to heighten or relax the feeling behind your design.

Launch Dreamweaver CS6 if you haven't already.

1. Go to File > Open and open the **07_csstransistions_work.html** file. Next, go to Window > CSS Transitions to open the CSS Transitions window.
2. Go back to the easing settings and try working with the different settings, try again without easing.

Working with Tables

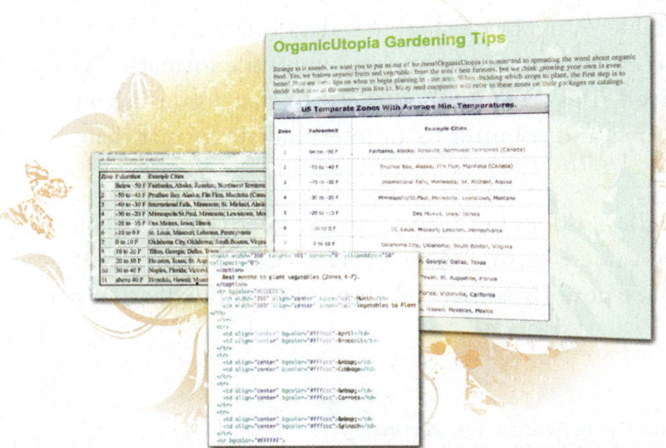

Key Terms

- CellPad
- CellSpace
- Cells
- Columns
- Merging Cells
- Rows
- Tables
- Tabular Data

Skill	Objective
Import tabular data to a web page	4.11

Business Case

Up until now, Organic Utopia owners have provided simple copy and images for the site. Now, they're providing information such as tabular data from spreadsheet programs and you need to incorporate this into your pages. This requires using HTML tables that are designed to display certain types of data into your web projects.

Introduction

Before starting, make sure that your tools and panels are consistent by resetting your workspace. See "Resetting the Dreamweaver workspace" in the Starting Up section of this book.

You will work with several files from the dw08lessons folder in this lesson. Make sure that you have loaded the dwlessons folder onto your hard drive. See "Loading lesson files" in the Starting Up section of this book.

Before you begin, you need to create site settings that point to the dw08lessons folder Go to Site > New Site, or, for details on creating a site, refer to Lesson 2, "Setting Up a New Site."

Using tables in web design

Tables are ideally suited for displaying tabular data. As discussed in Lesson 5, "Creating Page Layouts with CSS," in the beginning days of the Web, tables were the best tools available for designers when it came to layout. Over the years, Dreamweaver has steadily introduced a number of tools and visual aids to help people work with tables. Dreamweaver has mirrored the Web in that it has begun to shift its focus to CSS layout rather than table layout. Slowly, the table is reclaiming its original purpose: displaying tabular data.

In this lesson, you will learn how to automatically import and format existing data into a table. You will also explore how to modify rows and columns, style tables with CSS, and create new tables from scratch.

Importing table data

You'll get a chance right away to see tabular data in action by importing a .csv file into Dreamweaver. **Tabular data** refers to data that has been exported from a spreadsheet and can be formatted by Dreamweaver as a table. A majority of tabular data is exported from spreadsheet programs in the .csv (comma-separated values) and .txt (text) file formats. These are called comma, **tab**, or other **delimited files**. Essentially this means that a spreadsheet application converts the data within its rows and columns to an intermediate format that Dreamweaver can read.

Although Dreamweaver can open these files, it does not format them directly. With a comma-delimited file, for example, each column value is separated by a comma and each line break starts a new row. In Figure 8-1 you can see how Dreamweaver displays the raw .csv file that you are going to be working with:

```
Zone,Fahrenheit,Example Cities
1,Below -50 F,"Fairbanks, Alaska; Resolute, Northwest Territories (Canada)"
2,-50 to -40 F,"Prudhoe Bay, Alaska; Flin Flon, Manitoba (Canada)"
3,-40 to -30 F,"International Falls, Minnesota; St. Michael, Alaska"
4,-30 to -20 F,"Minneapolis/St.Paul, Minnesota; Lewistown, Montana"
5,-20 to -10 F,"Des Moines, Iowa; Illinois"
6,-10 to 0 F,"St. Louis, Missouri; Lebanon, Pennsylvania"
7,0 to 10 F,"Oklahoma City, Oklahoma; South Boston, Virginia"
8,10 to 20 F,"Tifton, Georgia; Dallas, Texas"
9,20 to 30 F,"Houston, Texas; St. Augustine, Florida"
10,30 to 40 F,"Naples, Florida; Victorville, California"
11,above 40 F,"Honolulu, Hawaii; Mazatlan, Mexico"
```

Figure 8-1: *The text editor's view of a comma-delimited file.*

When imported into Dreamweaver, this file will be translated accordingly into the rows and columns of a new table.

Step-by-Step

Follow these steps to import table data

1. In the Files panel, double-click the **tips.html** file to open it. This is a styled page for the tips section of the OrganicUtopia site. You will be inserting a .csv file with data on the vegetable-growing zones of North America.
2. Click after the last sentence in the main paragraph and press Enter (Windows) or Return (Mac OS) to make sure your cursor is below the text. Choose File > Import > Tabular Data. The Import Tabular Data dialog box opens.
3. In the Import Tabular Data dialog box, press the Browse button and locate the **temperate_zones.csv** file in your dw08lessons folder. Press Open.

4. Click on the Delimiter menu to see the various options that are available. In your case, you will be choosing Comma. In the Table width section, leave the Fit to data option selected as seen in Figure 8-2.

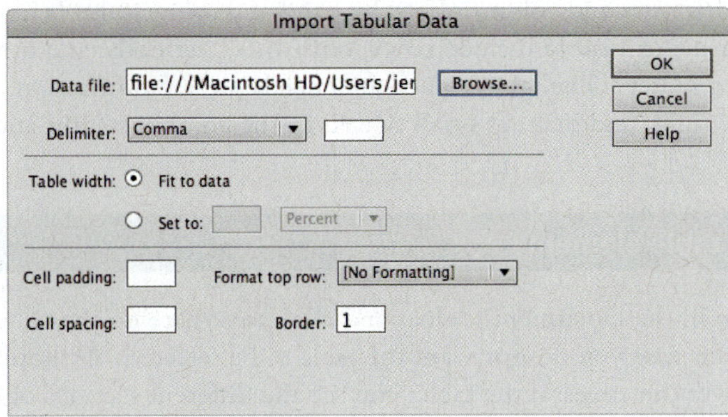

Figure 8-2: The settings in the Import Tabular Data dialog box affect the way a table is created.

Take Note...

You can either set a specific width for the generated table or let Dreamweaver construct the table automatically, based on the line-length of the incoming data.

5. Press OK and your table is imported into your document below the text. Your table is imported with 3 columns and 12 rows as seen in Figure 8-3. A quick way to confirm this is to look in the Property Inspector, where there is a field for columns and rows as well as other useful ways to work with tables.

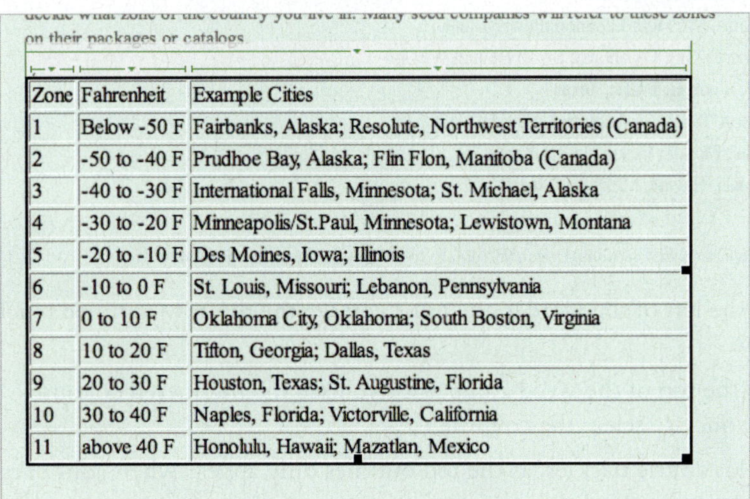

on their packages or catalogs

Zone	Fahrenheit	Example Cities
1	Below -50 F	Fairbanks, Alaska; Resolute, Northwest Territories (Canada)
2	-50 to -40 F	Prudhoe Bay, Alaska; Flin Flon, Manitoba (Canada)
3	-40 to -30 F	International Falls, Minnesota; St. Michael, Alaska
4	-30 to -20 F	Minneapolis/St.Paul, Minnesota; Lewistown, Montana
5	-20 to -10 F	Des Moines, Iowa; Illinois
6	-10 to 0 F	St. Louis, Missouri; Lebanon, Pennsylvania
7	0 to 10 F	Oklahoma City, Oklahoma; South Boston, Virginia
8	10 to 20 F	Tifton, Georgia; Dallas, Texas
9	20 to 30 F	Houston, Texas; St. Augustine, Florida
10	30 to 40 F	Naples, Florida; Victorville, California
11	above 40 F	Honolulu, Hawaii; Mazatlan, Mexico

Figure 8-3: A three-column and 12-row table generated by Dreamweaver from a comma-delimited file.

6. Press Dreamweaver's Code view button to see the code that makes up this table. It's safe to say that this is something you would not want to code by hand.

The table is now ready to be formatted according to your specifications. As you can see, you can save yourself a lot of time if your source data is properly formatted. Dreamweaver creates a table for you with all the data properly placed, eliminating the need for you to build a table, and type, or copy and paste, content into each cell.

Certification Ready 4.11

What are the different methods you can use to import tabular data?

Selecting table elements

It's worth taking a few moments to learn how to select the various elements of your table. Selecting a specific part of a table can be little tricky until you learn how. In this exercise, you'll look at ways to select a table's rows and columns both by hand and using controls in the Property Inspector. The components of a **table** include **rows**, **columns**, and **cells**, and other elements such as table headers and footers. The table you created needs some modification. It's rare that a table is created exactly right, and making small tweaks to the column widths and the row heights is the norm.

Step-by-Step

Follow these steps to select table elements

1. Press the Design view button in the Document toolbar and click anywhere on the background of the page. In this case you do **not** want the table to be selected. Without clicking, place your cursor over the edges of the table; you see the different sections of the table *light up* with a red border. Also notice that your cursor switches to a black arrow. The red border is Dreamweaver's visual cue for which part of the table you will be selecting, and the black arrow points in the direction of the row or column to be selected.
2. Place your cursor high in the upper-left corner until the entire table is outlined in red as seen in Figure 8-4. Click once, and the table is selected.

Zone	Fahrenheit	Example Cities
1	Below -50 F	Fairbanks, Alaska; Resolute, Northwest Territories (Canada)
2	-50 to -40 F	Prudhoe Bay, Alaska; Flin Flon, Manitoba (Canada)
3	-40 to -30 F	International Falls, Minnesota; St. Michael, Alaska
4	-30 to -20 F	Minneapolis/St.Paul, Minnesota; Lewistown, Montana
5	-20 to -10 F	Des Moines, Iowa; Illinois
6	-10 to 0 F	St. Louis, Missouri; Lebanon, Pennsylvania
7	0 to 10 F	Oklahoma City, Oklahoma; South Boston, Virginia
8	10 to 20 F	Tifton, Georgia; Dallas, Texas
9	20 to 30 F	Houston, Texas; St. Augustine, Florida
10	30 to 40 F	Naples, Florida; Victorville, California
11	above 40 F	Honolulu, Hawaii; Mazatlan, Mexico

***Figure 8-4**: A red border designates which section of the table you are selecting—in this case, the entire table.*

3. Place your cursor to the left of the word Zone until you see the top row outlined; click once to select the row.
4. Move your cursor to the top of the word Zone until you see the numbered column outlined in red; click once to select the column.

   Selecting a single cell is a little trickier, as the red outlines only appear when your cursor is on the edge of a table, not inside of one.
5. Click inside the cell with the word Zone. In order to select the cell, use the tag selector at the bottom-left of your document window. These tags are an alternative way to select parts of the table.

6. Click on the <table> tag first; this selects the table just as you did in step 2. Click on the <tr> tag next; this selects the table row. The <tr> tag appropriately stands for table row. Lastly, click on the <td> tag, and the cell itself is selected as seen in Figure 8-5; <td> is defined as a table cell in HTML. Note that in each of these cases the selected element is outlined in black.

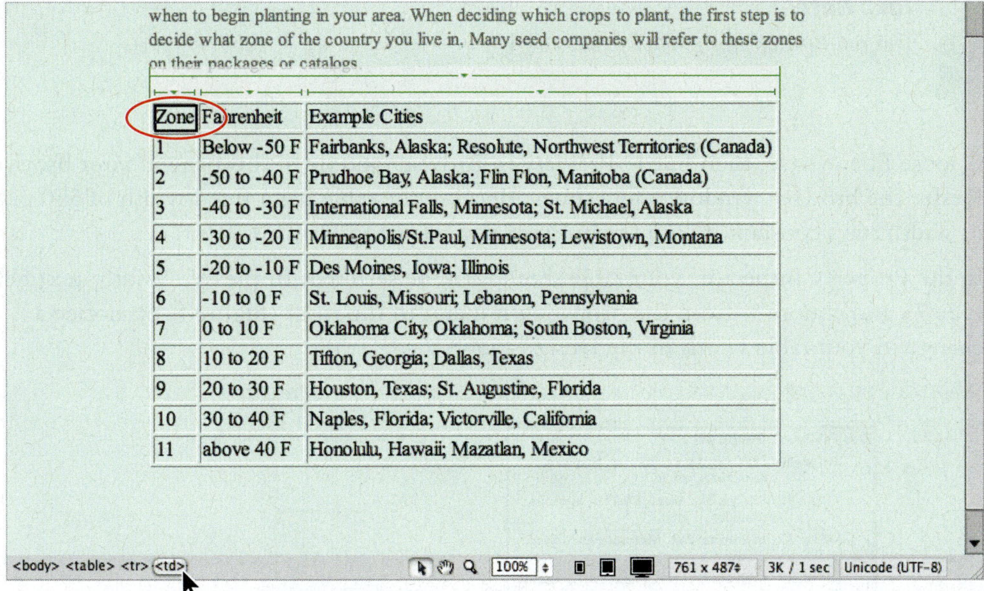

Figure 8-5: *Clicking on the appropriate table tag in the tag selector selects that part of the table.*

Some people prefer this method of selecting elements of their tables because it removes the chance that clicking on the table will move or modify it.

7. Click inside any cell in the table again, and choose Modify > Table > Select Table. This is yet another way to select tables. The Modify > Table command is one you'll be returning to. You can also select the table by right-clicking (Windows) or Ctrl+clicking (Mac OS) the table and choosing Table > Select Table from the contextual menu.

Modifying table size

Although importing tabular data from a text file is quick and easy, the data is seldom formatted perfectly. When you first imported the data, there was a choice to *Fit Table Width To Data.* The width of the table, when you choose this option, isn't always predictable due to the way Dreamweaver does its calculations. Although it is possible to set the width of the table during the import stage, this isn't always convenient if you don't know what the data looks like. Luckily, it's easy to change the size of tables in Dreamweaver. The first thing you'll do is set a fixed width for the table.

Follow these steps to modify the table size **Step-by-Step**

1. If your table is not currently selected, select it now using any of the methods you learned in the last exercise. In the Property Inspector, type **550** in the W text field and make sure the drop-down menu to the right is set to pixels, then press Enter (Windows) or Return (Mac OS). This expands the table to a width of 550 pixels.

Look closely at the top of your table; there is a visual guide outlined in green that displays the width of your table as well as the width of each column. This guide will come in handy when you are trying to create precisely measured tables, although it can also be turned off.

Take Note...

You can turn off this guide by choosing View > Visual Aids > Table Widths.

2. Choose File > Save, then File > Preview in Browser and open this page in your browser. Resize the browser window a few times. Because the table has a fixed width of 550 pixels, its width stays constant. Close the browser and return to Dreamweaver.

3. In the Property Inspector, your table should still be selected. In the W (Width) text field, type **75** and choose % from the drop-down menu to the right (Figure 8-6); notice a change in your table width in the Design view.

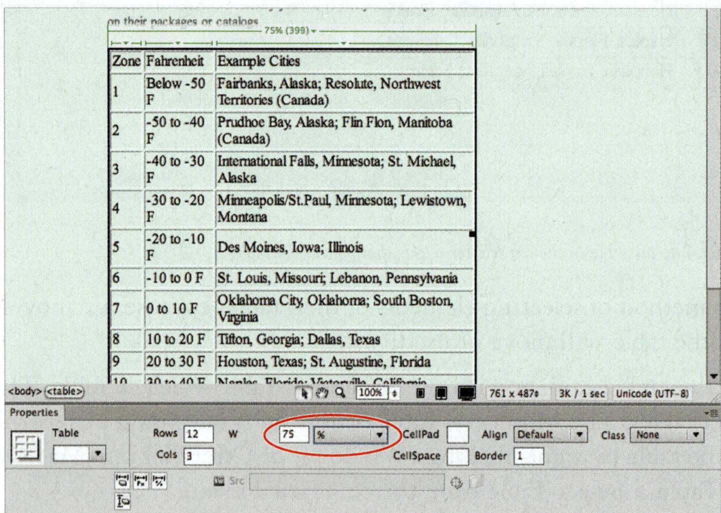

Figure 8-6: *You can set the table width to a percentage of the browser window by using the Property Inspector.*

Choose File > Save, then preview the page in your browser again and resize the browser window. The table width now resizes because you set it to be a percentage rather than a fixed width. Close the browser and return to Dreamweaver.

4. Reset your table to the original width by typing **550** in the W text field and choosing pixels from the drop-down menu.

   You also have the ability to resize the columns and rows in the Design view. You can do this manually using the Property Inspector

5. Place your cursor inside the table and then over the dividing line between the first column and the second column. Your cursor changes to a double-arrow. Click and drag slowly to the right to expand the width of the first column. N notice at the top of the two columns that there are blue numbers that update with the width of the columns. This has the effect of reducing the second column's width, although it leaves the third column's width alone.

6. Expand the first column to at least 50 pixels; the content in the second column breaks to the next line. Place your cursor on the dividing line between the second and third column, and click and drag slowly to narrow the width of the third column (thereby expanding the width of the second column). This example uses values of 390 pixels for the third column and 88 pixels for the second.

Take Note...
If you are mathematically inclined, you may have noticed that the three column values don't add up to 550. This is because there are additional factors of cell padding, cell spacing, and borders to consider.

Oftentimes, approximate column widths are not sufficient; Dreamweaver allows you to apply exact column widths in the Property Inspector.

7. Place your cursor above the first column until the red outline appears, and click once to select the column. The bottom half of the Property Inspector expands, allowing you to adjust the properties of only this column. Type **45** into the W text field. The width does not appear to change dramatically, but it is now 45 pixels (Figure 8-7).

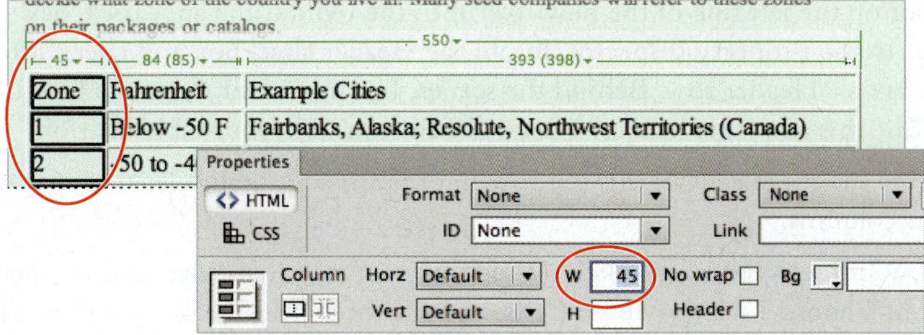

Figure 8-7*: Selecting a column and entering a specific width in the Property Inspector sets the column to that width.*

8. Click above the second column to select it. Type **100** into the W text field. Click above the third column and type **400** in the W text field. (This will have little effect on the appearance of the table.)

   You also have the ability to create a fixed height for rows.

9. Click on the left edge of the top row to select the whole row. In the Property Inspector, type **35** in the H text field, and press Enter (Windows) or Return (Mac OS) to apply the change.

Certification Ready 4.11

What are the different sizing methods used for tables?

Modifying table structure

In addition to modifying the width of columns and rows, the structure of a table often needs to be modified (for example, adding and deleting rows and columns, as well as **merging cells** in the column). First, you'll add a new row to the top of your table and then convert it to a header row. There are a few ways to add rows and columns in Dreamweaver, you'll begin with the Modify > Table command.

Modifying table structure

Step-by-Step

Follow these steps to insert rows and columns

1. Click inside any of the cells within the first row. Dreamweaver needs to have some frame of reference when adding a row.
2. Choose Modify > Table > Insert Rows or Columns. The Insert Rows or Columns dialog box opens.
3. The Insert Rows radio button should be selected. For Number of rows, leave the default value of 1. In the Where section, select *Above the Selection* as seen in Figure 8-8. Press OK to add the new row to the top of the table.

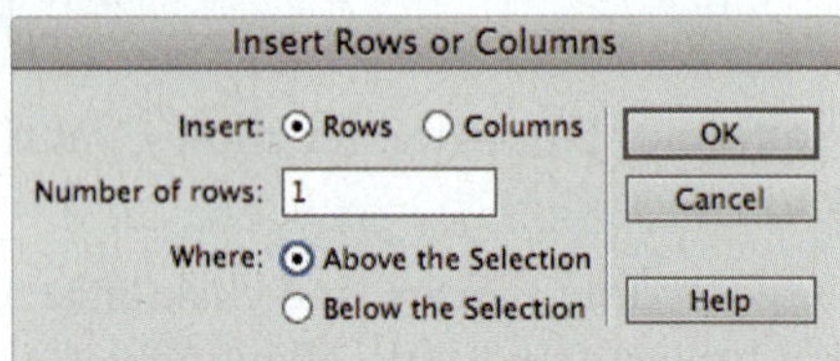

Figure 8-8: *Use the Insert Rows and Columns dialog box to add new rows or columns to an existing table.*

4. Place your cursor on the left side of the new row until the red outline appears. Click once to select it. In the Property Inspector, locate the Header checkbox and check it to designate this row as a Header row. Behind the scenes, Dreamweaver uses the HTML `<th>` tag to define this as a table header. This will help you style your table later on.

   Now you'll merge the three cells in this top row in order to add the header text that will span across your columns.

5. With the top row still selected, right-click (Windows) or Ctrl+click (Mac OS) to open a contextual menu. Choose Table > Merge Cells, and the three cells merge into one. This is referred to as columnspan.
6. Click inside this merged cell and type **US temperate zones with average min. temperatures**. (Figure 8-9)

US temperate zones with average min. temperatures.		
Zone	Fahrenheit	Example Cities
1	Below -50 F	Fairbanks, Alaska; Resolute, Northwest Territories (Canada)
2	-50 to -40 F	Prudhoe Bay, Alaska; Flin Flon, Manitoba (Canada)
3	-40 to -30 F	International Falls, Minnesota; St. Michael, Alaska
4	-30 to -20 F	Minneapolis/St.Paul, Minnesota; Lewistown, Montana
5	-20 to -10 F	Des Moines, Iowa; Illinois
6	-10 to 0 F	St. Louis, Missouri; Lebanon, Pennsylvania
7	0 to 10 F	Oklahoma City, Oklahoma; South Boston, Virginia
8	10 to 20 F	Tifton, Georgia; Dallas, Texas
9	20 to 30 F	Houston, Texas; St. Augustine, Florida
10	30 to 40 F	Naples, Florida; Victorville, California
11	above 40 F	Honolulu, Hawaii; Mazatlan, Mexico

Figure 8-9: *Merging cells creates a columnspan, allowing you to add header text.*

7. Choose File > Save to save your work.

Certification Ready 4.11

How do you set and change table, cell, row and column properties?

Certification Ready 4.11

How do you insert and delete columns and rows?

Certification Ready 4.11

How do you merge and split cells?.

Creating a table

In addition to creating a table from tabular data, you can also create a table from the ground up using Dreamweaver's Insert Table command.

Follow these steps to create a new table

Step-by-Step

1. Click to the right of your existing table, and then press Enter (Windows) or Return (Mac OS) two times. You will be placing a second table two lines below the first.
2. Choose Insert > Table, and the Table dialog box opens. Type **12** in the Rows text field, and **2** in the Columns text field. Type **550** in the Table width text field to match the width of your first table and make sure the drop-down menu is set to pixels. Set the Border thickness value to **1** if it is not already.

   The Cell padding and Cell spacing values should have no value (Figure 8-10); you'll return to these properties shortly.

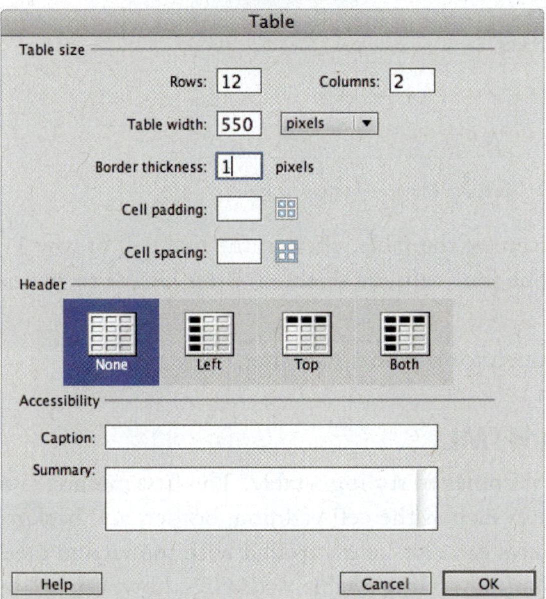

Figure 8-10: The Insert > Table command creates a new table.

3. In the Header section, select the third option, Top, in order to designate the top row as the header.
4. In the Caption field, type **Best months to plant vegetables (Zones 4–7)**. Table captions are a bit more specific than table headers. A table caption is a short description of the table contents and has its own `<caption>` element; by default, they are displayed centered and at the top of the table.

   Table captions are not required, but they are useful, especially from an accessibility perspective, as they supply useful information to screen readers and other devices. Press OK to insert the table.
5. Below the caption, in the first cell of the first column, type **Month**. In the first cell of the second column, type **Vegetables to Plant**. Your columns may shift; in order to adjust them, click on the divider between the two columns, and click and drag it as necessary to visually divide the two columns evenly.
6. In the second row of the *Month* column, type **April**, then five rows below, type **May**.

7. Below the *Vegetables to Plant* column, type **Broccoli**. Press the down arrow on your keyboard to move to the next row. Using this technique, first type **Cabbage** and then type each vegetable name in its own row—first **Carrots** and then **Spinach**. Skip one row and, making sure you are beginning in the same row as May, type **Corn**, **Tomatoes**, **Peppers**, **Cucumbers**.(Figure 8-11)

550

265 | 269

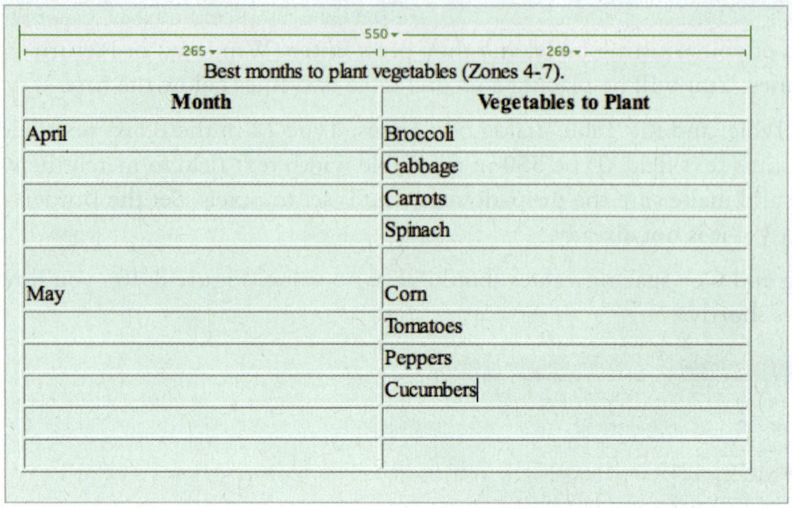

Best months to plant vegetables (Zones 4-7).

Month	Vegetables to Plant
April	Broccoli
	Cabbage
	Carrots
	Spinach
May	Corn
	Tomatoes
	Peppers
	Cucumbers

***Figure 8-11**: Press keyboard arrows to quickly move from one cell to another when typing text.*

8. To delete the two extra rows at the bottom of the table, click in the first cell of row 11, and then drag down and to the right. The four cells are selected. Press Delete to remove the rows.

9. Choose File > Save, and keep this file open for the next exercise.

Formatting and styling tables in HTML

There are two different paths to take when it comes to styling a table. The first method is to use HTML tag properties to modify attributes such as the cell padding, border, and background color in a table. However, these same attributes can also be controlled with the second method, CSS. It's fair to say that there are more options for styling a table with CSS; however, styling a table with HTML tags is faster for most people. Which method you choose often depends on the project specifications. You'll be learning both methods here so that you have the option to choose. You'll also get a chance to consider the pros and cons of both methods. First, you'll start off with the *traditional* method of styling tables with HTML tags and properties.

Follow these steps to style a table in HTML

Step-by-Step

1. In the second table you created (Best months to plant vegetables), click on the edge of the header row to select it. In the Property Inspector, click on the HTML category, if necessary, and then click the Bg (Background) color swatch. In the left column of swatches, choose the light gray (#CCCCCC). The background color of the header row changes to gray. (Figure 8-12)

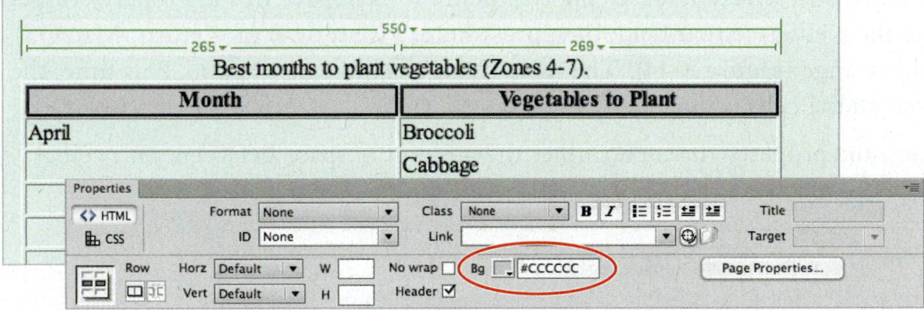

Figure 8-12: Select a row and click the Bg color swatch to apply a background color.

2. Click inside the April cell, then drag down and to the right until you reach the cell containing the text Spinach; this selects all the cells in these four rows and two columns.
3. Click in the Bg swatch text field and type **#FFFCCC**, a light yellow swatch in the lower-right corner. All four rows now have the same background color.
4. Click on the left edge of the empty row above the row labeled *May*. Click the Bg color swatch and choose white for this background color. Then click in the May cell and drag down and to the right to the last cell containing the text *Cucumbers*. Click the Bg color swatch and choose the light pink color swatch, #FFCCFF, in the bottom-right corner.

   Now, you will center the text in your columns.

5. Click at the top of the first column to select it. In the Property Inspector, from Horz (Horizontal) drop-down menu, select Center (Figure 8-13). Select the second column and repeat this step to center this text.

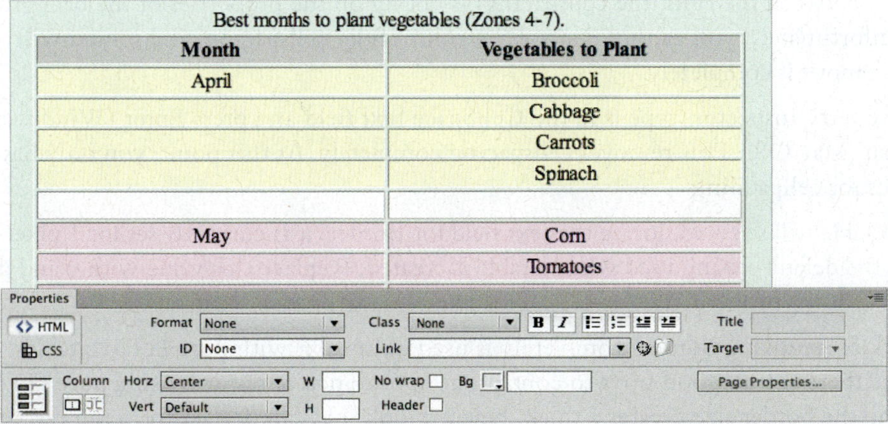

Figure 8:13: Select a column and click the Center option in the Horizontal menu of the Property Inspector.

6. Choose File > Save, then File > Preview in Browser. Your text is visually categorized by background color now, but it would be a stretch to say that this is a visually pleasing table. There are a few other properties that you can adjust to make this table look a bit better. Close the browser and return to Dreamweaver.

   You'll now examine the properties of cell padding.

7. Click in one of the corners of the table until the entire table is outlined in red. Then click on the table to select it. In the Property Inspector, locate the text field for CellPad and type **10**. Press Enter (Windows) or Return (Mac OS) to apply the change. There are now 10 pixels of space added to the inside of all cells. This has the effect of giving your text a bit more breathing room from the borders around it.

Cellpad is a property that determines the amount of space, measured in pixels, between the sides of a cell and its contents.

8. With your table still selected, locate the text field for CellSpace in the Property Inspector. Type **10** in the CellSpace text field, then press Enter (Windows) or Return (Mac OS) to commit the change (Figure 8-14). The table changes appearance again. This time, the width between the cells is increased.

Cellspace is the property that determines the amount of space between your cells.

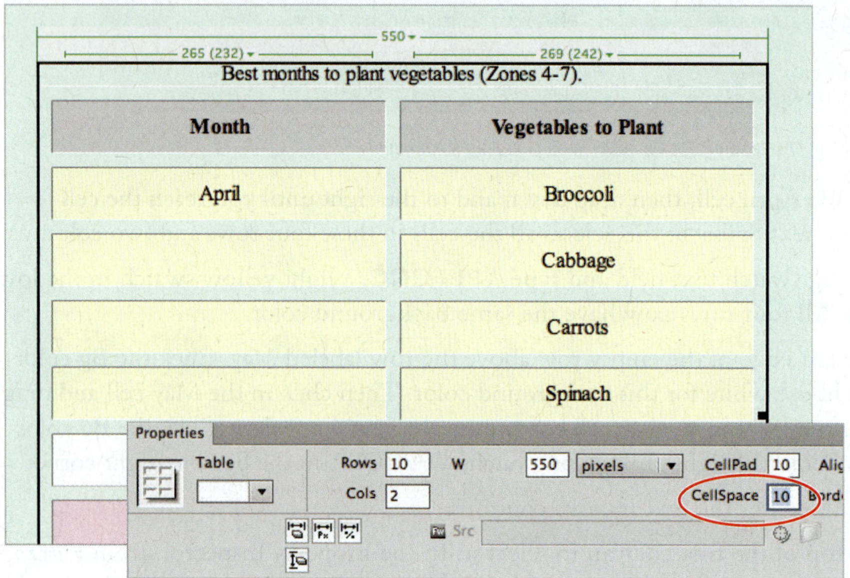

Figure 8-14: *A table with cellpadding of 10 pixels and cellspacing of 10 pixels.*

The space between the cells (the cellspacing) is taking on the properties of the background color. Unfortunately, you cannot control the color of the cellspacing, and so you will actually remove it completely.

9. In the Property Inspector, type **0** in the CellSpace text field and press Enter (Windows) or Return (Mac OS). This removes cellspacing completely. At this point, you only have properties for cellpadding.

10. With the table still selected, locate the text field for Border; it is currently set for 1 pixel, which is the default setting used when a table is created. Replace this value with 0 and press Enter (Windows) or Return (Mac OS). This removes the border completely.

This trick of removing borders completely is used quite a bit with pure HTML tables. This is because there are no good ways to control the appearance of borders using pure HTML. Increasing the border size creates a thick, beveled look that can detract from the rest of your page. Better control for borders exists in CSS.

11. Place your cursor on the small black square on the lower-right of the table until you see the double-arrow. Click and drag the table to the left to reduce its width. You can use the value at the top of the table if you choose, or just change the width until you're satisfied. The figure 8-15 below uses a new width of 350 pixels.

Best months to plant vegetables (Zones 4-7).

Month	Vegetables to Plant
April	Broccoli
	Cabbage
	Carrots
	Spinach
May	Corn
	Tomatoes
	Peppers
	Cucumbers

Figure 8-15: Click and drag the edge of a table to reduce the width.

12. With the table still selected, press the Split view button in order to see the code generated for this table (Figure 8-16). In the first line of the table, you see the settings for the width, height, border, and cell padding. In all the <td> or cells, you see the properties for alignment and background color repeated for every row. This extra code is part of the tradeoff for the easy application of the color and alignment. Part of the dilemma with this table now is that the alignment and background color settings, as well as the cellspacing, cellpadding, and border settings, are not linked to your CSS in any way.

Certification Ready 4.11

What are the table, cell, row and column properties?

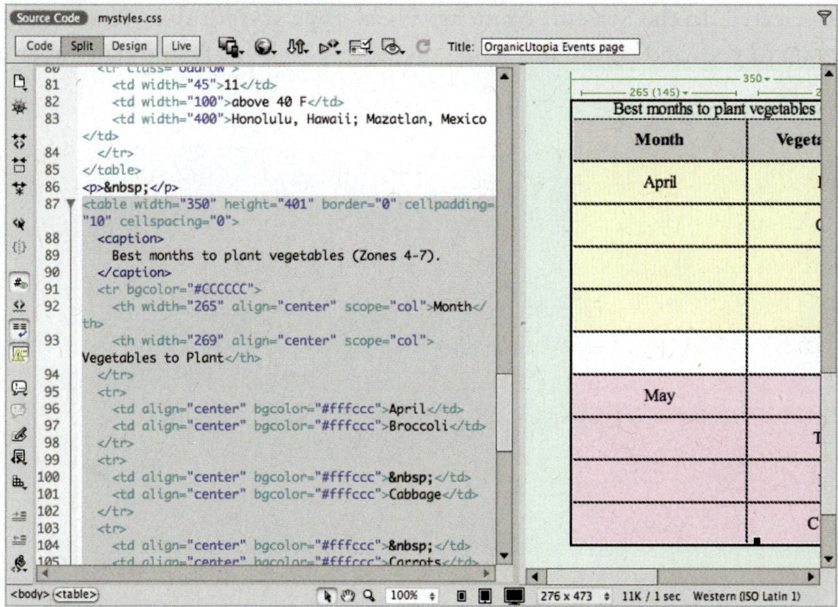

Figure 8-16: The visual styling of the table elements is combined with the structure.

One problem of creating pure HTML tables is the inability to quickly copy the style of one table and apply it to another. Because the content of the table and the style are intertwined, it's hard to separate one from the other. The larger problem is that pure HTML tables have none of the benefits associated with CSS. If your tables are not linked to any CSS, what happens when you redesign your website? As you saw in the last lesson, a simple change in CSS code can change the background color of your entire site. If the design of your tables clashes with your page, you have a lot of work to do as you locate each table and tweak it to fit.

Formatting and styling tables with CSS

In this exercise, you'll style your initial table using many of the same concepts covered in the previous exercise, such as padding and borders, but this time you'll do it with CSS. There is a little bit more work involved initially, but the result will be a table that not only is more visually appealing than an HTML-based table but also has a reusable style that can be applied to new tables. It's possible to create tag-based styles for all your tables—in other words, to create CSS rules for the various HTML table elements (`<td>`, `<tr>`, and so on). In fact, this is not a bad idea when creating a *default* style for tables in a website. In this example, however, you will be creating a class style that can readily be applied to different tables. It's not unusual to have three or four different styles of tables in a large website, each with their own CSS class definitions.

First you'll start by creating general rules for the background color, border, and font appearance of the table; then you'll create more specific rules as you drill down into the table.

Step-by-Step

Follow these steps to style a table using CSS

1. Press the Design View button to return to this view. Select the first table you created (US Temperate Zones...) by clicking on one of the corners when you see the red outline. If necessary, choose Window > CSS Styles to open the CSS Styles panel. In the CSS Styles panel, click on New CSS Rule button at the bottom of the panel; the New CSS Rule dialog box appears.
2. In the Selector Type drop-down menu of the New CSS Rule dialog box, leave the default choice of *Class* selected. In the Selector Name text field, type **styledtable**. Remember that class names are up to you, and choosing a name that is easy to identify and remember is the goal.

3. From the CSS Rule definition drop-down menu, select the **mystyles.css** external style sheet (Figure 8-17) . This is an important step because you would like to add these styles to your external style sheet rather than writing them to the tips.html page only.

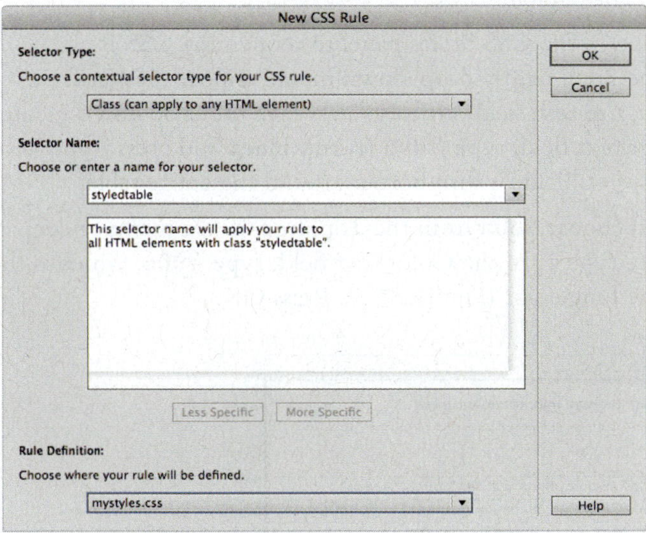

Figure 8-17*: Creating a new class for the style of the table and defining it in the external style sheet.*

4. Press OK, and the CSS Rule definition dialog box opens. Select the Background category and click the Background-color swatch. Choose the color white (#FFF) and press OK.

   You see no changes onscreen because you need to apply the `.styledtable` class to the table. You'll do that now, and then return to adding more styles.

5. Your table should still be selected; if it isn't, then select it now. In the Property Inspector, the table properties should be active. (If you are seeing the HTML and CSS properties, you have not selected the table.) On the right side of the Property Inspector, choose styledtable from the Class drop-down menu to apply the class as seen in Figure 8-18. The background of your table changes to white.

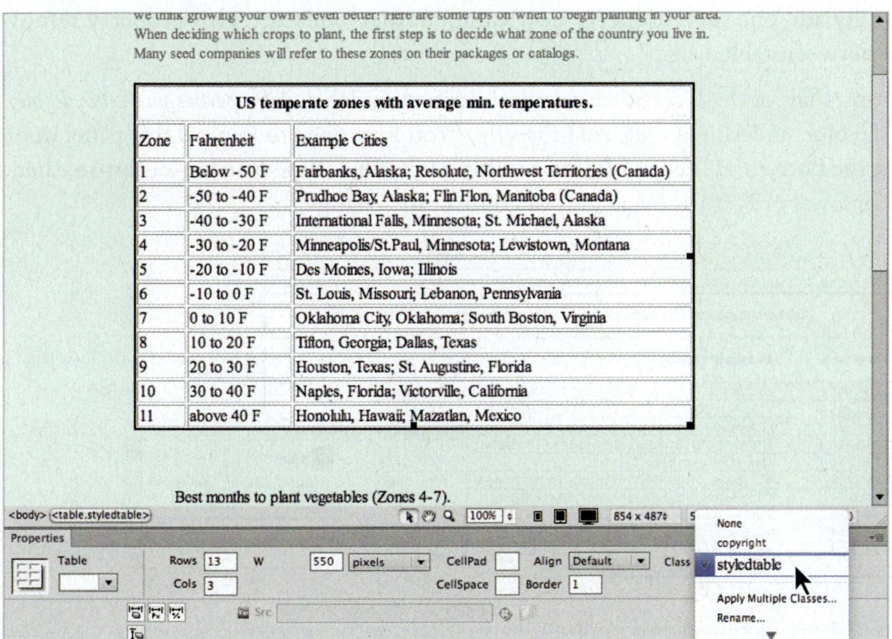

Figure 8-18*: Apply a class to a table by choosing the class name in the Property Inspector.*

Now you'll return to the styledtable class style and add additional properties. You could have created all your rules first and then applied the styledtable class; however, doing it this way allows you to preview your styling in real-time. Now you'll add some borders and change the font-styling for the entire table.

6. Double-click on `.styledtable` in the CSS Styles panel to reopen the CSS Rule definition dialog box. From the Font-family drop-down menu, choose the Verdana, Geneva, sans-serif. In the Font-size text field, type **10**, and leave the drop down menu to the right set to *px*. In the Color text field, type **#006** (a dark blue), and press Apply to see your changes to the table. Now you'll add a thin border around the entire table.

7. Select the Border category, and choose Solid from the Top drop-down menu under "Style." In the Width text field, type **1**. In the Color text field, type **#006**, which is the same dark blue you used for the font-color (Figure 8-19). Press OK.

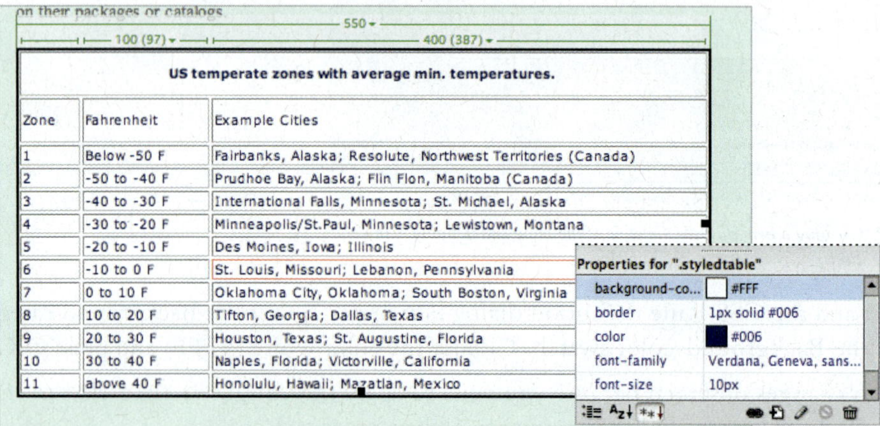

***Figure 8-19**: Your styled table with background-color, font styling and a border.*

The last property you'll add to the `.styledtable` class is one that is not available in the standard CSS Rule definition dialog box. It's important to realize that the language of CSS is quite large to begin with, and will continue to expand in the future. There are CSS properties that may not be used every day but nonetheless can be very useful. You'll semi-automatically add one such property now called border-collapse. This property removes the space between table cells.

8. In the bottom half of the CSS Styles panel in the section labeled *Properties for ".styledtable,"* click on the blue underlined text, *Add Property*. (You may need to expand this panel in order to see it at the bottom of the list.) In the resulting text field, type **border-collapse**, then press Enter (Windows) or Return (Mac OS) to commit the change.

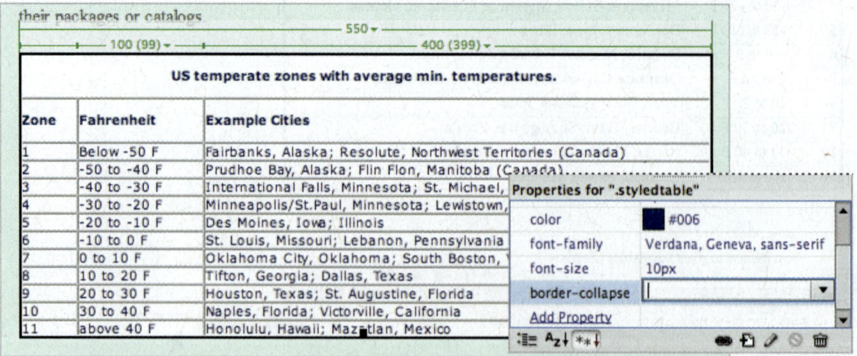

***Figure 8-20**: Click* Add Property *and type* **border-collapse** *to add a new CSS property.*

When it is typed correctly, Dreamweaver recognizes this property as part of the CSS language and makes the values available in the next field (Figure 8-20). (You can also click the Add Property menu to see the entire list of available properties.)

9. Click in the column to the right of the border-collapse property to activate the field. From the drop-down menu, choose *collapse*. You will not see an obvious change on screen; this property and value will help older browsers render the table correctly.

10. Choose File > Save All. Preview your page in your browser to see your styling. Close the browser and return to Dreamweaver.

Advanced CSS styling of tables

You have created a basic style for this table. You will now sharpen up the appearance of this table by adding a background image to the header, setting the text alignment and padding, and finally, creating subtle borders between each of the data cells.

Follow these steps to style a table with advanced CSS features

Step-by-Step

1. Click anywhere inside the header, and in the lower-left corner of your document window, click on the <th> tag to select the header. You defined this top row as a table header earlier in the lesson.

2. In the CSS Styles panel, press the New CSS Rule button (⊕) to open the New CSS Rule dialog box. In the Selector Type drop-down menu, the Compound option is listed (Figure 8-21). This is what you want because you are creating a specific rule for <th> tags, but only those found inside the styledtable class.

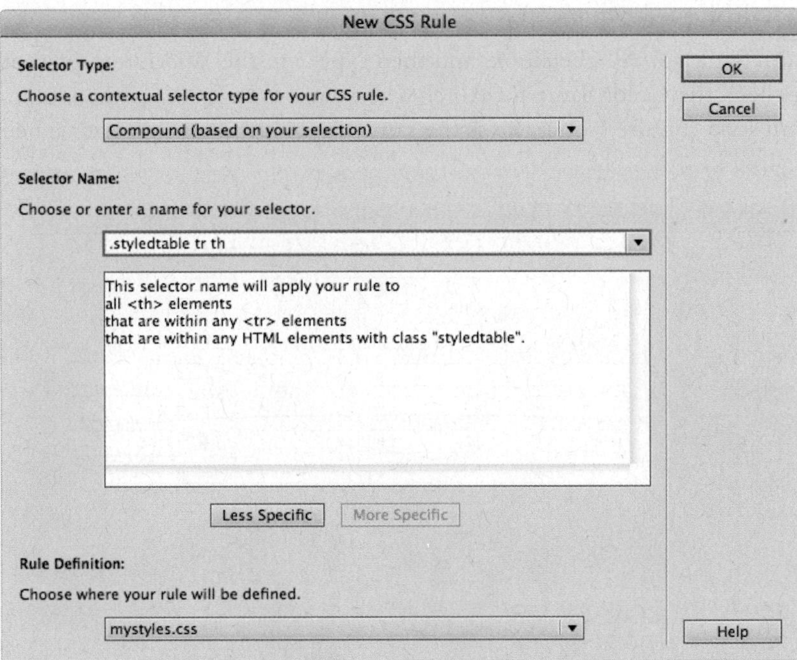

Figure 8-21: *Create a compound rule to style all header rows within the styledtable class.*

3. The Selector Name text field has been automatically populated as `.styledtable tr th`. Remember that compound rules are read from left to right. So, within the styledtable class, you are targeting table rows (`tr`) and specifically, table headers (`th`) within table rows.

4. Press OK and the CSS Rule definition dialog box opens. Select the Background category to access these options.

5. Press the Browse button to the right of the Background-image text field, and in the Select Image Source dialog box, locate the **bg_header.jpg** image and press OK (Windows) or Open (Mac OS).

6. From the Background-repeat drop-down menu, choose repeat-x from the list (Figure 8-22). The source image is a gradient that is designed to tile horizontally. Press Apply to see a preview of this effect on your table. You'll add a few other touches to this header row.

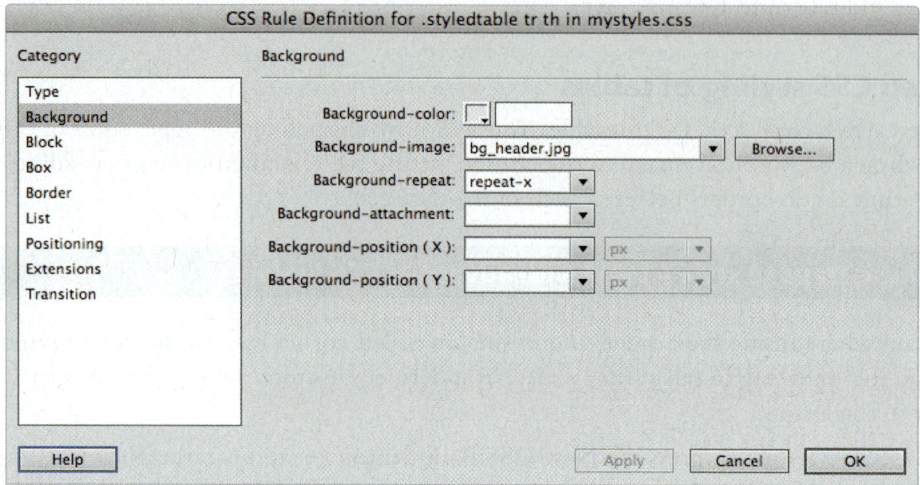

***Figure 8-22**: Choose a background image and tile it horizontally in the header row with* repeat-x.

7. Select the Border category and uncheck the Style Same for All checkbox. Choose Solid from the Bottom style drop-down menu.

8. Uncheck the Width Same for All checkbox, and then type **2** in the Width text field of the Bottom style. Uncheck the Color Same for All checkbox and type **#006** in the Color text field of the Bottom style (Figure 8-23); this is the same dark blue color that you've been using for other styling in this table.

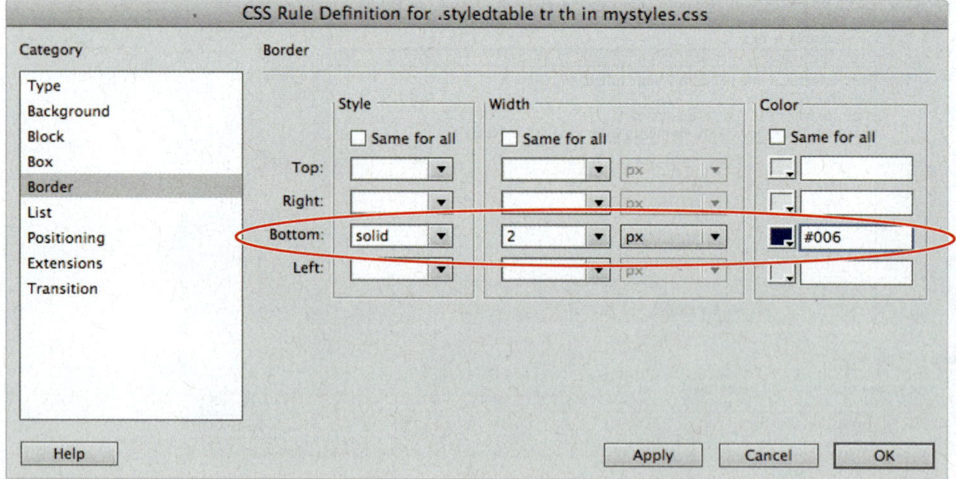

***Figure 8-23**: Applying a two-pixel-wide, solid, blue border to the bottom of the header row.*

9. Select the Type category, and type **14** into the Font-size text field to make the text slightly larger. From the Text-transform drop-down menu, choose capitalize. This property adds a capital letter to the beginning of each word.

10. Press OK to see your styled header seen here in Figure 8-24.

US Temperate Zones With Average Min. Temperatures.		
Zone	Fahrenheit	Example Cities
1	Below -50 F	Fairbanks, Alaska; Resolute, Northwest Territories (Canada)
2	-50 to -40 F	Prudhoe Bay, Alaska; Flin Flon, Manitoba (Canada)
3	-40 to -30 F	International Falls, Minnesota; St. Michael, Alaska
4	-30 to -20 F	Minneapolis/St.Paul, Minnesota; Lewistown, Montana
5	-20 to -10 F	Des Moines, Iowa; Illinois
6	-10 to 0 F	St. Louis, Missouri; Lebanon, Pennsylvania
7	0 to 10 F	Oklahoma City, Oklahoma; South Boston, Virginia
8	10 to 20 F	Tifton, Georgia; Dallas, Texas
9	20 to 30 F	Houston, Texas; St. Augustine, Florida
10	30 to 40 F	Naples, Florida; Victorville, California
11	above 40 F	Honolulu, Hawaii; Mazatlan, Mexico

***Figure 8-24**: Your header row is now styled.*

Choose File > Save All. Keep this file open as you will continue working on it in the next exercise.

Controlling cell alignment, padding, and borders with CSS

You'll now make the content within your table a bit more readable by aligning your text and padding your cells, as well as creating borders around each cell. Controlling borders and padding is much more flexible in CSS than in HTML; for example, the cellpadding values in HTML are uniform—there is no control over left, right, top, and bottom, as there is in CSS. The same applies to borders. However, before you begin styling padding with CSS, it's a good idea to remove these values from the HTML so that there are no surprises.

Follow these steps to modify cell alignment, padding, and borders with CSS | **Step-by-Step**

1. Click any corner of the table in order to select it. In the Property Inspector, notice the values for CellPad and CellSpace; they are empty, but this stands for default, not zero. You must specifically instruct Dreamweaver to use a value of zero.
2. For all three properties of CellPad, CellSpace, and Border, type **0** (Figure 8-25). Press Enter (Windows) or Return (Mac OS) when you have added the last value.

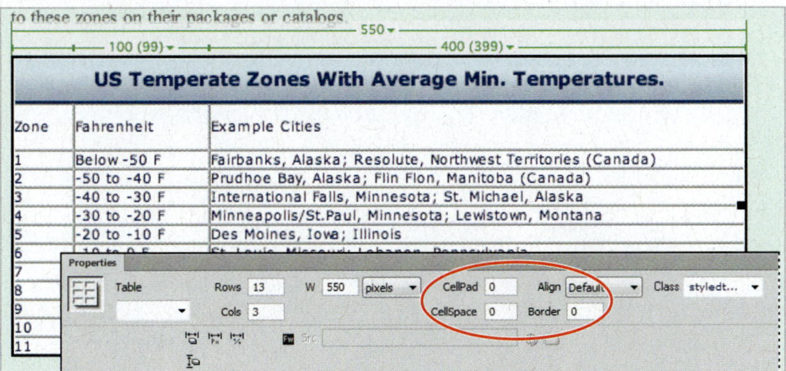

***Figure 8-25**: Type 0 for CellPad, CellSpace, and Border to make sure they are removed.*

3. Click inside any cell of your table, and in the bottom-left corner of your document window, click on the <td> tag to select a cell. You could also Ctrl+click (Windows) or Command+click (Mac OS) a cell to select it.

4. Press the New CSS Rule button (+) at the bottom of the CSS Styles panel, and the New CSS Rule dialog box appears. As in the last exercise, you are creating a Compound rule that applies only to cells within the `.styledtable` class. Your selector name reads `.styledtable tr td`. Click OK. The CSS Rule definition dialog box appears.
5. Select the Block category, then from the Text-align drop-down menu, choose center as seen in Figure 8-26. Press Apply to see this center.

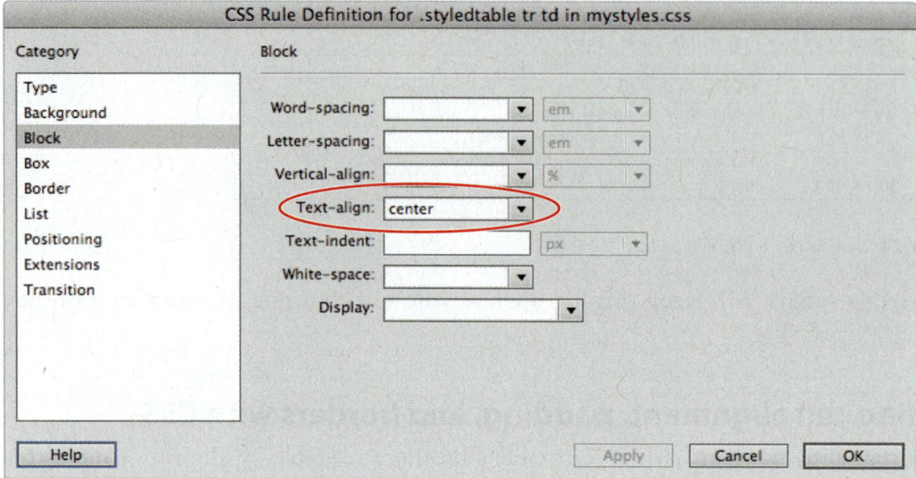

Figure 8-26: Applying a text-align of center to the <td> element centers all text in your cells.

6. Select the Box category, and in the Padding section, type **5** in the Top text field. Uncheck the Same for All checkbox. In the field for Left, type **2** and press Apply to see your text shift slightly. One of the main differences between HTML cellpadding and CSS cellpadding is the ability in CSS to control all four sides of a cell's padding individually.
7. Select the Border category, and in the Style section, choose Dashed from the Top drop-down menu.
8. Type **1** in the Width text field, and in the Color text field, type **#9AA8BD**, the hexadecimal number for a light blue-gray. Press OK to apply the style.
9. Select the row below the header row, and, if necessary, click on the HTML button in the Property Inspector, then press the Bold button to bold the text for Zone, Fahrenheit, and Example Cities.

10. Choose File > Save All. Then preview your page in your browser to see your table (Figure 8-27).

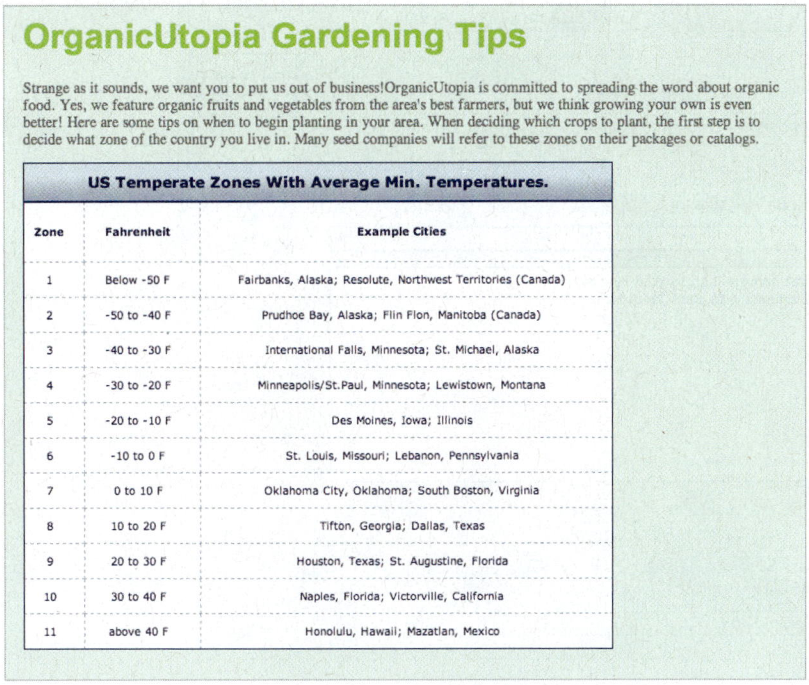

OrganicUtopia Gardening Tips

Strange as it sounds, we want you to put us out of business!OrganicUtopia is committed to spreading the word about organic food. Yes, we feature organic fruits and vegetables from the area's best farmers, but we think growing your own is even better! Here are some tips on when to begin planting in your area. When deciding which crops to plant, the first step is to decide what zone of the country you live in. Many seed companies will refer to these zones on their packages or catalogs.

US Temperate Zones With Average Min. Temperatures.

Zone	Fahrenheit	Example Cities
1	Below -50 F	Fairbanks, Alaska; Resolute, Northwest Territories (Canada)
2	-50 to -40 F	Prudhoe Bay, Alaska; Flin Flon, Manitoba (Canada)
3	-40 to -30 F	International Falls, Minnesota; St. Michael, Alaska
4	-30 to -20 F	Minneapolis/St.Paul, Minnesota; Lewistown, Montana
5	-20 to -10 F	Des Moines, Iowa; Illinois
6	-10 to 0 F	St. Louis, Missouri; Lebanon, Pennsylvania
7	0 to 10 F	Oklahoma City, Oklahoma; South Boston, Virginia
8	10 to 20 F	Tifton, Georgia; Dallas, Texas
9	20 to 30 F	Houston, Texas; St. Augustine, Florida
10	30 to 40 F	Naples, Florida; Victorville, California
11	above 40 F	Honolulu, Hawaii; Mazatlan, Mexico

Figure 8-27: *The table as rendered in a web browser.*

You're nearly finished. Now you'll add some final touches to your table to give it a little extra polish and readability. Close your web browser.

Creating alternate row styling with CSS

A common feature found in many tables is to alternate colors for every other row. When done correctly, this increases the contrast between the rows and allows the user to visually separate the content of the table. This is easily done in CSS by creating a new class solely for background color.

Follow these steps to create alternate row styling with CSS | **Step-by-Step**

1. Click on the edge of the row labeled 1 to select it. In the CSS Style panel, press the New CSS Rule button (⊕). The New CSS Rule dialog box opens.

Unlike the last few exercises, you will not be using a compound selection. Instead, you will be creating a new class. The reason for this is that you only want to style every other row. There is no automatic way to do this in CSS; after you create the class, it will have to be applied manually.

2. Choose Class from the Selector Type drop-down menu. In the Selector Name text field, type **oddrow** and press OK. (Figure 8-28).

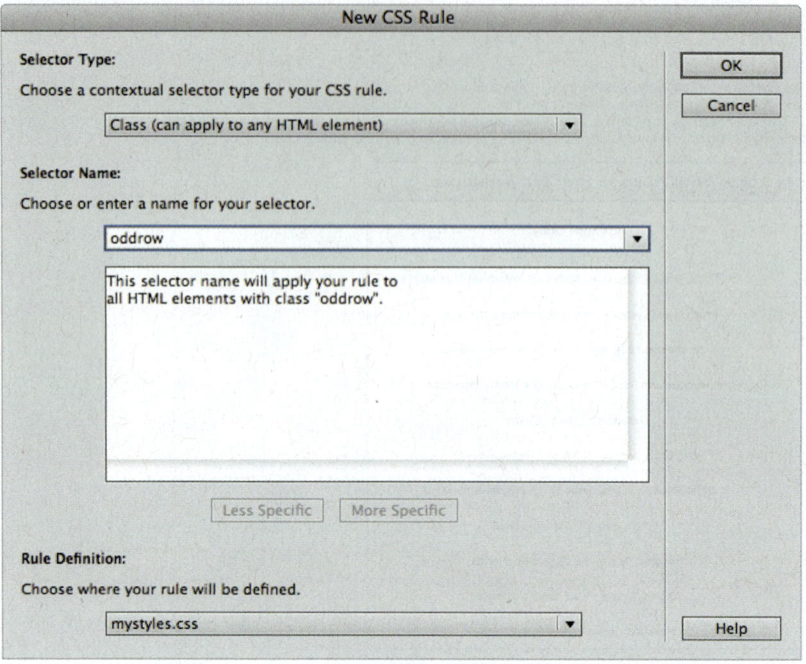

***Figure 8-28**: Create a new class named* oddrow *to style individual rows.*

3. Select the Background category, and type **#EAF1F4**, the hexadecimal color for a light blue, into the Background-color text field. Press OK. Now you will apply the oddrow class to every other row.

4. The row labeled *1* should still be selected; if not, do so now. In the Property Inspector, press the HTML button. From the Class drop-down menu, choose oddrow. The light-blue background color is applied.

5. Starting with the row labeled *3*, apply the oddrow class to all the odd-numbered rows as seen here in Figure 8-29.

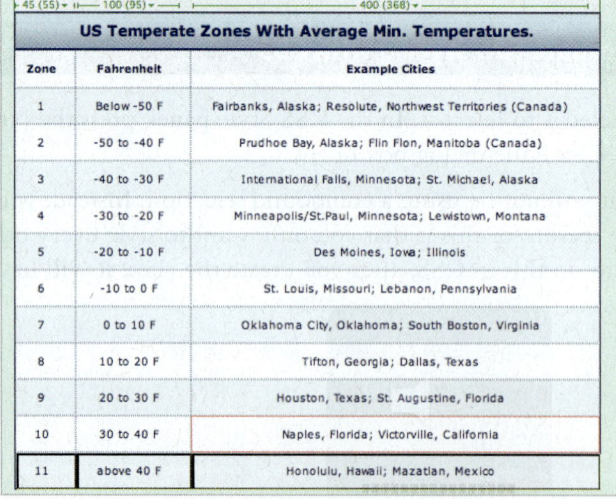

US Temperate Zones With Average Min. Temperatures.

Zone	Fahrenheit	Example Cities
1	Below -50 F	Fairbanks, Alaska; Resolute, Northwest Territories (Canada)
2	-50 to -40 F	Prudhoe Bay, Alaska; Flin Flon, Manitoba (Canada)
3	-40 to -30 F	International Falls, Minnesota; St. Michael, Alaska
4	-30 to -20 F	Minneapolis/St.Paul, Minnesota; Lewistown, Montana
5	-20 to -10 F	Des Moines, Iowa; Illinois
6	-10 to 0 F	St. Louis, Missouri; Lebanon, Pennsylvania
7	0 to 10 F	Oklahoma City, Oklahoma; South Boston, Virginia
8	10 to 20 F	Tifton, Georgia; Dallas, Texas
9	20 to 30 F	Houston, Texas; St. Augustine, Florida
10	30 to 40 F	Naples, Florida; Victorville, California
11	above 40 F	Honolulu, Hawaii; Mazatlan, Mexico

***Figure 8-29**: Styling alternating rows with a background color can improve readability.*

6. Choose File > Save All. Preview your page in the browser, then close the browser when you are finished.

Reusing CSS for other tables

As you have seen, CSS styling for tables is very powerful and capable of spicing up the appearance of tables without sacrificing their structure. Like CSS for text and layout, the real power is obvious when you apply and link the style to another table.

Follow these steps to reuse CSS with new tables

Step-by-Step

1. Double-click on the file **veggie_names.html**. This page is currently linked to the same external style sheet as the **tips.html** page, and includes an unstyled table. All that needs to be done is to apply the styledtable class you created to this table.
2. Click anywhere in the table, and then click the `<table>` tag in the lower-left corner of the document window to select the table.
3. In the Property Inspector, choose styledtable from the Class drop-down menu on the far right. The style is applied, and the appearance of this table matches the other. The style is flexible enough that, even though the top row has three cells, it has the header style applied (Figure 8-30).

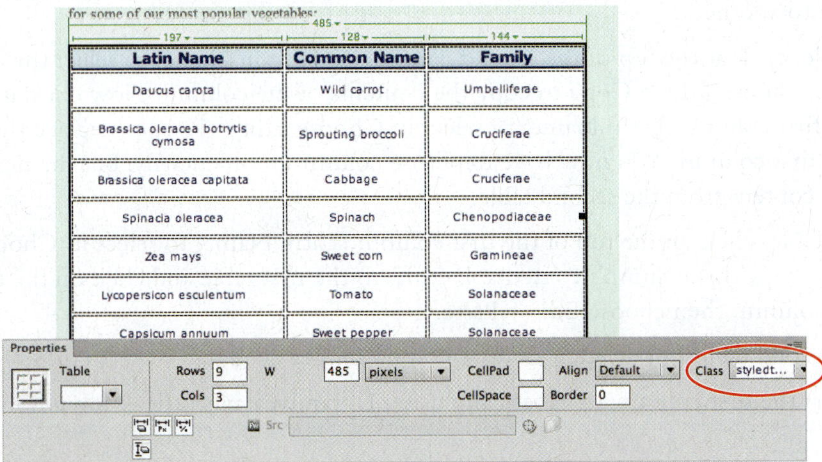

Figure 8-30: Applying the `styledtable` *class to a previously unstyled table.*

That's it! The hard work of creating the original style pays off when it comes time to creating new tables with identical style. Better yet, if you need to make a global change such as changing the background color or font color, changing a property in the external sheet will ripple through to all tables.

4. To add the alternating rows of color, click on the third row. In the Property Inspector, press the HTML button, and from the Class drop-down menu, choose oddrow. Repeat this step with every other row to add the style.

   The added benefit of having this class handy is that some tables benefit from this style more than others, and so it is your decision whether or not to use it.

5. Choose File > Save All. Keep this file open for the next exercise.

Sorting table data

There are a few other features related to managing tables that you may find useful. The structure of tables can be both a blessing and a curse. For example, take a look at the table from the previous exercise. What if you wanted to swap the order of the first two columns? There is no easy way to do this with a static HTML table. Another limitation of tables, especially tables created from tabular data where you may not have control over the order, is the difficulty of sorting the data. Dreamweaver has a feature that allows you to sort your data alphabetically by the column of your choice.

In the first part of the exercise, you will do some copy-and-pasting in order to switch the first two columns.

Step-by-Step

Follow these steps to sort tabular data

1. Click the edge of the table to select it. Choose Edit > Copy to copy the table.
2. Click to the right of the table, press Enter (Windows) or Return (Mac OS) twice, and choose Edit > Paste. You can copy and paste tables in Dreamweaver within a page, or from one page to another.
3. In the first table, click at the top of the second column (Common Name) to select the entire column. Choose Edit > Copy to copy the contents of the column. Now click at the top of the first column (Latin Name) to select it. Choose Edit > Paste to replace the content of the first column. You now have duplicate columns momentarily, but the next step is to copy content from the second table.
4. In the second table, click on the top of the first column (Latin Name) to select it. Choose Edit > Copy to copy this column's contents. Return to the first table and click on the top of the second column; then choose Edit > Paste.
5. Click on the second table and delete it now, as you no longer need it.

   Now you'll sort the first column alphabetically using Dreamweaver's little-known Sort Table feature.
6. Select the first table and choose Commands > Sort Table to open the Sort Table dialog box. You do not have to make any changes here because the default settings seen in Figure 8-31 fine, but take a quick look at the options. The Sort By menu allows you to choose which menu Dreamweaver will use to sort. The Order menu allows you to choose how the table should be sorted, either alphabetically or numerically. Alphabetically is correct for now.

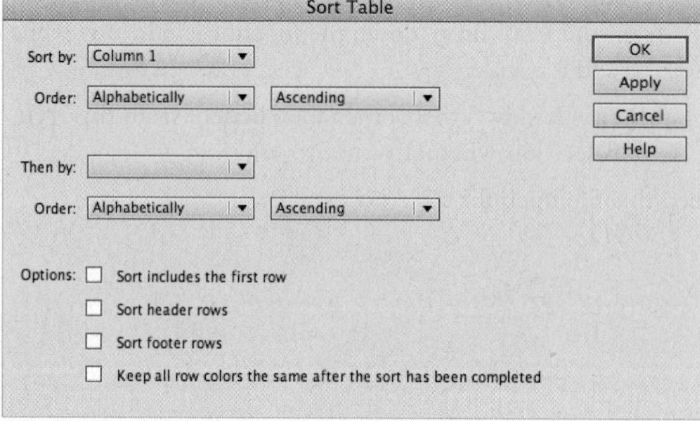

***Figure 8-31**: Choose Commands > Sort Table to sort a table alphabetically.*

7. Press OK, and the table is sorted, with the first column now in alphabetical order.
8. Choose File > Save All.

Congratulations, you have finished this lesson.

Skill Summary

In this lesson you learned how to:	Objective
Import tabular data to a web page	4.11

Knowledge Assessment

True/False

Circle T if the statement is true or F if the statement is false.

T F 1. Dreamweaver can import Microsoft Excel files (.xls or .xlsx) directly.

T F 2. Dreamweaver can import delimited text files directly.

T F 3. Dreamweaver can automatically create a table when you import a supported data file.

T F 4. You can resize a table by clicking on the border and dragging.

T F 5. You can change the color of cellspacing using the Property Inspector.

T F 6. Borders can be added to HTML using both HTML and CSS.

T F 7. You can control the cellpadding and text alignment of tables with CSS.

T F 8. You can best save and apply unique table styles with an external style sheet.

T F 9. There is an automatic method in Dreamweaver CS6 to create rows of alternating color with CSS.

T F 10. In order to sort table data you would use the Modify > Table command.

Multiple Choice

Select the best response for the following statements

1. The basic components of tables are rows, columns and ____
   a. footers
   b. borders
   c. squares
   d. cells

2. You are requesting spreadsheet data from a co-worker in order to convert it to a table in Dreamweaver. They can easily provide you the following file formats, but which of the following would be the best choice?
   a. An Excel document
   b. A tab delimited file
   c. A plain text file
   d. All of the above will do the same thing

3. In the Import Tabular Data window the default Table width option is ______
   a. Set to Percent
   b. Set to Pixels
   c. Fit to Data
   d. Prompt user to choose value

4. You might set the width of a table to a percentage value in order to do what?
   a. Ensure that the table data is mathematically accurate.
   b. Ensure that the table will expand or contract within a flexible container in your browser.
   c. Ensure that the width of the table remains constant.
   d. Remove the table from the default flow of HTML.

5. You need to add a new row to an existing table. Which of the following menu commands would you choose in order to do this?
   a. Edit
   b. Format
   c. Commands
   d. None of the above

6. Which of the following is the default style of a table caption?
   a. Captions at the top of a table with a centered alignment.
   b. Captions at the top of a table with a left alignment
   c. Captions at the bottom of a table with a centered alignment.
   d. Captions at the bottom of a table with a left alignment.

7. HTML tables whose appearance is set 100% by HTML attributes and values have which of the following problems?
   a. You cannot set a background-color using just HTML attributes and values.
   b. Copying the table from one page to another will result in a loss of the original style.
   c. It is time-consuming and inefficient to copy the table's style to another table in your site.
   d. All of the above

8. You need to create a style of alternating background colors for rows in a table. What is the most efficient way to do this.

   a. Select the row whose background color you would like to change. In the Properties panel set the BG color to the desired value. Repeat this process for every row you wish to style

   b. Create a CSS class with the name of your choosing and define a background color. Apply this class to every row you would like to style using the Properties panel

   c. Define a CSS style for the <tr> element and set the alternating colors using the background-color property

   d. Define a style for the <tr> element and set the alternating colors using the background-repeat property

9. Which of the following is a unique benefit of using CSS borders for a table?

   a. You can style any of the four sides of the table with a border.

   b. You can set the border width as a pixel value.

   c. You can choose either inside or outside border values.

   d. All of the above.

10. If you wanted to sort a table alphabetically in Dreamweaver's Design View, which of the following menu commands would you use in order to begin?

    a. Edit

    b. Modify

    c. Format

    d. Commands

Competency Assessment

Creating the structure of a table

Project 8-1

Your client is a Health Spa and they need a section of the page that clearly displays their services. A simple data table that lists them in rows and columns is a good choice for this and HTML tables are the easiest way to do this.

1. Choose File > New and from the New Document window choose Page Type: HTML and Layout: None. Save the page as **8-1.html**.
2. Click on the Design pane of the new page. Choose Insert > Table. In the Table dialog box, enter these values: Rows **5**, Columns **2**, Table width **330** pixels.
3. In the header section of the Table dialog box click the Top header option.
4. Click OK. Your table has been added.
5. First, you need to create the heading. Select the entire top row of the table you inserted and choose Modify > Table > Merge Cells to merge the two cells into one.
6. Click in the merged cell you just created, and type **Services**.
7. You have 4 more rows in your table; you will now add the following services to the first column of each row: **Swedish Massage**, **Shiatsu Massage**, **Therapeutic Massage**, and **Mud Bath**.
8. In the second column of your table, you now will add the following prices for each service: **$125**, **$100**, **$90**, and **$85**.
9. Choose File > Save. Keep this file open for the next exercise.

Project 8-2

Styling your table

You now will add a bit of color and font styling to the table you have created.

1. You should have the file **8-1.html** open from the last Project. If not, open it now.
2. Choose File > Save As and save the file as **8-2.html**.
3. In the CSS Styles panel click the New CSS Rule icon.
4. In the New CSS Rule window, click on the Selector Type menu and choose Tag. In the Selector Name section, click on the menu and scroll through the list of tags until you find "table" and then select it. Click OK.
5. In the CSS Rule Definition window that appears, click on Font-family and choose Verdana, Geneva, sans-serif;
6. Click on the Background category and then click on the Background-color swatch and select a light blue color from the swatches panel.
7. Click on the Block category and then click on the text-align menu and choose center. Click OK and your text will now be styled in Verdana and will be centered. Next you will add some space for all cells in the table in order to give your text some more breathing room.
8. In the CSS Styles panel click the New CSS Rule icon. In the New CSS Rule window, click on the Selector Type menu and choose Tag. In the Selector Name section, click on the menu and scroll through the list of tags until you find "td" and then select it. Click OK.
9. Click on the Box category and type **10** as the value for Padding (all 4 sides will be entered by default).Click OK to view your final table.

Proficiency Assessment

Project 8-3

Nesting Tables

You can place tables inside tables! Why would you do such a thing? Well, in case you want an image next to a data table but you don't want to alter the column structure of the data table.

Launch Dreamweaver CS6 if you haven't already.

1. Create a new blank HTML page.
2. Create a data table. Create a one column, one row table for an image, place an image in the table.
3. Create a one row, one column table and copy and paste the other two tables into the separate column cells.

Project 8-4

Tables and Accessibility

There are accessibility settings with relation to tables and how people using screenreaders may be affected. To see how the settings apply, you'll add them now.

Launch Dreamweaver CS6 if you haven't already.

1. Create a new blank HTML page and choose Insert > Table.
2. Add a Caption along with Summary information in the Accessibility section of the Table window.

Fine-Tuning Your Workflow

Key Terms

- Document tiling
- Favorites
- Grids
- Guides
- Panel Groups
- Panels
- Tag Selector
- Window Size
- Workspace Layout
- Zoom Level

Skill	Objective
Identify elements of the Dreamweaver interface	3.1
Use the Insert bar	3.2
Customize the workspace	3.6

Business Case

Since you've started developing websites, you got off to a good start by creating page layouts and including all the necessary content. Now, you feel the need to become more efficient with the application workspace. You'll find there are several ways of customizing the program and enabling you to configure the look and features in a way that suits your personal workflow. Let's change gears with a different project and focus a little more on reshaping the program to fit individual tastes while exploring other layout techniques...

Introduction

Before starting, make sure that your tools and panels are consistent by resetting your workspace. See "Resetting the Dreamweaver workspace" in the Starting Up section of this book.

You will work with several files from the dw9lessons folder in this lesson. Make sure that you have loaded the dwlessons folder onto your hard drive. See "Loading lesson files" in the Starting Up section of this book.

Before you begin, you need to create site settings that point to the dw9lessons folder. Go to Site > New Site, or, for details on creating a site, refer to Lesson 2, "Setting Up a New Site."

Customizing panels and panel groups

Panels can be moved, grouped, and docked to help keep everything you regularly use at your fingertips. In the next part of this lesson, you'll create a custom **workspace layout** for CSS layouts. You'll start by removing certain panels and repositioning the remaining panels.

Step-by-Step

Follow these steps to customize Dreamweaver panels

1. Make sure your dw09lessons folder has been defined as a site as described in the Starting Up section. This first exercise does not require any of the lesson files, as you will be focusing on the workspace.

   To ensure you are starting from the same workspace as we are, choose Window > Workspace Layout > Designer. Then choose 'Reset Designer,' You will now customize your panels.

2. Locate the Business Catalyst tab, click the panel menu in the top right, and then choose Close Tab Group.

3. Right-click or Control+click (Mac) the Adobe Browserlab tab and choose Close Tab Group.

4. Click once on the Files tab to expand this panel (seen in Figure 9-1). (To show a closed panel, click once. To hide it, double-click it.)

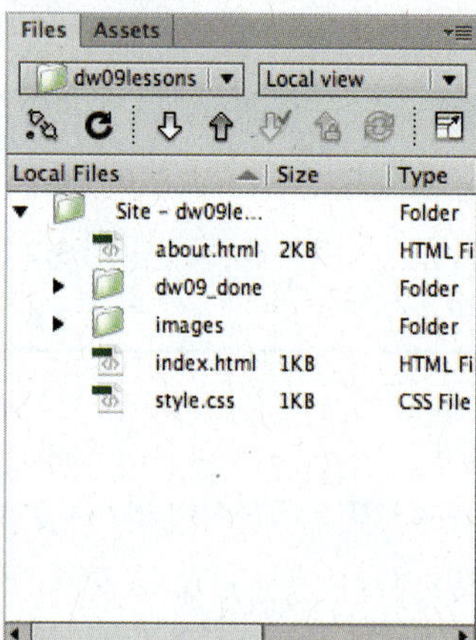

***Figure 9-1**: Click the Files tab to show the Files panel.*

There are two panels within the CSS **panel group**: CSS Styles and AP Elements. The AP Elements panel is currently hidden. In order to see both panels simultaneously, you'll drag the AP Elements panel out of the tab group.

5. Click and hold the AP Elements tab. Drag this tab into your workspace to remove it from the CSS panel group. This now becomes a floating window (seen in Figure 9-2) , which you can keep floating if you want. Many users prefer to have all their panels within a single column, so you'll add it back in now.

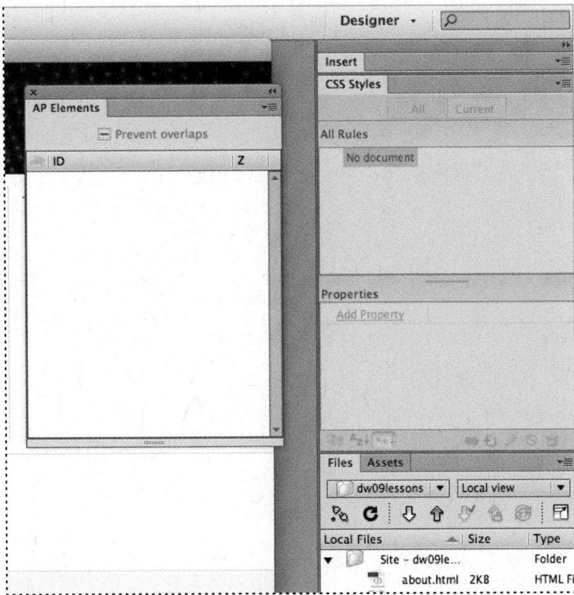

Figure 9-2: *Dragging the AP Elements panel out of the CSS panel group turns it into a floating window.*

6. To keep the AP Elements panel from interfering with your workspace, you can dock it with the other panels. Place your cursor over the AP Elements tab at the top of the panel, and click and hold.

7. Drag the AP Elements panel immediately above the title bar of the Files panel group. Be careful here: if the entire Files panel is highlighted blue, you will be *adding* to the group. You are looking for a thin blue line above the Files tab; this indicates that you are creating a new group. When a solid line appears above the Files panel group, release the AP Elements panel to snap it into place.

Customizing panels and panel groups

8. If necessary, adjust the width and height of the panels by placing your cursor on the edges of any panel group. When the black double-arrow appears, you can click and drag to adjust as needed. When you're finished, the panels should look similar to Figure 9-3. This configuration gives you quick access to the panels you'll use the most when creating the CSS-based layout in this exercise.

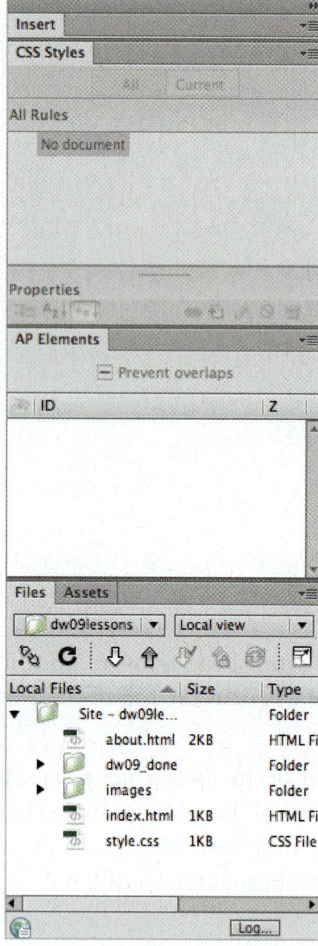

Figure 9-3: *The customized panels.*

Certification Ready 3.1

What is the Workspace Switcher?

Certification Ready 3.6

How do you open, minimize, collapse, close, resize, dock, and undock panels?

How do you access preset workspaces?

How do you change document views?

How do you save a custom workspace?

9. Dreamweaver CS6 also has the same Icon view as the other applications in the Creative Suite. Click the double-arrows on the top-right corner of the entire column of panels; they will collapse to the icon view.

10. Click the Files icon; that group will expand so you can work with it. This group will temporarily stay open until you start working on the document or click another icon.

    You can decide whether you prefer to work in the expanded panel view or the icon view. For now, you'll return to the panel view.

11. Click the double-arrows to return to the expanded panel view.

12. To save this workspace, choose Window > Workspace Layout > New Workspace. When the New Workspace Layout dialog box appears, type **CSS Layout** into the Name text field and press OK.

13. Choose Window > Workspace Layout > Designer to switch to the default workspace; then choose Window > Workspace Layout > CSS Layout to switch back to the custom workspace you just created.

Using the Favorites tab on the Insert bar

To help organize the many options available in the Insert panel, Dreamweaver groups similar items into categories. You may have already found yourself using some items more often than others. The **Favorites** category is a great way to group commonly used items into one place for quick access.

Follow these steps to edit the Favorites tab

Step-by-Step

1. Double-click the **index.html** file in the Files panel. In this exercise, you'll be inserting a number of images and AP Divs to create two pages in the Sounds of Nature website. These options are currently hidden within the insert panel, so you'll need to expand it.
2. Expand the Insert panel by clicking the Insert tab at the top of the panel. If necessary, adjust the heights of your available panels by dragging the borders between them.
3. If the menu at the top of the Insert panel is not currently set to Common, click on it and choose the Common option. Note that Images are one of the options here. Now click on the menu again and choose the Layout option and note the Draw AP Div object is listed here.

   The Insert panel has a number of different objects such as hyperlinks, form tags, Spry elements, media and other objects that you can click on to insert. However if you find yourself inserting the same objects over and over, you might want to group them. You can do this with the Favorite category of the Insert panel.
4. Click the Favorites category in the Insert panel's drop-down menu. Right-click (Windows) or Ctrl+click (Mac OS) in the empty gray area beneath the Favorite category, and choose Customize Favorites from the resulting contextual menu. The Customize Favorite Objects dialog box appears (Figure 9-4).

Certification Ready 3.2

Identify types of content that can be created or inserted by using the Insert bar.

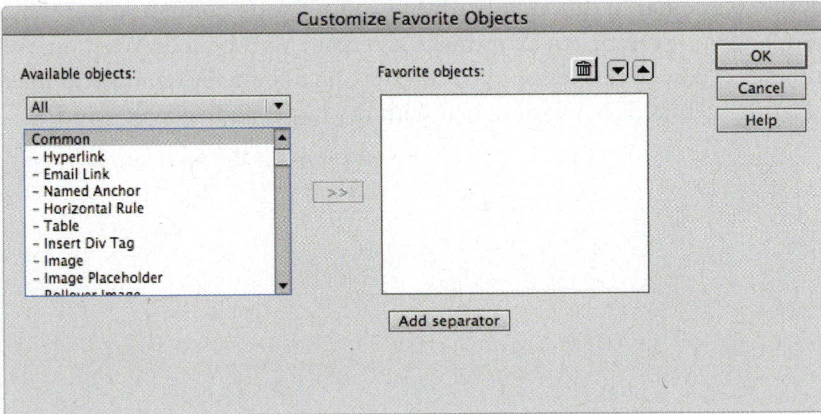

Figure 9-4: Right-click (Windows) or Ctrl+click (Mac OS) in the empty gray area beneath the Insert panel's Favorite category and choose Customize Favorites.

5. On the left side of the Customize Favorite Objects dialog box, the list of available objects is organized by the tabs, which indicate where each object can be found in the Insert bar. Select Image, then press the Add button (>>) in the middle of the dialog box (Figure 9-5).

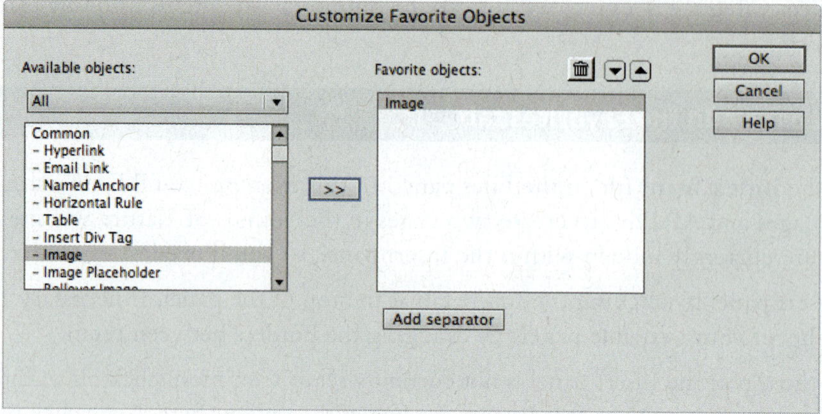

***Figure 9-5**: Select Image, and press the Add button.*

Certification Ready 3.2

What types of content can be created or inserted by using the Insert bar?

Certification Ready 3.2

How do you change between the categories on the Insert bar?

6. Click the Available Objects menu and choose the Layout category. Locate Draw AP Div from the list of available objects; then press the Add button. Press OK. The Favorites category now features the Image and Draw AP Div elements.

Resizing the document window

If you're familiar with any page layout or graphics programs, adjusting the size of the window in which you're working is probably something that you do regularly. However, when you're working on web pages in Dreamweaver, it's a good idea to think carefully about the size of your document. Because a number of different hardware and software configurations may be used to view your content, it can be tricky to make sure your website looks well on every user's computer. In the next part of this lesson, you'll resize the document window to make sure the Sounds of Nature website is being designed with the target audience in mind.

Follow these steps to resieze the Dreamweaver window

Step-by-Step

1. **Index.html** should still be open in your document window. If not, open it now. Also, make sure you're in the Design view. If necessary, press the Design View button in the Document toolbar.
2. Look at the very bottom of your document window; there are several controls relating to the **Window Size** on your screen (Figure 9-6).

Figure 9-6: ***A.*** *Mobile Size (480× 800).* ***B.*** *Tablet Size (768× 1024).* ***C.*** *Desktop Size (1000× 620).* ***D.*** *Window Size.*

Pay particular attention to the numbers 779 × 489 in our figure; this is the Window Size. It is quite likely your numbers will be different. This number represents the full width Dreamweaver is capable of displaying given the user's screen size. Because we are using a monitor set to 1024 × 768, this is as wide as Dreamweaver can display the page on *our* screen.

3. Click the Window Size numbers to access a menu. The default setting is actually set to the "Full Size" option. Dreamweaver calculates these numbers instantly.

   You will also that see there are other monitor size options in this menu. From the menu, choose the option that reads *1260× 875*. What happens on your screen depends on the size of your monitor. On our 1024 × 768 monitor, a scroll bar appears that allows us to scroll over to the right of the document. Generally speaking, you can leave this setting to Full Size unless you have a specific need to preview your page in different size screens.

Take Note...
The second value seen in this step, 1280× 1024 Maximized, refers to the "true" size of the page as if the user were maximizing their browser window to the fullest. The 1260× 875 number is a more realistic estimate of the available space a web browser would occupy on the screen (accounting for browser features, such as scroll bars).

There are three monitor icons that will allow you to change the window size to three different presets.

4. Click the first icon immediately to the right of the menu labeled 100% (Figure 9-7). This is the Mobile Size (480 × 800) preset.

Figure 9-7: *The Mobile Size preset changes the dimensions of the screen to 480 pixels wide by 800 high.*

This will set the window size to 480 pixels wide by 800 high and have the effect of cropping your current page. The goal here is to show you the window size as if you were viewing the site with a mobile device. Although this can be a useful feature, it's a bit deceptive. Dreamweaver is not trying to reproduce the behavior of a web browser on a smartphone, it's simply limiting the width and height of your current window.

A more sophisticated method of designing your pages for mobile devices is covered in Lesson 15, "Mobile Design and Layout," using the Multiscreen feature.

5. Click the next icon to the right, which is the Tablet Size. Note the change in the screen. Click the last icon, which is the Desktop view and is set to 1000 pixels by 620. All these settings can be useful if you want to see how your designs appear in these different size screens. Just remember that there is no substitute for seeing your design in a web browser.

6. Click the Window Size menu, and then click the "Full Size" option to set the screen back to the maximum amount of space on your monitor.

Changing the Zoom level

Changing the **zoom level** or magnification of a web page is very different than changing the window size as you did in the last exercise. You need to understand the difference between the two: changing the zoom level in Dreamweaver is very similar to zooming in an image program, such as Photoshop or Illustrator. In those applications, there are good reasons for changing the zoom level, since they are used for photography and illustration. On the Web, there's not as much of a need to examine objects at a magnified level.

Changing the magnification level in Dreamweaver can be helpful for exact positioning or viewing multiple documents at once, but we recommend that you return to 100 percent when you're finished. Now, you'll use the Zoom and Hand tools to navigate throughout your document.

Follow these steps to change the zoom level

Step-by-Step

1. At the bottom of the document **index.html** page, select the Zoom tool (🔍). Click twice inside the document window to zoom to 200 percent.
2. With the Zoom tool still selected, press and hold the Alt (Windows) or Option (Mac OS) key and click once inside the document window. The About page zooms out to 150 percent. These zoom shortcuts are standard across Adobe's applications.
3. At the bottom of the document window, select the Hand tool (✋) to the left of the Zoom tool. Click and drag the document in any direction within the document window. The Hand tool allows you to drag a document around in its window like a piece of paper. (Figure 9-8)

Figure 9-8*: Use the Hand tool to drag a document around in its window.*

4. Double-click the Zoom tool at the bottom of the document window to return to 100 percent. Now, choose 66% from the Set magnification drop-down menu to the right of the Zoom tool. Depending on the size of your monitor, this magnification level may allow you to see the entire About page. If not, use the Zoom tool or the Set magnification drop-down menu to find the appropriate size.

   Occasionally, this option will be useful if you have a lot of content on the page and you want to see the basic structure of the layout. Don't forget to set the view back to 100% when you are done.

5. Click the Selection tool (↖) in the bottom of the document window and choose 100% from the Set magnification drop-down menu.

Using guides

In Lesson 5, "Creating Page Layouts with CSS," you learned how AP Divs can be added to a page for precise layout. **Guides** are horizontal or vertical lines that you can add to Dreamweaver's Design view and can be a useful tool for AP Divs, as well as the other types of layout techniques. Guides allow you to line up and measure different elements on your page. In this exercise, you'll add an AP Div to index.html, and then place an image inside the div. First, you'll draw some guides to help you size and position the div.

Using guides

Step-by-Step

Follow these steps to create guides

1. If your rulers are hidden, choose View > Rulers > Show to turn them on.

Take Note...
Rulers can use inches, centimeters, or pixels in Dreamweaver. Because pixels are the most common unit of measurement on the Web, they are the default. If you prefer inches or centimeters, right-click (Windows) or Ctrl+click (Mac OS) on the rulers to access a context menu where you can choose your preferred unit. In this lesson, you'll be using pixels, so it's a good idea to stick with them for now.

2. Click inside the vertical ruler on the left side of your document window, and then drag a guide into the center of the page. Notice, as you drag, that a yellow box appears with the pixel number of your horizontal ruler. When you let go and move your cursor off the ruler, it will disappear.

   Dragging a guide manually is useful, but you can also set a guide's position precisely.

3. Double-click on this guide to open the Move Guide dialog box. From this dialog box, you can set an exact location for guides. This feature can be especially helpful when building a web page based on sketches or mockups.
4. Type **38** in the Location text field and press OK. The guide is repositioned 38 pixels from the left side of the document.
5. Create another vertical guide and set its position to 494 pixels, either by dragging it to this position or setting its value precisely.

   What if you wanted to determine the exact width between these two guides you just added? Instead of using a calculator, you can allow Dreamweaver to do it for you.

6. Press and hold the Ctrl (Windows) or Command (Mac OS) key and move your cursor across the three sections of your page as defined by the guides (seen in Figure 9-9). A blue line with arrows on either end indicates the distance between each of your guides, as well as the distance between guides and the edge of the document window. Between the two guides, you can now see that the width is exactly 456 pixels.

***Figure 9-9**: Hold down Ctrl (Windows) or Command (Mac OS) and hover over the vertical areas defined by guides.*

7. Drag two horizontal guides down from the ruler at the top of the document window. Double-click on each of them, and then use the Move Guide dialog box to position one of them 152 pixels from the top of the document, and the other 380 pixels from the top of the document.

8. Next, you'll draw an AP Div and start adding some content; but first make sure that Snap to Guides is turned on, by choosing View > Guides > Edit Guides. The Guides dialog box appears, with a number of options for customizing your guides.

   If you happen to be using a color in your web page that makes the guides hard to see, you can change their color here. Also, the Lock Guides option can be a helpful way to avoid accidentally repositioning guides. For now, make sure Snap to Guides is checked as seen in Figure 9-10 and press OK.

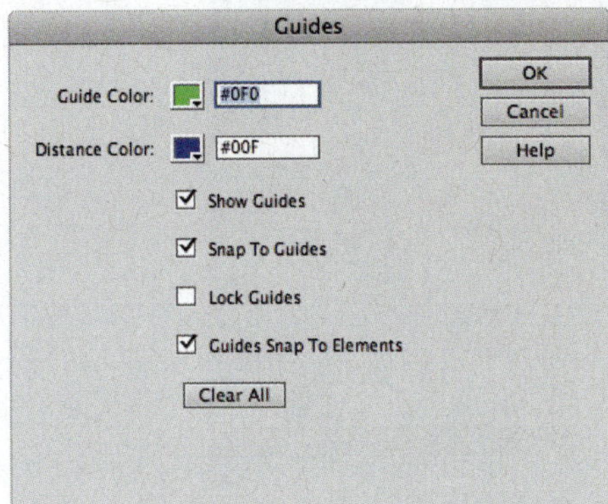

***Figure 9-10**: The Guides dialog box allows you to change the color of guides and turn snapping on and off.*

9. Now that your guides are set up, you're ready to add some content. With the Favorites category selected in the Insert panel, click the Draw AP Div object. Draw an AP Div inside the box created by your four guides.

10. The edges should snap to the guides easily. If they don't, select the div by clicking an edge and dragging it until it snaps to a guide.

11. Click inside the div to place your cursor, and then select the Image object in the Favorites category of the Insert panel.

12. In the Select Image Source dialog box, select **hp_photo.jpg** from the Images folder inside the dw09lessons folder, and press OK (Windows) or Open (Mac OS).

13. In the Image Tag Accessibility Attributes dialog box, type **Soothing Lakefront** into the Alternate text field and press OK. The **hp_photo.jpg** image fits nicely inside the div you created earlier (Figure 9-11).

***Figure 9-11**: The hp_photo.jpg placed inside of the AP Div.*

14. Choose File > Save and leave **index.html** open.

Using grids

Much like guides, **grids** are a visual aid used in Dreamweaver's Design View that consist of an overlay of vertical and horizontal lines on your page. In the next part of this lesson, you'll be adding AP Divs and images to the About page of the Sounds of Nature website. Creating a custom grid will help you align and evenly distribute these new elements on the page.

Step-by-Step

Follow these steps to create a custom grid

1. Double-click on the **about.html** file in your Files panel to open the About page. You may notice that this page has a white background and uses a default typeface. Later on, you'll use the tag selector to change this.
2. Choose View > Grid > Grid Settings to open the Grid Settings dialog box. Much like the Guides dialog box, the Grid Settings dialog box can be used to specify the grid color and turn on snapping. Type **#CCCCCC** in the Color text field and check Show Grid and Snap to Grid to turn the grid on and enable snapping.

3. For this layout, type **38** in the Spacing text field and make sure pixels are selected as the unit of measurement (Figure 9-12). Choosing a spacing of 38 pixels creates a series of squares that are 38 pixels high by 38 pixels wide. Press OK.

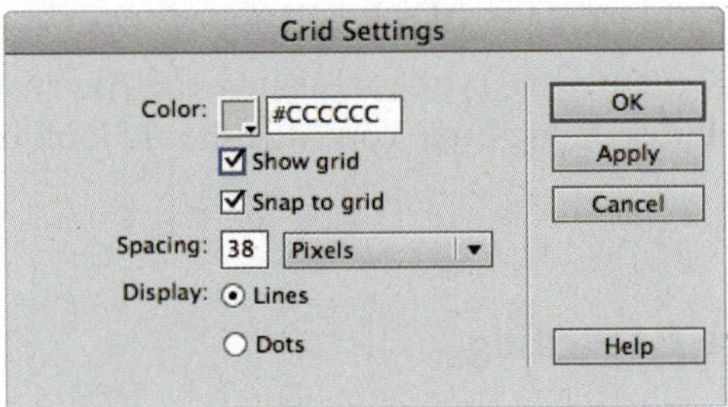

***Figure 9-12**: The Grid Settings dialog box.*

4. With the grid established, add the AP Divs that will house your images. Click the Draw AP Div object in the Favorites category of the Insert panel. Draw a square div that is 3 grid units wide and 3 grid units high. Use figure 9-13 for reference.

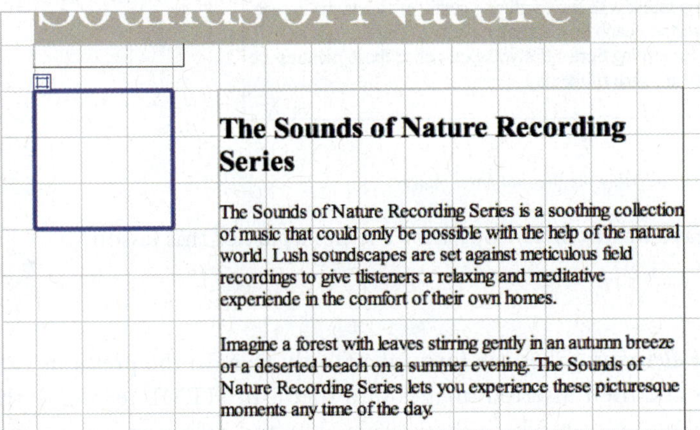

***Figure 9-13**: Draw a square AP Div.*

5. Press the Draw AP Div element in the Favorites category of the Insert panel again, and draw a second AP Div one grid unit below the first. Use Figure 9-14 for reference.

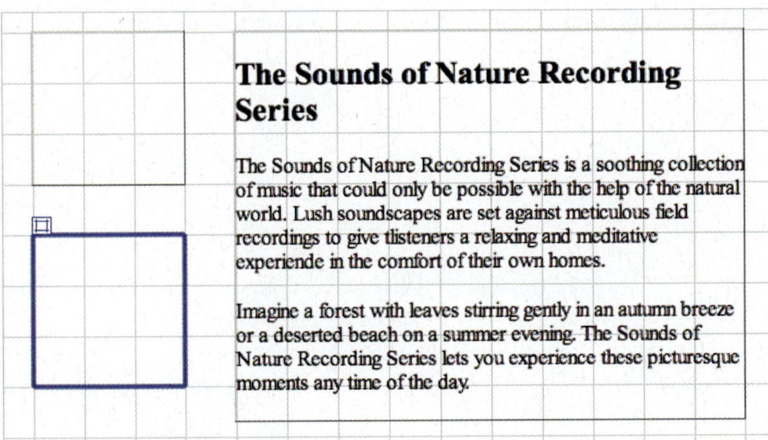

***Figure 9-14**: Draw a second AP Div one grid unit below the first.*

6. Click inside the first div to place the cursor, and then press the Image element in the Favorites category of the Insert panel.

7. In the Select Image Source dialog box, select **tree.jpg** from the images folder inside the dw09lessons folder, and press OK (Windows) or Open (Mac OS).
8. In the Image Tag Accessibility Attributes dialog box, type **tree** into the Alternate text field and press OK. The tree image is positioned inside the AP Div on your page.
9. Repeat steps 7 and 8 to add **forest.jpg** to the second div. Type **forest** into the Alternate text field of the Image Tag Accessibility Attributes dialog box. You page should look like Figure 9-15.

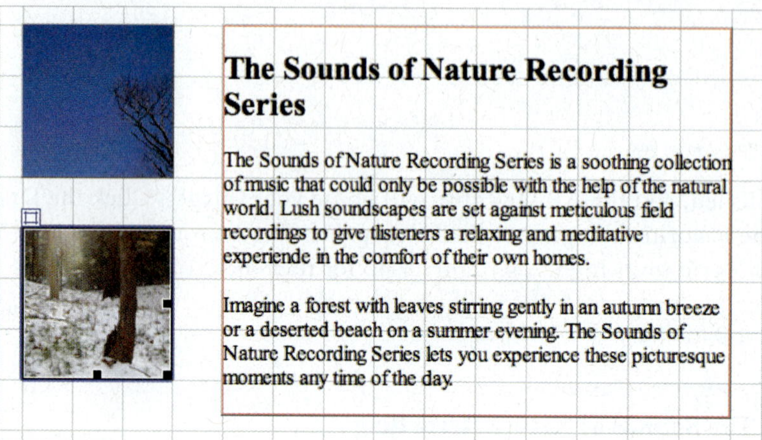

Figure 9-15: *The about.html page after inserting the tree and forest images.*

10. Choose File > Save and leave **about.html** open for the next part of this lesson.

The tag selector

In HTML, the organization of elements takes the form of a family tree. In the previous two exercises, you created AP Divs and then inserted images into them. In HTML terms, all these images are children of the AP Divs within which they reside. The **tag selector** is a feature of Dreamweaver that allows you to select HTML elements based on their relationship to one another. The tag selector has been used in previous sections of this book, but in this exercise you'll use it to apply a single style that will affect the entire about.html page.

Follow these steps to use the tag selector

Step-by-Step

1. With the About page open, click once on the forest image that you inserted at the end of the last exercise. At the bottom-left corner of the document window are a number of HTML tags. This is the tag selector. The `<img>` tag at the end of this line is highlighted to indicate that the **forest.jpg** image is selected. In addition, the Property Inspector displays information and options related to this image (Figure 9-16).

***Figure 9-16**: With the forest image selected, the <img> tag in the tag selector is highlighted and the Property Inspector displays information and options related to this image.*

2. In the tag selector, click on the `<div#apDiv2>` tag to the left of the `<img>` tag. Notice that the options in the Property Inspector change to reflect the selected div. In this case, you've selected the parent of the forest image.
3. To further illustrate this relationship, choose Edit > Select Child from the main menu. The `<img>` tag becomes highlighted in the tag selector, and the Property Inspector changes to reflect the selected element.
4. Now, select `<body>` on the far-left side of the tag selector. The Property Inspector displays options and information related to the `<body>` tag. Press the CSS button in the Property Inspector if necessary and then, from the Targeted Rule drop-down menu, choose body_style (Figure 9-17).

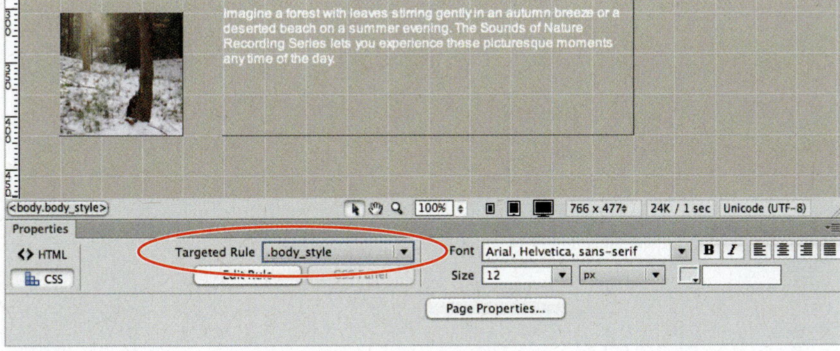

***Figure 9-17**: With the <body> tag selected in the tag selector, choose body_style from the Targeted Rule drop-down menu.*

Because many CSS properties are inherited throughout the document, it is possible to write generalized rules that will be applied to all the elements on a page. In this case, body_style changes the font and text color for the entire document because every element is a descendant of the body.

5. Choose File > Save and leave **about.html** open for the next part of this lesson.

Tiling documents

By default, Dreamweaver organizes open documents with a series of tabs in the upper-left corner of the document window. If you'd like to compare documents, or you simply prefer to use separate windows for each document, the tiling option provides an alternative for viewing open files. **Document tiling** allows you to place one or more pages side by side on your screen. Next, you'll use this feature to simultaneously view the index page and the about page of the Sounds of Nature website.

Step-by-Step

Follow these steps to view multiple documents using tiling

1. Both **index.html** and **about.html** should still be open. If they are not, open them now.
2. Choose Window > Tile Vertically (Windows) or Window > Tile (Mac OS). This will send the two pages into two windows side-by-side. This feature can be useful for dragging and dropping objects from one page to another or to work on both pages if you have a big enough monitor.

   The fastest way to group these two pages back together is different depending which platform you are on PC or Mac.
3. On the Mac, click the **index.html** tab, drag it to the **about.html** tab, and then release it. They will now be grouped as tabs again. On the PC, the best way to group the two document windows again is to click on the maximize button in the top right corner of one of the documents.

You have finished Lesson 9, "Fine-Tuning Your Workflow."

Skill Summary

In this lesson you learned how to:	Objective
Identify elements of the Dreamweaver interface	3.1
Use the Insert bar	3.2
Customize the workspace	3.6

Knowledge Assessment

True/False

Circle T if the statement is true or F if the statement is false.

T F **1.** Docked panels in Dreamweaver are permanently attached and are unable to be separated from one another.

T F **2.** Dreamweaver allows you to create and save your own workspace layouts.

T F **3.** Double-clicking on a ruler guide will open up the Move Guide dialog box.

T F **4.** There is a Lock Guides option in Dreamweaver used to avoid accidentally repositioning guides.

T F **5.** You cannot change the color of the Grid feature in Dreamweaver.

T F **6.** The tag selector is a feature in Dreamweaver that allows you to select HTML elements based on their relationship to one another.

T F **7.** Dreamweaver includes preset window sizes that allow you to preview what your page would look like in mobile devices and tablets, in addition to web browsers.

T F **8.** Images cannot be placed inside an AP Div, they are only used for text content.

T F **9.** CSS rules cannot be applied through the Property inspector; they can only be applied through the CSS panel.

T F **10.** Grids can be displayed as either lines or dots.

Multiple Choice

Select the best response for the following statements

1. You can organize the options available in the Insert Bar using which category?

a. Common
b. Data
c. Favorites
d. Layout

2. What is the default zoom value recommended for working in Dreamweaver?

a. 66%
b. Fit on screen
c. 100%
d. 75%

3. What units of measurement is the Dreamweaver ruler feature capable of?

a. Pixels
b. Inches
c. Centimeters
d. All of the above

4. Which of the following workspace layouts is best to work with in Dreamweaver?

a. Classic
b. Coder
c. Designer
d. It depends on the user and what they're doing

5. With 2 guides or more, and your mouse hovering over one of the guides, what is the keyboard modifier that needs to be held down in order to display the blue line that shows the distance between the guides?

a. Ctrl (Windows) or Command (Mac OS)
b. Shift
c. Alt (Windows) or Option (Mac OS)
d. None of the above

6. Which type of element can you click and drag on in order to move and place it according to pre-existing guides?

a. Table
b. Frame
c. Layout Box
d. AP Div

7. Of the preset display sizes, which one is geared specifically toward tablet devices?

a. 480 × 800
b. 768 × 1024
c. 1000 × 620
d. 1024 × 1220

8. Which menu in Dreamweaver allows access to changing Guide properties?

a. Window
b. Edit
c. View
d. Help

9. Which panel will allow you to access both HTML and CSS information?

a. Properties
b. CSS Styles
c. Assets
d. Snippets

10. Which of the following Grid Settings is not adjustable?

  a. Color
  b. Line thickness
  c. Spacing
  d. Display style

Competency Assessment

Changing the Physical Properties of a Div

Project 9-1

Something people forget about DIVs is that they can serve as a design element in addition to being a container. You'll add a DIV to a webpage to explore this concept more by using the CSS Styles panel.

1. Choose File > New > Blank Page > HTML > None to create a new empty webpage.
2. Using the Insert panel, choose the Layout category. Select the Draw AP Div tool.
3. Click and drag a AP Div on your webpage, don't worry about where you place it or how big it is.
4. Make sure the new AP Div is selected by clicking it on the webpage.
5. Choose Window > CSS Styles.
6. Click on the arrow to the left of <style> and then double-click the #apDiv1 element.
7. Use the Rule Definition panel to try out the various appearance options such as Background and Border. To keep the window open while experimenting, use the Apply button to view your changes. When you are satisfied with the results, click OK.
8. Save your file, name it **Lesson9_Project.html** and keep it open for the next exercise below.

Naming AP Divs

Project 9-2

You can be more specific about naming your AP Divs for both code purposes as well as organization.

1. Keep the file from Project 9-1 open.
2. Choose Window > AP Elements.
3. Select an AP Div on your page and use either the Properties panel or AP Elements panel to rename your AP Div to a more specific, descriptive name.

Proficiency Assessment

More Workspaces

Project 9-3

As you saw, you can create your own workspaces or use what's built in. Look further into the workspaces Dreamweaver has to offer to see more ways that you can establish your workspace.

Launch Dreamweaver CS6 if you haven't already.

1. Create a new blank HTML page.
2. Go to Window > Workspace Layout and try out the various layouts.

Project 9-4 Status Bar Window Settings

In the Document window you can of course adjust the monitor size you're trying to match to. But you can also add your own, custom values in there too; for example a specific laptop you're trying to target.

Get Ready. Launch Dreamweaver CS6 if you haven't already.

1. Create a new blank HTML page.
2. Choose Edit > Preferences (Windows) or Dreamweaver > Preferences (Mac OS). Go to the Status Bar to adjust the preset monitor settings.

Circling Back 2

As you saw earlier in the chapter, guides and grids are beneficial features that aid in the process of creating your layout. There will be occasions when you have a client who doesn't know the type of layout they want, and asks you to improvise. In such cases, you will need to design your own layout. Many new web designers will make the mistake of trying to design and create the layout at the same time. This isn't the best approach to take, especially when you're new to the program and the process. You can end up frustrated when trying to understand the features of Dreamweaver and trying to figure out design at the same time.

Project 1 Creating a Mockup

For the next exercise, you won't need a computer, just pencil and paper.

With pencil and paper in hand, open a web browser. Start visiting various websites that you find inspiring. If you need more direction, try *www.bestwebgallery.com* for some ideas. Make notes about the designs you like and why. Translate the visual design of the sites you find into a sketch. Use squares to abstractly mark up the numbers of columns, headers, footers, and navigation, and horizontal lines to represent text.

Once you have a sense of how other layouts are built, try one on your own. You don't need to be a great artist, just draw squares to represent images and straight lines to represent text content. This is how most websites by professionals start, with a simple drawing to represent where elements such as graphics, text, and media will be placed.

1. Draw at least 4 or 5 layouts to give yourself some options to choose from and explore design a bit.
2. Pick the one you like best for the next project.

Bringing Your Layout to Life

Project 2

Now that you have an idea of what your layout is in sketch form, you can focus on putting it together in Dreamweaver.

1. Open Dreamweaver and establish a new site and root folder called **Layout**.
2. Create a new HTML page in Dreamweaver and save it as **layout1.html**.
3. Using your drawings as a reference, recreate the basic layout structure using the guides as you did earlier in this lesson.
4. If you don't see the rulers, choose View > Rulers > Show. Double-check that the units are in pixels.
5. Start dragging out ruler guides to represent the layout you chose.
6. Once the guides are in place, add images and text using AP Divs.

Don't Forget to Customize!

Project 3

Remember that you can reconfigure your workspace to suit your needs. If you're unhappy with how the program is presented, change it and create your own workspaces.

1. Open Dreamweaver. Find panels that you like to use regularly and open them (e.g., Window > CSS Styles if you are using CSS heavily).
2. Drag and drop the panels you have open into a configuration you like.
3. Choose Window > Workspace Layout > New Workspace. In the dialog box that appears, type a name for the workspace (you can use your name) and click OK.
4. Find another task (or set of tasks) you do on a regular basis; open the panels that would go with the task or tasks (e.g., Snippets and Behaviors if you're doing code work) and set up a new workspace for that particular task.
5. Repeat as necessary to create your own custom workspaces.

Adding Flash, Video, and Sound Content

Key Terms

- Browser plug-in
- Flash Player
- Flash Video
- Progressive Download
- Quicktime
- Sound
- Streaming Video
- Windows Media
- Video

Skill	Objective
Use the Assets panel	3.4
Include video and sound in a web page	4.7
Add animation and interactivity to content	4.8

Business Case

The owners of Organic Utopia would like to add more exciting content to their site in the form of sound and video. Video is a must-have now to add more engaging visual elements and set your site apart from others. Once you understand some of the format considerations and how to use them, video becomes an indispensable tool that will take your site to a whole new level.

Introduction

Before starting, make sure that your tools and panels are consistent by resetting your workspace. See "Resetting the Dreamweaver workspace" in the Starting Up section of this book.

You will work with several files from the dw10lessons folder in this lesson. Make sure that you have loaded the dwlessons folder onto your hard drive. See "Loading lesson files" in the Starting Up section of this book.

Before you begin, you need to create a site definition that points to the dw10lessons folder. Go to Site > New Site, or, for details on creating a site definition, refer to Lesson 2, "Setting Up a New Site."

Making web content interesting

Adding video, sound, and animation to a web page is one way to make your pages more interesting and engaging. **Video**, for example, plays a key role in supplying interesting and varied web content. The barrier to creating original video has decreased dramatically in recent years as has the barrier to distributing these videos online. Videos allow individuals and companies to post commercials, speeches, and other content that otherwise would be difficult or cost-prohibitive to reach a large audience.

Sound allows you to enhance web pages by supplementing visual content with music or sound effects. Sound also inspires user interaction (as you'll see later in this lesson), thereby giving the user a more interesting online experience.

Animation gives web pages a whole new life by adding movement and effects to images that still pictures just can't match. Something moving on a web page automatically draws a visitor's eye. Movement is especially effective for banner ads, buttons, and whatever else you'd like your visitors to pay attention to.

Best Practices for Animation

Although animation can be a great addition to your pages, there are a few things to keep in mind:

- **Animations should not be distracting**. Users might enjoy your animation the first time, but if they are trying to read an article on your website, that animation might not be so enjoyable after the 40th time. Most animated content can be set to play one or two times, avoid animations that endlessly loop if at all possible.
- **Animations should add value**. Creating animations is a fun process for the designer, but it is easy to get carried away. Gratuitious animation can actually remove value from your site. Before adding any element with animation, take a step back and consider if it is truly useful for the user.
- **Keep it short**. Unless the animation is the only content on the page, try to keep your animations as short as possible.Your users may not have the patience for a long animation and longer animations will also be larger file size which translates to a longer download time.
- **Manage file size and be aware of technical limitations**. Animations will necessarily add file size to your page and this may affect those users with slower bandwidth (such as mobile users). In fact, your mobile users may not be able to view your animation at all depending on the technologies involved. For example, currently there is no support of the Flash plugin on Apple's iOS platform so your animations will not play on devices such as the iPhone and iPad.

Certification Ready 4.8

What are the best practices when including animation in a web page?

Inserting Flash movies

Adobe's Flash CS6 Professional application is used primarily to create animation and interactive projects. In terms of animation, you can use Flash to create animated web banners, buttons, splash pages, slide shows, and more. Inserting Flash animations into your web page is a great way to bring life to an otherwise static environment.

Web banners are a significant component of online advertising, and if a web banner includes moving elements, that movement automatically draws the user to the banner. In this exercise, you will add a flash banner to place on a website.

Follow these steps to insert a Flash movie

Step-by-Step

1. In the Files panel, navigate to the dw10lessons folder, and double-click the **banner.html** page to open it.
2. If the page opens in Split view, click on the Design view button.

Take Note...

If you have just finished Lesson 9, you may still have your grids and rulers turned on. They are not necessary for this lesson and you may turn them off by choosing View > Rulers and unchecking Show and choosing View > Grid > and unchecking Show Grid.

3. Click in the empty div element at the top of the sidebar on the right. A div element of 220 by 250 has been created for you seen here in Figure 10-1.

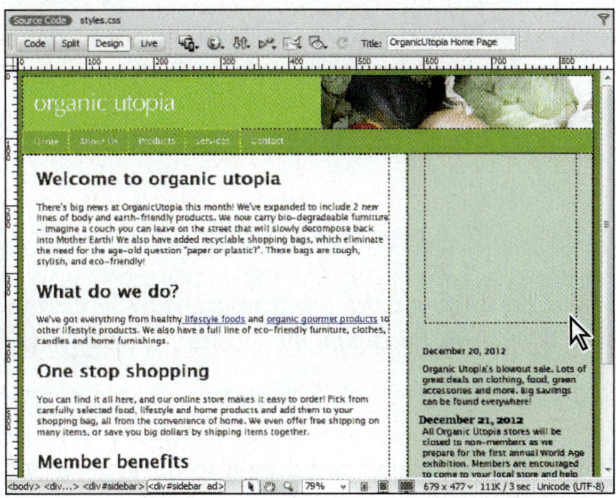

Figure 10-1: Click in the empty div element named `#sidebar _ ad`.

4. Click on the Assets tab of the Files panel, and locate the fourth button down, the Flash button, labeled SWF (Figure 10-2). Click on this button to see the list of .swf files in this site.

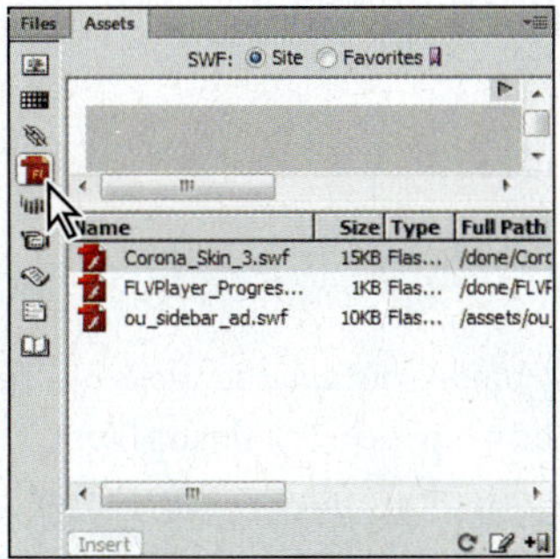

Figure 10-2: Press the Flash button in the Assets tab of the Files panel.

Learning More

Certification Ready 3.4

What are the Site and Favorites lists on the Assets panel used for and how can you edit them?

Site assets versus Favorite assets

The Assets panel contains a complete list of all recognized assets within a site (such as the 3 swf files in your current site), although initially very useful, imagine a site that had hundreds of SWF files (or any other category of Assets such as images or colors). Locating a particular file could take a while.

For this reason, Dreamweaver has a Favorites list to which you can add frequently used assets and group related assets together. You can also give them nicknames to remind yourself what they're for, and find them easily in the Assets panel.

Working with Favorites list

- Select one or more assets in the Site list of the Assets panel, then click the Add To Favorites button.
- To view Favorites click on the Favorites radio button at the top of the Assets panel.
- To place Favorite assets into a group click the New Favorites folder in the Assets panel, label the folder and then drag one or more Favorites into the folder.
- To remove a Favorite click the Remove from Favorites button

Take Note...

Favorite assets are not stored as separate files on your disk; they're references to the assets in the Site list. Dreamweaver keeps track of which assets from the Site list to display in the Favorites list.

Certification Ready 3.4

How do you apply assets from the Assets panel to a web page?

5. Click on the **ou_sidebar_ad.swf** file in the Assets panel and drag it to the sidebar_ad div to insert it.
6. Type **Organic Utopia sidebar ad** in the Title text field when the Object Tag Accessibility Attributes dialog box appears, then press OK.

   As you can see, inserting a Flash movie into a web page is much like inserting an image. The width and height of the .swf are automatically established based on the file's physical size, just as they are for images such as .jpeg and .gif files.

   The .swf file appears with a generic Flash icon on a gray image.

Take Note...

You must have **Flash Player***, which is available free from Adobe, installed to view an .swf file. If you don't have the application installed, visit* adobe.com/products/flashplayer *to download and install it. Note that visitors to your website also must have Flash Player installed to view your Flash content. A good rule of thumb when including Flash content on a website is to let visitors know as soon as they get to your site that they'll need to have Flash Player. Be sure to include the link to the Flash Player web page (the URL provided at the beginning of this paragraph) so that visitors can download the Flash Player, if necessary.*

7. To see the page in the browser choose File > Save, then File > Preview in Browser (Figure 10-3). If the Copy Dependent Files window appears, press OK. These are files that Dreamweaver automatically adds to the site. Included here is code to help users who may not have the Flash plug-in installed.

Figure 10-3: Your Flash web banner as seen in the browser.

8. After previewing, close the browser. There are other options in the Properties panel available for Flash files. If you have the Flash authoring program installed you could click on the Edit button, for example, and locate the .FLA authoring file connected with the .swf file. This would allow an easy link if you needed to update or modify your sidebar ad.

Certification Ready 4.8

How do you add SWF files to a web page?

9. You can also preview Flash animations directly within Dreamweaver by using Live view. Click the Live button and you will see your sidebar animation play. Press the Live button again to exit the Live view.

Certification Ready 4.8

How do you view SWF files in Live Mode?

Adding video

Adding video to a web page is relatively easy, assuming the video has already been optimized for the Web. A full discussion about the various file formats and how to convert digital video to a web optimized format is beyond the scope of this book. However, the decision to include web video should be based on an evaluation of your audience. The large file sizes associated with video can affect the experience of users who don't have high-speed Internet connections. In this section, you will learn how to integrate video into your web pages using three of the most popular formats: Flash Video, QuickTime, and Windows Media.

Flash Video

Flash video has been widely used for web video for a number of years, and is still the format of choice for a large number of sites. This is changing somewhat due to the rise of mobile devices (and specifically the lack of support for Flash video on these devices). Nevertheless, one of the primary advantages of Flash Video is that playback is enabled for any browser with the Flash plug-in. Since more than 95% of all desktop web browsers have some version of the plug-in installed, this means your video will find the widest possible audience. Again, this is not always true on mobile. Additionally, Flash video can be compressed to a reasonable size while maintaining image quality.

Different programs create Flash video, including the Adobe Media Encoder, Premiere Pro, and even Photoshop. Creating the video is a separate process, so you'll want to do your homework and learn as much as you can about how it works in order to get the best results. There are essentially two file formats that are used in Flash video: .flv and .f4v. The .flv format is the traditional flash video format and .f4v is a newer format. In this exercise, you'll add a pre-existing .flv video file into your page and add simple player controls to allow users to control the playback of the movie.

Follow these steps to insert a Flash video

Step-by-Step

1. Click the Files panel if necessary, then double-click the **flashvideo.html** file. In the Design view, click below the heading, *A look at our vegetables.*
2. Choose Insert > Media > FLV. The Insert FLV dialog box will appear (Figure 10-4). Make sure the video type is set to Progressive Download Video and then, to the right of the URL field, click Browse. The Select FLV window opens. Browse to your assets folder and select the **ou_veggies.flv** file and then press OK (Windows) or Open (Mac OS).

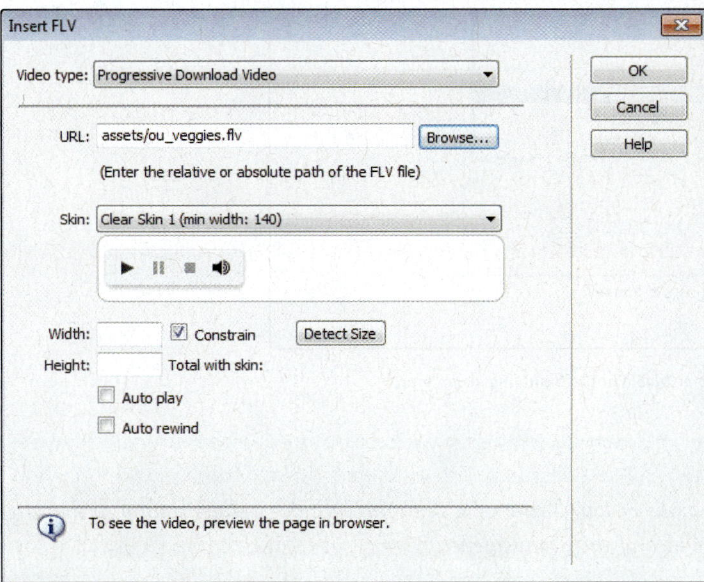

***Figure 10-4**: The Insert Flash Video dialog box.*

Take Note...

In this example, Progressive Download Video was chosen instead of Streaming Video because the former is the more common method among web developers. **Progressive Download** *Video works by downloading the video to the user's hard-drive; however, the video will start to play as soon as it is able. In other words, the user doesn't have to wait for the entire video to download in order to see it.* **Streaming Video** *streams video content and plays it on a web page after a short buffer period. The buffer period ensures smooth playback. The catch is that to enable Streaming Video, your videos must be accessible through a web streaming service such as Adobe Flash Media Server. If you want to learn more about the process, click the Help button on the Insert Flash Video dialog box.*

Next, you'll want to select a skin. A skin is a control panel that shows up on the bottom of the video, and allows the user to control video playback. In other words, this is where users can play, rewind, and fast-forward their videos.

3. Click on the Skin drop-down menu to examine your choices. You see a preview of the skin just below the menu. In Figure 10-5, we used Corona Skin 3.

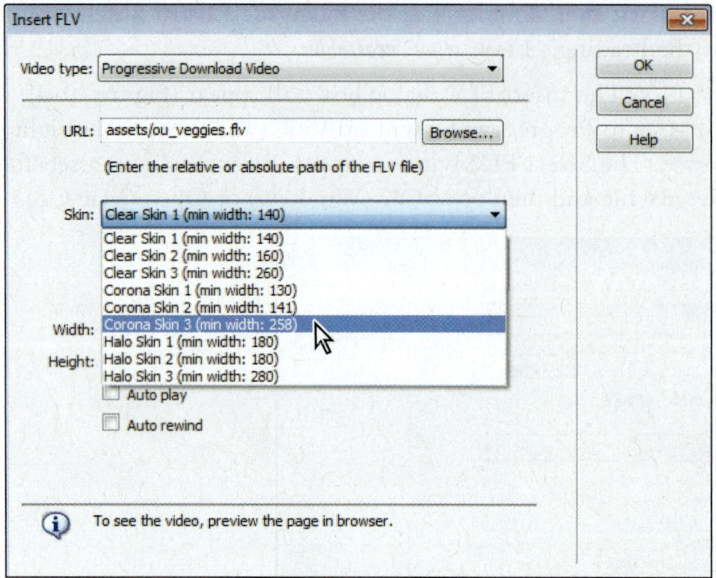

Figure 10-5: *A number of skins are available in the Skin drop-down menu.*

Take Note...

If your video is ten seconds or longer, choose a skin that includes a slider control so that users can scroll through the video at their convenience.

4. Click on the Detect Size button so that Dreamweaver can establish the physical space the video will occupy on the page. The size is based on the size of the actual video.

   You can manually type in a size, too, although be sure you are aware of the dangers here. Entering a size that's bigger than the original video will either blur or pixelate your video. Additionally, the width and height of a video is called the aspect ratio, and if you enter a width and height that do not match the original aspect ratio, then your viewers will see distorted video. In general, there's no reason not to let Dreamweaver detect the video size.

5. Press OK to insert the video.

   You can't see the video in Dreamweaver, so choose File > Save, then File > Preview in Browser to preview it in a web browser (Figure 10-6). This particular skin will allow you to scrub through your playback as well as mute and change the volume. Close the browser when you are finished previewing.

Figure 10-6:The Flash video and player controls on your page.

Learning More

Certification Ready 4.7

What are the benefits of using HTML5 to include video in a web page?

Certification Ready 4.7

What are the best practices when including HTML5 video in a web page?

Certification Ready 4.7

How do you add HTML5 video to a web page?

HTML5 Video

HTML5 video is a relatively new alternative to Flash video (and other plug-in based video such as Quicktime or Windows Media Video). It has become particularly popular for iOS devices such as the iPhone and iPod which do not support Flash (and by extension Flash Video). HTML5 video supports certain types of video in their native formats such as .MP4, .OGV and .WEBM and does not require a browser plug-in. A **browser plug-in** is a module of code that is not installed in a web browser by default, the most notable plug-in is perhaps Adobe's Flash Player. To add video to a page you can add the `<video>` tag and any browser that supports this tag (as well as the codec for the type of video being used) will play the video.

There are additional benefits to using HTML5 video: There are a set of native video controls (such as play, pause and volume) that can be added with a simple line of code and are keyboard accessible. Because of the architecture and specification of the `<video>` tag additional features such as text transcripts and/or captions can be added and in general HTML5 video is more searchable and discoverable by search engines because the code is exposed as an element with attributes (just like the paragraphs and headings on a page).

Adding HTML5 video to a web page

Unlike Flash Video, Dreamweaver CS6 does not have a specific command or object in the Insert menu allowing you to easily add HTML5 video. You must type the `<video>` element and any attributes in the Code view.

1. Choose File > New and in the New Document window make sure the page type is set to HTML and then click on the DocType menu and choose HTML5 and then click Create.

   A new untitled document is created.

2. Choose File > Save and save this file into the same folder as the video you would like to add (For this exercise we refer to an .mp4 video file and a .webm video file).
3. Click on the Code button to enter the code view and then locate the opening `<body>` tag and press return/enter to add space between the two `<body>` tags.
4. Add the following code:

```
<video autoplay controls tabindex="0">
<source src="my _ video.mp4" type='video/mp4;
codec="mp4a.40.2"'> <source src="my _ video.webm" type='video/
webm; codec="vp8"'> </video>
```

In this example you will need to replace the values my_video.mp4 and my_video.webm with the names of your own video files (as well as supply the video files themselves).

In this example, there are two video files being declared as the source. It is considered best practice to provide multiple video files when using HTML5 video because there is no single video format that is supported by all browsers. In this example .mp4 is supported by the most recent versions of Apple Safari and Internet Explorer and .webm is supported by the most recent versions of Mozilla Firefox and Google Chrome.

The attributes in the opening `<video>` tag are `autoplay`, `controls` and `tabindex="0"`. These are optional but very useful. The `autoplay` attribute begins the video automatically, the `controls` attribute adds basic player controls and the `tabindex` attribute ensures that the player is keyboard accessible.

QuickTime video and Windows Media

QuickTime and **Windows Media** are also common video formats used on the Web. In many ways they are similar; both offer compressed video with various levels of image and sound quality. When adding either file format to a page, the key thing to keep in mind is that viewers must have the necessary plug-in to view the video. Unlike Flash video, this is not necessarily a sure thing. QuickTime is traditionally Mac OS-based and Windows Media Video is traditionally Windows-based.

You can download QuickTime from *Apple.com/quicktime/download.* To view Windows Media files, you need Windows Media Player, which you can download at *Microsoft.com/windows/windowsmedia/download.* (At the time of this writing, there was no plug-in support from either Apple or Microsoft that allowed Windows Media Video to play on a Mac.)

QuickTime and Windows Media video are inserted into a page the same way as Flash Video. The difference between the video formats is that users create QuickTime and Windows Media video using different software applications, for example Adobe Premiere Pro and Apple Final Cut Pro.

The process for inserting either QuickTime or Windows Media Video is the same. In this example you may choose either format depending on your platform.

Follow these steps to insert a QuickTime or Windows Media Video

Step-by-Step

1. In the Files panel, open the **insertvideo.html** file. Click below the heading, *A look at our vegetables*, if necessary.
2. Go to the Assets panel and select the Movies button to show the videos available in your site.
3. Right-click (Windows) or Ctrl+click (Mac OS) on the **veggies.mov** file (or the **veggies.wmv** if in Windows), and choose Insert from the contextual menu to insert it into the page. You'll see a plug-in icon ( ) on the page, indicating that a plug-in is required to see the file.(Figure 10-7)

Figure 10-7: *Inserting QuickTime or Windows Media Video files creates a generic plug-in icon.*

4. When you insert a plug-in file, you need to manually enter the size of the file; Dreamweaver will not automatically detect it for you. You will also need to add 20 pixels to the height to make room for built-in player controls. The source video here is 320 by 240 so in the Property Inspector, type **320** in the W (width) window and **260** in the H (height) window.

   Again, you are using 260 for the height to allow space for the controller. QuickTime and Windows Media files already have a controller built in with the plug-in. You need to allow a little extra space for the video controls when you're entering a size manually.

5. To preview the file within Dreamweaver, choose File > Preview in Browser.

   If you see a message that Dreamweaver was unable to find the plug-in that handles this media type, it does not necessarily mean your system cannot play the video (although this is still possible). It only means that Dreamweaver can't find the correct plug-in. If this should happen, try to preview the video in your browser; you may find it works there.

Take Note...

The problem of playing video on your system may also have to do with the lack of a codec. Web video can get a little tricky because there are file formats (such as .mov or .wmv) and there are codecs. The codec does the job of actually compressing the frames of your video and there may be any number of codecs used for a particular file format. Both QuickTime and Windows Media Player are generally good at identifying which codec you or your users may be missing and then providing links to download and install the necessary codec.

Save your file if prompted and your video will now appear on your web page as seen in Figure 10-8.

Figure 10-8: *A Windows browser playing the WMV file.*

Other web video considerations

In addition to size, consider the following when you're preparing video for the Web:

Length: Unless you'll be offering video through a streaming video service, keep the video length down to keep the file size manageable and the progressive playback smooth.

Audio: Although stereo is nice, using stereo files on the Web is a little iffy, as many home users don't have stereo speakers hooked up to their computers. Stereo creates a larger file size and doesn't add that much to the quality of the sound unless you're doing some tricks with the balance between the speakers, which people without speakers won't hear anyway. Keep your video sound set to mono to help manage the file size a bit more effectively.

Movement, animated graphics, and effects: These things make a video look nice, but increasing the file size can interrupt playback.

Copywritten material: Be careful when choosing material for your video, especially when it comes to music. Pirating is a big issue today. Unless you have the rights to the music or you have permission from the music publisher and are paying royalties, you can't use music for promotional or commercial purposes when it comes to publishing material on the Web.

Learning More

Inserting sound

Sound is another element you can use to enhance your website. Sound has the same considerations as video: it can take a while to download and it requires a plug-in, such as QuickTime or Windows Media Player, to hear it.

Certification Ready 4.7

What are the best practices when including audio in a web page?

You can incorporate different types of sound files into a web page. Select a format that will run on any computer, whether the user is on the Windows or Mac OS platform. Three formats are common: .aif, .wav, and .mp3.

Files in the .aif or .wav format are similar; the main difference is where they originate. Windows is generally linked to the .wav format, and Mac OS is associated with the .aif format. The Windows and Mac OS platforms can read both formats. In addition, these files sound similar to one another: both are dynamic and depending on the settings can result in high-quality files.

You can also play .mp3 format files on both the Windows and Mac OS platforms. The big advantage to using an .mp3 file is that it's typically smaller in size than an .aif or .wav file. Depending on the compression settings, the .mp3 format may not reproduce full CD-quality sound, but it downloads faster and takes up less hard drive space. In this exercise, you'll add an mp3 file to your page.

Inserting sound

Step-by-Step

Follow these steps to insert a sound file

1. In the Files panel, double-click the **sound.html** file. Click in the empty paragraph just below the *What fruit is being eaten in this clip?* paragraph.
2. Choose Insert > Media > Plugin (Figure 10-10).

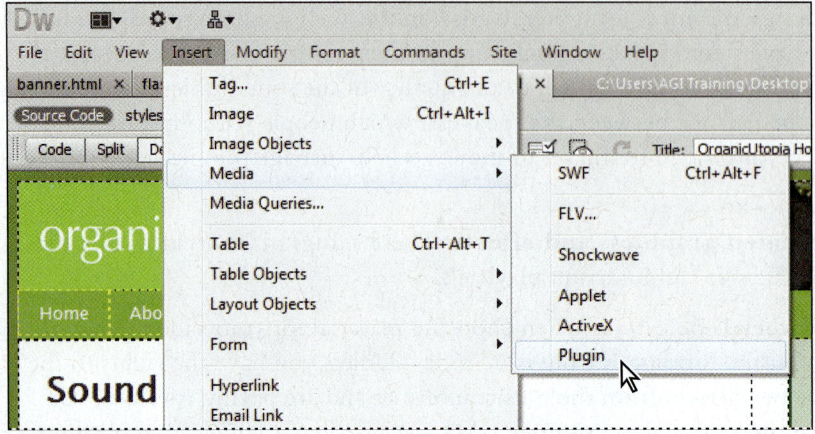

Figure 10-10: Choose the generic Plugin option to insert sound.

3. In the Select File dialog box, go to the assets folder located in the dw10lessons root folder. Choose the **crunch.mp3** file and click OK (Windows) or Open (Mac OS).

   A plug-in icon () appears in the table, indicating that a plug-in is required to hear the sound. This plug-in will play in the handler application set for .mp3s in your browser. On the Mac, for example this will be the QuickTime player and in Windows this will be the Windows Media player. Again, this may be the first time your system has encountered an MP3 file in the browser, and you may be prompted to download an additional plug-in.

   Even though there is no visual element to an audio file, by setting the width, you can allow the handler application to display a controller.

4. Click the edge of the plug-in icon and drag it to the right to extend it to approximately 150 pixels wide.
5. Choose File > Save, then preview the page in a browser by pressing the File > Preview in browser button. In most browsers, the sound will play automatically.

   To give users the ability to control the playback of the sound file you will need to change a parameter back in Dreamweaver.

6. Close the browser.

7. With the plug-in still selected, press the Parameters button in the Property Inspector. This opens the Parameters dialog box, it is located immediately below the Border field.

   In the Parameters dialog box, type **Autoplay** in the Parameter column and **False** in the Value column as seen in Figure 10-11. Press OK.

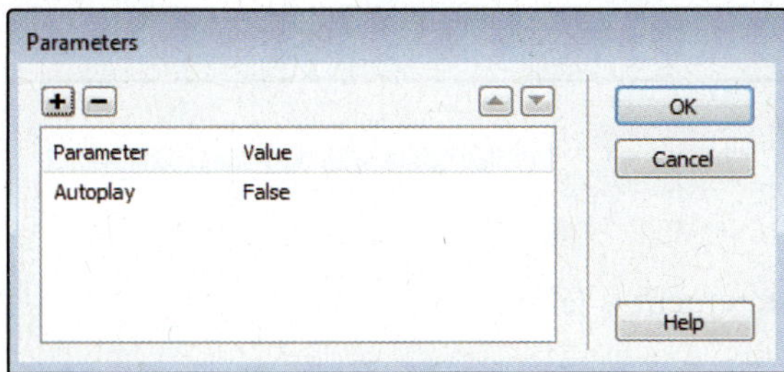

Figure 10-11*: The Parameters dialog box.*

8. Choose File > Save, then preview the page in a browser again, and note that you need to press the Play button in the plug-in application in order to hear the sound.
9. Close your browser.

Certification Ready 4.7

How do you add audio to a web page?

Preparing audio for the Web

Learning More

Audio has the same considerations as any other digital file type. You need to pay attention to file size while trying to maintain quality.

Various programs offer audio-editing and format capabilities. This includes programs such as Adobe Soundbooth, Apple Soundtrack Pro, and Audacity (which is available as a free download on the Web).

Once you've edited a sound to your liking, you need to set up certain technical specifications for the final file. This includes the type of file you'll output (.mp3, .aif, and so on), whether the sound is in stereo or mono, and a sample rate. For the Web, a good sample rate is in the 22kHz–32kHz range; 22kHz is at the low end of acceptable quality, and anything higher than 32kHz starts to weigh down the file size.

Stereo is nice, but unnecessary, unless you're moving sound from the left speaker to the right speaker and vice versa. You can save a significant amount of file space by keeping the sound file set to mono.

There are a number of compression choices when it comes to audio. Your best bet is to experiment and see what gives you the results you want. Creating audio files is very much like creating video for the Web: there are no definite answers, and you need to experiment to find the best balance between file size and quality.

Take Note...

To learn more about digital audio go to http://help.adobe.com/en_US/audition/cs/using/ *and select the Digital Audio Fundamentals link.*

Take Note...

For a look at the future of delivering multimedia and interactive content on the Web see the HTML5 Digital Classroom *book available in electronic and print formats.*

Skill Summary

In this lesson you learned how to:	Objective
Use the Assets panel	3.4
Include video and sound in a web page	4.7
Add animation and interactivity to content	4.8

Knowledge Assessment

True/False

Circle T if the statement is true or F if the statement is false.

T F **1.** You must have Flash Player to view an .swf file.

T F **2.** A .fla file is the file format that is the authoring file connected with the .swf file.

T F **3.** The two primary formats associated with Flash video are .flv and .mov.

T F **4.** Streaming Video is much more common than Progressive Download Video.

T F **5.** Unlike an .flv file, when you insert a plug-in file you must establish the physical size of the file on the page manually.

T F **6.** When establishing the size for a .mov or .wmv file you do not need to allow extra space for the built-in controllers of the files.

T F **7.** Unless you have the rights to the music or have the permission from the music publisher, you can't use music for promotional or commercial purposes when it comes to publishing material on the Web.

T F **8.** Stereo is a necessary component for audio on the Internet.

T F **9.** A plug-in is required to hear sound on the Internet.

T F **10.** .wav and .aif files are much smaller in file size than an .mp3.

Multiple Choice

Select the best response for the following statements.

1. Flash movies are labeled with which extension?

a. .swf
b. .mov
c. .wmv
d. .png

2. The video format that is used for the internet is:
   a. Flash Video
   b. Quicktime
   c. Windows Media
   d. All of the above

3. What is the name of the control panel that shows up at the bottom of a Flash video that allows the user to control video playback?
   a. Controller
   b. Control Bar
   c. Skin
   d. None of the above

4. The file format for sound on the Internet is:
   a. .aif
   b. .wav
   c. .mp3
   d. All of the above

5. With reference to video, a codec does what?
   a. Determines how the frames of a video will be compressed
   b. Specifies how audio will be controlled in the video
   c. Applies metadata information to the video
   d. Is used for search engine optimization

6. Which of the following is important to consider when preparing video for the Internet?
   a. Length of the video
   b. Audio
   c. Movement, animated graphics, and effects
   d. All of the above

7. To prevent a plug-in from playing automatically on a web page, you must set which of the following settings in the Parameters dialog box?
   a. Autoplay + True
   b. Autoplay + False
   c. Loop + Off
   d. Loop + False

8. Which of the following applications would be best suited for preparing audio for the Internet?
   a. Dreamweaver
   b. Flash
   c. Soundbooth
   d. After Effects

9. With regard to audio on the Internet, what is a good range to use for the sample rate?

a. 22kHz – 32kHz
b. 32kHz – 42kHz
c. 42kHz – 48kHz
d. 48kHz – 96kHz

10. To best prepare video and audio files for the Internet the best course of action is to:

a. Experiment and see what gives you the results you want.
b. Google the topic on the Internet and follow the instructions you find.
c. Download a video from the Internet and see what settings they used and copy them.
d. None of the above.

Competency Assessment

Project 10-1 Previewing in Different Browsers

It's important to preview your webpage in different browsers to see how they'll react to the design elements as well as the media. With Dreamweavers Preferences you can designate the browsers you'd like to preview your pages through.

1. Choose File > Open and locate the **insertvideo.html** document that you worked on earlier in this lesson. This file should have either a QuickTime movie or Windows Media Video movie embedded (depending on your platform).
2. Go to Edit > Preferences (Windows) or Dreamweaver > Preferences (Mac OS).
3. Select the Preview in Browser category.
4. Click the plus sign in the upper-left corner of the window to add a new browser from your computer. Add more than one if you like.
5. Click OK to commit the new browsers.
6. Try previewing your webpage in different browsers to see if there are any differences.

Project 10-2 Researching Copyright Law

The Internet has allowed people to share everything from pictures to logos to music to video. Unfortunately, many of these things are protected by copyright law and are not allowed to be so easily shared as the Internet provides. Many lawsuits have resulted in the sharing of such files, just ask Napster about their legal problems.

Fortunately there's a website where you can learn much more about the subject of copyright law as well as download the forms for yourself should you have a project that requires such protection.

Your assignment is to visit the following website to learn more about copyright law: *http://www.copyright.gov/.*

Proficiency Assessment

Trying on More Skins

Project 10-3

There are quite a few player options for your .flv file in terms of what the player controls look like. You can even create your own, but for now, let's examine some of the other pre-built skins that come with Dreamweaver.

Launch Dreamweaver CS6 if you haven't already.

1. Create a new blank HTML page.
2. Choose Insert > Media > FLV and take a look at the skin options.

Audacity

Project 10-4

Audacity is a free sound editing program that can be downloaded from the Internet You can find out more about the program and download it here: *http://audacity.sourceforge.net/.*

Maximizing Site Design

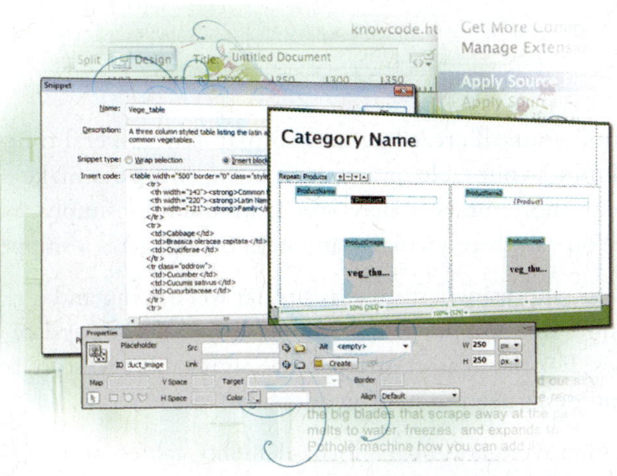

Key Terms

- Detach From Template
- Editable Regions
- Library Items
- Snippets
- Templates
- Template Objects

Skill	Objective
Create web page templates	5.5

Business Case

The Organic Utopia site is now growing in size. The company owners are intent on adding a lot more information that will require many more pages. The design of the site needs to remain uniform, but remain easy to update. Dreamweaver offers tools to streamline the process in the form of templates and library items.

Introduction

Before starting, make sure that your tools and panels are consistent by resetting your workspace. See "Resetting the Dreamweaver workspace" in the Starting Up section of this book.

You will work with several files from the dw11lessons folder in this lesson. Make sure that you have loaded the dwlessons folder onto your hard drive. See "Loading lesson files" in the Starting Up section of this book.

Before you begin, you need to create a site definition that points to the dw11lessons folder. Go to Site > New Site, or, for details on creating a site definition, refer to Lesson 2, "Setting Up a New Site."

Creating modular page elements

You may have heard the term *modular* before; whether referring to a prebuilt house that you can cart away and place on your property, or a well-built, scalable website. Modular refers to anything you can break down into standardized, reusable components.

Most websites contain common elements such as headers, footers, and menus that appear consistently across each page. The ability to convert these elements into reusable items is essential for maintaining a consistent look and feel across your pages. Add the ability to make components manageable from a single place and to make sitewide updates, and editing becomes a breeze.

Dreamweaver provides three modular features: snippets, library items, and templates. Each feature offers a different level of reusability, from simple code tidbits to entire pages, complete with navigation, content, and styling.

Introducing snippets

As you build pages and websites, you'll find yourself creating many similar items several times over. Whether you're creating a two-column layout table or a contact form, **snippets** make it possible to add any piece of code to a common library, where you can reuse it by simply dragging and dropping it into the page. You can store virtually any item on a page as a snippet.

The Snippets panel is like a super clipboard, and using a snippet is similar to copying and pasting an element onto your page. Changes to a snippet in the Snippets panel do not update snippets you've already used in your pages. For this reason, snippets are a great way to store and place any common page elements that you don't need to manage globally.

Examples of snippets might include common navigation bars, form elements, tables, and even JavaScripts. Snippets are stored as part of the Dreamweaver application, and they are not specific to any Dreamweaver site. You can add your own snippets directly within Dreamweaver, and they will be available for you to use at any time on any site.

The Snippets panel

The Snippets panel displays all available Dreamweaver snippets, broken down by category. You can add and edit snippets and categories directly from the Snippets panel. Using a snippet from the Snippets panel is as simple as locating it and dragging it from the panel to the page.

Dreamweaver provides many ready-to-use snippets that serve as great starting points for forms, lists, and navigation bars (to name a few); many of these require little more than text changes and some basic styling. In the following lesson, you will use some of these snippets to quickly build existing pages for the product display component of the Organic Utopia site.

Step-by-Step

Follow these steps to insert a snippet

1. Double-click the **home.html** file in the Files panel to open it. Choose Window > Snippets to launch the Snippets panel (you can also click on the Snippets tab). In the category list, locate the Text folder and click on the arrow to the left to expand it (Figure 11-1). You'll use the service mark snippet to add a service mark to this page.

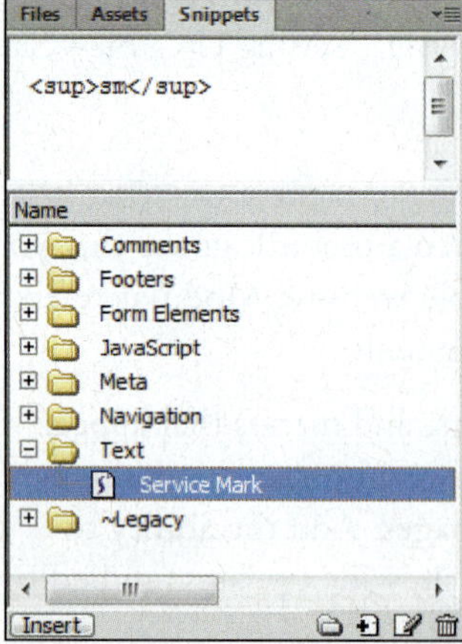

***Figure 11-1**: The Snippets panel contains many categories of pre-built snippets for your use.*

2. Click to the right of the heading, *Welcome to organic utopia*. Inside the Text folder, double-click the service mark snippet, and a superscripted *sm* appears in the heading.

3. At the top of the Snippets panel is a preview of the code that was inserted. In the Snippets panel, click on the panel menu (·≡) in the upper-right corner and choose Edit. The Snippets dialog box appears with a name, a description, the snippet type, and then the actual code (Figure 11-2). This snippet is using the `<sup>`, or superscript, HTML element.

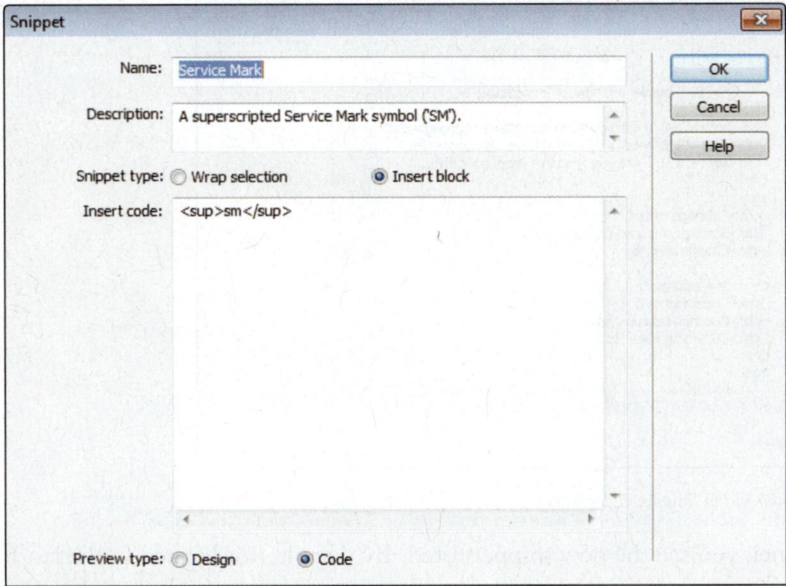

Figure 11-2: *The Snippet dialog box.*

4. Press Cancel, as you won't be making any changes at this time.

5. Choose File > Save.

Creating new snippets

Whenever you have something on a page that you'd like to reuse, creating a new snippet is a good option. You can create new snippets directly from the Snippets panel, and from any selected element(s) on a page.

In this section, you'll convert a pre-existing table to a snippet.

Follow these steps to create a new snippet

Step-by-Step

1. Choose File > Open, and choose the **gardentips.html** page. This page has a pre-styled table. Converting this table to a snippet will allow you to place it anywhere you like.

2. Click anywhere inside the table, and then choose Modify > Table > Select Table. You could also click on the edge of the table to select it.

3. For this next step, you need to make sure the Text folder within the Snippets panel is not selected. If the folder is still open, click the minus sign (-) (Windows) or arrow (Mac OS) to collapse it. This also ensures that the folder is no longer highlighted. At the bottom of the Snippets panel, click on the New Snippet icon (⊕). The Snippet dialog box opens, and all the code within the table is automatically copied into the *Insert before* window.

4. In the Name field, type **Vege_table**. In the Description field, type **A three column styled table listing the latin and family names of common vegetables**. For the Snippet type, select the *Insert block* option. For Preview type, select the *Design* option as seen in Figure 11-3 and then press OK.

Choosing the *Insert Block* option ensures that the table is inserted as a stand-alone element. Setting the Preview type to *Design* allows you to see a preview of the table in the Snippets panel, rather than the code.

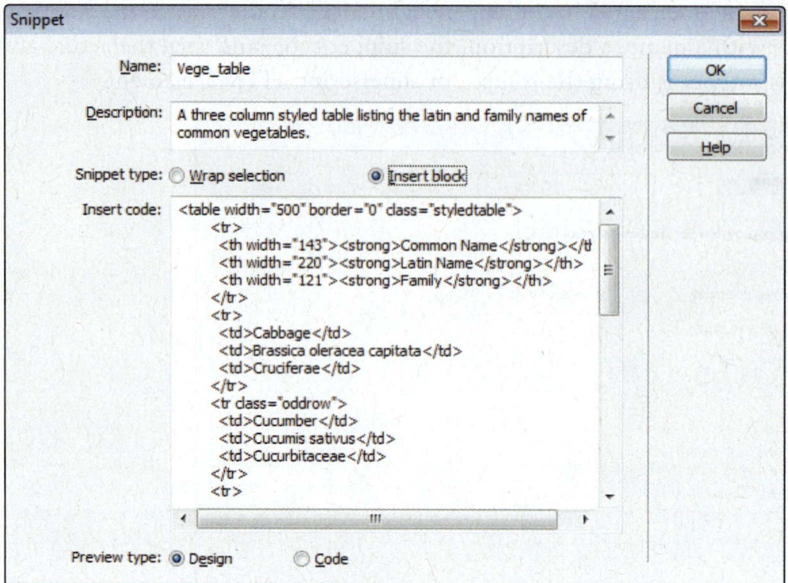

Figure 11-3: *Setting options in the Snippet dialog box.*

In the Snippets panel, you see the new snippet listed. By default, it is located in the last folder you used (Text). Before you do anything else, you'll organize your Snippets panel.

5. In the bottom of the Snippets panel, click on the New Snippet Folder icon (). A new folder appears; rename this folder **ou snippets**, then press Enter (Windows) or Return (Mac OS). Click on the **Vege_table** snippet and drag it on top of this new folder.

   Snippets are actually external files with the extension .csn and are stored deep within your operating system. If someone else has used your current computer to do this lesson, you may see this snippet already present. You may remove it by clicking on the snippet and then clicking the Remove icon () at the bottom of the Snippets panel.

6. Click once on the **Vege_table** snippet, if necessary. In the top half of the panel, there is a design preview of the table. It is most likely cropped. Depending on how much space you have, it may not be possible to view the entire table; however, you can expand this window by clicking on the dividing line of the panel, and dragging up or down until it resembles Figure 11-4.

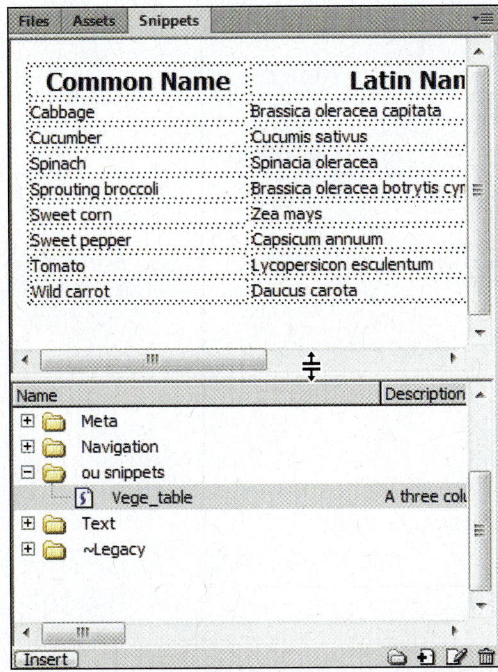

Figure 11-4*: Click and drag the dividing line in the Snippets panel to expand or contract the view.*

7. Choose File > Open, and choose the **latin_names.html** file. Click once below the Heading, Latin and Family names for common vegetables. In the Snippets panel, double-click the **Vege_table** snippet, and it is inserted into the new page.

   In many ways, a snippet is just a faster way to copy and paste. However, there are a few things to be aware of. Snippets only copy the HTML code and none of the associated CSS. If you look at the preview of the table snippet in the Snippets panel, you will see that it is unstyled. However, when you inserted it into the latin_names page, it appeared styled. This is because the Snippets panel only previews the raw HTML in the design view. The CSS rules for the table are being saved in an external stylesheet and all the pages in this site are already linked to this stylesheet. If you inserted this table into a blank page, it would appear unstyled until you attached the style sheet to the page.

8. In the Snippets panel, click on the panel menu in the upper-right corner and choose Edit. The Snippet dialog box appears. In the first line, change the table width value to **350** (Figure 11-5) and press OK. This has no effect on the current table because there is no link between the code in the Snippets panel and the code on your page. However, all future tables will use the new value.

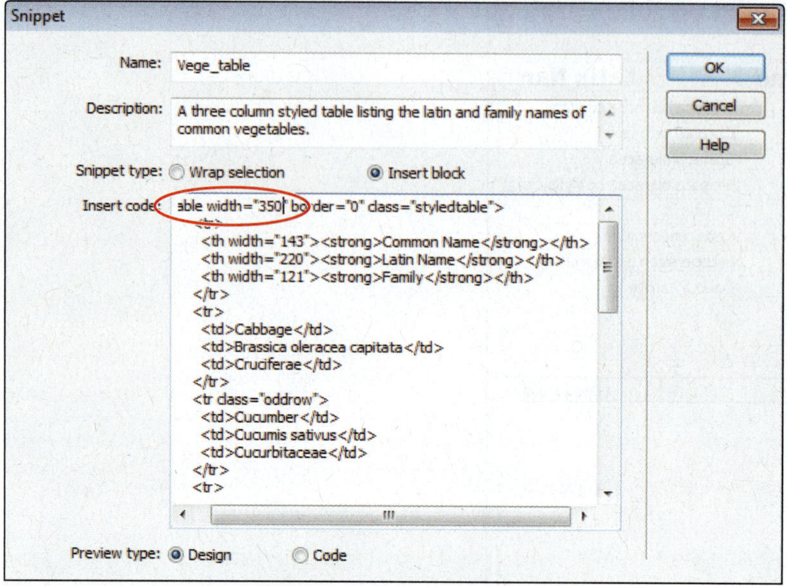

Figure 11-5: *Changing the table width when editing a snippet.*

9. Choose File > Save All. Keep this document open for the next exercise.

Take Note...

The Snippets panel lets you modify a snippet only through its HTML code. Here's a shortcut: if you make a change in the Design view, you can recreate the snippet by selecting it and then choosing New Snippet from the Snippets panel. If you select the folder containing the original snippet and save it under the same name, you will be prompted to replace it.

Introducing library items

While snippets are useful, they are perhaps most useful for items that will never change, like a person's name or a logo. However, a more powerful concept is an item that you can add to multiple pages and have linked to an original master item. This is where Dreamweaver library items come in.

With Dreamweaver **library items**, you can save any common element and manage it from a master copy in your site folder. When you place a library item on a page, the item remains attached to its master; any changes you make to the master automatically update any instances of the item placed throughout your site. Dreamweaver makes sure that any instances of a library item are synchronized.

Library items (unlike snippets) are specific to each Dreamweaver site, and they are stored as separate .lbi files in your site's Library folder.

Follow these steps to see how to use library items

Step-by-Step

1. Library items are located in the Assets panel. Choose Window > Assets, if it isn't already open, and then click the Library icon (📖) at the very bottom. The panel is empty because there are no library items in your site, yet (Figure 11-6).

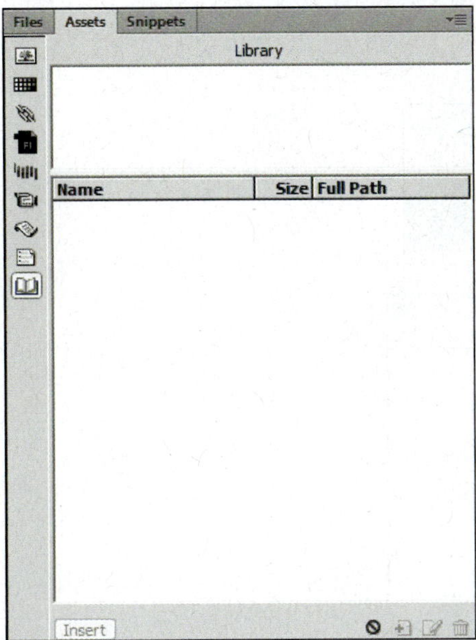

Figure 11-6*: The Library Items category of the Assets panel.*

You can add, edit, and manage all library items in your site directly from this panel. You will now convert the Global Navigation menu in your header to a library item.

2. Click on the **home.html** tab in the top of your document window to open this page. Click on the border of the GlobalNav <div> element in the upper-right corner to select it. (This is the small box that contains the "Site Map | Login" text.)

3. In the Assets panel, click the New Library Item button (). You will see a dialog box appear, warning you that this style sheet information will not be copied with this item. Press OK. The selected menu is added as a new library item; name it **GlobalNav**. If you're prompted to update links, choose Update. This ensures that any hyperlinks or references to image files are preserved. The GlobalNav div is now linked to the new library item you created. Note that your GlobaNav div is now highlighted in yellow (Figure 11-7) ; this is the visual indicator Dreamweaver uses for library items. Now you're ready to add this library item to other pages.

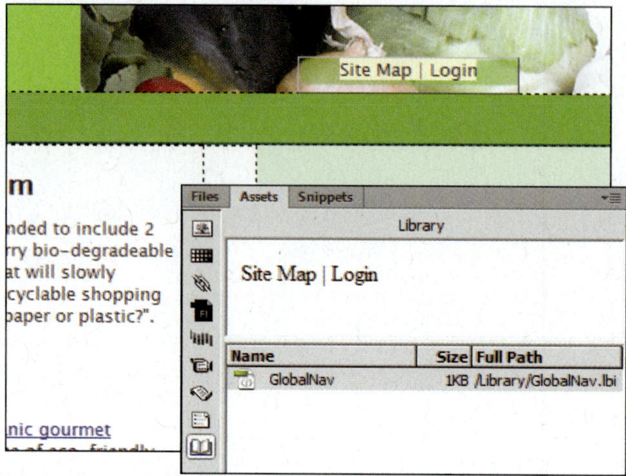

Figure 11-7: *The GlobalNav* `<div>` *element is highlighted yellow because it is now a library item.*

4. Click on the **gardentips.html** tab at the top of your document window to view this page (or open the file it if it is closed). Locate the GlobalNav library item in the Assets panel, and drag it onto the header of the page. An instance of the GlobalNav `<div>` element is placed.

5. Click on the **latin_names.html** tab (or open it if it is closed) from the Files panel. As you did in step 4, drag a copy of the GlobalNav library item from the Assets panel to the header section. Just as before, an instance of the GlobalNav `<div>` element is placed.

   The GlobalNav is now set in the exact location across three pages of your site. You will now modify your library item and all three pages will change.

Modifying and updating library items

The convenience and power of library items are apparent when you need to update a common item across several pages. Because all instances of a library item remain attached to a master copy, when the master item is edited from the library item list, every instance mirrors these changes.

You can edit library items from the Assets panel or by choosing the Open button from the Property Inspector when a library item instance is selected on the page.

Follow these steps to modify a library item

Step-by-Step

1. From the Library Items list in the Assets panel, double-click the GlobalNav library item to open it for editing. A new tab opens because the library item is actually a new file: **GlobalNav.lbi** (Figure 11-8).

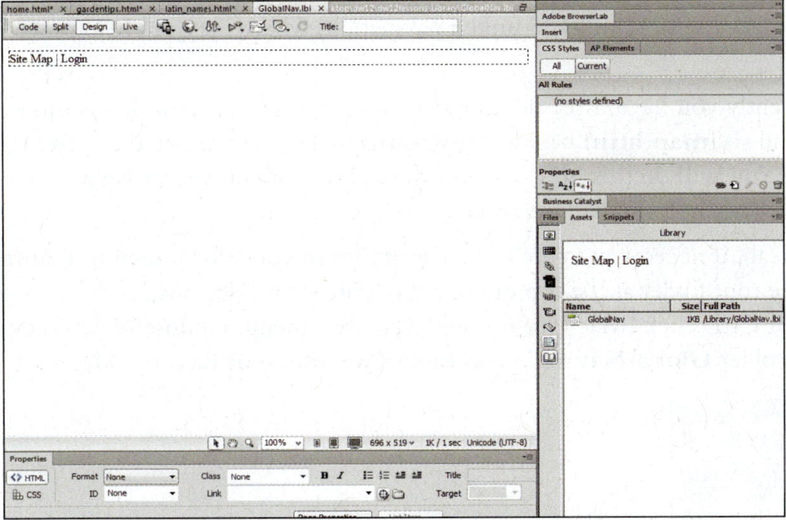

***Figure 11-8**: The GlobalNav library item opens as a separate document and has no style associated with it.*

It's important to realize that there is no style information associated with this file, as Dreamweaver warned you when you created the item. However, this is actually a good thing; it simply takes getting used to the idea that you are modifying the HTML content—all the style information resides in the style sheet.

2. Where it currently reads *Login*, select the text, then type **Your Account**. You will now link the text within the GlobalNav menu to the appropriate HTML pages. Select the text *Your Account*, then in the Property Inspector, click on the HTML button, if necessary. Next, click on the Browse for File folder icon (🗀) to the right of the link field. In the Select File window, choose **login.html**. Press OK (Windows) or Open (Mac OS).

3. Select the Site Map text. In the Property Inspector, click on the HTML tab if necessary, and click on the Browse for File icon (🗀) to the right of the link field. In the Select File dialog box, choose **sitemap.html**, then press OK (Windows) or Open (Mac OS).

4. Choose File > Save. The Update Library Items dialog box appears with a list of the three files (Figure 11-9). Whenever you modify a library item and save it, a list of all files using the item appears, and you are given the choice to update or not.

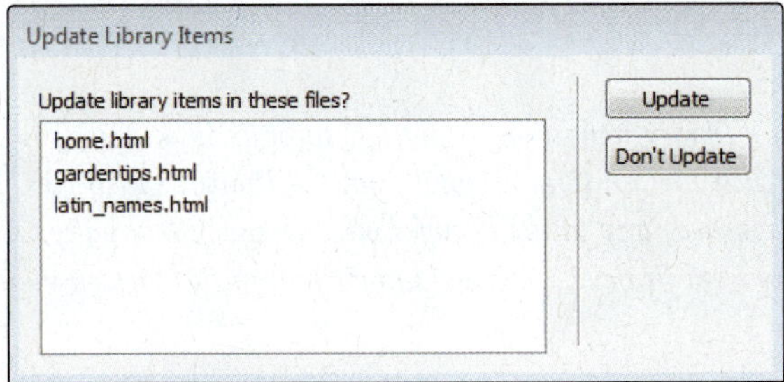

***Figure 11-9**: When saving library items, any pages affected will appear in the Update Library Items dialog box.*

5. Click Update. The files update and the Update Pages dialog box appears.

6. Click on the *Show Log* option in the Update Pages dialog box. A list of the files that were updated appears; this is where you can check to see if there were any problems and how many files were updated. Press Close.

7. Open **home.html**, **gardentips.html**, and **latin_names.html** if they were not already open, and you see that all instances of the menu have been updated in all three pages. Library items are tremendously powerful; the larger the site, the more useful they become. They are tremendously useful with hyperlinked navigation, where they can help prevent broken hyperlinks.

   For example, currently you have three documents all using a library item that is linked to the **login.html** and **sitemap.html** pages. But what happens if you move those two pages into a new folder? You will do this now so you can see how Dreamweaver keeps track of the move and prompts you to update the links.

8. Click on the Files tab, if necessary, to view the list of files in your site as seen in Figure 11-10. Click on the root folder at the top of the panel (Site – dw11lessons), and then right-click (Windows) or Ctrl+click (Mac OS) to open a context menu. Choose New Folder. Rename the new folder **GlobalNav** and press Enter (Windows) or Return (Mac OS).

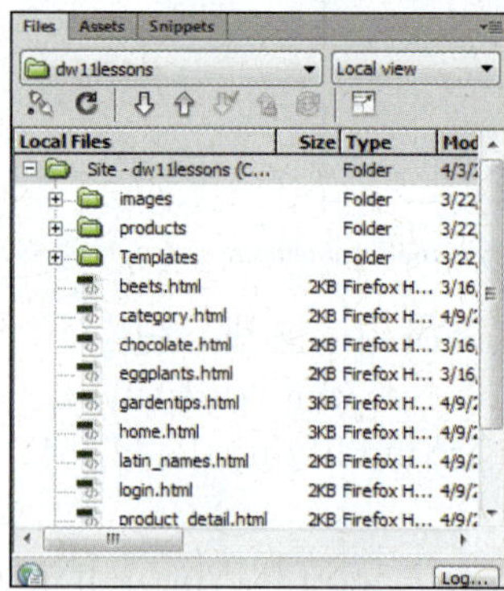

***Figure 11-10**: Right-clicking on the root folder allows you to create a new folder.*

9. In the Files panel, click and drag the **login.html** file into this new GlobalNav folder. As soon as you do, the Update Files dialog box appears with the list of all the files that need to be updated. This is a huge time-saver if you need to restructure your site. Traditionally, you would have to go to each page and relink everything that pointed to this page. Now click Update, and the links on each page are all updated behind the scenes.

10. Click and drag the **sitemap.html** file to the GlobalNav folder; press Update, and all the files are updated.

11. Choose File > Save All, update your pages if prompted, and then close all your open files.

Take Note...

Occasionally you may need to detach a library item from its master. In order to do this, you must select the library item and then click Detach from original from the Property Inspector. Just be aware that once a library item is detached, any future changes must be made manually. Also, it is sometimes easier to select a library item in the Code view rather than in the Design view.

Introducing templates

If you are creating several pages that need to share the same look and layout, Dreamweaver templates are for you. A Dreamweaver **template** is a master document from which other pages can be created; these pages inherit all the elements from the original template, but you can modify each page to include unique content and elements. As with library items, when you edit a template, all pages based on that template update to reflect your changes.

When you create a template, you specify editable regions, or areas of the page that you can modify. By default, all elements of a page created from a template are locked for editing. You can make changes only from the original master template. You can set sections of a page as editable so that you can add or modify content without accidentally (or intentionally) disturbing the original layout.

Templates are also a great mechanism for controlling access to pages on a site. If you need to provide editing ability to others, you can lock out important page elements and give users access to only certain sections of the page.

Templates are site-specific and are stored in a Templates folder under your site's root folder. You open, edit, or create templates from the Templates list in the Assets panel.

Take Note...

Dreamweaver templates work with Contribute, a basic but powerful web content management tool. You can design and manage templates that can be modified and published by Contribute users.

Creating a new template

For the Organic Utopia site, imagine that you need to create many different category and product detail pages for the products in the store. To do this, you'll set up templates for each page so that new pages can be easily created but will remain visually consistent with the master layout.

Follow these steps to create a new Dreamweaver template

Step-by-Step

1. In the Files panel (Window > Files), locate and double-click the **product_detail.html** page to open it for editing. This page has generic text and a placeholder image that will serve as your template.
2. Click on your Assets panel, and then click on the library item. As you did with the other pages, click and drag the **GlobalNav** item onto the header. This page will shortly serve as a template, and by including a library item, you are maximizing automation.

3. Save the **product_detail.html** page as a template by choosing File > Save as Template. The Save As Template dialog box appears as seen in Figure 11-11.

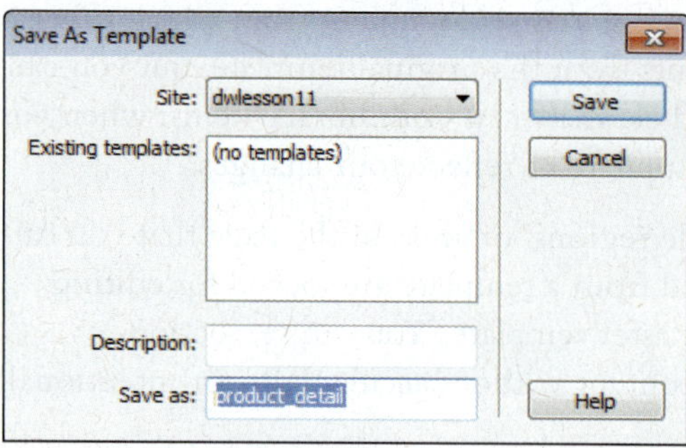

Figure 11-11: *Naming a new template.*

Certification Ready 5.5

How do you create a new Dreamweaver template?

Certification Ready 5.5

How do you save an existing HTML file as a Dreamweaver template?.

4. Choose Save to save the template. If prompted, allow Dreamweaver to update any links by choosing Yes from the dialog box.

Working with editable regions

Once you create a template, you have the ability to add **template objects** which are special features only available to this page type. The most common template object is the editable region. When new HTML pages are generated from templates, the **editable region** defines the section of a page you would like to be editable and all other areas will remain non-editable.

Step-by-Step

Follow these steps to create an editable region in a template

1. Select the placeholder text in the **product_detail** template that reads *Product Category*. Choose Insert > Template Objects > Editable Region. The New Editable Region dialog box appears.
2. Name the new editable region **ProductCategory** and click OK. The placeholder text now appears inside a black box with a blue tab at the top. This portion of the page and the content within it will now be editable in any pages created from this template.
3. Select the placeholder text in the **product_detail** template that reads *Product Name*. Choose Insert > Template Objects > Editable Region. The New Editable Region dialog box appears. Name this **ProductName** and click OK.
4. Select the image placeholder, then choose Insert > Template Objects > Editable Region. The New Editable Region window appears. Name this **ProductImage** (as seen in Figure 11-12) and click OK.

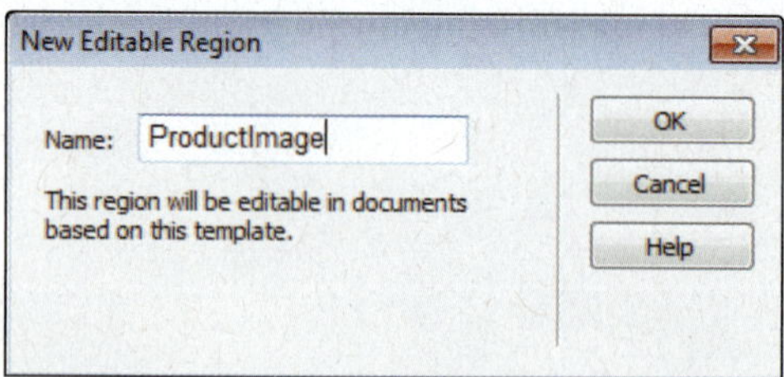

Figure 11-12: *Naming the Editable Region of the image placeholder.*

5. Finally, select all the text in the sidebar. Choose Insert > Template Objects > Editable Region. The New Editable Region dialog box appears. Name this **ProductDescription** and click OK.

6. Choose File > Save to save the template. You may see a warning about putting the editable region within a block tag; click OK.

   At this point, you can create any number of pages and manage them from this template. The editable regions you created will allow you to add content to any new pages based on this template, but will protect the main layout and page elements from unintended changes.

Certification Ready 5.5

How do you create and edit editable regions on a template?

Creating new pages from templates

Now you're ready to create multiple product pages that will be based on the new template you have built. You'll create two pages, enough to give you a sense of how templates work.

Follow these steps to create a new page using a template

Step-by-Step

1. Choose File > New. In the New Document dialog box, click the Page from Template option. The Site column lists all the sites you have defined; click the dw11lessons site. In the second column, the **product_detail** template should be selected. Press Create. This opens a new, untitled document based on the template. Choose File > Save. When prompted, navigate to the products folder in the dw11 lessons folder. Name this file **eggplants.html** and press Save.
2. Click inside the header of your page and notice that you are unable to select or move anything. This section is uneditable. Notice, in the upper-right corner, the yellow highlighted box that reads Template:product_detail. In a similar fashion to library items, this yellow highlight indicates that the page is based on a template.

   Dividing a page into editable and non-editable regions can be useful for any situation where the designer of the site would like some control over how the site is modified. Someone not familiar with Dreamweaver could easily learn to update the editable regions, and at the same time, there would be little risk that they click on something by accident and modify it.
3. Select the text inside the ProductCategory editable area and type **Vegetables**. Select the text in the ProductName area and type **Eggplants**. Select the Product_image placeholder, and in the Property Inspector, press the Browse for File button ( ) to the right of the Src text field (Figure 11-13).

   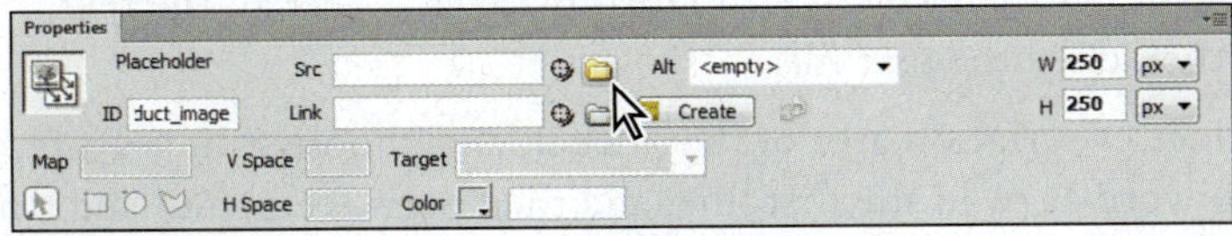

   Figure 11-13: Click on the Folder icon to locate the eggplant image.

   Navigate through your dw11lessons folder and locate the images folder. Select the **eggplant.jpg** image and press OK (Windows) or Open (Mac OS).
4. Double-click on the products folder in the Files panel to open it, and then double-click on the **eggplants.txt** file to open it in Dreamweaver. Select all the text, choose Edit > Copy, and then close the text file.
5. Select the text in the Product Description area of the sidebar, then choose Edit > Paste. Place your cursor after the word *Eggplant* in the first line, and then press Return to add a new line and separate the heading from the paragraph. Choose File > Save.

6. Choose File > New. In the New Document dialog box, click the *Page from Template* option. The Site column lists all the sites you have defined; click the dw11lesson site. In the second column, the **product_detail** template should be selected (Figure 11-14). Press Create; the new page is created.

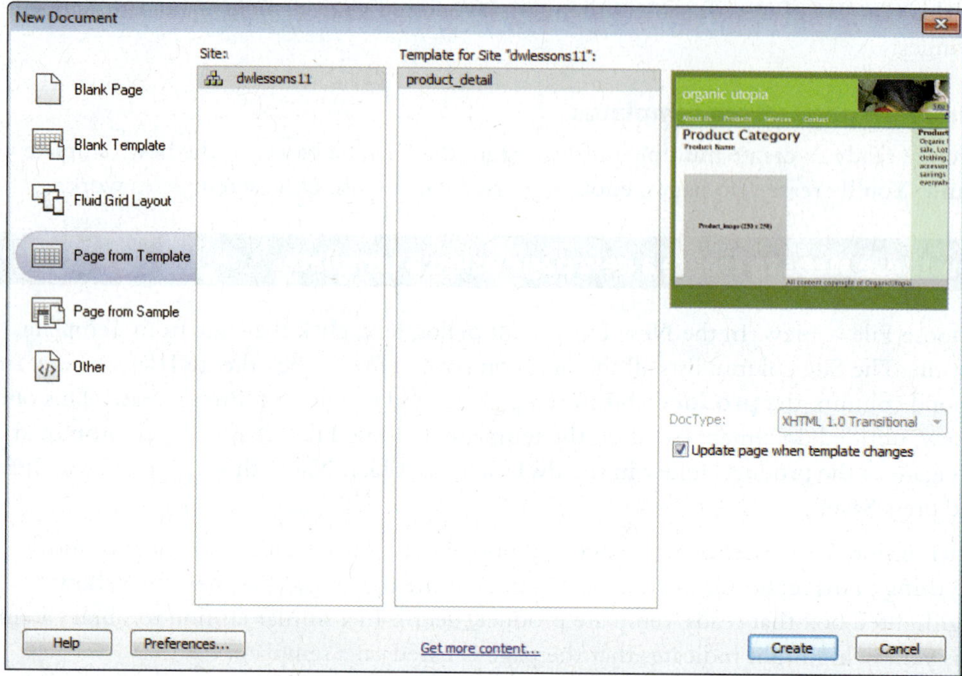

Figure 11-14: *Choose File > New, and then click the Page from Template option.*

7. Choose File > Save, and save this file as **beets.html** in your Products folder. Select the text inside the ProductCategory editable area and type **Vegetables**. Select the text in the ProductName area and type **Beets**. Select the Product_image placeholder, and in the Property Inspector, press the Browse for File button ( ) to the right of the Src text field.

   Navigate through your dw11lessons folder and locate the images folder. Select the **beets.jpg** image and press OK (Windows) or Choose (Mac OS).

8. In the Files panel, double-click on the products folder to open it, if it is not already open, and double-click on the **beets.txt** file to open it in Dreamweaver. Select all the text, choose Edit > Copy, and then close the text file.

9. Select the text in the Product Description area of the sidebar, and choose Edit > Paste. Place your cursor after the word *Beets* in the first line, and then press Return to add a new line and separate the description from the heading. Choose File > Save.

Certification Ready 5.5

How do you apply or build pages from templates and how do you detach a template from a page?

Detach from Template command

If you want to modify a template-based page beyond what the editable regions allow, you can use the Modify > Templates > **Detach from Template** command, which breaks the current page away from the master template, allowing you to edit it freely. Keep in mind that a page detached from a template will no longer be updated if you make any changes to the original template.

Modifying templates

In a similar fashion to library items, when you make changes to the original template, all linked pages are updated.

Follow these steps to modify an existing template

Step-by-Step

1. In the Templates list in the Assets panel, double-click the **product_detail** template to open it for editing. (You may need to select Refresh Site List from the Assets panel menu in order to see the product_detail template in the list.)
2. Place your cursor after the image placeholder, and press Enter (Windows) or Return (Mac OS) twice; then type **This vegetable is in season**.

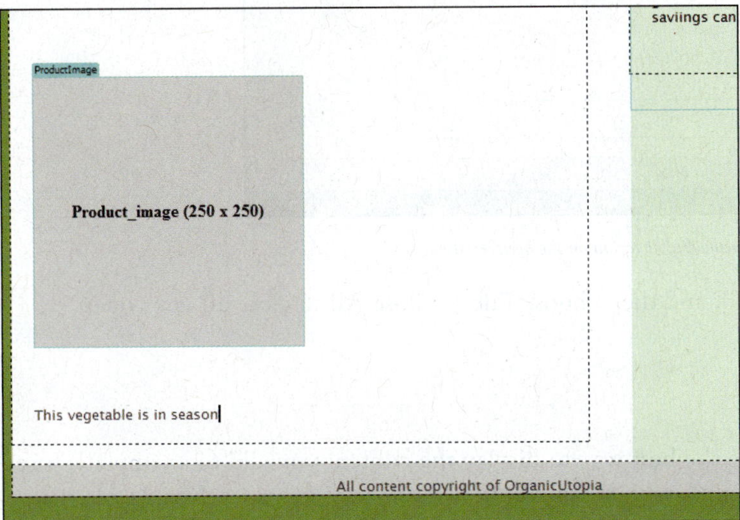

Figure 11-15: Insert text after the placeholder image.

3. If you were to save right now, your text would be updated on your two linked pages; however, you need to convert it to an editable item unless you want the text to be locked on those pages.
4. Select the text and choose Insert > Template Objects > Editable Region. Name this region **inseason** and press OK. Choose File > Save. (If you see the Editable Region warning, press OK.) The Update Files dialog box appears; any files linked to this template will now be changed. Press Update, then close the Update Pages dialog box.

Certification Ready 5.5

What are the main benefits of templates and how do you access them?

5. Click on the **beets.html** file; notice that it has automatically been updated. In the inseason editable region, update the text to read **This vegetable not in season**. (Figure 11-16)

***Figure 11-16**: Updating your new editable region on the beets.html page.*

6. Choose File > Save All, and then choose File > Close All to close all your open documents.

Repeating regions

A single region may not be the best way to display the content you add to a template-based page. You may require a template that can handle a number of items, such as a table that displays products in a category. If you need to build a flexible template that can hold any number of uniform items, you can add a repeating region to it.

Repeating regions allow you to define an element on a template as repeatable. When you create a page based on that template, you can increase, or repeat, the number of regions to accommodate the information. You'll also be able to reorder these repeated regions at any time without having to move the content. For example, you could set elements such as a table row, paragraph, or small display table as a repeating region, and then duplicate as many as you need to fit the content at hand.

A repeating region is not automatically editable. You need to set editable regions inside any repeating element in order to add to or edit its content.

In the following steps, you'll add a repeating region to your category.html page and convert it to a template so that you can use it to display any number of products in a specific category.

Follow these steps to add a repeating region to your template

Step-by-Step

1. Open the **category.html** page from the Files panel.
2. The table in the center contains one row with two columns, each containing a placeholder image and product title placeholder. Click on the edge of the table to select it.
3. Choose Insert > Template Objects > Repeating Region. Because you haven't saved this page as a template yet, a dialog box appears, letting you know that you need to convert the page to a template before you add regions. Press OK.
4. When the Repeating Region dialog box appears, assign the new region the name **Products**, as seen as in Figure 11-17 and press OK.

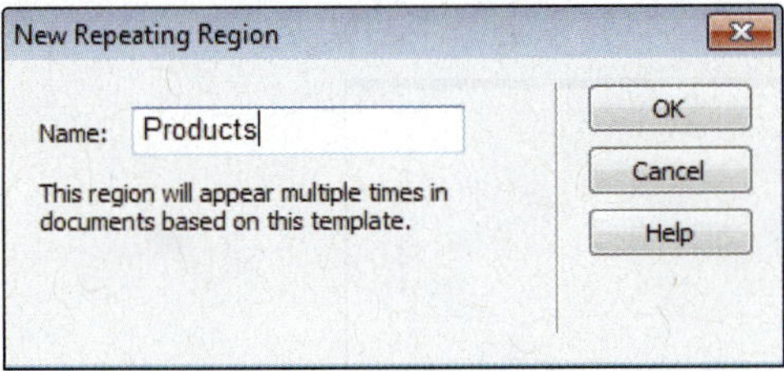

Figure 11-17: The row is now a repeating region, which you can duplicate in any page created from this template.

5. Choose File > Save As Template, and save the new template as **category_display**. Press Save and Update Links if asked.
6. In the left cell, highlight the Product text. Choose Insert > Template Objects > Editable Region. Name the new region **ProductName**, and press OK.
7. Select the placeholder image below the new editable region, and choose Insert > Template Objects > Editable Region. Name the new region **ProductImage**, and press OK.
8. In the right cell, highlight the Product text. Choose Insert > Template Objects > Editable Region. Name the new region **ProductName2**, and press OK.
9. Select the placeholder image below the new editable region, and choose Insert > Template Objects > Editable Region. Name the new region **ProductImage2**, and press OK.
10. Choose File > Save to save this template.

Take Note...

Templates can't contain duplicate region names. If you try to set two editable regions with the same name, Dreamweaver gives you an error message.

Repeating regions

Putting repeating regions into action

You're now ready to create a page from the new category_display template and see how repeating regions work.

Step-by-Step

Follow these steps to create a new page with a repeating region template

1. Open the Assets panel if necessary, then select the **category_display** template, and choose New from Template from the Assets panel menu.
2. Save the new document as **category_chocolate.html** in your site's root folder. Notice the new repeating region in the middle of the page—its tab features four buttons that allow you to add, remove, and shift repeating regions up or down in the stacking order (seen in Figure 11-18).

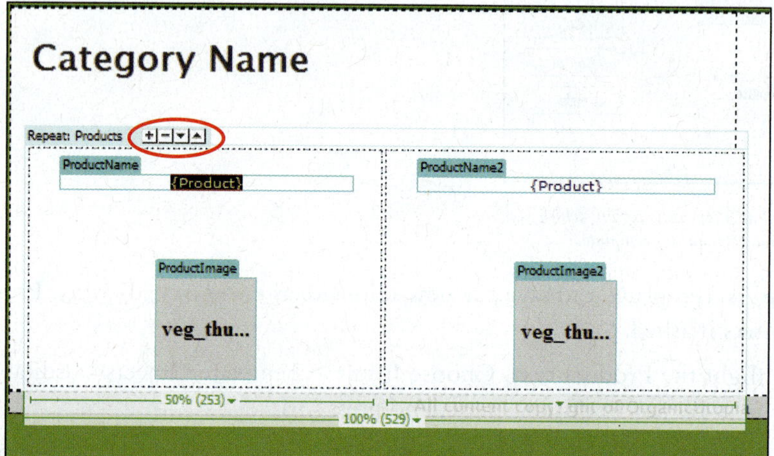

***Figure 11-18**: A repeating region has four buttons you can use.*

3. Click the plus sign button (+) on the top of the repeating region; a new table row with two more product display tables appears. Press the plus sign button two more times to see how it will automatically add new rows. Press the minus sign button to see how to remove a row. In the next step, you'll fill in the first four products with information to complete your page.
4. In the first row, type **Belgian Chocolate** in the ProductName text field and **French Chocolate** in the ProductName2 text field. In the second row, type **German Chocolate** in the ProductName text field and **Swiss Chocolate** in the ProductName2 text field.

   The four products now appear in the category page, and as an added benefit, if you wanted to reorder the rows you could do so using the repeating region toolbar.

5. Click on the up arrow in the repeating region toolbar to push the second row to the top (Figure 11-19). This feature is especially useful for repeating regions with many rows.

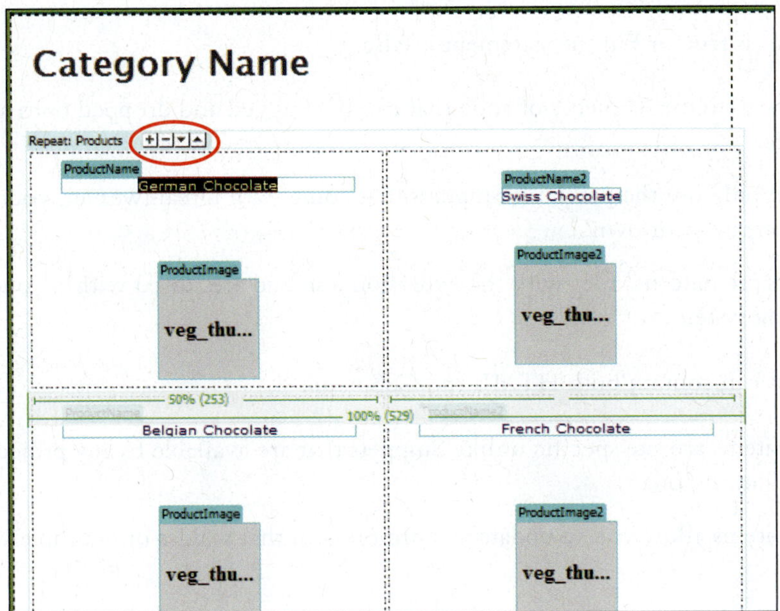

***Figure 11-19**: A repeating region has four buttons you can use.*

6. Choose File > Save All.

Congratulations! You have finished Lesson 11, " Maximizing Site Design."

Skill Summary

In this lesson you learned how to:	Objective
Create web page templates	5.5

Knowledge Assessment

True/False

Circle T if the statement is true or F if the statement is false.

T F 1. Snippets are reusable pieces of code that can be dragged and dropped onto a webpage.

T F 2. You can only use the pre-built Snippets that come with Dreamweaver, you cannot create your own.

T F 3. Snippets are external files with the extension .csn and are stored within your operating system.

T F 4. Snippets can contain both HTML and CSS code.

T F 5. Library items are site specific unlike Snippets that are available to any project you're working on.

T F 6. Library items allow you to update a common item that resides on multiple web pages.

T F 7. Library items are better used for small websites rather than large sites.

T F 8. A library item cannot be detached from the original it's based on.

T F 9. Pages built from a template inherit all of the elements from the original template.

T F 10. Only text can be placed inside an editable region.

Multiple Choice

Select the best response for the following statements

1. Snippets can be used for which of the following?
   - a. Forms
   - b. Lists
   - c. Navigation bars
   - d. All of the above

2. One key difference between a snippet and a library item is that library items:
   - a. Can be copied and pasted
   - b. Are linked to an original master item
   - c. Are not composed of code
   - d. There is no difference between the two

3. If you update and save a library item that's already been placed on numerous webpages, what will happen?
   a. It will only save the library item.
   b. Nothing happens.
   c. A list of all files using the item appears, and you are given the choice to update or not.
   d. You cannot change library items once they've been placed on a page.

4. If you need to create multiple webpages that have the same look and layout, the best item to start with is a:
   a. Template
   b. Library item
   c. Snippet
   d. Blank webpage

5. With reference to a webpage that's been built from a template, the areas of the page that can be modified are known as the:
   a. Open zones
   b. Editable regions
   c. Edit areas
   d. Modifiable modules

6. To update an item on a webpage that is in a non-editable region, you will have to:
   a. Open the original template the page is based on and then make the update.
   b. Double click on the item.
   c. All items are locked. No changes can be made.
   d. None of the above

7. When you make changes to a template:
   a. All linked pages are updated.
   b. You have to manually update each page the template is based on.
   c. You have to choose Save All from the File menu.
   d. You have to close any other open webpages first.

8. What is the name of the item that can be used to designate where an image will go without using an actual image?
   a. Image block
   b. Image placeholder
   c. Graphic template
   d. Code image

9. When you need a region that will appear multiple times in documents based on a template, it is best to use:
   a. Editable regions
   b. Cascading regions
   c. Repeating regions
   d. DIVs

10. If you want to modify a template-based page beyond what the editable regions allow, the most efficient approach would be to:
    a. Detach the page from the template.
    b. Unlock the page in the Properties panel.
    c. You cannot modify a page beyond the editable regions.
    d. Just start over and create the page from the ground up.

Competency Assessment

Project 11-1 Creating a Library Item from Scratch

You'll practice creating a library item from scratch since we supplied one to you last time. One thing to consider is what makes a good candidate for a library item, the menu you did earlier was a great example. This time, we'll do something a simpler that while it will only need to be updated once a year, it's a good choice for a library item since it is information that could be featured throughout the site.

1. Choose File > New > Blank Page > HTML > None to create a new empty webpage.
2. Type out **(Your Name or Company Here) Copyright 2012** on your webpage.
3. Save the page as **copyright.html**.
4. Go to Window > Assets, make sure the Library button has been selected.
5. Select the copyright text you just typed.
6. Click the New Library Item button at the bottom of the panel.
7. Name the library item **copyright**.
8. Place your new copyright text on separate pages or better still templates and update as needed!

Project 11-2 More Template Exploration

One of the more powerful ways to create an efficient workflow is to build your own templates of course. However, Dreamweaver does offer a starting point if you're looking for some layout ideas.

1. Choose File > New.
2. Choose the Blank Template category on the left followed by the HTML template for the Template Type.
3. Pick any one of the numerous layouts to explore. We recommend creating several and investigating the various layouts at your disposal and modifying them.

Proficiency Assessment

Another Look at Snippets

Project 11-3

Snippets offer some really convenient ways of applying code with a drag-and-drop style. Even some of the seemingly more complex operations are pretty easy to apply.

Launch Dreamweaver CS6 if you haven't already.

1. Create a new blank HTML page.
2. Choose Window > Snippets and take a look at the Navigation and JavaScript folders.

Connecting the Dots

Project 11-4

Now that you've learned the workflow of CSS, templates, library items and snippets, try putting them all together into one configuration to see how they work together.

1. Come up with a basic web project. Get some placeholder images and text content to work with.
2. Set up your site.
3. Build a template, connect a .css file to it, use the .css file to modify something from the Snippets that you add to the page. Make a library item of it and create other pages based on your template.

Working with Code-editing Features

Key Terms

- Code Hinting
- Coding Toolbar
- Comments
- Formatting Code
- Quick Tag Editor
- Tag Chooser
- Validating Code

Skill	Objective
Use basic HTML tags to set up an HTML document, format text, add links, create tables, and build ordered and unordered lists	5.6

Business Case

Up to now, the owners at Organic Utopia have loved your work. Unfortunately, they're working with a new programming expert who is quite adamant about the code format. However, you are not a code expert, so you cannot achieve cleaner code without having a strong programming background. Dreamweaver includes some great options that will help you achieve clean, organized code without having to be a professional developer.

Introduction

Before starting, make sure that your tools and panels are consistent by resetting your workspace. See "Resetting the Dreamweaver workspace" in the Starting Up section of this book.

You will work with several files from the dw12lessons folder in this lesson. Make sure that you have loaded the dwlessons folder onto your hard drive. See "Loading lesson files" in the Starting Up section of this book.

Before you begin, you need to create site settings that point to the dw12lessons folder. Go to Site > New Site, or, for details on creating a site, refer to Lesson 2, "Setting Up a New Site."

Working with code

Although Dreamweaver's traditional audience has been for those who prefer to work in the Design view and not with code, there are many good reasons to dive into the code editing view. In this lesson, you will look at some of the unique functions available in the Code view by taking a look at an older web page.

Accessing code with the Quick Tag editor

In this exercise, you will use a feature called the Quick Tag editor. This feature is generally for users who are more familiar with their code. The **Quick Tag editor** offers an easy way to add CSS class or ID names as well as attributes to your code without having to leave the Design view. The Quick Tag editor works in conjunction with the tag selector. In this exercise, you'll apply a CSS class to an image to float it to the right.

Step-by-Step

Follow these steps to use the Quick Tag editor

1. Open the **oldcode.html** file, and click on the image of the beets. In the bottom-left of the document window is the tag selector which now has the `<img>` tag selected.
2. Right-click (Windows) or Ctrl+click (Mac OS) the `<img>` tag in the tag selector. A contextual menu appears with all the code for the selected image. Choose Quick Tag Editor from the menu. The Quick Tag Editor appears as seen in Figure 12-1, displaying the code for this tag.

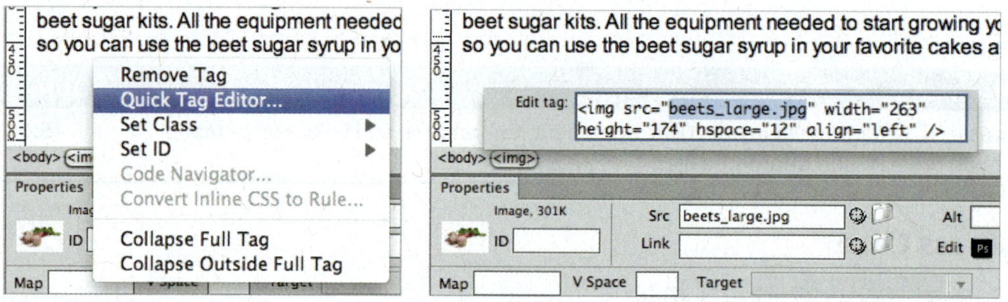

Figure 12-1: Viewing the attributes and properties of a tag in the Quick Tag Editor.

Instead of switching to the Code view to make changes to this code, you can make changes within the editor.

3. Click once after the `align="left"` code and press the spacebar. A code-hinting menu is triggered, allowing you to choose from a list of possible choices. Double-click the class option; the code will be written for you. Notice that the only option, `floatright`, is listed; press the Return (or Enter) key to apply this class. Your image now has the class applied and is floating to the right.

   You can also use the Quick Tag Editor to remove unnecessary code. For example, this page uses the older `<font>` tag to style text.

4. Click anywhere inside the main paragraph of your document. In the tag selector, click on the <font> tag and then right+click (Windows) or Ctrl-click (Mac OS) and from the context menu choose the Remove Tag option as seen in Figure 12-2.

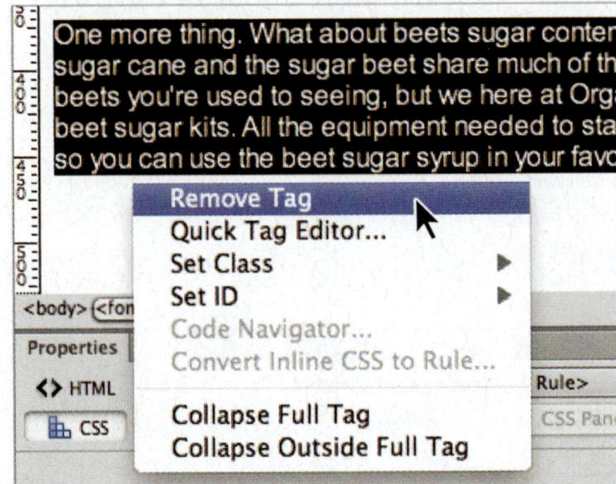

Figure 12-2: *Quickly remove a tag by choosing Remove Tag.*

This removes both the opening and closing font tags and the text now reverts to its default unstyled appearance.

Inserting tags with the Tag Chooser

Dreamweaver's **Tag Chooser** is a dialog box that allows you to insert any tag into your page with the Dreamweaver tag libraries—these include the Macromedia ColdFusion, ASP.NET, and PHP tag libraries among others. The Tag Chooser allows you to insert any tag from the Dreamweaver tag libraries in your page.

Follow these steps to insert a tag with the Tag Chooser — **Step-by-Step**

1. Switch to Code view by choosing View > Code or by pressing the Code View button on the Document toolbar.
2. Click in line 5 immediately before the <style> tag and press return. Now click back in the empty line 5. You will now add the title tag, which this document does not have.
3. Right-click (Windows) or Ctrl+click (Mac OS) and select Insert Tag. The Tag Chooser appears. The left pane contains a list of supported tag libraries, and the right pane shows the individual tags in the selected library.

4. Expand the *HTML tags* library if necessary, and then click the Page Composition subcategory; click the General category, and then click the `<title></title>` tag. Click the Tag Info button to expand this window (Figure 12-3). This info gives you a brief synopsis of the function of the tag and is a great way to learn more about HTML tags.

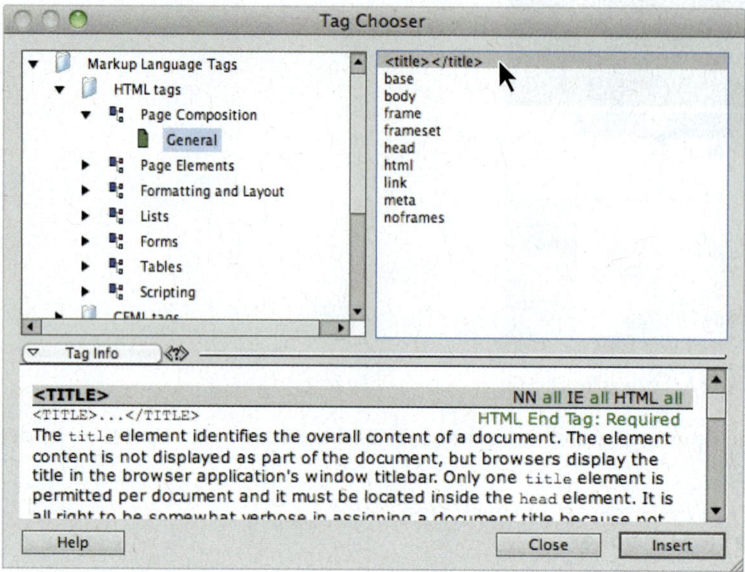

Figure 12-3: *Use the Tag Chooser to add from a list of tags. Click on the Tag Info button to learn more about the tag.*

5. Click the Insert button to add the tag to your code, then click the Close button. Your cursor is inside the `<title>` tags so type **The Lowly Beet**.

The Tag Chooser helps you categorize and use HTML tags

Although you have been working with HTML tags throughout the book, the Tag Chooser you just used is a great way to view and access all the tags available in HTML as well as learn more about their their exact function using the Tag Info description.

- The Page Composition section includes HTML tags such as the `html`, `head`, `body` and `title` tags
- The Formatting and Layout section includes HTML tags such as the `h1-h6`, `p`, `em`, and strong tags.
- The Lists section includes HTML tags such as `ol`, `ul`, `dl` and `li` tags.
- The Tables section includes HTML tags such as `table`, `tr` and `td`.

Certification Ready 5.6

Demonstrate knowledge of HTML tags

Inserting and editing comments

Comments are descriptive text that you insert in HTML code to explain the code or provide other information. By default, the text of the comment appears only in the Code view and is not displayed in a browser. You can also modify existing comments. In this exercise, you'll add your own comment to the HTML code, and edit a comment already in the the code.

Follow these steps to insert and edit an HTML comment

Step-by-Step

1. Go back into Design view by clicking on the Design view button in the Document toolbar. Click in front of the first character in the first paragraph and choose Insert > Comment.
2. Dreamweaver displays the Comment dialog box. Type **We need to add two or three links to other websites in the text below** as seen in Figure 12-4 and then press OK.

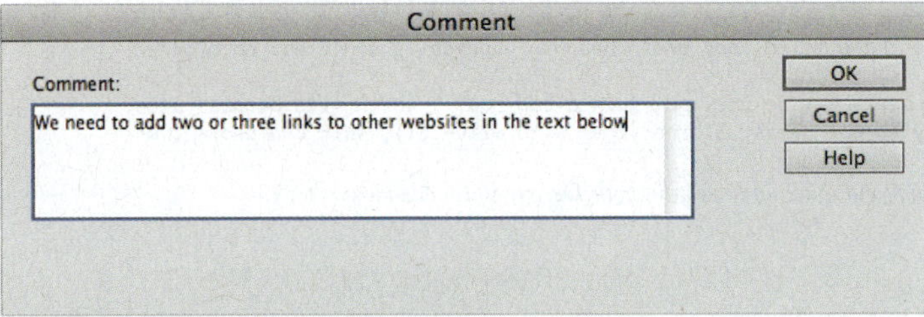

Figure 12-4: *Type the comment into the Comment dialog box.*

3. If you have not already set this up on your system, a box will appear warning that you will not be able to see comment markers in the Design view. If this message appears, select View > Visual Aids > Invisible Elements. Press OK. You will now enable the preference to view Invisible Elements.
4. Choose Edit > Preferences (Windows) or Dreamweaver > Preferences (Mac OS) and click on the Invisible Elements category. Check the box for Comments, and click OK. You now see a small icon with an exclamation point (!)—this is the visual representation of your comment. Click on the icon and the Properties panel will display the comments.

   Comments are a good way to communicate to members of a team who may be working on the same file. These comments are also visible in the Code view.
5. Switch back to the Code view by choosing View > Code or by pressing the Code view button on the Document toolbar.

In the line that corresponds to the location of your comment, Dreamweaver has inserted a comment tag (in gray, by default) that looks like Figure 12-5:

```
 7  #header {
 8     background-color: #9fcc41;
 9  }
10
11  .floatright {
12     float: right;
13  }
14  </style>
15  </head>
16
17  <body>
18  <div id="header"><img src="ou_logo.gif" width="210" height="41" /></div>
19  <img src="beets_large.jpg" width="263" height="174" hspace="12" align="left" class='
20  <h2><b>The Lowly Beet<b></h2>
21  <p><i>By Organic Utopia's founder Jonathon Applestone<i></p>
22  <p>
23    <!--We need to add two or three links to other websites in the text below -->
24    Give the beet a break. Beets suffer from an image problem. If there was a food ch
    very high. Of course there is no food chain because vegetables don't eat each other
25  </p>
26  <p>Now, back to the beet. Why do they get such a bad rap? I think it's because peop
    you my favorite way to eat beets. Slather them with olive oil, salt and pepper. Wr
```

Figure 12-5*: Comments inserted into your code can be seen in both Design and Code view.*

Take Note...

To delete a comment, select it in Design view and press Delete. In the Code view, highlight the entire line and delete it.

6. Choose File > Save to save your work.

Using HTML5 Code-hinting

The internal library of code that is available to Dreamweaver CS6 evolves as the language of the Web evolves. If you are working with the next generation of web pages, Dreamweaver has access to the latest HTML5 elements.

Step-by-Step

Follow these steps to use the code-hinting panel

1. In the Code view, locate the `<img>` element on or around line 20. Place your cursor immediately before the opening `<img>` tag and press Return (Mac OS) or Enter (Windows) to move this code to the next line.

Click once in the empty line you just created above the `<img>` element. You will now be adding a new HTML5 element.

2. Type a left angle bracket (<): Dreamweaver's code-hinting panel appears. **Code-hinting** is a feature that displays a list of every element that is a part of Dreamweaver's library of HTML tags.

Type the letters **fi**; notice that as you type, the list automatically narrows down to the available choices. Using the arrow keys on your keyboard, select the <figure> tag as seen in Figure 12-6 and press Return (Mac OS) or Enter (PC).

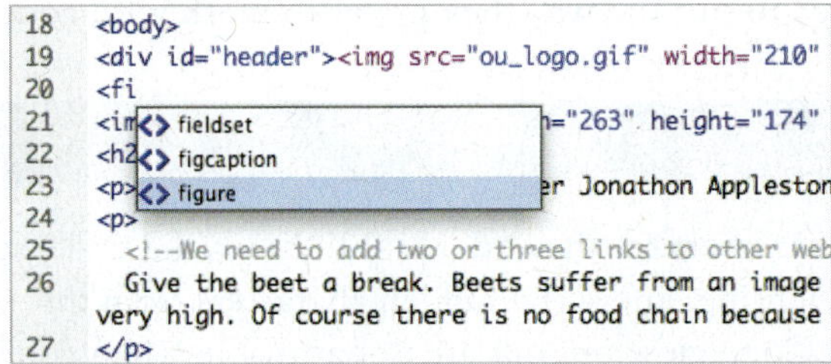

Figure 12-6: Use code-hinting to select the HTML5 figure tag.

3. Type the closing bracket. Dreamweaver will not automatically do it for you.

   The HTML5 <figure> element is designed to help structure your web pages by giving you a more specific way to define images on your pages. For example, you could add a common style for all figures on your page.

4. You need to add the closing tag for the figure element, so click once at the end of the line of the <img> code and press Return.

5. On this new line, type a left bracket and a forward slash: </. Dreamweaver will automatically complete (auto-complete) the rest of the tag as seen in Figure 12-7.

```
18 <body>
19 <div id="header"><img src="ou_logo.gif" width="210" height="41" /></div>
20 <figure>
21 <img src="beets_large.jpg" width="263" height="174" hspace="12" align="left" class="floatright" />
22 </figure>
23 <h2><b>The Lowly Beet<b></h2>
24 <p><i>By Organic Utopia's founder Jonathon Applestone<i></p>
```

Figure 12-7: Dreamweaver will auto-complete your closing tags.

Take Note...

You can choose to turn off the code-hinting and auto-complete options within your preferences. Choose Edit > Preferences (Windows) or Dreamweaver > Preferences (Mac OS). Select the Code Hints category. To turn off code-hinting, click to clear the Enable Code Hints checkbox. To prevent Dreamweaver from auto-completing your tags, select Never from the Close tags section.

Working in the Code view

As you've seen, the Code view is a hand-coding environment for writing and editing HTML and CSS. More experienced users who work in scripting languages such as JavaScript, PHP, and ColdFusion, can modify their workspace to suit the way they prefer to work with code.

Learning More

View options

You can set word wrapping, display line numbers for the code, highlight invalid code, set syntax coloring for code elements, set indenting, and show hidden characters from the View > Code View Options menu. The Code view options are not available when you are in the Design view, only when in Code or Split view.

Word Wrap: wraps the code so that you can view it without scrolling horizontally. This option doesn't insert line breaks; it just makes the code easier to view.

Line Numbers: displays line numbers along the side of the code.

Hidden Characters: displays special characters in place of white space. For example, a dot replaces each space, a double chevron replaces each tab, and a paragraph marker replaces each line break.

Highlight Invalid Code: causes Dreamweaver to highlight all HTML code that isn't valid in yellow. When you select an invalid tag, the Property Inspector displays information on how to correct the error.

Syntax Coloring: enables or disables code coloring.

Auto Indent: makes your code indent automatically when you press Enter or Return while writing code. The new line of code indents to the same level as the previous line.

Syntax Error Alerts: in Info Bar conveniently displays mistakes in your code.

Modifying the Code view workspace

You can view the source code for Dreamweaver documents in several ways. You can display it in the document window by switching to the Code view, you can split the document window to display both the visual page and its related code in Split view, or you can work in the Code Inspector, a separate coding window. The Code Inspector works like a detachable version of the Code view for the current page.

Step-by-Step

Follow these steps to modify your workspace

1. Choose View > Code and Design, to view the code and visually edit the page in the document window at the same time. By default the Code view is split with the Code on the left and Design view on the right.

2. From the View menu choose Design View on Left to swap the views (Figure 12-8).

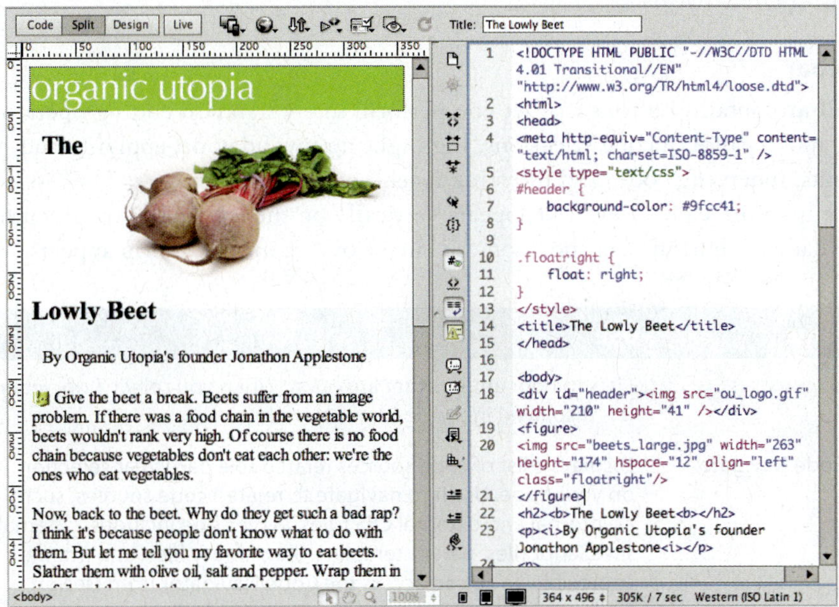

Figure 12-8: Choose Design View on Left to switch the location of the Code and Design views.

3. Place your cursor over the splitter bar between the Design view and the Code view. Click and drag the bar to the right and the Design view will expand as the Code view contracts.

4. Choose Window > Code Inspector (Figure 12-9). Working in the Code Inspector is just like working in the Code view, except that it is in a separate window. This might be useful, depending on how you choose to manage your workspace (for example, users who have two monitors could put this window in a separate window).

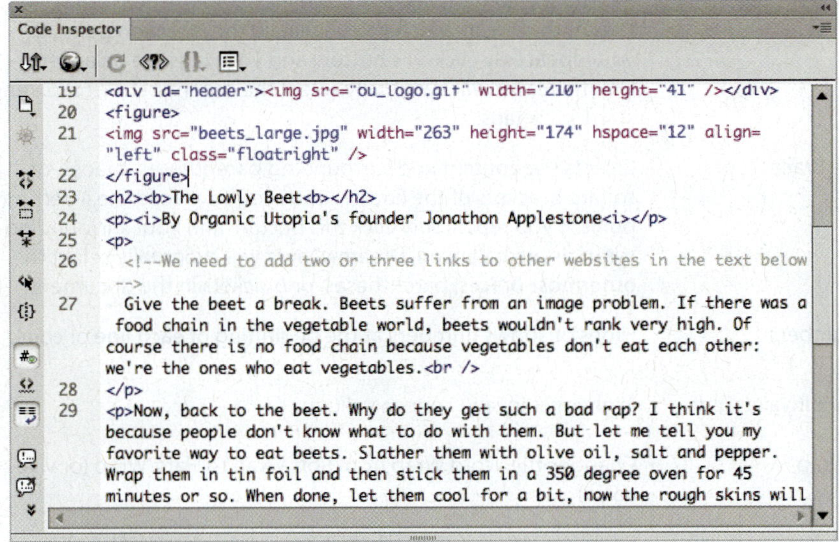

Figure 12-9: You can also view your HTML code in the Code Inspector window.

Press the Close button to close the Code Inspector for now. From the View menu, choose Design View on Left to return the split screen to its original orientation.

5. Choose View > Code. You will now look at some of the coding features available in the coding toolbar in Dreamweaver.

The Coding toolbar

The **Coding toolbar** contains buttons that let you perform many standard coding operations, such as collapsing and expanding code selections, highlighting invalid code, applying and removing comments, indenting code, and inserting recently used code snippets. The Coding toolbar is visible only in the Code view and appears vertically on the left side of the document window. To see what each button does, position the cursor over it until a tooltip appears.

Icon	Tool Name	Use
	Open Documents	Lists the documents that are open. When you select a document, it is displayed in the document window.
	Show Code Navigator	Displays a list of code sources related to a particular selection on your page. Use it to navigate to related code sources, such as internal and external CSS rules, server-side includes, external JavaScript files, parent template files, library files, and iframe source files. You can access the Code Navigator from Design, Code, and Split views, as well as from the Code Inspector.
	Collapse Full Tag	Collapses the content between a set of opening and closing tags (for example, the content between `<body>` and `</body>`). You must place the insertion point in the opening or closing tag and then click to collapse it.
	Collapse Selection	Collapses the selected code.
	Expand All	Restores all collapsed code.
	Select Parent Tag	Selects the content and surrounding opening and closing tags of the line in which you've placed the insertion point. If you repeatedly click this button, and your tags are balanced, Dreamweaver will eventually select the outermost `<html>` and `</html>` tags.
	Balance Braces	Selects the content and surrounding parentheses, braces, or square brackets of the line in which you've placed the insertion point. If you repeatedly click this button, and your surrounding symbols are balanced, Dreamweaver will eventually select the outermost braces, parentheses, or brackets in the document.
	Line Numbers	Hides or shows numbers at the beginning of each line of code.
	Highlight Invalid Code	Highlights invalid code in yellow.
	Word Wrap	Changes the Word Wrap from Soft Wrap to Hard Wrap (or vice-versa)
	Syntax Error Alerts in Info Bar	Enables or disables an information bar at the top of the page that alerts you to syntax errors. When Dreamweaver detects a syntax error, the Syntax Error Information bar specifies the line in the code where the error occurs. Additionally, Dreamweaver highlights the error's line number on the left side of the document in Code view. The info bar is enabled by default, but only appears when Dreamweaver detects syntax errors in the page.

Icon	Tool Name	Use
	Apply Comment	Wraps comment tags around selected code, or opens new comment tags.
	Remove Comment	Removes comment tags from the selected code. If a selection includes nested comments, only the outer comment tags are removed.
	Wrap Tag	Wraps selected code with the selected tag from the Quick Tag Editor.
	Recent Snippets	Inserts a recently used code snippet from the Snippets panel.
	Move or Convert CSS	Lets you move CSS to another location, or convert inline CSS to CSS rules.
	Indent Code	Shifts the selection to the right.
	Outdent Code	Shifts the selection to the left.
	Format Source Code	Applies previously specified code formats to selected code or to the entire page if no code is selected. You can also quickly set code formatting preferences by selecting Code Formatting Settings from the Format Source Code button, or edit tag libraries by selecting Edit Tag Libraries.

The number of buttons available in the Coding toolbar varies depending on the size of the Code view in the document window. To see all the available buttons, resize the Code view window or click the Show More arrow at the bottom of the Coding toolbar.

Collapsing and expanding tags and code blocks

Dreamweaver lets you collapse and expand code fragments so that you can hide and show various sections of your code. This can help reduce the amount of screen space that is taken up and also prevent mistakes since code that is collapsed cannot be edited. When you select code, Dreamweaver adds a set of collapse buttons next to the selection (minus symbols in Windows; vertical triangles in Mac OS). You can collapse code only in the Code view.

Follow these steps to collapse or expand tags and code blocks

Step-by-Step

1. Make sure you are in the Code view by pressing the Code view button on the Document toolbar. Scroll to the top of the screen if necessary and click anywhere between lines 6 and 14, which is the `<style>`, tag that contains all your CSS.
2. Click the Collapse Full Tag button in the coding toolbar. You can also choose Edit > Code Collapse > Collapse Full Tag. The `<style>` tag is now collapsed (Figure 12-10). This feature is useful for reducing the amount of screen space that your code occupies on the screen.

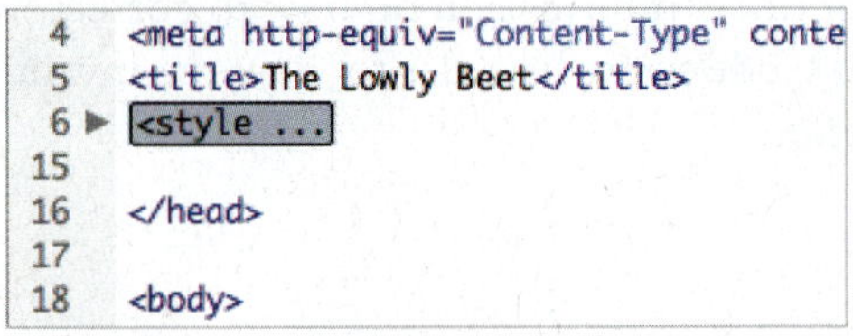

```
4   <meta http-equiv="Content-Type" conte
5   <title>The Lowly Beet</title>
6 ▶ <style ...>
15
16  </head>
17
18  <body>
```

Figure 12-10: *The Collapse Full Tag button collapses the relevant tag.*

Click on the plus sign (Windows) or arrow (Mac OS) on the left to expand the code again.

3. In the Coding toolbar click on the Select Parent Tag button. This will select the code that is nesting your existing selection. In this case, the parent is the <head> tag, which is now selected.

Take Note...
The Select Parent Tag button is a great alternative to selecting code by hand. Selecting by hand can often introduce mistakes; the Select Parent Tag will always be more reliable and faster.

4. In the Coding toolbar click on the Collapse Selection button to collapse the <head> tag and all its content. You could have also chosen Edit > Code Collapse > Collapse Selection.
5. Click anywhere within your document and note that you could begin to work in your HTML and the <head> tag will always remain collapsed until you need to access it.
6. Double-click the head tag to expand it again as seen in Figure 12-11.

```
3  <head>
4  <meta http-equiv="Content-Type" content="text/html; charset=ISO-8859-1" />
5  <title>The Lowly Beet</title>
6  <style type="text/css">
7  #header {
8      background-color: #9fcc41;
9  }
10
11 .floatright {
12     float: right;
13 }
14 </style>
15
16 </head>
```

***Figure 12-11**: Double-clicking collapsed code will expand it.*

Take Note...
To expand all code at once, you can also choose Edit > Code Collapse > Expand All. All your code fragments are now restored to their original view.

Validating your code

In addition to the many options available for formatting your code, you can also use Dreamweaver to find out if your code has tag or syntax errors; this is called **validating code**. Dreamweaver can validate documents in many languages, including HTML, XHTML, PHP, ColdFusion Markup Language (CFML), Java Server Pages (JSP), Wireless Markup Language (WML), and XML. You can validate the current document or a selected tag.

Highlighting and correcting invalid code

You can set Dreamweaver to highlight invalid code (in yellow) in the Code view. When you select a highlighted section, the Property Inspector offers information on how to correct the error. Invalid code is not highlighted by default in Code view. In order to view the invalid code, you must enable this option in the View menu.

Follow these steps to automatically highlight invalid code

Step-by-Step

1. Select View > Code View Options and turn on the Highlight Invalid Code option by selecting it from the menu.
2. Two tags become highlighted in yellow the <b> and the <i> tags (Figure 12-12).

```
18  <body>
19  <div id="header"><img src="ou_logo.gif" width="210" height="41" /></div>
20  <figure>
21  <img src="beets_large.jpg" width="263" height="174" hspace="12" align="left
22  </figure>
23  <h2><b>The Lowly Beet<b></h2>
24  <p><i>By Organic Utopia's founder Jonathon Applestone<i></p>
25  <p>
26    <!--We need to add two or three links to other websites in the text belo
27    Give the beet a break. Beets suffer from an image problem. If there was
    vegetable world, beets wouldn't rank very high. Of course there is no food
    vegetables don't eat each other: we're the ones who eat vegetables.<br />
```

Figure 12-12: Invalid code is highlighted in yellow in both the Design and Code views.

3. Click once on the first highlighted (invalid) code for the <b> tag. In the Property Inspector, this has been identified as invalid markup because there is an unclosed or overlapping tag as seen in Figure 12-13. (In this case, the author used two opening tags and no closing tags.)

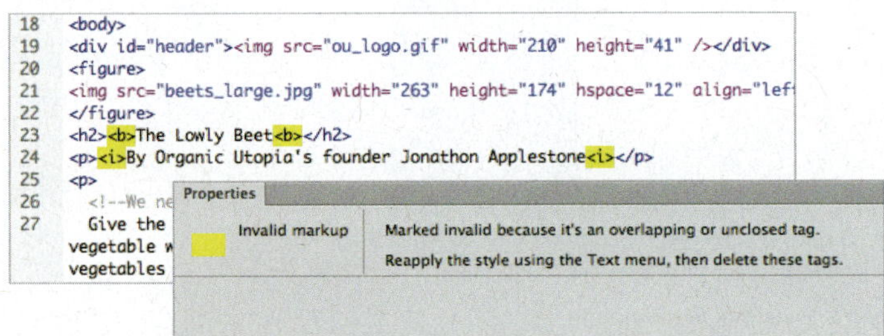

Figure 12-13: The Property Inspector identifies the invalid code and suggests how to correct it.

4. Correct the error by removing the incorrect markup. Individually select each of the four highlighted tags and then delete them. You can now style them correctly either in the Design view or the Code view; for now, you will leave them as is.

Running a Report

Site reports allow you to scan your code using a set of criteria. Code which doesn't fit the criteria is identified, allowing you to fix it. In this exercise, you'll run all the reports for HTML.

Step-by-Step

Follow these steps to run a report

1. Choose File > Save. Then choose Site > Reports and in the site Report window that appears, check all five boxes for HTML reports as seen in Figure 12-13. Be sure that the Report on menu is set to Current Document. You can also run reports sitewide, for certain files only or an entire folder.

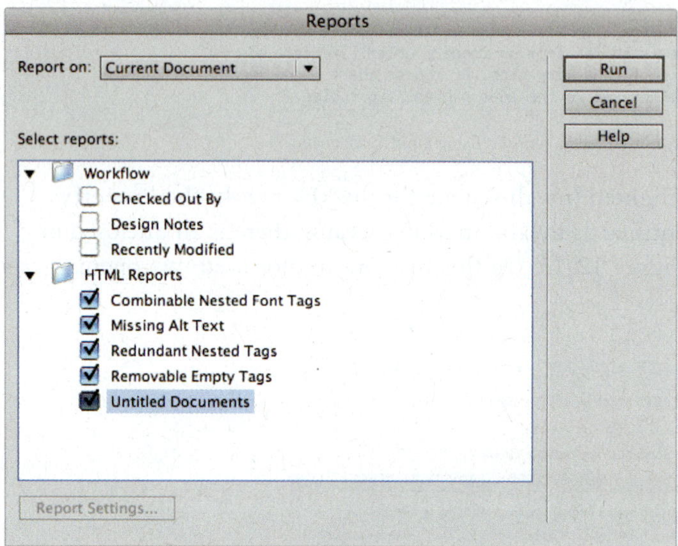

***Figure 12-13**: Check the HTML Reports you would like to run.*

2. Press Run; the results of the Report appear in a new Site Reports panel below the Properties panel. In this case, there are two warnings that the `alt` attribute is missing from your images. The alt attribute improves accessibility for images on your page for assistive devices, such as screenreaders. This is not technically required, but you should add them.

3. In the Site Reports panel, double-click the first warning. You will be sent directly to the code and the image will be selected. In the Properties panel, locate the Alt text field and type **Logo** as seen in Figure 12-14 nd then press Enter (Windows) or Return (Mac OS) to commit the change.

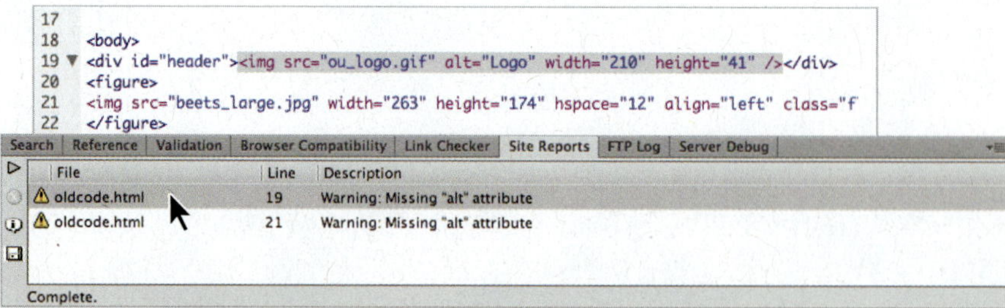

***Figure 12-14**: Clicking on a warning in the Site Reports panel sends you to this code.*

4. Repeat this step and double-click on the second warning. This will select your other image. Type **Beets** in the Alt text field, then press Enter or Return to commit the change.

5. Choose File > Save to save your file. You should also close the entire group of the report tabs. You can do this by clicking on the context menu at the top-right of the panel and choosing Close Tab Group.

Formatting code

Once you've validated your code, you can further change its look by formatting code. This is done by specifying formatting preferences, such as indentation, line length, and the case of tag and attribute names. Many developers who code by hand have certain conventions or preferences for the way their code appears on the page or for the formatting used. Dreamweaver helps automate certain code formatting tasks that would otherwise be time-consuming and tedious.

Follow these steps to set preferences for automating code formatting

Step-by-Step

1. Select Edit > Preferences (Windows) or Dreamweaver > Preferences (Mac OS).

2. When the Preferences dialog box appears, select Code Format from the Category list on the left. The Code Format preferences appear on the right as seen in Figure 12-15.

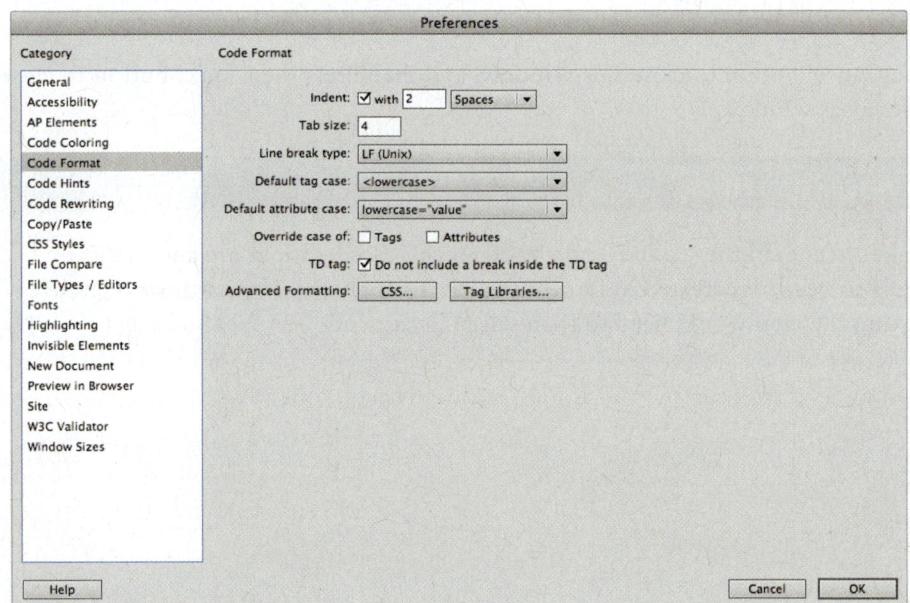

Figure 12-15: *Choose from the Code Format preferences to further change the look of your code.*

The Code Format preferences allow you to change the way code is written in Dreamweaver. For example, when you press the Tab key, your cursor indents four spaces. Using this preference window, you could increase or decrease the amount of the indent.

3. In the Advanced Formatting section, click the CSS button; the CSS Source Format Options window appears as seen in Figure 12-16. This window allows you to specify the way your CSS code is written.

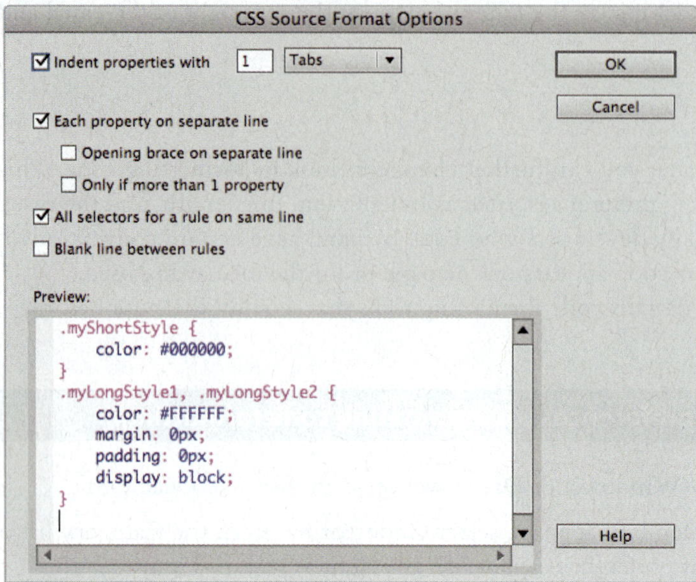

***Figure 12-16**: The CSS Source Format Options window allows you to change the way CSS syntax is written.*

Press the Cancel button to close this window, and then press the Cancel button to close the Preferences window.

Learning More

Apply Source Formatting

If you make changes in the Code Format preferences, those options are automatically applied only to new files created in Dreamweaver. To apply new formatting preferences to an existing file, you would need to then select Commands > Apply Source Formatting.

Indenting

Dreamweaver also offers indentation options for you as you write and edit code in the Code view or the Code Inspector. You can change the indentation level of a selected block or line of code, shifting it to the right or left by one tab.

Follow these steps to change the indentation level of code

Step-by-Step

1. In the Code view, click in front of the div element for the header and press the Tab key twice. Alternatively, you could select Edit > Indent Code or use the indent button on the Coding Toolbar.
2. To outdent the selected block of code, press Shift+Tab, or you can select Edit > Outdent Code.

Take Note...

You can also select multiple elements and Indent and Outdent them.

3. Choose File > Save to save your work, then close the file by choosing File > Close.

   Congratulations! You've finished Lesson 12, "Working with Code-editing Features."

Skill Summary

In this lesson you learned how to:	Objective
Use basic HTML tags to set up an HTML document, format text, add links, create tables, and build ordered and unordered lists	**5.6**

Knowledge Assessment

True/False

Circle T if the statement is true or F if the statement is false.

T F **1.** The Quick Tag editor allows you to edit code without having to leave the Design view.

T F **2.** Comments are used to explain code or provide information about code.

T F **3.** You cannot view code and the design of the webpage simultaneously.

T F **4.** Code that has been collapsed down in the code view cannot be edited until it has been re-expanded.

T F **5.** Dreamweaver can be set to highlight invalid code in the code view.

T F **6.** Tags that have not been closed are not considered an invalid markup error.

T F **7.** The way the CSS code is formatted in Dreamweaver cannot be changed in order to prevent code errors.

T F **8.** One of the benefits to site reports is that you can scan your code using a specific set of criteria.

T F **9.** Even though Alt text is not a technical requirement for a website, it still generates an error in the site report log if not entered with the image.

T F **10.** Not only will Dreamweaver highlight invalid code but it will even suggest how to correct it.

Multiple Choice

Select the best response for the following statements

1. The default color for comments in Dreamweaver is which color?

a. Blue
b. Pink
c. Gray
d. Yellow

2. Which area of Dreamweaver allows you to turn off code-hinting and auto-complete options?

a. Help
b. Site Manager
c. Preferences
d. Live View

3. Which feature in Dreamweaver allows you to open code in its own floating window?

a. Code Inspector
b. Snippets
c. Assets
d. CSS Panel

4. Which option is available in the Preferences for altering code?

a. Code Coloring
b. Code Format
c. Code Hints
d. All of the above

5. Which of the following options in the Preferences is specific to changing how the code is written?

a. Code Format
b. Code Hints
c. Code Rewriting
d. Code Spelling

6. Which of the following is available criteria to base a report on under the heading HTML Reports?

a. Missing Alt Text
b. Redundant Nested Tags
c. Removable Empty Tags
d. All of the above

7. With reference to validating your code, which of the following code languages is Dreamweaver unable to validate?

a. HTML
b. XML
c. PHP
d. COBOL

8. What happens when you double-click a warning line in the site report panel?

a. Nothing, it just selects the line.
b. The name of the line highlights, allowing you to rename it.
c. You will be sent directly to the code referenced in the line.
d. It closes the panel.

9. Which set of code formatting characteristics allows you to shift code blocks left and right?

a. Step Forward / Step Backward
b. Indent / Outdent
c. Adjust position
d. None of the above

10. Which of the following allows you to adjust the indent properties of CSS code?

a. Properties panel
b. The page panel
c. CSS Source Format Options
d. Project settings

Competency Assessment

Project 12-1 Further Exploration of the Tag Chooser — Inserting DIVs

You had a taste of inserting a tag earlier in this exercise. Now, let's try something you're familiar with but from a different vantage point. Here, you'll insert a DIV into an empty web page to see what kind of options the Tag Chooser offers as opposed to using the Insert DIV Tag button.

1. Choose File > New > Blank Page > HTML > None to create a new empty webpage.
2. Save the page as **insert-div.html**.
3. Choose Insert > Tag.
4. In the Tag Chooser, select HTML tags and then div, then click Insert.
5. Note the Tag Editor-div window: it offers access right away to properties such as alignment, style sheet attachment and accessibility, as well as interactive events.
6. Explore the window and options available and try attaching a style sheet of your own.
7. Leave the file open for the next exercise below.

Project 12-2 One More Time

Exploring the Tag Chooser is a great way to expand your methodology on your own. To stress this, we offer one more tag suggestion to try out.

1. Continue on the page from above.
2. Choose HTML Tags and then click on form this time.
3. Continue to explore tags you're familiar with as well as trying new ones to expand your methodology!

Proficiency Assessment

Testing Syntax Errors

Project 12-3

Something that's important to understanding code is understanding how to fix it when a problem comes up. If you're not familiar with syntax errors, you'll create one now.

Get Ready. Launch Dreamweaver CS6 if you haven't already.

1. Create a new blank HTML page. Add some content.
2. Go to the Code View and remove different pieces of the code.
3. Run a check for syntax errors to familiarize yourself with how the process works.

More on Code Tools

Project 12-4

If you feel the draw of wanting to work more and more on code, you should get more familiar with the tools coders use.

1. Open up a fully designed page in the code view and make a backup copy of it so you don't alter the original.
2. Start experimenting with the following code tools: Wrap Tag, the Comment tools, and Indent Code.

Building Web Forms

Key Terms

- Behaviors
- Checkbox
- File Upload Field
- <form> Tag
- Form Validation
- Forms
- Radio Button
- Radio Group
- Reset Button
- Submit Button
- Text Field
- Textarea

Skill	Objective
Create forms	4.13

Business Case

Organic Utopia owners have a requirement for their company's website to encourage customer interaction and collect customer data for future marketing campaigns. They'd like you to come up with forms for their website that will allow such actions. The form tools give you the ability to create text fields that users can use to input data and then e-mail that data to a specific source for collection.

Introduction

Before starting, make sure that your tools and panels are consistent by resetting your workspace. See "Resetting the Dreamweaver workspace" in the Starting Up section of this book.

You will work with several files from the dw13lessons folder in this lesson. Make sure that you have loaded the dwlessons folder onto your hard drive. See "Loading lesson files" in the Starting Up section of this book.

Before you begin, you need to create a site definition that points to the dw13lessons folder . Go to Site > New Site, or, for details on creating a site definition, refer to Lesson 2, "Setting Up a New Site."

The basics of HTML forms

HTML forms are commonly used for questionnaires, hotel reservations, order forms, data entry, and a variety of other applications. Users provide information by entering text, selecting menu items, and so on, and then submit that information to you through a server.

Figure 13-1 shows the simple form you will be creating that includes labels, radio buttons, and push buttons (used to reset the form or submit it):

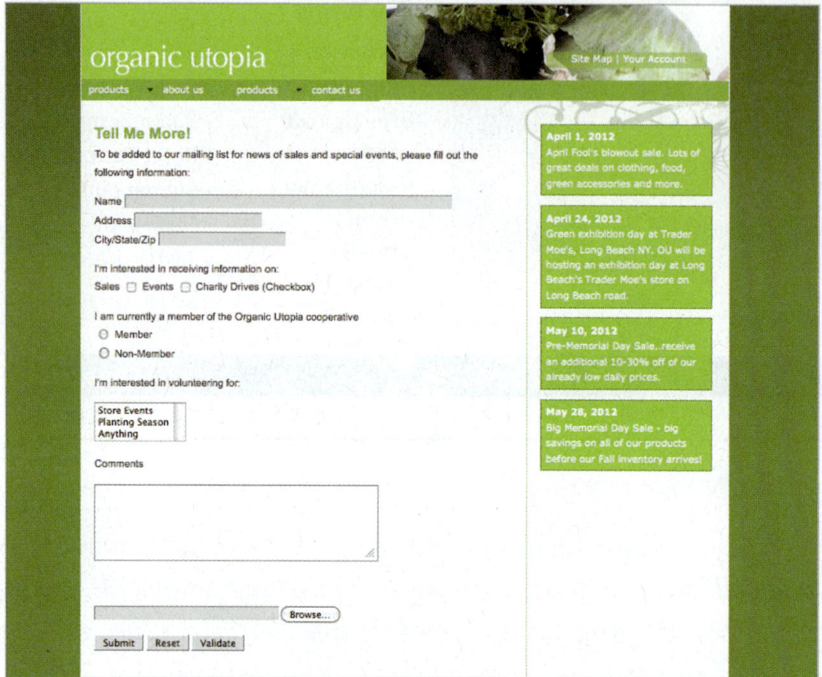

***Figure 13-1**: Forms are a great choice when you want to gather information from your audience.*

How forms work

An HTML **form** is a section of a document that often contains content such as text or images, markup, special elements called controls (checkboxes, radio buttons, and menus, among others), and labels on those controls. A form is completed when a user modifies its controls (by entering text and selecting menu items), and submits the form to an agent for processing.

When you add form controls in Dreamweaver, you are essentially creating the front-end of the form. A user can add all the data required on the page, but this data needs to saved and processed at a specific location when the user presses the Submit button. It's important to understand that Dreamweaver does not provide this location for you. You will need to work with your hosting provider or another service in order to have a system for accepting user data and then processing it in some way. You will learn more about this process a bit later in the lesson.

Building a contact form

In this lesson, you'll build a contact form for OrganicUtopia. This form allows users to be added to a mailing list for news of sales and special events, and it provides the site owners with relevant data, such as name, e-mail, and which information they would like to receive.

Inserting the <form> tag

The first step in building a form in Dreamweaver is to add a form element, which serves as a container for the form fields you'll be adding to it. In hand-coded HTML, you do this by inserting the **<form> tag** into your code. In the Design view, you can add a form element using the Form button.

Follow these steps to insert a <form> tag

Step-by-Step

1. Choose File > Open. When the Open dialog box appears, navigate to the dw13lessons folder. Select the **formbase.html** file and press Open. We have added most of the form content for you, but you will have to remove the placeholder text and add the proper form controls.
2. In the Design view, place an insertion cursor where you want your form to appear. Because this is an existing page, click with your mouse in the white area immediately to the left of the word *Name* as seen in Figure 13-2.

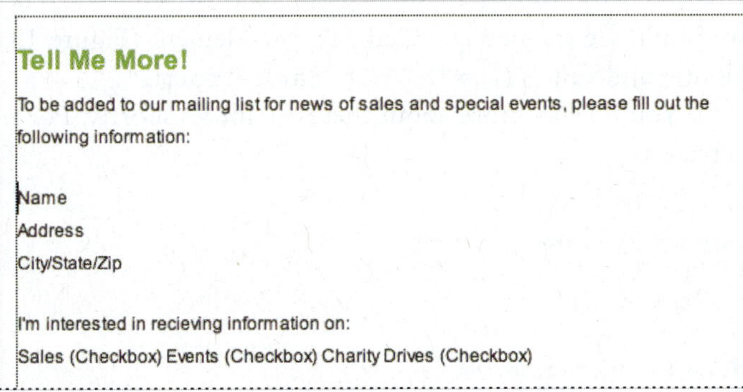

***Figure 13-2**: Insert your cursor before the Name text field label.*

3. In the Insert panel on the right side of your screen, choose the Forms category from the drop-down menu to display options for adding form elements to a page.
4. From the Forms category of the Insert panel, select the Form element (▢) as seen in Figure 13-3.

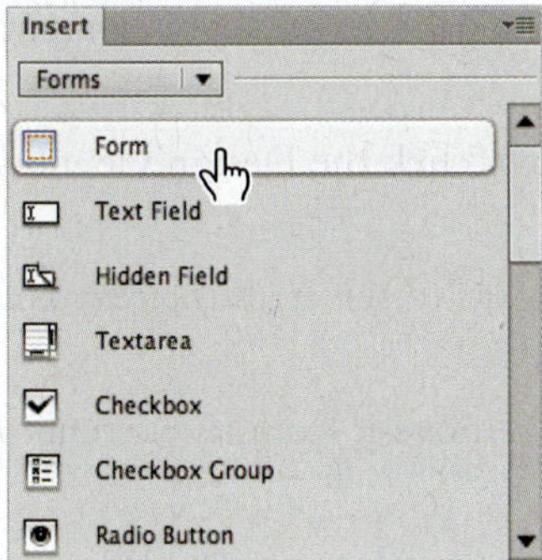

***Figure 13-3**: Options for adding form elements to a page are found in the Forms category of the Insert panel.*

5. You should now see a red outline on your page. This is how a form is displayed in the Design view. If you don't see this outline, choose View > Visual Aids > Invisible Elements to turn on the form element's visibility as seen in Figure 13-4.

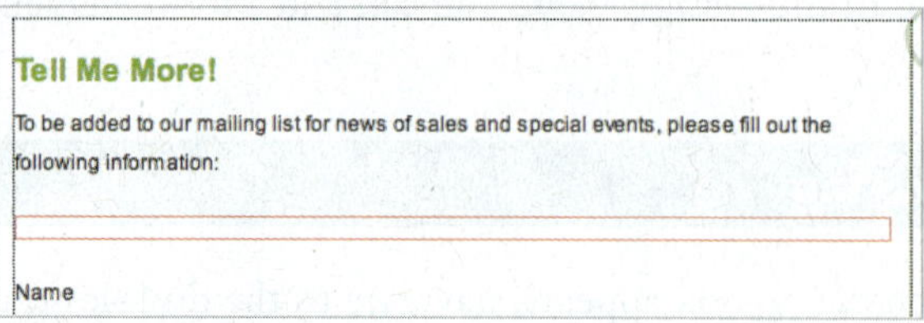

Figure 13-4: A dotted red outline on your page indicates a placed form element.

Now you'll take a look at the code generated by the steps you just completed in the Design view. This is for educational purposes to help you understand the foundations of how forms work.

6. In the Document toolbar just above your document window, click the Code view button to switch to your page's HTML code view.

7. In line 214 of your code, you should see the newly added `<form>` element (Figure 13-5). Take note of the default attributes and values (`ID="form1" name="form1" method="post" action=""`). You'll learn more about these attributes shortly. For now, simply note that these were created.

```
<form id="form1" name="form1" method="post" action="">
</form>
<p>Name<br />
Address<br />
City/State/Zip</p>
<p>I'm interested in receiving information on:<br />
Sales (Checkbox) Events (Checkbox) Charity Drives (Checkbox)</p>
<p>I am currently a member of the Organic Utopia cooperative<br />
  (Radio Button) Yes<br />
(Radio Button) No<br />
(Radio Button) Can't Remember</p>
```

Figure 13-5: In HTML code, a form element is added using the `<form>` tag.

Since this form element is currently empty, you'll need to move the existing content (Name, Address, and so on) from the current location on the page to the form element you just created.

8. In the Document toolbar just above your document window, click the Design view button to switch to your page's visual layout view.

9. Starting with the text labeled Name, click and drag downward to select all the text below your form element.

10. Choose Edit > Cut to copy the text to your clipboard and remove it from its current location on the page.

11. Click inside the red outline that represents your form element to place an insertion cursor there.

12. Choose Edit > Paste to place the text from the clipboard into your form element.

All the text for your element labels is now located inside the form element seen here in Figure 13-6.

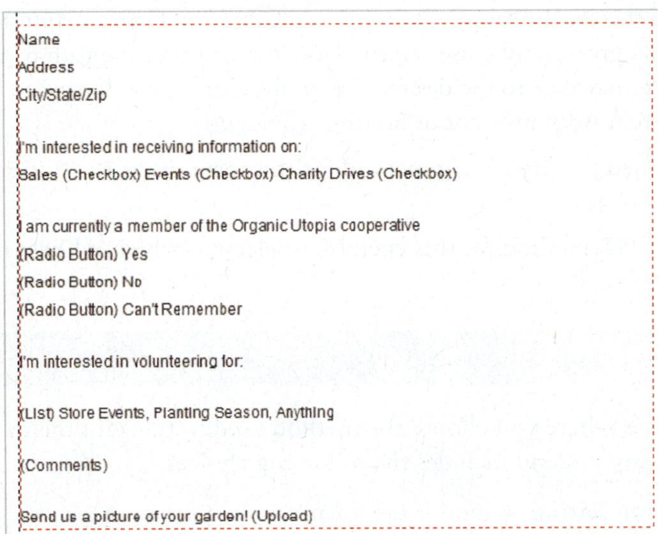

Figure 13-6: Cut and paste existing content from your page into the form element.

Setting form properties

As indicated previously, the <form> tag includes four different attributes and values by default. These attributes are listed as `ID`, `name`, `method`, and `action`, and they represent the HTML form element's properties. The default values for these attributes are not necessarily ideal, so you'll modify them.

Follow these steps to set form properties — Step-by-Step

1. Make sure the form element you added in the previous exercise is selected by clicking on the edge of its red outline. A form field element must be selected before you modify its properties.
2. In the Property Inspector at the bottom of your document window, you now have access to some of the properties associated with the <form> tag, seen her iin Figure 13-7.

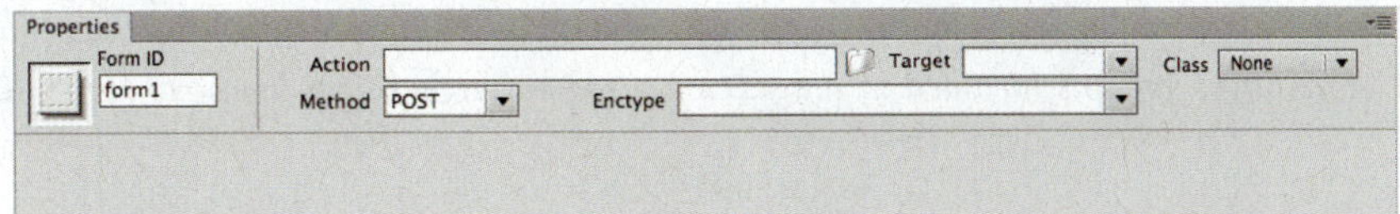

Figure 13-7: The fields in the Property Inspector reflect properties found inside the <form> tag in HTML code.

The Form ID makes it possible to identify and control the form with a script, as well as to style the form with CSS. It is also very important for form validation, which is discussed later in this lesson.

Take Note...

A form ID is the same ID attribute you have been using to style divs. This form, for example, would have the ID `#form1` by default, which is not a useful name.

3. In the Form ID text field, type the name **contact**. Press Enter (Windows) or Return (Mac OS).

   The Action field allows you to specify the script, for example, a Common Gateway Interface (CGI) script or a PHP page, that processes the user's form data. You can type the path to this file, or use the Browse button to navigate to the desired file. In most cases, you'll need to get this information from your system Administrator or hosting provider.

4. Because you have not yet defined the processing method for this form, leave the Action text field blank.

5. For method, make sure the POST method for this exercise is selected, which it likely is by default.

Learning More

The Method menu

The Method drop-down menu is where you choose the method used to transmit the data to a server. The Method drop-down menu includes the following choices:

Default uses the browser's default setting to submit the form data to a server. Most browsers use the GET method by default.

GET includes the form data as part of the URL of the request to the server. GET has a length limitation of 8,192 characters in the URL and is less commonly used to send long forms than the POST method.

POST is similar to GET, but it embeds the form data in the header of the server request instead of in the URL. Although the POST method is the most commonly used, be aware that pages sent by this method cannot be bookmarked and are not encrypted for security purposes.

Certification Ready 4.13

What are the methods used to transmit form data?

6. Choose *application/x-www-form-urlencoded* from the Enctype drop-down menu (Figure 13-8). The Enctype field defines the encoding type of the data being submitted to a server. Application/x-www-form-urlencoded is used in most situations, unless you're asking the user to upload a file, in which case you would choose multipart/form-data.

Take Note...

The optional Target property specifies the window or frame in which to display the data that is returned. The target value is included in the <form> tag only when you choose to specify it.

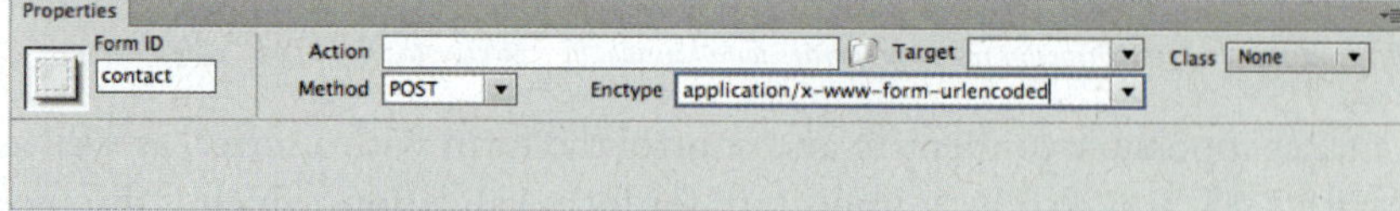

***Figure 13-8**: Form properties are set in the Property Inspector.*

Now that you've defined the properties of the form, you'll use options in the Insert panel's Forms section to add elements to the form.

Adding form elements

A Dreamweaver form is not a working form until you add the elements, or fields, that allow the user to provide information to you. Thankfully, the Forms category in the Insert panel (Figure 13-9) contains everything you need to insert any kind of form field into your page.

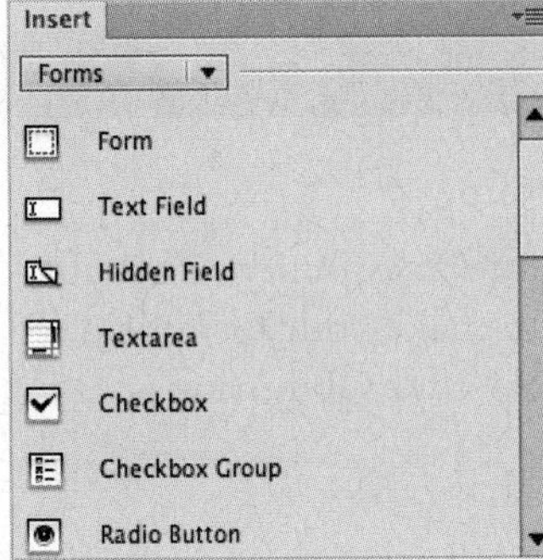

***Figure 13-9**: The Forms category in the Insert panel contains everything you need to add interactive fields to your form.*

Common form elements

Of the many form elements you can add using the Insert toolbar, these are the most commonly used ones:

Text fields accept alphanumeric text entries, in single- or multiple-line formats, or in a password (bulleted) format.

Checkboxes allow users to make as many choices as they want from a list of options.

Radio buttons allow only mutually exclusive choices in that selecting one radio button deselects all others in the group.

List menus permit the selection of single or multiple items from a scrolling list, whereas Jump menus allow you to set each option from a scrolling list to link to a document or file.

Buttons perform actions when clicked. You can assign the default Submit or Reset action to buttons, or define other processing tasks in a script.

A good way to understand all the options available in Dreamweaver for adding elements to a form is to add them to the form you created earlier.

Learning More

Certification Ready 4.13

Which form inputs are appropriate for collecting various types of information?

Adding text fields

The simplest and most common type of form field is the text field. Users can enter anything, from their name, to their credit card number, to their dog's name, into a text field. You control the formatting of their responses using the Property Inspector.

Step-by-Step

Follow these steps to add a text field to a form

1. Within your form, click immediately to the right of the word Name.
2. Press the Text Field button (▭) in the Insert panel. The Input Tag Accessibility Attributes dialog box opens (Figure 13-10), allowing you to set attributes to make your form field more accessible for users as well as whomever is receiving the data after submission.

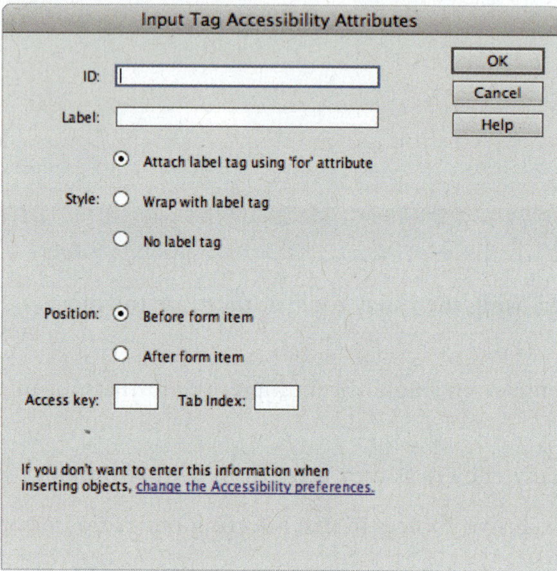

Figure 13-10: Make your form more accessible by changing your settings here.

3. In the Image Tag Accessibility Attributes dialog box, specify the following:

   In the ID section, type **Mailing_list_name**.

   In the Style section, choose No label tag. The label element in a form provides additional usability for the user. You will take a look at how to use the label tag shortly.
4. Press OK. A new text field appears within the form outline on your page as seen here in Figure 13-11.

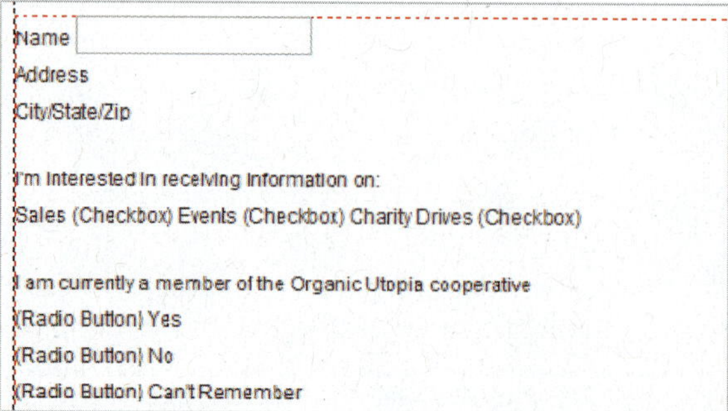

Figure 13-11: The settings you entered define the look of the Name text field as it's added to your form.

5. If it's not already selected, select the text field by clicking on it, and notice the options that are available in the Property Inspector.
6. Type **55** in the Char Width text field to set the text input area to a width of 55 characters.
7. Type **30** in the Max Chars text field to set the maximum number of characters that can be entered. For example, if this were a telephone number field, you probably would have limited it to ten characters.
8. Choose Single Line from the Type options. Choosing the Password option would cause the user's entry to appear as black dots, even though the correct value would be submitted to the server. The Multi-line option is discussed later, in the "*Adding a text area*" section.
9. Repeat steps 1 to 9 to add Address and City/State/Zip text fields beneath the Name field. When creating the Address text field, give it the ID **Mailing_list_address** and give the last text field the ID **Mailing_list_city_state_zip**. When naming form elements, you should stay away from using spaces between words. It is better to use underscores or hyphens instead.
10. Choose File > Save As. In the Save As dialog box, navigate to the dw13lessons folder and type **organicform.html** into the Name text field. Click Save.

    Now preview the open page in a browser by pressing the Preview/Debug in browser button on the Document toolbar. Your form should look like Figure 13-12:

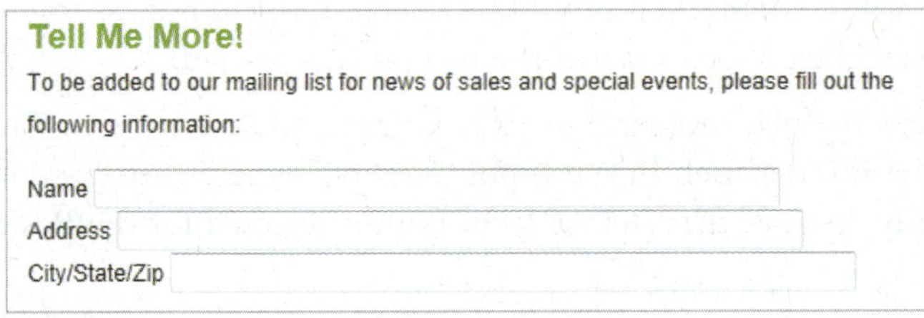

Figure 13-12*: This is what your form should look like with text fields added.*

11. Close the browser and return to Dreamweaver.

Certification Ready 4.13

How do you use Dreamweaver to insert various form elements on a page?

Adding checkboxes

Checkboxes are another valuable tool in your form control toolkit. They're valuable when you want to get specific responses from your users and you don't want to give them the opportunity to enter incorrect information into text fields. Again, you control the formatting of their responses using the Property Inspector. In this exercise, you will take a look at the use of form labels as well as the importance of setting the names of your form elements.

Follow these steps to add checkboxes to a form

Step-by-Step

1. Click and drag to select both the word Sales and the (Checkbox) placeholder text. Press Delete to remove it from your form and place an insertion cursor.
2. Click on the Checkbox element (☑) in the Insert panel. The Input Tag Accessibility Attributes dialog box opens.
3. In the Input Tag Accessibility Attributes dialog box, type **Sales** for ID, then type **Sales** for the Label. Choose the Wrap with label tag and make sure that Before form item is selected for the Position. The label tag is an optional element that adds an extra level of usability to your checkboxes. Users will now be able to click on the text (in addition to the checkbox) in order to make their selection. The Before and After form item options allow you to change the position of the checkbox.
4. Press OK. A new checkbox appears within the form outline on your page.

5. If it's not already selected, click to select the checkbox, and notice the options that become available in the Property Inspector (Figure 13-13).

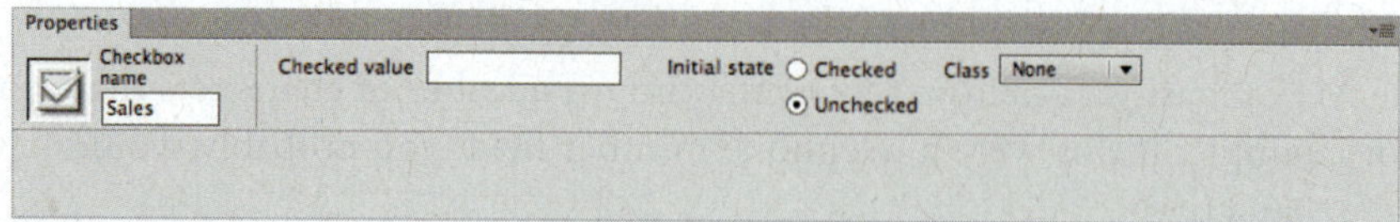

***Figure 13-13:** Settings that are specific to the checkbox you've just added to your form appear in the Property Inspector.*

6. In the Checkbox name text field on the left side of the Property Inspector, type **Receive_Info** and press Enter (Windows) or Return (Mac OS). It is important to understand what you are changing here. The *name* of the checkbox is different from the *ID* of a checkbox. An ID is used to style an element, the name is what gets passed when the user presses submit. The problem is that Dreamweaver automatically sets the name based on what you enter for ID back in the Input Tag dialog box, however this is not always a good choice. In the case of checkboxes, you want all the checkboxes to have the same name. To do this you will need to override Dreamweaver's default naming to make this field accessible for scripting and validation.

7. Type **Sales** in the Checked value text field to define the data that's passed to the server when the user checks this checkbox.

8. In the Initial State section, the value Unchecked should be selected; if it is not, do so now. This setting defines how the checkbox appears when the page is first loaded.

9. Next, select the word Events and the placeholder (Checkbox) text and delete them. Click on the Checkbox element in the Insert panel. In the Input Tag box, type **Events** and for Label, type **Events**. Additionally, be sure that Before form item is selected for the Position and click OK.

10. Click on the checkbox and change the checkbox name to **Receive_Info**. Because this name is the same as the first checkbox, users will be able to check both and have the values passed. In the Checked Value text field, type **Events** and press Enter or Return.

11. Repeat steps 9 and 10 with different values for the ID and Label to add a third checkbox for Charity Drives. Again, be sure to rename the checkbox, **Receive_Info**.

Now, preview the open page in a browser. Your form should look like figure 13-14:

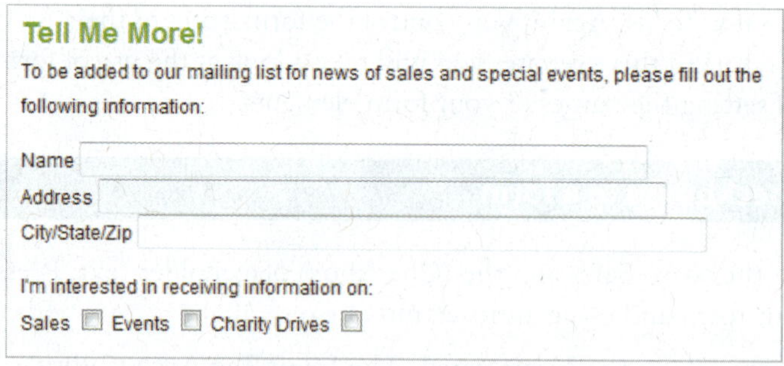

***Figure 13-14:** Your form, with checkboxes inserted, should look like this.*

12. With the page open in the browser, click the text next to the checkboxes; notice that this action selects the box. This is a function of the label tag. Try clicking on the text of your Name and Address text fields. They do not have the same behavior because they do not have labels.

Labels improve accessibility for all users, in particular for those who may be using screen readers or other devices.

13. Close your browser and return to Dreamweaver.

Adding radio buttons

When you add radio buttons to your form, you encounter the same settings in the Property Inspector as you do when you add checkboxes. The only difference between checkboxes and radio buttons is that from a group of radio buttons, only a single option can be selected. Checkboxes allow the selection of multiple options.

To make two or more individual radio buttons mutually exclusive, you select two or more radio buttons and give them the same name in the Property Inspector.

Creating a group of radio buttons by adding buttons one by one is often more time-consuming than it's worth. Thankfully, Dreamweaver offers a more efficient method for creating a list of mutually exclusive options: the radio group.

Adding radio groups

The **Radio Group** element in the Insert toolbar provides a quick and easy way to add a list of radio buttons to your form. The same rules regarding naming and values apply, but the Radio Group dialog box allows you to include several entries in a group at once.

Follow these steps to add radio groups to a form — **Step-by-Step**

1. Click and drag to select the three (Radio Button) placeholders and their labels (Yes, No, and Can't Remember). Press Delete to remove them from your form. You'll create your own labels for this group.
2. Click on the Radio Group button in the Insert panel. The Radio Group dialog box opens (Figure 13-15), and offers several property options.

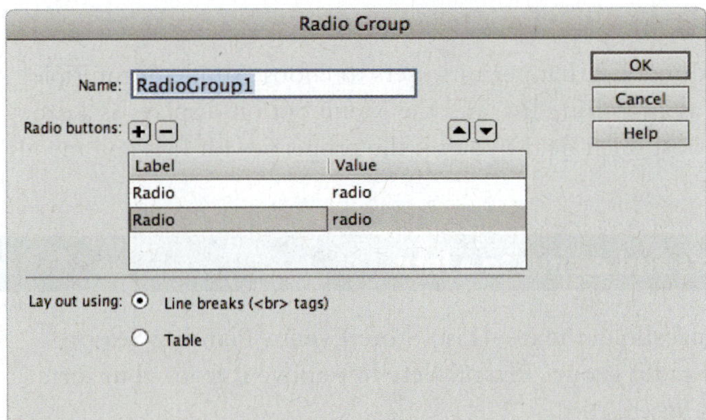

Figure 13-15: Set properties for your radio group in the Radio Group dialog box.

3. In the Name text field of the Radio Group dialog box, type **Membership Status** to give the group a name that associates all the radio buttons together.

   You will now create a unique label for each button.
4. Click on the first entry in the Label column and type **Member**.
5. In the Value column of the Radio buttons section, you assign a value to each button to be passed back to the server. Click on the first entry in this column and type **member**. This returns a value of member when the user clicks on the Member radio button.
6. Make sure Line breaks (`<br>` tags) is selected in the *Layout using* section at the bottom of the dialog box. This will place a hard return after each radio button.
7. Repeat steps 4 to 6, but this time create a label called **Non-Member** and a value of **nonmember**.

8. Click OK. Choose File > Save, and then preview the open page in a browser. Click on each of the two radio buttons and note that only one radio button can ever be selected (Figure 13-16). This is a function of a radio button group: for cases where you want more than one option to be selected and returned, you could use a checkbox.

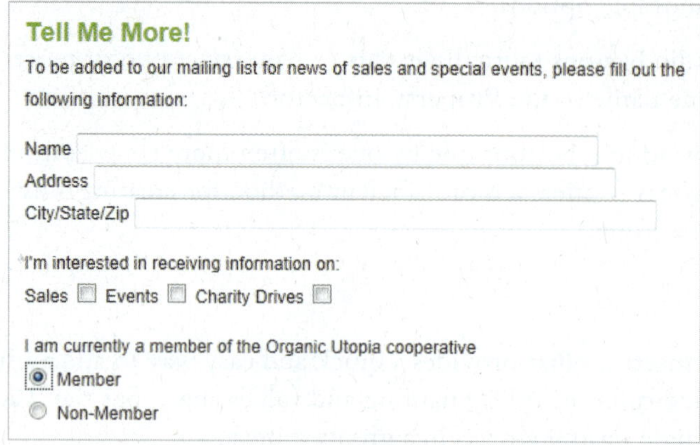

Figure 13-16: After adding the radio group, your form should look like this.

9. Close your browser and return to Dreamweaver.

Take Note...
Checkboxes can also be added as groups using the Checkbox Group option in the Insert panel.

Adding lists and menus

Lists and menus show choices within a list that permits users to choose single or multiple options. The List option displays as a scrolling list, and the Menu option displays as a drop-down menu. As is the case with most form fields, you set the properties for lists and menus in the Property Inspector.

Step-by-Step

Follow these steps to add lists and menus to a form

1. Click and drag to select the placeholder text—(List) Store Events, Planting Season, Anything—that follows your radio group. Press Delete to remove it from your form. You'll create your own labels for this list.
2. Press the Select (List/Menu) button (▤) in the Insert panel. The Input Tag Accessibility Attributes dialog box opens.
3. Type **Volunteer** in the ID text field and leave the additional settings as is, then press OK. A new list or menu appears within the form outline on your page.
4. Click the list menu control to select it, and notice the options that are now available in the Property Inspector (FIgure 13-17).

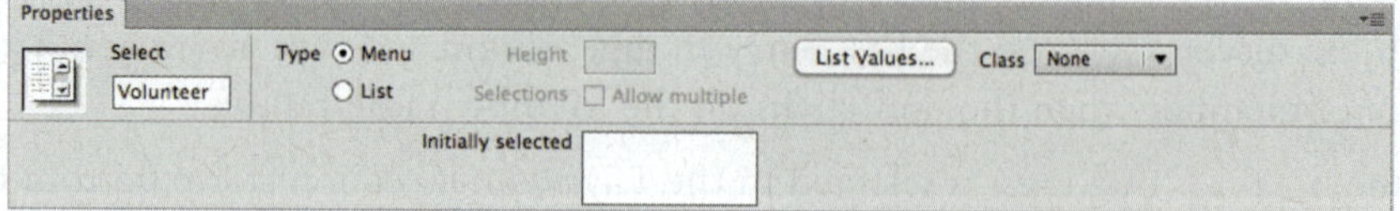

Figure 13-17: Enter the settings for your newly added list or menu in the Property Inspector.

5. The Type options let you define whether the field is displayed as a scrolling list or a drop-down menu. Click on the List radio button to choose this option. Notice that more settings become available on the right side of the Property Inspector.
6. Type **3** in the Height text field to set the number of items to be visible at any given time in the scrolling list.
7. Click in the checkbox to the right of the Selections option to allow multiple selections. With this feature activated, users can choose more than one option from your list at a time.
8. Click on the List Values button to enter items for your scrolling list. The structure of the List Values dialog box is identical to that of the Radio Group dialog box. Type **Store Events** as your first Item Label and **store_events** for the first value to be returned.

   Now you will add two more items to the list.
9. Click the Plus button (+) in the left corner of the List Values window, and type **Planting Season** as the second Item Label. Then click under the Events value and type **plantingseason**. Click the Plus button (+) again. Type **Anything** as the third Item Label, and, finally, click under the Planting value and type **anyevent** as seen in Figure 13-18. Click OK.

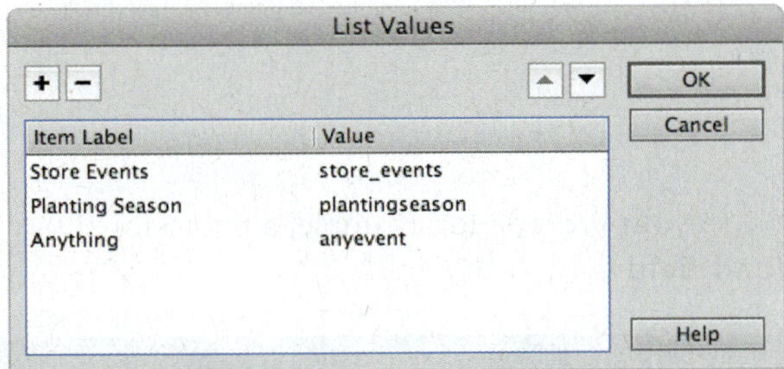

***Figure 13-18**: Adding the labels and values for a list control.*

10. Choose File > Save to save your work. Preview your page in the browser and click one of the labels to see how it is selected. Close your browser and return to Dreamweaver.

Adding a text area

Sometimes within a Dreamweaver form, you want to have a field that simply provides an open area into which users can enter text. For this form, you'll add a **textarea** element to provide a region for users to type in their comments about the site.

Follow these steps to add a text area to a form

Step-by-Step

1. Click and drag to select the placeholder text, (Comments), and retype it without the parentheses, to use as a label for this field.
2. Press Enter (Windows) or Return (Mac OS) to move your cursor to the next line.
3. Click on the Textarea element (▤) in the Insert panel. The Input Tag Accessibility Attributes dialog box opens.
4. In the ID text field, type **Comments**. In the Style section, select Wrap with label tag.
5. Click OK. A new text area appears within the form outline on your page.
6. Click the text area, and notice the options that are now available in the Property Inspector.
7. Type **40** in the Char width text field to set the text input area to a width of 40 characters.
8. Leave the Num lines text field set to 5, and leave Type set to Multi line.

9. Leave the Init Val and Class settings at their defaults and choose File > Save; then preview the open page in a browser (Figure 13-19). The text area will allow users to type inside of the box, and if the amount of text goes below the bottom of the text area, then a scrollbar will automatically appear.

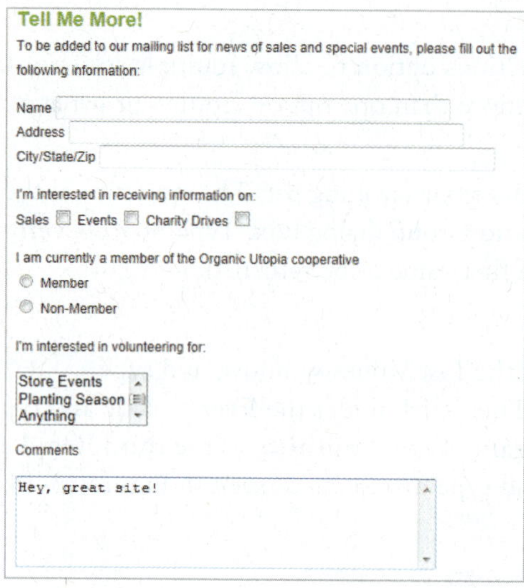

13-19: The form so far, as rendered by Mozilla Firefox.

Adding a File Upload field

If you want users to be able to upload a file to your server—for example, a photo for ID purposes—you'll want to add a **File Upload field**.

Step-by-Step

Follow these steps to add a file upload field

1. Close the browser and return to **organicform.html** in Dreamweaver. Click and drag to select (Upload), and delete it to place an insertion cursor next to your label.
2. Click on the File Field button ( ) in the Insert panel. The Input Tag Accessibility Attributes dialog box opens.
3. In the Input Tag Accessibility Attributes dialog box, type **filefield** for the ID. Additionally, make sure the Wrap with label tag field is selected.
4. Click OK. A new file field, with the Browse button included, appears within the form outline on your page.
5. Click to select the file field, and notice the options that become available in the Property Inspector.
6. Type **30** in the Char width text field to set the text input area to a width of 30 characters.
7. Type **30** in the Max chars text field as seen in Figure 13-20 to set the maximum number of filename characters that can be entered.

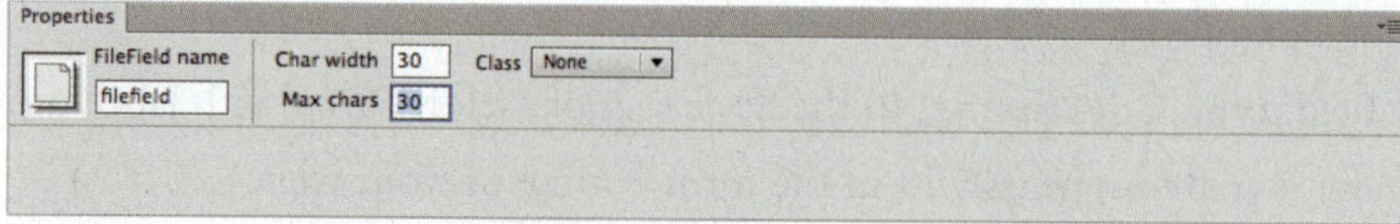

***Figure 13-20**: Set the properties for your File Upload field in the Property Inspector.*

8. The Class drop-down menu allows you to apply CSS to style this form field. Using CSS to style form fields is discussed in more detail later in this lesson.

   You are now finished with the file field section of your form. Users can now either enter the desired file name or click Browse to navigate to it.

Take Note...

For the file field element to actually upload a user's file to your server, you'll need to ask your server Administrator how the server is configured to accept files.

9. Choose File > Save, then preview the open page in a browser. Your form should look like Figure 13-21:

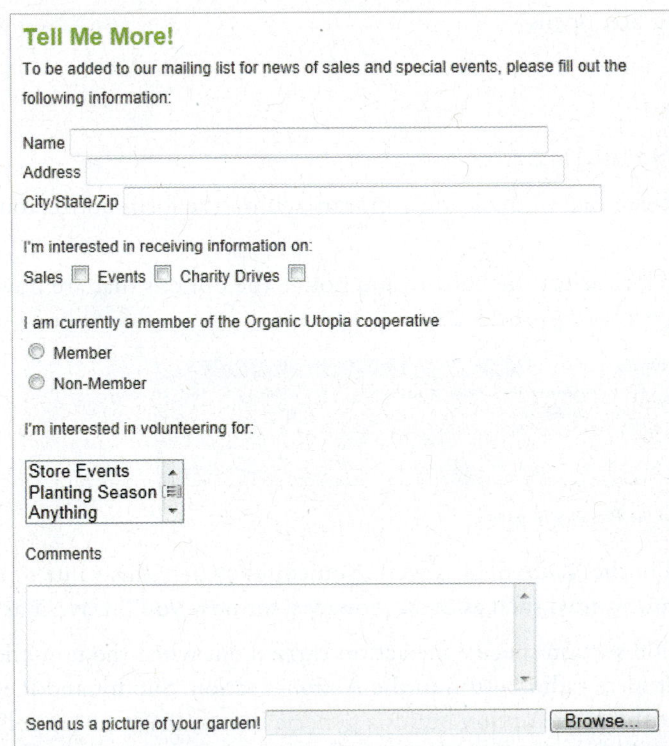

***Figure 13-21**: You're almost finished adding form fields to your form.*

10. Close the browser and return to Dreamweaver.

Creating Submit and Reset buttons

As you might expect, none of the field elements you've been adding to your form do any good if the user doesn't have a way to send the information to you. Buttons provide the means for the either to commit an action. A **submit button** provides the means for a user to submit form data and a **reset button** provides the means for a user to reset the fields and start the form over.

Step-by-Step

Follow these steps to create Submit and Reset Buttons on a form

1. Place your cursor after the Upload field, then press Enter (Windows) or Return (Mac OS) to specify where you want your button(s) to appear.
2. Click on the Button element (▭) in the Forms category of the Insert panel. The Input Tag Accessibility Attributes dialog box opens.
3. In the dialog box, specify the following:

   In the ID section, type **Submit**.

   In the Style section, choose No label tag.
4. Click OK. A new button, labeled *Submit* by default, appears within the form outline on your page.
5. If it's not already selected, click to select the button, and notice the options that are now available in the Property Inspector (Figure 13-22).

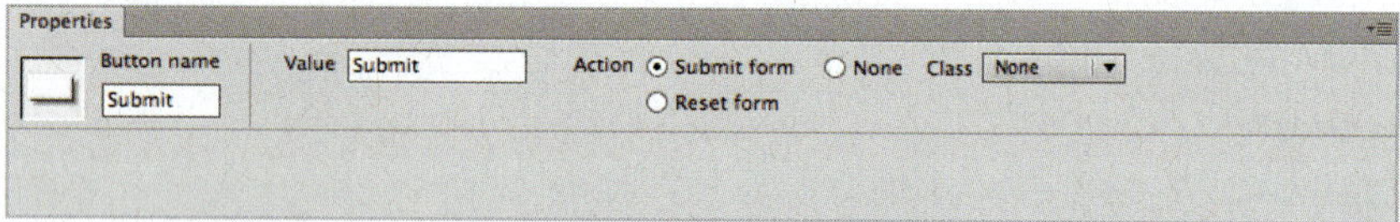

Figure 13-22: *Button properties are set in the Property Inspector.*

6. The word *Submit* is displayed in the Value field as well. You could change this value to a more user-friendly name if you wanted such as Send, however for now you'll leave it as is.
7. The three options in the Action section specify the action carried out when the user clicks this button. Select the Submit form radio button in the Actions section. Submit and Reset form are self-explanatory, but the None option builds a generic button that you can set to trigger a JavaScript behavior, which is discussed later in this lesson.
8. The Class drop-down menu allows you to apply CSS to style this form field—another technique that is covered later in the lesson.
9. Repeat steps 1 to 9 to add Reset and Validate buttons next to the Submit button. Choose Reset from the Action section in the Property Inspector for the Reset button, and None for the Validate button. Additionally, you will need to type Validate in the Value field to change the default value as seen in Figure 13-23.

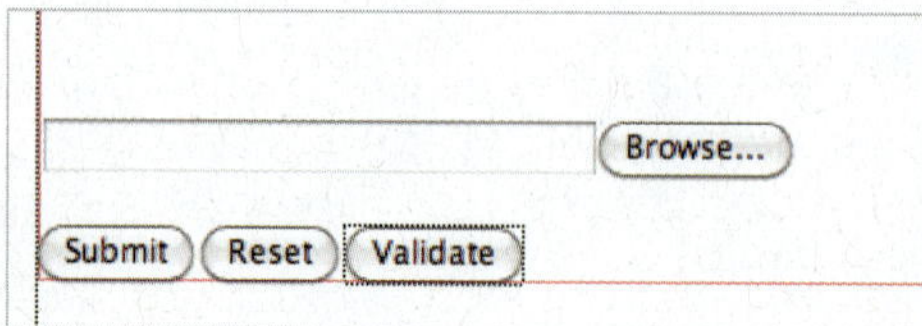

Figure 13-23: *The Submit, Reset, and Validate button are now placed in the form.*

10. Choose File > Save All to save your work.

Now that you've finished adding the necessary form fields to your Contact Form page, you'll add style to the form and its elements, using CSS.

Styling forms with CSS

In Lesson 4, "Styling Your Pages with CSS," you explored the many ways you can use CSS to format text and position content on an HTML page in Dreamweaver. However, the usefulness of CSS is not limited to static page content. Dynamic content, such as form fields, can also be successfully and creatively styled using CSS.

Attaching external styles

This exercise assumes you have already learned some of the basics of working with styles covered in previous lessons. You will now focus on applying some existing styles to the form elements that you've added in this lesson. The styles you apply have been created for you, but you must attach them to your form page in order to access them.

Follow these steps to attach an external style sheet

Step-by-Step

1. If your CSS Styles panel is not currently open, open it now by choosing Window > CSS Styles.
2. In the CSS Styles panel, click on the Attach Style Sheet button (⚭) in the lower-right corner of the panel. The Attach External Style Sheet dialog box opens (Figure 13-24).

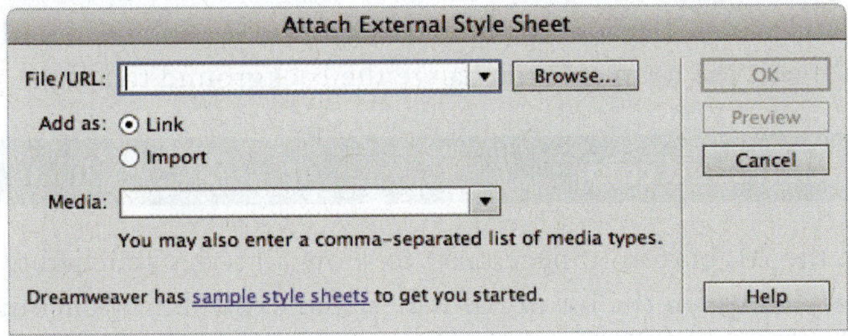

Figure 13-24: Select the CSS file you want to attach using The Attach External Style Sheet dialog box.

3. Next to the File/URL field, click the Browse button and select **formstyles.css** from the dw13lessons folder. Press OK (Windows) or Open (Mac OS) to exit the Select Style Sheet File dialog box.
4. In the Attach External Style Sheet dialog box, click the Link radio button to create a link `<href>` tag in the code for this page, and reference the location of the published style sheet. Most major web browsers support the link method.
5. In the Media drop-down menu, you can define the target medium for your style sheet. For this exercise, leave this setting at its default, which is blank.

Take Note...
For more information on media-dependent style sheets, see the World Wide Web Consortium (W3C) website at W3.org/TR/CSS21/media.html.

6. Press OK to attach the style sheet to this document.

Setting a background color

Once the formstyles.css style sheet is attached, the backgrounds of your form fields change to a light blue color as seen in Figure 13-25. This happens because formstyles.css contains a tag selector rule, which instructs the <form> tag you added earlier in the lesson to include a background color. The rule redefines the <form> tag, so the color is applied only to the background of the form fields themselves, and not to the entire body of the page.

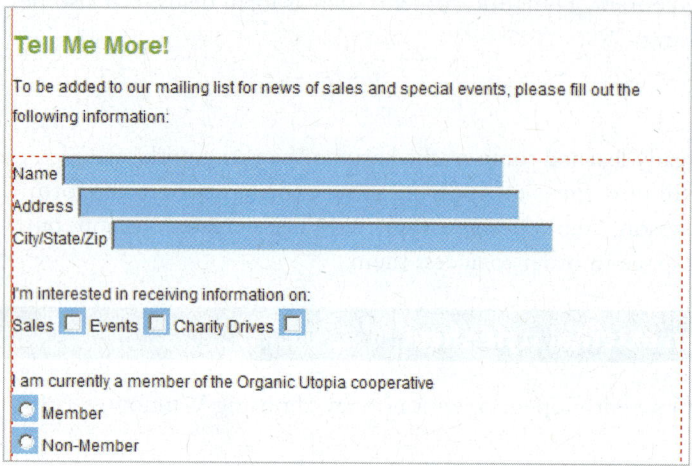

Figure 13-25: The formstyles CSS contains a rule that specifies a background color.

A major benefit of using CSS is that once you complete the initial styling, you can revisit the CSS file and change the included style rules. Because the blue background doesn't fit in with the color scheme of your site, you'll edit the form rule to change the background to a light gray.

Step-by-Step

Follow these steps to set a background color

1. In the CSS Styles panel, click the All button (if necessary) to show all styles attached to this document. Locate **formstyles.css** in the list of All Rules, and expand it by clicking on the Plus button (+) (Windows) or triangle button (▶) (Mac OS) to the left side. (You can collapse the <style> tag and the **SpryMenuGarHorizontal.css** style sheet to make more room in the panel.)

2. From the list of style rules included within **formstyles.css**, click on the input rule to select it for editing as seen in Figure 13-26.

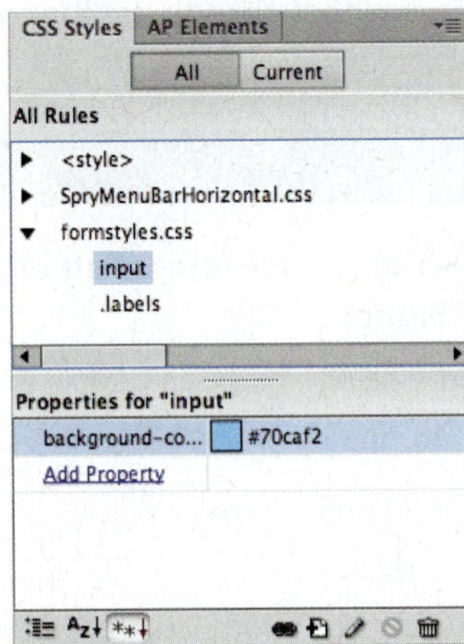

***Figure 13-26**: Selecting the input style in your formstyles.css style sheet reveals the style being used.*

3. Double-click the input style. The CSS Rule Definition dialog box opens.
4. Select the Background category to the left, and, in the Background color text field to the right, type the hexadecimal code **#d7d7d7**, to replace the current color (Figure 13-27).

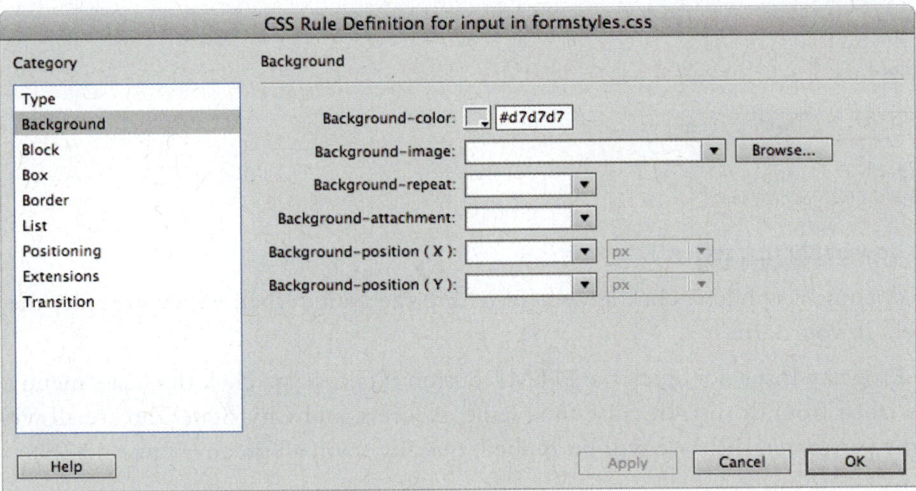

***Figure 13-27**: You've successfully changed the background color of your form fields by editing an attached CSS.*

5. To preview the change to the background color, press Apply. Press OK.

   You've just used a tag selector CSS rule to change the background color of your form. Next, you'll use a class style to change the appearance of the labels on your form fields.

Styling form elements

You may have noticed another CSS rule included in formstyles.css along with the `<form>` definition. It's a class style called `.labels`, and it contains properties that change the font, color, and weight of your form field labels.

Step-by-Step

Follow these steps to style form elements

1. In the CSS Styles panel, click the `.labels` CSS rule to select it; in the bottom half of the panel, you can see the properties currently set for the class (Figure 13-28).

   The `font-family` has been changed to Arial, Helvetica, sans-serif.

   The `font-weight` is set to bolder.

   The `color` has been set to a hexadecimal notation of #9FCC41, or green.

   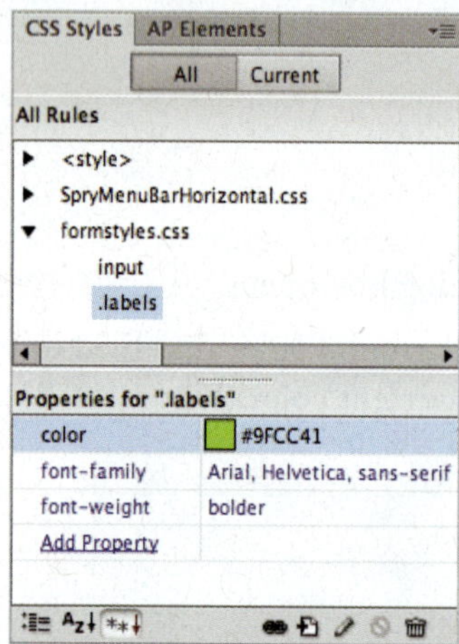

   Figure 13-28: The `.labels` rule can also be edited in the CSS Styles panel.

   You'll now apply this style.

2. In the document window, click anywhere within the Name label, which precedes the first text field in your form.
3. In the Property Inspector, click the HTML button if necessary; click the Class menu and choose labels from the list. Because the Name, Address, and City/State/Zip are all within the same paragraph, the style will be applied, making them all green (Figure 13-29).

   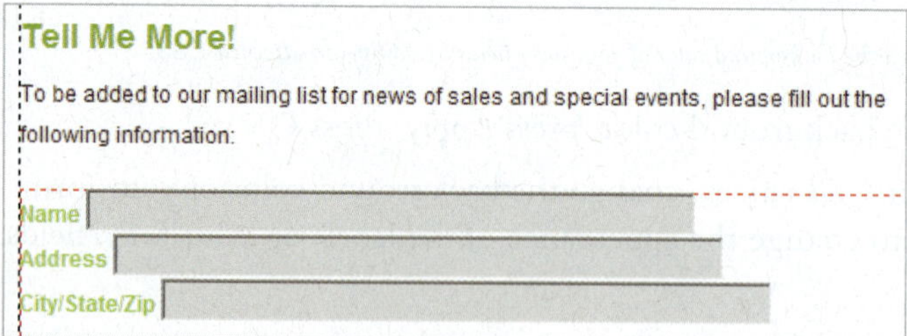

   Figure 13-29: The `.labels` class applied to your form.

These are just a few of the ways you can use CSS to style form elements. Experiment further with different properties to make your form more visually pleasing.

Form processing and validation

As attractive as CSS styling can make your form in Dreamweaver, you can't collect form data without using a server-side script or application (for example, CGI, PHP, ASP) to process the data.

CGI scripts are perhaps the oldest method of server-side scripting used to process form data. Several websites offer free CGI scripts that you can use. The hosting company for your website may also provide CGI scripts that perform many common tasks, such as collecting e-mail addresses or allowing visitors to send you comments through a web form. Other methods include the use of other scripting languages, such as PHP, ASP, and others. It is beyond the scope of this book to cover all the various ways to process form data.

It's also worth noting that **form validation**, a method for ensuring that the user has entered the correct type of data in the form's fields, also requires scripting to work correctly. Thankfully, Dreamweaver is capable of adding JavaScript code that checks the contents of specified text fields. This code is added through the use of the Validate Form behavior.

Adding form validation

The Validate Form behavior provides checks and balances for users when they complete forms on your site. You can make certain fields required, make sure a user has entered a value in a required field, or make sure a user has entered the correct type of information in a field. You can run validation on all fields in a form, or on individual fields contained in that form.

The first step, however, is to get to know the Behaviors panel.

A look at the Behaviors panel

Generally speaking, the **Behaviors** panel provides a means for you to add JavaScript code to your page without actually having to type in the code. The code it inserts adds interactivity to your site, and is usually triggered by some user action. For example, when the user clicks on or hovers over a link, the behavior performs a task. Behaviors are hardly limited to use with forms, as they're commonly used to add rollovers, open new windows, check for plug-ins, and add navigation elements, among other functions.

Specifically, you use the Behaviors panel to add, modify, and remove behaviors. Because you can apply multiple behaviors to the same object, you can also reorder them in the Behaviors panel.

Step-by-Step

Follow these steps to use the Behaviors panel

1. Access the Behaviors panel by choosing Window > Behaviors. It docks with the Tag Inspector panel on the right side of your screen. If necessary, expand the panel grouping and click on the Behaviors tab to bring it to the front as seen in Figure 13-30.

Figure 13-30: The Behaviors panel.

2. In the document window, click the Validate button you created earlier. You need to attach a behavior to objects on your page. For this exercise, the object you need to attach a behavior to is the Validate button.

3. Click the Plus button (+) at the top of the Behaviors panel to see the list of available options for the selected object (Figure 13-31). In this case, the menu displays options associated with a button element. If an option is grayed out, that action is not available for the selected object.

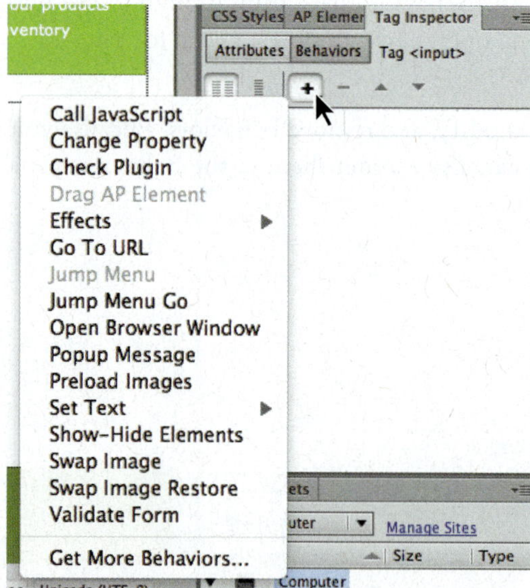

Figure 13-31: The list of available behaviors for your selected button element.

4. Select the Popup Message action. The Popup Message dialog box appears.

5. Type **Validate this form!** into the Message text field as seen in Figure 13-32, and click OK.

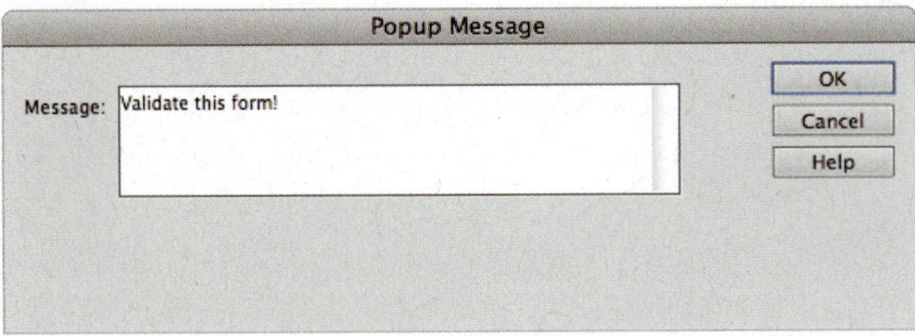

Figure 13-32: Enter text into the Popup Message dialog box to have it appear on the screen.

The behavior is set, but it needs an event, or trigger.

Setting an event or trigger

An event (or trigger) is generally a specific user action needed for the Popup Window (or other behaviors) to work. In this case, you'll set the window to appear when the user clicks the Validate button.

Follow these steps to set an event or trigger

Step-by-Step

1. In the top-left corner of the Behaviors panel, click on the Show All Events button (). The Show All Events button provides a complete list of all possible triggers for this behavior (Figure 13-33).

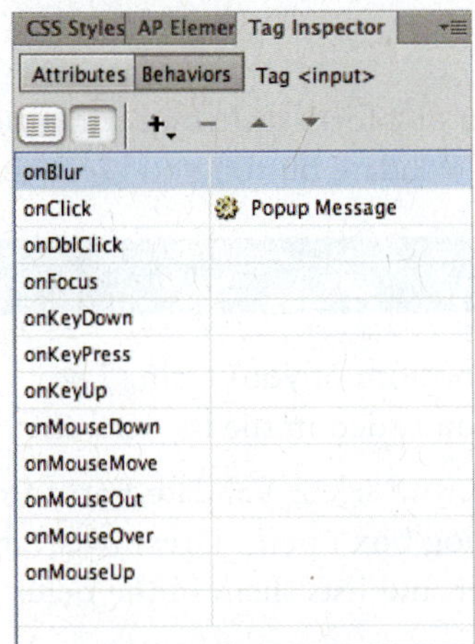

Figure 13-33: There are a number of choices for the event that triggers your specific behavior.

In this case, the default option "onClick" is the correct choice.

2. Choose File > Save All and preview your page in a browser.

3. Press on the Validate button at the bottom of your form. The pop-up message you set earlier appears (Figure 13-34).

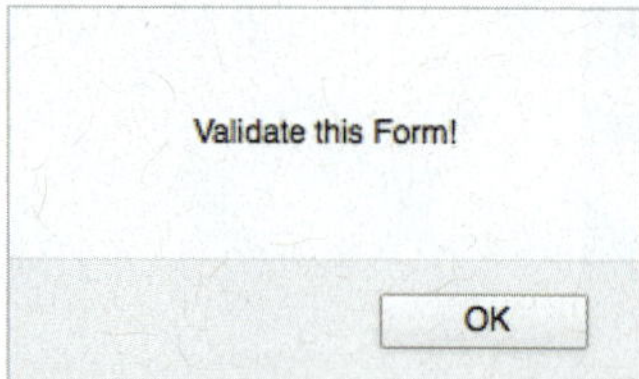

***Figure 13-34**: Use this feature to warn your viewers, or to guide them in a certain direction.*

Take Note...

Depending on the security configurations of your browser, you may be prompted to allow blocked content. If you'd like to change your preferences to avoid conflicts with scripts created in the Behaviors panel, refer to your browser's documentation for instructions on changing the default settings.

4. Press OK to close the message, and close your browser window and return to Dreamweaver.

   To further explore the Behaviors panel and its features, you'll add a Form Validation behavior to the same button.

Validating form fields

The Validate Form action allows you to prevent the submission of a form unless a certain field (or fields) is filled in by the user. You'll apply this action to the Validate button you created.

Step-by-Step

Follow these steps to validate form fields

1. In the document window, select the Validate button at the bottom of your form. The Behaviors panel should display the Popup Message action you added in the last exercise.
2. At the top of the Behaviors panel, click the Plus button (+), and select Validate Form from the drop-down menu that appears. The Validate Form dialog box opens. Dreamweaver automatically identifies the fields you have used on the page and lists them in the fields section.
3. Choose "Mailing_list_name," the first entry in the Fields list. Click the Required checkbox to require data entry into this field before the user can submit the form.

4. Click the Anything radio button so the field accepts any alphanumeric entry as seen in Figure 13-35. If you want to require that only numerical data be entered, you would select the Number radio button. If you want to check for an @ symbol within the entered data, you would click the Email address radio button. Finally, if you want to check for a number within a specific range, you could enter that range in the Number from and to fields.

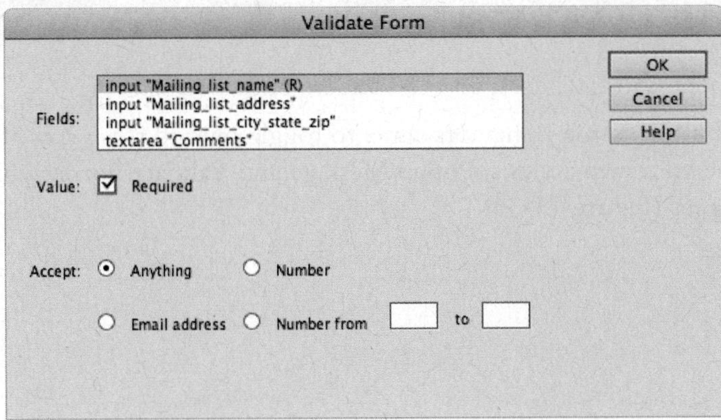

Figure 13-35: Specify which form elements get validated, and what is accepted.

5. Click OK to close the Validate Form dialog box.

6. Choose File > Save, then preview the form page in your browser. Leave the Name field blank, and click on the Validate button at the bottom of your form.

   Unfortunately, the Popup Message behavior you added earlier runs before the Validate Form behavior, requiring you to close the Popup Message window to see the results of your validation. After you dismiss the Popup Message you will see the error message stating that the Mailing list name is required.

   This means you have just a little more work to do; you'll now adjust the Validate Form behavior to correct these errors.

Changing a form field's behavior order

To keep the pop-up message from appearing before the results of your validation, you'll need to change the Validate Form behavior's position in the behavior order, delete it, and reapply it to the correct button.

Step-by-Step

Follow these steps to change a form field's behavior order

1. In the Dreamweaver document window, click on the Validate button to select it.
2. Click the Show Set Events button in the Behaviors panel to toggle over to this view (if necessary). You will now see your two actions, Popup Message and Validate Form, which share the same event, or trigger (Figure 13-36).

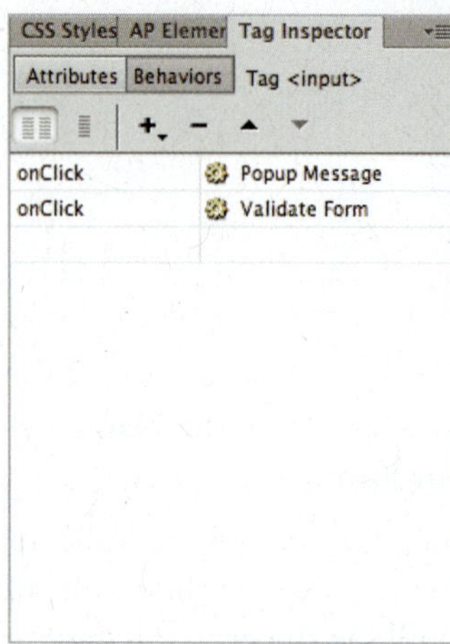

Figure 13-36*: Use the Behaviors panel to reorder behaviors and make them behave differently for the viewer.*

3. Click on the Validate Form behavior to select it, and click the up arrow at the top of the panel to move it to a position above the Popup Message behavior. Although this makes the Validate Form action run first, the pop-up message still appears after the validation window is closed. It actually makes more sense not to have the Validate Form behavior attached to the Validate button at all. You will now remove this behavior and attach it to the Submit button instead.
4. Click on the Minus button (–) to delete it from the behaviors associated with the Validate button.
5. Click on the Submit button at the bottom of your form to select it. Repeat steps 2-4 in the preceding exercise to add the validation action to the Submit button.

   Now it's time to see the fruits of your labor.

Verifying field contents

Now that you've adjusted the Validate Form behavior, you'll need to make sure the form functions as you expect it to.

Follow these steps to change field contents — Step-by-Step

1. Preview the open page in your browser, and click on the Validate button. This should now display only the pop-up message. Close it.
2. Click on the Submit button. Even though the data is not actually submitted (for lack of a CGI script), the Validate Form warns you that required fields have not been filled (Figure 13-37).

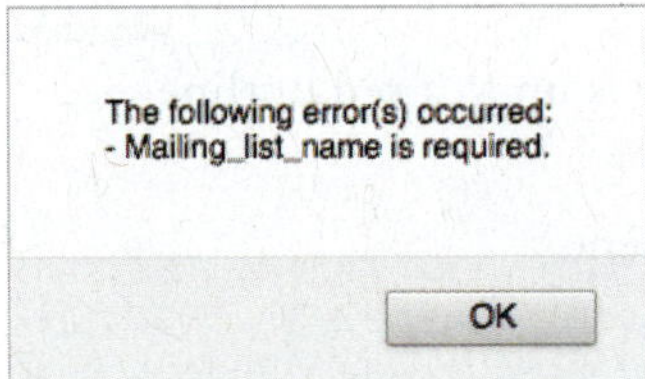

***Figure 13-37**: The Validate Form behavior functions as you originally intended, thanks to some editing in the Behaviors panel.*

You've successfully added validation to your form, and completed this lesson in the process. Congratulations!

Take Note...
For a more detailed look at adding modern forms to a website, see the HTML5 Digital Classroom *book available in electronic and print formats.*

Skill Summary

In this lesson you learned how to:	Objective
Create forms	4.13

Knowledge Assessment

True/False

Circle T if the statement is true or F if the statement is false.

T F **1.** An HTML form contains content such as text, images, markup, and special elements called controls.

T F **2.** Dreamweaver provides the location for form data when processed via the Submit button.

T F **3.** The first step in building a form in Dreamweaver is to add a form element which serves as a container for the form fields.

T F **4.** When you first add a form to a webpage, it shows up as a red outline.

T F **5.** Text cannot be cut and pasted into a form element.

T F **6.** A form ID makes it possible to identify and control the form with script.

T F **7.** The Method drop-down menu is where you choose the method used to transmit form data to a server.

T F **8.** Codes other than HTML such as CGI and PHP are often associated with regard to submitting form data.

T F **9.** Text fields will only accept single line formats with regard to inputing text. If you want additional lines of text to be inputted, you must add more text fields.

T F **10.** You can set a maximum amount of characters that a text field will accept, preventing the user from tying in more than the value you establish.

Multiple Choice

Select the best response for the following statements

1. Which of the following is a web form used for?

a. Questionnaires
b. Data entry
c. Hotel reservations
d. All of the above

2. In order to have a system for accepting user data from a form, you will need to:

a. Set up this system through Dreamweaver.
b. Set up this system with your hosting provider or another service.
c. Set up this system using Flash.
d. Configuring the settings through a search engine such as Google or Yahoo.

3. Which of the following is not an option from the Forms category of the Insert panel?
   a. DIV
   b. Text Field
   c. Hidden Field
   d. Radio Button

4. In HTML code, a form element is added using which tag?
   a. <element>
   b. <form>
   c. <form start>
   d. <start form>

5. Which of the following are all attributes of the <form> tag?
   a. Rotation
   b. Opacity
   c. Audio level
   d. None of the above

6. Which of the following is not an available option in the Method drop-down menu?
   a. FORWARD
   b. Default
   c. GET
   d. POST

7. Which button type will send all form data to the receiving server when clicked?
   a. Radio button
   b. Checkbox
   c. Submit button
   d. Reset button

8. Which of the following button types is used when you want the user to select only one option?
   a. Radio button
   b. Checkbox
   c. Tool button
   d. All of the above

9. Which of the following would be best to list all 50 of the United States for the address section of a form?
   a. List/Menu
   b. Text field
   c. Text area
   d. Form area

10. The File Field button is used when:

a. You want to place a logo on your form
b. You want to give the user the ability to upload a file
c. You want the webpage to accept form data from forms on another webpage
d. None of the above

Competency Assessment

Project 13-1 Examining more Behaviors

Behaviors are something that can really enhance the interactivity of your webpage for various reasons. Let's add another behavior, but don't forget to go back in there and keep trying out different options. Another way to find out more about Behaviors is to select Help from the panel flyout menu.

1. Choose File > New > Blank Page > HTML > None to create a new empty webpage.
2. Save the page as **behavior.html**.
3. Choose Window > Behaviors.
4. Click and hold the Add Behavior button and select Go To URL.
5. In the URL field, type: **http://www.adobe.com**.
6. Click OK and save the file. Once saved, preview in a browser to see what happens. Due to the onLoad trigger, your browser should jump to the Adobe website as you as you preview the page.
7. Leave the file open for the next exercise below.

Project 13-2 Examining the Code

Many behaviors are based on Javascript. When you add a behavior, the code is automatically added in the background. It's good to get familiar with what Javascript looks like in context to the other code you've been working with such as HTML and CSS. You'll take a look at and learn to identify Javascript below.

1. Continue with the page from above.
2. Choose the Code view.
3. Look for the line that starts `<script type="text/javascript">` and then the end tag `</script>`. Everything in between is the Javascript from the behavior you created above.

Proficiency Assessment

It's All in the Naming

Project 13-3

The reason you can only allow the user to pick one radio button is because they share the same name. If you want to understand the mechanics a bit more, follow this exercise.

Launch Dreamweaver CS6 if you haven't already.

1. Create a new blank HTML page.
2. Go to the Form tools in the Insert panel and select the Radio Group element.
3. Once you've added the group, select each button independently and change the name of each to something unique.
4. Test in a browser.

What's going on in the Background

Project 13-4

The form itself seems simple enough compared to what is actually processing the form in the background. Many form driven functions require security, such as a form that accepts credit card information. Understanding the security is an important aspect; CGI script is one of the types of code that is often used when securing form information.

1. Examine the following website to learn more about CGI: *http://www.cgiscript.net/*

Adding Interactivity with the Spry Framework

Key Terms

- AJAX
- Spry Accordion Panel
- Spry Assets
- Spry Collapsible Panel
- Spry Framework
- Spry Menu
- Spry Repeat List
- Spry Tabbed Panel
- Spry Widget
- Spry XML Data Set
- XML

Skill	Objective
Insert navigation bars, rollover images, and buttons created in a drawing program on a web page	4.9
Modify text and text properties	5.3

Business Case

The owners at Organic Utopia have asked you to make the site navigation and information more visually interesting. In order to do this easily, you can use Dreamweaver's Spry objects to create interactive user interface elements, such as accordion-style displays, customizable menu bars, and much more.

Introduction

Before starting, make sure that your tools and panels are consistent by resetting your workspace. See "Resetting the Dreamweaver workspace" in the Starting Up section of this book.

You will work with several files from the dw14lessons folder in this lesson. Make sure that you have loaded the dwlessons folder onto your hard drive. See "Loading lesson files" in the Starting Up section of this book.

Before you begin, you need to create site settings that point to the dw14lessons folder. Go to Site > New Site, or, for details on creating a site, refer to Lesson 2, "Setting Up a New Site."

Introducing the Spry Widgets

Introduced in Dreamweaver CS3, **Spry Widgets** give you the ability to create powerful, interactive navigation and user interface elements with easy-to-use insert bar objects. Spry Widgets include drop-down and accordion menus, expanding panels, and tabbed containers, all of which harness the power of CSS for easy customization and styling to match any project. They are a great way to enhance navigation, organize content, and add dynamic style to your web pages.

In addition, the Spry framework offers a set of data elements and display items that allow you to create dynamic page content that can read from an XML file. You can find the Spry Widgets in their own category on the Insert panel, and within the Layout category as well.

The Spry framework for AJAX

Developed by Adobe, **Spry Framework** is a JavaScript library and features data-driven and interface elements that can be easily added to a page and customized. Many of these elements can incorporate real-time data from XML or HTML files. These can be integrated into your existing pages to add features not available with HTML alone.

What is AJAX?

AJAX is an acronym for Asynchronous JavaScript and XML, and represents a combination of technologies: JavaScript, XML, and DHTML (more commonly referred to as DOM Scripting). AJAX is used to develop what is sometimes referred to as Rich Internet Applications (RIAs). RIAs are a great example of how the Web continues to evolve and progress beyond the static web page. RIAs exchange data behind the scenes and can easily update the appearance and display of the web page without the need to reload the page over and over again.

A great example of an RIA is Google's Gmail, which has the ability to update messages, create online chats, and retrieve address book contacts in real-time without the need to go to another page or even reload the existing one. Here, AJAX is used to send and retrieve XML-based data behind the scenes and updates the appearance and information on the page in real-time.

A look at the project

In this lesson, you'll be completing the OrganicUtopia home page by using and customizing different Spry Widgets. Before you get started, take a look at the completed version of the page to get an idea of what you'll be working toward.

If you haven't already created a site definition for this lesson in Dreamweaver, follow the instructions in Lesson 2, "Setting Up a New Site," to do so before moving ahead.

Step-by-Step

Follow these steps to view the finished project

1. In the Files panel, locate the **index_done.html** page, and double-click it to open it.
2. To view the Spry Widgets in action, choose File > Preview in Browser, and select a browser to preview the page. Depending on which browser you are using, you may see a message indicating that scripts are being blocked. Press the Allow Blocked Content button to allow the scripts to be run.

3. With the page open in a browser, move over the Navigation bar at the top. Notice that hovering over each menu item expands it to reveal more menu items as seen in Figure 14-1.

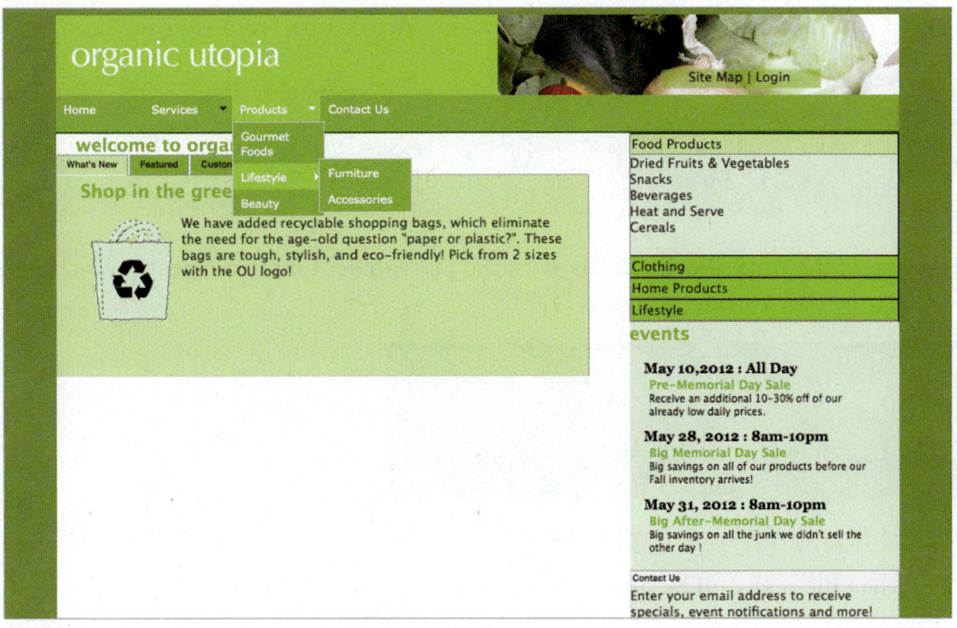

Figure 4-1: The completed Spry page contains numerous interactive elements.

4. On the right, click on the accordion-style menu to expand and contract different categories of products.
5. In the center of the page, locate the three tabs labeled featured, what's new, and testimonials. Click on each one to reveal a different content area—notice that the page doesn't refresh when you do this.
6. In the lower-right corner, click the Contact Us bar to reveal a signup box.
7. Close the browser and return to Dreamweaver. Then, choose File > Close to close the current file.

The Spry Menu bar

In Lesson 6, "Advanced Page Layout," you created your navigation bar from scratch using an HTML list styled with CSS. However, imagine that you are asked to create a more interactive menu, one which activates a drop-down menu of the sub-categories of your site. Although this is possible to do using CSS with perhaps some help from JavaScript, it is not necessarily easy or fast. The **Spry Menu** bar creates a multi-tiered horizontal or vertical menu that can be easily added as a master navigation element in your page(s). These menus are easy to add, and the Spry Menu bar is a great alternative.

The Spry Menu bar can be added from the Insert panel and customized using the Property Inspector and CSS Styles panel.

Step-by-Step

Follow these steps to add the Spry Menu bar

1. From the Files panel, locate and open the **index_start.html** file for editing.
2. Choose File > Save As, and save the page as **index_work.html** into your site's root folder.

Take Note...
If you can't locate your current site folder, click the Site Root button at the bottom of the Save As dialog box to automatically locate and set it as your save location.

3. At the top of the page, locate the div with the placeholder text that reads {*Menu Bar Here*} and select the text as seen in Figure 14-2.

Figure 14-2*: Locate the placeholder text where the menu bar will go.*

Now, delete the text, and be sure to leave your cursor in its place.

4. Open the Insert panel if necessary, and then select the Spry category from the drop-down menu at the top to display the Spry data objects and widgets.
5. Click the Spry Menu bar icon to insert a new menu bar at your cursor position. Choose Horizontal from the dialog box that appears, and click OK to add the menu bar to your page. The bar will be added with four generic navigation items as well as the default Spry Menu bar style which is a light gray background and black text (Figure 14-3). You will be restyling the appearance of the menu a bit later, but first you need to add new menu items.

Figure 14-3*: The inserted Spry Menu bar.*

Take Note...
To select an entire widget and make it active in the Property Inspector, click the blue tab that appears above its top-left corner.

6. The Property Inspector now displays all the options for the new widget. This includes three columns, each of which represents a new level of navigation for a drop-down menu. Locate the leftmost column, which lets you add and customize the top level links on the menu bar. Select the first item titled Item 1.

7. Locate the Text field on the right side of the Property Inspector. Type the name **Home** to rename the item (Figure 14-4). Press Enter (Windows) or Return (Mac OS).

Figure 14-4: Use the Property Inspector to modify and rearrange menu bar items and links.

8. Repeat steps 6 and 7 for Item 2, Item 3, and Item 4, renaming them **Products**, **Services**, and **Contact Us**, respectively.

   This covers the top level navigation for now; next, you will quickly add two more levels to your navigation. For each top-level menu item, you can add up to two additional tiers of menus.

9. Select the Products link in the leftmost column on the Property Inspector.

   Locate the plus sign above the second column, and click it to add a new submenu item as seen in Figure 14-5.

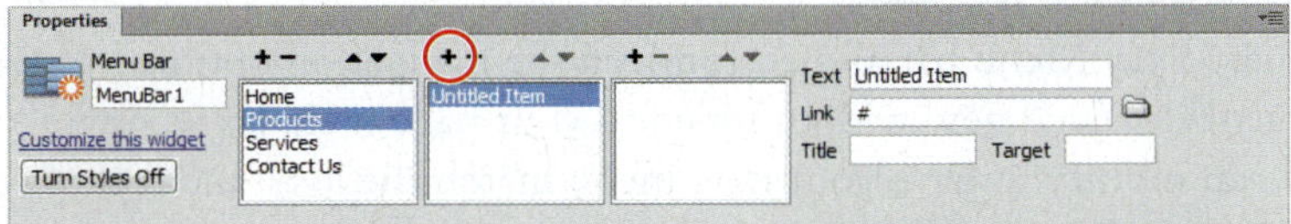

Figure 14-5: Add a second level to the menu by clicking the plus icon in the second column.

   Locate the Text field on the right, and rename the new item **Gourmet Foods**. Press Enter/Return.

10. Click the plus sign above the second column twice more to add two new submenu items. Rename them **Lifestyle** and **Beauty**. Next, you'll add a third tier by creating a submenu for the Lifestyle link you just added.

11. Select the Lifestyle link in the center column. Locate the plus sign above the rightmost column, and click it twice to add two new submenu items to the Lifestyle link.

12. Select each of the new items and use the Text field on the right side of the Property Inspector to rename them **Furniture** and **Accessories**, respectively. Press Enter/Return. In addition to adding levels, you can delete them as well. Your first link to Home has three sub-items that Dreamweaver added by default. You will delete them as they don't reflect your site structure.

13. In the leftmost column, select the top-level link named Home. Click on Item 1.1 and then press the minus icon to remove this link. Repeat this step for Item 1.2 and Item 1.3 so there are no sub-items.

    You'll now reorder some of the items in the Services menu.

14. In the Property Inspector, click on the Services link and then press the up arrow. This moves the item up one level and Services is now the second category (Figure 14-6).

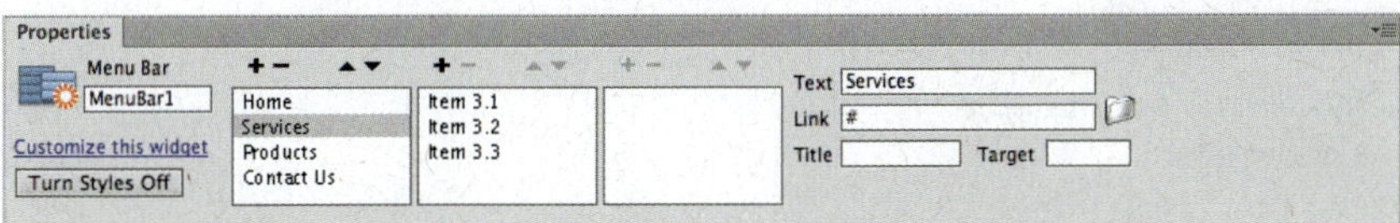

Figure 14-6: Use the up and down arrows above the first list to reorder the top-level links to set the final order.

15. Choose File > Save to save your page. The Copy Dependent Files dialog box appears to let you know that files will be copied to your site directory to support the new menu. Click OK to save the page.

Learning More

Spry Support Files

The first time you save a page that includes a Spry Widget, you are prompted to save new and necessary files to your site. If you look at your Files panel, you will notice that a new **Spry Assets** folder has been added to your site files. This folder contains essential JavaScript, CSS, and image files that style your new widget and make it work. *Be sure to copy this folder to your web server when publishing your site—your widgets will not work without it.*

16. Press the Live View button on the Document toolbar to test your new menu. Mouse over each menu item to see the rollover effects and submenus you created. Press the Live View button again to return to your editing view.

Customizing Spry Widgets with CSS

Now that you've added a new Spry Menu bar and customized the navigation options, you're ready to start giving it some style. Each new widget added to your page includes its own, attached CSS file that you can modify to have your new menu match the look and feel of your site. All CSS rules can be managed from the CSS Styles panel just like your existing page styles.

Step-by-Step

Follow these steps to customize Spry Widgets

Certification Ready 4.9

How do you insert navigation bars, rollover images and buttons?

1. Locate and, if necessary, expand the CSS Styles panel. Double-click the Insert panel to collapse it and give yourself more screen space. You have two groups of CSS styles in this page: styles.css is the external style sheet that contains the majority of the styles for the page, and SpryMenuBarHorizontal.css is the external style sheet for just the menu bar. Click the All tab to locate the attached **SpryMenuBarHorizontal.css** style sheet, and expand it to view all its rules.

   Click the minus sign (Windows) or down arrow (Mac OS) to the left of styles.css to collapse this list and view only the Spry menu styles as seen in Figure 14-7.

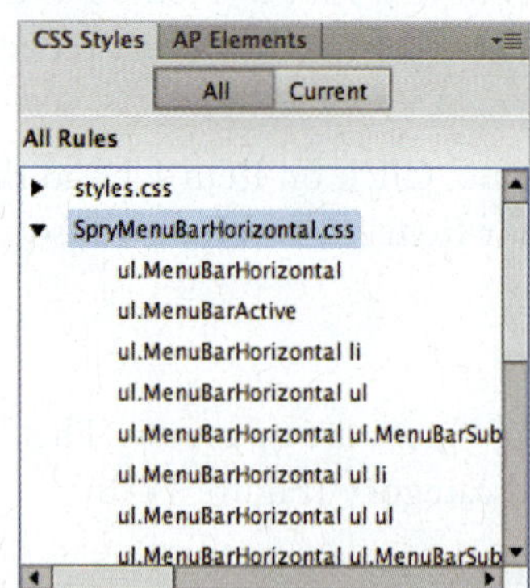

Figure 14-7: *A new style sheet has been attached to your page that controls the formatting of the Spry Menu bar.*

There are more than a dozen style rules for this menu; you will now modify a few of them in order to match your page design. A word of warning: the style names for these menu items are very similar and long, so you will need to pay careful attention to which style you are modifying. It may help you to expand the width of the CSS Styles panel in order to see the style names.

2. Select the `ul.MenuBarHorizontal` rule to view its properties (Figure 14-9). This rule controls the overall appearance and size settings for the menu bar.

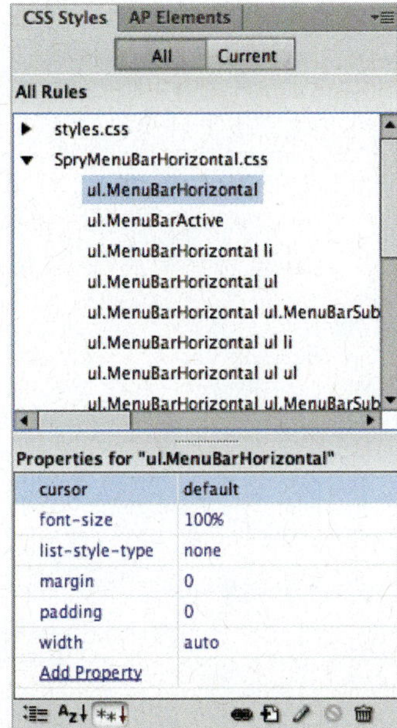

Figure 14-8: *Click Add Property to add a new CSS rule.*

3. Click Add Property at the bottom of the existing property listing. An empty field appears with a menu to the right.

   Note that depending on your workspace you may need to expand the Properties section of the CSS Styles panel to see the properties.

4. Click on the drop-menu and scroll down the resulting list to select the font-family property. This triggers a new field to the right. Click on this drop-menu and choose the Verdana, Geneva, sans-serif family.

5. Locate the font-size property, which has a default value of 100%. Click the 100% value and type 11, then click the rightmost drop-down menu and choose **px** for the unit value. This will have the effect of making the entire menu bar slightly smaller.

6. Select the `ul.MenuBarHorizontal a` rule to view its properties. In the Properties section, click on the value for `background-color` (#EEE) and type **#88B036** (green) as the new color and press Enter (Window) or Return (Mac OS) as seen in Figure 14-10. This sets the background color of the menu bar which happens to be the same shade as the navigation div.

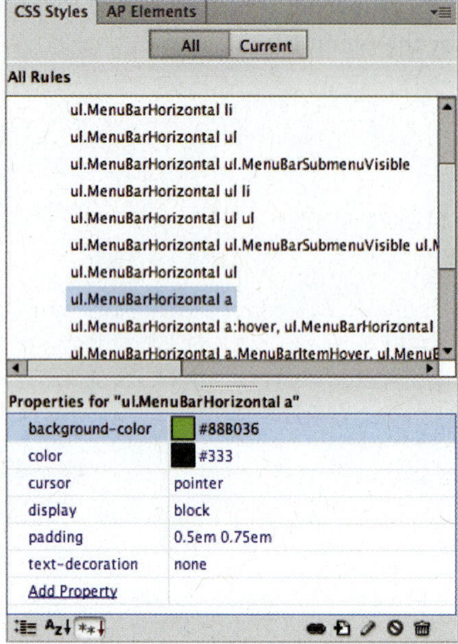

Figure 14-10*: Modify the* `background-color` *property of the rule to change the appearance of the menu bar items.*

7. Click the color swatch (currently set to #333) under the color property and change the color to **#FFFFFF** (white) and press Enter (Window) or Return (Mac OS). This changes the color of the hyperlinked text on each menu item.

8. In the list of rules, select the following to view its properties:

   `ul.MenuBarHorizontal a.MenuBarItemHover, ul.MenuBarHorizontal a.MenuBarItemSubmenuHover, ul.MenuBarHorizontal a.MenuBarSubmenuVisible` rule

   This rule controls the appearance of linked menu items as you roll over them in the menu; it is currently set to a dark blue.

Take Note...

Because this long CSS rule will be difficult to locate in the panel, you can count upward from the bottom of the rules. It is the seventh from the bottom and the default background color is #33C (blue).

9. Click the color swatch under the `background-color` property and type **#9FCC41** (light green) as the new color.

10. Click the Live View button on the Document toolbar to test your page and see the new style changes you've made (Figure 14-11).

Figure 14-11: Use Live View to preview the style changes and interactivity on your new menu.

11. Click Live View again to return to the standard view. Choose File > Save All to save your project. You'll now take a look at another navigation element: the tabbed panel.

The Spry Tabbed panel

The **Spry Tabbed panel** widget organizes content into several panels that you can toggle between by clicking on tabs. This is a great way to organize items on a page: it saves space and can improve usability when used correctly.

Editing the content of the tabbed panels is a bit easier to edit than the Spry Menu bar, instead of using the Property Inspector to add and modify content, you can type directly within the tabs or containers in the document window. Tabbed panels can contain almost any type of content, including text, images, video, and Flash movies.

You'll now add a Spry Tabbed panel to your page to display three pieces of featured content.

Follow these steps to add a Spry Tabbed panel

Step-by-Step

1. Near the top of your page, select the placeholder text that reads {tabbed panels here}, and delete it. Leave your cursor at this position.
2. Click the Insert panel if necessary to expand it. Locate and click the Spry Tabbed Panels button and click it to add a new tabbed panel set.

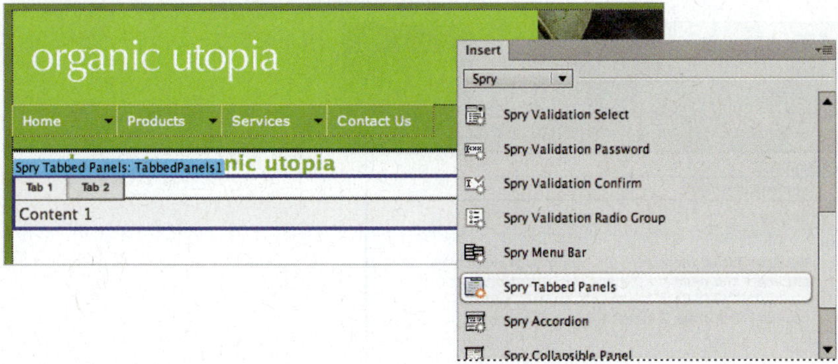

Figure 14-12: Add a new Spry Tabbed Panel at the top of the page, as shown.

3. Locate the Panels column in the center of the Property Inspector below. This shows you the current panels (and tabs) in your panel set, and lets you add new ones. Click the plus sign at the top of the column to add a third tab to your panel set.

   The new tab is out of order, so press the down arrow in the Panels section to move Tab 3 to the bottom of the list.

4. In the Property Inspector, click Tab 1 to activate it as seen in Figure 14-13. On the page and within the tab, select the text "Tab 1" and type **What's New** in its place.

***Figure 14-13**: Select the text inside Tab 1 and rename it to* **What's New**.

5. Select the text within Tab 2 and type **Featured**. Select the text within Tab 3 and type **Customer Testimonials**. Be careful as you move from one tab to the next: if the visibility icon appears and you click it, the tab will open up. For now, you just want to rename the tab headings.

   Next, you will add content into the areas inside each tab.

6. Below the tabbed panel, you'll see three paragraphs of content that you'll move and organize into the new panel group. Highlight the entire first paragraph, beginning with the headline Shop In the Green and be sure to include the recycle bag image. Choose Edit > Cut.

7. Select the placeholder text within the first tab (Content 1), then choose Edit > Paste to paste the content directly into the What's New panel. You will now place content into the Featured panel.

8. Place your cursor over the Featured tab but don't click yet.

9. Wait for the visibility icon to appear (Figure 14-14) and then click once to bring the tab to the front.

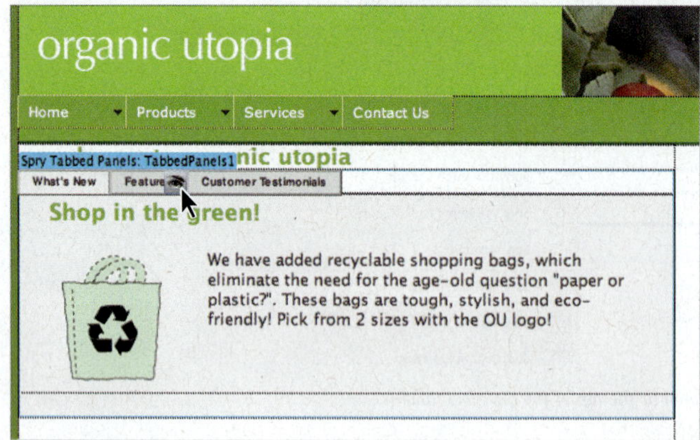

***Figure 14-14**: Clicking the eye icon will bring that tab to the front.*

10. Select the Featured Stuff! heading, paragraph and the image of the couch and choose Edit > Cut. Select the placeholder text Content 2 and then choose Edit > Paste.

11. Repeat steps 7, 8, and 9; cut the remaining content (Our loyal customers) from the page and paste it into the third panel (Customer Testimonials).

12. Click the Live View button on the Document toolbar to preview the tabbed panel so far (Figure 14-15). Click each of the three tabs in order to view the contents of each.

Figure 14-15: *Your new Spry Tabbed panels set after moving the page contents to each of the three tabs (shown in Live View).*

Click the Live View button again to return to Design view. Now it's time to style this panel to match your page theme.

Take Note...

If you want to change which panel is open by default, you can use the Default Panel drop-down menu on the Property Inspector to determine which tab and panel are loaded first.

13. In the CSS Styles panel, locate and expand the style sheet named **SpryTabbedPanels.css**, which was attached when you added the tabbed panel group. Like the Spry Menu bar, the tabbed panel has a dedicated style sheet that you can modify to change its appearance.

14. Select the rule named `.TabbedPanelsTab` to display its properties. Click on the background-color value, type **#88B036** (dark green), then press Enter (Windows) or Return (Mac OS) as seen in Figure 14-16. This changes the color of the non-active tabs.

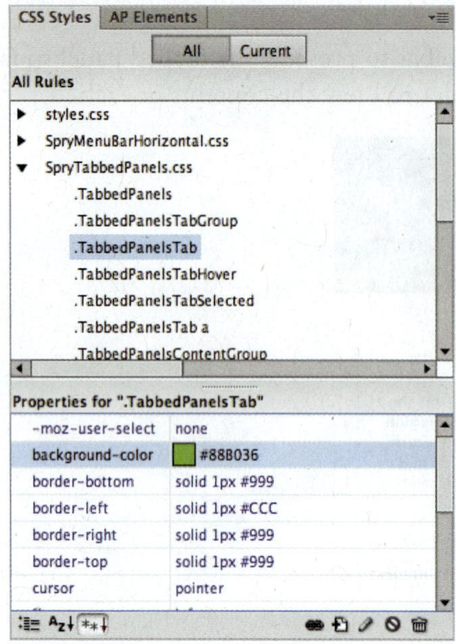

Figure 14-16: Modify the `.TabbedPanelsTab` *rule to change the appearance of non-active tabs.*

15. Select the rule named `.TabbedPanelsTabSelected`. Click on the background-color value, and type **#CF9** (light green), then press Enter/Return. This changes the color of the currently selected tab.

16. Select the rule named `.TabbedPanelsContentGroup`. Click on the background-color value (#EEE) and type **#CF9** and press Enter/Return. This sets the background color of the entire panel to the same shade of green as the tab.

The panels height is currently being defined by the amount of content. If you wanted to override this, you could set an explicit height for the panels.

17. Still within .TabbedPanelsContentGroup, click Add Property at the bottom of the properties list; this adds an empty field. Click the drop-down menu to the right and choose the height property. In the new field that appears, type **250** (make sure px is specified) and then press Enter/Return (Figure 14-17) . This increases the overall height of the content panels.

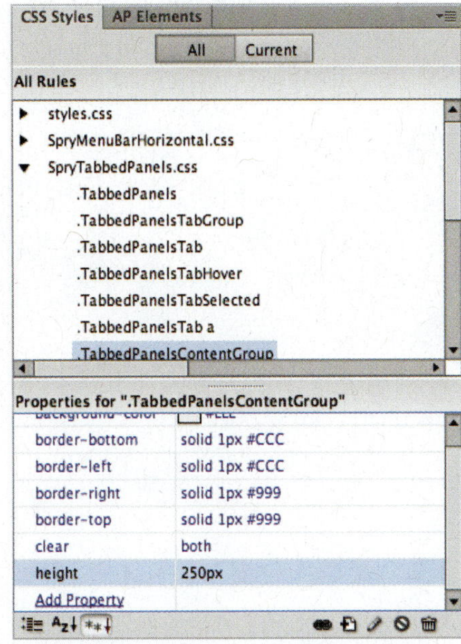

Figure 14-17: You can override the height of the panels by modifying the .TabbedPanelsContentGroup *style.*

18. Choose File > Save All. Then preview your page in the browser to see your tabs in action. The copy-dependent files dialog box will appear. Click OK to accept. There are a few other styles that you could modify here, but for now, you'll move on to the next Spry Widget: the Accordion Panel.

The Spry Accordion panel

At first glance, the **Spry Accordion panel** resembles a standard vertical menu bar. As the name suggests, however, each item contracts and expands to reveal a content panel where you can add text and images. The accordion panel allows you to have only one panel open at a time.

Accordion panels are great for navigation, tree-style navigation or lists, or organizing related content (such as a Frequently Asked Questions list) into a clean, panel-style format. As with the other Spry Widgets, the Spry Accordion uses its own style sheet, which you can easily modify to make it match your current theme.

The Spry Accordion panel

Step-by-Step

Follow these steps to add a Spry Accordion panel

1. In the right-hand column, locate the placeholder text that reads {accordion here}. Select and delete the placeholder text, and leave your cursor in place.
2. From the Insert panel, click and add a new Spry Accordion at the cursor position (Figure 14-18).

Figure 14-18*: The Spry Accordion added to the sidebar.*

The Property Inspector below now displays the properties for the new widget.

3. In the Property Inspector, you see a list of the panels currently in your accordion (Label 1 and Label 2). Click the plus sign (+) above the list twice to add two new panels for a total of four. A label displays above each new panel.
4. Click on Label 2 and then press the up arrow twice to push Label 2 back under Label 1. This step is not mandatory, but it helps to keep your label order straight.
5. On your page, highlight the Label 1 text. Delete it and type **Food Products** in its place as seen in Figure 14-19. Do ***not*** press Enter (Windows) or Return (Mac OS) after typing.

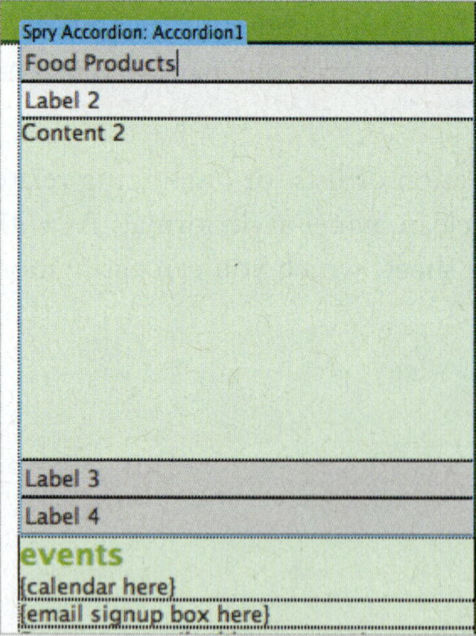

Figure 14-19*: Type directly within the accordion labels to rename them.*

6. Repeat step 5 for the labels 2, 3, and 4, renaming them **Clothing, Home Products**, and **Lifestyle**, respectively. Next, you'll add content to each panel that corresponds to its label.

7. In your Files panel, locate the text folder and expand it. Double-click and open the file named **accordiontext.html**. This contains the text you'll add to the accordion panel.

8. Select the text below the Food Products heading (don't include the heading itself), and choose Edit > Cut. Return back to your **index_work.html** page.

9. Click the blue tab labeled Spry Accordion: Accordion 1 to ensure it is selected; then, in the Properties panel, click the Food Products panel to open it (Figure 14-20).

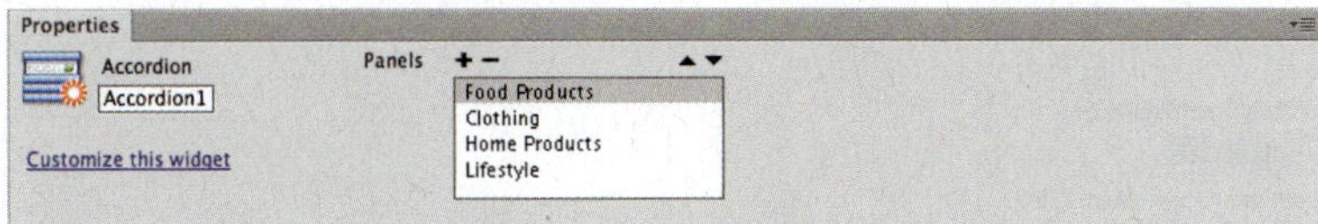

Figure 14-20: *Open the Food Products panel by clicking it in the Properties panel.*

Highlight the placeholder text on your page, and then choose Edit > Paste to paste it in the text from your content file.

10. Repeat steps 8 and 9 for the remaining paragraphs in the **accordiontext.html** file, pasting them into the Clothing, Home Products, and Lifestyle panels, respectively.

As with the other Spry Widgets, the default style will need to be changed to match the look and feel of your site.

11. Under the CSS Styles panel, locate the attached style sheet named **SpryAccordion.css**, and expand it to reveal its rules.

12. Select the `.AccordionPanelTab` rule. To the right of the background color property, click the color swatch and notice that your cursor is an eyedropper. Place the eyedropper in the green area immediately above the accordion, and click once to sample the green color from the header (Figure 14-21). This sets the background color to #88B036 (green).

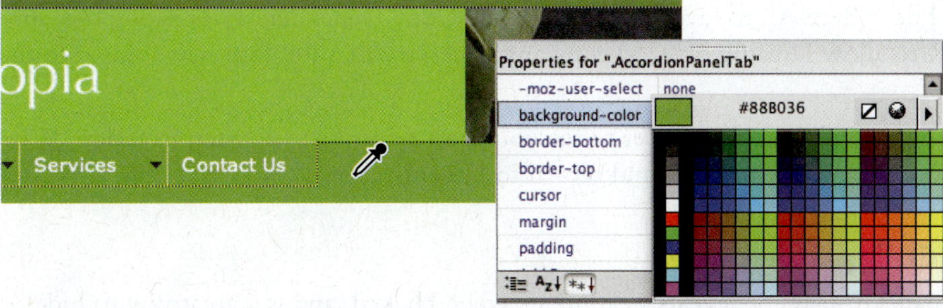

Figure 14-21: *Using the eyedropper, sample the green from the header to apply it as a background-color.*

13. Select the `.AccordionPanelOpen .AccordionPanelTab` rule. Click on the background-color value and type **#CF9**, then press Enter (Windows) or Return (Mac OS). This sets the open panel color to a light green,

14. Select the `.AccordionPanelContent` rule. Locate the height property shown in the Properties list, and change its value from 200px to **100px**. This changes the height of the content panels when shown.

There are a few more styles to change before you are done styling the accordion. One of the default styles for this widget is a Focused style which defines the appearance of the accordion when it is selected. By default, it is blue (although you cannot see this unless you preview in a browser), so you will change this now.

15. Select the `.AccordionFocused .AccordionPanelTab` style in the CSS Styles panel. Here you will match the background color you set in step 12. Click the color value for the background-color property and type **#88B036** as seen in Figure 14-22 then press Enter/Return to commit the change.

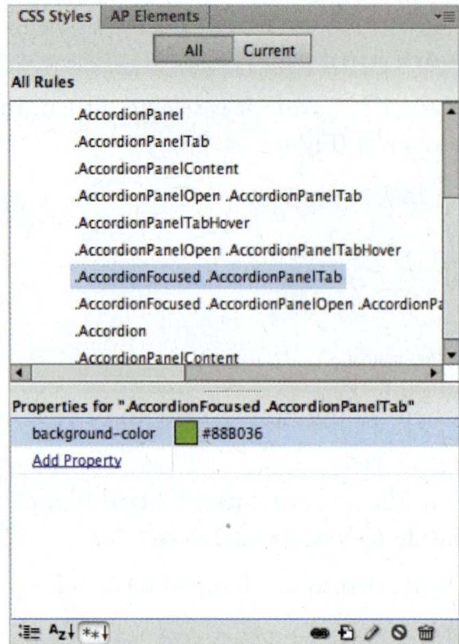

Figure 14-22: *Setting the* `.AccordionFocused .AccordionPanelTab` *style.*

16. Select the `.AccordionFocused .AccordionPanelOpen .AccordionPanelTab` style. This rule defines the appearance of any panel tab that is open. Click the color value for the background-color property and type **#CF9** to set it to the same light green used in step 12.

17. Choose File > Save All to save your page. If the Copy Dependent Files dialog box appears, press OK to allow Dreamweaver to copy any necessary files for your new widget to the site folder.

18. Choose File > Preview in Browser to see your new tabbed panel group in action. When you are done, close the browser and return to Dreamweaver.

The Spry Collapsible panel

This simple panel displays or reveals its contents when clicked, and is a great way to hide information that doesn't need to be visible at all times. You can think of the **Spry Collapsible panel** as a *piece* of the Spry Accordion that can only display a single panel and label.

You'll add a single Spry Collapsible panel to create a hidden e-mail signup form at the bottom of your page.

Step-by-Step

Follow these steps to add a Spry Collapsible panel

1. In the bottom half of the right column, locate the placeholder text that reads {Email signup box here}. Select and delete the placeholder text and leave your cursor positioned in its place.
2. On the Insert panel, locate and click the Spry Collapsible Panel button to add a button at your cursor position.

3. Select the text that reads Tab at the top of the panel, and type **Contact Us** in its place.
4. Below the panel, select the paragraph that reads Enter your e-mail address to receive specials, event notifications and more! and also select the form elements as seen in Figure 14-23.

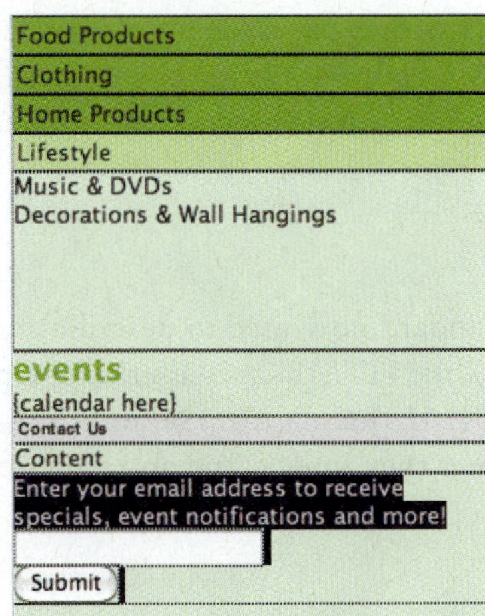

Figure 14-23: *Select all the content immediately below the Spry Collapsible panel.*

Choose Edit > Cut.

5. Select the word Content shown in the panel area of your collapsible panel, and paste the content you cut in its place. The text and form field now appear inside the panel.
6. In the CSS Styles panel, locate and expand the attached style sheet named **SpryCollapsiblePanel.css**. Select the rule named `.CollapsiblePanelTab` to display its properties.
7. Click the background-color value, and type **#88B036** to change the label's background color from gray to green.

   You can also define the default appearance of the collapsible panel; in this case, you would like it closed by default.
8. Click the blue tab above the Collapsible panel to select it. In the Property Inspector, choose Closed from the Display menu to close the panel. Choose Closed from the Default state menu as seen in Figure 14-24 so that the panel will appear closed by default until clicked.

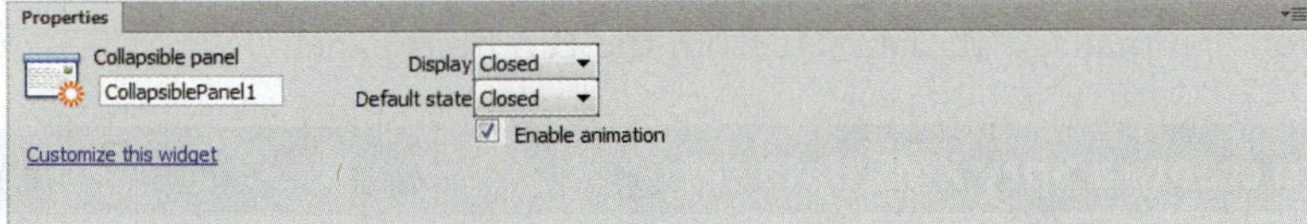

Figure 14-24: *Use the Property Inspector to set the new panel's Display State and Default appearance to Closed.*

9. Choose File > Save All to save your page. When the Copy Dependent Files dialog box appears, click OK to allow Dreamweaver to copy any necessary files to your site folder.
10. Choose File > Preview in Browser, and select a browser to test your page and see your new Collapsible panel in action. When you click the Contact Us label, the sign-up text and form appears—click it again to close it.
11. Close the browser and return to Dreamweaver.

Working with Spry Data Widgets

In addition to what you've seen so far, the Spry panel includes a whole group of powerful data widgets that can read from an external XML file. This is perfect for creating pages and page elements (such as calendars, news, and blogs) that otherwise would require manual formatting.

You can connect XML information to a pre-configured data widget from the Spry panel (such as the Spry Table), or build your own display components using common page objects such as lists, tables, and div tags. You can even use CSS to format Spry data widgets so they blend perfectly with your existing design.

What is XML?

XML stands for eXtensible Markup Language, and is the standard now used to describe and exchange data between seemingly unrelated systems. XML, like HTML, uses a series of tags—however, that's where the similarities end. Unlike HTML, XML doesn't use a series of pre-defined tags; instead, XML developers create tags using names they understand and that are relevant to the data they're trying to work with.

A typical XML document may look like the following:

```
<meeting>
    <attendee>
        <name>John Smith</name>
        <dept>Payroll</dept>
        <extension>2225</extension>
    </attendee>
</meeting>
```

Each tag is referred to as a node; the nodes and structure of an XML file are referred to as a schema.

XML can exist on a web server outside your local site, or as a local XML file. How this XML file is created, or where it comes from, is up to you, and this will be different for every project. Because XML documents are plain text, they can be created in Dreamweaver, as well as a variety of other popular text editors.

Creating a Spry XML data set

Before you can add a data widget to your page, you must first create a **Spry XML data set**. These are pointers to XML data sources (such as an XML file in your site folder) that let Dreamweaver know where the file is and what information it contains. A single page can use multiple data sets, and you can manage all data sets from the Bindings panel.

Step-by-Step | **Follow these steps to create a Spry XML data set**

1. Click the Spry Data Set button ( ) at the top of the Insert panel's Spry category. The Spry Data Set dialog box appears.
2. At the top, choose XML from the Select Data Type drop-down menu. Type **events** as the Data Set Name.
3. Click the Browse button next to the Specify Data File field. When the Select XML Source dialog box appears, navigate to the data folder in your site's root directory. Select the **events.xml** file in the folder and press OK (Windows) or Open (Mac OS).

The schema panel shown in Figure 14-25 displays the node structure of your XML document.

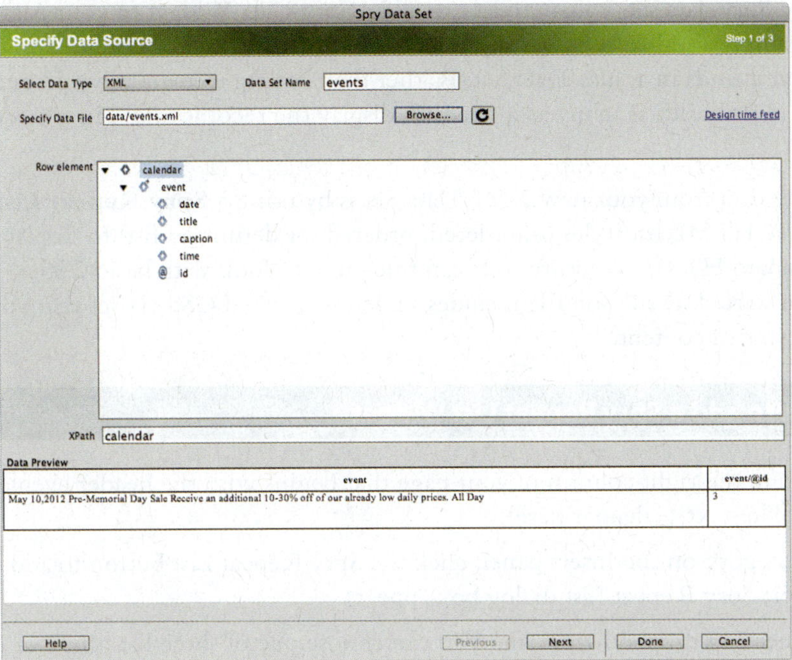

Figure 14-25: Pointing to the XML file to be used as a Data Set.

4. Click on the <event> node; the xData path at the bottom of the dialogue box should read calendar/event.

   This node is a *Row Element* which is a repeating node: this is appropriate because many events are held and they all have the same structure: Month, Date, Year.

5. Press Done to create the data set. You will now created data bindings to this data.

6. A new Bindings panel will now be visible as seen in Figure 14-26 (if not, choose Window > Bindings to display it). This is where you can view and manage your data sets and see the nodes that they contain. You may need to adjust the height of the Bindings panel or the surrounding panels to see the contents better.

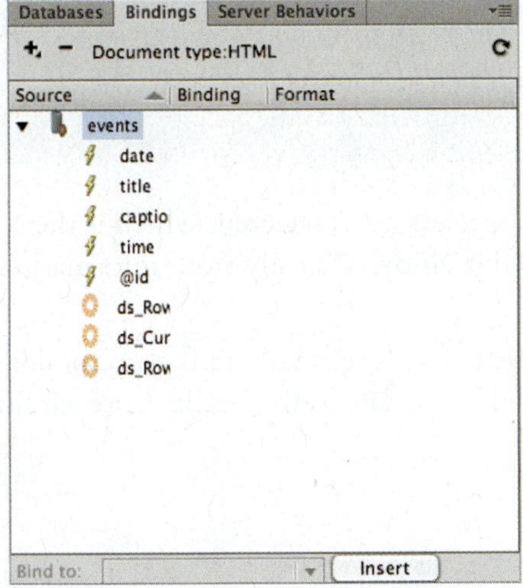

Figure 14-26: The Bindings panel displays the data set of your XML file.

7. Choose File > Save All to save your page. If you are prompted to Copy Dependent Files, press OK.

Certification Ready 5.3

What are ordered, unordered and definition lists?

Adding a Spry Data Widget: The Spry Repeat List

Once you've created a Spry data set, you are ready to add a Spry Data Widget to your page. A Spry Data Widget is simply an HTML structure (such as a list or table) that is designed to build itself from information it finds in a Spry Data Set. Rather than having to manually add bullet points or rows, the widget builds as many as it needs to display the records found in a specific data set.

An easy way to display data from your new XML Data Set is by using a **Spry Repeat List**, which uses one of three HTML list styles (unordered, ordered, or definition list) to display data. As with any standard HTML structure, you can fine-tune its look with basic CSS properties. To get you started, the lesson file includes some pre-created CSS classes that you will apply to your generated content.

Step-by-Step

Follow these steps to add a Spry Repeat List Widget

1. Locate the section in the right column of your page that begins with the header events. Select the placeholder text {calendar here}.
2. Under the Spry category on the Insert panel, click the Spry Repeat List button to add a new list. The Insert Spry Repeat List dialog box appears.
3. From the Container Tag drop-down menu, you can choose one of three list types, or even use a form SELECT menu. Select the DL (Definition List) as seen in Figure 14-27.

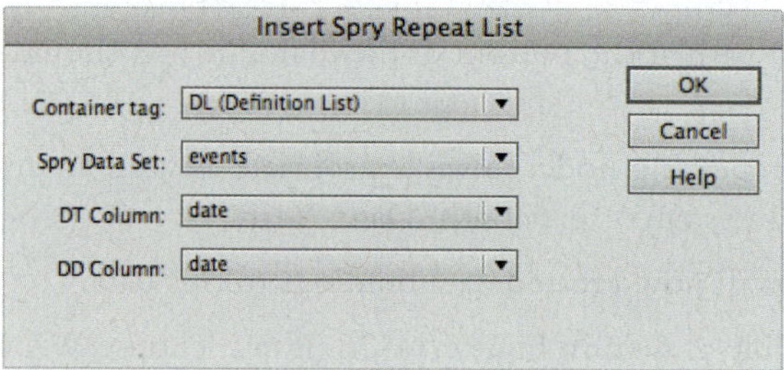

***Figure 14-27**: Choose the DL (Definition List) as your structure.*

Take Note...

A Definition List displays information in tiered Title/Definition sets. It is similar to a standard ordered or unordered list, except that each bullet contains a set of two pieces of information.

4. From the Spry Data Set drop-down menu, make sure events is selected, which is the XML data set you created earlier. The new list will build itself dynamically from information it finds in this dataset.
5. From the DT Column drop-down menu, make sure date is selected. This corresponds to the date node found in your data set, and will display the date as the header for each list item created.

6. From the DD Column drop-down menu, select title (Figure 14-28). This will display the event title below the date in each list item created.

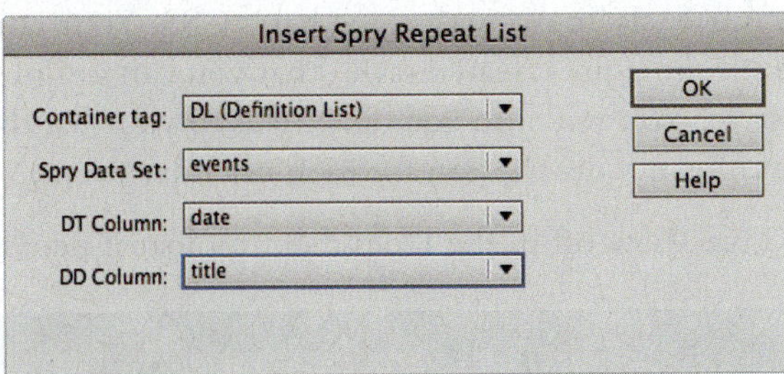

***Figure 14-28**: Choose the DL (Definition List) as your structure, and set it to display the date and title fields from your XML file.*

7. Click OK. If a dialog box appears prompting you to Add a Spry Region, make sure to press Yes. Without it, the data will not load into the widget.

Take Note...

If you forget to add a Spry Region, or need to recreate it, you can use the Spry Region button, found underneath the Spry category of the Insert panel. Just make sure that any Spry Data Widgets are placed inside the new region!

8. A new Spry Region is added to your page, as well as a new definition list. You will see placeholders for the information in your data set. Preview your page in the browser or Live View; these will be replaced with actual data from your data set as seen in Figure 14-29.

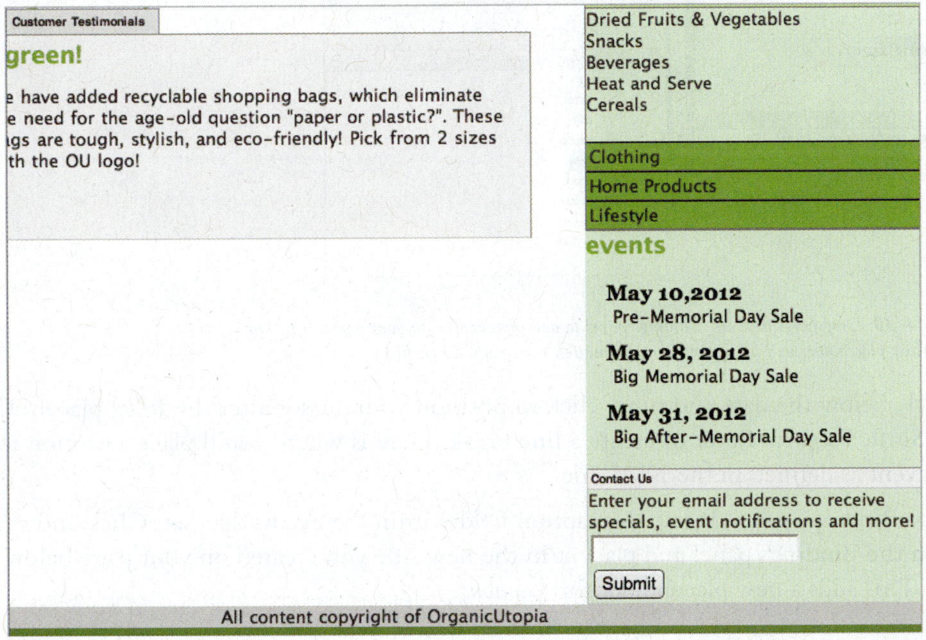

***Figure 14-29**: The Spry Region displays placeholders for your data from your events data set loads dynamically into the list when the page is previewed.*

Styling and fine-tuning data widgets

Once you've added a data widget, you can fine-tune it by adding additional data fields, rearranging the order of data fields, and of course, styling it with some basic CSS. Your current lesson file contains an attached style sheet with some pre-created styles that you can assign to your new Spry Repeat List to give it some style. You will also add data fields to your list that aren't currently being displayed, such as the time and description for each calendar event.

Before you begin, make sure that you turn Live View off in the Document toolbar if necessary.

Step-by-Step

Follow these steps to style a widget

1. Locate your new Spry Repeat List in the right-side column, and click to position your cursor directly after the *{date}* placeholder text.
2. Add a space, and type a colon (**:**). You'll follow this colon with the actual event time from your XML data set, which the list is not currently using.
3. If it is not currently visible, choose Window > Bindings to display your Bindings panel. You'll see your events data set listed, as well as the data fields below it. Locate and select the time data field in the list—this contains the time for each event.
4. Click and drag the time data field from the Bindings panel, and release it next to the *{date}:* text on the page. This adds a placeholder for the time to your repeat list. It should read *{date}:{time}* as seen in Figure 14-30.

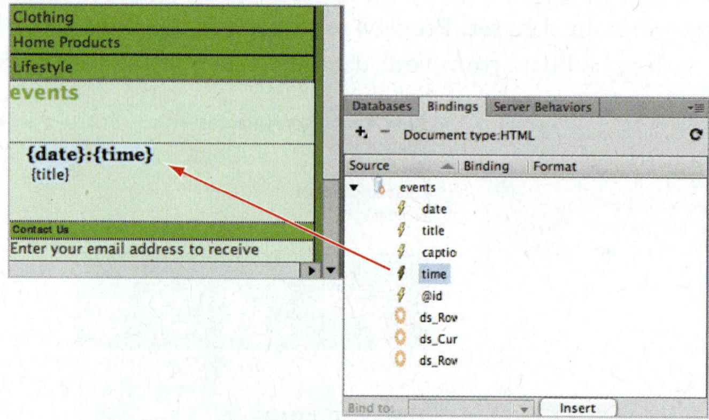

Figure 14-30: *Drag fields from the Bindings panel to add placeholders to your repeat list. The new* {time} *placeholder will fill in the time information from your XML file.*

5. Directly below the date and time, click to position your cursor after the *{title}* placeholder. Press Shift+Return/Enter to create a line break. Here is where you'll place a caption for each event as defined in the XML file.
6. On the Bindings panel, locate the caption field within the events data set. Click and drag it from the Bindings panel and place it in the new line you created on your page below the *{title}*. This adds a new placeholder for *{caption}*.

7. Now you'll use some pre-created CSS rules to dress up your list. Select the entire line in your list that reads *{date}:{time}*. On the left side of the Property Inspector, press the HTML button, if necessary, to switch to HTML view. Select .eventDate from the Class drop-down menu to apply it to the selected text (Figure 14-31).

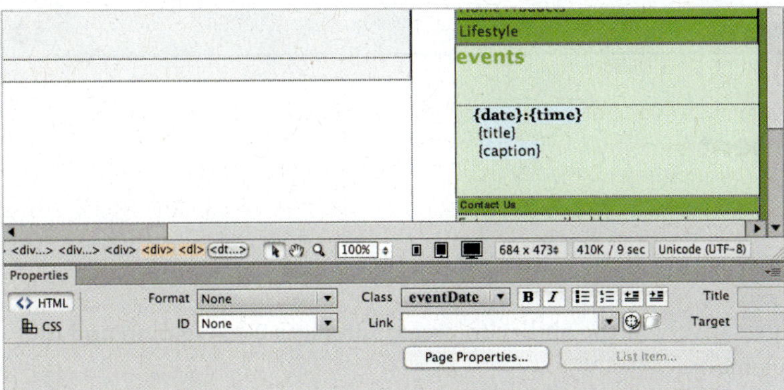

***Figure 14-31**: Select text in your repeat list and apply a class from the Property Inspector to style it.*

8. Select the text that reads *{title}*. Select `.eventTitle` from the Class drop-down menu to apply the rule to the selected text.

9. Highlight the text in your list that reads *{caption}*. Select `.eventCaption` from the Class drop-down menu to apply the rule to the selected text.

10. Choose File > Save to save your page. Click the Live View button on the Document toolbar to preview your list with the newly added data and CSS rules (Figure 14-32).

***Figure 14-32**: The finished and styled Spry Repeat List, shown in Live View.*

11. Click Live View again to turn it off.

    From this point, you can simply update the attached XML files without the need to modify the data widgets in any way. Because each Spry Data Widget populates dynamically, new data will flow into the widget each time the page is loaded.

12. Choose File > Close. You are done with this lesson!

Skill Summary

In this lesson you learned how to:	Objective
Insert navigation bars, rollover images, and buttons created in a drawing program on a web page	4.9
Modify text and text properties	5.3

Knowledge Assessment

True/False

Circle T if the statement is true or F if the statement is false.

T F **1.** Spry Widgets give you the ability to create interactive navigation and user interface elements.

T F **2.** Spry objects can be restyled using CSS code.

T F **3.** The Properties panel can be used to enter menu and submenu item information.

T F **4.** You have to manually attach CSS style sheets to Spry Widgets whenever a new widget is created.

T F **5.** You can only attach 1 CSS stylesheet to a Spry object.

T F **6.** Tabbed panels can contain almost any type of content including text, images, video, and Flash movies.

T F **7.** When placing multiple tabbed panels, you cannot determine which tab and panel is loaded first.

T F **8.** The Properties panel can be used to determine if a Collapsible panel is open or closed by its default state on the page.

T F **9.** A Spry Data Widget is designed to build itself from information it finds in a Spry Data Set.

T F **10.** Definition lists are very different from standard ordered and unordered lists.

Multiple Choice

Select the best response for the following statements

1. AJAX is a combination of which types of code?

a. JavaScript, XML, and DHTML
b. Java, XAML, and HTML
c. Actionscript, Java, and XML
d. Actionsctipt, JavaScript, and XAML

2. Spry Widgets offer which of the following options:
   a. Drop-down menus
   b. Expanding panels
   c. Tabbed containers
   d. All of the above

3. Which of the following panels allows you to format the appearance of a Spry Widget?
   a. AP Elements
   b. CSS Styles
   c. Insert panel
   d. Behaviors

4. XML tags are often referred to as:
   a. Nodes
   b. Code blocks
   c. Elements
   d. Snippets

5. Which panel can be used to view and manage your data sets and see the nodes that they contain:
   a. Server Behaviors
   b. Databases
   c. Bindings
   d. Assets

6. Which list structure is used by a Spry Repeat List?
   a. Ordered list
   b. Unordered list
   c. Definition list
   d. All of the above

7. Which of the following fields from the Bindings panel are available to add as placeholders to a repeat list?
   a. Date
   b. Time
   c. Caption
   d. All of the above

8. A Spry Data Widget is based on which code structure?
   a. XAML
   b. HTML
   c. CGI
   d. Perl

9. What should be turned off before you add Spry objects to your webpage?
   a. CSS styles
   b. Live View
   c. Templates
   d. Ruler guides

10. Once you've added a data widget, you can fine tune it by:
   a. Adding additional data fields
   b. Rearranging the order of data fields
   c. Styling with CSS
   d. All of the above

Competency Assessment

Project 14-1 Vertical Menus

As you've seen, Spry objects add some really engaging interactive elements to your pages while still serving practical functionality. Continue to practice adding and modifying Spry objects by creating a vertical menu.

1. Choose File > New > Blank Page > HTML > None to create a new empty webpage.
2. Save the page as **sprymenu.html**.
3. Go to the Insert panel and select the Spry category.
4. Click the Spry Menu Bar button to add a new menu.
5. Choose Vertical from the layout choices and click OK.
6. Open the CSS styles panel and start to modify the visual properties of the menu.
7. Save your work and preview the menu in a browser.

Project 14-2 Spry Form Objects

Beyond the menus and panels you've been working with, Spry objects extend into forms as well. Take a look and do some homework on your own to find out more.

1. Create a new webpage.
2. Go to the Insert panel and select the Spry category.
3. Start taking a look at the Spry form tools such as the Spry Validation Text area. Use the Help section to do research on the extended functionality of these objects.

Proficiency Assessment

Creating Your Own CSS Presets

Project 14-3

CSS is the main component that changes the look of your Spry Widgets. But since you're using CSS, you can save it and apply it to future Spry Widgets you may add later.

Launch Dreamweaver CS6 if you haven't already.

1. Create a new blank HTML page.
2. Add a Spry Widget such as a Spry Menu.
3. Modify it with CSS to your liking.
4. Save the style sheet as an external style sheet to apply to Spry menus you work with later.

Examining XML

Project 14-4

Understanding code elements is good when bringing in outside code documents. You don't have to be a coder to recognize how some of the objects are making the connections once you've had a chance to look at both the code and how the interface puts all the pieces together.

1. Go to the location on your computer where you've stored the lesson files for this book, find the dw14lessons folder.
2. Go inside the folder and open up the **events.xml** in a simple text editing program or Dreamweaver to take a look at the code.

Circling Back 3

You saw how dynamic Spry objects can be in terms of making your webpages more interesting to explore. Getting more familiar with the Spry objects that you have at your disposal could help you generate ideas for how to approach design. You'll practice adding various Spry components, and then modifying them using CSS.

Menu Bar

Project 1

Menus are a key component for navigation and design. You want the design to be interesting enough to compel someone to click it, but you also want to make sure users know where they're going. Creating a menu that's eye catching is part of what you'll be doing in the following exercise, but pay attention to how you're naming your topics and sub-topics. Remember, you're not designing this for site you, you're designing it for anyone who might visit your site, so be sure to name topics / sub-topics in such a way that users will know the section of the website they will end up on when exploring your menu.

1. Open Dreamweaver and establish a new site and root folder called **Spry**.
2. Create a new webpage and save it as **menu.html**.
3. Open the Insert panel and choose the Spry category.
4. Click to add a Spry Menu Bar. Choose Horizontal for the layout.

5. Instead of Item 1 to Item 4, rename the buttons to the following:

   Home

   About Us

   Services

   FAQ

6. Now modify and add sub-items you think are appropriate. For example:

   About Us

   > Contact Information

   > Company History

   > Staff

7. Choose Window > CSS Styles.
8. Open the properties for **SpryMenuBarHorizontal.css** and start to modify the visual properties of your new menu.
9. Repeat the process, but try it with a vertically-oriented menu instead.

Project 2 Tabbed Panels

Tabbed panels are a great way to visually organize your page. Placing content within a tab emphasizes the fact that it is conceptually different than other content on your site. HTML does not allow you to add panels, but you can add them with the help of the Spry Framework.

1. Continue to work in your Spry site and add a new page called **panels.html**.
2. Open the Insert panel and choose the Spry category.
3. Click to add a Spry Tabbed Panel.
4. Change the name of the tabs to represent a topic and sub-topic, for example, About Us and Contact Information.
5. Style the panels visually using the CSS Styles panel under the **SpryTabbedPanels.css** settings. Try different settings and explore design options.
6. Add some text content to each of the panels and test it in a browser.

Project 3 Accordion Panels

Screen space is always at a premium on the Web, especially with sites that feature large navigation structures. Accordion panels are one strategy at your disposal for maximizing screen space.

1. Continue to work in your Spry site and add a new page called **accordion.html**.
2. Open the Insert panel and choose the Spry category.
3. Click to add a Spry Accordion.
4. Change the name of the tabs to represent a topic and sub-topic, such as About Us and Contact Information.
5. Style the panels visually using the CSS Styles panel under the **SpryAccordion.css** settings. Try different settings and explore design options.
6. Add some text content to each of the panels, test in a browser, and compare the flow to your **panels.html** page.

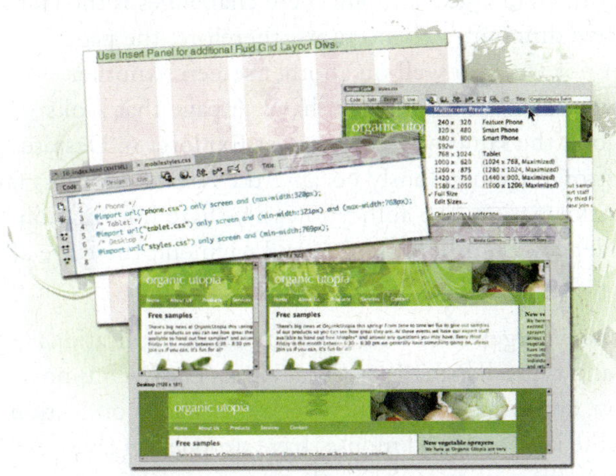

Mobile Design and Layout

Key Terms

- CSS3 Media Queries
- Fluid Grid Layout
- Mobile First
- Mobile Optimization
- Mobile Web
- Multiscreen Preview
- PhoneGap
- Tablet Layout

Skill	Objective
Produce website designs that work equally well on various operating systems, browser versions/configurations, and devices	2.2
Conduct technical tests	6.1

Business Case

One of the hot things right now is development toward mobile devices and tablets. Your client is aware of this and wants to use that technology for the Organic Utopia site. The trick is that the site will need to translate between three different modes of output, including home computers and laptops, tablets, and smart phones. Fortunately, Dreamweaver uses a fluid grid as the answer to multi-output considerations.

Introduction

Before starting, make sure that your tools and panels are consistent by resetting your workspace. See "Resetting the Dreamweaver workspace" in the Starting Up section of this book.

You will work with several files from the dw15lessons folder in this lesson. Make sure that you have loaded the dwlessons folder onto your hard-drive. See "Loading lesson files" in the Starting Up section of this book.

Before you begin, you need to create site settings that point to the dw15lessons folder. Go to Site > New Site, or for details on creating a site, refer to Lesson 2, "Setting Up a New Site."

Certification Ready 2.2

What are the different devices for viewing web content?

The rise of the mobile web

Creating websites has always presented certain challenges. Among these challenges is the fact that the people who visit your site might have different-size monitors; therefore, the page layout that works well on one screen might not work so well on another screen. Another challenge is the different versions of web browsers that users might have. A page that looks one way in Internet Explorer 9 might not look the same way on Internet Explorer 6. Despite these challenges, the Web has thrived and grown tremendously because the benefits it offers far outweigh the downsides. Instant access to information, the ability to easily share information through hyperlinks and e-mail, the convenience of online shopping and payment: these are all major benefits.

The **mobile web** is a broad definition for the emergence of websites and mobile applications that are designed to be viewed on portable and typically small screen devices. The Web is now portable. It is no longer tethered to a desktop, and is accessible wherever a user has a connection. In many cases, external peripherals, such as the keyboard and mouse, have dropped in favor of touchscreens' miniature keyboards. Built-in features such as GPS and cameras can also come into play, allowing the user to interact with the Web in new and different ways.

However, with all these benefits come new challenges. Portable screens also mean smaller screens. Consequently, your great desktop design suffers as it scales. Navigation that works well on the desktop may become difficult to click at ¼ the size. Other challenges include the still-limited bandwidth that currently exists when using a cellular network, the inability to play certain media such as Flash or web video, and web browser incompatibility, which is an issue that has not been quite resolved.

Dreamweaver tools for mobile layout

Dreamweaver CS6 has a few different tools for designers and developers who want to optimize their content for mobile devices. Before proceeding, you should learn about the different categories of the mobile web, which are explained next.

- **Native Applications**

  Smartphones, such as those on iOS, Android, and Windows Mobile platforms, have achieved a tremendous amount of growth and popularity since 2007 and the introduction of Apple's iPhone. Native applications, or "apps," live on a user's device. Apps are tightly integrated with the Web and display content from the Web, but they are not exclusively dependent on the Web. Dreamweaver CS6 is capable of creating native applications for iOS, Android, Blackberry, webOS, and symbian; however, it does so with the help of the Phonegap framework. With **PhoneGap** and Dreamweaver CS6, you start with an HTML and JavaScript document and are able to then build multiple apps for the different platforms. We do not cover PhoneGap functionality in this lesson or in this book.

For more information go to *phonegap.com*. You can also launch the PhoneGap service (Figure 15-1) in Dreamweaver CS6 by choosing Site > PhoneGap Build Service.

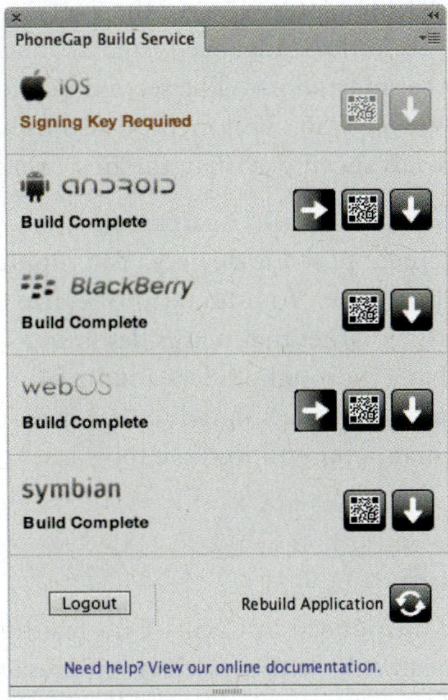

***Figure 15-1**: The PhoneGap service integrated with Dreamweaver CS6 allows you to build native applications for mobile devices.*

- **Websites**

  All websites that can be accessed on a desktop browser can also be accessed on a mobile browser; therefore, every web page is part of the mobile web. However, as you will soon see, when a mobile web browser visits a website, the appearance of that site might be different from the desktop version. There are a few different explanations for this:

  - The appearance of a web page on a mobile device might be different than the desktop version due to the scaling effect that the device's web browser applies. Apple's popular mobile Safari browser, for example, scales a web page to fit the screen and also allows for touch gestures such as pinch, zoom, or swiping in order to navigate through a page. Websites that were never intended for mobile viewing will still have these features because they are built-in to the browser itself.
  - The appearance of a web page on a mobile device might be different than the desktop version because the designer or developer has created a separate version designed for mobile. All web browsers, whether they are mobile or desktop, advertise themselves with something called a *user agent*. The creator of a website can let in all desktop user agents to their "standard site" and redirect all mobile users to a separate "mobile site."

Mobile website features in Dreamweaver

This lesson focuses on two methods for creating websites optimized for mobile. The first method focuses on using the Multiscreen feature and CSS3 Media Queries. In the exercise for this method, you will take the existing layout created in Lesson 6, "Advanced Page Layout," and create a layout optimized for a mobile device, such as a smartphone. The second method focuses on the new Fluid Grid Layout feature in Dreamweaver CS6. This method also uses CSS3 Media Queries, but in a slightly different and more advanced way than the first exercise.

Dreamweaver does its best to simplify the process used to create **mobile optimized** sites. These are websites designed to function well on smaller screen, portable devices. You should note that this is the most advanced and difficult lesson in this book. You should also realize that at the time of this writing, there is no application on the market that makes designing a website for multiple screens "easy." We firmly believe that a thorough understanding of the fundamentals of HTML, particularly CSS, is important when working with your sites. Therefore, once you have learned some of these fundamentals, you will find the tools in Dreamweaver to be extremely helpful and efficient.

Viewing your web page with the Multiscreen feature

Dreamweaver CS6 has improved the Multiscreen feature introduced in CS5.5. This feature helps you preview your pages in different screen sizes. Specifically, this **multiscreen** preview shows you your design in three different views by default: one for the desktop, and the other two for the smaller screens found in smartphone and tablet devices. Given that mobile device screens come in different sizes, you can also customize these views to any resolution you want. Additionally, Dreamweaver takes advantage of CSS3 Media Queries to let you build individual style sheets customized for each view. If you have not worked with Media Queries before, this exercise is designed to introduce you to the concept and also to help you learn how to use them in Dreamweaver.

Step-by-Step

Follow these steps to view a web page with the Multiscreen feature

Certification Ready 6.1

How do you preview a website for multiscreen designs?

1. In the Files panel, double-click the media_queries folder and then double-click **15_index.html** to open it. The basic design here is based on the one you created in Lesson 6 and uses floats and clears to create columns.
2. Choose File > Preview in Browser and select a browser. This page has a fixed-width size of 960 pixels and works well on most desktop monitor resolutions.

   To preview this page as it would appear on a mobile device such as a Smartphone or tablet device, you can use Dreamweaver CS6's Multiscreen option.

3. Return to Dreamweaver and click the Multiscreen icon immediately to the right of the Live button. A menu appears showing you the various sizes you can choose from as seen in Figure 15-2. Select Multiscreen Preview.

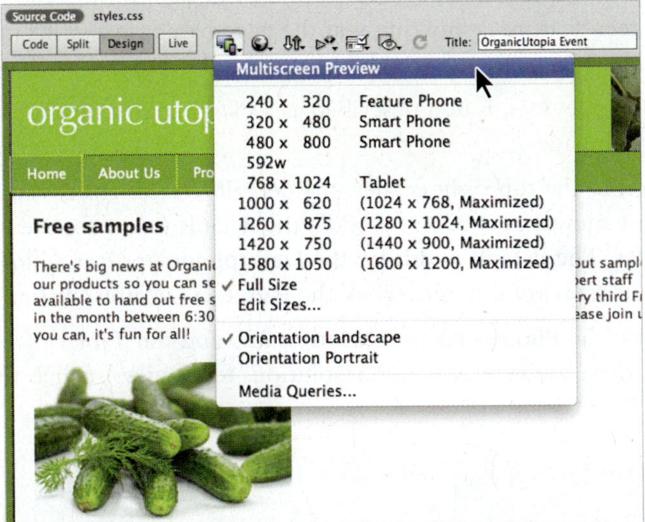

Figure 15-2: You can find Dreamweaver's Multiscreen Preview button next to the Live view button.

The Multiscreen Preview window appears (Figure 15-3). This window is divided into three different screen resolutions: Phone (320 × 300), Tablet (768 × 300), and Desktop (1126 × 181). Note that the height of the Desktop view may be different on your screen. This window adapts to the amount of space on your screen, which is dependent on your monitor resolution. In fact, if your monitor resolution is lower than 1280 pixels wide, you will have a difficult time working with Multiscreen Preview in general.

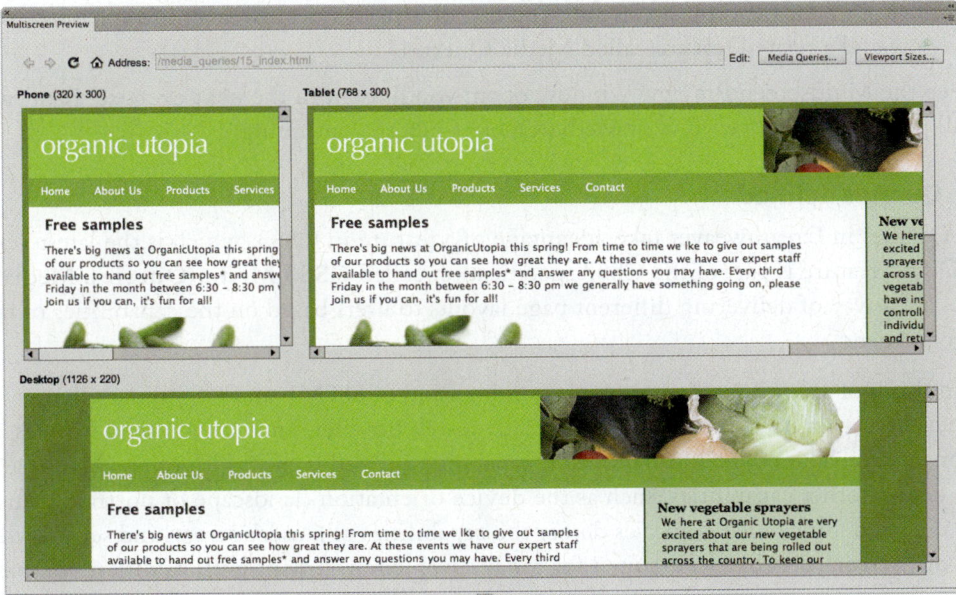

Figure 15-3: Dreamweaver's Multiscreen Preview shows three views by default: Phone, Tablet, and Desktop.

As you can see from the preview, the Phone view and the Tablet view are not wide enough to fit your fixed-width page. You should note that Multiscreen is not an emulator. (An emulator is software that attempts to imitate a hardware phone or other computer device.) Most modern smartphones would actually scale your entire page to fit in the browser window. The Multiscreen feature is showing you the page based on a strict interpretation of the *viewport*.

A viewport, as it relates to mobile devices, is best described as a viewing area on the screen through which a user views a web page.

4. Click the Viewport Sizes button in the top right corner; the default Viewport sizes appear. The default values for the Phone viewport is *320w by 300h*; the default values for the Tablet viewport is *768w by 300h*. The default width for the Desktop viewport is *1126w*, but no height is defined. (If your sizes are different, click the Reset to Defaults button.)

   These numbers are not arbitrary; the Phone viewport width is 320 and the Tablet viewport width is 768 because these are typical screen resolutions for devices such as the iPhone, iPad, and others.

Take Note...
Screen resolutions actually do vary among devices, but Dreamweaver has chosen these as standards.

5. Click Cancel. You can modify the viewport sizes to fit your needs; however, we recommend you use the default sizes until you become more familiar with the reasons for modifying the sizes.

   These viewport sizes are important because you can create unique style sheets that will only apply to viewports of a certain size. For example, for the smallest viewport you might want a layout that is only a single column, instead of the current three-column layout designed used for the desktop layout. You can do this in Dreamweaver using MultiScreen Preview and a related feature called Media Queries.

6. Keep the Multiscreen Preview window open; you'll use it in the next exercise. First, we will present a brief overview of Media Queries before continuing.

Certification Ready 2.2

What are CSS3 media queries?

Media Queries defined

Media Queries in Dreamweaver take advantage of a feature in CSS3, which is the latest version of CSS. This feature is part of the CSS3 specification called **CSS3 Media Queries**. Media Queries are a way of delivering different page layouts to users based on the capabilities of their screen or screens.

You can think of a CSS3 media query as a combination of HTML and CSS syntax that examines the capability of a user agent, typically a web browser, and lets you send it styles based on certain values. The most common capability queried is the width of a screen or a mobile device; other capabilities, such as the device orientation (landscape or portrait), can also be detected. Since media queries detect the capabilities of a user's screen and serve styles that fit that screen, they are well-suited for today's web environment with its different monitor resolutions. Figure 15-4 shows a simplified version of how media queries work: each device gets a specific style sheet based on the size of its screen.

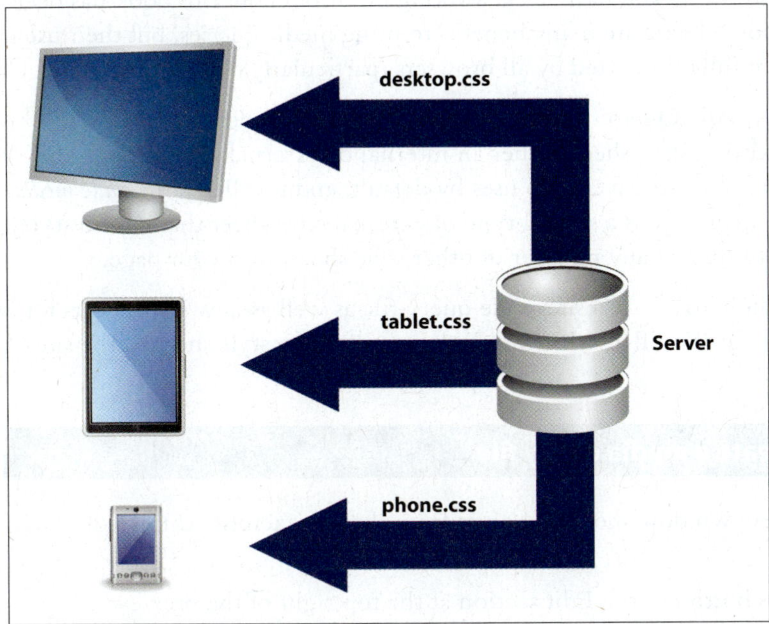

Figure 15-4: Unique style sheets are delivered to users depending on their screen capabilities.

Here is a different example: suppose a user has a smartphone with a screen resolution of 320 pixels wide by 480 pixels high, and the phone is in portrait mode (vertical). This user visits a website that uses media queries. When the user visits the site, the media queries built into the page detect the capabilities of the phone and serve it a specific style sheet with a single column layout. When the user rotates the phone into landscape position, the change is detected and the media queries send a style sheet designed for a 480 pixel-wide screen (the layout might have two columns instead of one).

From the perspective of users, they are simply getting the ideal layout for the screen size they are using. Users might notice this change in layout momentarily as they rotate their screen or visit the site on different devices, but the overall goal is to improve their experience on the site by improving aspects such as readability, navigation, and presentation of content.

Take Note...

For more details on the technical aspects of CSS Media Queries, visit http://www.w3.org/TR/css3-mediaqueries/.

Creating a site-wide media query file

As noted earlier, Media Queries are a relatively new advance in web design and are part of the CSS3 specification. (Most of the CSS you have been working on throughout this book has been part of the CSS2.0 specification.) There are many benefits to using media queries, but their use is a tradeoff because they are not fully supported by all browsers (particularly older browsers).

There are a few ways to add Media Queries to a page. The first method adds the Media Queries code within your existing style sheet (either an internal or external style sheet). The second method is the one that Dreamweaver CS6 uses by default, and is called a *site-wide media query* file. A site-wide media query file is a special type of external style sheet that has no style rules; instead, its only job is to import any number of other style sheets into your page.

In this exercise, you'll learn how to create a site-wide query file as well as new style sheets for a Phone layout and a Tablet layout. You'll also learn to link your existing style sheet to the site-wide media query file.

Step-by-Step

Follow these steps to create a media query file

1. Your Multiscreen Preview window should be open from the last exercise. If it is not, click the Multiscreen button.
2. Click the Media Queries button in the Edit section at the top right of the preview window. The Media Queries window appears (Figure 15-5).

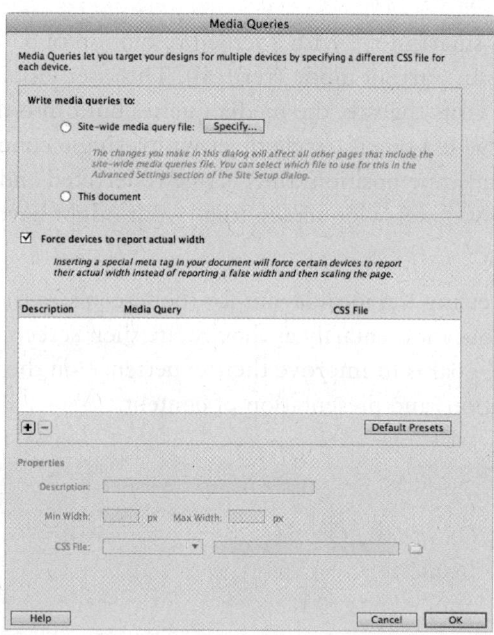

Figure 15-5: The Media Queries window in Dreamweaver CS6.

The site-wide media queries file you are about to create will function as a hub to import style sheets with rules designed for Phone and Tablet screens.

3. In the Write Media Queries to section, click the option button for Site-wide media query file, and then click the Specify button. In the window that appears, click the CSS File menu and choose Create new file. Type **mobilestyles** in the CSS File field as seen in Figure 15-6 and click OK.

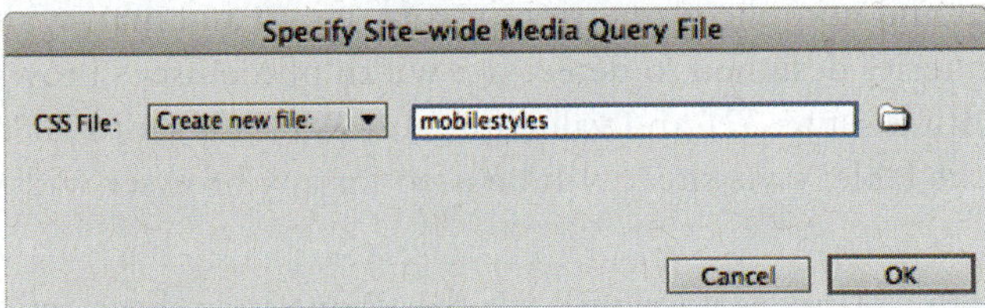

Figure 15-6*: Specify a new site-wide media query file.*

As noted earlier, this site-wide media query file has a very specific job: it imports external style sheets that contain styles for your different screen sizes. It's currently empty and so you will now create those style sheets.

Take Note...

After you have defined a site-wide media query file, the information is stored within your site definitions. To access it, choose Site > Manage Site. Choose your current site and click Edit. Click the Advanced Settings; the path to your site-wide media query file appears.

4. Make sure the "Force devices to report actual width" check box is selected. This option overrides a smartphone's default behavior of scaling a web page to fit the screen.

Take Note...

Selecting this option places the following line of HTML in the head section of your page: `<meta name="viewport" content="width=device-width" />`.

5. In the Media Queries window, click the Default Presets button; three media query presets appear in the middle window (Figure 15-7).

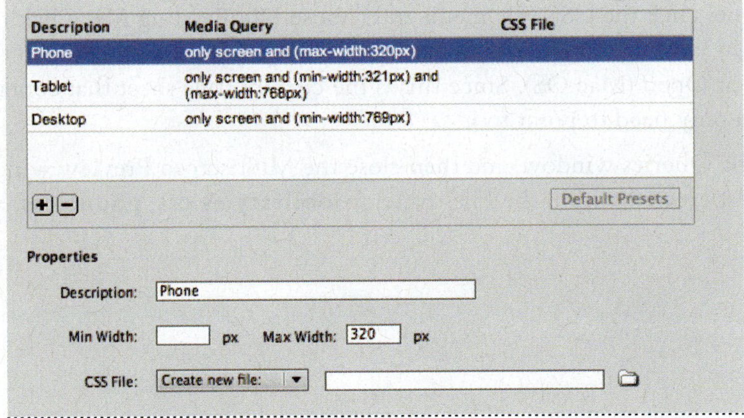

Figure 15-7*: The three default presets for Media Queries.*

The first preset is called Phone, and you can use it for screens up to 320 pixels wide. This preset is selected automatically; you can see the properties of this media query in the Properties section at the bottom. The important value here is max-width, which is set to 320px.

6. Locate the CSS File section and make sure Create new file is selected. Click the Folder icon on the far right and the Save File As window appears. Navigate to the media_queries subfolder in your dw15lessons folder, type **phone** in the File name field, and then click Save.

7. Click the second preset for Tablet and note the properties for min-width and max-width. These properties are the media queries designed to detect the width of the user's browser viewport; the value for Min Width is set to 321 and value for Max Width is set to 768. In practical terms, this means that the tablet style sheet will be used for any browser width between those two values.

   Furthermore, any browser *less* than 321 pixels wide will use the Phone style sheet defined in the last step.

8. Click the Folder icon on the far right side of the CSS File section (seen in Figure 15-8); the Save File As window appears. Navigate to the media_queries subfolder in your dw15lessons folder, type **tablet** in the File name field , and then click Save.

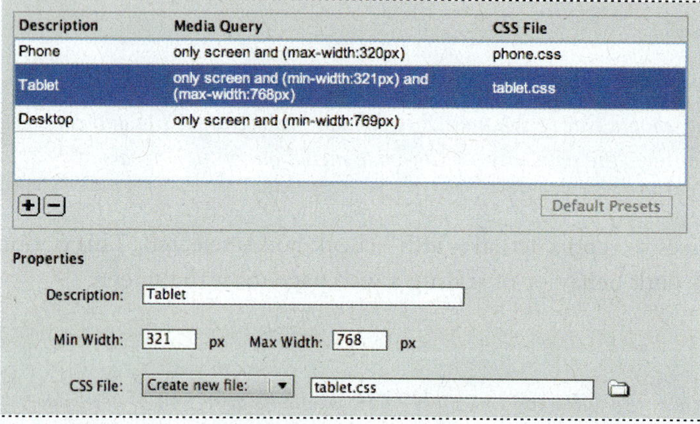

Figure 15-8: *Setting the media queries and style sheet for tablet devices.*

The last media query you need to add is for Desktop screens; in this case, any viewport wider than 768 pixels.

9. Click the Desktop preset. This preset has a min-width set to 769; there is no need to add a max-width. This time, click the CSS File menu and choose Use Existing file. Click the Folder icon, and within your media_queries folder, click the styles.css document, and then click OK (Windows) or Open (Mac OS). Since this is the current style sheet that contains your page's styles, you only need to point to it.

10. Click OK in the Media Queries window, and then close the Multiscreen Preview window. Locate the files you just created within the Files panel (**mobilestyles.css**, **phone.css**, and **tablet.css**).

11. In the Files panel, double-click the **mobilestyles.css** file to open it. This is the site-wide media query file you created in Steps 3 and 4. Note that it uses the `@import` syntax to link to the other three external style sheets (Figure 15-9). Keep this file open; you will modify it in the next exercise.

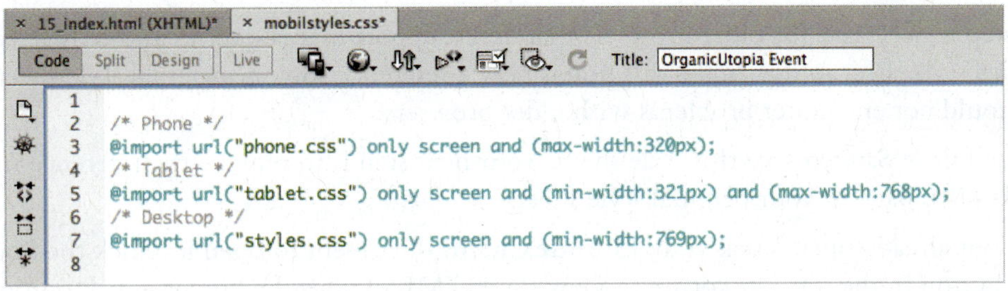

```
1
2  /* Phone */
3  @import url("phone.css") only screen and (max-width:320px);
4  /* Tablet */
5  @import url("tablet.css") only screen and (min-width:321px) and (max-width:768px);
6  /* Desktop */
7  @import url("styles.css") only screen and (min-width:769px);
8
```

Figure 15-9*: The site-wide media query file mobilestyles.css with the added media query files.*

The preceding steps might seem long, but you only need to do them the first time you set up media queries. Once you have them set up, you have a framework for creating unique styles for screens of different sizes.

Organizing your style sheets

Dreamweaver CS6's media queries feature simplifies complicated tasks when creating site-wide media queries, but it's not perfect. To ensure your style sheets are most effective, you need to manually fine-tune them. In this exercise, you will organize the style sheets you created in the last exercise.

Follow these steps to organize your style sheets — **Step-by-Step**

1. Your **mobilestyles.css** file should still be open from the last exercise. If not, open it by double-clicking the file in the Files panel.
2. Select the following code, and then choose Edit > Cut, Ctrl+X (Windows), or Cmd+X (MacOS).

```
/* Desktop */
@import url("styles.css") only screen and (min-width:769px);
```

3. Place your cursor on the first line, and then choose Edit > Paste, Ctrl+V (Windows), or Cmd+V (Mac OS) to paste the code at the top of your document as seen in Figure 15-10. This step is necessary to ensure that the desktop style sheet is used first, followed by the styles for the phone and tablet style sheets.

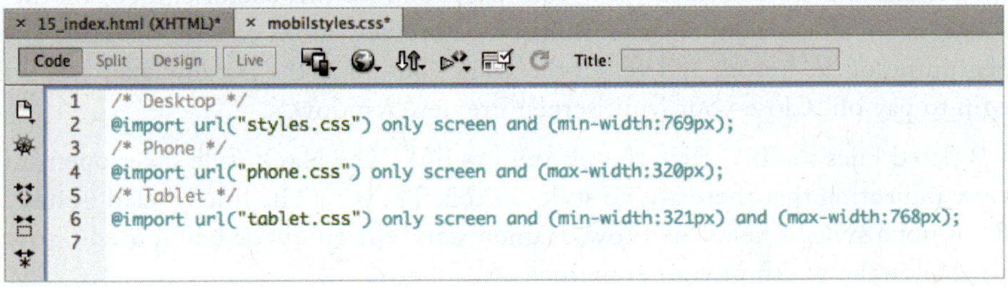

```
1  /* Desktop */
2  @import url("styles.css") only screen and (min-width:769px);
3  /* Phone */
4  @import url("phone.css") only screen and (max-width:320px);
5  /* Tablet */
6  @import url("tablet.css") only screen and (min-width:321px) and (max-width:768px);
7
```

Figure 15-10*: Your Desktop preset links to your original external style sheet.*

4. Next, select the following code (highlighted in red) and delete it. Do **not** delete the semicolon at the end of the line, or your styles will no longer work.

```
/* Desktop */
@import url("styles.css") only screen and (min-width:769px);
```

This step is necessary for older browsers that don't support media queries and only need a standard style sheet to use. Since this line is now a reference to your original style sheet, you should not encounter problems with older browsers.

5. Choose File > Save to save this style sheet. Your next step is to remove the reference in your HTML page to your original style sheet.

6. If it is not already open, click your **15_index.html** document to open it. Click the Source Code button in the top-left corner to view the HTML of your document. Click on the Code button to enter the Code view.

7. In the Code view, locate the following line in your head section (it should be on line 7):

```
<link href="styles.css" rel="stylesheet" type="text/css" />
```

Select this entire line and then press Delete to remove it.

This code is the original link to your style sheet, but you don't need it because you added a reference to this file in your mobilestyles.css document.

8. Choose File > Save All.

Creating a layout optimized for mobile

Now that you have prepared your site with a site-wide media query file and the associated style sheets, you can begin using them. The general principle of CSS3 Media Queries is that you use the exact same names for the style rules in your phone and tablet style sheets as the style rules in your desktop style sheet. By using the same names, you override the desktop style wherever needed. For example, you will first apply this rule with the ID style called `#container`. In your desktop style sheet, this ID style defines the width of the entire page as 960 pixels. In your phone style sheet, you will create another rule with the name `#container`, but you will set the width to 100% for this style.

In the following exercise, you will only work with the phone style sheet; use the tablet style sheet for practice.

Step-by-Step

Follow these steps to work with a phone style sheet

1. Click the Multiscreen button to preview your page, and for this exercise, focus on the Phone view. From all appearances, the multiscreen preview looks exactly the same as it did at the beginning of the lesson, and yet all the work you did in the last few exercises will now begin to pay off. Close your Multiscreen Preview window.

2. In your Related Files toolbar, click the **phone.css** link. The blank style sheet opens in the Code view indicating that there are no styles in this file, yet. (The line labeled `@charset "utf-8";` is not a style, it helps the browser understand the language being used.) Your first task is to change the width of your container.

3. In the CSS Styles panel, click the New CSS Rule button, and then in the Selector Type menu, choose ID. Click the Selector Name menu and choose container from the list (Figure 15-11).

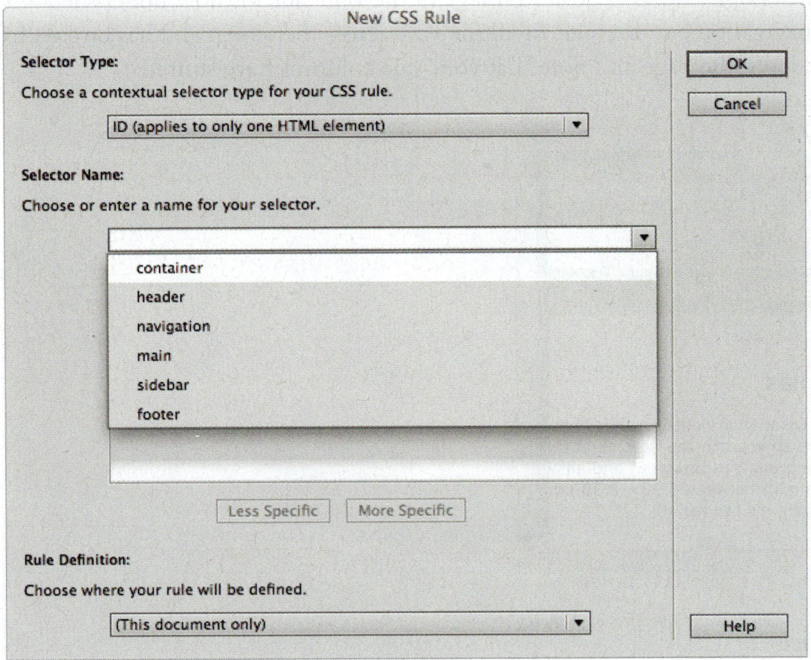

***Figure 15-11**: Creating a new rule for the container ID in your phone.css style sheet.*

4. Click OK. In the CSS rule definition window, click the Box category and type **100** in the width box. Click the menu to the right and change the value from px to %. Click OK.

   To see the effect this has on your phone style sheet, you will need to preview your page in the Multiscreen Preview.

5. Since you cannot open the Multiscreen Preview when you have a style sheet selected, click the Source Code button in your Related Files toolbar to switch to your HTML page. Now click the MultiScreen button to view your page.

6. When the Multiscreen Preview page opens, you will see your page has dramatically changed in the Phone viewport (Figure 15-12) . By setting the width of the container to 100%, it will only be as wide as the viewport and most of the content within will have shifted or is overlapping. For example, the background image of the vegetables is now under the logo. Also notice the navigation bar does not fit all the way across the screen and has broken to the next line. Scroll down the page and note that your side columns have shifted.

***Figure 15-12**: The Phone view shows the effect of changing the container width to 100%.*

As you can see, creating a page optimized for mobile is not as simple as setting the container width to 100%. The page has changed, and you will need to modify it. The layout elements inside the container need to be addressed as well, since most of them have height or width values set as pixels. Also, some of the elements are floating. To fix the rest of the page, you will add rules that remove floats and override any explicit pixel width or height value. The goal is to create a single column layout.

Learning More

Tips and strategies for optimizing pages for mobile

The following is a list of tips and strategies to consider when designing pages for mobile. Navigating and using websites on smaller screens or screens that are touch-enabled is very different from the desktop, and you should take it into consideration.

- Navigation should be at or near the top of the screen to be easily accessible. Repeat navigation at the bottom of all your pages so the user does not have to scroll up after reading a page.
- For touchscreen devices, use a large target size for navigation links to prevent accidental clicking.
- Touchscreen devices do not always have a hover capability as triggered by the mouse cursor on desktops. Plan your styles accordingly and avoid rollover styles.
- Avoid image-based navigation; use list-based navigation styled with CSS.
- Single-column layout is much easier to navigate and read on a smaller screen. A general strategy for accomplishing this with media queries is by removing floated elements and most layout containers with fixed width and height pixel values.

7. Close your Multiscreen Preview; you'll now add more styles to your phone.css style sheet and create a single-column layout.

Take Note...

Since the Multiscreen Preview is large, it can become cumbersome to constantly open it and close it. If you have dual monitors, you can drag this window to a second monitor. Alternatively, you can collapse the Multiscreen Preview window by clicking the double arrows in the top-right corner. Click the arrows again to expand it.

8. Click the **phone.css** button in the Related Files toolbar. You'll now add styles for the header section.
9. In the CSS Styles panel, click the New CSS Rule button, and then in the Selector Type menu, choose ID. In the Selector name box, click the Selector Name menu and choose header.
10. Click OK. In the CSS rule definition window, click on the Background category. Click the Background-image menu, and then choose none as seen in Figure 15-13. Click OK. We will remove the image of the vegetables, which works well in the desktop version, but not in the phone version.

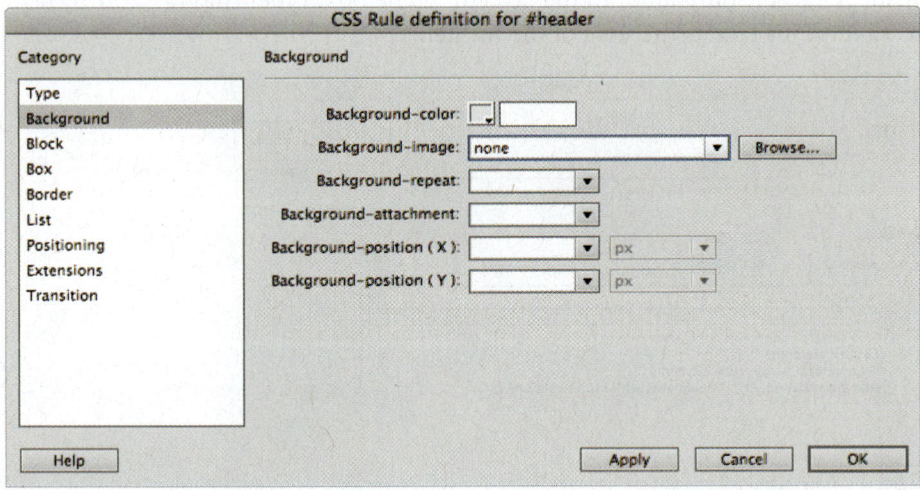

Figure 15-13*: Setting the background-image to none removes the image of the vegetables from the header.*

11. Choose File > Save all. Choose Source Code and then click the Multiscreen button to see your progress. The background image no longer appears in the header for the Phone viewport. Close your Multiscreen Preview window.

Your next step is to address the styles of the navigation bar. Typically, CSS navigation bars have a few different rules that you need to modify.

Creating styles for navigation and a single-column layout

Creating easy-to-use mobile navigation is very important because you want users to read your content and not be frustrated by content that's difficult to access. The *hit target* for mobile navigation should be large enough for touchscreens, and easy to read. You'll add these styles now.

Step-by-Step **Follow these steps to create styles for easy-to-use mobile navigation**

1. Click the **phone.css** button in the Related Files toolbar. In the CSS Styles panel, click the New CSS Rule button, and then in the Selector Type menu, choose ID. In the Selector name box, type **#navigation** and click OK.

   In the CSS rule definition window, click the Font-size menu and choose the keyword medium to override the 36 pixel value set in the original style sheet. This action prevents issues when there are differences between device screen resolutions.

2. Click the Positioning category, click the Height menu, and choose auto to override the fixed height of 36 pixels from the original style sheet. Click OK to create these styles.

   You will need to do more work to make the navigation look better. There are often different rules for CSS navigation menus, so you also need to modify these.

3. In the CSS Styles panel, click the New CSS Rule button, and then in the Selector Type menu, choose Compound. In the Selector name box, type **#navigation ul li** (Figure 15-14).This targets the style of the list items.

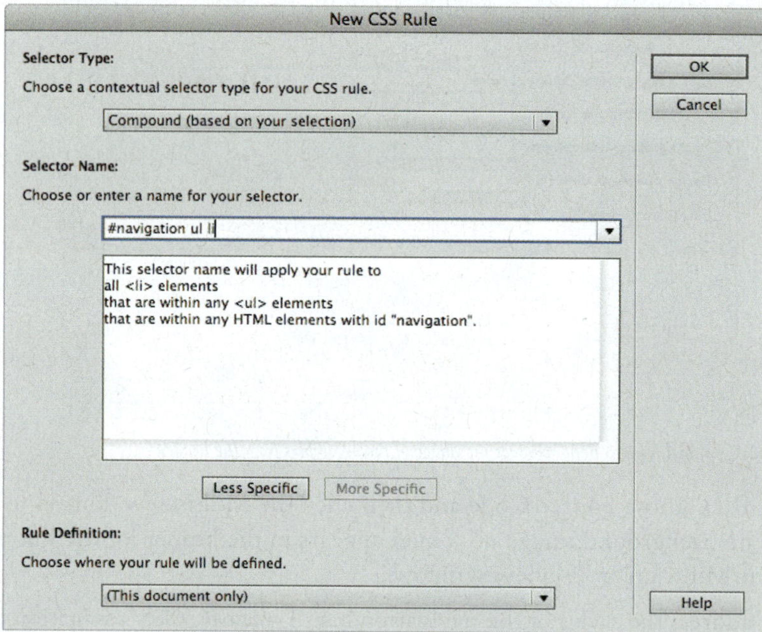

***Figure 15-14**: Create a compound selector to make a style for the navigation list items.*

   Click OK. In the CSS rule definition window, click the Box category, click the Float menu, and choose none. This overrides the float:left rule set in your original style sheet. Click OK.

4. Click the Source Code button to switch to your HTML page, and then click the Multiscreen button. Notice that by setting the float property of the list items to none, the list reverts to its default positioning, which is vertical (Figure 15-15).

Figure 15-15: Changing the float value of list items to "none" creates a vertical navigation instead of a horizontal one.

Your page is starting to improve: the navigation is now a single column. Place your cursor over the links and notice that the original hover styles are still present. One of the benefits of CSS3 Media Queries is that the original styles that have no overrides are still used.

Scroll down and notice that you still need to improve other areas: the main content and the sidebar still appear broken, but this is relatively easy to fix.

5. Close the Multiscreen Preview window, and then click the **phone.css** button in the Related Files toolbar.

6. In the CSS Styles panel, click the New CSS Rule button, and then in the Selector Type menu, choose ID. Click the Selector name menu and choose the main ID.

   Click OK. In the CSS rule definition window, click the Box category, click the Float menu, and choose none. This overrides the `float:left` property and value set in your original style sheet.

7. Click the Width property menu and choose auto as seen in Figure 15-16.

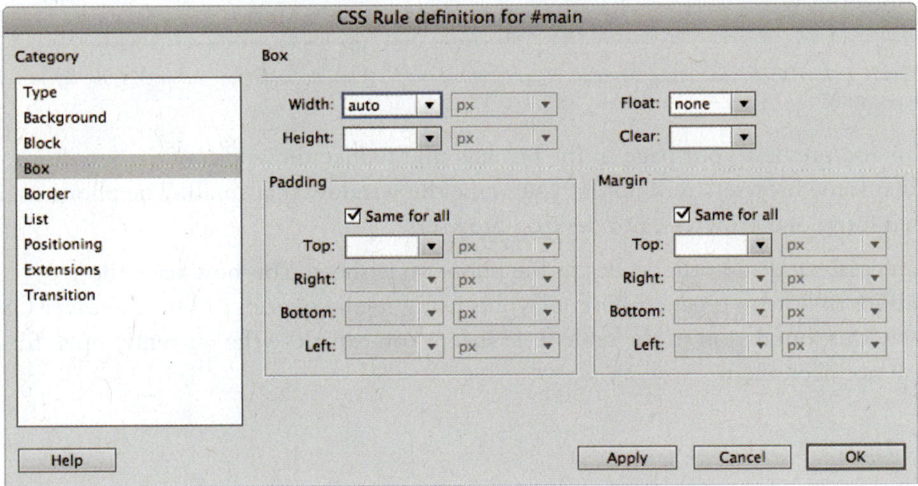

Figure 15-16: Set the float value of the main column to none and the width to auto.

8. Click OK and repeat Steps 6 and 7, but use the Selector name sidebar instead of main.

9. Choose File > Save All Related Files, click the Source Code button, and click the Multiscreen button. Scroll down your page and notice that your content section and sidebar now fill the screen from edge to edge. Also, notice that by removing the floats, your sidebar is now located below the main content.

10. Close the Multiscreen Preview menu window. You can also test your page in Dreamweaver's Live view. First, click the Design button to switch to this view. Then click the Live view button. Live view uses the WebKit rendering engine, which is the same as Apple Safari and Google Chrome browser.

11. Click the Window Size menu located on the bottom right of your document window, and from the list that appears, choose 320 × 480 Smart Phone as seen in Figure 15-17; your window will automatically adjust to this size and your media query file will be applied. This will also work in the Design view; however, you should place your cursor over the navigation. Note that in Live view the rollovers are active.

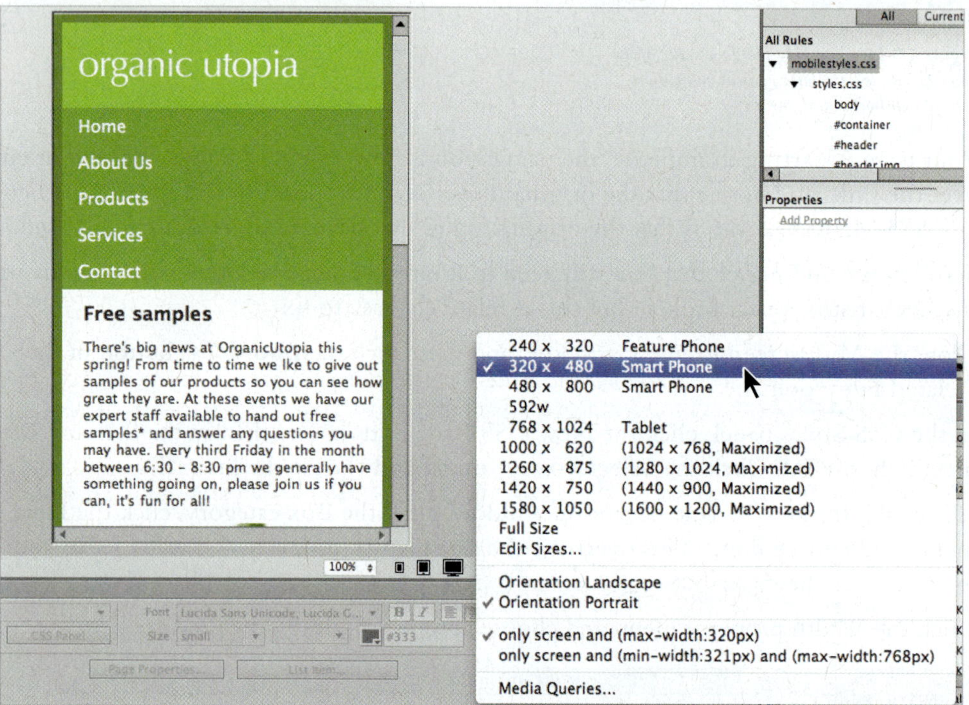

Figure 15-17: *In Live View, you can see the values of your window width. When the width is less than 321, the layout switches to the phones.css styles.*

You can also preview your page in the browser and reduce the width of the window. Note that some browsers will not let you make the window that small. The phone.css is designed for phone browsers, not desktop browsers.

You can create and add other styles to the phone style sheet. You now have the foundations of how to create different layouts using media queries in Dreamweaver CS6, and apply this foundation to the table style sheet. You can close the currently open files; you will not need them.

The basics of Fluid Grid Layout

Dreamweaver's **Fluid Grid Layout** expands on the concept of media queries. To understand fluid grids, think about page layout. Remember that the layout you began working with at the beginning of this lesson was a "fixed-width" layout set to a width of 960 pixels wide. Fixed-width layouts are very common on the Web because they are reliable to work with and control. However, one of the downsides of fixed-width layouts is that they do not respond well to different size screens. Many designers feel that fixed-width layouts do not reflect the nature of the Web and that "flexible" or "fluid" layouts are better suited for content. Flexible layouts generally use percentages or em units to define the various sections on the page. For example, the width of a sidebar might be defined as 33% of the page rather than 450 pixels.

Take Note...

If you would like to see the results of this exercise before you begin, navigate to the done folder within the fluidgrid folder, open the index.html file within a browser that supports media queries and resize the browser window.

Follow these steps to create a Fluid Grid layout

Step-by-Step

1. Chose File > New Fluid Grid; the New Document window appears with the Fluid Grid Layout settings on the screen (Figure 15-18).

   The first major change that you will see is that Fluid Grids actually create three layouts at a time: Mobile, Tablet, and Desktop. Each of these layouts is defined as media queries; in this way, the settings are very similar to the ones you saw in the last exercise. However, notice that fluid grids use media queries, *and* they add grid structure to help you align content on the page.

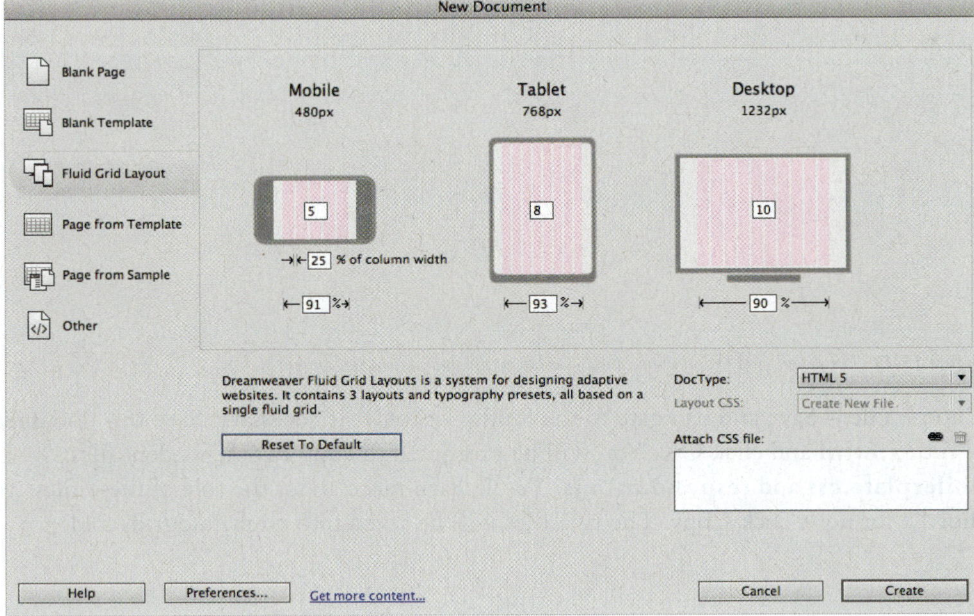

Figure 15-18*: The Fluid Grid Layout has layout settings for mobile, tablet, and desktop.*

Each of the three layouts has a number of columns that will be created by default. The Mobile layout has five columns, the **Tablet layout** has eight columns, and the Desktop layout has ten columns. You can type any number of columns you want for each type of layout, but for now, you will use the defaults. Notice that the mobile layout has a unique setting, "25% of column width." This represents the space between each of the columns, otherwise known as the *gutter width*. Additionally, each of the three layouts has a default page width listed at the bottom. For mobile, this is 91%; for tablet, this is 93%; and for the desktop, this is 90%. This means all the layouts will have a small amount of padding on the left and right sides.

Take Note...

If you do not see these values, click the Reset to Default button.

2. Click Create; you will be prompted to generate a new external style sheet. Navigate to your dw15lessons folder, locate the fluidgrid folder, save this style sheet as **base.css**, and then click OK. A new document opens; you are in the unique fluid grid mode with a five-column layout and a default grid layout div element with placeholder text (Figure 15-19). You'll learn more about both of these features shortly. For now, we'll discuss the structure of this page and the related files created for Fluid Grid Layouts.

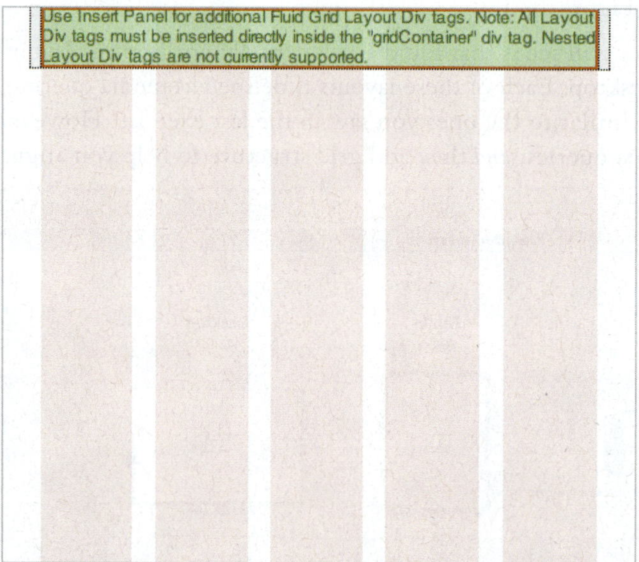

***Figure 15-19**: The default grid layout with a fluid grid layout div and placeholder content.*

3. Choose File > Save and navigate to the fluidgrids folder if necessary. Save this document as **index.html** and click OK. You will be prompted to copy two dependent files: **boilerplate.css** and **respond.min.js**. You'll learn more about the role of these files shortly; for now, click Copy. The two files will be saved into your fluidgrids folder.

Working with Fluid Grids is different from what you might be used to. This initial view of five columns is the Mobile view for your web page. There are two other views as well: Tablet and Desktop. These views can be accessed by clicking any of the three icons (Figure 15-20).

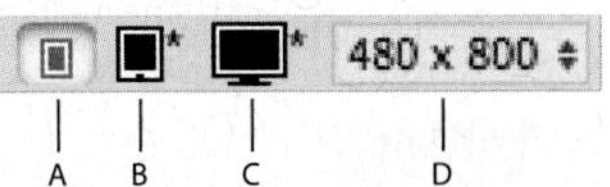

Figure 15-20: ***A.*** *Mobile size (480 × 800).*
B. *Tablet size (768 × 1024).*
C. *Desktop size (1000w).* ***D.*** *Window Size.*

4. Click the Tablet Size icon; the size of the window changes to 768 by 1024 and displays 8 columns.

5. Click the Desktop Size icon; the size of the window changes to 1000 wide; the height is set to the vertical space on your screen.

Regardless of the view you are in, you should note that the columns are visual aids only and are designed to help you align the Fluid Grid Layout Divs.

6. Choose View > Visual Aids and select the Fluid Grid Layout Guides option to turn off the guides. The reason for turning off the guides is to see your page design better; however, these guides are key to working with the Fluid Grid feature, so choose View > Visual Aids and select Fluid Grid Layout Divs to turn them back on.

7. Click the Mobile Size icon to return to the default five-column view. Dreamweaver opens this view initially because one of the foundations of Fluid Grid Layout is a concept called "mobile first." The basic idea is that when designing a website from scratch, you start with the mobile design and layout first, and then move upward to the larger tablet and desktop sizes.

The foundations of "mobile first" design

Learning More

Mobile first is a concept in web design that has been gaining popularity among designers in recent years. The basic idea is that when you are creating a new website design, you begin working with the mobile design first, and then move on to your larger screen designs. The rationale is that technique forces you to identify your most important or "core" features first, thus ensuring that they are folded into the mobile experience for your users.

The traditional technique of starting with your complex desktop layout and removing or restyling parts until you arrive at your mobile layout can lead to design compromises and inefficient styles. By incorporating mobile first concepts into Fluid Grid Layouts, Dreamweaver is helping to promote the adoption and importance of designing for different size screens.

Creating your mobile layout

In the first half of this lesson, you covered the basics of using site-wide media query files. Note that you are still using media queries with Fluid Grid Layouts. However in this case, rather than dividing your media queries into separate style sheets, the rules for your three layouts are gathered in one style sheet (in this case, base.css). Specifically, as you begin to create the styles for the single column layout in this exercise, keep in mind that all these styles will automatically be applied to your larger tablet and desktop layouts.

Step-by-Step

Follow these steps to create a mobile layout

1. Click in the default div that was created by Dreamweaver. In the Properties panel, locate the Div ID field, select the default value, and type **header**. (Figure 15-21)

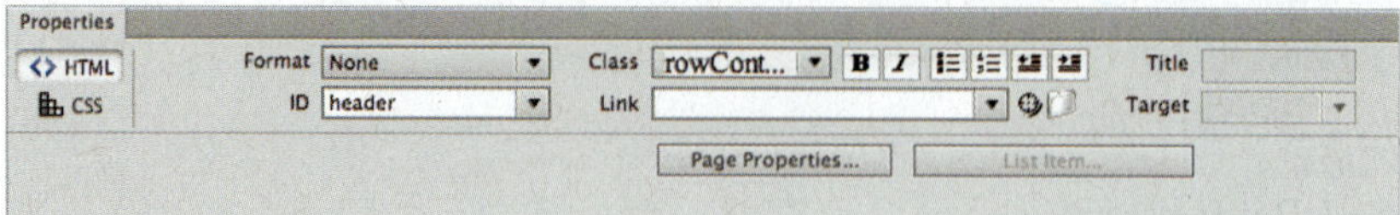

***Figure 15-21**: Change the name of the default fluid grid layout div to "header."*

2. Select the placeholder text inside the header and delete it. Choose Insert > Image. Navigate to the images folder inside the fluidgrid folder and locate the **ou_logo.png** file. Click Open (Mac OS) or OK (Windows). Type **logo** in the Alternate Text field, and then click OK.

   You just added the image to a "Fluid Grid Layout Div Tag." Dreamweaver always adds a Fluid Grid Layout Div Tag to your page when you start a new Fluid Grid Layout. You can add new ones to your page as needed.

3. Click the edge of the header div if necessary to make sure it is selected. Then, in the Insert panel, click the Insert Fluid Grid Layout Div Tag object; a dialog box appears. Make sure that the Start new row check box is selected, type **introcontent**, and then click OK.

   A new fluid grid layout div appears below the header. Select the placeholder text and then press delete to remove it.

4. In your files panel, double-click the **intro_content.html** document. Select everything on the page by pressing Cmd+A (Mac OS) or Ctrl+A (Windows) and then copy it. Toggle back to your index page, click inside the introcontent div, and press Cmd+V (Mac OS) or Ctrl+V (Windows) to paste it (Figure 15-22).

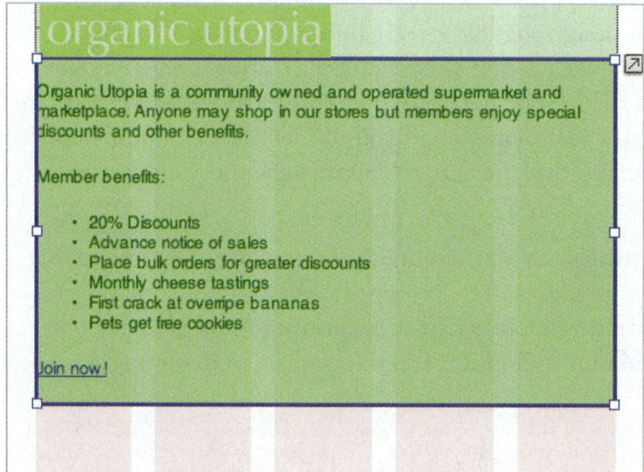

***Figure 15-22**: The introcontent fluid grid div with content.*

5. Click the edge of your introcontent div to select it. Then, in the Insert panel, click the Insert Fluid Grid Layout Div Tag object; a dialog box appears. Type **secondarycontent** and click OK.

   A new fluid grid layout div appears below the header. Select the placeholder text that appears and delete it.

6. In your files panel, double-click the **secondary_content.html** document. Select everything on the page by pressing Cmd+A (Mac OS) or Ctrl+A (Windows) and then copy it. Toggle back to your index page, click inside the secondarycontent div, and press Cmd+V (Mac OS) or Ctrl+V (Windows) to paste it.

7. Click the edge of your secondarycontent div to select it. Then, in the Insert panel, click the Insert Fluid Grid Layout Div Tag object; a dialog box appears. Type **events** and click OK.

8. In your files panel, double-click the **events.html** document. Select everything on the page by pressing Cmd+A (Mac OS) or Ctrl+A (Windows) and then copy it. Toggle back to your index page, click inside the events div, and press Cmd+V (Mac OS) or Ctrl+V (Windows) to paste it (Figure 15-23).

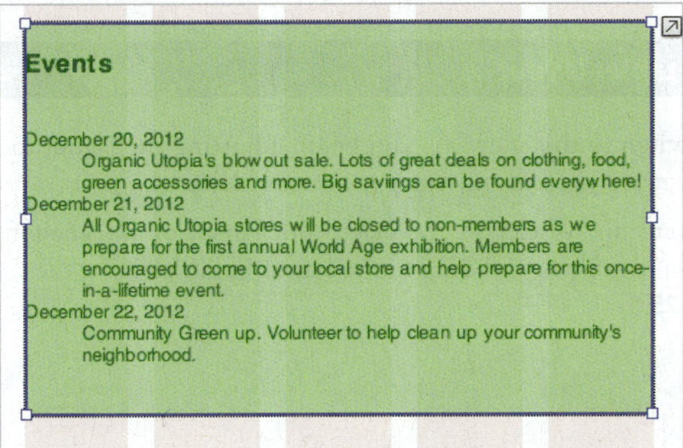

***Figure 15-23**: The events fluid grid layout div is located below* `secondarycontent`.

9. Click the edge of your events div to select it. Then, in the Insert panel, click the Insert Fluid Grid Layout Div Tag object; a dialog box appears. Type **footer** and click OK. You'll leave the placeholder content in here for now.

10. Within the secondarycontent div, click below the heading "Celebrate Vegetables." Choose Insert > Image. Navigate to your images folder, select **beets_fluid.jpg**, and click Open (Mac OS) or OK (Windows). Type **beets** in the Alternate Text field and click OK. The image is inserted below the heading as seen in Figure 15-24.

***Figure 15-24**: An image added below your heading.*

11. Choose File > Save All.

    This is the foundation of a mobile layout. There is much more you could do in regards to styling, but now that you have a basic layout with content, you'll take a look at the way Fluid Grid Layouts work with additional layouts.

Creating a tablet layout

You have seen the three views that are part of Fluid Grid layouts, and you just created a simple single-column layout for a mobile device. Note that Dreamweaver created styles for the mobile view, the tablet view, and the desktop view. In fact, it has placed these styles in three separate media queries (one for mobile, one for tablet, one for desktop). You'll now modify your mobile layout so that it is better suited for a tablet device.

Step-by-Step **Follow these steps to create a tablet layout**

1. Click the Tablet Size icon to switch to this view. As you begin adjusting the layout to two columns, keep in mind that *the new styles will only apply to the tablet layout.*
2. Click the edge of the introcontent div to select it and place your cursor on the anchor point located on the right of the div. Click and drag to the left to begin resizing the container as seen in Figure 15-25.

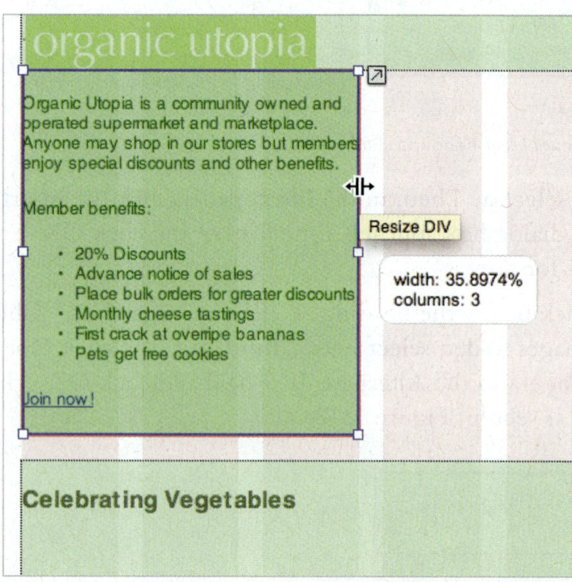

Figure 15-25: *Resize a fluid grid div by clicking and dragging the right edge.*

   Note as you drag that the indicator shows you the width and how many columns you have. Drag until you reach three columns and approximately 35% width.

3. Click the edge of the secondarycontent div to select it and notice on the top-right corner there is an arrow. Hover over this for a moment, and the tool tip indicates the arrow will move the edge up a row. Click the arrow; notice that the edge doesn't shift position. This is because you need to resize the div in order to fit in the space above.
4. Place your cursor on the resize anchor point (on the right edge of the div) and drag to the left. When the div width reaches five columns, it will jump up into the space above. Keep resizing the div until it is four columns wide.

5. Now place your cursor on the anchor point on the left edge of this div and wait for the tooltip. This indicates that it will shift the div. Click and drag to the right until the right edge of the div snaps to the furthest column as seen in Figure 15-26.

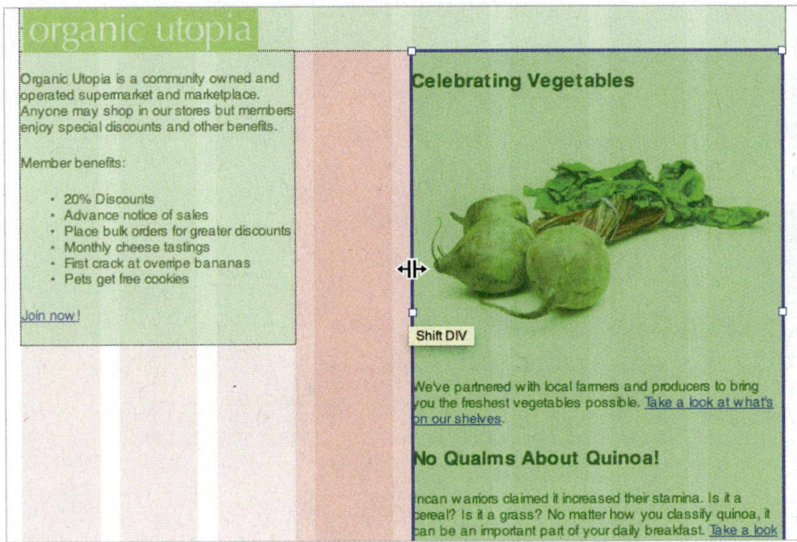

Figure 15-26*: Resize a fluid grid div by clicking and dragging the right edge.*

At this point, you have the basics of a two-column layout, but for the tablet view only.

6. Click the Mobile Size icon to switch back to this view; note that the mobile layout has remained in its single-column view. Click the Tablet Size icon to see the two-column view you just created, and then click the Desktop view. This view is still using the single-column layout; it has not been affected by the changes made in the Tablet view.

7. Choose File > Save All to save your work, but keep this document open. In the next exercise, you will build a three-column layout for the desktop.

Creating a three-column fluid layout for the desktop

In keeping with the mobile first philosophy, the desktop is the last design you will work on.

Follow these steps to create a three-column fluid layout

Step-by-Step

1. Click the Desktop view icon if you are not currently in this view.

2. Click the edge of the introcontent div to select it, and place your cursor on the anchor point located on the right of the div. Click and drag to the left to begin resizing the container. Resize this div until you reach three columns.

3. Click the edge of the secondarycontent div to select it and click the arrow on the top right. This will attempt to move the div up a row, but because it is too wide, you have to resize it in order to fit in the space above.

4. Place your cursor on the anchor point located on the right of the div and drag it to the left. When the div is narrow enough, it will jump up into the space above. Continue resizing the div until it snaps to four columns (Figure 15-27), which is a width of approximately 38.7%.

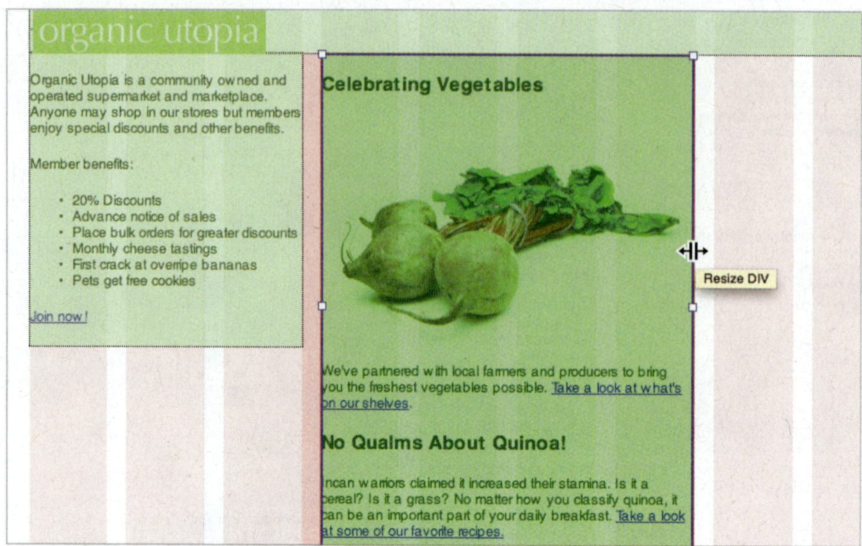

Figure 15-27: *Resize a fluid grid div by clicking and dragging the right edge.*

5. Click the edge of the events div to select it, and click the arrow at the top right to move it up a row. As with the other divs, you need to resize it in order to fit into the available space.

6. Place your cursor on the anchor point located on the right side of the div and drag to the left. When the div is narrow enough, it will jump up into the space above. Continue resizing the div until it snaps to three columns, which is a width of approximately 28.5%.

7. Choose File > Save All. At this point you have the foundations of a fluid and adaptive layout.

8. Click the Live button to see your layout in the Live View (Figure 15-28). When using Fluid Grid Layouts, the Live View behaves a bit differently. Typically, the Live View acts as a web browser and only allows you to view your content, not edit it. However, you can see that the Visual Aids are still visible. Additionally, if you click the edge of any of your divs, it will become active and you can then adjust their size or shift them as needed.

Figure 15-28*: In the Live view, the Fluid Grid layout is still visible and the layout divs can be adjusted as well.*

If you need to see your layout in action, the browser is still the best place.

9. Choose File > Preview in Browser; your page will load in the three column layout view (most likely). Slowly reduce the width of your web browser and note how the columns of text begin to resize. This is the "fluid" part of fluid layouts: because your columns are defined by percentages, not pixels, this is the expected behavior. At the same time, the amount of space between these columns also remains proportional.

10. Keep reducing the width of the browser; it will eventually switch to the two-column layout. Continue reducing the width of the browser until it switches to the single-column Mobile layout.

11. Continue resizing your browser window back and forth between the three views, and pay particular attention to the image in the middle column (Figure 15-29). This image is also fluid; in other words, it will resize according to how much space it has available. This is most obvious in the single-column mobile view.

Figure 15-29: *The images added to your layout will be fluid or responsive by default.*

This fluid image behavior is actually made possible by the inclusion of the boilerplate.css support file that all Fluid Grid Layouts include by default. (You saw these dependent files created in step 1 of the first exercise.)

12. Close your browser and return to Dreamweaver. You will now take a look at how to style your pages.

Learning More

Looking deeper into the dependent files

When you create a fluid grid layout, the two dependent files that are created are boilerplate.css and respond.js. For the most part, you will not touch any of these files. If you are familiar with what they do and need to modify them, you can.

boilerplate.css: This is a popular framework for modern websites that has been customized and modified for Dreamweaver's fluid grid layout documents. Essentially, you can think of this as a well-tested and documented CSS reset file that pays special attention to the formatting of page styles in older browsers and supports some of the newer media query features. For detailed information on this page, visit *http://html5boilerplate.com/docs/The-style/.*

respond.min.js: This external JavaScript file provides support for CSS3 media queries in web browsers that do not support them natively. For detailed information on what this code does, visit *https://github.com/scottjehl/Respond.*

Styling elements in your fluid grid layout

The layout you created is fairly minimal at the moment. The method of creating and applying styles is not new when working with Fluid Grids; however, there is added complexity you have to take into account. Remember that every time you create a style, it is not just created in one place, but three. To see how to manage this, you'll style the header of your page.

Follow these steps to style elements in a fluid grid layout | **Step-by-Step**

1. Click the Mobile size icon to view your single-column layout.
2. Look within your CSS Styles Panel and click the All tab, if necessary. Expand the base.css external style sheet to see all the rules. You might also need to expand the All Rules section of the panel as seen in Figure 15-30.

***Figure 15-30**: The list of rules within your base.css style.*

3. Starting at the top of the list, scroll down until you find the first `#header` style. After you locate it, keep scrolling down the list to find a second `#header` rule. Continue scrolling down through the list to find the third `#header` style.

   Although it is not immediately obvious, the first header rule sets the style for the mobile styles, the second header sets the style for the tablet, and the third header rule sets the style for the desktop.

3. Double-click the first `#header` rule. In the CSS Rule definition window, click the background category. In the Background-color field, type **#b1d564** as seen in Figure 15-31. This is the same shade of green as the background color of the organic utopia logo. Click OK to apply it.

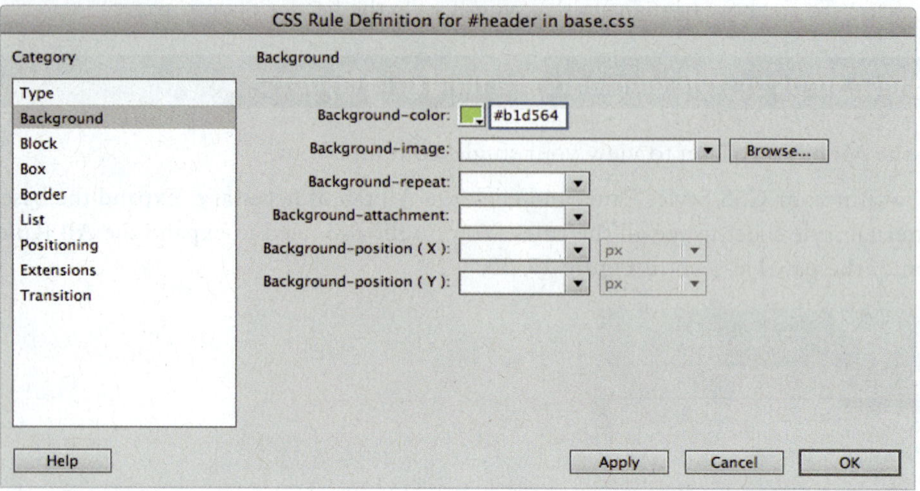

***Figure 15-31**: Applying a background color to the header.*

4. In the Design view, note that your header is now the same color as the background. Click the Tablet and Desktop views, and note that they have inherited the same background color.

   Generally, this is not a problem since you don't want to style the header three different times. However, there might be times when you do want the style of an element to be different in your tablet or desktop views.

5. In your CSS styles panel, double-click the second `#header` style (the one for the tablet). Click the background category, then click the Background-color swatch, and then choose a dark red (the exact shade is not important). Click OK.

   This header style is now specific only to the Tablet view. Click the Tablet view to see it.

6. Choose File > Save All, and then preview your page in the browser. Resize your browser window until it switches to the tablet view layout. You will see the background color of the header change (Figure 15-32).

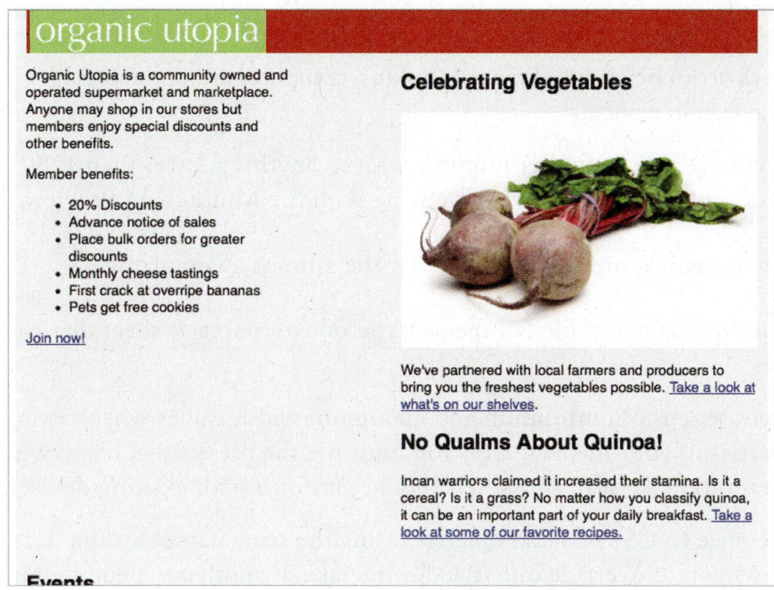

Figure 15-32: *The header in your tablet view has a different background color style.*

Typically, you wouldn't change the background color style of a header. This exercise was just a demonstration of how to apply styles for specific layouts.

7. Close your browser and return to Dreamweaver. Double-click the second #header rule in the CSS Styles panel, click the background color property, and remove the color you added in Step 5. Click OK.
8. Choose File > Save All to finish the lesson.

Congratulations, you have finished Lesson 15, "Mobile Design and Layout."

Skill Summary

In this lesson you learned how to:	Objective
Produce website designs that work equally well on various operating systems, browser versions/configurations, and devices	2.2
Conduct technical tests	6.1

Knowledge Assessment

True/False

Circle T if the statement is true or F if the statement is false.

T F **1.** Websites that can be accessed from a desktop computer are not accessible through a mobile device.

T F **2.** If your own desktop computer monitor is set to anything lower than 1280 pixels wide, you may have trouble working with the Multiscreen Preview.

T F **3.** The Multiscreen feature functions exactly the same as an emulator.

T F **4.** A site-wide media query file is a special type of external style sheet that has no style rules.

T F **5.** You cannot set custom minimum and maximum width values when setting up the properties of your media query, you must use the presets that come with the program to make sure all the settings are uniform with existing devices.

T F **6.** With reference to CSS3 Media Queries, using the same names for the style rules allows you to override one style for the sake of another depending on the device.

T F **7.** Fluid Grids create three layouts at a time.

T F **8.** With reference to Fluid Grids, every time you create a new style, it is not just created in one place, but three.

T F **9.** Using Live View with the Fluid Grid feature works exactly the same as when you're not using a Fluid Grid.

T F **10.** Fluid Grids have eliminated the need for entering Alternate Text information.

Multiple Choice

Select the best response for the following statements

1. Dreamweaver allows you to preview which of the following with the Multiscreen Preview feature?

a. Smart Phones
b. Tablet devices
c. Various desktop sizes
d. All of the above

2. CSS3 Media Queries function as:

a. A way of delivering different page layouts to users based on the capabilities of their screens.
b. A way to update old CSS code to the new CSS3 standards
c. A bridge between HTML, Java, JavaScript, Actionscript and CSS3
d. A way to automatically style your webpages without having to input any settings yourself

3. Which of the following is the code below used for?

```
/* Desktop */
@import url("styles.css") only screen and (min-width: 769px);
```

a. To ensure that the style sheet is connected to the desktop computer
b. To import style sheets that will used for importing and connecting other style sheets
c. It's necessary for older browsers that don't support media queries so they have a standard style sheet to use
d. All of the above

4. Which of the following statements should you take into consideration when designing pages for mobile?

a. Navigation should be at or near the top of the screen to be easily accessible.
b. For touchscreen devices, use a large target size for navigation links to avoid accidental clicking.
c. Avoid image-based navigation, use list-based navigation styled with CSS.
d. All of the above.

5. Which of the following is not an option when choosing the size of your document window?

a. 240 × 320 Feature Phone
b. 768 × 1024 Tablet
c. 1260 × 875 (1280 × 1024, Maximized)
d. 1350 × 950 (1350 × 1050, Maximized)

6. Fluid Grids use which unit of measurement generally?

a. Pixels
b. Inches
c. Percentage
d. Centimeters

7. The space between columns is otherwise known as:

a. Gutter width
b. Spacing width
c. Vertical width
d. Empty width

8. The concept of "mobile first" design refers to:

a. The concept that mobile device design is ultimately way more important than designing toward a desktop computer.
b. A design trend that was started in Europe and is now becoming popular in the US.
c. Forcing the designer to identify the more important or "core" features first.
d. All of the above.

9. What component is added automatically by Dreamweaver whenever you start a new Fluid Grid Layout?
   a. A Fluid Grid Table
   b. A Fluid Grid Layout DIV tag
   c. A PHP formatting page
   d. None of the above

10. When you create a fluid grid layout, the two dependent files that are created automatically are:
    a. boilerplate.css and respond.min.js
    b. bolierplate.js and respond.css
    c. placeholder.css and boilerplate.js
    d. This does not actually occur

Competency Assessment

Project 15-1 Column Values for the Fluid Grid

You worked with some files we provided and had a chance to work with the default values of the Fluid Grid Layout. Another good thing to practice is to get the feel of how changing the column values will effect the flow of your design when it's seen on different platforms.

1. Choose File > New Fluid Grid.
2. When the New Document window appears, try changing the column values for each of the layouts.
3. Click Create and follow the instructions for saving the CSS files, name them descriptively to your liking.
4. Add some content both in terms of text and images and save your work.
5. Preview the page in the various device layouts.
6. Keep creating new Fluid Grid Layouts and trying different settings to keep experimenting.

Project 15-2 Seeing for Yourself

It's hard to translate visually how each device will translate a page, even though Dreamweaver does a pretty good job things are still a simulation. Your device screens and the environment you're in also have an impact on the effectiveness of your design with relation to how the device displays it.

1. Use your own smart phone or tablet, or borrow one from a family member or friend.
2. Look at a website you designed for various devices using Dreamweaver.
3. Look at some older websites that haven't been optimized using HTML5 and take note of the differences.

Proficiency Assessment

Experimenting with Media Content

Project 15-3

Still images and text are one thing when it comes to creating a webpage for mobile content, but adding sound and video is another big consideration.

Launch Dreamweaver CS6 if you haven't already.

1. Create a new blank HTML page.
2. Set up your page as your normally would according to the exercises you just completed.
3. Add some video and sound content to see how it translates to other devices.

Backgrounds in the Header

Project 15-4

Headers allow some great design choices in terms of creating a colorful banner for your webpage. You can also use background patterns or pictures as well. You'll need to have an image handy to work with.

1. Set up a Fluid Grid layout page and go to the CSS elements.
2. Go to the Background category of the Header element in the CSS panel. Use your image as the background for the header.

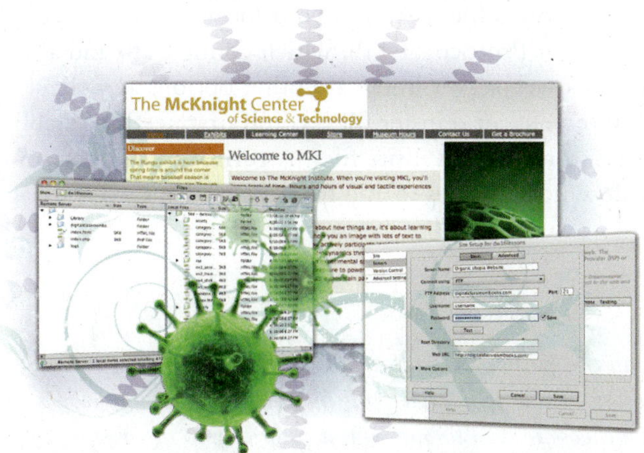

Managing your Website: Reports, Optimization, and Maintenance

Key Terms

- Check In/ Check Out
- Check Links
- Design Notes
- Get
- Metatags
- Put
- Reference Panel
- Remote Connection
- Remote Web Server
- Search Engine Optimization
- Site Reports

Skill	Objective
Demonstrate knowledge of website accessibility standards that address the needs of people with visual and motor impairments	1.4
Produce website designs that work equally well on various operating systems, browser versions/configurations, and devices.	2.2
Communicate with others (such as peers and clients) about design plans	2.6
Add head content to make a web page visible to search engines	5.7
Conduct technical tests	6.1
Identify techniques for basic usability tests	6.2
Identify methods for collecting site feedback	6.3
Manage assets, links, and files for a site	6.4
Publish and update site files to a remote server	6.5

Business Case

You're at the point where you need to learn what needs to be done to get a website ready for publishing to the web. Troubleshooting steps such as checking for code problems and collaborating with others on a project are all concepts you need to learn.

Introduction

Before starting, make sure that your tools and panels are consistent by resetting your workspace. See "Resetting the Dreamweaver workspace" in the Starting Up section of this book.

You will work with several files from the dw16lessons lesson folder in this lesson. Make sure that you have downloaded the dwlessons onto your hard drive.

Creating a remote connection and publishing files to the Web

You've already used the Files panel throughout this book to locate and open files within your site projects. In addition to serving as a useful file browser, the Files panel also serves as a full-featured file transfer application and synchronization tool. From the Files panel, you can upload your site to a web server, synchronize local and remote files, and manage files and notes between multiple designers.

Establishing a remote connection

The Files panel uploads, retrieves, and synchronizes files between your local site and a web server. Typically, this is done using File Transfer Protocol (FTP), which connects to and allows interaction between your local machine and a web server (there are other options as well, including SFTP, WebDav, and more). Before you can transfer files, you'll first need to establish a remote connection to the web server that stores your website files. A **remote connection** is a method used to enable the upload and download of files to and from your web server, using Dreamweaver.

Take Note...

You will not be able to proceed with this portion of the lesson if you do not have FTP information available for a web server. If you do not have this information or do not have a connection to the Internet, you can choose to read through the steps or skip to the Testing Site Integrity exercise in this lesson.

Before you start this lesson, make sure you have the following:

- **The FTP address of the web server and specific directory.** This would be provided by your web-hosting provider as part of your account details, or from your company or organization's IT department. A typical FTP address looks like *ftp.mysite.com*.
- **A user login and password for access to the server.** Most web servers require a user login and password for access. This information should be available from your web-hosting provider as part of your account details, or from your organization's IT department.
- **The specific directory to which your files should be uploaded.** In many cases, this is the main directory or folder that appears when you connect to your web server. However, in certain cases, you'll need to upload files to a specific directory other than the main directory.
- **The web address (URL) or IP address where you can view your uploaded files on the server.** Sample addresses would be *www.mysite.com/*, *www.mysite.com/2007/*, or *http://100.0.0.1*.

Learning More

Certification Ready 6.4

What is the relationship of a FTP server to a Dreamweaver site?

Web server connection options

FTP is still the default choice in Dreamweaver CS6; however, FTP is an aging protocol. Many people are wary of security concerns related to FTP because data sent over FTP is not encrypted.

SFTP stands for "SSH File Transfer Protocol" and represents a more secure version of FTP.

FTP over SSL/TLS is another more secure version of FTP that relies on encryption. For this option, a server must have previously been specifically set up as trusted.

Local/Network allows you to define a remote folder on a network drive you may be connected to. Depending on the setup, this network may or may not also be connected to the Internet

WebDav is a technology that allows file access to a remote server. It is often used collaboratively with multiple users allowed access to the same file system.

RDS is a security component of ColdFusion Server that permits users to access files and databases through a remote HTTP connection.

Follow these steps to create a remote connection

Step-by-Step

1. Choose Site > New Site. Name the site **dw16lessons** and choose the dw16lessons folder for the Local Site Folder.
2. The Site Setup window appears, as shown in Figure 16-1. In the Site Setup window, click on the Servers button to access the server setup screen, then click on the Plus button in the lower left.

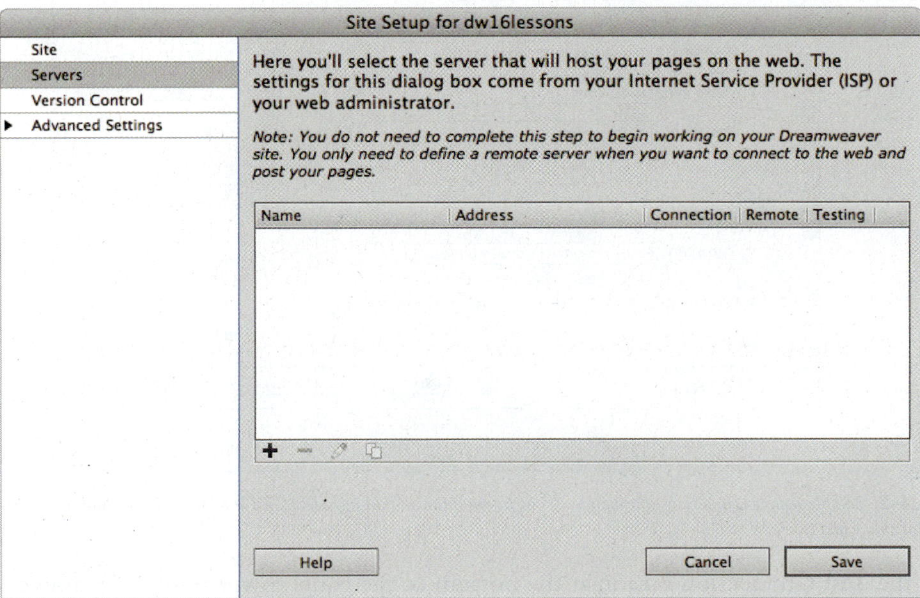

Figure 16-1: *Press the Add new Server button.*

This opens up the Basic tab where you will need to add the required information to access your server.

3. Enter your specific FTP information in the text fields. In Figure 16-2, we have used sample data. The Server Name should be a common sense label that will help you identify which site you are modifying. The FTP Address, Username, and Password are the mandatory pieces of information.

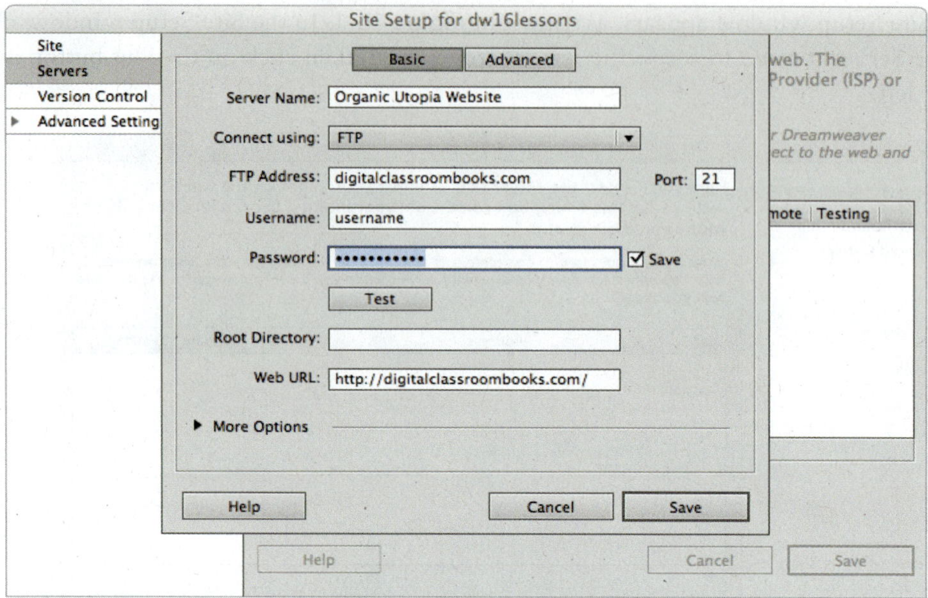

Figure 16-2: Sample remote connection information. Your information should include an FTP address, login, and password, with a possible folder name.

4. Click the Test Connection button at the bottom of the panel to verify that Dreamweaver can connect to your server. If the information you've provided is valid and you have a live Internet connection, a dialog box appears, as shown in Figure 16-3, confirming that Dreamweaver has successfully connected to your web server.

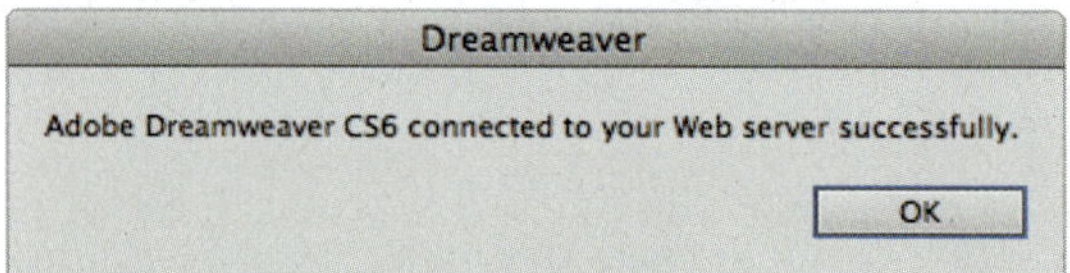

Figure 16-3: A dialog box lets you know if your connection was successful. If you receive an FTP error, double-check your FTP information, and make any necessary corrections.

Take Note...

Certain servers may require a passive FTP connection to connect successfully. If you are certain your FTP information is correct, but experience a long delay or failure when connecting, check the Use Passive FTP checkbox in the Advanced tab, Remote Info category, and try again.

5. Press the Save button and you will see your site listed in the Server window, as you see in Figure 16-4.

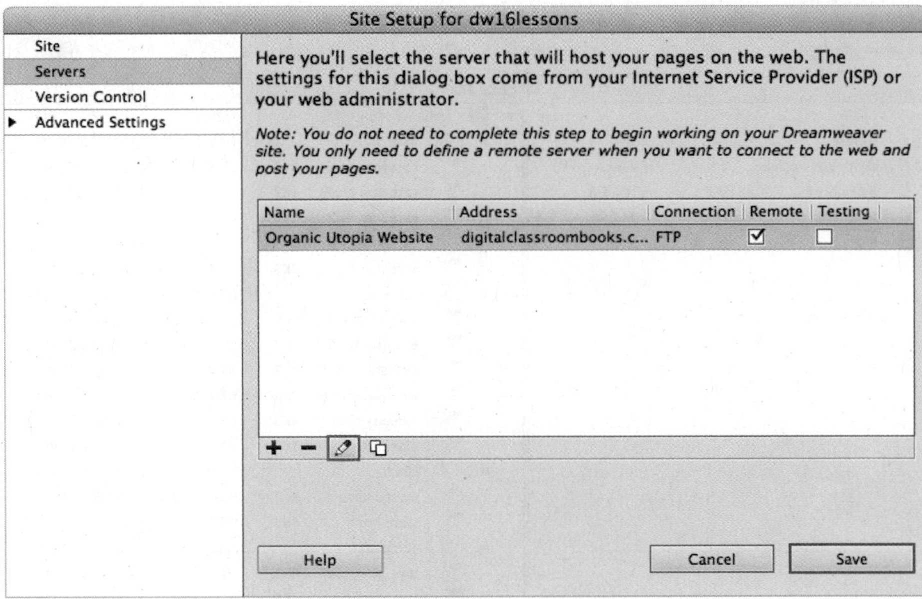

Figure 16-4: Your site is now listed in the Server window.

6. Press the Save button in the Site Setup window. This may trigger an activity window that updates your site settings. Press Done in the Manage Sites dialog box, as you're now finished editing the site definition.

Certification Ready 6.5

How do you set up a connection to a server?

Viewing files on a remote web server

A **remote web server** is a location where site files are hosted so that people can view them online. Once you've established a connection to your web server, you can expand the Files panel for a split view that displays both your remote and local files. You can easily drag and drop between both sides to upload or download files and update existing files.

Follow these steps to view files on a remote server

Step-by-Step

1. If necessary, choose Window > Files to open the Files panel. Click the Expand button (▣) at the top of the Files panel to ungroup and expand it to full view.
2. Locate and click the Connect button (⚇) above the left-hand column at the top of the panel. Dreamweaver attempts to connect to your remote server, and, if successful, displays all its files on the left side of the Files panel, as shown in Figure 16-5.

   It's important to note that web servers can be configured in many different ways, and you may need to edit your site settings again once you have made a successful connection (in particular, the folder information). A discussion of the different ways that web servers

Certification Ready 6.4

How can you expand and collapse the Files panel in order to access features such as the site map, get and put, check in and out?

might be configured is outside the scope of this book; if you have specific questions regarding your site, you should contact an IT professional or your web-hosting company.

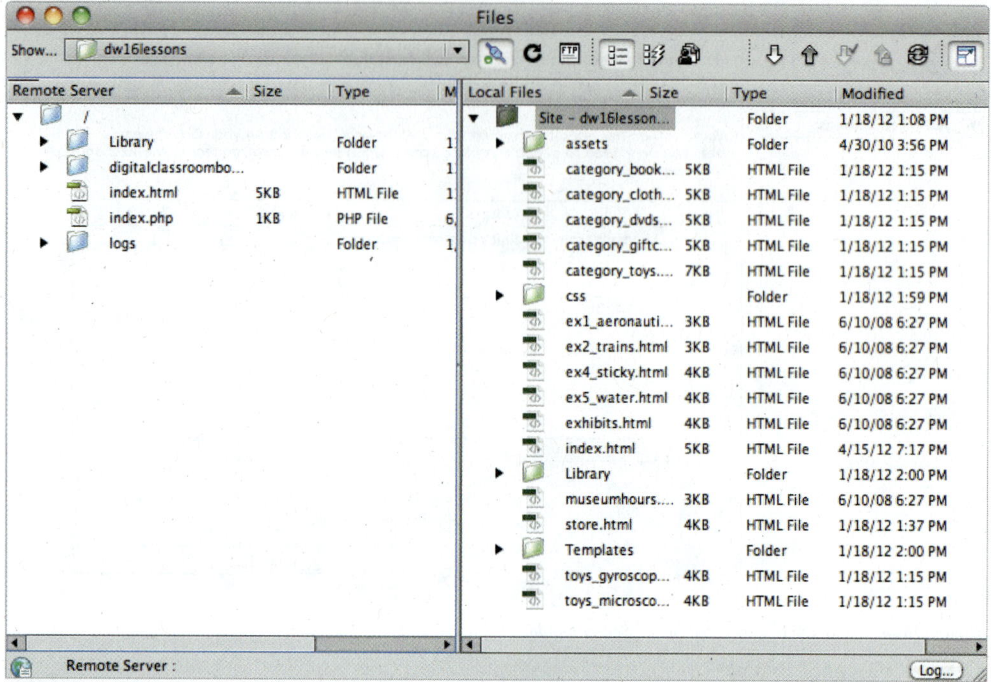

Figure 16-5: Click the Connect button to view files on your remote server in the left column of the Files panel.

Step-by-Step

Follow these steps to transfer files to and from the server

The built-in FTP and file transfer functionality of the Files panel makes it a snap to place files on your remote server or download files onto your local machine. This can be accomplished using the **Get** and **Put** buttons, or by dragging and dropping files between the Remote and Local file listings in the Files panel. Please note again, this exercise involves publishing your sample documents to a remote server, and therefore publishing them to the Internet; be very careful not to overwrite any pre-existing files that may be crucial to your website.

1. Make sure you've connected to the remote server as described in the previous exercise, and that you can see your remote files in the left-hand column of the Files panel.

2. Select the **index.html** file from the local file listing on the right side of your Files panel, as you see in Figure 16-6, and press the Put button ( ) at the top of the panel. Choose *No* when asked if you would like to include dependent files.

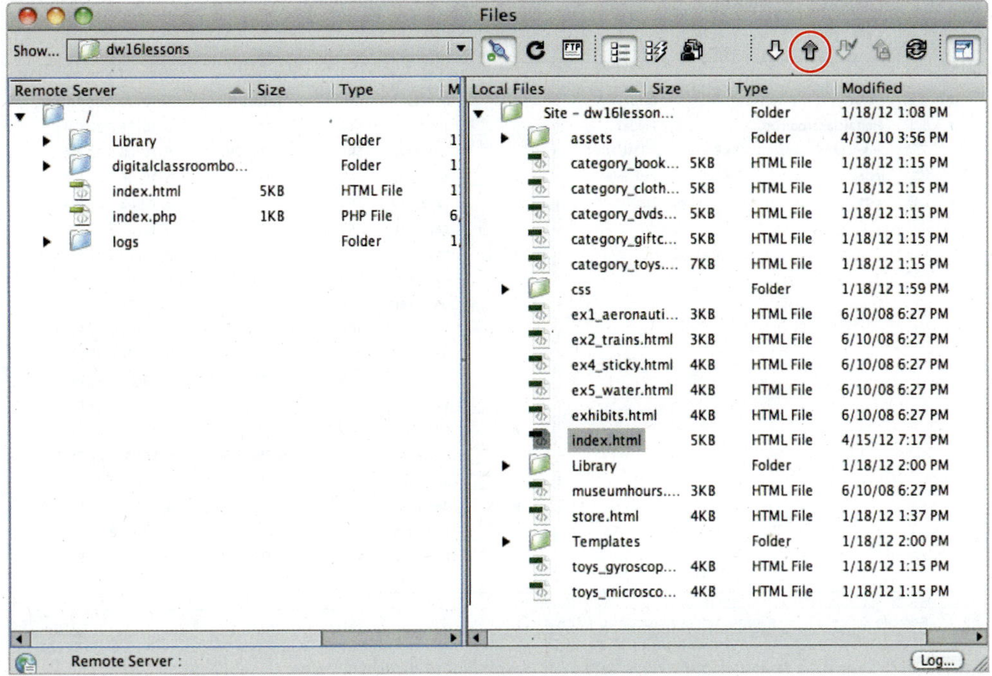

Figure 16-6: *Select a file and click the Put button to upload it to the remote server.*

Take Note...

When you transfer a document between a local and remote folder, a window may open, offering you the option of transferring the document's dependent files. Dependent files are images, external style sheets, and other files referenced in your document that a browser loads when it loads the document. This feature can be very useful: think of it as a way to make sure that any files which are linked to a particular document come along for the ride, however, for the purposes of this exercise, it will be unnecessary to transfer dependent files.

Viewing files on a remote web server

Alternatively, you can click and drag a file from the right, Local Files column, to the left, Remote Server column. See Figure 16-7.

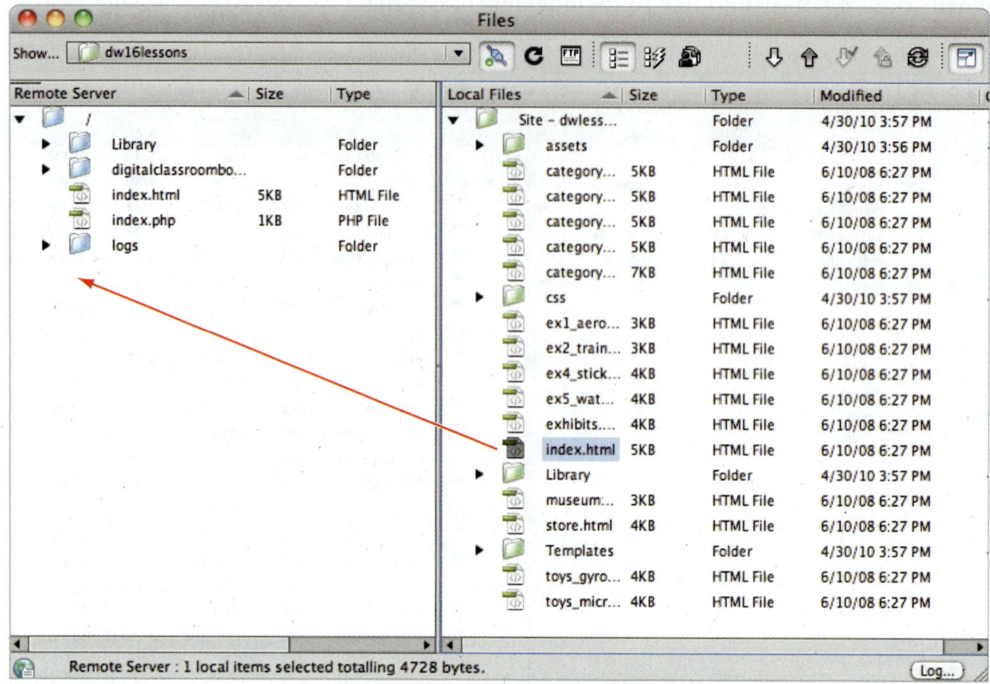

Figure 16-7: *Drag a file from the right column to the left to upload it to the remote server.*

Certification Ready 6.5

How do you publish files to a remore server?

Certification Ready 6.5

How do you use the Files panel to connect to and disconnect from a remote site?

How do you upload and download files from a remote site.?

Follow these steps to get (download) a file from the remote server:

1. Make sure you've connected to the remote server as described in the previous exercise, and that you can see your remote files in the left-hand column of the Files panel.
2. Select the **index.html** file from the remote file listing on the left side of your Files panel, and press the Get button (⇩) at the top of the panel. Note that in your case this does not make a lot of sense since you just uploaded your index.html document.

Take Note...

You can update the local or remote file listing at any time by clicking the Refresh button (C) at the top of the Files panel.

Using Check In/Check Out and Design Notes

If you're collaborating with others on a project, you'll want to set up an environment where everyone can edit files independently without overlapping or overwriting someone else's work. For these situations, the Check In/Out and Design Notes features can help you to manage workflow and communicate with others on a Dreamweaver site project.

Check In and Check Out

Dreamweaver's **Check In/Check Out** feature is a way of letting others know that you are working on a file and don't want it disturbed. When Check In/Check Out is enabled, a document that you're editing becomes locked on the remote server to prevent others from modifying the same file at the same time. If you attempt to open a file that's been checked out by another user, you see a warning that lets you know that the file is in use and who is currently working with it. Check In/Check Out doesn't require any additional software to run, and other Dreamweaver users can check out files if they also have Check In/Check Out enabled in their site definition.

Take Note...

The Check In/Check Out system does not work with a testing server. To transfer files to and from a testing server (if one is set up), use the standard Get and Put commands.

Follow these steps to enable Check In/Check Out — **Step-by-Step**

1. Choose Site > Manage Sites. Select the Dreamweaver site that you want to enable Check In/Check Out for and choose Edit.
2. In the Site Setup window, click on the Servers button, then select your site and click on the pencil icon at the bottom to edit the server settings.
3. Click on the Advanced button and then click on the Enable file check-out checkbox.
4. Type your name and e-mail, as you see in Figure 16-8. This information will appear to other Dreamweaver users who attempt to retrieve a file that you have checked out. Press Save and then press Save again to exit.

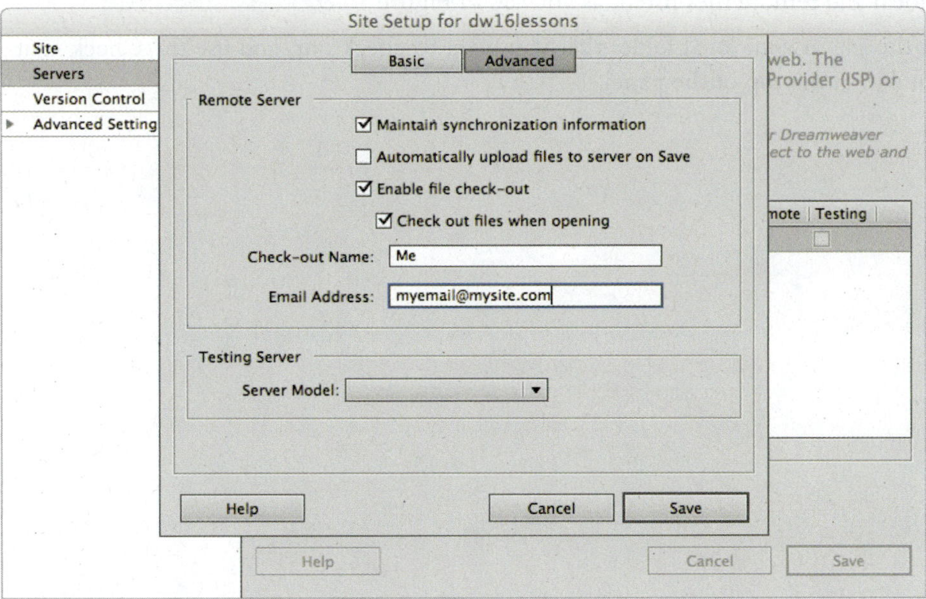

Figure 16-8: Enable check in/check out in the Site Definition panel to manage workflow between several users.

Learning More

What is Check In and Check Out?

Dreamweaver creates a lock (LCK) file for every document that is checked out; this basic text file contains the name and e-mail address of the user who has checked out the file. LCK files are written to both the remote server and local folder using the same name as the active file. When files are checked back in, the LCK files are deleted from both the remote server and local folder.

Although LCK files are not visible in the Files panel, they work behind the scenes to let Dreamweaver know what's checked out and what isn't. Checked-out files appear on both the local and remote file listings with a check mark next to them. Note that a colleague not using Dreamweaver can potentially overwrite a file that's checked out—however, LCK files are visible in applications other than Dreamweaver, and their appearance alone can help avoid any overwriting issues.

Take Note...
A user will be allowed to override your lock and switch checkout status to themselves. Make sure you establish rules with others about how to share and manage locked files.

Checking files in and out

When you check a file out, you are downloading it from the remote server to your local root folder, and placing a lock on the remote copy. Both your local copy and the remote copy appear with check marks next to them, which indicates that the file is currently checked out for editing. When you check a file back in, you are uploading the modified version to the remote server, and removing any locks currently on it.

Step-by-Step

Follow these steps to checking out a file

1. Launch the Files panel and click the Expand button to expand it so that you can see both your local and remote files listed, as you see in Figure 16-9.
2. Select the file in your local folder that you want to check out, and use the Check Out button (⇩✓) at the top of the panel.

Note that Dreamweaver overwrites your local copy of the file, as it needs to get the remote file from the server. The local and remote versions of the file appear with check marks next to them in the Files panel.

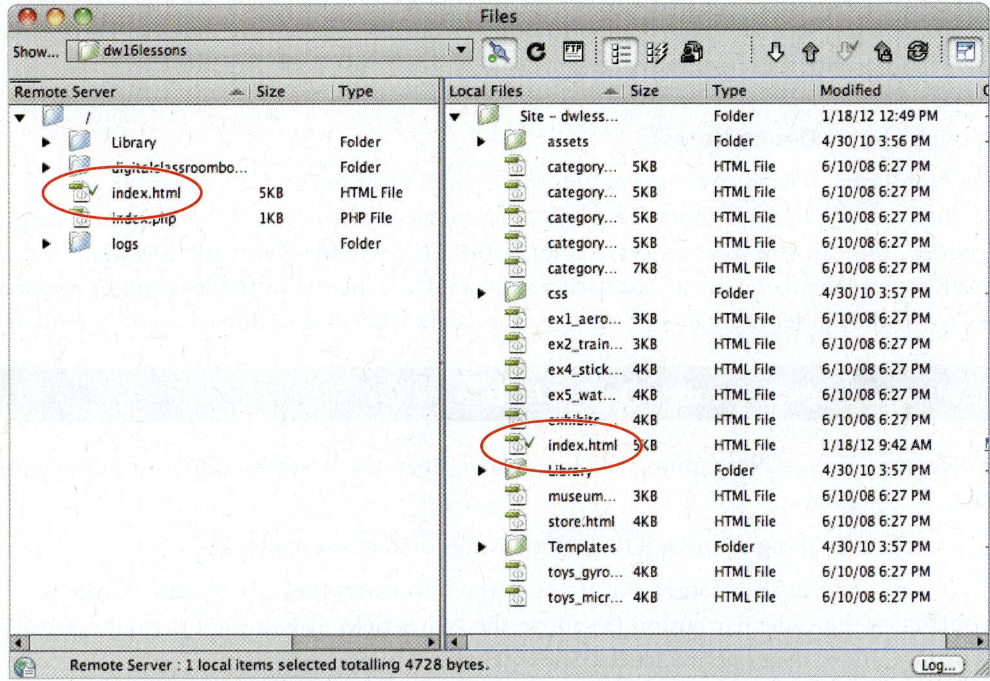

Figure 16-9: *Check files out before modifying them so other users won't accidentally overwrite your work.*

3. Open the checked file from your Local Files panel for editing. Make any necessary changes to the file, then save and close it.

4. From the Files panel, select the file again in the local Files panel and check it back in, using the Check In button ( ) at the top of the panel. The file is uploaded to—and unlocked on—the remote server.

Take Note...

When you transfer a document between a local and remote folder, a window may open offering you the option of transferring the document's dependent files. Dependent files are images, external style sheets, and other files referenced in your document that a browser loads when it loads the document. For this exercise, it won't be necessary for you to transfer dependent files.

Certification Ready 6.4

How do terms Get, Put, Check In, Check Out, Publish, and Remote Server apply to managing files and publishing a website?

Your local copy becomes read-only, and appears with a padlock icon next to it. Next time you open the file for editing, Dreamweaver will automatically check out and get the latest copy from the server.

5. Collapse the Files panel to return it to the dock.

Using Design Notes

Design Notes store additional information about a file or media object in your Dreamweaver site. These notes can be for your own use, or they can be shared with others using the same root folder. Design Notes can be set to appear automatically when the file is opened, making it easy to display up-to-date information to others working on the same site. All Design Notes are stored as separate files in a *_notes* folder inside of your site's root directory.

What can be put in Design Notes?

Design Notes can contain any information that is important to the file or project; you can store design instructions, updates about the project, or contact information for project managers and supervisors. You can also store sensitive information that you ideally would not want in the file itself, such as the name of the last designer to work on the file or the location of important assets. You can even set the status of the file to indicate what stage of the revision the file is in.

Step-by-Step

Follow these steps to create a Design Note

1. To create a Design Note, under the Files panel, open the **store.html** file from the current site.
2. Choose File > Design Notes. The Design Notes dialog box appears.
3. Type a message in the Notes field. If you wanted to insert the current date stamp, you could click the Calendar button () above the Notes field. If you want the note displayed when the file is next opened, check Show when file is opened.

   The Status menu is used to set the document status; this can be useful in letting other collaborators know the revision stage of the current document.
4. Press OK to create the Design Note.

   To view a Design Note, choose File > Design Notes when a file is open in the document window. As mentioned earlier, you can also choose to have Design Notes automatically appear when the file is first opened.

> ***Take Note...***
> *Design Notes can also be created or viewed directly from the Files panel; right-click (Windows) or Ctrl + click (Mac OS) a document in the files list and choose Design Notes from the contextual menu.*

Sharing Design Notes

By default, Design Notes are stored only in the local site folder, and are not automatically copied to the remote server. However, you can share Design Notes with other collaborators by having Dreamweaver automatically upload and update them on the remote server.

Follow these steps to share a Design Note

Step-by-Step

1. Choose Site > Manage Sites. Select your site from the Sites panel and choose Edit. The Site Setup window appears.
2. Click on the Advanced Settings options and choose Design Notes from the left.
3. Under the Design Notes panel, shown in Figure 16-10, check Enable Upload Design Notes for sharing. Design Notes are now copied and updated on the remote server so that other users can share them.

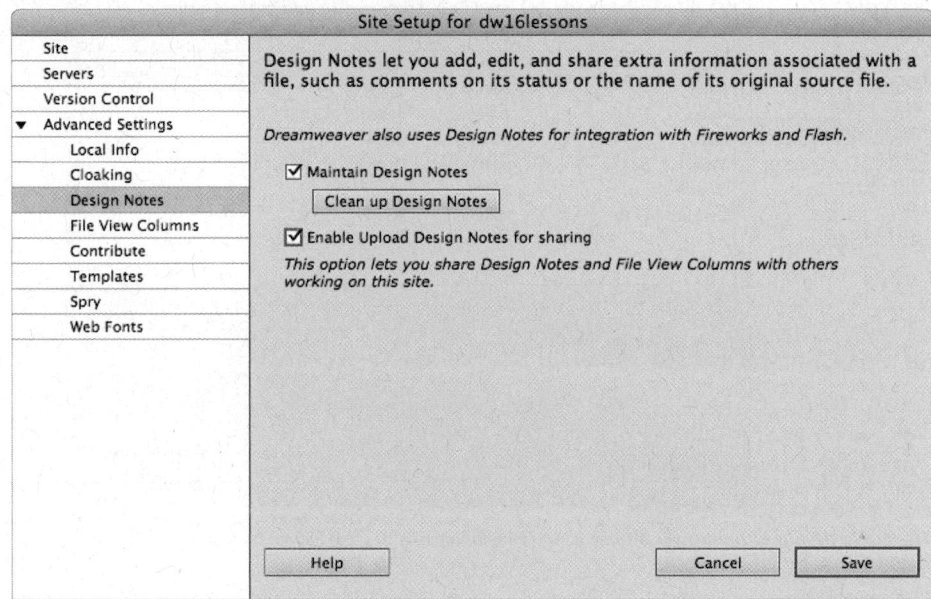

Figure 16-10: *Set up Design Notes for sharing so other Dreamweaver users can see and modify Design Notes on the remote server.*

4. Choose Save to update the site definition, then press Done to close the Manage Sites dialog box.

Displaying Design Notes in the Files panel

A convenient way to view and access Design Notes is by enabling the Design Notes column in the Files panel. An icon that can be used to open and edit Design Notes accompanies documents that have an associated Design Note. This feature also allows you to see all available Design Notes at a glance.

Step-by-Step

Follow these steps to display Design Notes in the Files panel

1. Choose Site > Manage Sites. Select your site from the Sites panel and choose Edit. The Site Setup for dw16lessons dialog box appears, as shown in Figure 16-11. In Advanced Setting options, choose File View Columns.

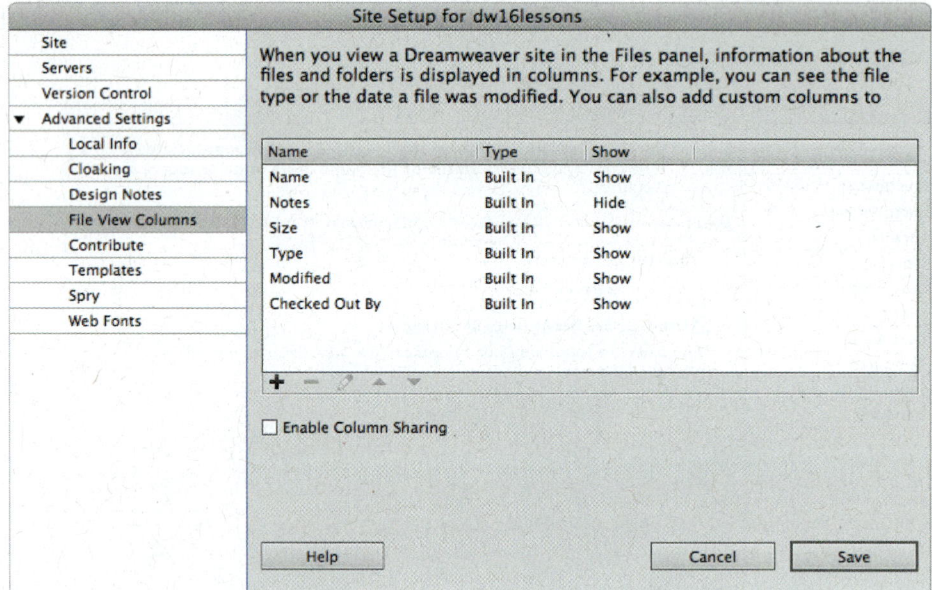

Figure 16-11: *Use the Site Definition panel's File View Columns category to show Design Notes in both the local and remote file listings.*

2. Double-click the Notes item from the list and click the Show checkbox and then press Save.

Certification Ready 2.6

What techniques do you use for gathering feedback on design plans?

3. Choose Save to update the site definition, then press Done to close the Manage Sites dialog box. You will likely see the Background File Activity window appear, wait for this to complete. A Notes column appears in the Files panel; a Notes icon ( ) is displayed next to each file that currently is associated with a Design Note.

Testing site integrity

Catching potential issues on a page before your visitors do is key to ensuring success from the start. Broken links, display issues, or unreadable pages can make the difference between a great first impression and a poor one. To look for and address problems before you publish your site, Dreamweaver provides many useful tools that can point out potential hazards and, in some cases, help you find the solution.

Using Check Links

The **Check Links** feature detects any broken links between pages in your local site and will identify orphaned files that are not linked to or used by any document within the site.

Follow these steps to check links on a page | **Step-by-Step**

1. From the Files panel, double-click and open the **index.html** document.
2. Choose File > Check Page > Links, as you see in Figure 16-12.

Figure 16-12: Choose File > Check Page > Links to check for broken links in the current document.

3. The Link Checker panel appears; you see one listing here, as shown in Figure 16-13. A link to the exhibits.html page is misspelled; you need to fix the error.
4. Click the misspelled "exhbits.html" item under the Broken Links column. The link name becomes editable.

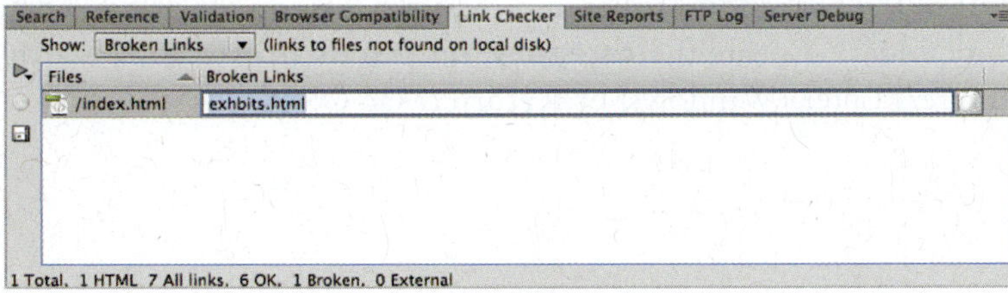

Figure 16-13: Clicking on the link in the Broken Links column allows it to be edited.

5. Click on the folder icon to the far right. A Select File dialog box appears. Select the file **exhibits.html** and then press Choose. In the Link Checker tab, press Enter (Windows) or Return (Mac OS), and the broken link disappears.

6. Close the Link Checker panel by right-clicking (Windows) Ctrl+clicking (Mac OS) the Link Checker tab and choosing Close Tab Group. Save and close the current document.

Checking links sitewide

Check Links can be used on a single document, multiple documents (through the Files panel), or an entire local site at once.

Step-by-Step

Follow these steps to check Links site-wide

1. Choose Site > Check Links Sitewide.

2. The Link Checker panel appears, as shown in Figure 16-14. By default, any broken links are displayed. All the broken links here are referencing the same incorrect link to **category_books_cds.html**. This could have happened if you or a collaborator on the site changed the name of the file within the operating system or another web editor.

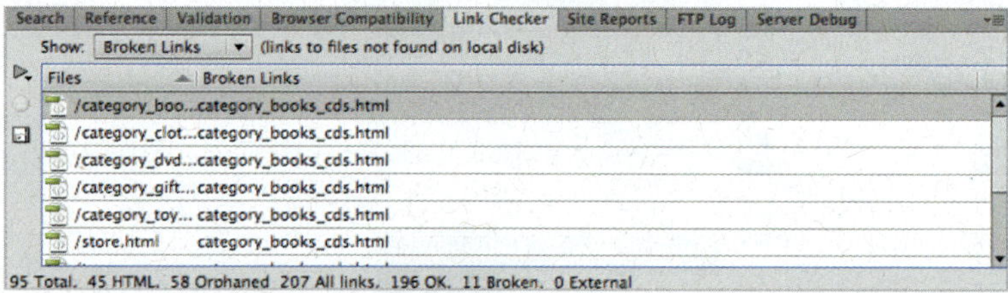

Figure 16-14: *Choose Site > Check Links Sitewide to check for broken links throughout the current local site. The Link Checker panel opens and displays any broken links found.*

3. To view external links, choose External Links from the Show drop-down menu at the top of the panel. This site will have none, but any links to outside web pages that you have on your site would be listed.

Take Note...

External links are displayed, but aren't validated by Dreamweaver. The Link Checker can only validate links between local documents and files.

4. To view orphaned files, choose Orphaned Files from the Show drop-down menu at the top of the panel. In this site, a number of files will appear. Orphaned files are files that are not currently being linked to in your site. This may include stray multimedia files that have not been added to a page yet. You will not be doing anything with these files at this moment.

5. Choose Broken Links from the Show drop-down menu to return to the broken links report. Click on the first of the broken links shown to edit it. Click on the folder icon and browse through your site folder to locate the **category_bookscds.html** file. Select this file, press OK and then press Enter (Windows) or Return (Mac OS).

6. A dialog box appears, as shown in Figure 16-15, asking if you'd like to make the same correction throughout the entire current local site.

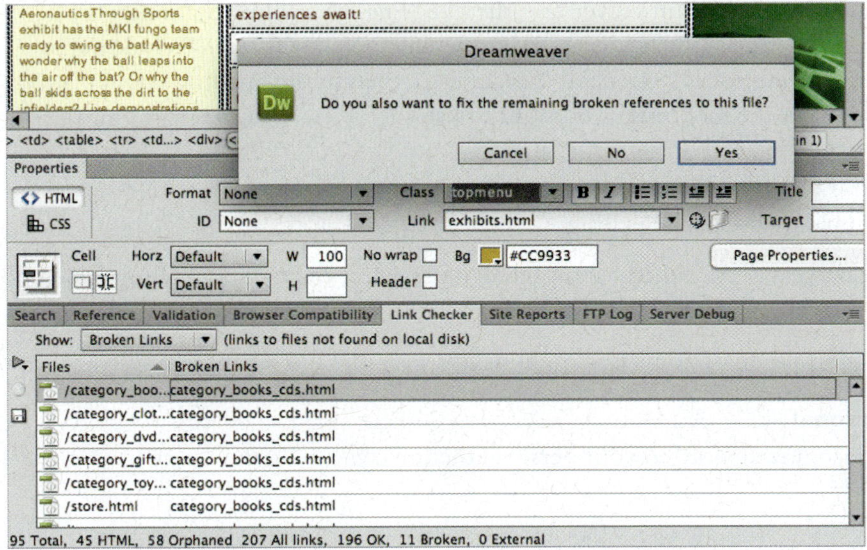

Figure 16-15: *Adjust a link directly from the Link Checker panel to correct it across the site.*

Press *Yes*. Behind the scenes Dreamweaver will go through all the pages and automatically update the correct link. This feature is an amazing timesaver as you don't even have to open the files to make the changes!

Link Checker results

If and when the Link Checker returns results, you can jump to any problem document to view and fix any issues. The Link Checker panel's Show menu (located at the top of the panel) toggles between three different Link Checker reports: Broken Links, Orphaned Files, and External Links.

Broken Links lists links that point to files not found within the local site. To jump to a page that contains a broken link, double-click the filename shown in the left column of the Link Checker panel. To correct a link directly from the Link Checker panel, click the link shown under the Broken Links column of the panel to edit it. Type in the proper page name or use the folder to browse to the proper file. If you edit a broken link this way, Dreamweaver can apply the same correction throughout other pages on your site.

Orphaned Files are any pages, images, or media files not linked to, referenced, or used by any files in your site. This report can be useful in identifying unused files that can be cleaned up from the local site, or pages that should be linked to (like a site map) but were overlooked.

External Links lists any links to outside websites, pages, or files; and like the Broken Links panel, allows you to directly edit them or jump to the page that contains them. It's important to note, however, that Dreamweaver does not validate external links—you will still be responsible for double-checking these links on your own. You'll also notice that e-mail (mailto:) links are included in this list.

Learning More

Certification Ready 6.1

How do you test links using the Check Links Sitewide command?

Learning More

Spellchecking a page

The spelling checker in Dreamweaver uses the U.S. English spelling dictionary by default. To change the dictionary, select Edit > Preferences > General (Windows) or Dreamweaver > Preferences > General (Macintosh), then in the Spelling Dictionary pop-up menu select the dictionary you want to use.

To Check Spelling of a page

- Select Commands > Check Spelling
- When Dreamweaver encounters an unrecognized word, the Check Spelling dialog box appears.
- Select the appropriate option based on how you want the discrepancy handled.

Add To Personal
Adds the unrecognized word to your personal dictionary.

Ignore
Ignores this instance of the unrecognized word.

Change
Replaces this instance of the unrecognized word with text that you type in the Change To text box or with the selection in the Suggestions list.

Ignore All
Ignores all instances of the unrecognized word.

Change All
Replaces all instances of the unrecognized word in the same manner. irectly from the Link Checker panel, click the link shown under the Broken Links column of the panel to edit it.

Certification Ready 6.1

How do you test links using the Check Links Sitewide command?

Generating site reports

Dreamweaver's **site reports** feature is an indispensable asset for detecting potential design and accessibility issues before publishing your site to the Web. Reports can be generated in several categories to give you a virtual picture of health, and the opportunity to locate and fix minor or major issues across an entire Dreamweaver site. These issues can include missing alternate text or titles, CSS issues, and recommendations for better accessibility practices, based on the W3C's Web Consortium Accessibility Guidelines (WCAG).

Reports can be generated for a single page, selected documents, or the entire current local site. Any results open and display in the Results panel, where you can see a list of issues and the pages on which they are located.

Follow these steps to run a Site Report

Step-by-Step

1. To run a site report, choose Site > Reports. The Reports dialog box opens, displaying two categories of reports: Workflow and HTML.

Take Note...
It is not necessary to have a document open in order to run sitewide reports.

Workflow reports display information about Design Notes, check in and check out operations, and recently modified files. HTML reports display potential design, accessibility, and display issues, based on best practices and W3C/WCAG accessibility guidelines.

2. In the Reports panel, check all the reports under the HTML category. At the top of the panel, select Entire Current Local Site from the Report on drop-down menu, as shown in Figure 16-16.

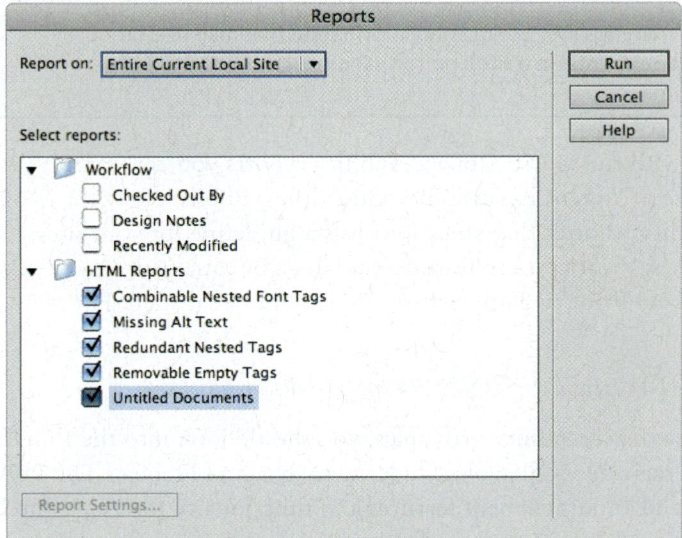

Figure 16-16: *Choose Site > Reports, and select the reports you'd like to run in the Site Reports dialog box.*

3. Click Run in the top-right corner of the Reports panel. The Results panel appears, displaying any potential issues. Note that depending on the size of your site and number of issues found, it may take a few moments for all results to display.

4. Leave the Results panel open, as you see in Figure 16-17. You'll learn how to read and address issues in the next exercise.

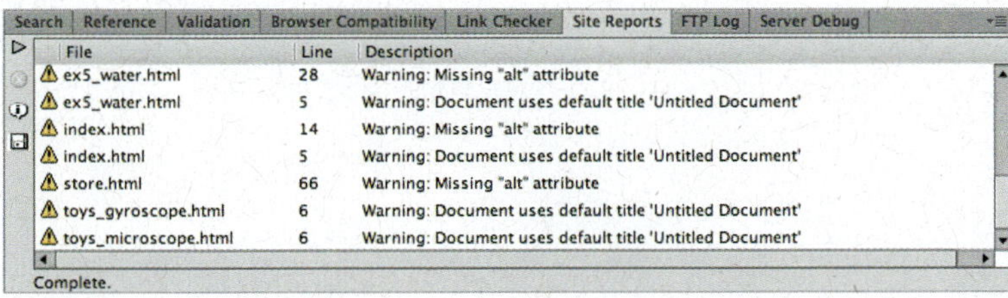

Figure 16-17: *The Results panel displays issues found across your entire current local site.*

Understanding report results

At first glance, you may be overwhelmed at the amount of information returned by site reports. Keep in mind that many of the listings returned are recommendations or possible issues that should be looked into, not necessarily items that will prevent a site from working. Learning to read these site reports a little more closely will enable you to decide which items are crucial to your site's performance, requiring immediate action. Listings are displayed with three distinct icons.

Icon	Name	Use
?	Question Mark	These listings suggest possible accessibility issues that should be investigated. Many of these issues have a reference to a specific W3C/WCAG guideline.
✗	Red X	These listings indicate a failure to meet a certain guideline or requirement. Possible listings could include missing header information, deprecated HTML markup, or page titles that are not defined properly.
⚠	Warning Sign	Warnings indicate missing information that may be potentially detrimental to a site's performance, such as missing ALT text for images.

To further familiarize yourself with the specifics of accessibility reports you can consult the Checklist of Checkpoints for Web Content Accessibility Guidelines. Published by the W3C this is large checklist of accesibility features that you can use as a guideline for your sites. There are three levels of priorities: Priority 1 are features that must be satisified, Priority 2 are features that should be satisfied and Priority 3 are features that could be satisfied. For a full listing of the checklist visit:

http://www.w3.org/TR/1999/WAI-WEBCONTENT-19990505/full-checklist

Certification Ready 1.4

What are the W3C Priority 1 Checkpoints and the W3C Priority 2 POUR principles for making a website accessible?

If you would like a broader view of accessibility principles, you should look into the POUR principles (POUR stands for Perceivable, Operable, Understandable, and Robust) The POUR principles can help you understand and implement features and functionalty for users who have visual or auditory disabilities. For a full explanation of the principles, visit:

http://webaim.org/articles/pour/

Using Site Reports

Although the value of site reports increases with larger websites, features such as the Link Checker are one of the main reasons that Dreamweaver is used in a production workflow. Without this feature, identifying broken links would be extremely time-consuming. In addition, because Dreamweaver allows you to fix any broken links without needing to open the pages, even more time is saved.

Addressing a listed item

After you've sifted through the report results, you'll want to use the Results panel to address items listed in the Site Reports tab.

Follow these steps to address items in a Site Report

Step-by-Step

1. Go to the Site Reports tab on the Results panel, shown in Figure 16-18. Click the Description column header to sort the results. Scroll to the bottom of the page as needed, and locate the **store.html** listing.

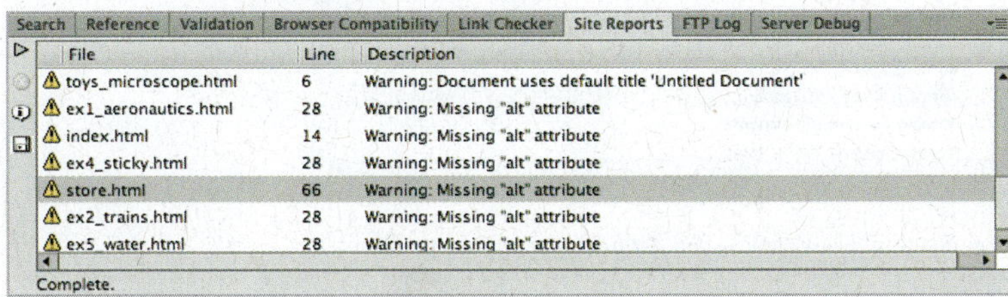

Figure 16-18: *Select a listing and click the More Info button to display a detailed description about the issue found.*

The Description column shows that an image on this page is missing the ALT attribute and alternate text. This attribute can potentially affect accessibility of your site; you don't need to fix it, but we highly recommend you do.

2. Double-click the **store.html** listing to open the page for editing. Your document window divides into the Code view and Design view; the image appears selected in the Design view and highlighted in the Code view.

3. In the Property Inspector, shown in Figure 16-19, type **MKI Gift Cards are now available!** in the Alt field and press Enter (Windows) or Return (Mac OS).

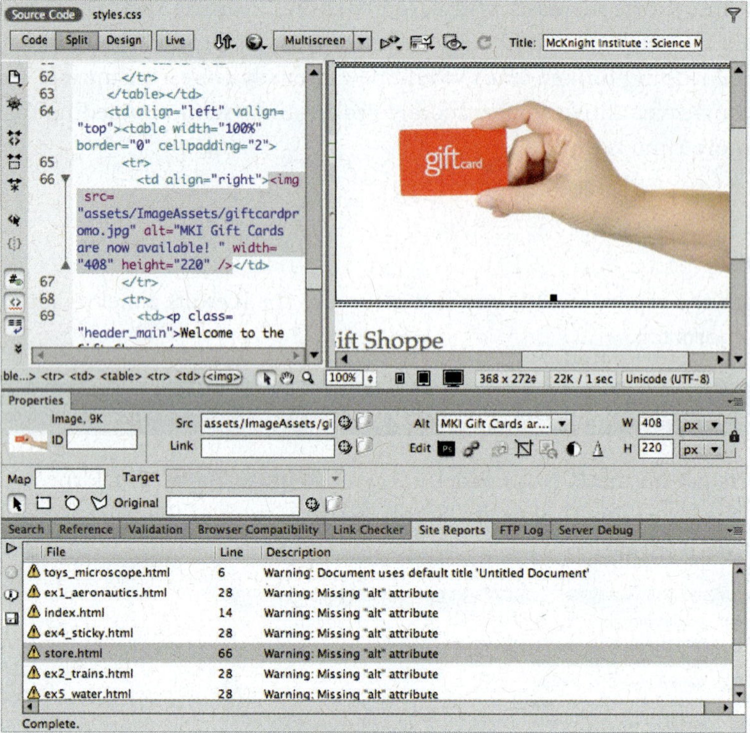

Figure 16-19: *Select the problem image and enter text in the Alt field to rectify the problem.*

Multiple Results

Whenever you have multiple results as you do here, you might want to save them for future reference. Reports can be saved as XML for import into databases, existing template files, and archival files. You can sort report results using the Results panel before saving them.

1. Click the Save Report button (▣) on the left edge of the Results panel. When the Save Report dialog box appears, assign the report a name, and choose a location for the file.
2. Save and close the page, and close the Results panel.

Take Note...

A full listing of accessibility guidelines, or WCAG, for web page designers and developers is available at the World Wide Web Consortium (W3C) website at W3.org.

Identifying and labeling accessible areas of your page

Although accessibility has come a long way since the beginning of the Web, it still has a long way to go. Although Dreamweaver's site reports help identify areas of your page that can be read by screen readers, much of this information is gathered by experience (alt tags, headers, page titles, and captions for example, are all read by screen readers).

A relatively new initiative aimed at standardizing accessibility practices is currently in development and is known as the Accessible Rich Internet Applications Suite (WAI-ARIA for short). One portion of the specification, called *landmark roles*, is specifically designed to be used with HTML and XHTML elements. A landmark role is a way of categorizing and identifying different parts of a web page. For example, a role called *banner* identifies the region that contains the primary heading of the page. You can add this role as an attribute for the HTML5 <header> element, for example:

```
<header role="banner">
```

Some of the landmark roles have direct equivalents to HTML elements. For example, the `role="form"` attribute is used for form elements and the `role="navigation"` is used for the HTML5 `<nav>` element. You can use landmark roles today, but you might need to review your code in the future to ensure that it is aligned with the specification when it is finalized.

You can learn more about WAI-ARIA and landmark roles here:

http://www.w3.org/WAI/PF/aria/usage#usage_intro

http://www.w3.org/WAI/PF/aria-practices/

The aria-practices page above also includes sample code and best practices for adding landmark roles into your web pages.

Learning More

Certification Ready 1.4

What elements of an HTML page are readable by screen readers?

Certification Ready 1.4

What is Web Accessibility Initiative's Accessible Rich Internet Applications specification?

Specific techniques for addressing usability

Throughout this book we have attempted to point out cases where Dreamweaver paves the way for improving accessibility. For example, by now you should be aware of how inserting an image onto a page will always trigger the Image Tag Accessibility Attributes window and remind you to add an Alt tag. However, a full commitment to making your pages accessible to as many users as possible requires a lot of work. Here are some of the techniques to consider:

- Have a good sense of which elements of a web page are not read or could be confusing for someone using a screen readers such as graphics without alt tags, hyperlinks without title attributes, text that is embedded as an image, imagemaps, buttons and rich media such as Flash, video or sound.

Take Note...
For more information on Screen Reader Compatibility visit http://webaim.org/techniques/screenreader/

- Although there are certain default keyboard conventions (such as pressing the Tab key to navigate from field to field) you can control the order in which fields are activated by changing the tab index value in the dialog box for form elements.
- CSS fonts and CSS3 web fonts. This issue is covered in multiple locations throughut the book, but essentially the guidelines are to use only the most common web fonts if using standard CSS and to be aware of browser compatibility for the latest CSS3 web fonts functionality.

Certification Ready 6.2

What elements are involved in conducting a website usability test?

The Browser Compatibility Check

When you format page content or create layouts with CSS, you'll want to be certain that your pages appear consistently across a variety of browsers. Some combinations of HTML and CSS can unearth some nasty display bugs in specific browsers. In fact, some browsers may not support certain CSS properties at all. To seek out and fix any potential CSS display problems, you'll use Dreamweaver's Browser Compatibility Check (BCC) reports in conjunction with the CSS Advisor.

Optimizing pages for launch

Although page optimization is discussed at this point in the book, it is by no means an afterthought. A big part of preparing a site for success involves making it accessible to users with special needs, such as those who are visually impaired, or preparing it for indexing by various search engines. In addition to clean design and well-written content, pages can be optimized through the use of keywords, descriptions, and often-overlooked tag attributes, such as alternate text (alt) for images and a page's Title area. Combined, these pieces of information facilitate site usability and visibility in several essential ways.

Search engine visibility and Search Engine Optimization

A big part of a website's success stems from its visibility. Visibility comes through good advertising, networking with other sites, and, above all, proper indexing and listings on the Web's major search engines. Search engines can be a key to generating business and visits to your site, but only if your website can be easily found. Major search engines such as Google (which powers AOL, MySpace, and Netscape searches), Yahoo! (which powers AltaVista and others), and LiveSearch (formerly MSN Search) use a variety of factors to index and generate listings for websites. Many of these factors start at home, or more appropriately, on your home page.

Titling your documents with the `<title>` tag

Each document's head area contains a `<title>` tag, which Dreamweaver automatically inserts with any new HTML/XHTML document. At its most basic, the `<title>` tag sets a display title for a page in the browser window. You can modify the `<title>` tag contents using the Title text field that sits at the top of your document window. By default, each new document is issued the default title of Untitled Document. The `<title>` tag and its contents, however, can be a powerful and effective way to assist search engines in indexing your page.

What makes a good title?

A good document title ideally should include keywords that describe your site's main service, locale, and category of business or information. In addition to the obvious—your company's name—think about the categories you would want your site to appear under on a web directory or as the result of a web search. For instance, the McKnight Institute would ideally want users looking for science museums or exhibits in the Philadelphia, Pennsylvania, area to find them first. A possible title could be: The McKnight Institute: Science Museum, Educational Exhibits and Attractions, Philadelphia, Pennsylvania.

This title contains several important keywords that describe the Institute's offerings, and features the Institute's name and location. In addition, reshuffling these phrases and words produces several other search terms that could be beneficial to the Institute, such as:

- Science Exhibits
- Philadelphia Museum
- Pennsylvania Attractions

Take Note...

Avoid the rookie mistake of including only your company name in the document title. Remember, web searchers who haven't used your business before will only search by terms that apply to the service they are seeking (for example, wedding photographers, Washington, D.C.). Even the most recognized names on the Web such as eBay and Amazon, include generic search terms in their page titles.

Follow these steps to add a title to your web page

Step-by-Step

1. From the Files panel, select and open the **index.html** document to open it for editing.
2. Locate the Title text field at the top of the document window, as shown in Figure 16-20. It currently displays the default title of Untitled Document. Select its contents and type **The McKnight Institute: Science Museum, Educational Exhibits and Attractions, Philadelphia, Pennsylvania** and press Enter (Windows) or Return (Mac OS).

Figure 16-20: *Add a well-constructed title to the index.html page to make it more search-engine and bookmark friendly.*

3. Choose File > Save to save the document, and then choose File > Preview in Browser > [Default browser] to open the document in your system's primary browser.

4. Note, in Figure 16-21, that the title now appears in the bar at the top of the browser window. Close the browser window and return to Dreamweaver.

Figure 16-21: *The most basic purpose of the <title> tag is to display a title at the top of the browser window. If used properly, it can also be used as a powerful hook for search engines.*

Take Note...

While there is technically no limit to title length, the W3C's Web Consortium Accessibility Guide recommends that page titles be a maximum of 64 characters to be considered "well-defined." Titles exceeding this length may generate warnings in the Site Reports Results panel. Longer titles may also appear truncated (cut off) when displayed in some browser windows.

Learning More

What determines the Bookmark or Favorite name?

It's common for users to bookmark a site or specific page they've found so that they can easily return to it. Every browser has a bookmark feature, which allows users to mark and display favorite sites in an organized list; sometimes, favorite sites are listed in a Bookmarks bar in the browser window.

The document title determines the text that appears with a bookmark, so it's important to consider this when creating a good document title. Using a vague or non-descriptive title (or even worse, the default Untitled Document text) can make it impossible for a user to remember which bookmark is yours. A good title appears as a descriptive bookmark in a browser's Favorites list or Bookmarks bar.

Adding meta keywords and descriptions

While Search Engine Optimization (SEO) is a broad topic that's far beyond the scope of this book; good SEO methods begin at the design level. **Search Engine Optimization** is defined as the process of structuring the HTML and CSS code of your site in order to best expose the content to search engines. Search engines use a variety of factors to rank and list web pages. Keywords and descriptions can help specify the search terms that are associated with your site and how it's listed. The HTML **<meta> tag** enables you to associate any page with a specific list of search terms, as well as a brief description of the page or the website itself. Like the `<title>` tag, `<meta>` tags are placed in the `<head>` section of a page, and can be added from the Common Insert bar on the right side of your workspace.

Follow these steps to add a keyword to your metatags

Step-by-Step

1. If it's not already open, choose File > Open and locate and open the **index.html** document for editing.
2. From the Common Insert bar, choose the Keywords button from the Head tags group.
3. When the Keywords window appears, as shown in Figure 16-22, add a comma-separated list of search keywords that you'd like associated with this page, or the site in general. While there is no general consensus on the limit of how many keywords you can use, common sense says that you should be able to categorize your site in roughly 20 keywords or fewer. For example, type **museum, technology exhibits, attractions, family attractions, philadelphia, pennsylvania museums**. Press Return (Windows) or Enter (Mac OS) to add the keywords.

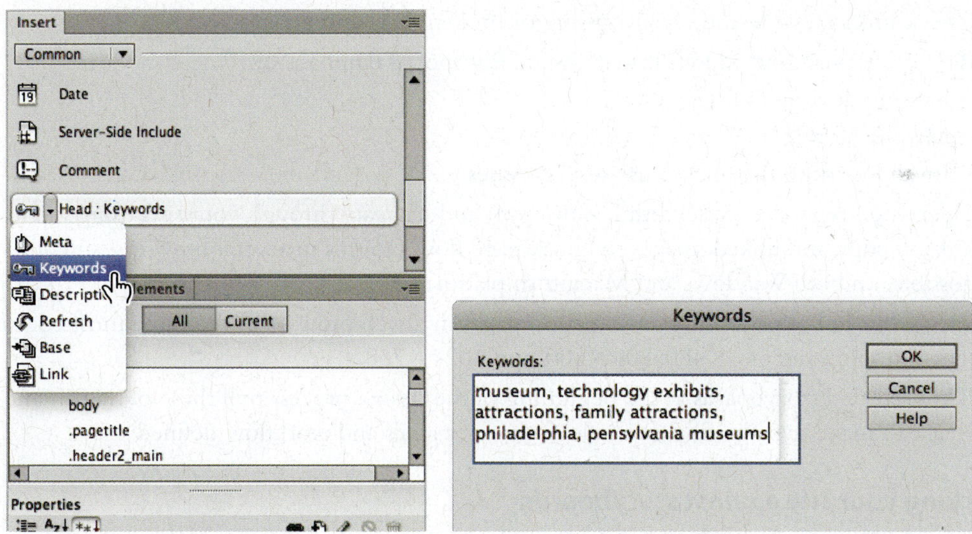

Figure 16-22: From the Common category of the Insert bar, choose the Keywords object from the Head tags group and enter a list of keywords in the resulting dialog box.

Certification Ready 5.7

What is head content, meta tags and the tag inspector?

4. Now you'll add a description that a search engine can use to summarize your page when creating a listing for it. Choose the Description button from the Head tags group on the Common Insert bar.

5. When the Description dialog box appears, see Figure 16-23, type in a brief descriptive paragraph (fewer than 250 characters, including spaces). For example, type **The McKnight Center is a family-oriented education center and museum that explores the history of technology and scientific discovery through hands-on exhibits and events**. Press OK.

Certification Ready 5.7

How do you add and edit head content using the Common category in the Insert bar?

Certification Ready 6.2

What elements are involved in conducting a website usability test?

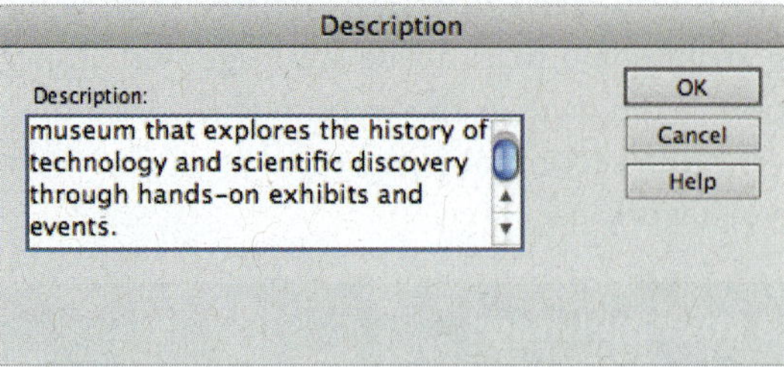

Figure 16-23: *Add a short description that search engines can use to display a caption for your site listing.*

6. Choose File > Save, then choose File > Close to close the file.

Launching your site

Before launching your site for the public—and to ensure that your site works at, and looks, its best—take a moment to go over this pre-flight checklist.

Site Launch Checklist

- Enter FTP or upload information and test your FTP connection.
- Check links sitewide and repair missing or broken links and images.
- Run site reports and address crucial issues. Put special emphasis on:
  - Missing document titles
  - Missing alt text
  - Invalid markup that may cause display issues
- Open the homepage (index.html, and so on) and navigate through your site, using menus, links in copy, and linked images to check page flow. Do this in several browsers, and, if possible, on both Windows and Macintosh platforms.
- View your home page and major section pages in a web browser in the three most common screen resolutions: 640 × 480, 800 × 600, and 1024 × 768.
- If you created storyboards at the beginning of the design process pull these out again and check to make sure the final site reflects the user goals and workflow defined

Certification Ready 6.1

How do you test a website against a storyboard?

Checking your site against storyboards

In Lesson 1, "Dreamweaver CS6 Jumpstart," you learned about the role of storyboards in the planning stage of site design. A storyboard consists of number of pages that describe a site's navigation, each pages may have a list of related links, a functional description of the page, images, text and some notes on content for that page. You can do a comparison of your final website to the storyboard by using it as a checklist of sorts. Does the functionality and content of the final site reflect the functionality and content of the storyboard? If not, then why not? Was the content removed (or never delivered?) In the end, if the storyboards were well thought out, this step is a good measure of success. Were you able to include all the features you had originally planned? Maybe you ended up adding more, in which case you should ask for a raise!

Browser testing

Certification Ready 2.2

What web page elements may not appear the same in different browsers, operating systems or on different devices?

A web browser is a program that renders HTML, CSS, and JavaScript files according to a set of rules built into the application. Although web browser manufacturers use the recommended guidelines of the Word Wide Web Consortium's specifications for HTML and CSS, they can interpet these rules as required for their own purposes. Browser manufacturers can also add their own rules to the specifications to add features to their browsers that are not available in others.

Throughout this book we have attempted to stay away from techniques that result in web page elements that may not look the same on different browsers and operating systems (or at least make it clear what the differences are and how to account for this). Here is a quick review of the page elements that are historically worth investigating:

- Form elements that have no styling look different on Mac versus PC. Controls such as buttons and scrollbars will use the operating system's default user interface. To a certain extent, CSS styles can standardize most of these controls.
- Rich media such as audio and video is dependent on the capabilities of the operating system and therefore may either use a different user interface for controls (such as a volume slider) or may simply not appear. Media that depends on a plug-in for functionality (such as Flash and/or Flash video) may not have support in the mobile environment.
- CSS styles that are not supported in specific browsers. There are a number of CSS selectors or properties that do not work consistently across all browsers, although Dreamweaver's browser compatibility reports can help identify these, the ultimate test is to check your pages in multiple browsers.
- CSS fonts and CSS3 web fonts. This issue is covered in multiple locations throughut the book, but essentially the guidelines are to use only the most common web fonts if using standard CSS and to be aware of browser compatibility for the latest CSS3 web fonts functionality.

Adobe BrowserLab

No matter how thorough your knowledge is of the various web page elements that might look different in different browsers, the ultimate test is to check for yourself. Typically, this is accomplished by using a separate machine than the one you have been working on. If you develop on a Mac, you can a use a PC and vice-versa. The problem with this approach is that it does not cover all the bases. It is impractical to have multiple browsers (and multiple versions of these browsers) on a machine.

This is where Adobe Browserlab enters the picture. Adobe BrowserLab is an online service that you can use as a stand-alone product or in conjunction with Adobe applications, such as Dreamweaver CS6. BrowserLab lets you preview your page in a number of different browsers and platforms, so you are not limited to Mac or PC.

1. Open a page you would like to test in multiple browsers. Open the Adobe BrowserLab panel if it is not currently open.
2. Click on the Preview button. BrowserLab is an online service that Adobe provides and the first time you use it you will have to enter an Adobe ID and password (or create one if you haven't already). Because the service requires your pages to be uploaded to Adobe's server, you will have to give permission for this by clicking Accept (Or Deny if you do not wish to give permission).

Certification Ready 2.2

How do you conduct cross-browser compatibility with the BrowserLab online service?

3. Your default web browser will automatically launch the BrowserLab site and begin to load the selected page. This may take a few moments as the site is converting your page to a static screenshot. Once the page is loaded you will see your page in a target web browser, for example Internet Explorer 6 on Windows. You can change the browser to use by clicking on the menu and choosing another option.

Take Note...

Because BrowserLab is a web-based service you should read the official documentation to learn all the features currently available, it may have changed since the time of this writing. http://help.adobe.com/en_US/cslive/cs/using/WS58a04a822e3e5010-7b304dbd1263439ac1b-8000.html

Step-by-Step

Follow these steps to create and upload files to your site

From this point forward, the exercise assumes that you have access to a remote FTP server.

1. If you're ready to upload your site to the remote web server, make sure that the Files panel is open. It is located under Window > Files.
2. Click the Expand button ( ) at the top of the Files panel to display it in two-column expanded view.
3. Click the Connect button ( ) above the left (remote view) column to connect to your remote web server.

Take Note...

To upload your site you need to have created a valid connection, as described earlier in the lesson.

Once a successful connection is made, the remote files (if any) display in the left-hand column.

4. In the right column, click and select the Folder icon at the very top of the file listing. This should be the root folder, and displays the current site definition title which is dw16lessons.

5. Click the Put button at the top of the Files panel to copy the entire current local site and all included files to the current directory on the remote server. As you can see in Figure 16-24, a dialog box appears with the message, *Are you sure you wish to put the entire site?*

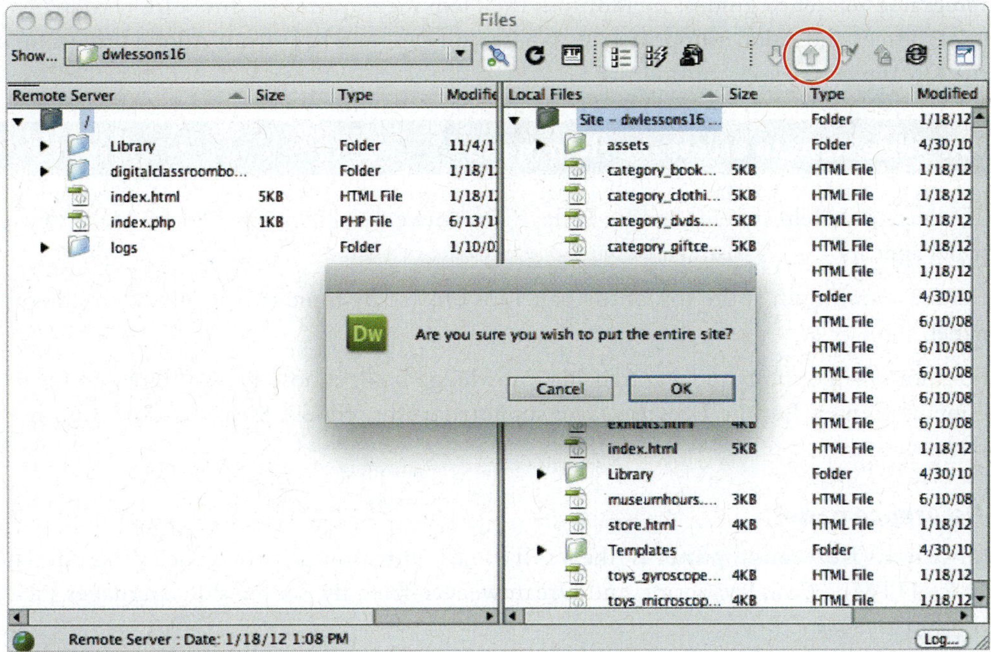

Figure 16-24: Select the root folder of your local site, and click the Put button to upload the entire site to the web server.

6. Press OK to begin copying the files to the remote server. The Background File Activity window appears, shown in Figure 16-25, with a progress bar and a list of the files being transferred.

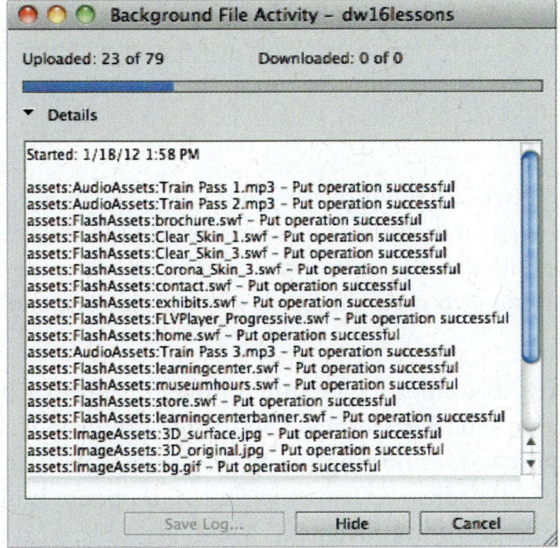

Figure 16-25: Files being transferred in the Background File Activity window.

7. Collapse the Files panel to return it to the dock. Your site is now live!

Getting help and using the reference guides

Whether you are seeking a solution to a Dreamweaver-specific problem, or looking up the appropriate CSS rule to format a page item, you can use Dreamweaver's built-in Help system and integrated reference guides. In addition, the Help menu provides direct links to many online resources and Adobe support areas where you can seek help from Adobe professionals and the Dreamweaver user community.

Step-by-Step

Follow these steps to access the Help menu

1. To access the Help system, choose Help > Dreamweaver Help. The Adobe Help Viewer panel appears.
2. Enter a search term at the top of the panel, or browse by topic on the left-hand side of the panel.
3. For more help options and a searchable knowledge base, choose Help > Dreamweaver Support Center. For the Dreamweaver support forums, choose Help > Adobe Online Forums.

The Reference panel

Dreamweaver's **Reference panel** is like a full library of technical books, including reference guides for HTML, CSS, JavaScript, and Dreamweaver-friendly, server-side languages such as ColdFusion and JSP.

Step-by-Step

Follow these steps to access the Reference panel

1. To open the Reference panel, choose Help > Reference.
2. From the menu at the top left corner of the panel, select the *Usablenet Accessibility Reference* from the Book menu.
3. Click on the Rule menu and a list of various guidelines to help you make your websites more accessible is listed. Choosing any topic reveals detailed information in the window below.

Site feedback and testing

Congratulations on launching your first Dreamweaver site project! There's nothing more exciting than having your hard work on the Web, and available for the world to see. The important thing to remember is that your website should not be static; part of maintaining a successful website requires continuously evolving it to meet the needs of your viewers, and keeping the content fresh and new.

Certification Ready 6.3

What are the methods for collecting view feedback and site evaluation information to determine if the site meets intended goals and user needs?

Whether your site is for business, pleasure, or self-promotion, be sure to solicit feedback from friends, family, and colleagues after you've launched. Alert a small and trusted group about the launch by sending out an e-mail, mailing a postcard, or posting a notice on a blog (sometimes this is referred to as the 'beta' stage). Feedback and constructive criticism (a little praise is okay, too) are the best ways to objectively know what needs improvement. You'll probably receive more feedback and suggestions than you can handle, so focus on points that are common across multiple users, and address any major issues before making a more public launch (for instance, to your entire client base).

Focus on focus groups

Focus groups are an excellent way to get non-biased feedback on a major new site or product launch, and they have been a regular practice in product marketing and research for years. A focus group is composed of a group of individuals who are brought together to analyze, try out, and comment on a specific product—in this case, your website—for the purpose of obtaining feedback and testing the product's effectiveness.

Groups can be guided through certain portions or processes on the site, or may be encouraged to navigate it on their own. Afterwards, they are polled with specific questions about their experience, and the results are put together to form a picture of the site's usability, effectiveness, and impact. This may include questions such as the following:

- Did you feel the website was easy to navigate? On a scale from 1 to 10, how would you rate the difficulty level in locating specific pages or topics?
- Did the design, including graphics and color themes, effectively help communicate the website's offerings?
- On a scale from 1 to 10, how would you rate the quality of the written content on the site?

Focus groups are often interactive, encouraging participants to talk with each other and share their opinions. In some cases, a moderator may be used to regulate group discussions, and hand out questionnaires. Participants can be composed of a focused demographic group (for instance, 25- to 35-year-old technology professionals), or they can represent a diverse professional and demographic range.

Focus groups are reasonable for any size company to organize—even if it's just you and five friends—and are a highly effective way to find out what's currently working and what's not. Give it a try; you may find the results encouraging, surprising, or even slightly discouraging. The trick is to use this feedback wisely toward the main purpose of making a better website, and you'll be glad you did.

Certification Ready 6.2

What are the elements involved in conducting a website usability test?

Website design resources

There is a vast amount of information, and many tutorial-based websites, covering topics from web page standards to advanced CSS design. Here is a small sampling of some useful sites that can help you take your skills and knowledge further. Use these in conjunction with Dreamweaver's built-in reference guides and Adobe's online support forums:

- W3C (World Wide Web Consortium)—*www.w3.org*
- W3Schools—*www.w3schools.com*
- A List Apart—*http://alistapart.com/*
- Adobe's Dreamweaver Developer Center—*www.adobe.com/devnet/dreamweaver/*
- CSS Zengarden—*www.csszengarden.com/*
- maxdesign—*http://css.maxdesign.com.au/*
- CSSplay—*www.cssplay.co.uk/www*

Skill Summary

In this lesson you learned how to:	Objective
Demonstrate knowledge of website accessibility standards that address the needs of people with visual and motor impairments	1.4
Produce website designs that work equally well on various operating systems, browser versions/configurations, and devices.	2.2
Communicate with others (such as peers and clients) about design plans	2.6
Add head content to make a web page visible to search engines	5.7
Conduct technical tests	6.1
Identify techniques for basic usability tests	6.2
Identify methods for collecting site feedback	6.3
Manage assets, links, and files for a site	6.4
Publish and update site files to a remote server	6.5

Knowledge Assessment

True/False

Circle T if the statement is true or F if the statement is False.

T F **1.** The site setup window allows you create a remote connection to a server.

T F **2.** The only way to connect to a remote server in Dreamweaver is via FTP.

T F **3.** After defining a remote server you can begin to transfer files using the Files panel.

T F **4.** It is optional that you test your connection after defining a remote server.

T F **5.** To upload files to a remote server you can only use the "Put" button.

T F **6.** Design Notes can be shared with other collaborators of a website.

T F **7.** Orphaned files are documents that are not linked to or used by any document within a site.

T F **8.** The Site Reports panel only lists technical issues discovered in your site, it does not allow you to fix them.

T F **9.** The Link Checker feature allows you to check for broken links on both the local and remote server.

T F **10.** Dreamweaver will allow you to view and validate external hyperlinks on your site.

Multiple Choice

Select the best response for the following statements.

1. When creating an FTP remote connection which of the following is optional?
- **a.** user login
- **b.** user password
- **c.** FTP address
- **d.** Web URL

2. SFTP stands for _______
- **a.** SSH File Transfer Protocol
- **b.** Secure File Transfer Protocol
- **c.** Security File Transfer Protocol
- **d.** Server File Transfer Protocol

3. You can view the files on your remote server by doing which of the following?
- **a.** Pressing the Connect button in the Files panel
- **b.** Pressing the Test button in the Site Setup window
- **c.** Pressing the Refresh button in the Files Panel after you have defined a testing server
- **d.** None of the above

4. When you upload an html file from your local server to a remote server for the first time, what message are you likely to receive?
- **a.** A message asking you to enter a user login and/or password.
- **b.** A message prompting you to Save All site files
- **c.** A message asking if you would like to include dependent files.
- **d.** A message asking if you would like to run the Link Checker.

5. Which of the following features can you display in the files panel?
- **a.** Design Notes
- **b.** Broken Links
- **c.** Invalid document
- **d.** Orphaned Files

6. When you run a report the results you receive can fall into which of the following sets?
- **a.** Question Mark, Red X, Warning Sign
- **b.** Red light, Yellow light, Green ligh
- **c.** Error, Possible problem, Recommendation
- **d.** Invalid, Valid, Warning

Competency Assessment

You are about to go live with your website and want to be sure that it is as optimized for search engines as possible.

Search Engine Optimization — Project 16-1

1. Open the **toys_gyroscope.html** file.
2. Choose Insert > HTML > Head Tags > Keywords.

3. You need to add approximately 9–10 words that customers might use in a search engine that would take them to this page. Type the following keywords separated by commas: **physics, fun, science, toys, museum, gyroscope, learning, science toys, physics toys, store, science store**.
4. Choose Insert > HTML > Head Tags > Description.
5. You need to write a short description of this page. Think of how the description would allow potential customers to understand what is on the page if they were to read the description in search engine results. Type the following in the description field: **Our museum gift shop offers many fun science toys including the Super Gyroscope, it makes physics cool!** Click OK when done.
6. Save the file.

Project 16-2 Collaborating with team members

You are one member of a team working on a website. Your other team members are working on multiple projects and some of them work remotely. You need to establish an easy way to communicate the changes that have been done (or need to be done).

1. Open the **ex1_aeronautics.html** file from the current site.
2. Choose File > Design Notes. The Design Notes dialog box appears.
3. Type the following in the Notes field: **Hi Jane, this page has a number of typos, can you fix them and check the other pages when you have a chance? Thanks!**
4. Check the Status menu and choose Needs Attention. Also check the Show when file is opened checkbox.
5. Press OK to create the Design Note.
6. To make sure the Design Note works, close this document and reopen it. The Design Note window will appear. Click OK and then close your document.

Proficiency Assessment

Project 16-3 Defining a site for remote access

You are beginning the process of starting a new website and need to setup a site for remote connection.

1. Using the Site Setup window define a new site named Museum. The folder you should use for this site is named "Museum_Proficiency" and is provided in the dw16lessons folder.
2. Define a server for this site and enter in the following information for the FTP server: **mcknight-center.org**, username: **admin** and password: **90120**. (This information is fictional and for assessment purposes only.)

   Leave Dreamweaver open for the next exercise.

Project 16-4 Checking Links

You have a nearly-finished site that is about to launch, but you need to check all the pages and make sure there are no broken links.

1. If necessary, open the Museum_Profiecency site defined in the last project.
2. Locate all the broken links on these pages and fix them automatically.

   Close Dreamweaver.

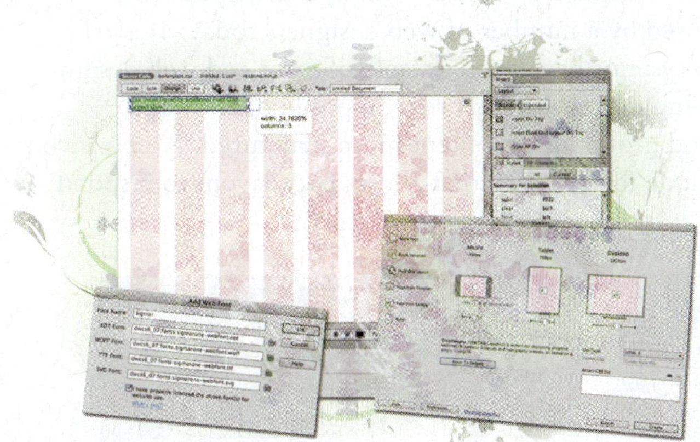

Dreamweaver CS6 New Features

Key Terms

- @font-face
- jQuery Mobile Framework
- jQuery Mobile Swatches
- W3C Validation
- World Wide Web Consortium

Business Case

Your performance review is coming up shortly, and one of the questions that will be asked is how you are keeping up with current technology. In order to answer this, you should have a familiarity with the latest features in Dreamweaver CS6.

What's new in Dreamweaver CS6?

The version of Dreamweaver prior to CS6 was Dreamweaver CS5.5; the fact that Adobe released a ".5" version might indicate that Adobe is increasing the speed at which it releases updates. This increase in speed makes sense for a program such as Dreamweaver, due to the speed at which web technology evolves. In fact, most of the major additions in 5.5 were new features for the rapidly evolving landscape of mobile design, including the Multiscreen feature (with support for CSS3 media queries), support for jQuery mobile, and support for the development of iOS and Android applications using the Phonegap Framework, among others.

Some of the new features in 5.5 have been integrated into the exercises in this book, most notably in Lesson 15, "Mobile Design and Layout." However, given that many users might have upgraded directly to Dreamweaver CS6 from CS5, we cover the 5.5 features in a separate section at the end of this lesson.

Dreamweaver CS6 introduces three major new features: Fluid Grid Layout, CSS3 Transitions, and Web Font Integration. These features have also been integrated into some of the lessons in this book, primarily in Lesson 15, "Mobile Design and Layout" and Lesson 7, "CSS3 Transitions and Web Fonts." In addition to these major new features, there are a few upgrades to pre-existing features such as Business Catalyst, jQuery Mobile, and PhoneGap.

Fluid Grid Layout

Dreamweaver's new Fluid Grid Layout feature (Figure 17-1) is essentially a combination of two advanced layout techniques currently used by a number of web designers today: 1) a grid system; and 2) responsive web design. Grid systems have been a staple of print and web design for many years, and involve the designer using a "grid" structure (composed of rows and columns) on a page to make the aligning and grouping of content more structured. Responsive web design is a relatively new layout technique for the Web that allows page layout to respond or adapt based on the user's screen size.

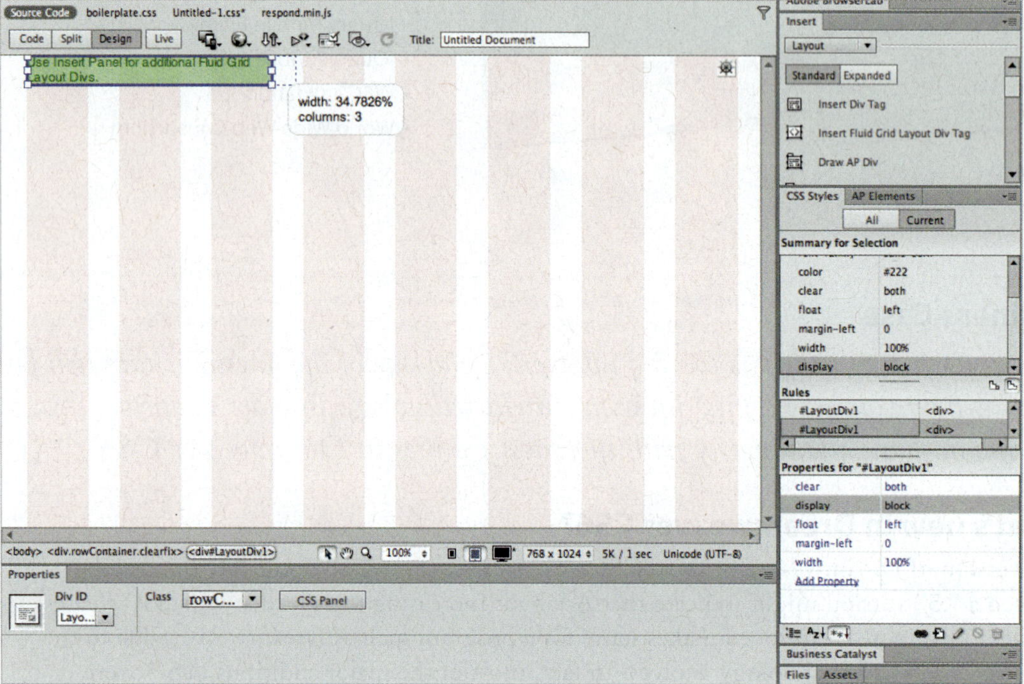

Figure 17-1: An empty Fluid Grid Layout page with its default columns.

Fluid Grid Layout allows a designer or developer to build a new page with an empty grid, and then add Fluid Grid Layout Divs into which they can add content such as text and images. These layout containers are unique in that they snap to the grid columns (Figure 17-2), but just as importantly, you can also control the way the layout containers appear based on the size of the user's screen. For example, you could create a five-column layout for users with extremely wide desktop monitors; and users with small screen sizes, such as mobile phones, would see just a single-column layout.

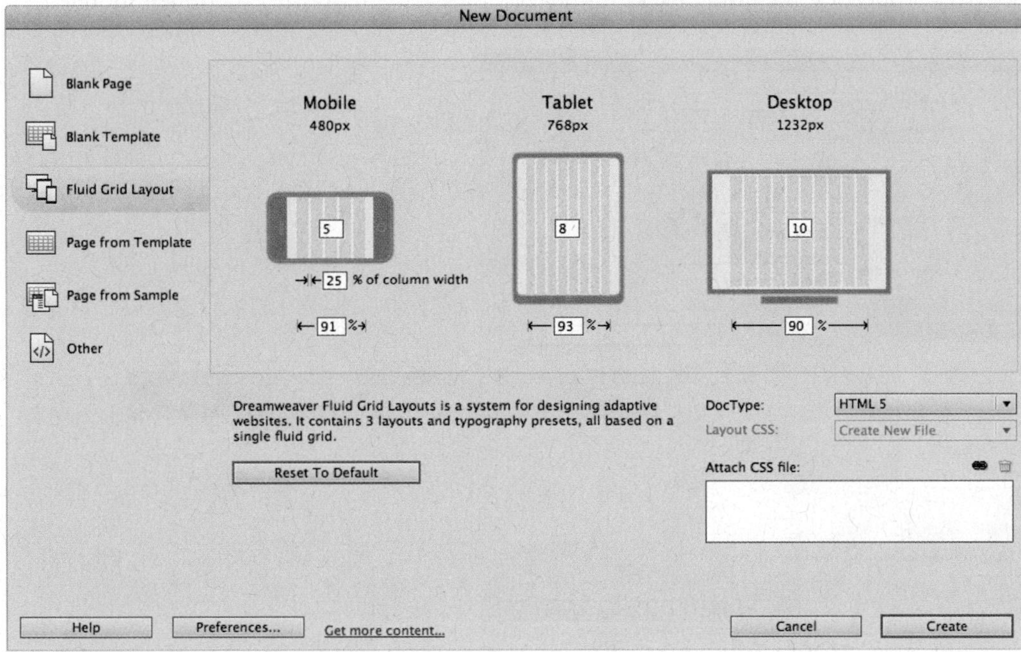

***Figure 17-2**: The Fluid Grid feature creates three layouts by default: one for mobile screens, one for tablets, and one for desktops.*

The goal of Fluid Grids is to allow your website to respond or adapt to the user's screen while maintaining the degree of structure and composition that a grid layout provides.

CSS transitions

Dreamweaver CS6 has a new CSS Transitions feature that includes the ability to add animation effects to objects on your page. An example of a transition is a button that gradually changes color when the user hovers over it, known as a rollover effect (Figure 17-3). In previous versions of Dreamweaver, you had to use some form of JavaScript to create a rollover effect, perhaps even use one of the Spry effects (which are JavaScript). CSS Transitions in Dreamweaver are built with CSS3 syntax that allows you to set the duration, delay, and easing of many CSS properties, including background-color, opacity, font-size, and much more.

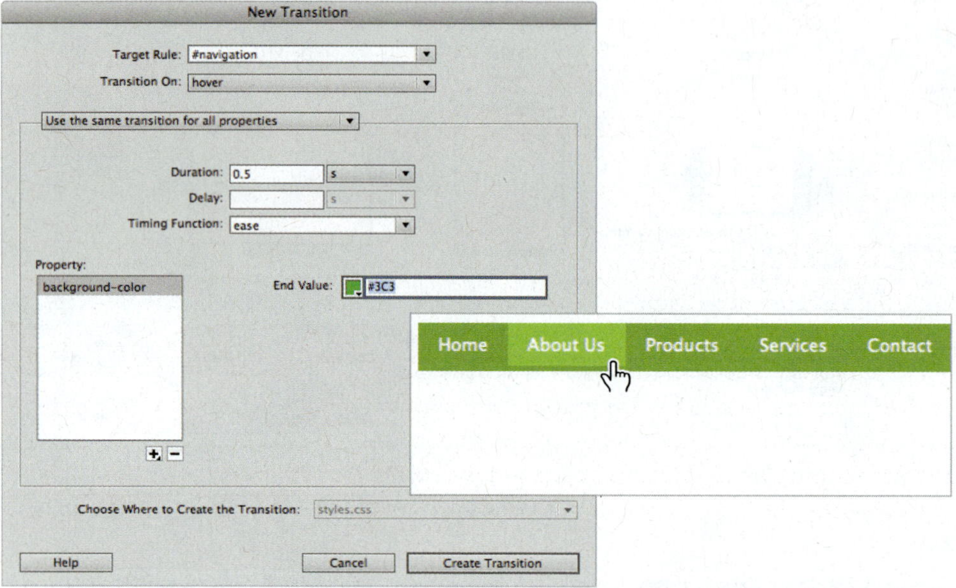

***Figure 17-3**: CSS Transitions allow you to add effects, such as an animated navigation menu with fade effects.*

One of the benefits of CSS Transitions is that you can create basic visual effects within Dreamweaver without JavaScript or Flash. A good use of transitions, for example, is to create a smooth fading effect on the user interface, such as menus.

Web fonts

Dreamweaver CS6 takes major steps toward addressing the lack of choice in fonts to use on the Web with the new Web Fonts feature (Figure 17-4). This feature takes advantage of the `@font-face` property in CSS3 to give Dreamweaver users a much easier way to add new fonts to their page. When you choose Modify > Web Fonts, the Web Fonts Manager appears, allowing you to link to any commercially-licensed web font you want to embed on your page.

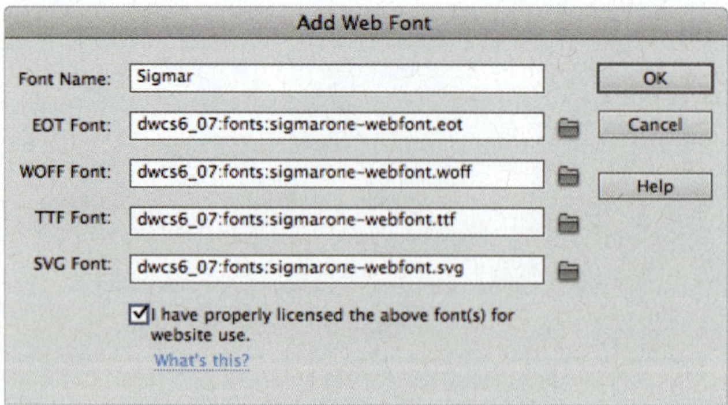

***Figure 17-4**: Adding a web font to your site requires linking to the font files in your local folder.*

After you embed a specific web font on your page, you can easily apply the style of the font using the Property Inspector. The addition of web fonts in Dreamweaver means it is quite easy to add unique styles to page elements such as headings and still maintain the benefits of CSS (Figure 17-5).

***Figure 17-5**: A heading with a Web Font style applied.*

jQuery Mobile Swatches

Dreamweaver CS5.5 introduced support for jQuery Mobile (see the following section New Features in Dreamweaver CS5.5 for a full description). In addition to the features found in the previous version, there is now the addition of **jQuery Mobile Swatches** in CS6. This feature allows you to quickly style jQuery layout elements as well as user interface elements by dragging and dropping color swatches onto your page. You can choose from a preset number of element themes within Dreamweaver as well as download additional themes for your use. This feature is accessed within a jQuery site by choosing Window > jQuery Mobile Swatches.

PhoneGap Build Service

This feature is an upgrade of the PhoneGap integration introduced in Dreamweaver CS5.5 (see the following section New Features in Dreamweaver CS5.5 for a full description). The PhoneGap Build Service allows you to connect with your online PhoneGap account in order to build native applications for the following mobile operating systems: iOS, Android, Blackberry, webOS and symbian. This integration dramatically reduces the complexity involved in compiling these applications and also provides online emulators as well as the ability to download your compiled applications from your PhoneGap account. This feature can be accessed by choosing Site > PhoneGap Build Service.

New Features in Dreamweaver CS5.5

The Multiscreen Preview option and the related CSS3 Media Queries are perhaps the biggest change in Dreamweaver CS5.5, but there are several other new additions, many of which are related to mobile design and development.

CSS3 and HTML5 authoring support

Dreamweaver CS5.5 has added to its internal library of code many of the new HTML5 elements and CSS3 styles. Examples of HTML5 elements now available include `<header>`, `<nav>`, `<aside>`, and others (Figure 17-6). In previous versions of Dreamweaver, there was no code that indicated the use of these elements. Users could still add the elements, but they were not readily available in Dreamweaver's code-hinting interface.

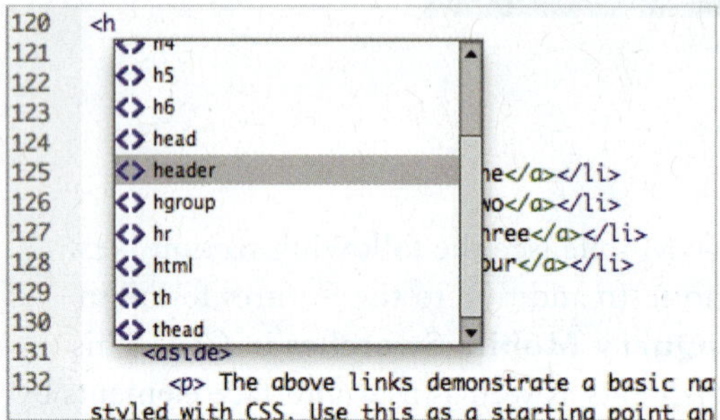

Figure 17-6: *You can easily create HTML5 pages in Dreamweaver with code-hinting support for the new HTML5 elements.*

Similarly, CSS3 includes several new styles to help you enhance your pages, including features such as rounded corners, gradients, border images, and more. These CSS3 properties are now readily available in Dreamweaver's code-hinting library (Figure 17-7). (This library also includes the vendor-specific prefixes needed to ensure that styles are visible on specific browsers, such as Firefox, Chrome, Safari, and Internet Explorer.)

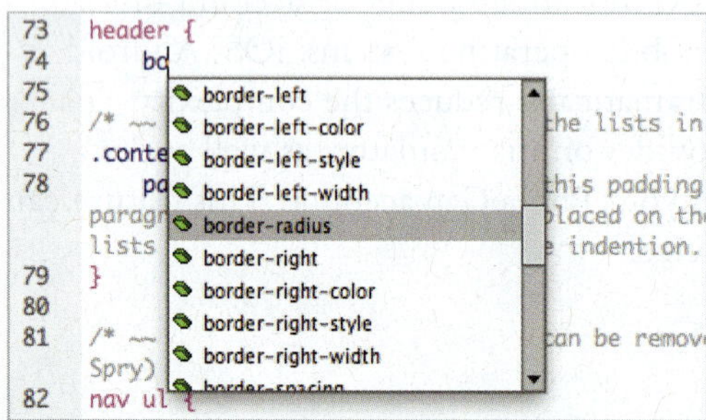

Figure 17-7: *You can easily add CSS3 styling in Dreamweaver with code-hinting support for the new CSS3 styles.*

jQuery Mobile integration

Designers and developers who need to create web pages and user interfaces optimized for mobile devices can create Dreamweaver projects using the jQuery Mobile Framework. jQuery is generally used for desktop applications to enhance websites with the reliable JavaScript code included in this open-source JavaScript library. The **jQuery Mobile Framework** is a relatively new addition that lets you add features such as animations and components for touchscreen interfaces, form field validation, pattern matching, and more.

You can create a site optimized for mobile by choosing File > New Page From Sample > jQuery Mobile to open a layout that has placeholder content and several built-in user interface features (Figure 17-8). Some examples of these built-in interface features are a multi-page design with styles formatted for mobile, animated pages and collapsible panels, and buttons designed for the touch-sensitive capabilities of smartphones, tablets, and other touch-enabled screens.

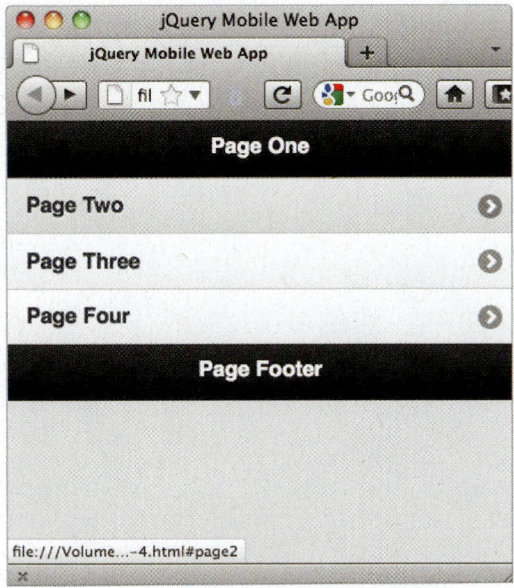

***Figure 17-8**: The default layout for a jQuery Mobile project includes page elements targeted for touchscreen interfaces.*

Support for building native mobile apps for iOS and Android with PhoneGap

In addition to the jQuery Mobile support, designers and developers can now use Dreamweaver to build native applications for iOS and Android applications with help from the **PhoneGap Framework**. This framework packages HTML, CSS, and JavaScript files into native applications to let designers and developers with limited or no programming nowledge build native apps.

You can build an entire site as a native application by choosing Site > Mobile Applications > Build. For the Android operating system, Dreamweaver helps install the necessary SDKs on your system using the Easy Install option. For iOS, you need to manually install Apple's Xcode or the Apple iOS SDK to compile the applications from Dreamweaver.

Take Note...
You can create native applications for Android or iOS with Dreamweaver CS5.5 or CS6 and support from the PhoneGap framework.

W3C Validation

Designers and developers have long used the **World Wide Web Consortium** (W3C) as a resource to help troubleshoot problems. The W3C provides a free service that checks HTML, XHMTL, and CSS documents for syntax errors. In the past, you would have had to go to the W3C website and either upload your file, or copy and paste your code into their web interface. Starting with the release of CS5.5, Dreamweaver now allows you to send your file directly by clicking the W3C button at the top of your document window. The results then appear within a W3C Validation window in Dreamweaver. **W3C Validation** is a built-in validation engine in Dreamweaver allowing authors of an HTML document to check for conformance to HTML or XHTML standards.

Adobe Web Communication Using Dreamweaver CS6 Objectives

Skill	Objective	Lesson
Setting Project Requirements	1	
Identify the purpose, audience, and audience needs for a website	1.1	1
Identify web page content that is relevant to the website purpose and appropriate for the target audience	1.2	1
Demonstrate knowledge of standard copyright rules (related terms, obtaining permission, and citing copyrighted material)	1.3	3
Demonstrate knowledge of website accessibility standards that address the needs of people with visual and motor impairments	1.4	3, 16
Make website development decisions based on your analysis and interpretation of design specification	1.5	1
Understand project management tasks and responsibilities	1.6	1
Planning Site Design and Page Layout	2	
Demonstrate general and Dreamweaver-specific knowledge of best practices for designing a website, such as maintaining consistency, separating content from design, using standard fonts, and utilizing visual hierarchy	2.1	1, 4, 5, 6
Produce website designs that work equally well on various operating systems, browser versions/configurations, and devices	2.2	15, 16
Demonstrate knowledge of page layout design concepts and principles	2.3	6
Identify basic principles of website usability, readability, and accessibility	2.4	3
Demonstrate knowledge of flowcharts, storyboards, and wireframes to create web pages and a site map that maintain the planned website hierarchy	2.5	1
Communicate with others (such as peers and clients) about design plans	2.6	16
Understanding the Adobe Dreamweaver CS6 Interface	3	
Identify elements of the Dreamweaver interface	3.1	1, 2, 9
Use the Insert bar	3.2	9
Use the Property Inspector	3.3	3
Use the Assets Panel	3.4	1, 10
Use the Files panel	3.5	2
Customize the workspace	3.6	9

Skill	Objective	Lesson
Adding Content by Using Dreamweaver CS6	4	
Demonstrate knowledge of Hypertext Markup Language	4.1	3
Define a Dreamweaver site	4.2	2
Create, title, name, and save a web page	4.3	1, 2
Add text to a web page	4.4	1, 3
Insert images and apply alternative text on a web page	4.5	1, 3
Link web content, using hyperlinks, e-mail links, and named anchors	4.6	3
Include video and sound in a web page	4.7	10
Add animation and interactivity to content	4.8	7, 10
Insert navigation bars, rollover images, and buttons created in a drawing program on a web page	4.9	14
Build image maps	4.10	3
Import tabular data to a web page	4.11	8
Import and display a Microsoft Word or Microsoft Excel document to a web page	4.12	3
Create forms	4.13	13
Organizing Content by Using Dreamweaver CS6	5	
Set and modify document properties	5.1	2, 4
Organize web page layout with relative and absolutely-positioned div tags and CSS styles.	5.2	4, 5, 7
Modify text and text properties	5.3	3, 4, 7, 14
Modify images and image properties	5.4	3
Create web page templates	5.5	11
Use basic HTML tags to set up an HTML document, format text, add links, create tables, and build ordered and unordered lists	5.6	12
Add head content to make a web page visible to search engines	5.7	16
Use CSS to implement a reusable design	5.8	4, 6
Evaluating and Maintaining a Site by Using Dreamweaver CS6	6	
Conduct technical tests	6.1	3, 6, 15, 16
Identify techniques for basic usability tests	6.2	16
Identify methods for collecting site feedback	6.3	16
Manage assets, links, and files for a site	6.4	1, 2, 3, 16
Publish and update site files to a remote server	6.5	16

Glossary

@font-face Special syntax within CSS3 that enables you to embed web fonts in a page.

<form> Tag The element used to define a section of the page that contains one or more form elements.

A

Absolute Positioning A CSS term that refers to the manner in which an element is positioned relative to its first positioned ancestor element.

Absolute Hyperlink Absolute hyperlink paths provide the complete URL of the linked document, including the protocol (usually http:// for web pages). You must use an absolute path to link to a document or asset on another server.

AJAX Acronym for Asynchronous JavaScript and XML.

AP Div A feature in Dreamweaver that creates an absolutely positioned (AP) div element on the page for layout purposes.

B

Behaviors A feature within Dreamweaver that allows you to add scripting events to the elements on your Web page.

Border property A CSS property that allows you to set a border width, color and style for any or all four sides of a box.

Box Model The CSS box model refers to the fact that all HTML elements can be styled as a box with four sides. Any (or all) of these four sides can also use the following properties: margin, padding and border.

Browser Font Support The ability of a desktop browser to support font embedding via the `@font-face` CSS declaration. Specifically the ability to support one of the four available font formats (.ttf, .eot, .woff, .svg).

Browser plug-in A set of software components that adds specific abilities to a web browser. Examples include Flash Player, Quicktime and Windows Media Player.

C

Cascading Style Sheets see **CSS**.

CellPad Refers to space inside of a table cell (commonly referred to as "padding) between your element and the sides of the table

Cells A component of an HTML table. The The `<td>` tag defines a standard cell in an HTML table.

CellSpace Refers to the space between table cells.

Check In/Check Out A feature in Dreamweaver that allows users in a collaborative web environment to download files from a remote web server and lock them in order to prevent other users from modifiying them.

Check Links A feature that checks a page or series of pages for hyperlinks that have incorrect paths.

Checkbox A component of an HTML form used to allow the user to select several options.

Clear Property A property in CSS often used in conjunction with HTML elements that have the CSS float property applied.

Elements that have been "cleared" do not allow floated elements to either the left, right or both sides.

Code Hinting A feature within Dreamweaver's Code View that displays code from a specific code library as the user begins to type.

Code Navigator Allows you to see the CSS files and rules that are affecting the current selection within the Design/Code View and jump directly to the code.

Code View A view in Dreamweaver which displays the source code of a document.

Coding Toolbar The collection of code-specific icons and features available for use when in Dreamweaver's Code View.

Column Layouts The broad term used to describe web page layout, most often by using a combination of div elements that have been assigned CSS styles.

Columns Can refer to table columns or css columns. There is no HTML tag or CSS property for a column.

Comments A comment is descriptive text that you insert in HTML code to explain the code or provide other information.

Contextual Selectors A specific CSS rule that consists of two or more simple selectors separated by a white space. Used to specifically target an HTML element. For example the contextual selector `#main h1` would allows you to style only the heading 1 elements within the ID named "main."

Cross-browser Compatibility The technique for identifying HTML or CSS code that could cause potential browser-support problems. A web page is said to be "cross-browser compatible" when there are no significant visual differences between a baseline browser and specified comparison browsers.

CSS (Cascading Style Sheets) is a simple language that works alongside HTML to apply formatting to content in web pages, such as text, images, tables, and form elements.

CSS Class styles Class styles can be applied to any HTML element in a document. All class styles are displayed in the CSS Styles panel with a period [.] preceding their name and in the Style pop-up menu of the text Property inspector. Unlike ID styles, Class styles can be reused multiple times per page.

CSS Floats Refers to the CSS float property which is often used to position div elements in order to create layout columns.

CSS IDs ID styles can be applied to any HTML element in a document. All class styles are displayed in the CSS Styles panel with a hash tag [#] preceding their name and in the Style pop-up menu of the text Property inspector. Unlike Class styles, ID styles can only be used one time per page.

CSS Rules A CSS rule automates the formatting of HTML tags or a range of text identified by class or ID attributes.

CSS Selector CSS selectors are used to select the element(s) you want to style within an HTML document.

CSS Styles The broad term generally used for the collection of CSS rules and properties affecting a page element.

CSS Transitions A component of CSS3 that allows you to create animated effects with various CSS properties such as width, height, background-color and many others.

CSS Web Fonts A component of CSS3 that allows you to embed custom fonts in a page. Unlike the standard CSS font property, users do not have to have fonts installed on their system in order to view them.

CSS3 Cascading Style Sheets 3.0. Refers to the latest features available for web page design. Includes multiple categories such as media queries, transitions, web fonts and many others. Not all features of CSS3 are supported in current browsers.

CSS3 Media Queries Web technology that allows a browser to detect the user's screen capabilties and send them a custom style sheet for the screen size.

D

Design The creative process used to convey a specific message (or messages) to an audience. In the context of the Web, it is referred to as the combination of typography, visual elements and page layout that creates the look and feel of a web page or website.

Design Notes A feature in Dreamweaver that allows users in a collaborative environment to add a virtual note to an HTML document in order to communicate information.

Detach From Template A feature of Dreamweaver templates that allows you to remove an attached HTML page from a master template. Pages that are detached are completely editable and are no longer updated when the master template is modified.

Div Tags The div tag in html (`<div>`) is often combined with a CSS class or ID style in order to create layout blocks of content that are positioned and styled in your document.

Document Tiling The ability to align multiple documents in Dreamweaver either vertically or horizontally.

E

Easing An term used to describe the ability to accelerate or decelerate animations. Most typically used in Dreamweaver with CSS3 transitions.

Editable Regions A feature of Dreamweaver templates that allows you to define areas of the attached HTML files as editable. Areas that are not editable cannot be modified.

External Style Sheets The collection of CSS rules that define the appearance HTML elements. The location of these rules are located in an external file with the extension .css. This document is referred to as an "eternal style sheet" and is linked to one or many HTML pages.

F

Favorites A category within the Insert panel that allows you to add various items of the Insert panel into a single group.

File Upload Field A component of an HTML form that allows the user to browse their system and upload a file.

Flash Player Adobe's cross-platform, browser plug-in that provides viewing of Flash content.

Flash Video A container file format used to deliver video over the Internet using Adobe Flash Player.

Fluid Grid Layout A feature of Dreamweaver CS6 that allows you to create a fluid layout HTML5 based site optimized for phone, tablet and desktop.

Font Licensing Refers to the legal terms of a font that is being used in a published web page. A font that a user has purchased may be licensed for print, may not be licensed for web use, particularly when using Dreamweaver's Web Font feature.

Form Validation The process of checking the contents of specified form fields to ensure that the user has entered the correct type of data. Typically accomplished with Behaviors (JavaScript) in Dreamweaver.

Formatting Code The process of automatically aligning or rewriting code according to a set of rules. In Dreamweaver this can be done by choosing Commands > Apply Formatting.

Forms A collection of form elements on a page. Typically include a mechanism to process data your visitors submit on a page.

FTP Stands for File Transfer Protocol. A system used to transfer documents from your local system to a remote server (and vice-versa).

G

Get The term used in Dreamweaver when downloading files from a remote site.

Grids A visual aid in Dreamwaver's design view used to assist in layout such as aligning page elements.

Guides A guide is a thin horizontal or vertical line often used as a visual aid for layout.

H

Hexadecimal color The default method for specifying colors on a web page. A hexadecimal value is preceded by a hash sign. Hexadecimal numbers use some combination of the digits 0–9 and the letters A–F and are either 3 digits or 6 digits long.

HTML Hypertext Markup Language. Provides the structure of a web document.

Hyperlinks The technique used to create connections from your documents to other documents in HTML.

I

Image Formats There are a number of of graphic file formats in existence, but three are generally used in web pages—GIF, JPEG, and PNG.

Image Resolution Image resolution refers to the number of pixels, on a linear inch of an image. Often referred to as PPI (or occasionally DPI), web graphics are set to 72 PPI.

Inheritance In CSS inheritance refers to the fact that certain properties in a style sheet inherit the values of their parent. For example if the body style defines text color as red, a paragraph nested within the body will also be red.

Internal Style Sheets The collection of CSS rules that define the appearance HTML elements. The location of these rules are located in the head section of an HTML document and apply to that document alone.

J

jQuery Mobile Framework Integrated support in Dreamweaver for documents that use the open source jQuery Mobile ibrary for sites designed for mobile.

jQuery Mobile Swatches Integrated support for a theming system that allows you to style elements of a page using the jQuery Mobile Framework.

L

Library Items A feature in Dreamweaver that allows you to reuse a section of code throughout your websites. If one or more library items have been added to a page they can be updated by editing the original.

List Item A single item in an HTML unordered or ordered list. Also known as the `<li>` tag.

List-based Navigation A common technique that creates site navigation using a combination an HTML list and CSS styling.

Lists In HTML you can create numbered (ordered) lists, bulleted (unordered) lists, and definition lists from existing text or from new text as you type in the Document window.

Live View Allows you to preview a web page (or pages) as it would appear in a browser, without leaving Dreamweaver.

M

Margins In the CSS box model the margin property adds space to the outside of a box (on any or all sides).

Markup language System for annotating (marking up) a document in syntax that is different than the plain text.

Merging Cells The act of combining two or more cells within a row in order to create a larger single cell

Metatags Special HTML tags located in the head section and using the `<Meta>` tag. Are read and used solely by web browsers and robots and are not rendered on the page.

Mobile First The practice of designing a website for a mobile device first and then adding features for larger screens such as tablet and deskop.

Mobile Optimization The process of customizing the appearance of a page (typically with CSS) for a particular mobile screen size.

Mobile Web The generic term for websites that are optimized for devices with smaller screens such as smartphones and tablets.

Multiscreen Preview A feature in Dreamweaver that allows you to preview a web page in multiple screen resolutions and initiate the process of creating media queries for each.

P

Padding In the CSS box model the padding property adds space to the inside of a box (on any or all sides).

Page Properties A dialog box that allows you to specify the default font family and font size, background color, margins, link styles, and other aspects of page design.

Panel Groups A set of related panels docked together below one heading.

Panels A section of the Dreamweaver workspace dedicated to a single feature such as the CSS Styles panel.

PhoneGap A service that allows you to compile HTML, CSS and JavaScript web pages into native applications for mobile devices including iOS and Android.

Preview in Browser A command in Dreamweaver that allows you to preview a page in a browser at any time (without the need for uploading it to a server).

Progressive Download Describes the transfer of digital media files from a server to a client. The consumer can play the media before the download is complete and the video file is saved on the user's computer.

Property Inspector Allows you to examine and edit the most common properties for the currently selected page element, such as text or an inserted object. The contents of the Property inspector vary depending on the element(s) selected.

Pseudo-class A pseudo-class selectors in CSS is typically associated with hyperlinks and allows you to create styles for the different "states" of a hyperlink, specifically `a:link`, `a:visited`, `a:hover`, and `a:active`.

Put The term used in Dreamweaver when uploading files from a remote site.

Q

Quick Tag Editor A feature in Dreamweaver used to to select, edit, or remove HTML tags without leaving Design view.

QuickTime Apple's proprietary container file format used to deliver video.

R

Radio Button A component of an HTML form used to allow the user to select only one item from a group of options.

Radio Group A component of an HTML form in that combine multiple radio buttons into a single entity.

Reference Panel A panel in Dreamweaver that contains reference documentation on HTML tags, JavaScript objects, and CSS styles.

Relative Hyperlink Usually best for local links in your websites. They're used when the current document and the linked document or asset are in the same folder and are likely to remain together.

Relative Positioning A CSS term that refers to the manner in which element is positioned relative to its normal position.

Remote Connection The method used to enable the upload and download of files to and from your web server, using Dreamweaver.

Remote Folder The remote folder that holds the files that users access on the Internet and is typically on the computer where your web server is running. Dreamweaver refers to this folder as your "remote site" in the Files panel.

Remote Web Server The location where site files are hosted so that people can view them online.

Reset Button A component of an HTML form that will clear existing form data when activated by the user.

Root Folder Stores the files you're working on referred to in Dreamweaver as your "local site." Typically on your local computer, but it can also be on a network server.

Rows A component of an HTML table. The `<tr>` tag defines a row. A row is divided into one or more cells.

Rule Definition The CSS rule definition dialog box displays CSS styles by category and allows you to add style options for a new CSS rule or modify and/or delete style options for existing CSS rules.

S

Search Engine Optimization The process of structuring the HTML and CSS code of your site in order to best expose the content to search engines.

Selector CSS syntax that defines which HTML elements you are going to be manipulating with CSS code. A selector needs to have at least one property and one value to have an effect in your document.

Server / Web Hosts In the context of the Web, a server is a computer program used to serve the requests of other programs, such as a web browser client. A web host is the company or entity that maintains the server for a website.

Server Name A field located in the Server section of the Site Setup dialog box that identifies which server the site definition belongs to.

Site In Dreamweaver refers to a local or remote storage location for the documents that belong to a website.

Site Management Allows you to create a new site, edit an existing site, duplicate a site, remove a site, or import/export a site's settings.

Site Reports A Dreamweaver feature that tests and troubleshoots your entire site based on a number of criteria.

Sound Allows you to enhance web pages by supplementing visual content with music or sound effects.

Snippets A feature in Dreamweaver that allows you to reuse a section of code throughout your websites Once a snippet has been added to a page there is no way to automatically update it.

Split View The view in Dreamweaver that displays the Design view and the Code view side by side.

Spry Accordion Panel One of Dreamweaver's Spry Widgets that allow you to create an interactive container with multiple sections that expand horizontally when activated.

Spry Assets The folder created and saved in the root folder whenever a Spry Widget is added to a page. The Spry Assets folder contains items including .js, .css and image files needed in order for the Spry Widget to work correctly.

Spry Collapsible Panel One of Dreamweaver's Spry Widgets that panel allows you to store content in a compact space. Users hide or reveal the content stored in the Collapsible Panel by clicking the tab of the widget.

Spry Framework Adobe's JavaScript library that allows you to add interactive elements (Spry Widgets and Spry Effects) to your web pages.

Spry Menu One of Dreamweaver's Spry Widgets that allow you to create an interactive navigation menu.

Spry Repeat List A data object that is part of a Spry Region. The Repeat list can display data from an XML data source file and be styled with CSS.

Spry Tabbed Panel One of Dreamweaver's Spry Widgets that allow you to create two or more interactive tabbed sections within a page.

Spry Widget A page element that enables user interaction such as menus and accordion panels. A Spry Widget consists of HTML for structure, CSS for style and JavaScript for user initiated events.

Spry XML Data Set A JavaScript object that you can use to display data from an XML data source file on a web page.

Streaming Video Describes the transfer of digital media files from a server to a client. The consumer can play the media before the download is complete but the video file is not saved on the user's computer.

Submit Button A component of an HTML form that sends form data to a server for processing.

Syntax The rules that define how a particular language such as HTML, CSS or JavaScript should be written and formed.

T

Tables Refers to the HTML `<table>` tag. Intended to display data aligned in rows, columns and cells.

Tablet Layout An option within Dreamweaver's Fluid Grid Layout that is optimized for tablet device screen sizes.

Tabular Data Refers to data that has been exported from a spreadsheet and can be formatted by Dreamweaver as a table.

Tag In Dreamweaver, commonly used name for HTML tags. There are opening and closing tags and a pair of tags is referred to as an element.

Tag Chooser Allows you to insert any tag from the Dreamweaver tag libraries in your page.

Tag Selector A feature in Dreamweaver that exposes the HTML element hierarchy and allows you to click on a tag in order to select it.

Template Objects A command in the Insert menu that allows you to add components of a template such as Editable or Repeating regions.

Templates Dreamweaver uses the .dwt extension for templates.You can create multiple HTML pages based on a template, any changes made to the template will update the attached HTML pages

Text Field A component of an HTML form used for collecting text data from the user.

Textarea A component of an HTML form that allows a user to add multiple lines of text.

Timing Function The ability found in the CSS transition feature that allows you to control the speed of an animated transition as it progresses.

V

Validating Code The act of validating your HTML documents for conformance to HTML or XHTML standards. Dreamweaver has built-in code validation that can be switched on.

Video Allows individuals and companies to post commercials, speeches, and other content that otherwise would be difficult or cost-prohibitive to reach a large audience.

W

W3C Validation The built-in validation engine in Dreamweaver allowing authors of an HTML document to check for conformance to HTML or XHTML standards.

Window Size A menu in the Dreamweaver within the document window that allows you to resize your document window to various preset or custom pixel dimensions.

WIndows Media Microsoft's container file format used to deliver video.

Workspace The arrangement of document windows and panels.

Workspace Layout The arrangement of Dreamweaver panels, bars, and windows. There are default workspaces as well as the ability to create a custom workspace.

World Wide Web Consortium Commonly referred to as the W3C. The organiziation that defines the standards for web technologies such as HTML, CSS and much more.

X

XHTML 1.0 Transitional The default document type for new documents in Dreamweaver CS6.

XML A markup language that defines a set of rules for encoding documents in a format that is both human-readable and machine-readable.

Z

Zoom Level The currrent magnification within Dreamweaver's document window. The default zoom level is 100%.

Index

E

M

N

O

U

V

X

Y

Z

Credits

All of the photos in this book were printed with permission—including those credited below—or were created by the authors of the book:

Front matter

Page vii, Three Beets on White: © Sean McDermid/iStockphoto

Page xxiii, gears: © Milos Luzanin/iStockphoto

Page xxiii, Cellular Fertilization: © Dieter Spears/iStockphoto

Page xxiv, Three Beets on White: © Sean McDermid/iStockphoto

Page xxv, Three Beets on White: © Sean McDermid/iStockphoto

Page xxvii, Healthy Eating Variety of Fresh Vegetables in Arrangement: © Joanna Pecha/iStockphoto

Page xxxi, Three Beets on White: © Sean McDermid/iStockphoto

Page xxxii, Healthy Eating Variety of Fresh Vegetables in Arrangement: © Joanna Pecha/iStockphoto

Page xxxiii, Healthy Eating Variety of Fresh Vegetables in Arrangement: © Joanna Pecha/iStockphoto

Page xxxiii, Healthy Eating Variety of Fresh Vegetables in Arrangement: © Joanna Pecha/iStockphoto

Page xxxiv, Future design technology I: © dinn/iStockphoto

Page xxxiv, 3d virus: © Sebastian Kaulitzki/iStockphoto

Lesson 1

Lesson opener (page 1), gears: © Milos Luzanin/iStockphoto

Lesson opener (page 1), Cellular Fertilization: © Dieter Spears/iStockphoto

Figure 1-3 (page 4), Healthy Eating Variety of Fresh Vegetables in Arrangement: © Joanna Pecha/iStockphoto

Figure 1-5 (page 6), Healthy Eating Variety of Fresh Vegetables in Arrangement: © Joanna Pecha/iStockphoto

Figure 1-6 (page 7), Healthy Eating Variety of Fresh Vegetables in Arrangement: © Joanna Pecha/iStockphoto

Figure 1-8 (page 9), Healthy Eating Variety of Fresh Vegetables in Arrangement: © Joanna Pecha/iStockphoto

Figure 1-11 (page 11), Healthy Eating Variety of Fresh Vegetables in Arrangement: © Joanna Pecha/iStockphoto

Figure 1-12 (page 12), DNA Strands (XXL): © Kyu Oh/iStockphoto

Figure 1-12 (page 12), Future design technology I: © dinn/iStockphoto

Figure 1-12 (page 12), gears: © Milos Luzanin/iStockphoto

Figure 1-12 (page 12), Cellular Fertilization: © Dieter Spears/iStockphoto

Lesson 2

Lesson opener (page 41), Three Beets on White: © Sean McDermid/iStockphoto

Figure 2-14 (page 56), Healthy Eating Variety of Fresh Vegetables in Arrangement: © Joanna Pecha/iStockphoto

Figure 2-18 (page 60), Three Beets on White: © Sean McDermid/iStockphoto

Lesson 3

Lesson opener (page 67), Three Beets on White: © Sean McDermid/iStockphoto

Figure 3-18 (page 96), Three Beets on White: © Sean McDermid/iStockphoto

Figure 3-20 (page 98), Cucumbers Composition: © small_frog/iStockphoto

Figure 3-21 (page 100), Eggplants: © MARIA TOUTOUDAKI/iStockphoto

Figure 3-22 (page 101), Eggplants: © MARIA TOUTOUDAKI/iStockphoto

Figure 3-24 (page 103), Cucumbers Composition: © small_frog/iStockphoto

Lesson 5

Lesson opener (page 149), Healthy Eating Variety of Fresh Vegetables in Arrangement: © Joanna Pecha/iStockphoto

Figure 5-3 (page 153), Healthy Eating Variety of Fresh Vegetables in Arrangement: © Joanna Pecha/iStockphoto

Figure 5-19 (page 164), Healthy Eating Variety of Fresh Vegetables in Arrangement: © Joanna Pecha/iStockphoto

Figure 5-23 (page 168), Healthy Eating Variety of Fresh Vegetables in Arrangement: © Joanna Pecha/iStockphoto

Figure 5-27 (page 172), Healthy Eating Variety of Fresh Vegetables in Arrangement: © Joanna Pecha/iStockphoto

Figure 5-29 (page 174), Healthy Eating Variety of Fresh Vegetables in Arrangement: © Joanna Pecha/iStockphoto

Lesson 6

Figure 6-21 (page 201), Healthy Eating Variety of Fresh Vegetables in Arrangement: © Joanna Pecha/iStockphoto

Lesson 7

Figure 7-11 (page 221), Healthy Eating Variety of Fresh Vegetables in Arrangement: © Joanna Pecha/iStockphoto

Figure 7-14 (page 224), Healthy Eating Variety of Fresh Vegetables in Arrangement: © Joanna Pecha/iStockphoto

Figure 7-15 (page 226), Healthy Eating Variety of Fresh Vegetables in Arrangement: © Joanna Pecha/iStockphoto

Figure 7-19 (page 230), Healthy Eating Variety of Fresh Vegetables in Arrangement: © Joanna Pecha/iStockphoto

Lesson 10

Figure 10-1 (page 291), Healthy Eating Variety of Fresh Vegetables in Arrangement: © Joanna Pecha/iStockphoto

Figure 10-3 (page 293), green leaf: © Vladimir Vladimirov/iStockphoto

Figure 10-6 (page 297), Healthy Eating Variety of Fresh Vegetables in Arrangement: © Joanna Pecha/iStockphoto

Lesson 11

Figure 11-7 (page 316), Healthy Eating Variety of Fresh Vegetables in Arrangement: © Joanna Pecha/iStockphoto

Figure 11-14 (page 322), Healthy Eating Variety of Fresh Vegetables in Arrangement: © Joanna Pecha/iStockphoto

Figure 11-16 (page 324), Three Beets on White: © Sean McDermid/iStockphoto

Lesson 12

Lesson opener (page 333), Three Beets on White: © Sean McDermid/iStockphoto

Figure 12-1 (page 334), Three Beets on White: © Sean McDermid/iStockphoto

Figure 12-8 (page 341), Three Beets on White: © Sean McDermid/iStockphoto

Lesson 13

Lesson opener (page 355), Healthy Eating Variety of Fresh Vegetables in Arrangement: © Joanna Pecha/iStockphoto

Figure 13-1 (page 356), Healthy Eating Variety of Fresh Vegetables in Arrangement: © Joanna Pecha/iStockphoto

Lesson 14

Lesson opener (page 387), Healthy Eating Variety of Fresh Vegetables in Arrangement: © Joanna Pecha/iStockphoto

Figure 14-1 (page 389), Healthy Eating Variety of Fresh Vegetables in Arrangement: © Joanna Pecha/iStockphoto

Figure 14-3 (page 390), Healthy Eating Variety of Fresh Vegetables in Arrangement: © Joanna Pecha/iStockphoto

Figure 14-12 (page 395), Healthy Eating Variety of Fresh Vegetables in Arrangement: © Joanna Pecha/iStockphoto

Figure 14-13 (page 396), Healthy Eating Variety of Fresh Vegetables in Arrangement: © Joanna Pecha/iStockphoto

Figure 14-14 (page 396), Healthy Eating Variety of Fresh Vegetables in Arrangement: © Joanna Pecha/iStockphoto

Figure 14-15 (page 397), Healthy Eating Variety of Fresh Vegetables in Arrangement: © Joanna Pecha/iStockphoto

Figure 14-21 (page 401), Healthy Eating Variety of Fresh Vegetables in Arrangement: © Joanna Pecha/iStockphoto

Figure 14-32 (page 409), Healthy Eating Variety of Fresh Vegetables in Arrangement: © Joanna Pecha/iStockphoto

Lesson 15

Lesson opener (page 415), Healthy Eating Variety of Fresh Vegetables in Arrangement: © Joanna Pecha/iStockphoto

Figure 15-2 (page 419), Healthy Eating Variety of Fresh Vegetables in Arrangement: © Joanna Pecha/iStockphoto

Figure 15-2 (page 419), Cucumbers Composition: © small_frog/iStockphoto

Figure 15-3 (page 419), Healthy Eating Variety of Fresh Vegetables in Arrangement: © Joanna Pecha/iStockphoto

Figure 15-3 (page 419), Cucumbers Composition: © small_frog/iStockphoto

Figure 15-12 (page 428), Healthy Eating Variety of Fresh Vegetables in Arrangement: © Joanna Pecha/iStockphoto

Figure 15-24 (page 437), Three Beets on White: © Sean McDermid/iStockphoto

Figure 15-26 (page 439), Three Beets on White: © Sean McDermid/iStockphoto

Figure 15-27 (page 440), Three Beets on White: © Sean McDermid/iStockphoto

Figure 15-28 (page 441), Three Beets on White: © Sean McDermid/iStockphoto

Figure 15-29 (page 442), Three Beets on White: © Sean McDermid/iStockphoto

Figure 15-32 (page 445), Three Beets on White: © Sean McDermid/iStockphoto

Lesson 16

Lesson opener (page 451), Future design technology I: © dinn/iStockphoto

Lesson opener (page 451), 3d virus: © Sebastian Kaulitzki/iStockphoto

Figure 16-12 (page 465), Future design technology I: © dinn/iStockphoto

Figure 16-15 (page 467), Future design technology I: © dinn/iStockphoto

Figure 16-19 (page 472), Giving Gift Card: © spxChrome/iStockphoto

Figure 16-21 (page 476), Future design technology I: © dinn/iStockphoto